Microsoft®

OFFICE 97
PROFESSIONAL
6-IN-1

Step by Step

Other titles in the *Step by Step* series:

Microsoft Access 97 Step by Step
Microsoft Excel 97 Step by Step
Microsoft Excel 97 Step by Step, Advanced Topics
Microsoft Exchange 5.0 Step by Step
Microsoft FrontPage 97 Step by Step
Microsoft Internet Explorer 3.0 Step by Step
Microsoft Office 97 Integration Step by Step
Microsoft Outlook 97 Step by Step
Microsoft Team Manager 97 Step by Step
Microsoft Windows 95 Step by Step
Microsoft Windows NT Workstation version 4.0 Step by Step
Microsoft Word 97 Step by Step
Microsoft Word 97 Step by Step, Advanced Topics

Step by Step books are available for the Microsoft Office 95 programs.

Microsoft®

OFFICE 97
PROFESSIONAL
6-IN-1

Step by Step

Catapult

Perspection

Microsoft Press

PUBLISHED BY
Microsoft Press
A Division of Microsoft Corporation
One Microsoft Way
Redmond, Washington 98052-6399

Library of Congress Cataloging-in-Publication Data pending.

Printed and bound in the United States of America.

5 6 7 8 9   WCWC   2 1 0 9

Distributed to the book trade in Canada by Macmillan of Canada, a division of Canada Publishing Corporation.

British Cataloging-in-Publication Data pending.

Microsoft Press books are available through booksellers and distributors worldwide. For further information about international editions, contact your local Microsoft Corporation office. Or contact Microsoft Press International directly at fax (425) 936-7329.

FoxPro, FrontPage, Microsoft, Microsoft Press, MS, MS-DOS, PivotTable, PowerPoint, Visual Basic, Windows, and Windows NT are registered trademarks and ActiveX, AutoSum, MSN, and Outlook are trademarks of Microsoft Corporation. Other product and company names mentioned herein may be the trademarks of their respective owners.

Companies, names, and/or data used in screens and sample output are fictitious unless otherwise noted.

Acquisitions Editor: Casey D. Doyle
Project Editor: Laura Sackerman
Technical Editor: Robert Lyon
Production: Frog Mountain Productions

Catapult, Inc., Perspection, Inc., & Microsoft Press

Microsoft Office 97 Professional 6-in-1 Step by Step has been created by the professional trainers and writers at Catapult, Inc., and Perspection, Inc., to the exacting standards you've come to expect from Microsoft Press. Together, we are pleased to present this self-paced training guide, which you can use individually or as part of a class.

Catapult, Inc. is a software training company with years of experience in PC and Macintosh instruction. Catapult's exclusive Performance-Based Training system is available in Catapult training centers across North America and at customer sites. Based on the principles of adult learning, Performance-Based Training ensures that students leave the classroom with confidence and the ability to apply skills to real-world scenarios.

Perspection, Inc. is a technology training company committed to providing information to help people communicate, make decisions, and solve problems. Perspection creates software training books, and designs and develops interactive multimedia applications for Windows-based and Macintosh personal computers.

Microsoft Office 97 Professional 6-in-1 Step by Step incorporates Catapult's and Perspection's training expertise to ensure that you'll receive the maximum return on your training time. You'll focus on the skills that increase productivity the most while working at your own pace and convenience.

Microsoft Press is the independent—and independent-minded—book publishing division of Microsoft Corporation. The leading publisher of information on Microsoft software, Microsoft Press is dedicated to providing the highest quality computer books and multimedia training and reference tools that make using Microsoft software easier, more enjoyable, and more productive.

Table of Contents

Table of Contents

Table of Contents

*Quick*Look Guide

Windows 95 and Windows NT

Getting help,
see page 37

**Controlling
Windows 95
with the mouse**,
see page 5

**Managing
windows on
the Desktop**,
see page 16

**Opening
recently used
documents**,
see page 33

**Using menus,
commands, and
dialog boxes**,
see page 10

**Manipulating
windows with
the taskbar**,
see page 34

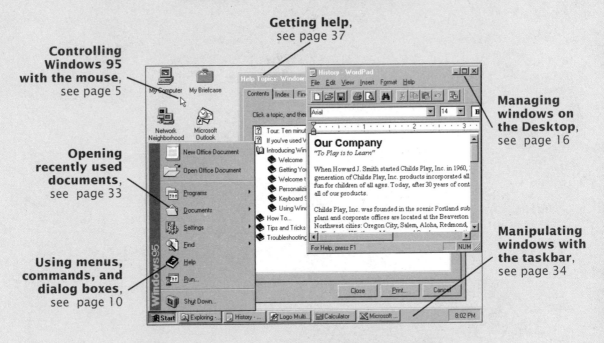

Using shortcuts,
see page 52

**Customizing
your display**,
see page 62

**Customizing
your Start
menu**,
see page 48

**Customizing
your mouse**,
see page 66

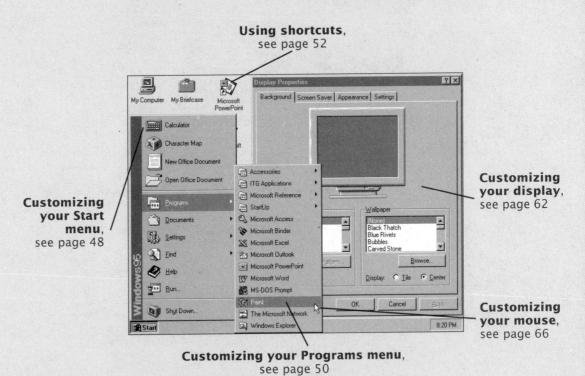

Customizing your Programs menu,
see page 50

Windows 95 and Windows NT

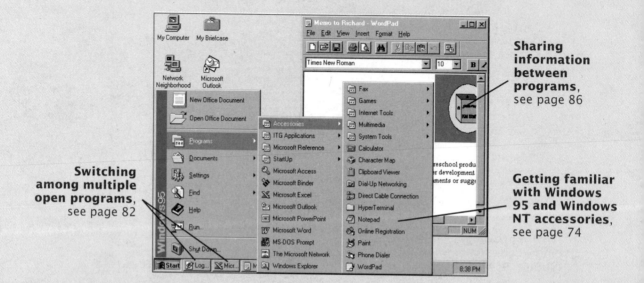

Sharing information between programs, see page 86

Switching among multiple open programs, see page 82

Getting familiar with Windows 95 and Windows NT accessories, see page 74

Managing disks, see page 113

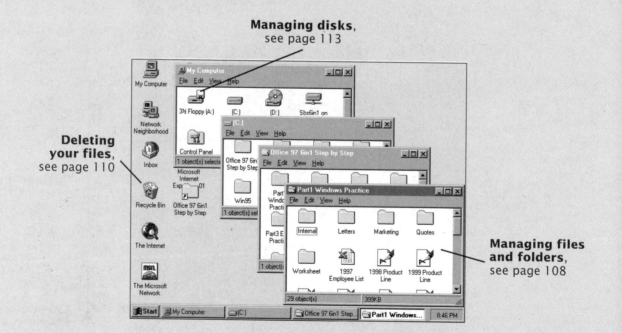

Deleting your files, see page 110

Managing files and folders, see page 108

Word 97

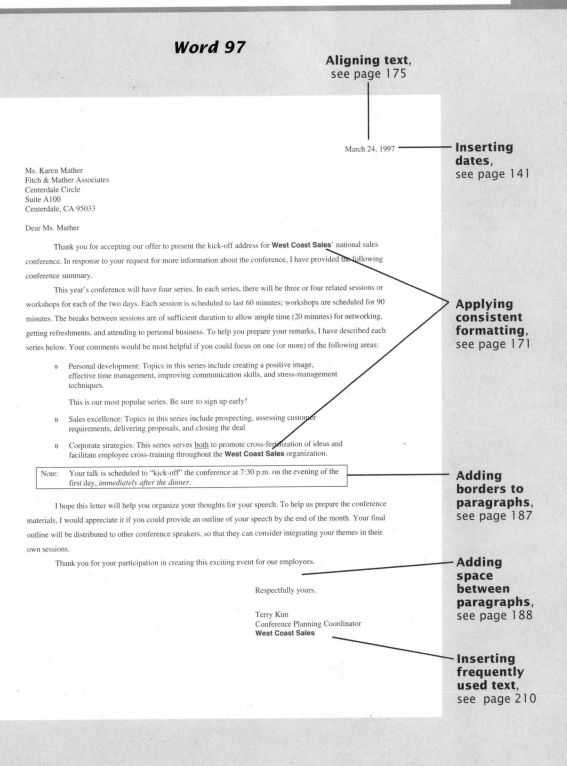

Aligning text,
see page 175

Inserting dates,
see page 141

Applying consistent formatting,
see page 171

Adding borders to paragraphs,
see page 187

Adding space between paragraphs,
see page 188

Inserting frequently used text,
see page 210

March 24, 1997

Ms. Karen Mather
Fitch & Mather Associates
Centerdale Circle
Suite A100
Centerdale, CA 95033

Dear Ms. Mather

Thank you for accepting our offer to present the kick-off address for **West Coast Sales**' national sales conference. In response to your request for more information about the conference, I have provided the following conference summary.

This year's conference will have four series. In each series, there will be three or four related sessions or workshops for each of the two days. Each session is scheduled to last 60 minutes; workshops are scheduled for 90 minutes. The breaks between sessions are of sufficient duration to allow ample time (20 minutes) for networking, getting refreshments, and attending to personal business. To help you prepare your remarks, I have described each series below. Your comments would be most helpful if you could focus on one (or more) of the following areas:

θ   Personal development: Topics in this series include creating a positive image, effective time management, improving communication skills, and stress-management techniques.

This is our most popular series. Be sure to sign up early!

θ   Sales excellence: Topics in this series include prospecting, assessing customer requirements, delivering proposals, and closing the deal

θ   Corporate strategies: This series serves <u>both</u> to promote cross-fertilization of ideas and facilitate employee cross-training throughout the **West Coast Sales** organization.

Note: Your talk is scheduled to "kick-off" the conference at 7:30 p.m. on the evening of the first day, *immediately after the dinner.*

I hope this letter will help you organize your thoughts for your speech. To help us prepare the conference materials, I would appreciate it if you could provide an outline of your speech by the end of the month. Your final outline will be distributed to other conference speakers, so that they can consider integrating your themes in their own sessions.

Thank you for your participation in creating this exciting event for our employees.

Respectfully yours,

Terry Kim
Conference Planning Coordinator
West Coast Sales

Word 97

Using the ruler,
see page 181

Moving and copying text,
see page 158

Formatting text,
see page 168

Creating bulleted and numbered lists,
see page 178

Displaying document views,
see page 156

Selecting text,
see page 158

Searching for specific objects,
see page 214

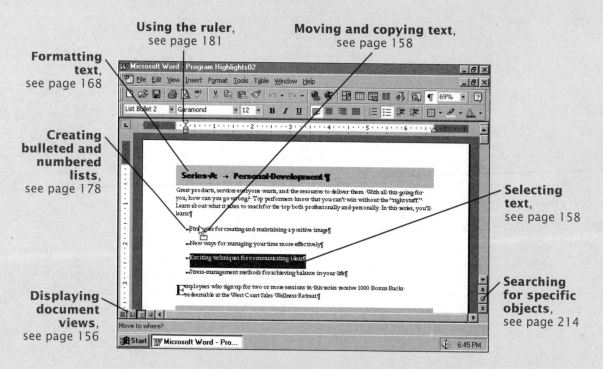

Previewing a document,
see page 194

Inserting section breaks,
see page 230

Adding headers and footers,
see page 224

Changing page orientation,
see page 222

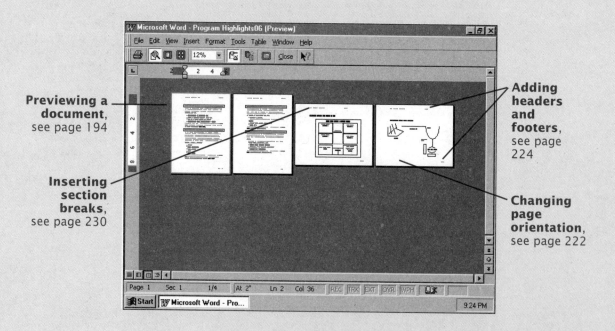

Excel 97

Creating embedded charts,
see page 327

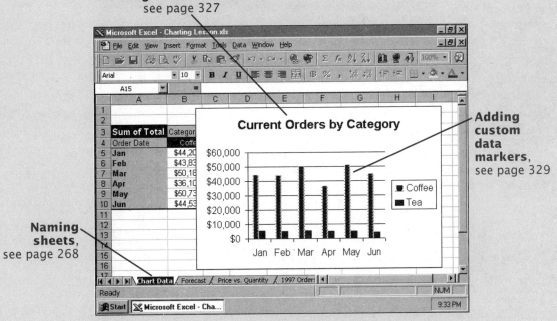

Adding custom data markers,
see page 329

Naming sheets,
see page 268

Writing formulas with AutoSum,
see page 286

Filtering records,
see page 316

Writing a SUBTOTAL formula,
see page 320

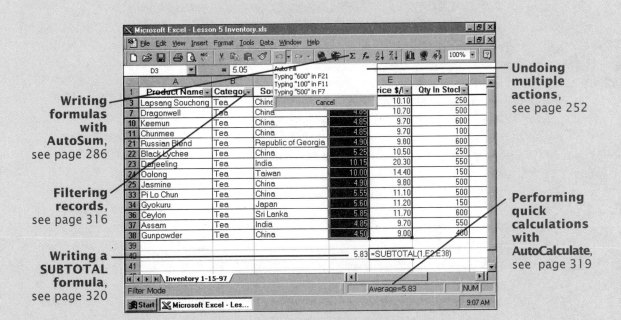

Undoing multiple actions,
see page 252

Performing quick calculations with AutoCalculate,
see page 319

Excel 97

Viewing a worksheet in Page Break Preview, see page 340

Changing page breaks by dragging, see page 341

Changing page printing order, see page 343

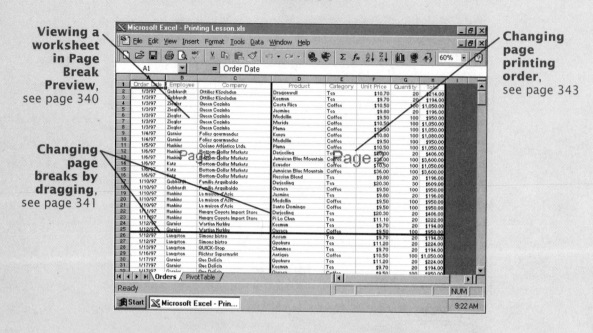

Applying custom number formatting, see page 304

Writing formulas using worksheet labels, see page 289

Setting data validation rules, see page 275

Applying cell borders, see page 299

Navigating with ScrollTips, see page 247

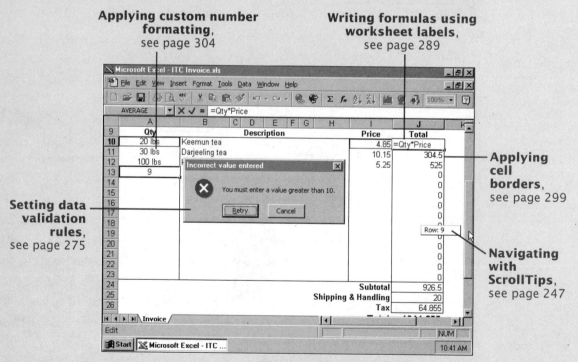

PowerPoint 97

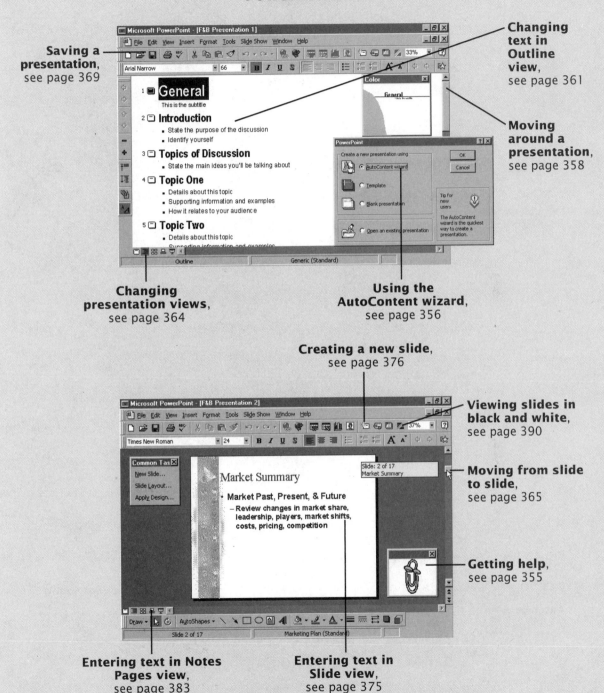

Saving a presentation, see page 369

Changing text in Outline view, see page 361

Moving around a presentation, see page 358

Changing presentation views, see page 364

Using the AutoContent wizard, see page 356

Creating a new slide, see page 376

Viewing slides in black and white, see page 390

Moving from slide to slide, see page 365

Getting help, see page 355

Entering text in Notes Pages view, see page 383

Entering text in Slide view, see page 375

PowerPoint 97

Checking spelling,
see page 412

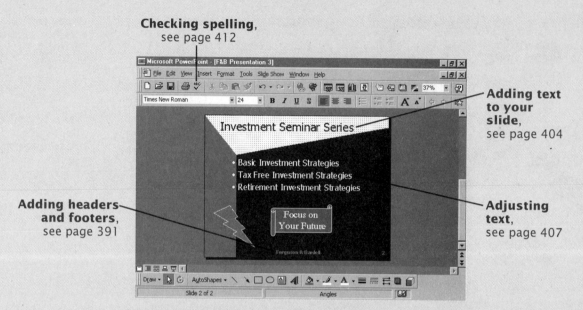

**Adding text
to your
slide**,
see page 404

**Adding headers
and footers**,
see page 391

**Adjusting
text**,
see page 407

Adjusting text indent markers,
see page 429

Applying templates,
see page 420

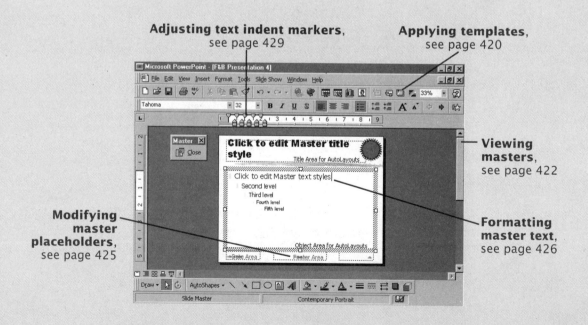

**Viewing
masters**,
see page 422

**Modifying
master
placeholders**,
see page 425

**Formatting
master text**,
see page 426

Access 97

Opening a table, see page 465

Viewing and creating relationships, see page 523

Linking to external databases, see page 557

Creating a new table, see page 511

Relating tables, see page 524

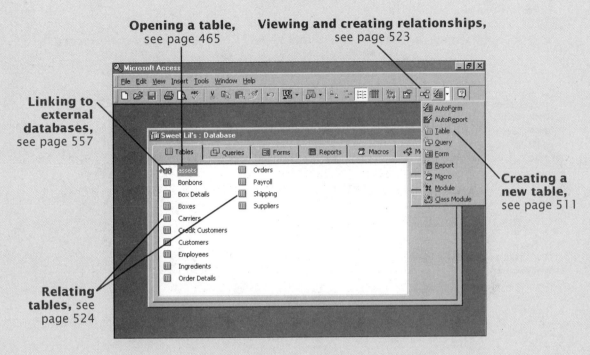

Sorting in Datasheet view, see page 495

Filtering by selection, see page 496

Creating a new table by adding data to a blank datasheet, see page 515

Setting and changing field properties, see page 520

Moving to different records, see page 463

Adding new records, see page 513

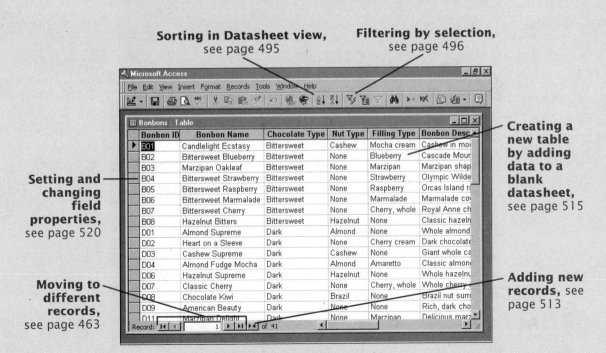

*Quick*Look Guide

Access 97

Sorting a query in Datasheet view, see page 575

Finding specific records, see page 488

Switching views with the View button, see page 574

Basing a report on a parameter query, see page 498

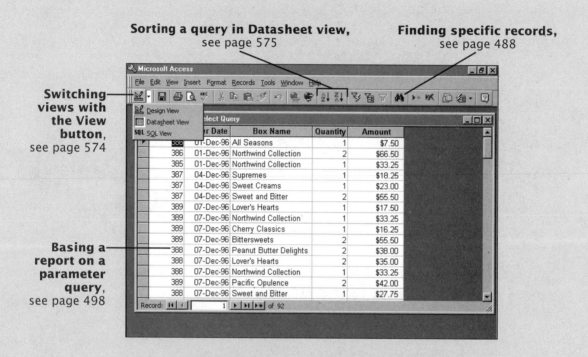

Using junction tables to join two tables, see page 552

Joining tables in a query, see page 580

Setting query criteria, see page 574

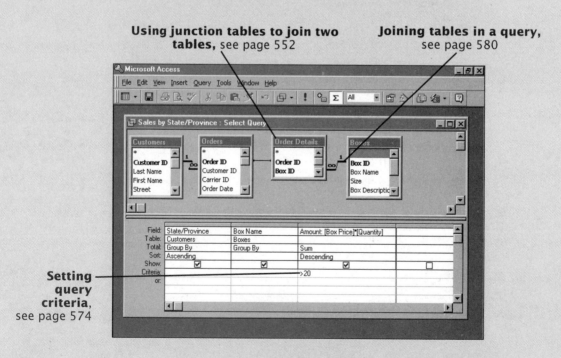

Outlook 97

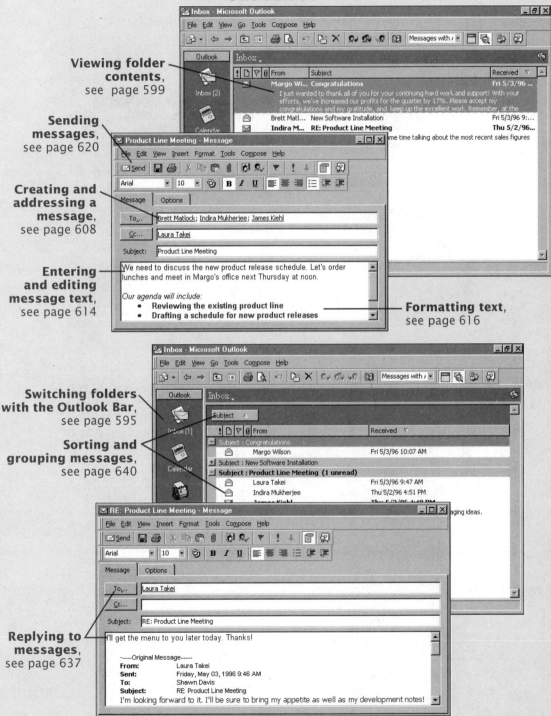

Viewing folder contents, see page 599

Sending messages, see page 620

Creating and addressing a message, see page 608

Entering and editing message text, see page 614

Formatting text, see page 616

Switching folders with the Outlook Bar, see page 595

Sorting and grouping messages, see page 640

Replying to messages, see page 637

Outlook 97

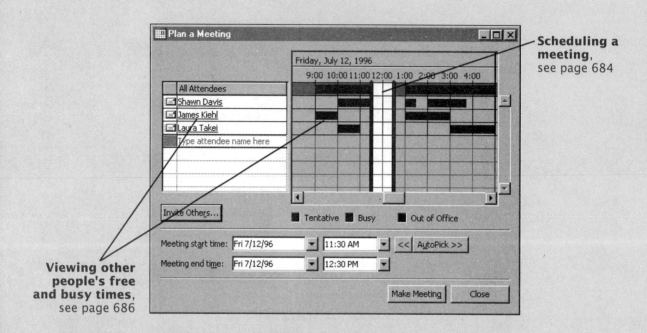

Scheduling a meeting, see page 684

Viewing other people's free and busy times, see page 686

Adding events to your schedule, see page 674

Adding and editing appointments, see page 660

Setting tentative appointments, see page 669

Setting reminders, see page 668

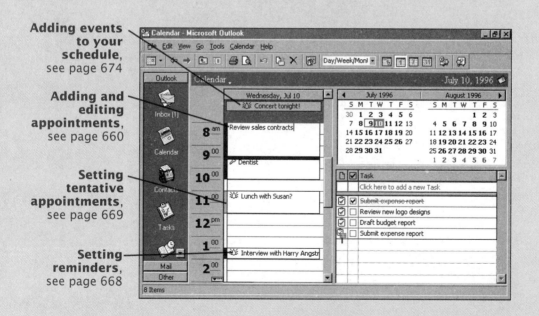

Finding Your Best Starting Point

Microsoft Office is a powerful family of integrated programs that you can use to produce sophisticated documents. *Microsoft Office 97 Professional 6-in-1 Step by Step* shows you how to use Microsoft Office 97 plus Windows 95 or Windows NT to streamline your work and increase your productivity.

 IMPORTANT This book is designed for use with Microsoft Office 97 Professional Edition for the Windows 95 and Windows NT version 4 operating systems. To find out what software you're running, you can check the product package or you can start the software, click the Help menu, and click About Microsoft for the Office 97 program you are using. If your software is not compatible with this book, a Step by Step book for your software is probably available. Many of the Step by Step titles are listed on the second page of this book. If the book you want isn't listed, please visit our World Wide Web site at http://mspress.microsoft.com or call 1-800-MSPRESS for more information.

Finding Your Best Starting Point in This Book

This book is designed for readers who are learning Office 97 for the first time and for more experienced readers who are switching from other programs or earlier versions of Office. Use the following table to find your best starting point in this book.

If you are	Follow these steps
New... to computers to graphical (as opposed to text-only) computer programs to Windows 95 or Windows NT to Microsoft Office programs	**1** Install the practice files as described in "Installing and Using the Practice and Camcorder Files." **2** Become acquainted with the Windows 95 or Windows NT operating system by working through Part 1. **3** Work through the other parts in any order.

If you are	Follow these steps
Switching... from Lotus SmartSuite from Corel Office	**1** Install the practice files as described in "Installing and Using the Practice and Camcorder Files." **2** Work through Parts 2 through 6 in any order.

If you are	Follow these steps
Upgrading... from Microsoft Office 95 from a previous version of Microsoft Word, Microsoft Excel, Microsoft PowerPoint, or Microsoft Access	**1** Install the practice files as described in "Installing and Using the Practice and Camcorder Files." **2** Complete the lessons that cover the topics you need. You can use the table of contents and the *Quick*Look Guide to locate information about general topics. You can use the index to find information about a specific topic or a feature from Microsoft Office 95.

If you are	Follow these steps

Referencing...

this book after working
through the lessons

1 Use the index to locate information about specific topics, and use the table of contents and the *Quick*Look Guide to locate information about general topics.

2 Read the Lesson Summary at the end of each lesson for a brief review of the major tasks in the lesson.

New Features in Windows 95 and Windows NT Workstation version 4

If you have used previous versions of Microsoft Windows or Microsoft Windows NT, you'll see that the features in Windows 95 and Windows NT version 4 are significantly improved. The following table identifies the new features that are covered in this book.

To learn how to	In Part 1, see
Explore the new Windows 95 and Windows NT Desktop.	Lesson 1
Use Help.	Lesson 2
Start programs and documents with the Start button.	Lesson 2
Manage and manipulate your open windows with window controls and the taskbar.	Lesson 2
Customize your menus and Desktop.	Lesson 3
Create shortcuts to programs, folders, and documents.	Lesson 3
Open and use new accessories, including new Desktop tools, system utilities, and games.	Lesson 4
Find and run programs.	Lesson 4
Organize your files and folders using My Computer and Windows Explorer or Windows NT Explorer.	Lesson 5
Move, copy, and rename files and folders using new techniques.	Lesson 6
Delete and recover files and folders using Recycle Bin.	Lesson 6

New Features in Microsoft Word 97

The following table lists the major new features in Microsoft Word that are covered in this book.

To learn how to	In Part 2, see
Find answers to your questions about Microsoft Word with the Office Assistant.	Lesson 1
Insert AutoText entries provided by Microsoft Word	Lesson 1
View document headings alongside document text using the Document Map	Lesson 2
Highlight important ideas in a document using AutoSummarize	Lesson 2
Use new font formatting options	Lesson 3
Identify and correct grammatical errors as you work	Lesson 5
Use new options on the Headers And Footers toolbar	Lesson 6

New Features in Microsoft Excel 97

The following table lists the major new features in Microsoft Excel 97 that are covered in this book.

To learn how to	In Part 3, see
Get help with specific procedures from the Office Assistant	Lesson 1
Enter lists of data in a worksheet efficiently using AutoReturn	Lesson 1
Undo multiple actions and redo multiple undone actions	Lesson 1
See the range reference where dragged cells will be dropped using ScreenTips	Lesson 1
Write formulas using the Formula palette	Lesson 1
Select formulas from the formula list in the Name box	Lesson 1
See which cells a formula refers to by looking at the color-coded cell references in a formula	Lesson 1
Use the new interface to name a worksheet	Lesson 2
Add worksheet comments with an automatic user name	Lesson 2
Ensure that an entry contains valid data by using data validation	Lesson 2

To learn how to	In Part 3, see
Use worksheet labels in formulas	Lesson 3
Open a file using Microsoft Outlook	Lesson 5
Apply new fill effects to chart elements	Lesson 6
Switch an embedded chart to a chart sheet and vice versa	Lesson 6
View a worksheet's page layout using Page Break Preview	Lesson 7
Set and change page breaks easily using Page Break Preview	Lesson 7

New Features in PowerPoint 97

The following table lists the major new features in Microsoft PowerPoint 97 that are covered in this book.

To learn how to	In Part 4, see
Use the new and improved AutoContent Wizard to create informal, formal, and Internet presentations.	Lesson 1
Find, insert, rearrange, and catalog slides.	Lesson 2
Spell check different languages.	Lesson 4
Look up references in Microsoft Bookshelf and other CD-ROM reference tools.	Lesson 4
Create animated slides and custom slide shows.	Lesson 6

New Features in Microsoft Access 97

The following table lists the major new features in Microsoft Access that are covered in this book.

To learn how to	In Part 5, see
Work with Office Assistant	Lesson 1
Switch between views of an object with the View button	Lesson 3
Create a hyperlink to jump to another part of the database	Lesson 6

Visit Our World Wide Web Site

We invite you to visit the Microsoft Press World Wide Web site. You can visit us at the following location:

http://mspress.microsoft.com

You'll find descriptions for all of our books, information about ordering titles, notice of special features and events, additional content for Microsoft Press books, and much more.

You can also find out the latest in software developments and news from Microsoft Corporation by visiting the following World Wide Web site:

http://www.microsoft.com

We look forward to your visit on the Web!

Installing and Using the Practice and Camcorder Files

The companion CD-ROM inside the back cover of this book contains practice files that you'll use as you perform the exercises in the book. For example, when you're learning how to check the spelling in a Word 97 document in Part 2 of the book, you'll open one of the practice files—a partially completed letter—and then use the Spelling feature. By using the practice files, you won't waste time creating the samples used in the lessons—instead, you can concentrate on learning how to use Microsoft Office 97. With the files and the step-by-step instructions in the lessons, you'll also learn by doing, which is an easy and effective way to acquire and remember new skills.

The companion CD also contains Camcorder files to help you better understand how to perform certain tasks in Office 97. Camcorder files are short audiovisual demonstrations of how to do tasks in Office 97. You will need a sound card and speakers to hear the audio part of the Camcorder movies.

 IMPORTANT This book is designed for use with Microsoft Office 97 Professional Edition for the Windows 95 and Windows NT version 4 operating systems. To find out what software you're running, you can check the product package or you can start the software, click the Help menu, and click About Microsoft for the Office 97 program you are using. If your software is not compatible with this book, a Step by Step book for your software is probably available. Many of the Step by Step titles are listed on the second page of this book. If the book you want isn't listed, please visit our World Wide Web site at http://mspress.microsoft.com or call 1-800-MSPRESS for more information.

Install the practice files and Camcorder files on your computer

Follow these steps to install the practice files and/or Camcorder files on your computer's hard disk so that you can use them with the exercises in this book.

1 If your computer isn't on, turn it on now.

2 If you're using Windows NT, press CTRL+ALT+DELETE to display a dialog box asking for your username and password. If you are using Windows 95, you will see this dialog box if your computer is connected to a network. If you don't know your username or password, contact your system administrator for assistance.

3 Type your username and password in the appropriate boxes, and then click OK. If you see the Welcome dialog box, click the Close button.

4 Remove the companion CD from the package inside the back cover of this book.

5 Insert the CD in the CD-ROM drive of your computer.

6 On the taskbar at the bottom of your screen, click the Start button.

The Start menu opens.

7 On the Start menu, click Run.

The Run dialog box appears.

8 In the Open box, type **d:setup** (if your CD-ROM drive is a different letter, be sure to use that letter instead; for example **e:setup**). Don't add spaces as you type.

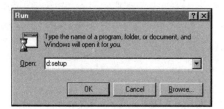

9 Click OK and the Welcome dialog box appears.

10 Click OK and the Select Practice and Camcorder Files dialog box appears.

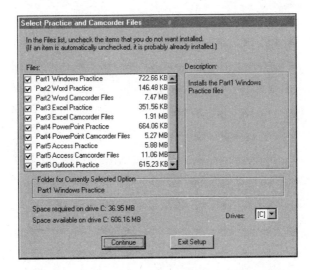

11 When you run the Setup program for the first time, all the items in the Files list are checked by default, so uncheck the items that you do not want installed.

All checked items will be installed. Remember to scroll down in the Files list to display all the items. If an item is automatically unchecked, it is probably already installed. You may want to install only the items for the parts of the book you will be working on. If you want to install additional items at a later time, you can just run this Setup program again at that time.

 NOTE If you try to install items that have already been installed, you will receive Confirm File Replace messages. Therefore, if you want to reinstall an item, it is recommended to first uninstall that item, and then run Setup again to install it. See "Uninstalling the Practice and Camcorder Files" later in this section for instructions for uninstalling items.

If you install all of the practice and Camcorder files for all six parts of the book, about 40 MB of hard disk space will be required. The following list shows your choices and the space required:

- Part1 Windows Practice (0.8 MB)

- Part2 Word Practice (0.2 MB)

- Part2 Word Camcorder Files (7.9 MB)

- Part3 Excel Practice (0.4 MB)

- Part3 Excel Camcorder Files (2 MB)

- Part4 PowerPoint Practice (0.7 MB)

- Part4 PowerPoint Camcorder Files (5.6 MB)
- Part5 Access Practice (6.2 MB)
- Part5 Access Camcorder Files (11.6 MB)
- Part6 Outlook Practice (0.7 MB)
- Part6 Outlook Camcorder Files (3.1 MB)

 NOTE The Camcorder files are not required to complete the step-by-step lessons. Therefore, if you have limited hard disk space on your computer, you might choose not to install the Camcorder files.

12 From the Drives drop down list, select the drive you want to install to, and then click the Continue button.

13 An installing dialog box appears, indicating the progress of the files being installed on your computer. Once all the selected files have been installed, a Finished dialog box appears.

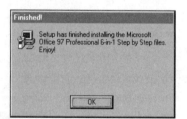

14 Click OK and remove the companion CD from your drive and replace it in the package inside the back cover of the book.

During the installation, a new folder was created on your hard disk. The folder is named Office 97 6in1 Step by Step and it contains all of the practice and Camcorder files you chose to install.

Office 97 6in1
Step by Step

Microsoft
Press
Welcome

 NOTE In addition to installing the practice and Camcorder files, the Setup program created two shortcuts on your Desktop. You can double-click the Office 97 6in1 Step by Step shortcut to view the practice and Camcorder files copied to your hard disk. If your computer is set up to connect to the Internet, you can double-click the Microsoft Press Welcome shortcut to visit the Microsoft Press Web site. You can connect to the Web site directly at http://mspress.microsoft.com.

Using the Practice Files

Each lesson in this book explains when and how to use any practice files for that lesson. When it's time to use a practice file, the book will list instructions for how to open the file. The lessons are built around scenarios that simulate a real work environment, so you can easily apply the skills you learn to your own work.

The screen illustrations in this book might look different from what you see on your computer, depending on how your computer has been set up. To help make your screen match the illustrations in this book, please follow the instructions in the Appendix, "Matching the Exercises."

 NOTE This book was written using the English version of Microsoft Windows 95, Microsoft Windows NT version 4, and Microsoft Office 97. If you are using a non-English version of Windows 95, Windows NT, or Office 97, you may notice small differences or errors in the lessons.

Using the Camcorder Files

Some of the lessons in this book refer to Camcorder files that you can view to see a demonstration on how to do a certain task. To view these Camcorder files, first double-click the Office 97 6in1 Step by Step shortcut on your Desktop. Depending on which files you chose to install, you will see folders for the practice files and folders for Camcorder files for parts of the book. Double-click the folder for the Camcorder files you want to view. In the window that is displayed, double-click the Camcorder file you want to view. If you have a sound card with speakers, you will see and hear a short movie about a certain task.

For example, if you installed the Part2 Word Camcorder Files folder and you wanted to view the Camcorder file demonstrating how to insert page breaks, these are the steps you would follow:

Office 97 6in1
Step by Step

1 Double-click the Office 97 6in1 Step by Step shortcut on the Desktop.

2 In the window that is displayed, double-click the Part2 Word Camcorder Files folder.

3 In the window that is displayed, double-click the Camcorder file Inserting Page Breaks. The demonstration will play.

Need Help with the Practice or Camcorder Files?

Every effort has been made to ensure the accuracy of this book and the contents of the companion CD. If you do run into a problem, Microsoft Press provides corrections for its books through the World Wide Web at

http://mspress.microsoft.com/mspress/support/

We also invite you to visit our main Web page at

http://mspress.microsoft.com

You'll find descriptions for all our books, information about ordering titles, notices of special features and events, additional content for Microsoft Press books, and much more.

Uninstalling the Practice and Camcorder Files

Use the following steps when you want to delete the practice and Camcorder files added to your hard disk and the shortcuts added to your Desktop by the Setup program.

1 Click Start, point to Settings, and then click Control Panel.

2 Double-click the Add/Remove Programs icon.

Add/Remove
Programs

The Add/Remove Programs Properties dialog box is displayed.

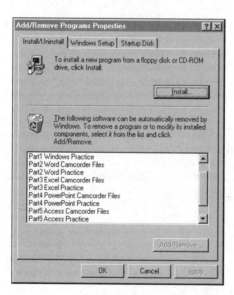

3 Select which item you want to uninstall from the list. The items listed depend on which parts you chose to install with the Setup program. If you chose to install the files for all six parts of the book, the following would be listed on the Install/Uninstall tab of the Add/Remove Programs Properties dialog box:

- Part1 Windows Practice
- Part2 Word Camcorder Files
- Part2 Word Practice
- Part3 Excel Camcorder Files
- Part3 Excel Practice
- Part4 PowerPoint Camcorder Files
- Part4 PowerPoint Practice
- Part5 Access Camcorder Files
- Part5 Access Practice
- Part6 Outlook Camcorder Files
- Part6 Outlook Practice

4   After you have selected a part you want to uninstall, click the Add/Remove button.

A confirmation message appears, asking you if you want to continue.

5   Click Yes.

The files for that part are uninstalled.

6   If you want to uninstall additional parts, repeat steps 3 through 5.

7   When finished uninstalling, click the OK button in the Add/Remove Programs Properties dialog box.

8   Close the Control Panel window.

If you would like to delete the Office 97 6in1 Step by Step and the Microsoft Press Welcome shortcuts on the Desktop, follow these steps.

Office 97 6in1
Step by Step

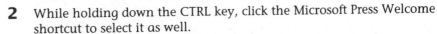

Microsoft
Press
Welcome

1   On the Desktop, click the Office 97 6in1 Step by Step shortcut to select it.

2   While holding down the CTRL key, click the Microsoft Press Welcome shortcut to select it as well.

3   Press the DELETE key, and the Confirm Multiple File Delete dialog box appears.

4   Click Yes.

Both shortcuts are moved to the Recycle Bin.

Removing the Part 6 Practice Profile

When you go through the lessons in Part 6, "Microsoft Outlook 97," you create a practice user profile for a fictional person, Shawn Davis. Use the following steps when you want to remove the Shawn Davis profile from your Outlook configuration.

1 Click Start, point to Settings, and then click Control Panel.

Mail and Fax

2 Double-click the Mail icon or the Mail And Fax icon.

3 Make sure the Services tab is selected, and click Show Profiles.

4 On the General tab, click the Shawn Davis profile in the Profiles box.

5 Click Remove.

6 In the dialog box asking you if you want to remove this profile, click Yes.

7 Close the Mail dialog box, and close the Control Panel window.

If the Choose Profile dialog box is displayed each time you start Outlook and you do not want it to appear, follow these steps to eliminate its appearance:

1 Double-click the Microsoft Outlook shortcut on the Desktop.

2 In the Choose Profile dialog box, select the profile you normally use from the drop-down list and click OK.

3 In the Microsoft Outlook window, choose Options from the Tools menu.

4 In the Options dialog box, click the General tab.

5 In the Startup Settings area, click the Always Use This Profile option button.

6 In the drop-down list to the right of the Always Use This Profile option button, select the profile you want to always use.

7 Click OK.

The next time you start Outlook the Choose Profile dialog box will not be displayed.

Conventions
and Features
in This Book

You can save time when you use this book by understanding, before you start the lessons, how instructions, keys to press, and so on, are shown in the book. Please take a moment to read the following list, which also points out helpful features of the book that you might want to use.

Conventions

- Hands-on exercises for you to follow are given in numbered lists of steps (1, 2, and so on). An arrowhead bullet (▶) indicates an exercise with only one step.
- Text that you are to type appears in **bold**.
- A plus sign (+) between two key names means that you must press those keys at the same time. For example, "Press ALT+TAB" means that you hold down the ALT key while you press TAB.

The following icons identify the different types of supplementary material:

	Notes labeled	Alert you to
	Note	Additional information for a step.
	Tip	Suggested additional methods for a step or helpful hints.
	Important	Essential information that you should check before continuing with the lesson.
	Troubleshooting	Possible error messages or computer difficulties and their solutions.
	Warning	Possible data loss and tell you how to proceed safely.
	Demonstration	Skills that are demonstrated in audiovisual files available on the practice files CD.

Other Features of This Book

- You can learn about techniques that build on what you learned in a lesson by trying the optional "One Step Further" exercise at the end of the lesson.
- You can get a quick reminder of how to perform the tasks you learned by reading the Lesson Summary at the end of a lesson.
- You can quickly determine what online Help topics are available for additional information by referring to the Help topics listed at the end of each lesson.

Part 1

Microsoft Windows 95 and Microsoft Windows NT

Working with Desktop Tools

Estimated time
40 min.

In this lesson you will learn how to:

- Control window elements using the mouse.
- Give commands using the mouse and menus.
- Specify options and properties in dialog boxes.
- Move and size a window on the screen.

If you were to begin working at a new job, one of the first things you might do is become familiar with your environment and the tools available to you. Perhaps a co-worker would help you learn how to use these tools.

In this lesson, you'll start to become familiar with the Microsoft Windows 95 or Microsoft Windows NT screen, and you'll be introduced to the basic tools you need to manage your work in Windows 95 or Windows NT. This includes understanding the different elements you see on the screen and using the mouse to control the computer.

Getting to Know Your Desktop

When you look at the Windows 95 or Windows NT screen for the first time, you see a few items displayed, such as the My Computer picture in the upper-left corner and the Start button in the lower-left corner. You might also see the Welcome To Windows 95 or Welcome To Windows NT window. Another name for your Windows 95 or Windows NT screen is the *Desktop*. Just like an actual desk,

3

the items that are on your Desktop might depend on your current tasks and projects. The contents of your Desktop can change as your work changes.

Unless otherwise noted, screens from Windows 95 are shown in Part 1 of this book. The corresponding screens from Windows NT are the same or very similar.

Icon

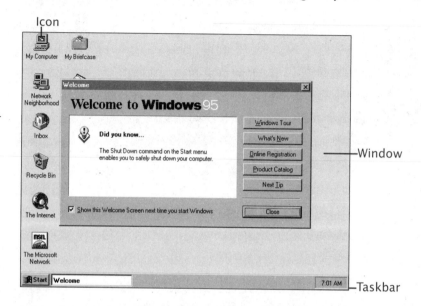

Window

Taskbar

A *window* is a rectangular, bordered element on the screen. You can have multiple windows open at the same time on your Desktop, with each window running a different program or displaying a different document.

The rectangular bar that runs horizontally across the bottom of your screen is called the *taskbar*. The taskbar includes the Start button, which is the starting point for your work on the computer. The taskbar also shows the current time. When you start working, you'll see other items listed on the taskbar. These items show you the names of the windows currently open on your Desktop. You'll learn more about the taskbar later in this lesson.

The named pictures along the left side of your screen are *icons*. Icons graphically represent items you use in your work or play in Windows 95 or Windows NT. For example, the My Computer icon represents all the programs, documents, and other resources available to your computer system.

You'll learn more about how to work with icons in Lesson 2, "Getting Around in Windows 95 or Windows NT."

A *menu* is a list of commands that appears on your Desktop. For example, when you click the Start button on the Desktop, the Start menu appears. A command is an order you can give to the computer. You choose a command to start an activity, such as running a program, opening a document, or closing a file. Menus organize commands into categorized groups. For example, commands that you use to start programs are on the Programs menu. Commands that you use to control files are on the File menu. You'll learn more about menus and commands later in this lesson. The following illustration shows the Start menu.

Menu

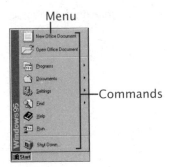

—Commands

Using the Mouse

You use the mouse to select icons, buttons, or other elements on your Desktop. Using the mouse is intuitive, because you're using hand movements to select, move, and activate objects you see on the screen.

There are four basic mouse actions to help you carry out different functions, such as displaying a menu, choosing a command, or opening a file. The following table summarizes these mouse actions.

For this action	**Do this**
Point	Place the mouse pointer in a specific location on the screen by moving the mouse.
Click or single-click	Press and release a mouse button.
Double-click	Press and release a mouse button two times in rapid succession.
Drag	Point to an item on the Desktop, hold down a mouse button, slide the mouse to a different place, and then release the mouse button.

 NOTE If you already know how to do these four actions with the mouse, you can skip ahead to the next section.

Most of the time, the mouse pointer looks like an arrow. However, the mouse pointer can change shape, depending on where you place the mouse pointer on the screen. The mouse pointer shape might also change when you choose certain commands.

If you are left-handed, refer to Lesson 3, "Customizing Your Desktop for the Way You Work," for instructions on switching the mouse button setup.

With Windows 95 or Windows NT, you use two mouse buttons: the left button and the right button. If you use a three-button mouse, you can ignore the middle button. The primary mouse button is initially set as the left mouse button and is used for most mouse actions. The secondary mouse button, the one often used for special shortcuts, is set initially as the right mouse button. This setup is more comfortable for right-handed users.

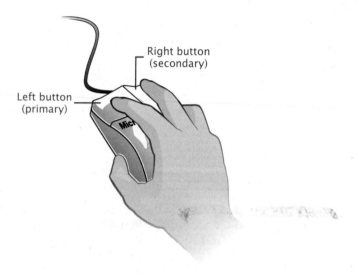

Right button (secondary)

Left button (primary)

 NOTE   Throughout this book, any reference to a mouse button means the primary button, unless otherwise specified.

Making Desktop Choices with the Mouse

When you set up your practice files, you used the mouse to move the pointer on the Desktop and click commands. In the next two exercises, you'll learn more about selecting Desktop elements using both the left and right mouse buttons.

Select Desktop objects with the mouse

In this exercise, you'll get more practice with pointing and clicking by using the mouse.

If you have reconfigured your mouse to a left-handed setup, click the right mouse button instead.

1   Move the mouse until the tip of the pointer is positioned somewhere on the My Computer icon.

2   Click the left mouse button by pressing and releasing the button once. Be careful not to move the mouse while you're clicking the button.

The My Computer icon changes color, indicating that it is selected for further action.

3   Pull the mouse toward you until the tip of the pointer is positioned somewhere on the My Briefcase icon, which is displayed on the left side of your Desktop.

4   Click the left mouse button once.

The My Briefcase icon changes color, indicating that it is now the selected icon.

5   Point to the Start button in the lower-left corner of the Desktop, and then click the left mouse button once.

The Start menu opens, as shown in the following illustration.

6   Move the mouse pointer to an empty area of the Desktop, away from the Start menu, and then click the left mouse button once.

The Start menu closes.

Pointer

7   Move the mouse pointer until the tip of the arrow is touching the top edge of the taskbar.

The mouse pointer changes to a two-headed arrow. As you complete various tasks throughout the lessons in this book, you will learn about other instances in which the mouse pointer changes shape.

8   Move the mouse pointer to any empty area on the Desktop.

The mouse pointer changes back to the standard arrow.

Open pop-up menus with the mouse

In certain areas on your Desktop, you can click the right mouse button to open a *pop-up menu.* The menu lists shortcut commands that directly relate to the action you are performing. In this exercise, you'll see that pop-up menus are context-sensitive, which means that the list of commands on each menu changes depending on where you click.

If you have reconfigured your mouse to a left-handed setup, click the left mouse button instead.

1 Point to an empty area of the Desktop, and click the right mouse button once.

A pop-up menu appears, listing shortcut commands for the Desktop.

2 Point to the My Computer icon, and click the right mouse button once.

The first pop-up menu closes, and a second pop-up menu appears, listing shortcut commands for the items stored in My Computer.

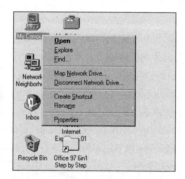

3 Use the left mouse button to click an empty area of the Desktop.

The pop-up menu closes.

Performing Actions by Double-Clicking with the Mouse

You can perform some actions quickly by *double-clicking* the left mouse button while the pointer is at a location on your Desktop. You double-click to quickly open an object, such as an icon or a file.

Open icons by double-clicking the mouse

1   Move the mouse until the pointer is positioned on the My Computer icon.

You can adjust the double-click speed. For more information, see Lesson 3, "Customizing Your Desktop for the Way You Work."

2   Double-click the My Computer icon by pressing and releasing the left mouse button twice in rapid succession. Be careful not to move the mouse and pointer while you're double-clicking.

The My Computer window appears. You should still see the My Computer icon on the left side of the screen. The name of the window also appears as a button on the taskbar.

3   Double-click the My Briefcase icon.

The My Briefcase window opens, and its name also appears as a button on the taskbar. If the Welcome To The Windows Briefcase wizard appears, click Finish.

4   Double-click the Recycle Bin icon.

The Recycle Bin window opens, and its name appears as a button on the taskbar. Your screen should look similar to the following illustration.

With Recycle Bin, you can delete files you no longer need. You'll learn more about Recycle Bin in Lesson 6, "Managing Files and Disks."

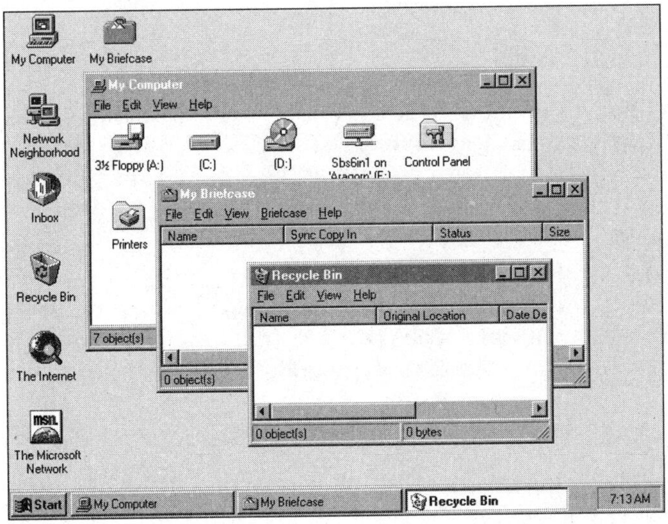

If your screen looks different from this illustration, refer to the Appendix, "Matching the Exercises."

9

Moving Items by Dragging with the Mouse

You can move and resize objects on your Desktop by *dragging* with the mouse. For example, you can drag to move a window or an icon, or to change a window's size.

Move Desktop objects by dragging with the mouse

1   Position the mouse pointer on the words "Recycle Bin" at the top of the Recycle Bin window.

2   Holding down the left mouse button, drag the window about one inch to the right, and then release the mouse button.

   The Recycle Bin window moves to the right.

3   Position the mouse pointer on the Recycle Bin icon on the Desktop.

4   Holding down the left mouse button, drag the icon to an empty space on the Desktop, and then release the mouse button.

   The Recycle Bin icon now appears in the new location.

5   Drag the Recycle Bin icon downward to its original location.

Telling Windows 95 or Windows NT What To Do

Windows 95 and Windows NT are sophisticated tools that can help you perform work on the computer. As the user of one of these tools, you can control the way it operates. You specify the kind of work you want to do, and how you want it done, by choosing commands from a menu.

In the previous section, you clicked the Start button and the Start menu appeared, displaying a list of commands. In this section, you'll learn more about menus and commands, which you use to direct Windows 95 or Windows NT to do what you want. You'll also learn about *dialog boxes*, which are a type of window in which you can specify additional details for a command activity.

Opening and Closing Menus

When you go to a restaurant, you usually read a menu to see the restaurant's bill of fare, and then you make your choice from that menu.

In a similar way, Windows 95 and Windows NT provide a variety of menus you can use to choose and perform different tasks. The most frequently used menu is the Start menu. When you have a particular task in mind that you want to accomplish with your computer, you begin by clicking the Start button. This tells Windows 95 or Windows NT to start working.

When you click the Start button, the Start menu presents a list of commands from which you can choose. From here, you can choose a command that indicates the direction you want to go to start doing your work. This might be to run a program, open a document, write an electronic mail message, play a game, look for a file, or any number of other activities.

In addition to the Start menu, there are many windows and programs that have their own sets of menus and commands.

Open and close menus

You can also open the Start menu by pressing CTRL+ESC or ALT+S. You can close any open menu by pressing ESC.

1 Click the Start button.

The Start menu opens.

2 Click an empty space on the Desktop.

The Start menu closes.

3 On the taskbar at the bottom of the Desktop, click My Computer.

The My Computer window appears on top of any other open windows. Across the top of the My Computer window is a list of menu names: File, Edit, View, and Help. This list is called the *menu bar*.

4 On the menu bar on the My Computer window, click View.

The View menu opens. Your screen should look similar to the following illustration.

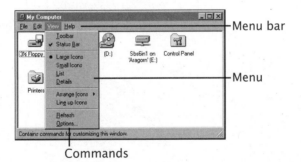

Commands

5 On the My Computer window's menu bar, point to Help.

The View menu closes, and the Help menu opens.

6 Click an empty space in the My Computer window.

The Help menu closes.

 TIP You can activate the menu bar in an active (selected) window by pressing the ALT key. When you press the ALT key, the first menu in the menu bar is highlighted. You can use the arrow keys on the keyboard to move to the different menus in the menu bar, and then press ENTER to open the selected menu.

Choosing Commands

Back at the restaurant, when you have looked over the menu and made your decision, you tell the waiter what you have chosen, and the waiter carries out your order. You can think of Windows 95 or Windows NT as your waiter, taking orders based on your choices from a menu. The command you choose depends on which task you want Windows 95 or Windows NT to perform. While the menus list all the available commands, clicking the command actually carries it out. If a command opens another menu, you might only need to point to the command. However, to choose most other commands, you must click the command.

Open menus by pointing

1 Click the Start button.

The Start menu opens. If a menu item has a right-pointing arrow after its name, this means it opens another menu—a *cascading menu*.

2 Point to Programs.

The Programs menu, which is a cascading menu, opens to the right of the Start menu.

You can also press the right arrow key on the keyboard to open the cascading menu to the right.

3 On the Programs menu, point to Accessories.

The Accessories menu opens to the right of the Programs menu.

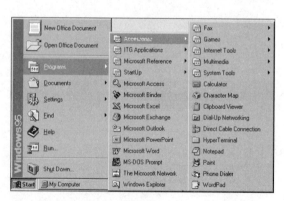

4 On the Start menu, point to Settings.

The Accessories and Programs menus close, and the Settings menu opens to the right of the Start menu.

5 Click an empty area of the Desktop.

The Start and Settings menus close.

Choose commands by clicking

1 Click the Start button.

The Start menu opens. Each item that does not have a right-pointing arrow after its name is a command that you can perform by clicking the command name.

You can also press the DOWN ARROW key to move the highlighted selection down the open Start menu.

2 Click Shut Down.

The Shut Down Windows dialog box opens, so you can make choices about shutting down Windows 95 or Windows NT.

3 Click the No button.

The Shut Down dialog box closes without shutting down Windows 95.

4 On the My Computer window, click File in the menu bar.

The File menu opens.

5 On the File menu, click Close.

The My Computer window closes.

6 On the Recycle Bin window, click File.

7 On the File menu, click Close.

The Recycle Bin window closes. Your Desktop should look similar to the following illustration.

You can also use the DOWN ARROW key on the keyboard to move down the open menu and then press ENTER to choose the command you want.

Specifying Options in Dialog Boxes

When you give your meal order in a restaurant, sometimes the waiter needs more information about your meal choices, such as whether you want soup or salad, what kind of salad dressing you prefer, or whether you want rice or baked potato.

In the same way, some commands require more information from you before they can be carried out. For example, when you choose the Help command on the Start menu, Windows 95 or Windows NT needs more information about the topic for which you want Help. Even when you choose the Shut Down command, you are asked what kind of shutdown you want. You specify this additional information through windows called *dialog boxes*. When you choose a command followed by an ellipsis (...), a dialog box appears.

Dialog boxes can take many different forms, but they always display choices or areas in which you select or enter the required additional information. As soon as you specify the required information, the program can continue carrying out your command. The following table summarizes the most common ways to respond to the options in a dialog box.

To use this dialog box option	Do this
Check box A small square next to a word or phrase. 	Click in the square to activate or deactivate the option. When a checkmark or an "X" appears, the option is active.
Command button A rectangular button labeled with a command. 	Click the button to carry out the command. This action often closes the dialog box. Many dialog boxes include three command buttons labeled OK, Cancel, and Help.
List box A box containing a list of items. A list box sometimes includes an arrow that makes the list drop down. 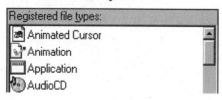	Click the desired item to select it. If it is a drop-down list box, you can click the arrow first to display the option list.

To use this dialog box option	Do this
Option button A round button next to a word or phrase that represents one option in a set of mutually exclusive options. 	Click the button to activate or deactivate the option. When a black dot appears, the option is active. Only one button in a set can be selected at one time.
Text box A rectangular box in which you can enter text (letters, numbers, or symbols) from the keyboard. 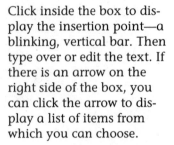	Click inside the box to display the insertion point—a blinking, vertical bar. Then type over or edit the text. If there is an arrow on the right side of the box, you can click the arrow to display a list of items from which you can choose.

Specify options in a dialog box

1   Click Start.

The Start menu appears.

2   Click Run.

The Run dialog box appears. This dialog box includes three command buttons. The Browse button ellipsis indicates that clicking this button will open another dialog box.

You'll learn more about the Run command in Lesson 4, "Using Programs and Accessories To Do Your Work."

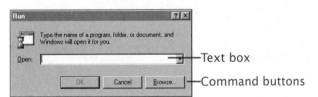

3   Click the Browse button.

The Browse dialog box appears. This dialog box includes three list boxes, a text box, and the Open and Cancel command buttons.

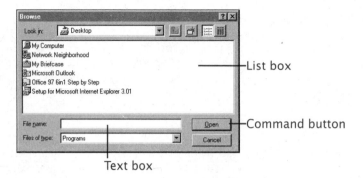

List box

Command button

Text box

4   Click the Cancel button.

The Browse dialog box closes, and the Run dialog box can be seen again.

5   If there is text in the text box, be sure the text is completely selected (highlighted), and then press the DELETE key to clear it.

If the text is not selected, drag the mouse pointer across the text to highlight it.

6   Type **calc** in the text box, and then click the OK button.

The Calculator accessory starts, as shown in the following illustration.

Managing the Windows on Your Desktop

Just as you might have several pieces of paper or file folders lying on your desk, you can have several different windows open on your Desktop at the same time. You can manage the size, position, and visibility of these multiple windows so that you can quickly see and work in the window you want.

Although the window looks like a simple rectangle with information in it, it is a flexible object. There are several graphic controls on every window that let you manage its position and size. The following illustration and table detail these controls.

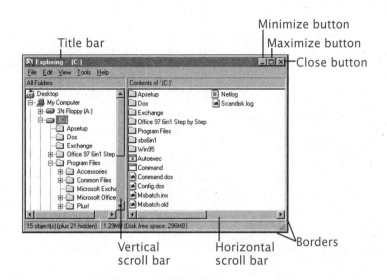

The bar at the top edge of all windows, showing the window's name.

Window element	Description and function
Title bar	The bar at the top edge of all windows, showing the window's name. By dragging this bar, you can move the window around the Desktop. When the title bar is highlighted, the window is active.
Minimize button	A button in the upper-right corner of most windows. The Minimize button looks like a single line. Clicking this button hides the window, but the program continues running. The window can be restored by clicking the button with its name on the taskbar.
Maximize button	A button in the upper-right corner of most windows. The Maximize button looks like a single window. Clicking this button enlarges the window to fill the entire screen.
Restore button	A button in the upper-right corner of a maximized window. This button looks like two overlapping windows. Clicking this button sets the window to the size and position it was before it was maximized.
Close button	A button in the upper-right corner of all windows. The Close button has an "X" on it. Clicking this button closes the window, removes the corresponding button from the taskbar, and might end the program that was running in the window.

Window element	Description and function
Borders	The visible lines surrounding all sides of a restored (not maximized) window. Dragging a side of the border changes the height or width of the window. Dragging a corner changes the height and width of the window simultaneously.
Horizontal scroll bar	The horizontal bar that appears along the bottom of any window when the window contains information that is wider than the window's current width. The scroll bar moves the display of the window's contents horizontally, without changing the window's size or location.
Vertical scroll bar	The vertical bar that appears along the right side of any window when the window contains information that is longer than the window's current length. The scroll bar moves the display of the contents in a window vertically, without changing the window's size or location.

In the following exercises, you'll practice with each of the window controls so that you can successfully manage the windows on your Desktop.

Sizing and Moving Windows

Sizing and moving windows is especially useful when you have two or more windows open on your Desktop and you want to view a window that's obscured by another window, or when you want to view two windows side by side.

Maximize and restore a window

1   Double-click the My Computer icon. If necessary, drag the Calculator title bar to move the Calculator window out of the way.

The My Computer window appears.

Maximize

2   Click the Maximize button.

The My Computer window enlarges to fill the entire Desktop. The Maximize button changes to the Restore button.

Restore

3   Click the Restore button.

The My Computer window returns to its previous size.

Minimize and restore a window

Minimize

You'll learn more about the taskbar in Lesson 2, "Getting Around in Windows 95 or Windows NT."

1 On the upper-right corner of the My Computer window, click the Minimize button.

The My Computer window disappears, but its name remains on the taskbar at the bottom of the screen.

2 Click the My Computer button on the taskbar.

The My Computer window returns to its previous size and location on the Desktop.

Resize a window

1 Position the mouse pointer on the right border of the My Computer window.

The pointer shape changes to a two-headed arrow pointing left and right.

2 Drag the border approximately one inch to the left to make the window smaller.

3 Point to the top border of the My Computer window.

The pointer shape changes to a two-headed arrow pointing up and down.

4 Drag the border approximately two inches downward to make it smaller.

5 Point to the lower-left corner of the My Computer window.

The pointer shape changes to a two-headed diagonal arrow.

6 Drag the border diagonally, approximately one inch upward and one inch to the right.

Your window size changes in the direction that you just dragged.

Move a window

1 Point to the words "My Computer" in the title bar.

2 Drag the title bar of the My Computer window until the window is positioned in the upper-left corner of the Desktop.

3 Drag the title bar of the My Computer window until the window is positioned about in the center of the Desktop.

Scrolling a Window's Contents

If a window is large enough to display its entire contents, the window is surrounded only by a title bar and borders. However, when you add more to the contents of the window, or when you decrease the size of the window, portions of the window contents can become hidden. When this happens, a set of scroll bars appear on the right or bottom edges of the window. You can use these bars to bring hidden portions of the window contents into view.

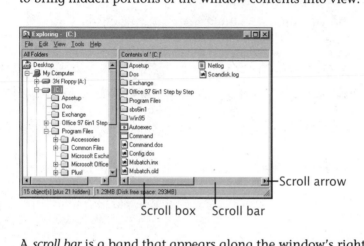

Scroll box · Scroll bar

A *scroll bar* is a band that appears along the window's right edge for vertical scrolling, or along the bottom edge for horizontal scrolling. Each scroll bar contains scroll arrows and a scroll box. When a scroll bar appears on your window, this indicates that you have more information in the window than is currently visible.

The *scroll arrows* appear on either side of the scroll bar. You can use these arrow buttons to move the scroll box in either direction.

The *scroll box* is the rectangle that appears inside the scroll bar. Its relative location on the scroll bar indicates the position of the window's visible contents relative to its total contents. You can drag the scroll box to scroll the window contents in larger increments than with the scroll arrows.

Scroll a window

1   Drag the lower-right corner of the My Computer window until the window is about two inches square.

Vertical and horizontal scroll bars appear on the My Computer window, as shown in the following illustration.

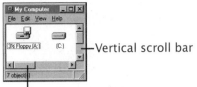

Vertical scroll bar

Horizontal scroll bar

2 On the vertical scroll bar, click the down arrow twice.

Other items in the My Computer window come into view.

3 On the horizontal scroll bar, click the light gray scroll bar area to the right of the scroll box.

Other items in the My Computer window come into view.

4 Drag the horizontal scroll box to the left.

5 Continue to experiment with the vertical and horizontal scroll bars, boxes, and arrow buttons.

6 Drag the borders of the My Computer window until the window is close to the size it was when you first opened it.

One Step Further: Organizing Windows on Your Desktop

In addition to managing individual windows on your Desktop, you can quickly organize all the windows on your Desktop by using the Desktop pop-up menu.

1 Use the right mouse button to click an empty area of the taskbar.

A pop-up menu appears, displaying commands for arranging windows on your Desktop.

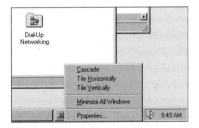

2 If you're using Windows 95, click Cascade. If you're using Windows NT, click Cascade Windows.

All open windows are arranged on the Desktop in a cascading fashion, with the title bar of each window showing.

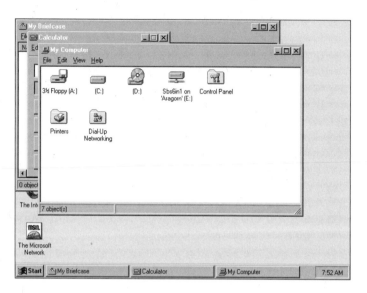

3 Use the right mouse button to click an empty area of the taskbar.

4 On the pop-up menu, click Tile Horizontally if you're using Windows 95 or Tile Windows Horizontally if you're using Windows NT.

All open windows are arranged in rectangles, as shown in the following illustration.

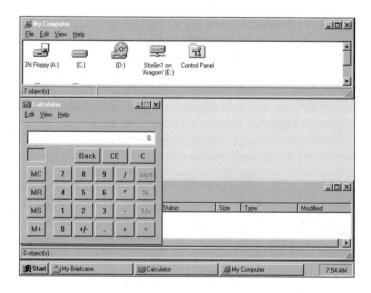

5   Use the right mouse button to click an empty area of the taskbar.

6   On the pop-up menu, click Minimize All Windows.

All open windows are minimized.

7   Click the buttons of each window name on the taskbar to restore the minimized windows.

Finish the lesson

Close

1   On the upper-right corner of the My Computer window, click the Close button.

The My Computer window closes.

2   On the Calculator window, click the Close button.

3   If any other windows are open, click the Close button.

4   If any window is minimized, use the right mouse button to click the window's taskbar button, and then click Close.

You are now ready to start the next lesson, or you can work on your own.

5   If you are finished using Windows 95 or Windows NT for now, on the Start menu click Shut Down, select the appropriate option bar, and then click Yes.

Lesson Summary

To	Do this
Move the mouse pointer on the Desktop	With your hand on the mouse as it sits on a flat surface next to your keyboard, move the mouse.
Click with the mouse	Press and release the mouse button.
Double-click with the mouse	Press and release the mouse button twice in rapid succession.
Drag an item on the Desktop	Point to the item, hold down the mouse button, slide the mouse to the new location, and then release the mouse button.
Open a menu	Click the menu name on the menu bar.
Close a menu without executing a command	Click an empty area on the Desktop. *or* Press ESC on the keyboard.

To	Do this	Button
Choose a command	Click a command on a menu.	
Maximize a window to fill the Desktop	Click the Maximize button on the window.	
Restore a maximized window to its previous size	Click the Restore button on the window.	
Minimize a window	Click the Minimize button on the window.	
Restore a minimized window	Click the item's name on the taskbar.	
Resize a window	Drag one of the window's borders or corners.	
Move a window	Drag the window's title bar.	
Scroll a window's contents	Drag the scroll box. *or* Click the scroll arrows.	
Close a window	Click the Close button on the window.	

You'll learn more about online Help in Lesson 2, "Getting Around in Windows 95 or Windows NT."

For online information about	From the Help dialog box, click Index and then type	
	Windows 95	Windows NT
Using the mouse	**mouse**	**mouse**
Using menus	**menus**	**menus, taskbar**
Using dialog boxes	**dialog boxes, using**	**dialog box Help**
Controlling a window's appearance	**window**	**windows**

Lesson

2

Getting Around in Windows 95 or Windows NT

Estimated time

30 min.

In this lesson you will learn how to:

- Locate and start documents and programs stored on your computer and on a network.
- Activate and control documents and programs using the taskbar.
- Look up topics and learn about Windows 95 or Windows NT using the online Help system.

At a new job, once you feel comfortable with your immediate working area, you might take a tour of your building. You'd probably learn where the supplies are, where the coffee is, who's who, and what's the best way to get things done.

In Lesson 1, you learned how to manage the individual windows and other objects that appear on your Desktop, and how to give commands to the computer. Now you're ready to go beyond your Desktop and learn more sophisticated techniques. In this lesson, you'll explore how to find and open the documents and programs on your computer system. These documents and programs are the files you use to do your everyday work.

Starting Programs

When you work, you use different tools and equipment to accomplish the tasks associated with your job. When you work on a computer, you use a variety of programs to create different types of documents and to do different kinds of work. A *program* is a detailed set of logical instructions to the computer, telling it to perform a specific task or a group of related tasks. For example, the job of one simple program might be to display the time on your Desktop. The job of a more complex program, such as the Microsoft Excel spreadsheet program, might be to perform calculations and draw graphs based on numeric data. Microsoft Windows 95 and Microsoft Windows NT come with a number of built-in programs, called *accessories*, that can be used for different purposes. One easy way you can find and start many of these programs is to use the Start button on the taskbar at the bottom of your screen.

Unless otherwise noted, screens from Windows 95 are shown in Part 1 of this book. The corresponding screens from Windows NT are the same or very similar.

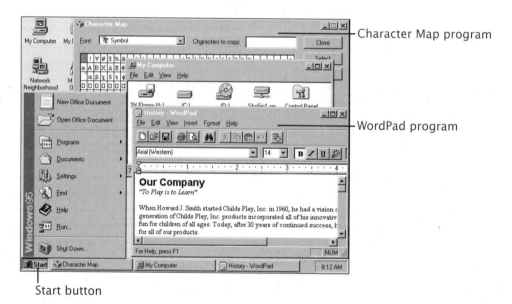

— Character Map program

— WordPad program

Start button

Start and use a program

Suppose you need to write a memo. In this exercise, you'll start WordPad, a simple text editing program that is a Windows 95 and Windows NT accessory.

1 Click the Start button.

The Start menu appears.

2 On the Start menu, point to Programs.

As soon as you point to Programs, the Programs menu appears in a cascading fashion.

3 On the Programs menu, point to Accessories.

When you point to Accessories, the Accessories menu appears.

4 On the Accessories menu, click WordPad.

WordPad opens. The title of the WordPad window also appears on the taskbar at the bottom of your Desktop. At this point, you could write your memo.

If your screen looks different from this illustration, refer to the Appendix, "Matching the Exercises."

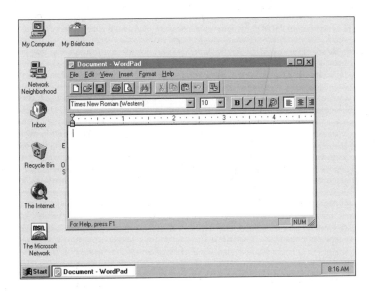

Finding Documents

To find information, such as a letter, in your computer, you need to understand how computers store information. All information on a computer is stored in *files*, individually named sets of information. When you enter information, like a letter, into the computer using a program, you store this information in a *document file* (usually just called a *document*). The documents you create might include letters, reports, presentations, tables, graphics, charts, and detailed lists.

You'll learn more about organizing your documents and folders in Lesson 5, "Setting Up a Filing System," and Lesson 6, "Managing Files and Disks."

As you work, you will probably create a lot of documents. You can keep these documents organized in *folders*. Folders are comparable to file folders in a filing cabinet. Each folder can hold one or more documents. Your folders are stored on the *hard disk*, which is like a huge filing cabinet inside your computer. Your folders and documents can also be stored on a *floppy disk*. A floppy disk is like a small, portable filing cabinet for your computer.

You probably think of your work in terms of the end product, such as a letter, rather than the program that created that letter, such as Microsoft Word. In Windows 95 and Windows NT, you can find the various documents you create and then open them directly, without first having to find and open the program that created them. With your documents stored in different folders, disk drives, or even in different computers on your network system, you can use one of these tools to find your documents:

■ Windows Explorer or Windows NT Explorer

■ My Computer and Network Neighborhood icons

■ Documents menu

In the following sections, you'll try out these tools.

Finding Documents Using Explorer

With *Windows Explorer* or *Windows NT Explorer*, you can search through and get into all the computers, disk drives, folders, and files in your computer and network system. Although you'll be learning more about Windows Explorer in Lesson 5, "Setting Up a Filing System," the next exercise is a quick preview.

Open documents using Explorer

In this exercise, you'll look for a document file stored on your system that outlines the history of Childs Play, Inc. You'll use Explorer to browse through your system.

1   Click Start.

The Start menu appears.

2   On the Start menu, point to Programs.

The Programs menu appears.

3   On the Programs menu, click Windows Explorer or Windows NT Explorer.

Explorer starts, and the title in the title bar begins with the word "Exploring." A button for this program appears on the taskbar at the bottom of your Desktop. Explorer is divided into two windows. The left window lists the computers, disk drives, and folders on your system. The right window lists the contents of what you have selected in the left window.

If you have not installed the Part1 Windows Practice files, refer to "Installing and Using the Practice and Camcorder Files," earlier in this book.

4   In the left window of Explorer, titled All Folders, find the Office 97 6in1 Step by Step folder, and click it. You might need to use the scroll bar to find the folder.

The contents of the Office 97 6in1 Step by Step folder appear in the right window, displaying the names of other files and folders stored there.

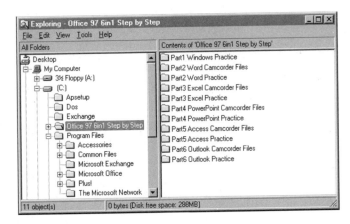

5 In the right window, find the Part1 Windows Practice folder, and double-click it.

The contents of the Part1 Windows Practice folder appear in the right window, displaying the names of other files and folders stored there.

6 In the right window, which shows the contents of the Part1 Windows Practice folder, find the WordPad document called History, and double-click it.

The History document appears in WordPad.

TROUBLESHOOTING If an error message appears when performing step 6, click OK to close the message box, close the WordPad window, and then see the Troubleshooting section in the Appendix.

Close

7 Click the Close button in the upper-right corner of the History - WordPad document window.

The History document and WordPad close.

Minimize

8 Click the Minimize button in the upper-right corner of the Exploring window, and then in the Document - WordPad window.

TIP You can also start a program in Explorer. To do this, find the program file and double-click its name. For example, to start Microsoft Excel without opening an existing workbook, use Explorer to find the folder in which the Microsoft Excel program file is stored. Double-click the program file name (in this case, EXCEL.EXE), and the program opens with a blank sheet for you to start entering your data.

29

Getting Around in the Computer Community

My Computer

Windows 95 and Windows NT display a few standard icons on your Desktop to graphically organize the files on your computer system. These icons are labeled My Computer, Network Neighborhood, Recycle Bin, and Inbox.

Network Neighborhood

Inbox (Microsoft Exchange)

> **NOTE** If your computer system does not include an installed network, you probably will not see the Network Neighborhood icon. If your computer system does not include an installed modem with some type of communication software, you probably will not see the Inbox icon.

The icons on the left represent your computing community. You can think of the My Computer icon as your home base, the computer on which you're actually working. When you open My Computer, you can view the folders and files that are stored on your own computer's disk drives. You can also see any other disk drives and computers on your network to which you have an active connection.

Recycle Bin

If My Computer is home base, then Network Neighborhood represents the outside community that provides different types of services to which you have access. When you open Network Neighborhood, you can view the folders and files that are stored on other computers in your network of computers.

The Internet

You'll learn more about My Computer, Network Neighborhood, and the Recycle Bin in Lesson 6, "Managing Files and Disks." However, you can orient yourself to where your files are stored with the following exercises.

View the files in the available computers

Suppose you're looking for a particular file that's stored somewhere on your computer system, but you're not sure exactly where. The first thing you would do is browse through the files stored on your computer system. In this exercise, you'll open My Computer and Network Neighborhood to see the files and folders stored there.

1 Double-click the My Computer icon.

A new window opens, listing the icons and names of the disk drives and CD-ROM drive on your computer. There are also folders for Control Panel, Printers, and Dial-Up Networking.

When you double-click an icon...

*If you don't see
the Dial-Up Net-
working folder,
but you do have
a modem in-
stalled, refer to
the Appendix,
"Matching the
Exercises."*

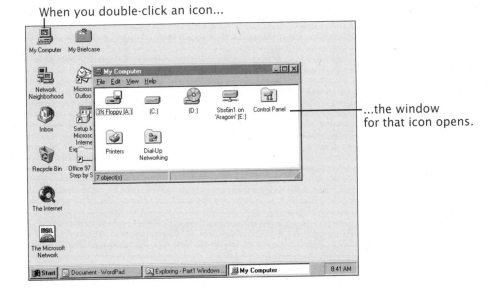

...the window
for that icon opens.

2   If you see the Network Neighborhood icon, double-click it. Otherwise,
proceed to the next exercise.

If necessary, move the My Computer window out of the way by dragging
the title bar. You'll see a list of the various computers, disks, and public
folders for your workgroup. You'll also see the Entire Network icon.

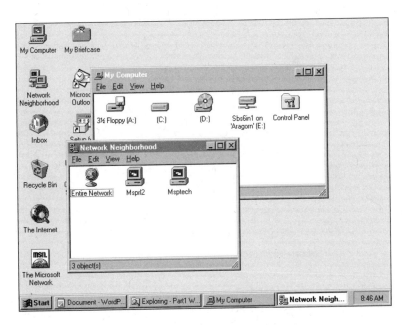

Close

3   Click the Close button to close the Network Neighborhood window.

31

Change drives and folders in My Computer

Maybe you think that the file you're looking for is on a CD-ROM instead of the hard disk. In this exercise, you'll change disk drives to browse through the files that you have on a CD-ROM.

1 Be sure that the My Computer window is active. You know a window is active when the title bar is highlighted.

If another window is active, on the taskbar, click My Computer.

2 Insert the Microsoft Office 97 Professional 6-in-1 Step by Step CD-ROM into your CD-ROM drive.

3 Double-click the CD-ROM icon in the My Computer window to switch to it.

A new window opens displaying the contents of your CD. Your screen should look similar to the following illustration.

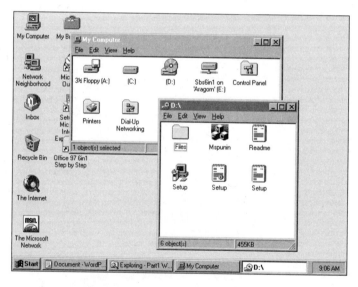

4 Double-click the Files folder.

A new window opens, displaying the contents of the Files folder.

5 Close the Files window by clicking its Close button.

6 Close the CD-ROM window by clicking its Close button.

7 Remove the CD from your CD-ROM drive.

☒

Close

Open documents and programs in My Computer

After browsing through My Computer, suppose you find the file you've been looking for. In this exercise, you'll open the logo file from a window in My Computer.

1 In the My Computer window, double-click the (C:) icon.

The (C:) window appears, displaying the names of the files and other folders stored on your hard disk.

2 Double-click the Office 97 6in1 Step by Step folder, and then double-click the Part1 Windows Practice folder.

The Part1 Windows Practice folder appears, displaying the names of its files and folders.

3 Double-click the Logo Yellows file.

The Logo Yellows file opens in the Paint program, as shown in the following illustration.

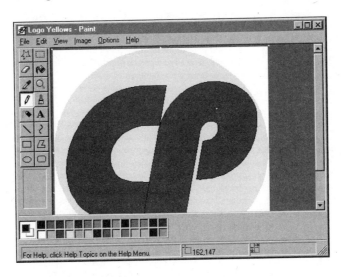

Paint is a drawing program that you can use to draw and view graphics files. Paint is provided as a Windows 95 and Windows NT accessory.

Opening Your Recently Used Documents

In the course of doing your work, you might often return to the same documents in successive work sessions. Perhaps it takes several days to complete a certain document, or maybe there are documents that you refer to while doing other work. Instead of having to search for these documents using My Computer or Windows Explorer each time you need them, you can use the Documents menu to open your recently used documents. The Documents menu remembers the last 15 documents you opened, regardless of where they are stored.

Open your recent work

Maybe you want to open the History document you referred to earlier in this lesson to make a few changes and then print it. In this exercise, you'll use the Documents menu to find the document file quickly.

1 Click Start. On the Start menu, point to Documents.

The Documents menu appears.

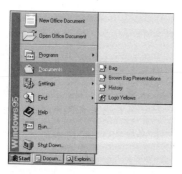

2 On the Documents menu, click History.

The History document opens in WordPad. You can now make changes and print the document.

 TIP To completely clear your Documents menu so that a new documents list will be created, click Start, point to Settings, and click Taskbar. In the Taskbar Properties dialog box, click the Start Menu Programs tab, and then under Documents Menu, click the Clear button. Click OK.

Managing Multiple Windows

In a typical day, you might often work on two or three projects at the same time. Or, you might refer to one project while working on another. With Windows 95 or Windows NT, you can work on multiple projects at the same time, with each project running in its own window. And with the taskbar, it's easy to find all your open windows.

The taskbar lists any open documents or programs, whether or not their windows are visible. You can use the taskbar to manipulate the various programs you are running. The taskbar is always visible on the edge of your Desktop, unless you explicitly hide it.

As soon as you start a program or open a window of any kind, its name appears on the taskbar. If you open another window, and then want to view the first window again, you can click its name on the taskbar.

Manage multiple windows with the taskbar

You now have several documents and programs open, as you might have in a typical workday. In this exercise, you practice using the taskbar to view what you need when you need it.

Minimize

1   Be sure that the History - WordPad document window is the active window on top of your Desktop. If it is not, click its button on the taskbar.

2   Click the Minimize button near the upper-right corner of the History window.

The History window is reduced to its button on the taskbar. The History - WordPad document no longer appears anywhere on your Desktop. However, the presence of its button on the taskbar indicates that the program is still running.

As you add more windows to your Desktop, the taskbar buttons become smaller and the names more abbreviated. When you point to an abbreviated taskbar button, its full name appears.

3   Click the Minimize button on the Logo Yellows Paint window.

The Logo Yellows Paint window disappears, but its button remains on the taskbar.

4   On the taskbar, click History - WordPad.

The History window is restored as the active window on top of your Desktop. Whether a window is minimized or just behind other windows, clicking the window's button on the taskbar always brings it to the top of your Desktop so that you can work with it again.

5   On the taskbar, click Document - WordPad.

The blank WordPad window becomes the active window.

6   On the Document - WordPad window, click the Close button.

The document closes, and the WordPad button disappears from the taskbar.

Close

If you use the right mouse button to click an empty space on your taskbar, a pop-up menu appears that includes commands for arranging all your windows on the Desktop.

7   On the taskbar, click Exploring - Part1 Windows Practice.

Explorer becomes the active window.

8   Quit Explorer by clicking its Close button.

Explorer closes. Its button is also removed from the taskbar.

Hiding and Showing the Taskbar

Suppose you need to see your entire page on your screen and you don't want your taskbar using up some of that screen space. If you prefer, you can hide the taskbar. This keeps your Desktop as open and available as possible.

Hide the taskbar

Imagine that you're working on a dense document for which you need every square inch of space on your Desktop. In this exercise, you hide the taskbar so that you can see the entire screen.

1 On the taskbar, click History - WordPad.

2 On the History - WordPad window, click the Maximize button.

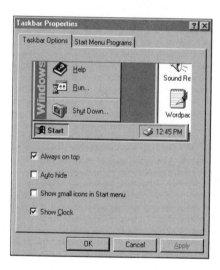

Maximize

3 Click Start. On the Start menu, point to Settings.

4 On the Settings menu, click Taskbar.

The Taskbar Properties dialog box appears. This dialog box is "tabbed" at the top, letting you choose between two categories of options.

You can also open the Task-bar Properties dialog box with a pop-up menu. Use the right mouse button to click an empty space on the taskbar, and then click Properties.

5 The Taskbar Options tab should already be active. If it is not, click the Taskbar Options tab.

6 Select Auto Hide, and then click OK.

Your taskbar is hidden from view.

View a hidden taskbar temporarily

When your taskbar is hidden, you still might need to use it from time to time. In this exercise, you'll bring the hidden taskbar into view temporarily.

1   Move your mouse pointer close to the bottom edge of your Desktop.

   The hidden taskbar reappears.

2   Click Start. On the Start menu, point to Programs, and then click Windows Explorer or Windows NT Explorer.

   The taskbar remains visible until Explorer appears. Then the taskbar disappears.

Show a hidden taskbar

In this exercise, you'll restore your taskbar so that it always appears on your Desktop again.

1   Move your mouse pointer close to the bottom edge of your Desktop.

   The hidden taskbar reappears.

2   Click Start. On the Start menu, point to Settings.

3   On the Settings menu, click Taskbar.

   The Taskbar Properties dialog box appears. Be sure that the Taskbar Options tab is active.

4   Click the Auto Hide check box to clear it, and then click OK.

   Your taskbar appears again at the bottom of your Desktop.

Restore

5   On the History - WordPad window, click the Restore button.

   The document is restored to its original size.

Getting Help with Windows 95 or Windows NT

When you're at work and you want to find out more information about how to do a project, you might ask a co-worker or consult a reference book. When you need information about a procedure or how to use a particular feature on your computer, the online Help system is one of the most efficient ways to learn. The online Help system for Windows 95 or Windows NT is available from the Start menu, and you can choose the type of help you want from the Help dialog box.

For instructions on broad categories, you can look at the Help contents. Or, you can search the Help index for information on specific topics. The Help information is short and concise, so you can get the exact information you need quickly. There are also shortcut buttons in many Help topics that you can use to directly switch to the task you want to perform.

Viewing Help Contents

The Help Contents tab is organized like a book's table of contents. As you choose top-level topics, or chapters, you see a list of more detailed topics from which to choose. Many of these chapters have special "Tips and Tricks" subsections that can help you work more efficiently.

Find Help on general categories

Suppose you want to learn more about using Calculator, a program that comes with Windows 95 and Windows NT. In this exercise, you'll look up information in the online Help system.

If you have used a previous version of Windows, you might be interested in the Help topic named "If you've used Windows before."

1 Click Start. On the Start menu, click Help.

The Help Topics dialog box appears. If this is the first time you've opened Help since you set up Windows 95 or Windows NT, you might need to wait a minute while the Help system is set up.

2 If necessary, click the Contents tab to make it active.

3 Double-click "Introducing Windows" or "Introducing Windows NT."

A set of subtopics appears.

4 Double-click "Using Windows Accessories."

5 Double-click "For General Use," and then double-click "Calculator: for making calculations."

A Help topic window appears.

6 Click the Maximize button on the Help window.

The Help window fills the entire screen.

Close

7 Click the Close button to close the Help window.

Finding Help on Specific Topics

There are two methods for finding specific Help topics: the Index tab and the Find tab. The Help Index tab is organized like a book's index. Keywords for topics are organized alphabetically. You can either scroll through the list of keywords or type the keyword you want to find. One or more topic choices are then presented.

With the Find tab, you can also enter a keyword. The main difference is that you get a list of all Help topics in which that keyword appears, not just the topics that begin with that word.

Find Help on specific topics using the Help index

In this exercise, you'll use the Help index to learn how to change the background pattern of your Desktop.

1 Click Start. On the Start menu, click Help.

The Help dialog box appears.

2 Click the Index tab to make it active.

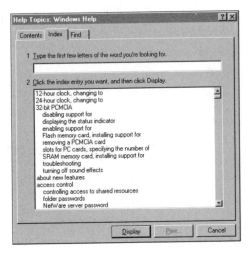

3   In the text box, type **desktop**

A list of Desktop-related topics appears.

4   If you're using Windows 95, double-click the topic named "background pictures or patterns, changing." If you're using Windows NT, double-click the topic named "patterns."

5   If you're using Windows 95, double-click the topic named "Changing the background of your desktop." If you're using Windows NT, double-click the topic named "To change the background of your desktop."

6   Read the Help topic.

7   Click the jump button in Step 1 of the Help topic.

Jump

The Display Properties dialog box appears. If you want, you can immediately perform the task you were looking up in Help.

8   Click the Close button on the Display Properties dialog box.

9   Click the Close button on the Help window.

> **TIP**   You can print any Help topic. Click the Options button in the upper-right corner of any Help topic window, and then click Print Topic.

Find Help on specific topics using the Find tab

In this exercise, you'll use the Find tab to learn how to change your printer's settings.

1   Click Start. On the Start menu, click Help.

The Help dialog box appears.

2   Click the Find tab to make it active.

3   If you see a Find Setup Wizard, be sure that the Minimize Database Size (recommended) option button is selected, and then click Next. Click Finish to exit the wizard.

The wizard creates a search index for your Help files. This might take a few minutes. The next time you use Find, you won't have to wait for the index to be created. The Find tab appears.

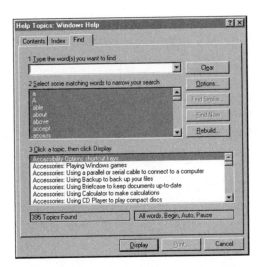

4   In the first box, type **print**, and then in the second box, click "printer."

All topics that have to do with printers are displayed in the third box.

5   If you're using Windows 95, in the third box, click the "Changing pointer settings" topic, and then click Display. If you're using Windows NT, in the third box, click the "To change printer settings" topic (use the scroll bar to find it), and then click Display.

The Help topic appears.

6   Read the Help topic.

7   Click the Close button on the Help window.

Find Help on a dialog box

Almost every dialog box includes a question mark button in the upper-right corner of its window. When you click this button and then click any dialog-box control, a Help window appears that explains what the control is and how to use it. In this exercise, you'll get help on specific elements in a dialog box by using pop-up Help.

1   Click Start. On the Start menu, click Run.

The Run dialog box appears.

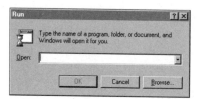

Help

2   Click the Help button.

The mouse pointer changes to an arrow with a question mark.

3   Click the Open text box.

A Help window appears, providing information on how to use the Open text box.

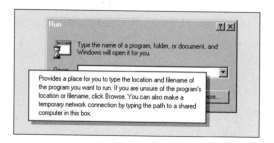

4   Click anywhere on the Desktop, or press ESC to close the Help window.

5   Click the Help button again, and then click Browse.

Help displays information about the Browse button.

6   Click Browse.

The Browse dialog box appears.

7   Click the Help button, and then click the Files Of Type list box.

The Help window appears with information for the list box.

8   Click Cancel.

9   In the Run dialog box, click Cancel.

TIP   You can change the font size in Help topic windows. Click the Options button in the upper-right corner of any Help topic window, and then point to Font to change the font size.

One Step Further: Move and Change the Size of the Taskbar

You can move your taskbar to any of the four sides of your Desktop. You can also make the taskbar wider if you like.

1   Move your mouse pointer to an empty space on your taskbar.

2   Drag the taskbar to the right edge of your Desktop.

   The taskbar is docked along the right side of your screen. You can move the taskbar to any of the four edges of your Desktop by dragging it in this manner.

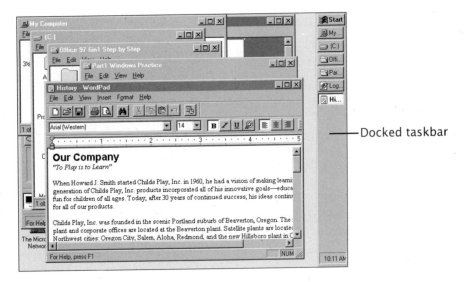

—Docked taskbar

3   Drag the taskbar to the top of your Desktop.

   The taskbar docks at the top of your screen.

4   Drag the taskbar back to the bottom of your Desktop.

   The taskbar docks in its original position.

5   Move the mouse pointer to the inside edge of the taskbar so that its shape changes to a two-headed arrow.

6   Drag the edge of the taskbar upward to widen it.

   You can make the taskbar wider or narrower by dragging its inside edge.

7   Drag the edge of the taskbar downward to return it to its original size.

Finish the lesson

Close

1 Close all open windows by clicking the Close button in the upper-right corner of each window.

2 If any window is minimized, use the right mouse button to click the window's taskbar button, and then click Close.

You are now ready to start the next lesson, or you can work on your own.

3 If you are finished using Windows 95 or Windows NT for now, on the Start menu click Shut Down, select the appropriate option button, and then click Yes.

Lesson Summary

To	Do this
Start a program	Click Start, point to Programs, and then click the program. *or* From Explorer, find the program, and then double-click its icon.
Start Explorer	Click Start, point to Programs, and then click Windows Explorer or Windows NT Explorer.
Open a document	From Explorer, find the document, and then double-click its icon.
Open a recently used document	Click Start, point to Documents, and then click the document name.
View and open the contents of disks, CD-ROM, folders, or files on your computer	Double-click the My Computer icon. Double-click succeeding disk, CD-ROM, folder, or file icons.
View and open the contents of computers, disks, or public folders on the network	Double-click the Network Neighborhood icon. Double-click succeeding disk, folder, or file icons.
Manage multiple windows with the taskbar	Click the Minimize button of any open window to reduce the window to a taskbar button. Click any taskbar button to restore or activate its window.
Hide the taskbar	Click Start, point to Settings, and then click Taskbar. Click the Taskbar Options tab, select Auto Hide, and then click OK.

To	Do this	Button
Temporarily view a hidden taskbar	Move the mouse pointer close to the edge of the Desktop where the taskbar was last docked. If you're not sure where the taskbar was docked, move the mouse pointer to all four edges of the Desktop until the taskbar appears.	
Show a hidden taskbar	Click Start, point to Settings, and then click Taskbar. Click the Taskbar Options tab, clear the Auto Hide check box, and then click the OK button.	
Find Help on a general topic	Click Start, click Help, click the Contents tab, and then double-click the topic you want.	
Find Help on a specific topic	Click Start, click Help, click the Index or Find tab, type a keyword, and then double-click the topic you want.	
Find Help on a dialog box	Click the Help button on the dialog box, and then click the dialog box control for which you want help.	🔲

For online information about	From the Help dialog box, click Index and then type	
	<u>Windows 95</u>	<u>Windows NT</u>
Opening programs using the Start button	**opening, programs**	**opening: programs**
Opening documents using the Start button	**opening, files**	**opening: files**
Using the My Computer icon	**My Computer**	**My Computer**
Using the Network Neighborhood icon	**Network Neighborhood**	**Network Neighborhood**
Managing documents and programs using the taskbar	**taskbar**	**taskbar**
Referencing online Help	**Help**	**Help**

Lesson

3

Customizing Your Desktop for the Way You Work

In this lesson you will learn how to:

Estimated time
40 min.

- Access frequently used programs by adding commands to your Start and Programs menus.
- Create shortcuts to frequently used files, and display these shortcuts as Desktop icons.
- Set the computer date and time.
- Customize your display to suit your preferences.
- Configure your mouse to reflect the way you work.

People often tailor their work areas with an eye toward comfort and efficiency. Sometimes this involves arranging furniture, adding plants, or hanging artwork on the walls. It's also convenient to have within reach the tools, equipment, and supplies you use most often.

In Microsoft Windows 95 and Microsoft Windows NT, you can change various aspects of your computer work environment. You can customize your menus to quickly start the programs you use most. You can create shortcuts to documents you frequently open. You can also individualize your display and your mouse. In this lesson, you'll find out how you can create an environment that reflects your individual style and working patterns.

Customizing Your Menus

If you use your telephone, fax machine, stapler, or tape dispenser on a regular basis, you probably have them on or near your desk for easy and convenient access. In Windows 95 and Windows NT, you can add a command for any installed program to your Start or Programs menu. Then you always have quick access to the accessories or other programs that you use most often.

You can also remove items that you rarely use from your Start and Programs menus.

Unless other-
wise noted,
screens from
Windows 95 are
shown in Part 1
of this book.
The correspond-
ing screens
from Windows
NT are the
same or very
similar.

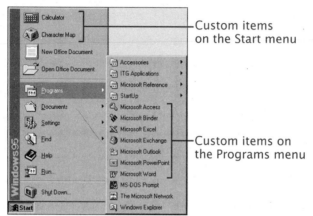

Custom items
on the Start menu

Custom items on
the Programs menu

Adding Commands to Your Start Menu

Adding a command to your Start menu is an efficient way to open any program you have set up on your computer system. For example, if you use the Calculator accessory often, you can add the Calculator command to your Start menu. Then, whenever you need Calculator, you can just click the Start button and then click Calculator. This is more direct than clicking the Start button, pointing to Programs, pointing to Accessories, and then clicking Calculator.

Or, suppose you have set up a new program, such as Microsoft Access, on your computer system. If you use Microsoft Access every day, it might be convenient to add Microsoft Access to your Start menu.

NOTE   Adding a command to your Start menu makes the command more readily available to you. However, the command does not automatically execute when you start Windows 95 or Windows NT. See "One Step Further: Starting Programs Automatically" later in this lesson for more information about starting programs automatically.

Add commands to your Start menu

Character Map is an accessory used mainly for inserting special characters and symbols into your documents. Suppose you use Character Map almost every day. Because you're constantly referring to it, you want it to be more easily accessible. In this exercise, you'll add Character Map to your Start menu.

1 Click Start. On the Start menu, point to Settings.

Another way to open the Taskbar Properties dialog box is to use the right mouse button to click an empty area of the taskbar and then click Properties.

2 On the Settings menu, click Taskbar and then click the Start Menu Programs tab to make it active.

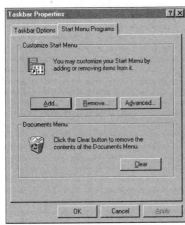

3 Under Customize Start Menu, click Add.

The Create Shortcut dialog box appears.

4 In the Command Line text box, type **charmap** and then click Next.

The Select Program Folder dialog box appears.

If you don't know the filename of a command you want to add, you can search for it by clicking Browse.

5 Click the Start Menu folder, which is the second item in the list, and then click Next.

6 When prompted for the name of the program, type **Character Map** and then click Finish.

7 Click OK, and then click the Start button.

The Character Map command, along with its associated icon, appears at the top of the Start menu. Items you add to the Start menu appear in alphabetical order above the default Start menu items.

You can learn more about Character Map in online Help.

8 On the Start menu, click Character Map.

Character Map starts.

9 Click the Close button on the Character Map window to close it.

Adding Commands to Your Programs Menu

When you first start using Windows 95 or Windows NT, the Programs menu includes a few important programs, such as Windows Explorer or Windows NT Explorer. However, you can customize the Programs menu to contain the startup commands of all your installed programs, or the programs you use most frequently. Adding program commands to the Programs menu is very similar to adding commands to the Start menu. The result is similar as well—the command appears on the Programs menu rather than on the Start menu. Where you add the command—on the Programs menu or the Start menu—is simply a matter of how you prefer to organize your menus.

You can also remove program commands from the Programs menu. You might, for example, want to remove commands for programs you don't use very often. When you remove a command from the menu, the program itself is still available. Its command is just not available from the Programs menu. You can remove any Programs menu command you want, even if you didn't add it in the first place.

The program commands you will most likely add to your Programs menu will be for installed programs beyond those that came with Windows 95 or Windows NT—for example, Microsoft Publisher. In the following exercises, however, you'll practice with two accessories.

NOTE Unlike the Start menu or Programs menu, your Documents menu cannot be customized. Whenever you open a document, a shortcut to the document is automatically added to the Documents menu. The Documents menu lists shortcuts to the last 15 documents you have opened.

Add program commands to your Programs menu

Let's say that you want to add your frequently used programs to the Programs menu. In this exercise, you'll add Paint to the Programs menu.

1 Using the right mouse button, click an empty area of the taskbar.

A pop-up menu appears.

2 On the pop-up menu, click Properties.

The Taskbar Properties dialog box appears.

3 Click the Start Menu Programs tab to make it active, and then click Add.

If you don't know the name of a command you want to add, you can search for it by clicking Browse.

4 In the Command Line text box, type **pbrush** and then click Next.

5 Click the Programs folder, and then click Next.

6 When prompted for the name of the shortcut, type **Paint**, click Finish, and then click OK.

7 Click Start. On the Start menu, point to Programs.

The Paint command appears on the Programs menu in alphabetical order with the other commands.

8 On the Programs menu, click Paint.

Paint starts.

9 Click the Close button on the Paint window to close it.

Remove program commands from your Programs menu

Suppose that later you decide that you will not be using Paint as frequently as before, and you don't want it to appear on the Programs menu. In this exercise, you'll remove the Paint command from the Programs menu.

1   Use the right mouse button to click an empty area of the taskbar.

A pop-up menu appears, listing commands for the taskbar.

2   Click Properties.

The Taskbar Properties dialog box appears.

3   Click the Start Menu Programs tab to make it active, and then click Remove.

4   In the next window, click Paint, and then click Remove. If you are asked to confirm that you want to delete Paint, click Yes.

Paint is deleted from the Programs menu.

5   Click Close, and then in the Taskbar Properties dialog box, click OK.

6   Click Start. On the Start menu, point to Programs.

Paint no longer appears as a command on the Programs menu. However, you can still open it from the Accessories menu.

7   Click anywhere else on the Desktop to close the menus.

 TIP   You can remove any command you want from the Programs menu, even if it is a default command. If you change your mind, you can always add it back again.

Using Shortcuts

As part of your standard Desktop setup, you always see the My Computer and Recycle Bin icons on your Desktop. If your computer has a network system installed, you'll have the Network Neighborhood icon available to you. If your computer includes modem capabilities along with mail or fax capabilities, you will also see the Inbox icon on your Desktop.

While this setup is clean and spare, you might find it useful to add *shortcuts*, icons that graphically represent programs, folders, or documents that you use frequently. For example, you might use a spreadsheet program every day. Or, maybe you often access a certain public folder on the network. Perhaps there is a document you refer to or update every two or three days. Any of these is a good candidate for a shortcut that you can access directly from your Desktop.

Default icons

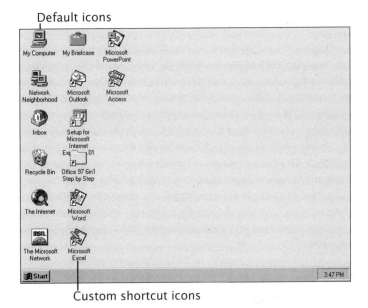

Custom shortcut icons

Creating New Shortcuts

A shortcut represents and functions as a pointer to the actual item, wherever it might be stored on your hard disk. When you double-click the icon to open the shortcut, you're opening the actual item to which the shortcut is pointing.

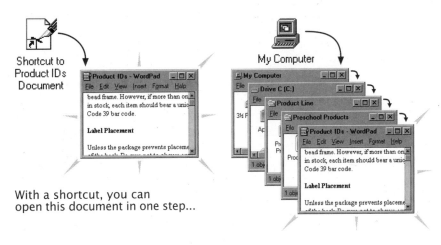

Shortcut to Product IDs Document

My Computer

With a shortcut, you can open this document in one step...

...instead of five steps.

Suppose you create a shortcut to a commonly used network folder. The shortcut is represented by an icon on your Desktop. A shortcut icon is identified by a little arrow in its lower-left corner. When you double-click the shortcut icon to open it, you are actually opening the network folder, which is stored out on the network server on another computer. This is quite convenient, because it saves time that you would have spent browsing through disk drives and perhaps several folders to find the file you need.

Create a shortcut to a program

In this exercise, you'll use the Find command to locate where WordPad is stored and then create a shortcut to WordPad on the Desktop.

1 Click Start. Point to Find, and then click Files Or Folders.

The Find dialog box appears. Be sure that the Name & Location tab is active.

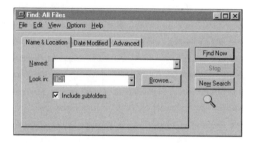

2 In the Named box, type **wordpad**

3 Click the Find Now button.

A list appears, showing all files with wordpad in their names.

4 Use the right mouse button to drag the Wordpad application file (not the CNT or Help file) to the Desktop.

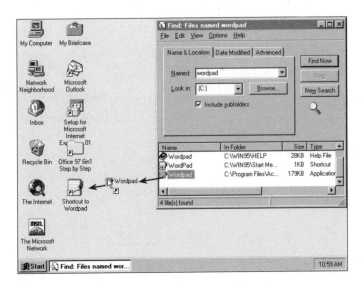

5 On the pop-up menu, click Create Shortcut(s) Here.

The Shortcut To WordPad icon appears on your Desktop.

6 Close the Find dialog box.

Create shortcuts to a folder and document

In this exercise, you'll create shortcuts for two items that you use often: the Marketing folder, and a logo document file.

1 Double-click the Office 97 6in1 Step by Step folder shortcut on the Desktop.

2 In the Office 97 6in1 Step by Step window, double-click the Part1 Windows Practice folder.

The Part1 Windows Practice folder opens.

3 Use the right mouse button to drag the Marketing folder to the Desktop.

A pop-up menu appears.

4 On the pop-up menu, click Create Shortcut(s) Here.

The Marketing folder shortcut appears on your Desktop.

If you drag a folder or document with the left mouse button, the folder or document is moved to the Desktop, rather than a shortcut linked to the folder or document.

5 In the Part1 Windows Practice folder window, use the right mouse button to drag the Logo Multicolored file to the Desktop.

6 On the pop-up menu, click Create Shortcut(s) Here.

The Logo Multicolored shortcut appears on your Desktop.

Rename the shortcuts

In this exercise, you'll close the open windows, and then rename the three shortcut icons.

1   Close all open windows until your Desktop is clear of all windows.

Your screen should look similar to the following illustration.

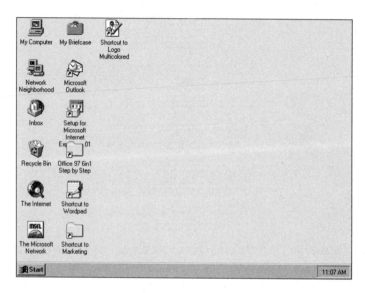

2   Use the right mouse button to click the Shortcut To WordPad icon.

A pop-up menu appears.

3   On the menu, click Rename.

The name "Shortcut To WordPad" is highlighted, and a blinking insertion point appears.

4   Type **WordPad** to replace the selection, and then press ENTER.

The WordPad shortcut is renamed.

5   Use the right mouse button to click the Shortcut To Marketing folder icon, and then click Rename.

6   Type **Childs Play Marketing** and then press ENTER.

7   Use the right mouse button to click the Shortcut to Logo Multicolored document icon, and then click Rename.

8 Type **Color Logo** and then press ENTER.

Use the shortcuts

In this exercise, you'll use the shortcuts you created to start WordPad, open the Marketing folder, and then open the Color Logo file.

1 Double-click the WordPad shortcut.

WordPad starts, as if you had started it from the Accessories menu.

2 Double-click the Childs Play Marketing folder shortcut. If necessary, drag the WordPad title bar to move its window out of the way.

The Childs Play Marketing folder opens, displaying its contents. This has the same effect as if you had opened My Computer, opened the hard drive (C:), opened the Office 97 6-in1 Step by Step folder, opened the Part1 Windows Practice folder, and then opened the Marketing folder. With the shortcut, the process of opening this folder is much quicker.

3 Double-click the Color Logo shortcut.

The Color Logo graphic opens in Paint. This is the same document that is stored in the Part1 Windows Practice folder.

4 If not already maximized, click the Maximize button on the Paint window to see the entire logo.

5 Close all open windows, until your Desktop is clear again.

Managing Your Shortcuts

You can make your Desktop as spare or as robust as you like. When you add more icons to your Desktop, there are additional tools that can help you manage, arrange, and work with the icons.

If you decide you no longer need a shortcut, you can remove the icon from your Desktop without deleting the object to which the shortcut is pointing. You're only deleting the pointer, not the actual item.

Arrange your icons on the Desktop

You now have several icons on your Desktop. In this exercise, you'll arrange the icons in an orderly scheme.

1   Use the right mouse button to click an empty area of the Desktop.

    A pop-up menu appears, including commands for arranging your icons.

2   Point to Arrange Icons, and then click By Name.

    Your shortcut icons are arranged in alphabetical order on your Desktop, after the default icons.

3   Use the right mouse button to click the Desktop again, point to Arrange Icons, and then click By Date.

    Your icons are arranged in date order.

Drag a shortcut onto the Start menu

You might want to make WordPad and the Childs Play Marketing folder available on your Start menu. In this exercise, you'll add the shortcuts to WordPad and the Marketing folder to the Start menu.

1   Drag the Wordpad icon until it is on top of the Start button.

2   Click the Start button.

    You'll see that the Wordpad command is added to the top of the Start menu.

3   Close the Start menu by clicking elsewhere, or by pressing ESC.

4   Drag the Childs Play Marketing folder icon to the Start button.

5   Click the Start button again.

    The Childs Play Marketing folder is now added as a command to the Start menu.

6   From the Start menu, choose Childs Play Marketing.

    The Marketing folder opens. This command is a shortcut to the folder that is actually stored on the hard drive (C:) in the Part1 Windows Practice folder.

7   Close the Marketing folder window.

Remove shortcuts from your Desktop

Suppose that some time has passed and you're busy working on other projects. Because of this, you no longer need these three shortcuts on your Desktop. In this exercise, you'll delete the shortcuts using three different methods. Deleting the shortcut does not delete the item to which the shortcut is pointing.

1   Drag the WordPad shortcut to the Recycle Bin icon.

     The WordPad shortcut is removed from the Desktop and placed inside Recycle Bin.

2   Use the right mouse button to click the Childs Play Marketing folder shortcut, and then click Delete.

3   In the Confirm File Delete dialog box, click Yes.

     The Childs Play Marketing folder shortcut is removed from the Desktop.

4   Click the Color Logo shortcut, and then press DELETE.

5   In the Confirm File Delete dialog box, click Yes.

     The Color Logo shortcut is removed from the Desktop.

 TIP   If you change your mind and want the deleted WordPad short-cut back, you can double-click the Recycle Bin icon to open it, and then drag the shortcut onto the Desktop again. Items in Recycle Bin stay there until you explicitly empty Recycle Bin. You'll learn more about using Recycle Bin in Lesson 6, "Managing Files and Disks."

Reset your Start menu

In this exercise, you'll remove Character Map and your other shortcuts from your Start menu to return it to the default setup.

1   Use the right mouse button to click an empty area of the taskbar.

     A pop-up menu appears, listing commands for the taskbar.

2   Click Properties.

     The Taskbar Properties dialog box appears.

3   Click the Start Menu Programs tab to make it active, and then click Remove.

4   In the Remove Shortcuts/Folders window, click Character Map, which is probably toward the bottom of the list, and then click Remove. If you are asked to confirm the deletion, click Yes.

5   Click WordPad, and then click Remove. If you are asked to confirm the deletion, click Yes.

6   Click Childs Play Marketing, and then click Remove. If you are asked to confirm the deletion, click Yes.

7 Click Close, and then click OK.

8 Click Start.

The three shortcuts that you added to the Start menu in this lesson are no longer listed as commands on the Start menu.

9 Press ESC to close the Start menu.

 NOTE In the Start menu, you can remove only those commands that you have added. You cannot remove the default Start commands.

Setting Up Your Environment

Although you can leave your Windows 95 or Windows NT environment at all the default settings, you might like to customize it to suit your own preferences. With Control Panel, you can change the date and time, the look of your display, the performance of your mouse, and more.

Setting the Date and Time

Whenever you save a document file, it is "stamped" with the current date and time. This is useful, for example, when you want to see which version of a file is the most current. Because of this date and time stamping, you want to be sure that the date and time settings in your computer are correct.

If you send electronic mail to users on other computers, your mail message is also stamped with the date and time as set in your computer. The time also appears on the right side of your taskbar. Twice a year, you might need to change the time for Daylight Savings Time.

To change the computer's date or time settings, you can use the Date/Time control in Control Panel.

Set the date and time

Suppose that your computer's date and time are set incorrectly. In this exercise, you'll change the date to August 22, and you'll change the time to 10:45am.

1 Click the Start button. On the Start menu, point to Settings.

The Settings menu appears.

Another way to open Control Panel is to double-click the My Computer icon, and then double-click the Control Panel folder.

2 On the Settings menu, click Control Panel.

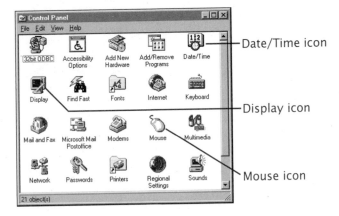

Date/Time icon

Display icon

Mouse icon

3 In the Control Panel window, double-click the Date/Time icon.

The Date/Time Properties dialog box appears. Be sure that the Date & Time tab is active.

Date/Time

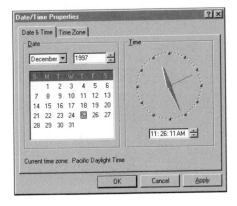

Make a note of the actual date and time so that you can quickly reset them in the next exercise.

4 In the Months list box, click the down arrow to open the list, and then click August.

5 On the calendar, click 22.

6 In the Time box, double-click the hour, and then type **10**

You can also click the up arrow or down arrow until 10 appears. The analog clock changes accordingly.

7 In the Time box, double-click the minutes, and then type **45**

You can also click the up arrow or down arrow until "45" appears. The analog clock changes accordingly. If necessary, click PM and type **AM**, or click the up arrow or down arrow once.

8 Choose the OK button.

The time change appears on the taskbar.

Reset the date and time

In this exercise, you'll change the date and time back to the current date and time.

1 With Control Panel still open, double-click the Date/Time icon.

2 In the Date/Time Properties dialog box, change the month and day back to today's date.

3 Change the hour and minutes to the current time.

4 If necessary, change the AM/PM designation.

5 Choose the OK button.

The current time appears on the taskbar.

Customizing Your Display

From the Control Panel, you can design your display like the way you decorate your office. You can choose color schemes for different window elements, such as the menu bar, the title bar, and selected text. You can choose a particular pattern for your Desktop background to make a more interesting environment for yourself while you work on your computer. To protect your monitor from possible damage caused by prolonged display of the same image, you have a wide variety of *screen-saver* patterns from which to choose.

Customize your display colors

In this exercise, you'll select a color scheme for your window elements using the Appearance tab in the Display Properties dialog box.

Display

1 With the Control Panel window open, double-click the Display icon.

2 Click the Appearance tab.

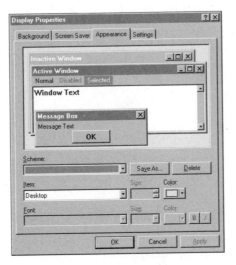

3 In the Scheme list box, click Plum (high color).

The colors in the sample display change to the Plum color scheme.

4 In the Scheme list box, click Teal (VGA).

The colors in the sample display change to the Teal color scheme.

5 Click the Apply button.

Your Desktop colors change to the Teal color scheme.

6 Sample and then select the color scheme you want, and then click OK.

 TIP If you want to change the color of an individual Desktop element, click it in the Item list box, and then select the color you want from the Color list box. You can also change Desktop element fonts, where applicable. You can even create and save entirely new color schemes in this way.

Choose your background

In this exercise, you'll set the background pattern and the wallpaper—two different sets of options for the Desktop background.

63

You can also open the dialog box by using the right mouse button to click an empty area of the Desktop and then choosing Properties.

1 With the Control Panel window still open, double-click the Display icon.

The Display Properties dialog box appears. Be sure that the Background tab is active.

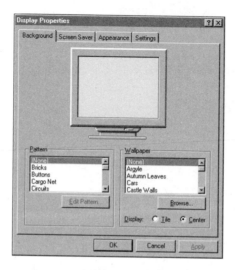

2 In the Wallpaper list box, if you're using Windows 95, click Waves. If you're using Windows NT, click Winnt.

The sample shows the graphic centered in the display. With Wallpaper, you often have the choice between a single design in the center of the Desktop, or a repeating design tiled across the display.

3 Click Tile.

The sample shows the graphic tiled across the display.

4 Click Apply.

The graphic is tiled across your actual display.

5 Click Center, and then click Apply.

6 In the Pattern list box, click Thatches.

Pattern is somewhat similar to Wallpaper. The sample display shows the Thatches pattern with the Waves or Windows NT graphic still in the center.

7 Sample and then select the pattern or wallpaper you want, and then click OK.

NOTE You can choose a wallpaper graphic that sits on top of your background pattern, as in this exercise. However, if the wallpaper fills your screen, the pattern will be completely hidden. This is because the wallpaper always sits on top of the pattern.

Choose a screen saver

A *screen saver* is a continually moving pattern that protects your monitor from damage when you're not actively using the computer. In this exercise, you'll view the screen savers that come with Windows 95 or Windows NT and then choose one you like. You'll also change the screen saver wait time.

1 With the Control Panel window still open, double-click the Display icon, and then click the Screen Saver tab.

The Screen Saver tab appears.

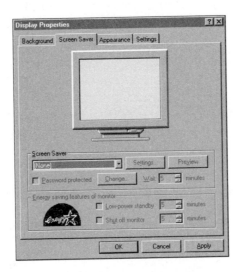

2 In the Screen Saver list box, select Flying Windows, if you're using Windows 95, or Mystify, if you're using Windows NT.

The sample display shows what the screen saver looks like.

3 In the Screen Saver list box, select Flying Through Space, if you're using Windows 95, or Starfield Simulation, if you're using Windows NT.

The sample changes to the new screen saver.

4 Click the Preview button.

The screen saver appears on your entire screen. It will stay there until you move your mouse or press any key.

5 Move your mouse or press any key to stop the screen-saver preview.

6 Click the Settings button.

A setup options dialog box appears, in which you can change the speed and density in the screen saver. Most of the screen savers have elements like this that you can set up according to your own preferences.

65

7 Change the Warp Speed value, and then choose the OK button.

The sample demonstrates the screen saver's new speed.

8 Sample the other screen savers, explore their settings, and then select the screen saver you want to use.

9 In the Wait box, type the number of minutes that the computer should be inactive before the screen saver starts, and then choose the OK button.

NOTE Your screen saver will start whenever your computer is idle for the number of minutes you specified in the Wait box. The moving image of the screen saver temporarily takes over your screen and obscures your previous work. When you want to use your computer again, press any key on the keyboard, or move the mouse. Your screen is restored and looks exactly as you left it.

Customizing Your Mouse

The way your mouse and pointer respond to your hand and finger actions can determine the efficiency with which you can control the graphical elements in Windows 95 or Windows NT. If you are not completely comfortable with the default settings for your mouse, you can change various mouse characteristics in Control Panel. If you are left-handed, you can switch the left and right button configuration. You can increase or decrease the speed, or sensitivity, with which the pointer responds to mouse movements. You can also adjust how fast or slow your double-click action can be.

Change your mouse pointer speed

Perhaps your mouse pointer seems to move slowly in relation to moving the mouse itself and you want to increase the speed of the pointer to make it more responsive to your slightest hand movements. In this exercise, you'll use the Mouse Properties dialog box to increase the mouse pointer speed.

Mouse

1 With Control Panel still open, double-click the Mouse icon.

The Mouse Properties dialog box appears.

2 Click the Motion tab.

The Motion tab appears.

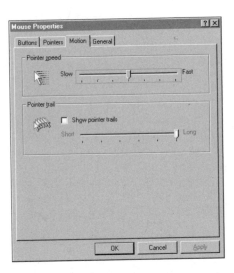

3   Drag the Pointer Speed slider a little to the right, to make the mouse pointer a little faster, and then click Apply.

As you move your mouse around the screen, you will notice a difference in the mouse pointer response. Make any further adjustments you want.

4   Click OK.

Change the mouse button setup

Perhaps you're left-handed and you want to change the primary button to the right button, and change the secondary button to the left button. In this exercise, you'll change your mouse button setup.

 NOTE   If you like your mouse button configuration the way it is, you can skip this exercise, or you can experiment with this exercise and then return the mouse to its original setup afterward.

---

1   In the Control Panel window, double-click the Mouse icon.

2   In the Mouse Properties dialog box, be sure that the Buttons tab is active.

3   Click the Left-Handed option button.

4 Click OK.

The mouse is reconfigured to a left-handed setup. The right mouse button is now the primary button.

5 Use the right mouse button to click the Close button on the Control Panel window.

6 Unless you prefer a left-handed button configuration, change the configuration back to its original setting.

Remember, you'll have to use the right mouse button to open and make selections in the Mouse Properties dialog box.

One Step Further: Starting Programs Automatically

If you want a certain program to start as soon as Windows 95 or Windows NT starts, you can add a shortcut to the program to your StartUp folder.

Find the file for a new StartUp shortcut

Suppose you like to make some notes in Notepad before you start working each day. In this exercise, you'll browse through your files to find the Notepad program file. Then you can add Notepad to your StartUp folder so that it starts automatically each time you start Windows 95 or Windows NT.

1 Click Start. On the Start menu, point to Settings, and then click Taskbar.

The Taskbar Properties dialog box appears.

2 Click the Start Menu Programs tab.

3 Click Add.

The Create Shortcut dialog box appears.

4 Click Browse.

The Browse dialog box appears. Be sure that the Look In text box indicates your hard drive (C:). If it does not, click the down arrow next to the list box, and then click (C:).

5 If you are using Windows 95, double-click Windows. If you are using Windows NT, double-click Winnt. Be aware that your Windows or Winnt folder may be named something different.

The contents of the Windows or Winnt folder appear.

6 Scroll through the list until you find the Notepad program file.

7 Double-click the Notepad icon.

The Create Shortcut dialog box appears again, with the Notepad information in the command-line text box.

8   Click Next.

The Select Program Folder dialog box appears.

Add a shortcut to your StartUp folder

Now that you have located the Notedpad program, you can add it to your StartUp folder. Any program in your StartUp folder starts as soon as you start Windows 95 or Windows NT.

1   In the Select Program Folder dialog box, click the StartUp folder, which is near the bottom of the list, and then click Next.

2   In the next window, click Finish.

The Taskbar Properties dialog box appears.

3   Click OK.

4   Click Start, point to Programs, and then point to StartUp.

The StartUp menu lists any items that will start up as soon as Windows 95 or Windows NT starts. In Windows 95, Notepad will be in this list. In Windows NT, items added to the StartUp menu don't appear until after you restart your computer.

Also, if you are using Windows NT, you should check the top StartUp menu folder.

   NOTE   If you are using Windows NT, you may have noticed that there are two StartUp menu items listed in the Programs menu. Items in the top StartUp folder are startup items for a particular user, while the bottom one is a startup folder for all users of this computer.

Restart Windows 95 or Windows NT

In this exercise, you'll restart Windows 95 or Windows NT and see how Notepad starts automatically.

1   Click Start. On the Start menu, click Shut Down.

2   In the Shut Down Windows dialog box, click Restart The Computer, and then click Yes.

Windows 95 or Windows NT restarts with Notepad running. If the Welcome window appears, click Close.

3   Type some text in Notepad if you like.

Click the Help menu and then click Help Topics for details on how to use Notepad.

4   When you have finished, close Notepad.

Remove a shortcut from your StartUp folder

In this exercise, you'll remove Notepad from your StartUp folder so that it will no longer start automatically.

1   Click Start. On the Start menu, point to Settings.

2   On the Settings menu, click Taskbar.

3   In the Taskbar Properties dialog box, click the Start Menu Programs tab.

4   On the Programs tab, click Remove.

5   In the Remove Shortcuts/Folder dialog box, double-click the StartUp folder.

6   Under the StartUp folder, click the Notepad shortcut, and then click Remove. If you are asked to confirm that you want to delete this shortcut, click Yes.

7   Click Close.

8   In the Taskbar Properties dialog box, click OK.

The Notepad shortcut is removed from the StartUp folder.

Finish the lesson

Close

1   Close all open windows by clicking the Close button in the upper-right corner of each window.

2   If any window is minimized, use the right mouse button to click the window's taskbar button, and then click Close.

You are now ready to start the next lesson, or you can work on your own.

3   If you have finished using Windows 95 or Windows NT for now, on the Start menu click Shut Down, select the appropriate option button, and then click Yes.

Lesson Summary

To	Do this
Open the Taskbar Properties dialog box	Use the right mouse button to click an empty area on the taskbar, and then click Properties.
Add a command to the Start menu or Programs menu	Open the Taskbar Properties dialog box. On the Start Menu Programs tab, click Add. Type the name of the program in the Command Line text box, and then click Next. Click the Start Menu or Programs folder, and then click Next. Type the name you want the shortcut command to have, and then click Finish. Click OK.
Remove a command from the Start menu or Programs menu	Open the Taskbar Properties dialog box. On the Start Menu Programs tab, click Remove. In the next window, click the item to remove, and then click Remove. Click Yes to confirm deletion. Click Close, and then click OK.
Add a shortcut icon to the Desktop	Find where the item is stored. Use the right mouse button to drag the item to the Desktop, and then click Create Shortcut(s) Here.
Rename a shortcut	Use the right mouse button to click the shortcut icon. On the pop-up menu, click Rename. Type the new name, and then press ENTER.
Add a shortcut to the Start menu	Drag the shortcut icon to the Start button.
Remove a shortcut from the Desktop	Drag the shortcut icon to the Recycle Bin icon. *or* Use the right mouse button to click the icon, click Delete, and then click the Yes button.

To	Do this
Open Control Panel	Click Start, point to Settings, and then click Control Panel. *or* Double-click My Computer, and then double-click the Control Panel folder.
Set the date and time	Open Control Panel. In the Control Panel window, double-click the Date/Time icon. In the dialog box, click the Date & Time tab. Make your selections and click OK.
Customize your display, including the background, screen saver, and colors	Use the right mouse button to click the Desktop, and then click Properties. In the Display Properties dialog box, click the appropriate tab and then select the settings you want.
Customize your mouse	In Control Panel, double-click the Mouse icon. In the Mouse Properties dialog box, click the appropriate tab, and then select the settings you want.

For online information about	From the Help dialog box, click Index and then type	
	Windows 95	Windows NT
Customizing your Start menu and Programs menu	**customizing, the Start menu**	**customizing: Start menu**
Creating and using shortcuts	**shortcuts**	**shortcuts**
Customizing your setup with Control Panel	**Control Panel**	**Control Panel**

Using Programs and Accessories To Do Your Work

In this lesson you will learn how to:

- Locate and start Windows 95 or Windows NT accessories.
- Locate and start programs.
- Switch among a variety of open programs.
- Share information between different programs.

Estimated time
35 min.

In your work area, you might keep various types of supplies, resources, and equipment handy to help you do your everyday work. Your supplies might include a notepad and briefcase. Your equipment might include your calculator, telephone, fax machine, and tape recorder. Likewise, in Microsoft Windows 95 or Microsoft Windows NT, you have a variety of accessory programs that act as supplies, resources, and equipment for your everyday work on your computer.

The work you do will likely require that you use other specialized programs that can do specific types of tasks for you. Such programs might include word processing, spreadsheet, database, graphic design, project management, or page layout capabilities. You must acquire these programs separately—they do not come with Windows 95 or Windows NT. However, Windows 95 or Windows NT provides the foundation for and the environment in which these programs can operate. In this lesson, you'll learn how to locate and start the different programs that are set up on your computer. You'll also learn how to switch among multiple open programs and how to share information between different programs.

Looking at Your Accessories

Although the WordPad word processing program and the Paint graphics program might be the two most commonly used programs that come with Windows 95 and Windows NT, there are many more. In fact, there is an entire set of computer programs that are built in to Windows 95 and Windows NT. These built-in programs are called *accessories* and are sometimes referred to as *components*.

In addition to WordPad and Paint, there are accessory programs called Calculator, Phone Dialer, CD Player, HyperTerminal, and many more. These accessories all have specific jobs to do, and they can either help you do your work more efficiently or help you use your computer more effectively.

You might use some of these accessories every day. Others are more technical system utilities that you might use only when you need to do some kind of computer system maintenance or monitoring, or you might never need to use them at all. Still other accessories are used only if you have certain types of equipment, such as multimedia or telecommunication hardware, installed with your computer.

Windows 95
Accessories menu

Windows NT
Accessories menu

The following table lists the Windows 95 and Windows NT accessories by category and describes their functions. Some accessories require appropriate hardware to be available, such as a modem or CD-ROM device.

NOTE Some of the accessories or components listed in the following table may not have been installed when Windows 95 or Windows NT was installed. For information on how to add or remove accessories or components, see the Appendix, "Matching the Exercises," or consult the Windows or Windows NT Help.

Desktop accessory		Function	Windows 95	Windows NT
📟	Calculator	Displays a calculator that you can use to perform simple, scientific, and statistical calculations.	✓	✓
🔧	Character Map	Displays special characters that you can insert into your documents.	✓	✓
📋	Clipboard Viewer	Displays the contents of your Clipboard, showing items you have cut or copied while you work in programs.	✓	✓
🕐	Clock	Displays a clock in its own window.		✓
🖼	Imaging	An accessory to assist in scanning.		✓
📦	Object Packager	An accessory you use to create a package that you can insert into a document.		✓
📝	Notepad	Allows you to create or view short, unformatted text documents.	✓	✓
🎨	Paint	Allows you to create, edit or view pictures.	✓	✓
📄	WordPad	Allows you to create, edit, format, or view short documents.	✓	✓

Telecommunication accessory		Function	Windows 95	Windows NT
💬	Chat	Allows you to communicate with someone on another computer		✓
📁	Dial-Up Networking	Uses modems and telephone lines to connect your computer to another computer that you call. You can share information between the two computers, even when you're not on a network. Both computers must be running Windows 95 or Windows NT.	✓	✓

Telecommunication accessory		Function	Windows 95	Windows NT
	Direct Cable connection	Physically connects your computer to another computer with a cable. You can share information between the two computers, even when you're not on a network. Both computers must be running Windows 95 or Windows NT.	✓	✓
	HypterTerminal (folder)	Connects to a remote computer using a modem. Sends and receives files, connects to online services, bulletin boards, and other information programs. Connects to computers running different operating systems. Any connections you set up are stored in the folder.	✓	✓
	Phone Dialer	Places telephone calls from your computer, using your modem or another Windows telecommunication device.	✓	✓
	Telnet	Allows you to connect to a remote computer.		✓

Fax accessory		Function	Windows 95	Windows NT
	Compose New Fax	Displays an editing screen in which you can write a fax message.	✓	
	Cover Page Editor	Allows you to write a cover page for a file to be faxed.	✓	
	Request a Fax	Allows you to call a fax information service and retrieve a document a file.	✓	

Multimedia accessory		Function	Windows 95	Windows NT
	CD Player	Plays audio compact discs from a CD-ROM drive connected to your computer.	✓	✓
	Media Player	Plays audio, video, or animation files. Controls multimedia hardware devices. This is available if your hardware setup includes a sound card.	✓	✓

Multimedia accessory	Function	Windows 95	Windows NT
Sound Recorder	Allows you to create, play back, edit, and insert sound clips into documents.	✓	✓
Volume Control	Controls the volume and balance of your sound card.	✓	✓

System accessory	Function	Windows 95	Windows NT
Backup	Copies files from the hard disk to floppy disks, tape, or another computer on the network to back up your files. Restores back-up files.	✓	
Disk Defragmenter	Optimizes your disk so that files and unused space are used efficiently.	✓	
DriveSpace	Compresses data on hard and floppy disks, creating more free space.	✓	
Inbox Repair Tool	Scans a personal folder file for errors.	✓	
Net Watcher	Lists the names of users who are currently using resources on your computer and who have used them in the past. Manages shared folders to your computer. Disconnects users from your computer.	✓	
Resource Meter	Monitors your computer's system resources.	✓	
Scan Disk	Checks a disk for logical or physical problems, and then marks the bad areas so that data is not written to those areas.	✓	
System Monitor	Shows a graph that reflects the current, real-time use and activity of your computer's internal core processor (central processing unit).	✓	

Games accessory		Function	Windows 95	Windows NT
	FreeCell	Displays a solitaire game.	✓	✓
	Hearts	Displays a group card game.	✓	
	Minesweeper	Displays a strategy board game.	✓	✓
	Pinball	Displays a pinball game.		✓
	Solitaire	Displays a solitaire game.	✓	✓

The following illustraton shows a few accessories open on the desktop.

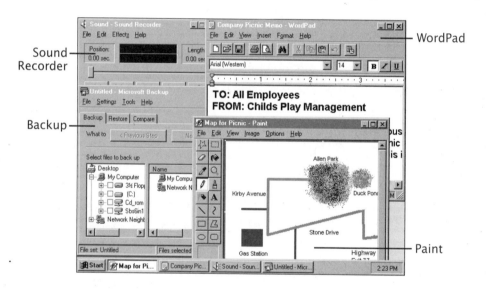

Finding and Exploring Programs

It's likely that you'll need to use programs besides the accessories to do some of your work. When this is the case, you would typically buy the program you need from a computer store, catalog, or other resource, and then you would set up the program on your computer. Examples of such programs include Microsoft Access, WordPerfect for Windows, Microsoft PowerPoint, and Adobe PageMaker.

Regardless of the type of program you have, or who developed it, programs for Windows 95 and Windows NT tend to have certain elements in common, as illustrated below. You can count on these characteristics as you move among programs for Windows 95 and Windows NT.

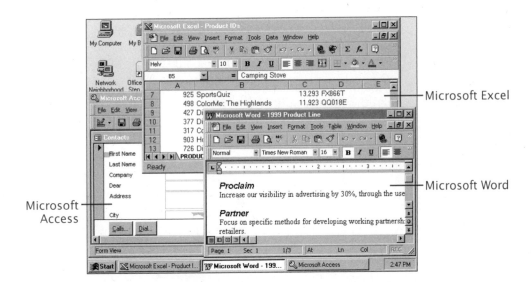

When a program opens in its window, you see the familiar window controls, including the Minimize, Maximize, and Close buttons. If the contents of the window extend beyond the window's boundaries, you'll also see the horizontal and vertical scroll bars.

Each program has a menu bar across the top of its window, from which you can choose commands to control the program. Many programs also use one or more toolbars, on which you can click a button that acts as a command shortcut.

To start a program, you can browse through My Computer or Windows Explorer to find the program file and then double-click the filename. If you prefer to run the program by clicking an icon or a command, you can create a shortcut to the program on the Start menu, Programs menu, or Desktop.

In the following exercises, you'll find and start the same program using two different methods.

Start a program by browsing through My Computer

You can also start a program by clicking Start and then clicking Run. In the Run dialog box, type the path and program name, and then click OK. The program starts.

Suppose you have set up a new software program on your computer's hard disk, and now you want to run it. In this exercise, you'll browse through your files to find and start a program.

1 Double-click the My Computer icon.

2 Double-click the hard disk (C:) icon.

3 Double-click the Office 97 6in1 Step by Step folder. Use your scroll bar if necessary.

4 Double-click the Part1 Windows Practice folder.

5 Double-click the Quotes folder.

The Quotes folder contains a program named Quotables, along with a text file.

Quotables

6 Double-click the Quotables program file icon.

The Quotables program starts, and it displays the text of a famous quote. Although the quote might be different, your screen should look similar to the following illustration.

If your screen looks different from this illus-tration, refer to the Appendix, "Matching the Exercises."

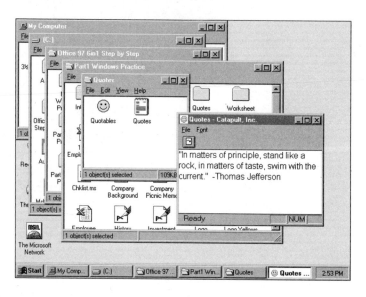

7 Click the Next Quote button.

Next Quote

The next quotation appears.

8 Click the Close button to close the window and shut down the Quotables program.

Start a program with the Find command

Suppose you know that you have a type of quotation program on your hard disk somewhere, but you don't know where and you don't know the exact name of the program. In this exercise, you'll find and start a program using the Find command.

1 Click Start. On the Start menu, point to Find, and then click Files Or Folders.

The Find dialog box appears. Be sure that the Name & Location tab is active.

2 In the Named text box, type **quot**

Because you know the program has "quot" somewhere in its name, you narrow your search by specifying to find only those files that have "quot" somewhere in their filename.

3   Click the Advanced tab.

The Advanced tab of the Find dialog box becomes active, as shown in the following illustration.

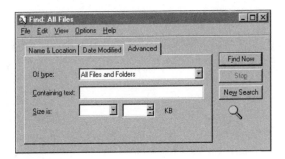

4   Open the Of Type list box by clicking its down arrow.

A list of all available file types appear.

Application is another term for program.

5   Click Application.

When you specify a search with the Application file type, only program files will be found.

6   Click Find Now.

A list of program files that meet your criteria appears at the bottom of the dialog box. The Quotables program file should be among them. If you have a large hard disk with many files stored, the search might take a minute or so.

7   Double-click the Quotables program file in the Find list.

The Quotables program file starts.

8   Close the Quotables program window.

9   Close the Find dialog box.

Create a shortcut to a program

You can also add program shortcuts to your Start and Programs menus. See Lesson 3, "Customizing Your Desktop for the Way You Work," for more information.

Let's say you use the Quotables program frequently. In this exercise, you'll make the Quotables program more readily available by creating a shortcut to it on your Desktop.

1   With the Quotes folder still open, use the right mouse button to drag the Quotables program file to any empty area on your Desktop.

A pop-up menu appears.

2 Click Create Shortcut(s) Here.

An icon named "Shortcut To Quotables" appears on your Desktop.

3 Close all open windows.

4 Double-click the Shortcut To Quotables icon.

The Quotables program starts.

5 Close the Quotables window.

Switching Among Multiple Open Programs

When working at a desk, you often have several documents or project folders available at one time. While you might be actively using one project, you know you can reach for and refer to another project right there on your desk.

In the same way, you can keep several programs open at the same time, each one running in its own window on your Desktop. While one window is always active and visible on top of the other windows, you can always quickly switch to and work in any of the other windows.

Suppose you've just created a drawing in Paint and you need to write a memo to accompany the drawing. While writing your memo, you find you need to make some calculations. In the following exercises, you'll switch among Paint, WordPad, and Calculator by using the taskbar.

Switch between Paint and WordPad using the taskbar

In this exercise, you'll write a memo to accompany your drawing.

1 Click Start. Point to Programs, point to Accessories, and then click Paint.

Paint starts.

2 On the File menu, click Open.

The Open dialog box appears.

3 Click the down arrow in the Look In drop-down list box. Click the hard disk (C:).

The contents of your hard disk appear.

4 Double-click the Office 97 6in1 Step by Step folder. Use the scroll bar if necessary.

5 Double-click the Part1 Windows Practice folder.

6 Double-click the Toys Logo.

The Toys Logo drawing opens in the Paint window.

7 Click Start again. Point to Programs, point to Accessories, and then click WordPad.

WordPad starts.

For instructions about how to use WordPad, click the Help menu in Word-Pad, click Help Topics, and then double-click the topics you want to read about.

8 In WordPad, type the following note.

TO: Gwen Lehua, Advertising

FROM: Craig Armand, Marketing

Attached is a logo concept I sketched for our new preschool product line. Please develop the logo based on these ideas. Note that we are working on a budget of

You now need to make a calculation of your budget.

Switch between Calculator and WordPad

In this exercise, you'll switch between WordPad and Calculator to compute numbers you need in your WordPad memo.

1 Click Start. Point to Programs, point to Accessories, and then click Calculator.

Calculator starts.

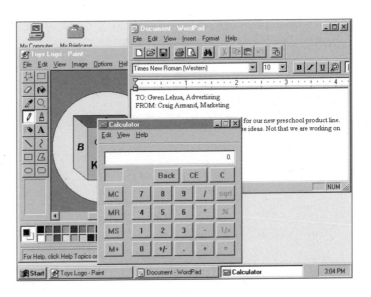

83

2 Use Calculator to figure 15% of 3500. Do this by typing the numbers and operators with the numeric keypad on your keyboard, or by clicking the numbers and operators with your mouse on Calculator. Enter the formula as **3500 * 15%** using the Percent (%) function on Calculator.

Your result should be 525.

3 On the taskbar, click Document - WordPad.

WordPad becomes the active window.

4 Finish typing your memo where you left off, as follows.

$525.00 for this task. Let's meet next Tuesday to discuss this project in more detail. Thank you!

Save

5 On the WordPad Standard toolbar, click the Save button.

The Save As dialog box appears. Be sure that the Part1 Windows Practice folder appears in the Save In box.

6 Select the contents of the File Name box, type **Preschool Toys Memo.wri** and then click Save.

The memo is saved on your hard disk in the Part1 Windows Practice folder.

Switch between programs using the keyboard

Just as you can switch to a different program by clicking its name on the taskbar, you can switch between programs using the keyboard. In this exercise, you'll switch among Paint, WordPad, and Calculator by using the keyboard.

1 With the WordPad window still active, hold down the ALT key and press TAB. Do not release ALT yet.

A dialog box appears in the center of the screen, with icons that represent each of your open windows. The selected window is named at the bottom of the window.

2 Continue to hold down ALT and press TAB repeatedly until the Paint icon is highlighted, and then release the ALT key.

Now Paint is the active window.

NOTE Pressing ALT+ESC switches among items listed on the taskbar in sequence. If the task is currently open, it comes to the top of the Desktop. If the task is currently minimized, you can select it with ALT+ESC and then press ENTER to restore its window on the Desktop.

Arrange windows on the Desktop

Perhaps you want the WordPad and Calculator windows visible at the same time on your screen. In this exercise, you'll arrange, or *tile*, the two program windows side by side. You'll also arrange your windows in a cascading fashion across the Desktop.

1 Minimize the Paint window.

2 Minimize any other windows that might be open on the Desktop except the WordPad and Calculator windows.

3 Use the right mouse button to click an empty space on the taskbar.

A pop-up menu appears, listing commands for arranging the open windows on the Desktop.

If you want to restore your tiled windows to their previous sizes and shapes, use the right mouse button to click an empty space in the taskbar, and then click Undo Tile.

4 On the menu, if you're using Windows 95, click Tile Vertically. If you're using Windows NT, click Tile Windows Vertically.

The two open windows are arranged side by side on your Desktop.

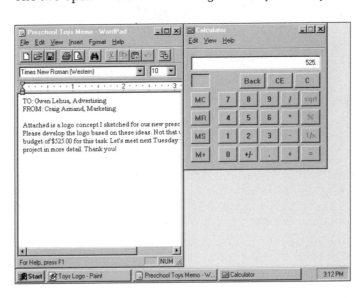

5   On the taskbar, click the Toys Logo - Paint button.

The Paint window appears on the Desktop.

6   Use the right mouse button to click an empty space in the taskbar.

7   On the pop-up menu, if you're using Windows 95, click Cascade. If you're using Windows NT, click Cascade Windows.

The three open windows are arranged in a cascading fashion across your Desktop, and you can see the title bar of each window.

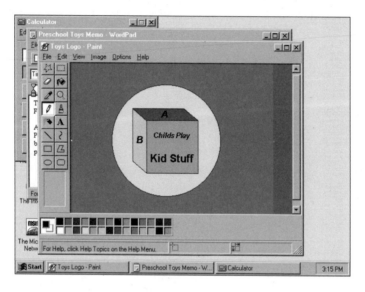

8   Close all open windows.

Sharing Information Between Different Programs

You have probably worked with paper documents in which one document had information you wanted to include in another document. To avoid the inconvenience of copying by hand, you might have used scissors to cut information from one document and then used tape or paste to place that information in another document.

In Windows 95 and Windows NT, you can electronically cut or copy information from one program and then paste the information into another program, for example, from Paint to WordPad, or from Microsoft Excel to Microsoft Word.

Find and open a Paint and a WordPad document

Imagine that you have used Paint to draw a map to the company picnic site. In this exercise, you'll open the map drawing in Paint and the picnic memo in WordPad. In a later exercise, you will add the map to the memo.

1   Double-click the Office 97 6in1 Step y Step folder shortcut on the Desktop.

   The Office 97 6in1 Step by Step window opens.

2   Double-click the Part1 Windows Practice folder.

   The Part1 Windows Practice folder opens.

3   Double-click the Company Picnic Memo file. Use your scroll bar if necessary.

   The Company Picnic Memo file opens in a WordPad window.

4   On the taskbar, click the Part1 Windows Practice folder button.

5   In the Part1 Windows Practice folder, double-click the Map For Picnic file. Use your scroll bar if necessary.

   The Map For Picnic file opens in a Paint window.

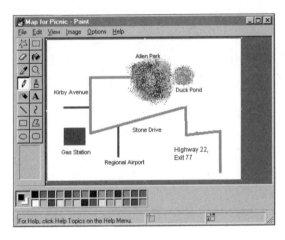

6   Maximize the Paint window.

Copy and paste from Paint to WordPad

In this exercise, you'll copy the map and paste it into your picnic memo.

Select

1   In Paint, click the Select tool.

2   Use the Select tool to drag a dotted rectangle around the entire map.

3   On the Edit menu in Paint, click Copy.

   Although nothing appears to change on your screen, the map is temporarily copied into the *Clipboard*, which is the temporary holding place for items that have been cut or copied.

4   On the taskbar, click Company Picnic Memo - WordPad.

   The WordPad window appears.

87

5 Maximize the WordPad window.

6 Click at the end of the document, after "See you there!" Press ENTER twice to add two blank lines.

Paste

7 On the WordPad toolbar, click the Paste button.

The map drawing appears in your memo.

Save

8 On the toolbar, click the Save button.

Print the document with the copied drawing

1 Be sure that your printer is on.

If you do not have an active printer that can print graphics, skip to step 3.

Print

2 On the toolbar in WordPad, click the Print button.

The memo prints with the inserted map.

3 Click the Restore button on the WordPad window.

4 Click the Restore button on the Paint window.

5 Close all open windows.

One Step Further: Embedding and Updating a Graphic That Is Part of a Memo

You can insert, or *embed*, a copy of an object created in another program (the *source* program) into a document in your current program (the *destination* program). When you embed an object, you can use the resources of the source program to edit the embedded object without leaving the program you are in. This provides you with double the resources in just one document.

In the following exercises, you will create a new memo, embed an existing Paint drawing into the memo, and then update the embedded drawing.

Create a new WordPad document

You can embed an object into a new or existing WordPad document. In this exercise, you'll create the memo in which you want to include the embedded drawing.

1 Click Start. On the Start menu, point to Programs, point to Accessories, and then click WordPad.

WordPad starts.

2 Maximize the WordPad window.

3 Type the following text into the WordPad writing area.

TO: Richard Tashi

FROM: Craig Armand

This is the rough logo concept for our new preschool product line. I have sent this idea to Advertising for further development and refinement. Let me know if you have any comments or suggestions. Thank you.

4 On the toolbar, click the Save button.

The Save As dialog box appears. Be sure that the Part1 Windows Practice folder appears in the Save In box.

5 Select the contents of the File Name box, type **Memo to Richard.wri** and then click Save.

Embed a Paint drawing into a WordPad document

In this exercise, you'll embed an existing drawing into your WordPad memo.

1 Press ENTER three times to move the insertion point downward and add three lines.

2 On the Insert menu, click Object.

The Insert Object dialog box appears with the Create New option selected.

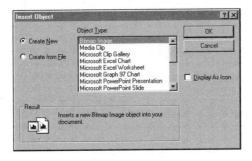

3 Click the Create From File option button.

A dialog box appears in which you can browse through your files and select an existing file to embed as a separate object into your current document.

4 Click Browse.

The Browse dialog box appears. Be sure that the Part1 Windows Practice folder appears in the Look In box.

5 Click Toys Logo, and then click Insert if you are using Windows 95. If you are using Windows NT, click Open.

The Insert Object dialog box appears again, with the path and filename for Preschool Toys Logo inserted into the File text box.

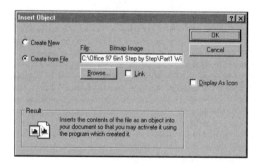

6 In the Insert Object dialog box, click OK.

The Toys Logo drawing appears in your memo. Your screen should look similar to the following illustration.

7 Click anywhere outside the Paint object window.

WordPad redraws the document.

Save

8 On the toolbar, click the Save button.

Update the embedded drawing

In this exercise, you'll open the embedded Paint drawing and edit it using the resources of the Paint accessory without leaving WordPad.

1 Double-click the embedded logo drawing in the memo.

The WordPad menu and toolbars change, and they are temporarily replaced with the Paint menu, toolbox, and color box.

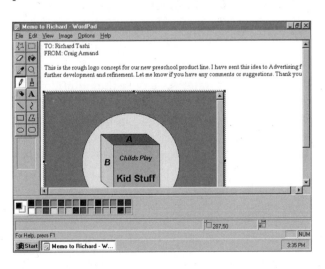

Line

2   Click the Line tool.

3   Drag a line from any point of the circle outward toward the edge of the drawing area.

4   Drag several more lines from other points around the circle outward to simulate rays of sunshine.

The drawing should look similar to the following illustration.

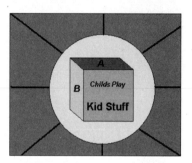

5   Click anywhere outside the Paint object window in the WordPad document.

The Paint menu and tools return to those of WordPad. The changes you made in Paint are reflected in the Paint logo.

6   On the toolbar, click the Save button.

7   On the WordPad window, click the Restore button.

Save

Finish the lesson

In the following steps, you will return your computer to the settings it had when you started this lesson. You will also close any open windows.

1   Close all open windows by clicking the Close button in the upper-right corner of each window.

2   If any window is minimized, use the right mouse button to click the window's taskbar button, and then click Close.

Close

3   Delete the Shortcut To Quotables from the Desktop. Click it, press DELETE, and then click Yes; or drag it to Recycle Bin.

You are now ready to start the next lesson, or you can work on your own.

4   If you are finished using Windows 95 or Windows NT for now, on the Start menu click Shut Down, select the appropriate option button, and then click Yes.

Lesson Summary

To	Do this
Start and use accessories	On the Start menu, point to Programs, and then point to Accessories. Click the accessory you want to start.
Find a program by browsing	Browse through files with My Computer or Explorer.
Find a program with Find File	Click Start, point to Find, and then click Files or Folders. Click the Advanced tab. In the Of Type list box, click Application. Click Find Now. All programs on the hard disk are found and listed.
Start a program	Double-click the program icon.
Start a program with the Run command	Click Start, and then click Run. In the Open text box, type the path, or click Browse to find the program path and filename. Click OK.
Switch among open programs	Click the program name on the taskbar. *or* Hold down ALT and press TAB. While continuing to hold down ALT, continue pressing TAB until you cycle to the program you want to open. Then release both keys. *or* Hold down ALT and press ESC.
Tile open windows on the Desktop	Use the right mouse button to click an empty space on the taskbar. On the shortcut menu, if you're using Windows 95, click Tile Horizontally or Tile Vertically. If you're using Windows NT, click Tile Windows Horizontally or Tile Windows Vertically.
Cascade open windows on the Desktop	Use the right mouse button to click an empty space on the taskbar. On the shortcut menu, if you're using Windows 95, click Cascade. If you're using Windows NT, click Cascade Windows.

To	Do this
Copy and paste information between different programs	Use the Copy command to copy the information in the first program. Switch to the second program. Use the Paste command to paste the information in the location you want.
Embed a Paint drawing into a WordPad document	On the Insert menu of the WordPad document, click Object. Click the Create New option button. Click the Bitmap Image object type, and then click OK. *or* On the Insert menu of the WordPad document, click Object. Click the Create From File option button. Type in the path and filename or Browse for the file, and then click OK.

For online information about	From the Help dialog box, click Index and then type	
	Windows 95	Windows NT
Opening and using accessories	**the accessory name**	**the accessory name**
Adding or removing accessories or components	**accessories, installing**	**components, adding or removing**
Locating program files	**programs, finding**	**programs: finding**
Switching between different open programs	**switching, between running programs**	**programs: finding switching: to**
Copying and pasting information between different programs	**copying, information from one document to another**	**copying: between programs documents**
Embedding information between different programs	**OLE**	**OLE**

Setting Up a Filing System

In this lesson you will learn how to:

- Browse through your computer's filing system.
- Set up the information you want to see in your computer's filing system.
- Organize your files on your disks and in folders.
- Manage your files and folders by moving them where you want.

Estimated time
20 min.

After you work at a job for a while, paperwork can start to accumulate into one or more piles on your desk and around your office. This might be okay—until you can't find items you need right away. Your solution might be to organize your paperwork into different categories, and then place the appropriate papers into labeled file folders. You might then place the folders into a filing cabinet. As you continue to work and accumulate more papers, you can put these papers exactly where they belong.

In the same way, after you work at your computer for a while, your files can accumulate in various places on your computer. You can organize your files into different categories, and put them in specific places on your computer so that you can easily find them later. You can use My Computer or Windows Explorer to carry out these file management tasks.

In this lesson, you'll learn how to set up and maintain a computer filing system that suits the way you like to organize your files.

Understanding Files and Folders

Whenever you create a new document in a program such as Paint or Microsoft Word, you store, or *save*, the document as a *file* in your computer. When you save a file, you give the file a name. The filename can be as long as you want it to be (up to 255 characters), and it can include spaces.

For more information about disk drives, see Lesson 6, "Managing Files and Disks"

When you save a file, it is recorded, or written, onto a disk in your computer, in much the same way as music is recorded on magnetic tape. The file is identified by the name you have specified, and it occupies a specific location on the disk. When you retrieve, or *open*, the file again, the disk drive finds the file you want and then displays it on the screen.

To help you organize your computer files into specific categories, you create *folders*. Folders can hold any number of individual files. When you save a *document file* that you have created, you can choose the folder in which to store the file. You can also move files from one folder to another. By organizing your files in different folders, you can follow your own logic in specifying file locations. You can then find your files later when you want to open them again.

Program files are also stored in folders on your computer. When you set up a program on your computer, the setup process creates a new folder on your hard disk. All the program files that make the new program run are copied into that folder. The program files for one program are usually separated from the program files for another program. Because of this, even if you have a new computer, you probably already have a folder structure for your programs.

Just as you can have several manila file folders within a hanging file folder, you can have folders within folders on your computer system. With multiple levels of subfolders, you can organize your files precisely and efficiently.

Viewing Your Filing System

Whether you have a new computer system, or you've been using your computer for a while, you might be interested in taking a look around to see what files you have on your computer and how they're organized. After you have examined the files stored on your computer, you'll better understand how to use the computer, how you might want to organize your files, and where you can find the files you want.

You can use My Computer to browse through your filing system. You can also change how you view the information in the My Computer windows.

Disk Drive

CD-ROM Drive

Network Drive

Unless otherwise noted, screens from Windows 95 are shown in Part 1 of this book. The corresponding screens from Windows NT are the same or very similar.

Folder

Browse through your filing system with My Computer

In this exercise, you'll use My Computer to investigate which folders, files, and other resources you have on your computer. You'll also see how they're organized.

1   Double-click the My Computer icon.

The My Computer window appears. All drives on your computer are represented by a drive icon and name. If there are any established connections to other computers on the network, those computers are represented by a network drive icon and name.

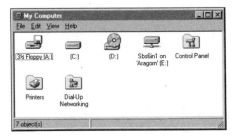

2   Double-click the hard disk (C:) icon.

A new window appears, showing all top-level folders and files stored on the hard disk. Top-level folders and files are those that are not stored in any other folders.

97

3 Double-click the Office 97 6in1 Step by Step folder. If necessary, use your scroll bars. The Office 97 6in1 Step by Step window appears.

4 Double-click the Part1 Windows Practice folder.

A new window appears, showing all folders and files stored in the Part1 Windows Practice folder. Folders, which hold other files, are represented by folder icons and names. Files are represented by filenames and the program icons in which the files were created.

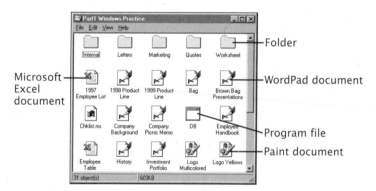

5 Double-click the Internal folder.

A new window appears, showing all files stored in the Internal folder. As you continue to open folders within folders, new windows open, listing each new folder's contents.

If the icons in your window look different from these, click Large Icons on the View menu of the Part1 Windows Practice window. Then, on the View menu, point to Arrange Icons, and click Auto Arrange if it is not selected.

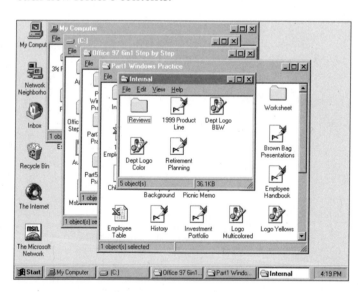

6 Close all open windows by clicking the Close button on each window.

Change the view of the My Computer windows

You can set up each of the My Computer windows to show only the information you want to see. In this exercise, you'll change the display of folders and files in any My Computer window.

1 Double-click the My Computer icon.

2 Double-click the hard disk (C:) icon.

3 Click the View menu of the hard disk (C:) window. If Toolbar is not selected, click Toolbar. If Toolbar is selected, press ESC to close the menu.

The toolbar appears in the hard disk (C:) window. This toolbar provides shortcuts for performing certain tasks and for changing window views. You can set each My Computer window to show or hide the toolbar. This setting remains in effect even after you close the window. If you cannot see the entire toolbar, drag the left or right side of the window to make the window wider.

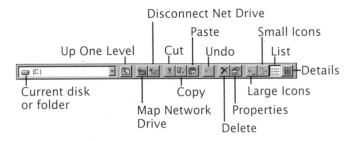

4 On the toolbar, click the Large Icons button.

Large Icons

You can also click Large Icons on the View menu.

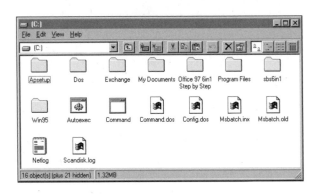

Small Icons

You can also click Small Icons on the View menu.

5 On the toolbar, click the Small Icons button.

The view changes from large icons to small icons. This way, you can see more information in one window, as in the following illustration.

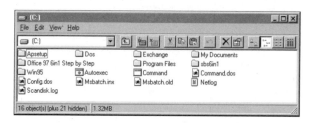

Details

*You can also
click Details on
the View menu.*

6 On the toolbar, click the Details button.

Details about each file or folder are listed in columns across the window. The details include the type of file it is and when the item was last modified.

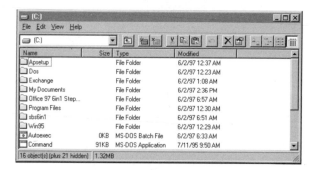

 TIP All files include a three-letter filename extension that identifies the file type. For example, files created with Paint have an extension of ".bmp," while files created with Microsoft Word have an extension of ".doc." In Windows 95 and Windows NT, you typically don't need to see the filename extensions, so they're hidden. However, if you want to see all the filename extensions, on the View menu of either My Computer or Explorer, click Options. In the Options dialog box, click the View tab. If you're using Windows 95, click Hide MS-DOS File Extensions For The File Types That Are Registered to clear it. If you're using Windows NT, click Hide File Extensions For Known File Types to clear it. Click OK. All files will show their filename extensions.

Organizing Your Files Within Folders

Depending on the nature of your work and the way you like to organize it, your filing scheme can take different forms. You might have a separate folder for each type of project, for example, letters, status reports, and budget forecasts. If you work with different clients, you might prefer to designate a separate folder for each client. If several individuals use one computer, as in a family or small business setting, you might want to set up a separate folder for each user. You can move files into the folders you create. You can also move or create folders within other folders. By adopting and adhering to a particular organizational scheme, you can keep your files in logical order for quick and easy access.

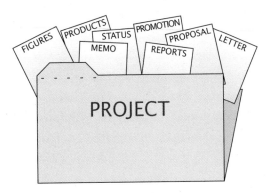

If you're having trouble finding your files in a folder...

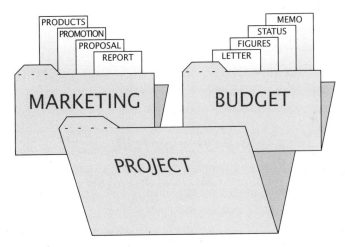

...you can organize your files into additional
subfolders within the original folder.

Create folders for your new filing system

Suppose that after browsing through your computer filing system, you think of a more efficient way to organize your files. You decide to group related files by tables, employee information, and product line information. In this exercise, you'll create these three folders for your new file organization scheme.

1   With the hard disk (C:) window still open, double-click the Office 97 6in1 Step by Step folder icon.

The Office 97 6in1 Step by Step folder window opens.

2   Double-click the Part1 Windows Practice folder icon. The Part1 Windows Practice folder window opens.

3   On the File menu of the Part1 Windows Practice window, point to New, and then click Folder.

A new folder, named New Folder, appears at the bottom of the window. The name is selected, so you can replace it with the name you want.

4   Type **Tables** and then press ENTER.

The name of the folder changes to Tables.

5   Click an empty space in the Part1 Windows Practice window.

This removes the selection from the Tables folder icon and allows you to create another folder. You cannot create a new folder when any item in the window is selected.

6   On the File menu, point to New, and then click Folder.

Another new folder appears in the window.

7   Type **Employee Information** and then press ENTER.

8   Following the same steps, create a new folder named **Product Line** within the Part1 Windows Practice folder.

9   On the View menu, point to Arrange Icons, and then click By Name.

This rearranges all of your new icons, so the folders appear in alphabetical order at the top of the window.

Move files into your new folders

Now suppose that you want to move files into the folders you just created. In this exercise, you'll move files from the Part1 Windows Practice folder into the appropriate folders, using menu commands as well as the mouse.

1   With the Part1 Windows Practice folder still open, click the Personnel Letter file icon once to select it. Use your scroll bar if necessary. All files are listed in alphabetical order.

You can also press CTRL+X to cut the selected file.

2   On the Edit menu, click Cut.

The Personnel Letter icon is dimmed, indicating that it's in the middle of a move operation.

3   Double-click the new Employee Information folder to open it. Use your scroll bar if necessary.

The Employee Information window appears.

You can also press CTRL+V to paste the selected file.

4 On the Edit menu of the Employee Information window, click Paste.

The Personnel Letter file appears in the Employee Information folder and disappears from the Part1 Windows Practice folder.

5 On the taskbar, click Part1 Windows Practice.

The Part1 Windows Practice folder appears.

6 In the Part1 Windows Practice window, drag the 1998 Product Line icon to the Tables folder until the Tables folder changes color.

1998 Product Line moves to the Tables folder and is no longer listed in the Part1 Windows Practice folder.

7 Double-click the Tables folder icon.

The Tables window appears, along with the moved file.

You can use these same procedures to move a folder into another folder.

8 Either use the Cut and Paste commands on the Edit menu or drag with the mouse to move the following files into the indicated folders. You might want to rearrange your windows or scroll through them to do this more easily.

Move this file	To this folder
Investment Portfolio	Employee Information
Employee Table	Tables
Product IDs	Tables
Employee Handbook	Employee Information
1999 Product Line	Product Line
Product Descriptions	Product Line

9 Close all open windows.

One Step Further: Browsing with Windows Explorer or Windows NT Explorer

Just as you can browse through your filing system with My Computer, you can also browse with *Explorer*. Explorer provides a different view of the same information presented in the My Computer windows. You can create new folders and move files between folders in a similar manner as in the My Computer windows.

Browse through your filing system with Explorer

In this exercise, you'll browse through your computer system files with Explorer. You'll also display the same toolbar you use in the My Computer windows and change the view of folders and files in the same way.

1   Click Start. On the Start menu, point to Programs, and then click Windows Explorer or Windows NT Explorer.

The Exploring window appears. As shown in the following illustration, the left window displays your computer's entire file structure, including any disk drives, folders, and established network connections in your computer system. The right window displays the names of the files and folders stored in the item selected in the left window.

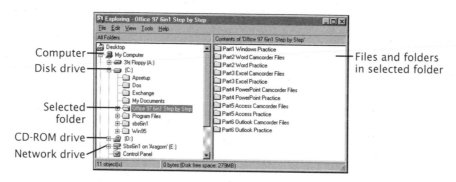

If the icons in your window look different from those illustrated above, on the View menu of the Exploring window, click List to change the view.

2   In the left window, click the hard disk (C:).

The right window displays the names of the files, as well as any folders, stored there.

3   In the left window, double-click the Office 97 6in1 Step by Step folder. If necessary, use the scroll bar.

4   In the left window, double-click the Part1 Windows Practice folder. If necessary, use the scroll bar.

The left window displays all folders stored in the Part1 Windows Practice folder. The right window displays these folders as well as the names of the files stored in the Part1 Windows Practice folder. These are the same folders and files you saw listed in My Computer.

5   In the left window, click the Marketing folder.

The right window displays all files stored in the Marketing folder.

6   On the Explorer View menu, click Large Icons.

The display of folders and files in the right window changes to large icons.

7   On the View menu, click Toolbar to turn on the toolbar display.

The toolbar appears on the Exploring window. Drag the sides to make the window wider, if necessary, to view all the buttons on the toolbar.

Details

8   On the toolbar, click the Details button.

The display of folders and files in the right window changes to display a list of the files with small icons, along with detailed information about each file.

Finish the lesson

In the following steps, you will return your computer to the settings it had when you started this lesson. You will also close any open windows.

Small Icons

1   Double-click the My Computer icon, and then double-click the hard disk (C:) icon. On the toolbar, click Small Icons.

2   Close all open windows by clicking the Close button in the upper-right corner of each window.

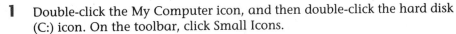

Close

3   If any window is minimized, use the right mouse button to click the window's taskbar button, and then click Close.

You are now ready to start the next lesson, or you can work on your own.

4   If you are finished using Windows 95 or Windows NT for now, on the Start menu click Shut Down, select the appropriate option button, and then click Yes.

Lesson Summary

To	Do this
Browse through your computer filing system with My Computer	Double-click the My Computer icon. Double-click any drives and folders in which you want to browse for files.
Browse through your computer filing system with Explorer	Click Start, point to Programs, and then click Windows Explorer or Windows NT Explorer. In the left window, click the drive or any folders in which you want to browse. In the right window, view the files stored on the drive or folder selected in the left window.
Change the view of the My Computer or Explorer window	On the My Computer or Explorer window, click the View menu, and then select how you want to view the contents of the window.
Create a new folder	Open the drive or folder in which you want the new folder to be stored. On the File menu, point to New, and then click Folder. Type a name for the new folder, and then press ENTER.
Move a file to another folder	Click the name of the file to be moved. On the Edit menu, click Cut. Open the folder in which you want to move the folder. On the Edit menu, click Paste. *or* Drag the file to the folder in which you want to move the file.

For online information about	**From the Help dialog box, click Index and then type**	
	<u>Windows 95</u>	<u>Windows NT</u>
Browsing with My Computer or Explorer	**browsing, through folders on your computer**	**browsing: files, folders, programs**
Creating and using folders	**folders, creating**	**folders: creating**
Moving files and folders	**moving, files or folders**	**moving: files, folders**

Managing Files and Disks

**Estimated time
25 min.**

In this lesson you will learn how to:

- Rename and copy your files and folders.
- Delete unwanted files and folders.
- Format new floppy disks to prepare them for use in your computer.

Even the best organization and filing systems are refined periodically. One adjustment might be to change the label on a file folder to make it more descriptive or easy to find. Another change might include photocopying a file in one folder so that it can be included in another folder. An important change can simply mean throwing away documents that are no longer needed.

In the same way, your computer filing system might need periodic adjustments to suit your changing needs. You can rename a file or folder. You can copy a file to another folder or to another disk. Or you can discard unused or outdated files that are taking up valuable space on your hard disk.

In this lesson, you'll learn how to manage your files, folders, and disks by renaming, copying, or deleting them. You'll also learn how to copy files to floppy disks for portability and safekeeping.

Managing Your Files and Folders

To maintain your computer filing system, you can use Microsoft Windows 95 or Microsoft Windows NT tools to rename, copy, and delete files. This keeps your filing system as efficient and usable as possible for your purposes.

Renaming and Copying Files and Folders

You can rename your files to make the filenames more descriptive or to take advantage of the long filenames you can use in Windows 95 and Microsoft Windows NT. You can also copy files to other folders or to the Desktop.

Rename files and folders

Suppose you want to rename several files to make the filenames consistent with a new file naming scheme you've developed. In this exercise, you'll rename the Company Background file to Childs Play History. You'll also rename the Bag file to Brown Bag Lunch.

1 Double-click the Office 97 6in1 Step by Step shortcut folder on the Desktop.

2 Double-click the Part1 Windows Practice folder.

3 Click the Company Background file once to select it.

4 On the File menu, click Rename.

On the Company Background file icon, the filename is highlighted and an insertion point appears at the end of the filename.

5 Type **Childs Play History** to change the filename, and then press ENTER.

6 Use the right mouse button to click the Bag WordPad file.

The file is selected, and a pop-up menu appears.

7 On the pop-up menu, click Rename.

An insertion point appears at the end of the selected filename.

You can use these same procedures to rename a folder.

8 Type **Brown Bag Lunch** and then press ENTER.

The filename changes.

 TIP You can also rename files with Explorer. In the right window, click the file you want to rename, and then from the File menu, click Rename. Or, use the right mouse button to click the file, and then click Rename.

Copy files to another folder

Suppose you have files in one folder, and you want to put an exact copy of these files in another folder. In this exercise, you'll copy files between folders.

1 With the Part1 Windows Practice folder still open, click the Sports Products List file icon to select it. Use the scroll bar if necessary.

You can also press CTRL+C to copy. Or, use the right mouse button to click the file, and then click Copy.

2 On the Edit menu, click Copy.

The Sports Products List file is copied to the computer's memory, but nothing changes on the screen.

3 Double-click the Marketing folder. Use the scroll bar if necessary.

4 On the Edit menu of the Marketing window, click Paste.

A copy of the Sports Products List file appears in the Marketing folder.

You can also press CTRL+V to paste. Or, use the right mouse button to click the window, and then click Paste.

5 If the icons appear jumbled, on the View menu point to Arrange Icons, and then click By Name.

If you want your icons to always be neatly arranged in a window, on the window's View menu, point to Arrange Icons, and then click Auto Arrange.

6 On the taskbar, click Part1 Windows Practice and then click an empty area in the Part1 Windows Practice window to deselect the Marketing folder icon.

7 In the Part1 Windows Practice folder, hold down CTRL and drag Chklist.ms to the Letters folder until the folder icon changes color.

While you're dragging, your mouse pointer displays a plus sign. The plus sign appears when you hold down CTRL, indicating that you are copying, rather than moving, the file as shown in the following illustration.

If your screen looks different from this illustration, refer to the Appendix, "Matching the Exercises."

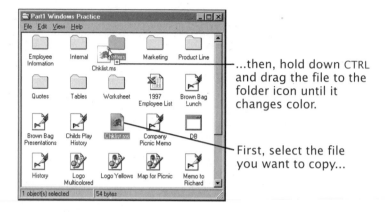

...then, hold down CTRL and drag the file to the folder icon until it changes color.

First, select the file you want to copy...

You can use these same procedures to copy a folder into another folder.

8 Double-click the Letters folder.

The Letters folder opens, and it now includes the Chklist.ms file.

 TIP You can also copy files with Explorer. In the right window, click the file you want to copy, and then from the Edit menu, click Copy. In the left or right window, click the folder where you want to place the copied file, and then from the Edit menu, click Paste. Or, you can hold down CTRL and drag the file to the folder.

Deleting Files and Folders

Another aspect of organizing and managing your files and folders is cleanup. You can delete old files you don't use anymore, and you can delete backup or temporary files to free up space on your hard disk.

Any deleted files or folders are placed in Recycle Bin. When you drag a file or folder to the Recycle Bin icon, it is ready to be deleted from your disk. If you change your mind before you empty Recycle Bin, you can "recycle" the item and reuse it by retrieving it from Recycle Bin.

Delete files

Let's say you have some files that are old duplicates, and you don't need them in your folders anymore. In this exercise, you'll delete files and an entire folder by using Recycle Bin.

1 On the taskbar, click Part1 Windows Practice.

The Part1 Windows Practice window becomes active.

2 Drag the 1997 Employee List to the Recycle Bin icon on your Desktop. If necessary, position or minimize windows to move them out of the way.

The 1997 Employee List file no longer appears in the Part1 Windows Practice window. You have just moved it to Recycle Bin, a holding area for files and folders you no longer need.

3 In the Part1 Windows Practice window, use the right mouse button to click the Retirement Planning Backup file.

A pop-up menu appears.

4 On the pop-up menu, click Delete.

The Confirm File Delete dialog box appears.

You can also delete a file by selecting it and pressing DELETE on your keyboard.

5 Click Yes.

The Retirement Planning Backup file disappears from the Part1 Windows Practice window and is placed in Recycle Bin.

6 From the Part1 Windows Practice window, drag the Worksheet folder to the Recycle Bin icon.

The Worksheet folder is deleted. Deleted items stay in Recycle Bin until you explicitly empty it. You might prefer to keep deleted items as insurance against accidental deletions or other mishaps.

You can follow the same process to delete files and folders from Explorer.

Recover deleted files from Recycle Bin

Suppose you changed your mind about a file or folder you have deleted. If you have not yet emptied Recycle Bin, you can retrieve and re-use any item stored there. In this exercise, you'll recover deleted files from Recycle Bin.

1 Double-click the Recycle Bin icon.

The Recycle Bin window appears, listing all files, folders, and other items deleted since the last time Recycle Bin was emptied.

To recover the last item deleted, you can also click the Undo Delete command on the Edit menu of the Recycle Bin window.

2 From the Recycle Bin window, drag 1997 Employee List back to the Part1 Windows Practice folder.

The 1997 Employee List file appears in the folder again, and you can use it as if it were never deleted.

111

3 Close the Recycle Bin window.

 TIP Another way to recover files from Recycle Bin is to click the item and then on the Recycle Bin File menu, click Restore. The file returns to whatever folder it was deleted from, even if the folder is not currently open.

Empty Recycle Bin

Items in Recycle Bin take up space on your hard disk. If you're deleting files and folders to make more room on your hard disk, you'll need to empty Recycle Bin. In this exercise, you'll delete selected files in Recycle Bin from the hard disk. You'll also empty all the items in Recycle Bin.

1 Double-click the Recycle Bin icon.

Recycle Bin opens, displaying a list of all items deleted since the last time Recycle Bin was emptied. The status bar at the bottom of the Recycle Bin window indicates the number of objects in Recycle Bin, and how much disk space they occupy.

You can select multiple adjacent items by holding down SHIFT, clicking the first item, and then clicking the last item in the series. All items between the first and last item are selected.

2 Hold down CTRL and click any three nonadjacent items in the list.

Recycle Bin			
File Edit View Help			
Name	Original Location	Date Deleted	Type
Advertising	C:\Office 97 6in1 St...	6/2/97 5:14 PM	Write
Calculator	C:\WIN95\Start Menu	6/2/97 10:25 AM	Shor
Character Map	C:\WIN95\Start Menu	6/2/97 10:25 AM	Shor
Childs Play Marketi...	C:\WIN95\Desktop	6/2/97 11:17 AM	Shor
Childs Play Marketi...	C:\WIN95\Start Menu	6/2/97 11:19 AM	Shor
Color Logo	C:\WIN95\Desktop	6/2/97 11:18 AM	Shor
Marketing Costs	C:\Office 97 6in1 St...	6/2/97 5:14 PM	Write
Marketing Proposal	C:\Office 97 6in1 St...	6/2/97 5:14 PM	Write
Marketing Status R...	C:\Office 97 6in1 St...	6/2/97 5:14 PM	Write

3 object(s) selected   22.0KB

By holding down CTRL, you can select several nonadjacent items at one time in any list.

3 On the File menu of Recycle Bin, click Delete.

The Confirm Multiple File Delete dialog box appears.

To empty Recycle Bin without opening it, use the right mouse button to click Recycle Bin, and then click Empty Recycle Bin.

4 Click Yes to delete the three items from Recycle Bin and from your hard disk.

5 On the File menu, click Empty Recycle Bin.

6 In the Confirm Multiple File Delete dialog box, click Yes.

All the contents of Recycle Bin are removed from your hard disk.

7 Close all open windows.

Managing Your Disks

Although your hard disk is probably the primary storage device you use every day, you might use floppy disks as well. It's wise to copy your document files onto a floppy disk periodically so that you have a backup in case your hard disk malfunctions. In addition, you might have document files stored on floppy disks that you want to transfer onto your hard disk. You can use My Computer or Explorer to manage the information on your disks in these ways. You can also format a new floppy disk to prepare it for use.

Understanding Disk Storage

Two types of disks are generally used: hard disks and floppy disks. You can think of your *hard disk* as being like a room full of filing cabinets built into your computer system. Likewise, *floppy disks* are like file boxes that you can transport.

A floppy disk is like...   ...a file box.

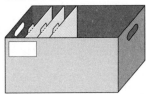

It holds a limited amount of information, but it can easily be transported between computers.

A hard disk is like...

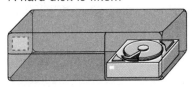

...a room full of file cabinets.

Although a hard disk is not portable, it can store hundreds of times more information than a single floppy disk.

The hard disk is used to store the files that make Windows 95 or Windows NT and all your other programs run. It is often used to store your document files as well. Floppy disks are used to transfer information from one computer to another and to make backup copies of information stored on the hard disk.

The *disk drive* is the mechanism that reads and writes information to and from the disk. Floppy disk drives are usually built into the system unit of the computer, and the floppy disks are inserted into the disk drive slots. The hard disk drive is also built into the system unit, but it is not accessed from the outside. You might have one or more floppy disk drives in your system. You can also have more than one hard disk drive.

Each disk drive has a name that you use to identify which drive you want to use. The first floppy disk drive is typically referred to as Drive A. The second floppy disk drive is typically referred to as Drive B. The hard disk is typically referred to as Drive C. These names can be changed by the person who configures the computer system. There can be any number of additional disk drive designations for other storage devices, such as CD-ROM drives, tape drives, and network drives.

There are two physical sizes for floppy disks: 3.5-inch and 5.25-inch. There are also two densities possible for either size of disk: high density and double density. Each of the four types of floppy disks can hold a different amount of information, measured in *bytes*, the unit of measure for information stored in a computer.

Floppy disk type	Storage capacity in bytes
5.25-inch double density (DD)	360 kilobytes
5.25-inch high density (HD)	1.2 megabytes
3.5-inch double density (DD)	720 kilobytes
3.5-inch high density (HD)	1.44 megabytes

In English, one byte equals about one character. One *kilobyte* (KB) is approximately one thousand bytes. One *megabyte* (MB) is approximately one million bytes.

Backing Up Files onto a Floppy Disk

You can use floppy disks to make backup copies of the files stored on your hard disk. If you copy your files onto a new, blank floppy disk, you must first be sure that it is formatted. Then you can copy the files from your hard disk onto the floppy disk.

Format a new floppy disk

Suppose you have just bought a box of unformatted floppy disks. In this exercise, you'll learn how to format a new floppy disk to prepare it for use in your computer. A disk needs to be formatted only once.

⚡ **WARNING**   The formatting process erases any information previously stored on the floppy disk.

1   Place a new floppy disk (or a used one containing information you can discard) in the appropriate floppy disk drive (3.5-inch or 5.25-inch).

Be sure you know whether it is a double-density or high-density floppy disk. Most floppy disks are labeled "DD" for double density or "HD" for high density.

2   Double-click the My Computer icon.

The My Computer window appears.

3   Click the icon for the drive that contains the floppy disk you want to format.

Be sure to click just once to select the icon, rather than open the disk.

You can also use the right mouse button to click the drive icon, and then on the pop-up menu, click Format.

4   On the File menu, click Format.

The Format dialog box appears.

Format dialog box in Windows 95   Format dialog box in Windows NT

The Quick (Erase) option erases all information from a formatted floppy disk. Copy System Files Only copies system files to a formatted floppy disk.

5   In the Capacity list box, specify the capacity of the floppy disk.

The capacity depends on whether the floppy disk is a high-density (HD) or double-density (DD) disk.

6   If you're using Windows 95, under Format Type, click Full. If you're using Windows NT, click the File System box down arrow to specify the File System. Click the Allocation Unit Size box down arrow to specify the allocation unit size.

7   If you're using Windows 95, under Other Options, be sure that Display Summary When Finished is checked.

8   Click Start. If you see a warning dialog box, click OK.

To format a disk and then copy system files onto it, click Copy System Files under Other Options.

In the Formatting bar at the bottom of the Format dialog box, tic marks indicate the status of the formatting process, which might take a couple of minutes. When the bar is filled in, the formatting is complete. If you're using Windows 95, the Format Results dialog box appears.

If you're using Windows NT, a small message box appears telling you that the format is complete.

9 If you're using Windows 95, in the Format Results dialog box, click Close. If you're using Windows NT, in the Formatting message box, click OK.

The Format dialog box appears again. If you wanted to format several floppy disks of the same size and capacity, you could now remove the formatted floppy disk, insert another floppy disk, and click Start again. This is useful when you're formatting an entire box of new floppy disks.

10 In the Format dialog box, click Close. Remove the floppy disk from the drive, and label it "Disk and Briefcase Practice." Then, reinsert the disk for use in the next exercise.

 TIP You can also format floppy disks with Explorer. In Explorer, use the right mouse button to click the name of the floppy disk drive in the left window. From the pop-up menu, click Format.

Copy from the hard disk to a floppy disk

Now that your floppy disk is formatted, you're ready to copy files onto it from your hard disk. You do this to make a backup of your files in case of a malfunction or to transfer files to another computer. In this exercise, you'll copy files from the Part1 Windows Practice folder (on the hard disk) onto your floppy disk.

To duplicate floppy disks, select the icon in the My Computer window for the floppy disk you want to copy, and then click Copy Disk from the File menu.

1 Open the hard disk (C:), then open the Office 97 6in1 Step by Step folder, and then open the Part1 Windows Practice folder.

2 In the Part1 Windows Practice folder, click Brown Bag Lunch.

3 On the File menu, point to Send To, and then click the appropriate drive.

The Brown Bag Lunch file is copied to the floppy disk drive.

4 On the taskbar, click My Computer, and then double-click the floppy disk drive icon, either Drive A or Drive B.

The Drive window appears and displays the icon for the Brown Bag Lunch file.

5 On the taskbar, click the Part1 Windows Practice button.

The Part1 Windows Practice window appears.

6 Arrange the floppy drive window so that at least part of it is visible under the Part1 Windows Practice window.

7 From the Part1 Windows Practice window, drag the Brown Bag Presentations file to the floppy disk window.

When dragging between two folders on the same disk, the item is automatically moved. To copy an item between folders rather than move it, hold down CTRL while dragging.

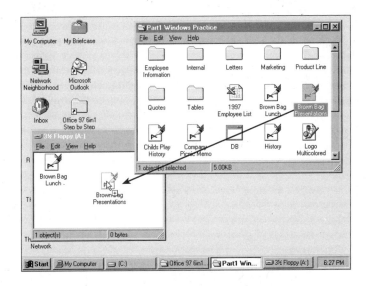

The plus sign on your mouse pointer indicates that you're copying the file to the floppy disk. When dragging between a floppy disk and the hard disk, the item is automatically copied rather than moved. To move, rather than copy, hold down SHIFT while you drag.

You can use these same procedures to copy files and folders from a floppy disk to your hard disk or to copy or move a folder into another folder.

8 Close all open windows.

TIP   You can also copy files between the hard disk and floppy disk drive with Explorer. In Explorer, select the file to be copied. From the File menu, click Send To, and then click the floppy disk drive name. Or, drag the file to the drive icon.

One Step Further: Searching for Files with Find File

Up to this point, you've been locating your files by browsing through My Computer or Windows Explorer. When you know the general vicinity of a file—that is, which folder a file might be in—browsing like this is probably the most convenient way to find the files you're looking for. But what do you do if you know part of the filename, but you don't have any idea where it might be on the hard disk?

You can use the Find File command to search your computer for files. By searching, you can locate either *program files* or *document files*. Program files are responsible for running your programs such as WordPad, Paint, and Microsoft PowerPoint. Document files are the work, or data, you create when you use one of these programs.

Find a document file

Suppose you have created a document file, but you don't remember the folder in which you saved it. In this exercise, you'll find and open a document file using the Find command.

1   Click Start. On the Start menu, point to Find.

2   On the Find menu, click Files Or Folders.

The Find dialog box appears.

3   Be sure that the Name & Location tab is active.

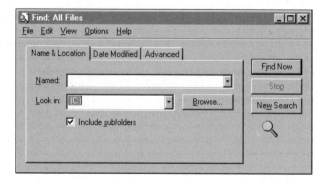

The Named list box maintains a list of your previous search operations.

4 In the Named box, type **logo** and then click Find Now.

All files throughout your hard disk that have "logo" as part of their filenames are listed at the bottom of the dialog box. Also listed are the folders in which the files are stored, the file sizes in kilobytes (KB), the file types and the date and time modified.

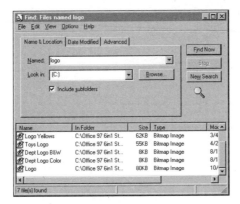

5 In the resulting list of files, scroll to Dept Logo Color and double-click it.

The Paint program starts, and then the Dept Logo Color file appears in the Paint window.

6 On the taskbar, use the right mouse button to click the Find button.

7 On the pop-up menu, click Close.

The Find dialog box closes.

8 Minimize the Paint window.

Find a program file

Suppose you have set up a new program, but you have not added a shortcut to it on the Programs menu or the Desktop, and now you don't know where the program is. In this exercise, you'll find a program file and then start the program.

1 Click Start. On the Start menu, point to Find.

2 On the Find menu, click Files Or Folders.

The Find dialog box appears.

3 Be sure that the Name & Location tab is active.

4 In the Named box, type **wordpad**, and then click Find Now.

All files throughout your hard disk that have "WordPad" as part of their filename are listed at the bottom of the dialog box. Among these is the WordPad program, the one listed with the Application file type. *Application* is another word for program.

5   Double-click the name of the WordPad application program file in the Find dialog box.

WordPad starts.

6   Minimize WordPad.

Find a file by its file type

You can search for a file by *file type*. The file type is the category of file, such as a bitmap image file, application (program) file, Briefcase file, folder, shortcut, or WordPad document. In this exercise, you'll search for application files and bitmap image files.

1   With the Find dialog box still open, click the New Search button, and then click OK.

This clears the search criteria from your previous search. Any criteria specified on any of the three tabs are cleared.

2   Click the Advanced tab to make it active.

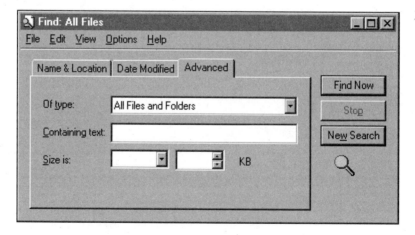

3   In the Of Type list box, click the down arrow to open the list.

A list of file types appears.

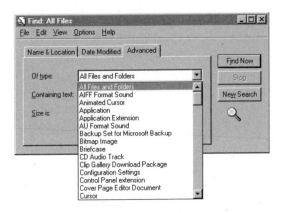

4   Click Application, and then click Find Now.

Windows 95 or Windows NT searches throughout the disk specified in the Name & Location tab (probably the hard disk, drive C:), and lists all application program files found there.

5   In the search list, scroll to and then double-click Charmap, which is the program file for the Character Map accessory.

The Character Map starts, as shown in the following illustration.

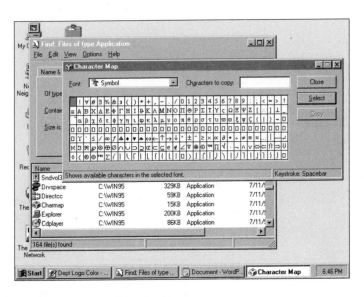

6   On the taskbar, click the Find button.

The Find dialog box appears again.

7 Open the Of Type list box again, click Bitmap Image, and then click Find Now.

All bitmap image files, such as the logo files in the Part1 Windows Practice folder, are listed. If you want, you could double-click a file to open it in Paint.

Finish the lesson

Close

1 Close all open windows by clicking the Close button in the upper-right corner of each window.

2 If any window is minimized, use the right mouse button to click the window's taskbar button, and then click Close.

3 If you are finished using Windows 95 or Windows NT for now, on the Start menu click Shut Down, select the appropriate option button, and then click Yes.

Lesson Summary

To	Do this
Rename a file or folder	Use the right mouse button to click the file you want to rename. On the pop-up menu, click Rename. Type the new name, and then press ENTER.
Copy a file to another folder	Hold down CTRL and drag the file you want to copy to the new location.
Delete a file	Drag the file to the Recycle Bin icon on the Desktop. *or* Click the file, press DELETE, and then click Yes.
Recover a deleted file	Open Recycle Bin, and then drag the file you want to recover to a folder, drive, or Desktop. *or* Open Recycle Bin, click the file you want to recover, and then on the Recycle Bin File menu, click Restore.
Empty Recycle Bin	Open Recycle Bin, and then from the File menu, click Empty Recycle Bin.

To	Do this
Format a new floppy disk	Insert the floppy disk, and use My Computer or Explorer to select the drive. On the File menu, click Format. Specify the capacity of the floppy disk. If you're using Windows 95, click Full. Click Start.
Copy files and folders from the hard disk to a floppy disk	In My Computer or Explorer, select the files or folders you want to copy. On the File menu, point to Send To, and then click the appropriate drive.
Find a document file	Click Start, point to Find, and then click Files Or Folders. On the Name & Location tab, type all or part of the filename in the Named box, and then click Find Now.
Find a program file	Click Start, point to Find, and then click Files Or Folders. On the Name & Location tab, type all or part of the name of the program in the Named box. Click the Advanced tab. In the Of Type list box, click Application, and then click Find Now.

For online information about	From the Help dialog box, click Index and then type	
	Windows 95	Windows NT
Copying files and folders	**copying, files or folders**	**copying: files**
Deleting files and folders	**deleting, files or folders**	**deleting: files**
Using Recycle	**Recycle Bin**	**Recycle Bin**
Formatting floppy disks	**formatting, disks**	**formatting disks**

Microsoft Word 97

Creating and Saving Documents

In this lesson you will learn how to:

**Estimated time
45 min.**

- Start Microsoft Word.
- Use toolbars and other basic features in the document window.
- Type text in a new document window.
- Correct spelling errors using automatic spell checking.
- Insert, delete, and replace text.
- Name and save your document.

In Microsoft Word, it's easy to create documents and make them look the way you want. In this lesson, you will type a short letter that you'll use to help you become familiar with the AutoCorrect feature (which corrects your spelling as you type) and learn how to edit text by deleting, replacing, and inserting words and phrases. You will also save your work by storing the document on your computer hard disk.

Using Microsoft Word to Customize Your Documents

You use word processing software when you want to create a new document—such as a letter, memo, or report—or when you want to modify a document that you or someone else created. You can use Microsoft Word to type in text, edit existing text, and format text to add emphasis, clarify ideas, and arrange text attractively on the page. You can also use Microsoft Word to insert graphics, tables, and charts, as well as to check your document for spelling and grammatical mistakes. In addition, you can use Microsoft Word to create and modify Web pages that you can display on the Internet.

In addition to these features, Microsoft Word offers other capabilities that make creating documents a snap. Below is a summary of the features you will probably use most often.

- The AutoCorrect feature corrects your spelling of certain words as you type. In addition, you can use Microsoft Word to identify words not found in the Word dictionary; a wavy red underline indicates words that might be misspelled. This feature helps you quickly locate and correct errors. Similar features are available to correct grammatical errors as you type and to identify grammatical errors in your document.

- If you use hyphens as list bullets, fractions, ordinal arabic numbers (such as 3RD), and trademarks or other symbols in your documents, the AutoFormat feature automatically inserts the correct symbol as you type.

- If you need to arrange text in a grid of rows and columns, Word's table feature helps you format your text quickly and attractively. If your table contains numbers, you can use the table feature to format your numbers as in a spreadsheet, and you can use MS Graph to display the numbers in a chart.

- To store and insert frequently used text and graphics, you can use the AutoText feature. In addition, Word already provides many AutoText entries for common expressions and phrases.

- To store and apply formatting combinations easily, consistently, and accurately, you can create and apply styles.

- To create form letters, envelopes, and labels, you can use the Mail Merge feature.

- To create attractively formatted documents quickly, you can use the variety of document wizards and templates provided in Word. These templates and wizards give you a great head start in the formatting of your documents. Use a wizard to create a document based on your responses to a series of questions, or use a template to begin creating a document right away.

 TIP   If you are already familiar with previous versions of Microsoft Word, be sure to review the "Finding Your Best Starting Point" section earlier in this book for a list of the features that are new in this version of Microsoft Word.

An Introduction to the Office Assistant

While you are working with Microsoft Office 97, an animated character called the *Office Assistant* pops up on your screen to help you work productively. The Office Assistant offers helpful messages as you work. You can ask the Office Assistant questions by typing your question, and then clicking Search. The Office Assistant then shows you the answer to your question.

You can close any Office Assistant tip or message by pressing ESC.

You will sometimes see a lightbulb next to the Office Assistant—clicking the lightbulb displays a tip about the action you are currently performing. You can view more tips by clicking Tips in the Office Assistant balloon when the Office Assistant appears. In addition, the Office Assistant is tailored to how you work—after you master a particular skill, the Office Assistant stops offering tips.

Clippit, an Office Assistant, in action

The Office Assistant appears in the following situations:

- When you click the Office Assistant button on the Standard toolbar.
- When you choose Microsoft Word Help on the Help menu or when you press F1.
- When you type certain phrases. For example, you might see the Office Assistant when you type the text **Dear Ms. Rasmussen:** and press ENTER.

Office Assistant

The Office Assistant is a shared application—any settings that you change will affect the Office Assistant in other Office 97 programs. You can customize the Office Assistant in two ways. You can:

Determine when you want to see the Office Assistant

Use the right mouse button to click the Office Assistant and click Options to open the Office Assistant dialog box. You can then define when you want the Office Assistant to appear, and what kind of help you want it to offer.

Change your Office Assistant character

Use the right mouse button to click the Office Assistant and click Options to open the Office Assistant dialog box. Click the Gallery tab.

Starting Microsoft Word

You can start Microsoft Word from the Programs menu, which is available when you click the Start button.

If you have not installed the Part2 Word Practice files, refer to "Installing and Using the Practice and Camcorder Files," earlier in this book.

Start Microsoft Word from the Programs menu

1 On the taskbar, click Start.

2 On the Start menu, point to Programs, and then click Microsoft Word.

IMPORTANT If the Office Assistant appears, click the Start Using Microsoft Program option. If the User Name dialog box appears, fill in your name and initials, and then click OK. On the Office Assistant, click the Close button.

For the purposes of this book, the Office Assistant will not appear in the illustrations. If you want to match the illustrations, any time the Office Assistant appears, use the right mouse button to click the Office Assistant, and then click Hide Assistant. If you want to leave Office Assistant on top to help guide you, but it is in your way, simply drag it to another area on the screen.

Maximize

3 If the window is not already maximized, click the Maximize button. Your screen should look similar to the following illustration.

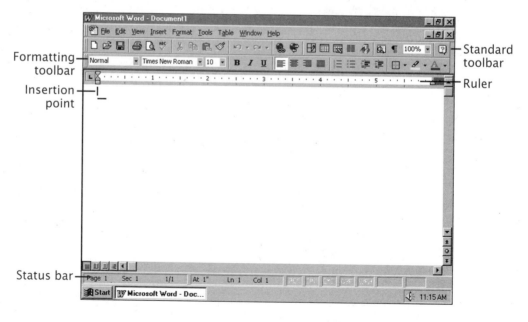

Exploring the Microsoft Word Document Window

When you start Microsoft Word, a new blank document appears in a *document window*. The document window is the Microsoft Word equivalent of a sheet of paper in a typewriter—it is where you type your text. The buttons and ruler you see at the top of the window offer easy ways to work on your documents.

Using Toolbars to Perform Basic Operations

The first row of buttons below the Microsoft Word menu bar is the Standard toolbar. This toolbar contains buttons for performing basic operations, such as opening, saving, and printing a document, in Microsoft Word. It is generally much faster to click a button on a toolbar than to select a command from a menu.

There are several toolbars in Microsoft Word; you can display or hide these toolbars depending on your needs. Each toolbar is composed of buttons that perform related tasks. For example, you use the Formatting toolbar (located below the Standard toolbar) to enhance the appearance of your document, including the style and size of the type.

When you click certain toolbar buttons—for example, the Print button—Microsoft Word carries out the corresponding command using the command default options. A *default* is a setting or option that is in effect if you do not specify another choice. Clicking other buttons turns features on and off. For example, the Show/Hide ¶ button displays or hides nonprinting characters, such as spaces between words and paragraph marks between paragraphs. Still other buttons, such as the Open button, perform in the same way as their corresponding menu commands. The instructions in this book emphasize using buttons whenever possible.

Take a quick tour of the Standard toolbar

Undo

Take a moment to familiarize yourself with the buttons on the Standard toolbar. If you accidentally click a button, you can click the Undo button on the Standard toolbar.

> Move the mouse pointer over a button, and wait.

After a moment, a ScreenTip, which is an on-screen description of an element on the screen, appears. If you do not see the button name, on the Tools menu, choose Customize, and then click the Options tab. Click Show ScreenTips On Toolbars.

ScreenTip

Typing Text

As the communications manager at West Coast Sales, your duties include developing a wide variety of documents. The key to your success has been your effectiveness at getting the message out to employees and customers by creating attractive and professional-looking documents. Using Microsoft Word will help you develop the documents you need both quickly and with a minimum of effort. One of your major projects this year is to coordinate a national sales conference for West Coast Sales employees. After an initial telephone call to a motivational speaker who has expressed interest in delivering the keynote address, you decide to follow up with a letter.

You can begin typing in the empty document window, just as you would begin typing on a clean sheet of paper. The blinking insertion point, which is already positioned for you at the top of the window, shows where the text you type will appear. For the next exercise, you'll start by typing the salutation. Later, you will insert the date and inside address. Whenever you see the name "Terry Kim," you can type your own name in the document.

Type text in a letter

1   Type **Dear Ms. Mather:** and press ENTER.

> **NOTE**   If the Office Assistant asks you if you would like to use the Letter Wizard, click the option to create a letter without the Letter Wizard (the second option). Working without the Letter Wizard for now will help you focus on typing and simple editing. If you would like to try creating a letter with the help of the Letter Wizard, you can complete the One Step Further exercise at the end of this lesson.

Pressing ENTER places the insertion point at the start of a new blank line. If a red, wavy underline appears below a word you type, it means that the automatic spell checking feature is enabled and the word is identified as misspelled or unknown. You will learn more about this feature later in this lesson.

2   Press ENTER to create another blank line.

Type a paragraph of text

When you type sentences that are longer than one line, you do not need to press ENTER at the end of each line. Instead, you can just keep typing. When the insertion point approaches the right margin, it automatically moves to the beginning of the next line as you continue typing. This feature is known as *wordwrap*. You press ENTER when you want to begin a new paragraph or to create a blank line.

➤   Type the body paragraph below without pressing ENTER. If you make a typing mistake, either press the BACKSPACE key to delete the mistake and then type the correct text, or ignore the mistake and correct it later.

Thank you for agreeing to present the opening address for our company's national sales conference next year. Supporting the professional development of our employees is a long-standing priority at our company. A reflection of that commitment is our desire to present the highest quality speakers at our next year's conference.

Correcting Mistakes as You Type

If you tend to make certain kinds of spelling or typographical errors, you might notice that Microsoft Word automatically makes the necessary corrections as you type. This is the AutoCorrect feature. For example, some common spelling mistakes, such as typing "adn" instead of "and," are corrected as soon as you type the first space after the word. Similarly, with the exception of certain abbreviations, if you type two capitalized letters in a row, the program automatically changes the second character to lowercase as you continue typing. Word also changes a lowercase character immediately following a period to uppercase.

If you misspell a word that is not corrected right away, or you type a word that is not in the Word dictionary, the program underlines the word with a red, wavy line. Repeated words (such as "the the") are also identified by a red, wavy underline. This feature is known as Automatic Spell Checking. After you finish typing, you can place the mouse pointer on the underlined word, and click the right mouse button to open a shortcut menu of correction options. You can:

■ Choose the correct spelling from the suggested words at the top of the list.

■ Choose Ignore All to remove the underlining and ignore every occurrence of the word.

■ Choose Add to add the word to the dictionary. This means that in the future, Microsoft Word will no longer identify the word as misspelled or unknown.

133

- Choose the Spelling command to display the Spelling dialog box in which you can specify additional spelling options.
- If no suggested spelling appears on the shortcut menu, click the word and edit it to correct the spelling.

Correct typing errors

1 Use the right mouse button to click the word "Mather."

The Spelling shortcut menu opens. Your screen should look similar to the following illustration.

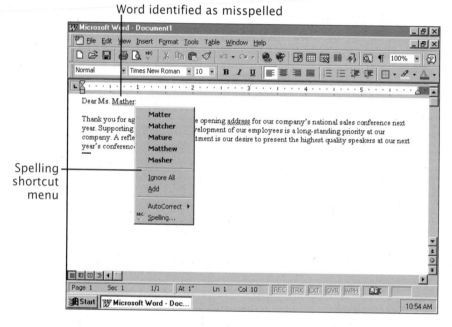

2 Click Ignore All to ignore all occurrences of this word in the document.

3 Use the right mouse button to click any other words underlined with a red, wavy line to display the Spelling shortcut menu. Then, click the correct spelling of the word, or click Ignore All. If you repeated a word, click Delete Repeated Word.

For now, do not click Add or Spelling. You will learn how to use these options in Lesson 5, "Increasing Editing Productivity."

Deal with a potential grammatical error

Grammatical errors, or errors in punctuation or usage, are identified with green, wavy underlines. In the same way you can click the right mouse button on a possible spelling error to correct it, you can use the right mouse button to correct possible grammatical errors. If you do not see the green underlines, you can skip this exercise.

1 Use the right mouse button to click the word "address."

In this case, this usage of the word "address" is correct.

2 Click Ignore Sentence to ignore all possible errors in this sentence.

> **NOTE** The Automatic Spell Checking feature is enabled by default. If you wish to turn the feature off or hide the red, wavy underlines in your document, on the Tools menu, click Options. Click the Spelling & Grammar tab to bring it to the front. Under the Spelling section, click the Check As You Type check box to clear it. Automatic Spell Checking will be turned off until you select the feature again. You can hide the red, wavy underlines by clicking the Hide Spelling Errors In This Document check box to select it. To hide any green, wavy underlines, click the Hide Grammatical Errors In This Document check box to select it.

Displaying Special Characters

In Microsoft Word, any amount of text that ends with a paragraph mark is treated as a paragraph. Even a blank line is a paragraph. Microsoft Word also displays small dots that represent the spaces between words; these dots appear when you press the SPACEBAR, if nonprinting characters are being displayed. Paragraph marks and space dots do not appear in printed documents.

Display paragraph marks and special symbols

When you typed the salutation for the letter, Microsoft Word inserted a paragraph mark (¶) each time you pressed ENTER. You can display or hide paragraph marks and space dots by clicking the Show/Hide ¶ button. When nonprinting characters are displayed, you can see how many paragraph marks are between lines of text and the number of spaces between words. In this exercise, you display these nonprinting characters.

Show/Hide ¶

➤ On the Standard toolbar, click the Show/Hide ¶ button if your paragraph marks are not already displayed. Your screen should look similar to the following illustration.

Nonprinting characters

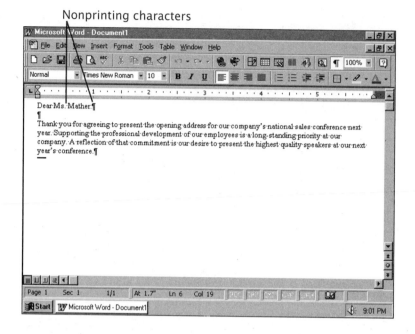

Type additional paragraphs of text

In this exercise, you will add text to the body of your letter. The AutoFormat feature makes ordinal numbers easier to read by changing them to superscripts as you type the dates.

1 Place the insertion point at the last paragraph mark, and then press ENTER twice to create another blank line.

2 Type:

We are still in the planning stages of this conference, so our schedule is still flexible at this point. So far, we have discussed your availability on two tentative dates: October 21st and 22nd. In addition to paying your travel expenses to the conference site (the Park View Center) and your accommodations, we are offering an honorarium of $1500.

3 Press ENTER twice to create another blank line.

4 Type:

If these terms are agreeable to you, please sign both copies of the attached contract and return them to me as soon as possible.

5 Press ENTER twice to create another blank line.

Type a nonbreaking space

When you type words that you want to appear together, you can insert a nonbreaking space between each word. By using a nonbreaking space between words, you prevent the wordwrap feature from separating words at the end of a line. In this exercise, you want to ensure that all the words in the company name appear together.

1   Type **I would like to extend my personal thanks for considering our offer. On behalf of the entire West**

2   Press CTRL+SHIFT+SPACEBAR, and then type **Coast**

3   Press CTRL+SHIFT+SPACEBAR, and then type **Sales organization, I look forward to your timely confirmation.**

4   Press ENTER twice to create another blank line.

5   Type **Terry Kim** and press ENTER.

6   Type **Conference Planning Coordinator** and press ENTER.

7   Type **West Coast Sales** and press ENTER.

Improving Document Creation by Using AutoText Entries

There are certain common words and phrases most people use in letters and documents. The Microsoft Word AutoText feature provides a fast way to insert such frequently used text. Using AutoText entries not only saves you time, but it also prevents typing mistakes. With the AutoText command, you can insert AutoText entries for many common words, phrases, and expressions.

Insert an AutoText entry

Instead of typing "Respectfully yours" at the closing of a letter, you can insert these words by choosing them from the AutoText menu.

1   Click to position the insertion point in front of the name in the signature block.

2   On the Insert menu, point to AutoText.

If a menu item has a right-pointing arrow after its name, this means it opens another menu—a *cascading menu*.

3   On the cascading menu, point to Closing, and then click Respectfully yours.

Word inserts the text in the document.

4   Press ENTER twice.

NOTE Although Word provides AutoText entries for some of the more common words, phrases, and expressions, you can also create your own AutoText entries for your own frequently used text and graphics. You will learn how to create your AutoText entries in Lesson 5, "Increasing Editing Productivity."

Inserting and Deleting Text to Edit Your Document

Editing text simply means making changes by inserting new text, removing (*deleting*) existing text, or replacing text by removing old text and inserting new text in its place.

Insert text in a sentence

You can easily insert new text anywhere in a document.

1 Press CTRL+HOME to position the insertion point at the beginning of the document.

2 Position the pointer just before the word "professional" in the second sentence, and then click immediately to the right of the space character.

3 Type **training and** and then press the SPACEBAR to insert a space between the words.

Delete extra spacing between paragraphs

You can delete text one character at a time using either BACKSPACE or DELETE. Use BACKSPACE to remove characters to the left of the insertion point. Use DELETE to remove characters to the right of the insertion point.

1 Click before the first word ("I") of the last body paragraph to position the insertion point—the last paragraph in the main body of the document.

2 Press BACKSPACE twice to delete the paragraph marks.

3 Press the SPACEBAR to insert a space between the two sentences.

Edit text in a sentence

Pressing DELETE removes characters to the right of the insertion point. After removing text, you can insert new text in its place.

1 Click before the number 5 in $1500 to position the insertion point.

2 Press DELETE, and then type **7**

Select and delete a word

Of course, it would be cumbersome to backspace a letter at a time through an entire document. You can delete as much text as you want by selecting the text first.

1 In the second sentence of the second body paragraph, double-click the word "tentative" to select the word and the space that follows it.

Selected text is highlighted so that you can easily distinguish it from text that is not selected. Double-clicking to select words maintains the correct spacing after you delete a word.

2 Press DELETE to remove the word from the text.

The text in the document moves to fill the space left by the deleted word.

Select text and replace it

Double-clicking a word selects only that word, but you can select any amount of text by dragging across it with the mouse. When text is selected, the next text you type—regardless of its length—replaces the selected text. In this exercise, you select and replace text.

1 In the first body paragraph, place the insertion point in front of the first o in the text "our company's."

2 Drag the pointer across the next two words, so that both "our" and "company's" are highlighted.

3 Type **West Coast Sales**

4 Check the spacing before and after the new text you typed. If you need to add a space, click where you need to add the space to position the insertion point, and then press the SPACEBAR.

Undoing Your Changes

A useful feature in Microsoft Word is the Undo button, which you can use to reverse your changes. For example, in the next exercise, you use the Undo button to remove the new text and restore the original text to your document.

 NOTE You can undo most Microsoft Word commands; operations that cannot be undone include saving, printing, opening, and creating documents.

Undo the last change

Undo

You can also press CTRL+Z to undo the most recent change.

➤ On the Standard toolbar, click the Undo button to undo your last change.

If this action did not remove the new text and restore the original text, you might have pressed another key before you clicked the Undo button. Clicking Undo once reverses only the last change. Click the Undo button again until the original text is restored.

Undo more changes

You can also click the Undo down arrow to see a list of the actions you can reverse. For example, if you wanted to return the document to the way it looked before you made the last three changes, you would scroll to the last of the three changes listed in the Undo list and select it. This action would undo all three changes. In this exercise, you'll see how this works.

➤ On the Standard toolbar, click the Undo down arrow, and then select the third change in the list to undo your last three actions: deleting the word "tentative," typing a 7, and deleting the 5 in $1500.

All the changes you made are reversed. The changes in the Undo list appear so that your most recent change is at the top of the list, with each previous change appearing below it. Because several changes in sequence often depend on preceding changes, you cannot select an individual action on the list without undoing all the actions that appear above that action.

Change your mind again

The Redo button on the Standard toolbar allows you to reverse an undo action. You can reverse the results of the last change by clicking the Redo button. In this exercise, you redo your actions.

Redo

➤ On the Standard toolbar, click the Redo button to redo your last undo action.

The 5 is again deleted from $1500.

Redo all changes

➤ On the Standard toolbar, click the Redo down arrow, and then select the bottommost change in the list to redo all actions.

Your document should look like the following illustration.

140

Inserted text   Replacement text
Deleted text

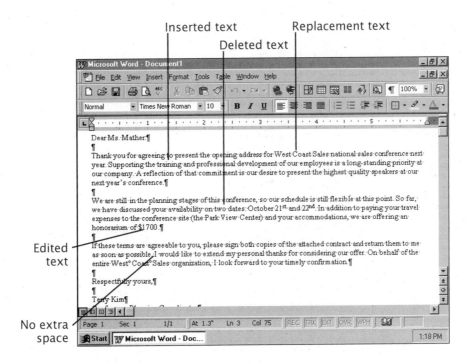

Edited
text

No extra
space

Inserting Dates Quickly

The Microsoft Word Date And Time command provides a fast way to include today's date in a document. With the Date And Time command you can select from a variety of date and time formats. Using this command saves time and eliminates errors. In these exercises, you insert the date and an address.

Insert today's date

1   Press CTRL+HOME to place the insertion point at the top of the document.

2   On the Insert menu, click Date And Time.

    The Date And Time dialog box appears.

3   In the Available Formats list box, click the fourth date format from the top, and then click OK.

    The current date is inserted at the insertion point. This date is based on your computer's date and time setting.

4   Press ENTER twice.

Insert the inside address

1 Type **Ms. Karen Mather** and press ENTER.

2 Type **Fitch & Mather** and press ENTER.

3 Type **1800 Centerdale Circle** and press ENTER.

4 Type **Centerdale, CA 95033** and press ENTER twice.

Saving Your Documents

To keep your work for future use, you must give the document a name and save it. After you save it, the document is available each time you want to use it.

It is best to name and save a document soon after you start working on it. After that, it's a good idea to save a document every 15 minutes or so to minimize the amount of work you could lose if power to your computer is interrupted. The Save button on the Standard toolbar makes this quick and easy to do.

 NOTE The first time you save a document, clicking either Save or Save As on the File menu will open the Save As dialog box, because the first time you save, you need to name the document.

Save the document

When you save a document, you must give it a name and specify where you want to store it. Although you can specify the drive and folder where you want to save your documents, for now save the letter in the same folder as the Step by Step practice files.

 TIP The AutoRecover feature saves the document periodically so that it can be automatically restored in the event of a loss of power. You can specify how often Word saves your document on the Save tab when you choose the Options command on the Tools menu. The AutoSave feature does not eliminate the need for saving the document yourself.

Save

1 On the Standard toolbar, click the Save button.

The Save As dialog box appears the first time you save a document. The dialog box should look like the following illustration.

Current folder   Up One Level button
Look In Favorites button

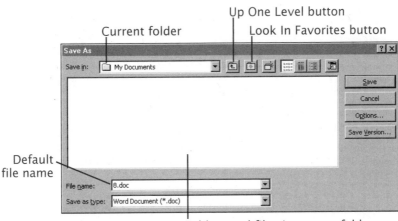

Default file name

Folders and files in current folder

Look In
Favorites

2   If the Part2 Word Practice folder is not currently displayed in the Save In box, click the Look In Favorites button, and then double-click the Part2 Word Practice folder.

3   Be sure the text in the File Name box is selected, and type **Mather Letter01**

You can enter a filename that is up to 255 characters long. You can also use spaces and other characters as part of the name. You can enter a name in lowercase or uppercase letters; however, text in mixed case (for example, a capital first letter, and lowercase for the following letters) is usually easier to read than text in all capital letters.

You can also press ENTER.

4   Click the Save button to close the dialog box and save the document as you've specified.

Your letter is saved with the name Mather Letter01 in the Part2 Word Practice folder.

5   On the File menu, click Close.

NOTE   If you'd like to build on the skills that you learned in this lesson, you can do the One Step Further. Otherwise, skip to "Finish the lesson."

One Step Further: Creating a Letter by Using the Letter Wizard

Wizards can be a big help when you want to create a new document. You simply choose the kind of document you want to create—such as a letter, brochure, report, or fax—and the document wizard prompts you to answer a series of questions. You can choose the style of document and select other options. Then

Microsoft Word creates a professionally designed document based on the selections you made, but without you having to do any of the formatting yourself. With the basics of the document established, you just type the text and edit the document as you wish.

Start the Letter Wizard

In your role as a conference planner you must arrange for the equipment needed by presenters at the conference. To follow up on an attractive bid from a contractor who provides this service, you decide to write a quick letter that summarizes your requirements. In this exercise, you use the Letter Wizard to get a head start on your letter.

New

1 On the Standard toolbar, click the New button.

   You must have a document open in order to select Letter Wizard from the Tools menu.

2 On the Tools menu, click Letter Wizard.

   The Letter Wizard dialog box and the Office Assistant appear. The Letter Wizard looks like the following illustration.

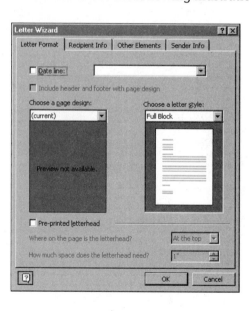

Format the letter

If you are using preprinted letterhead, click the Pre-Printed Letterhead check box and specify the location and size of the letterhead on the page.

On the Letter Format tab, you specify the overall appearance of the letter. The Preview area of the dialog box shows you what the document will look like as you make your selections.

1   On the Letter Format tab, click the Date Line check box.

2   Click the Date Line down arrow, and be sure that the third date format is selected.

3   Click the Choose A Page Design down arrow, and select Contemporary Letter.

4   Click the Choose A Letter Style arrow, and choose Modified Block.

Enter recipient information

On the Recipient Info tab, you can specify information about the individual to whom the letter is addressed.

1   Click the Recipient Info tab.

The Recipient Info tab looks like the following illustration.

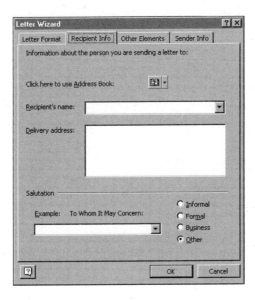

2   In the Recipient's Name box, type **Mr. Eric Bustos**

3 In the Delivery Address box, type the following information:

Bits, Bytes & Chips, Inc.
1001 Industrial Drive
Centerdale, CA 95033

Inserting Addresses from Your Address Book

Using the Insert Address button that is available in some dialog boxes (including the Recipient Info tab in the Letter Wizard), you can insert name and address information that is stored in your Microsoft Outlook Address Book or in your Schedule+ Contact List. Simply click the Address Book button, and select the Address Book you want to use. Then double-click the name you want to insert.

4 In the Salutation area, click the Business option button.

Enter subject information

On the Other Elements tab, you can specify subject, reference line, mailing instructions, and attention information.

1 Click the Other Elements tab.

The Other Elements tab looks like the following illustration.

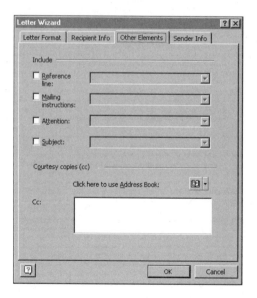

2 Click the Subject check box.

3 In the Subject box, type **West Coast Sales Conference Equipment Proposal**

Enter sender information

On the Sender Info tab, you can specify information about the sender, including the closing and how your name should appear in the signature block. In this exercise, you set up your closing.

1 Click the Sender Info tab.

The Sender Info tab looks like the following illustration.

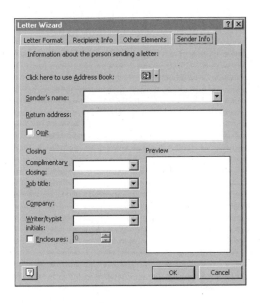

If your letter includes enclosures, click the Enclosures check box and specify the number of enclosures that will accompany this letter.

2 Click the Sender's Name down arrow, select your name if listed, or type it in.

3 Click the Omit check box so your address will not appear in the letter.

4 For a closing, click the Complimentary Closing down arrow, and then select Yours truly.

5 Click the Job Title down arrow, choose your title if listed, or type it in.

6 Click the Company down arrow, choose your company's name if listed, or type it in.

7 Click the Writer/Typist Initials down arrow, choose your initials if listed, or type them in.

8 Click OK.

The Letter Wizard creates a letter formatted according to your selections.

Type the text of the letter

With the basic formatting of the letter established, you are ready to type the text of the letter.

 Type:

As I mentioned on the phone this morning, my management is quite pleased with your proposal. We would like to accept your bid to provide the equipment needs for the West Coast Sales conference as specified in your proposal. We have processed your invoice that represents your retainer fee for the week of the conference. If there is anything else you require to begin the project, please let me know.

Save the letter

Save

1   On the Standard toolbar, click the Save button.

    The Save As dialog box appears.

2   Be sure that Part2 Word Practice is in the Save In box.

    If the folder is not in the Save As box, click the Look In Favorites button, and then double-click Part2 Word Practice.

*Look In
Favorites*

*You can also
press ENTER.*

3   If the text is not selected, drag to select all the text in the File Name box, and then type **Equipment Letter01**

4   Click Save in the dialog box to close the dialog box and save the file.

    Your file is saved with the name Equipment Letter01 in the Part2 Word Practice folder.

Finish the lesson

1   To continue to the next lesson, on the File menu, click Close for each document you have open.

2   If you are finished using Microsoft Word for now, on the File menu, click Exit.

Lesson Summary

To	Do this
Start Microsoft Word	On the taskbar, click Start, point to Programs, and then click Microsoft Word.
Create a new paragraph or a blank line	Press ENTER.

To	Do this	Button
Display or hide paragraph marks	Click the Show/Hide ¶ button.	¶
Insert frequently used text	Choose Insert, and then click AutoText and choose an entry.	
Insert text into existing text	Click to position the insertion point at the place where you want to insert the text, and start typing.	
Remove characters	Press BACKSPACE to remove characters to the left of the insertion point. Press DELETE to remove text to the right of the insertion point.	
Select a word	Double-click the word. *or* Drag across the word.	
Select any amount of text	Drag to highlight text.	
Replace text	Select and type over text.	
Undo the most recent action	Click the Undo button immediately after the action.	
Undo multiple actions	Click the Undo down arrow, and then select the appropriate number of changes.	
Reverse the most recent undo action	Click the Redo button.	
Reverse multiple undo actions	Click the Redo down arrow, and then select the appropriate number of changes.	
Save a new document	On the File menu, click Save or Save As.	

For online information about	Use the Office Assistant to search for
Creating a new document	**Create document**, and then click Create A New Document
Saving documents	**Saving documents**, and then click Save A Document
Using Undo	**Undo**, and then click Undo Mistakes

Moving and Copying Text

In this lesson you will learn how to:

Estimated time
45 min.

- Open an existing document and save it with a new name.
- Display a document in Page Layout view.
- Move text to a new location in a document.
- Copy text to a new location in a document.
- Use the Clipboard to move and copy text.

In Microsoft Word, it's easy to edit your documents. If you want to edit a document but you want to keep the original document unchanged, you can open the document and save it with a new name. That is, you can keep the original document unchanged while you make changes in the new document. By moving and copying text, you can take advantage of work you've already done. For example, you can copy text, move it to a different location, and edit it. To get a better idea of how your document looks, and to edit it easily, you can work in Page Layout view. In this lesson, you'll move and copy text within a document—by dragging text and dropping it in new locations and by using the Clipboard.

Opening a Document

A new, blank document window opens when you start Microsoft Word. You can also open an existing document and modify that document in the same way you would a new document.

Start Word and open a practice file

In this exercise, you'll open the practice file called 02Lesson and then save the file with a different name, Program Highlights02. This process creates a duplicate of the file that you can work on and modify during the lesson. The original file, 02Lesson, is unchanged so that you can practice the lesson as many times as you wish.

1 On the taskbar, click the Start button.

2 Point to Programs, and then click Microsoft Word.

Open

3 On the Standard toolbar, click the Open button.

The Open dialog box appears. In the Open dialog box, you select the folder and document you want to open. The Look In box shows the folder that is currently selected.

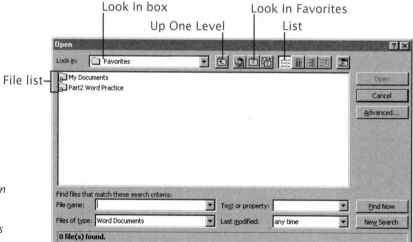

Depending on how your system is configured, your Open dialog box might look different from this illustration.

List

*Look In
Favorites*

Preview

4 On the toolbar of the Open dialog box, verify that the List button is selected.

The names of all folders and files within the selected folder appear in the file list.

5 Be sure that the Favorites folder is in the Look In box, as shown in the illustration in step 3.

If a folder name other than Favorites appears in the Look In box, click the Look In Favorites button on the toolbar.

6 In the file list, double-click the Part2 Word Practice folder.

7 On the toolbar of the Open dialog box, click the Preview button.

A portion of the document appears in the dialog box, so you can preview the document before you open it.

Preview of document

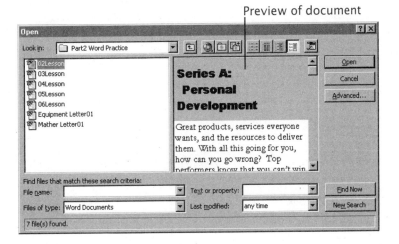

8 In the file list, double-click the 02Lesson file.

The Open dialog box closes, and the 02Lesson file opens in the document window.

 TIP When you click Start on the taskbar and point to the Documents menu, you can see the filenames of the last 15 documents you have opened. When you click a document on the Document menu, the correct program opens and displays the document. At the bottom of the Word File menu, you can see a filename list of your four most recently opened documents.

153

Searching for Documents by Using the Open Dialog Box

In the Open dialog box, you can search for a document even if you can't recall the entire document name. You can enter a partial filename in the File Name box, and Word will locate all the documents with filenames containing the characters you typed. You can also locate a document based on other factors, such as a word or phrase in the document or when the document was last modified.

1   On the Standard toolbar, click the Open button.

2   In the File Name box, type part of the filename.

- To locate files that begin with the text you type, type an asterisk (*) after the text.

- To locate files that end with the text you type, type an asterisk (*) before the text.

- To locate files based on a word or phrase stored in the document, type the text in the Text Or Property box.

- To locate documents based on when the document was last modified, choose a time period in the Last Modified box.

3   Click Find Now.

     The filenames that match the text you type (or any other specifications you entered) appear in the Name area of the Open dialog box.

4   Double-click the document you want to open.

Save the practice document with a new name

When you save a file, you give it a name and specify where you want to store it. The name you give a document can contain up to 255 characters, including spaces and numbers. For each file you use in Part 2 of this book, you'll usually save it in the 6in1 Word folder with a new name; therefore, the original practice file remains unchanged, and you can repeat the exercises as many times as you want. In this exercise, you will create the 6in1 Word folder and then save the document in that folder.

*Look In
Favorites*

1   On the File menu, click Save As.

     The Save As dialog box appears.

2   In the Save As dialog box, click the Look In Favorites button.

3   Click the Create New Folder button.

*Create
New Folder*

4   In the New Folder dialog box, type **6in1 Word**

5 Click OK to create a new folder.

The 6in1 Word folder is created within the current folder, Favorites.

6 Double-click 6in1 Word to make it the new current folder in the Save In box.

7 If the text is not selected, drag to select all text in the File Name box, and then type **Program Highlights02**

You can also press ENTER.

8 In the Save As dialog box, click Save to close the dialog box and save the file.

Your file is saved with the name Program Highlights02 in the 6in1 Word folder. When the dialog box closes, the original document is no longer open; the new document, Program Highlights02, is open, and the name Program Highlights02 appears on the title bar.

Opening Documents Using Microsoft Outlook

If you use Microsoft Outlook, you can easily find and open your documents directly from Outlook. To open a document using Microsoft Outlook:

1 On the taskbar, click the Start button, point to Programs, and click Microsoft Outlook.

2 On the Outlook Bar, click the Other shortcut bar.

3 On the Outlook Bar, click the folder you want to open.

4 In the Information viewer, double-click the document you want to open.

Disabling Automatic Spell Checking and Automatic Grammar Checking

Whenever Automatic Spell Checking is enabled, the misspelled or unknown words in a document are underlined with red, wavy lines. When Automatic Grammar Checking is on, grammatical errors are underlined with green, wavy lines.

Turn off Automatic Spell Checking and Automatic Grammar Checking

The Program Highlight02 document is a draft of the program for next year's West Coast Sales national sales conference. As the conference coordinator, you are responsible for completing the program and preparing it for distribution.

In this exercise, to help you focus on moving around in the document (rather than on misspelled words, unknown words, or grammatical errors), you will disable Automatic Spell Checking and Automatic Grammar Checking.

1 On the Tools menu, click Options, and then click the Spelling & Grammar tab.

2 In the Spelling area, click the Hide Spelling Errors In This Document check box to select it.

There should be a check mark in the check box. Selecting the Hide Spelling Errors In This Document option hides the red, wavy underlines in the document.

3 In the Grammar area, click the Hide Grammatical Errors In This Document check box to select it.

Selecting the Hide Grammatical Errors In This Document option hides the green, wavy underlines in the document.

4 Click OK to close the dialog box and return to the practice document.

The misspelled or unknown words and grammatical errors are no longer underlined.

Display nonprinting characters

To make it easier to see exactly where to move text around in the document, you can display nonprinting characters.

Show/Hide ¶

➤ If paragraph marks are not already displayed, click the Show/Hide ¶ button on the Standard toolbar.

Selecting the Best View for Examining Your Document

In the document window, there are several display options, known as *views*, for examining your document. In each view, you can focus on different parts of the editing process. For example, you will probably most often use the default, Normal view. In Normal view, you can see basic text and paragraph formatting, which makes Normal view ideal for focusing on text and revising your document. On the other hand, Page Layout view is the best view to use when you want to see the arrangement of text and graphics on the page while you edit text. For example, in Page Layout view, you can see text formatted in columns, but in Normal view, you cannot. Outline view is great for organizing ideas and establishing a structure for your document, because you can easily see the structure and organization of the headings in the document. You can switch between these three views quickly by using the View buttons located to the left of the horizontal scroll bar.

In addition, you can use the Online Layout view, which is ideal for reading documents on the Internet. Another view, called the Document Map, is a convenient way to move through a long document.

Switch to Page Layout view

To help you get a better idea of the formatting used in your Program Highlights document, you decide to display the document in Page Layout view.

Page Layout View

1 Make sure you are in Page Layout view. If not, click the Page Layout View button.

2 Click the scroll down arrow at the bottom of the vertical scroll bar to view the contents of the first page.

You can now see the special formatting applied to the first character of some of the paragraphs.

Next Page

3 Click the Next Page scroll button at the bottom of the vertical scroll bar until the third page of the document is in the document window.

Using the scroll down arrow, you can now see that parts of the document are formatted in multiple columns. You also see where graphics appear in relation to text on the page. Your document should look similar to the following illustration.

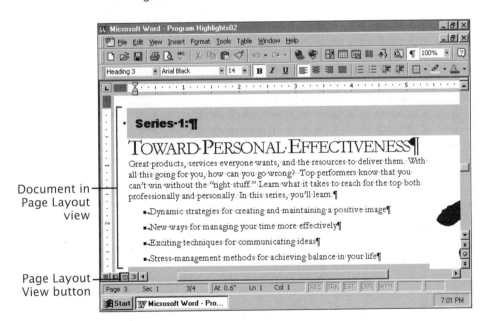

Remain in Page Layout view as you move and copy text in the next part of this lesson.

Adjust magnification

When you want to copy or move text, if you can see the place to which you want to move the material, dragging is the most efficient method of making your changes. Depending on the size and resolution of your monitor, you might not be able to see all the text on a line without scrolling to the right first. If so, you can change the magnification, which adjusts the size of the display so that all the text fits in the window.

Zoom

➤ On the Standard toolbar, click the Zoom down arrow, and then click Page Width.

Moving and Copying Text by Dragging

For a demonstration of how to drag and drop text, double-click the Camcorder file named Moving Text By Dragging in the Part2 Word Camcorder Files folder. See "Installing and Using the Practice and Camcorder Files," earlier in this book for more information.

You can reuse and rearrange text in your documents by using the drag-and-drop feature in Microsoft Word. By dragging selected text, you can quickly copy or move text to a new location. When you can see the final destination for the text on the screen, dragging is the most efficient way to copy or move selected text.

Select a line of text

At the left of every paragraph, there's an invisible selection bar. By clicking in the selection bar, you can select an entire line. You can also drag the mouse pointer down the selection bar to select several lines at once. In this exercise, you will select a line in a list.

TIP If you are selecting a large amount of text, it is easier to click where you want the selection to begin and then, while holding down the SHIFT key, click where you want the selection to end. Microsoft Word selects everything between the first place you clicked and the second place you clicked. This technique is especially useful when you want to select text that spans more than one screen.

---

1 Press CTRL+HOME to move to the beginning of the document. Position the mouse pointer to the left of the line that begins "Exciting techniques."

When the mouse pointer is in the selection bar, the pointer changes to a right-pointing arrow.

2 Click to select the line.

When the line is selected, the text changes to white text on a black background. Your screen should look similar to the following illustration.

Selection bar   Selected line

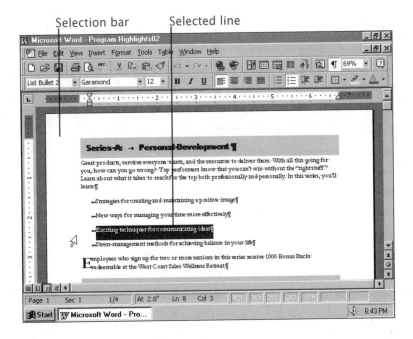

Drag to move text

Next, you'll move the selected line to the start of the list.

1   Position the mouse pointer over the selection until the pointer turns into a left-pointing arrow.

2   Hold down the left mouse button. A small, dotted box and a dotted insertion point appear. Drag up until the dotted insertion point is at the beginning of the line that starts with the word "Strategies," as shown in the following illustration. Then, release the mouse button.

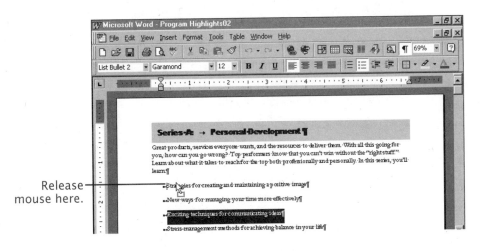

Release mouse here.

159

3   Click anywhere outside the selected text to clear the selection.
Your screen should look like the following illustration.

Moved text ──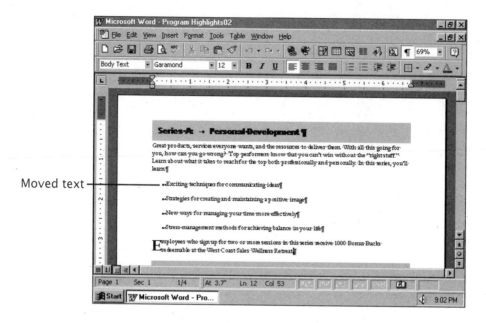

Copy text using the mouse

Copying text by using the mouse is similar to moving text by using the mouse.
If you have to repeat the same text many times in a document, copying not
only saves you time and effort—it also helps you maintain consistency and
guard against typographical errors. In this exercise, you will copy the words
"your customers," and then insert them at another location in the sentence.

1   Scroll to the paragraph below the heading "Series B: Organizational
Strategies."

2   Drag to select the words "your customers" in the second sentence.

3   Hold down the CTRL key on the keyboard, point to the selected text, and
then hold down the mouse button.

4   Drag to position the dotted insertion point immediately after the word
"prepare" in the next sentence. Release the mouse button, and then
release CTRL.

A copy of the selected text is inserted; the original text is unchanged.

5   Click anywhere outside the selected text to clear the selection.

Copying and Moving Text Using Buttons

You can also select text, use the right mouse button to click the selected text, and click Copy or Cut.

You can use the Copy and Paste buttons to copy or move text that is not visible on the screen. When you copy (or cut) text, Microsoft Word stores the copy on the *Clipboard*—a temporary storage area that you can't see on the screen. The text remains on the Clipboard, so you can insert the same text multiple times. The contents of the Clipboard remain the same until you cut or copy other text, or until you shut down your computer.

The following illustration shows how you can use the Copy and Paste buttons on the Standard toolbar to insert text in a new location.

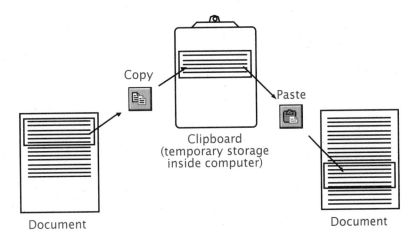

Copying Text Over a Long Distance

When you copy text using the Clipboard, the original text remains in its original location; you copy the Clipboard contents to new locations in the document. To quickly move to different parts of a document without scrolling, you can switch to Document Map view. In this view, you see the major headings of the document in the left side of the window, and the entire document in the right side of the window. By clicking a heading on the left side, you can quickly move the insertion point to that heading in the document on the right side of the window. By clicking the plus or minus sign, you can expand or collapse the heading to display or hide its subheadings.

Switch to the Document Map

Document Map

➤ On the Standard toolbar, click the Document Map button.

Your screen looks like the following illustration.

161

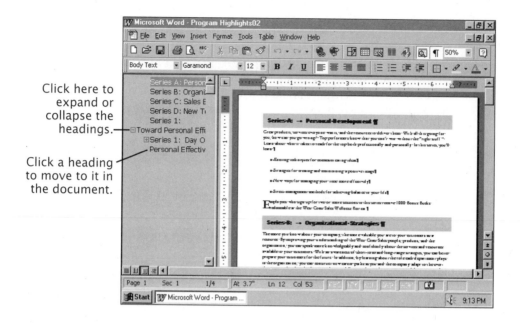

Click here to expand or collapse the headings.

Click a heading to move to it in the document.

Copy a heading

If you copy the heading "Series 1: Day One" and insert the text in a new location, you need to change only one word to create a new heading, "Series 1: Day Two." The formatting of the new heading is identical to that of the original heading.

1   In the left side of the window, click the heading "Series 1: Day One – Aspen Room."

The insertion point moves to this heading in the right side of the window.

2   Select the text in the heading and be sure to include the paragraph mark, but not the section break, in your selection.

3   On the Standard toolbar, click the Copy button.

Copy

You'll see no change in the document, but a copy of the selected text is placed on the Clipboard.

4   Scroll to the bottom of page 3, and place the insertion point in front of the line "Section Break (Continuous)."

5   On the Standard toolbar, click the Paste button.

Paste

A copy of the heading is inserted.

Edit the new heading

➤ Double-click "One" in the new heading, and then type **Two**
The word "Two" replaces the word "One."

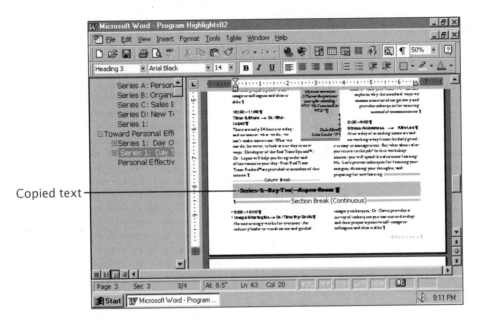

Copied text —

 IMPORTANT If the word "Two" does not replace the word "One" but instead appears next to "One," be sure that the Typing Replaces Selection check box is selected on the Edit tab of the Options dialog box of the Tools menu. For more information, see the Edit Options section in the Appendix, "Matching the Exercises."

Moving Text Over a Long Distance

Moving text over a long distance within a document is similar to copying text over a long distance. The Standard toolbar makes moving text easy. The difference is that instead of copying the text, you *cut* the text from its original place in the document and store the text on the Clipboard. Then, you scroll to where you want to insert the text and paste it into the document.

163

Move text from the end of the document to the middle

You decide that people attending the first day of the conference might overlook the last three paragraphs after the schedule for Day Two. You decide to change the layout of the scheduling information. In this exercise, you'll move the last two paragraphs so that they appear at the end of the first day's schedule, on page 3.

1 In the left side of the window, click the heading "Personal Effectiveness Hospitality Room Aspen Room Annex."

The insertion point moves to this heading in the right side of the window.

2 Select the two-line heading and the following paragraph. Do not select the last paragraph mark in the document.

3 On the Standard toolbar, click the Cut button.

The text is removed from the document and stored on the Clipboard.

4 Click the Previous Page scroll button at the bottom of the vertical scroll bar to move quickly to the previous page.

5 Scroll downward, if necessary, and place the insertion point at the start of the heading "Series 1: Day Two – Aspen Room."

6 On the Standard toolbar, click the Paste button to insert the text from the Clipboard.

Cut

Previous Page

Paste

Close the Document Map

➤ On the Standard toolbar, click the Document Map button.

Document Map

Save the document

➤ On the Standard toolbar, click the Save button.

Microsoft Word saves the changes you made in this document.

Save

 NOTE If you'd like to build on the skills that you learned in this lesson, you can do the One Step Further. Otherwise, skip to "Finish the lesson."

One Step Further: Summarizing a Document

To get an idea of the contents of a long document, you can have Word summarize the document for you. By using the AutoSummarize command on the Tools menu, you can identify the kind of summary you want and how you want to view the summarized information. If you choose to view a highlighted summary in the document window, you can adjust the amount of detail you want to see.

Summarize a document

Your colleagues at West Coast Sales contributed to this document, but it was assembled by an assistant, so you are not familiar with its contents. In this exercise, you use the AutoSummarize feature to learn more about the information in the document.

1   On the Tools menu, click AutoSummarize.

After summarizing the document, Word displays the AutoSummarize dialog box.

AutoSummarize options

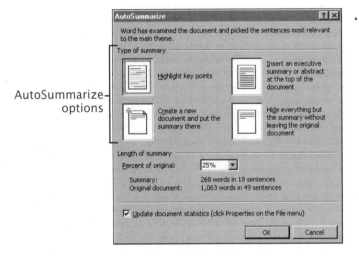

You can also display only the summarized text, add summarized text to the start of the document, or create a new document that contains the summarized text.

2   Double-click the first box to see a highlighted summary of the document.

The important ideas and text are highlighted in the document window. The AutoSummarize toolbar allows you to hide or display only the summarized text and to change the amount of detail highlighted.

3   Scroll through the document to review the highlights.

4   On the AutoSummarize toolbar, click the Close button.

Finish the lesson

1   To continue to the next lesson, on the File menu, click Close.

If you are prompted to save your changes, click Yes.

2   If you are finished using Microsoft Word for now, on the File menu, click Exit.

Lesson Summary

To	Do this	Button
Open an existing document	Click the Open button, and in the File Name list, double-click the document name. If you don't see the document name, check to make sure that the correct drive and folder are selected.	
Display the document headings	On the Standard toolbar, click Document Map button.	
Preview a document before opening it	In the Open dialog box, click the Preview button.	
Adjust the magnification of the screen	On the Standard toolbar, click the Zoom down arrow, and then select your magnification preference.	100%
Move or copy text to a location not currently visible	Select the text, and click the Cut or Copy button on the Standard toolbar. Scroll to the new location, and click. Click the Paste button to insert the selection.	
Display a document in different views	Click the appropriate view button located to the left of the horizontal scroll bar.	

For online information about	Use the Office Assistant to search for
Opening documents	**Opening documents,** and then click Open A Document
Moving and copying text	**Moving and copying text,** and then click Move Or Copy Text And Graphics
Scrolling through a document	**Scrolling,** click See More, and then click Move Around In A Document
Saving documents	**Saving documents,** and then click Save A Document

Changing the Appearance of Text

In this lesson you will learn how to:

- Apply formatting.
- Change the magnification of the document window.
- Set paragraph indents.
- Create numbered lists and bulleted lists.
- Align text in columns with tabs.
- Add a border around a paragraph.
- Change the line spacing within and between paragraphs.

Estimated time
60 min.

Changing the appearance of your text allows you to enhance the look of your document. More than mere aesthetics, the appearance of your documents can make the material easier to read and can help your reader quickly locate important ideas. In this lesson, you'll learn about using the buttons on the Formatting toolbar to emphasize and align text. You will also indent paragraphs, add a border around a paragraph, and add bullets and numbers to lists. You'll increase the space between lines within a paragraph and between paragraphs. And you'll learn to adjust the magnification of the document window to see more of the page at one time.

Start the lesson

Do the following steps to open the practice file called 03Lesson, and then save the file with the new name Speaker Letter03.

Open

Look In Favorites

1 On the Standard toolbar, click the Open button.

2 Make sure the Part2 Word Practice folder is in the Look In box.

You can click the Look In Favorites button to display the Part2 Word Practice folder, and then double-click the Part2 Word Practice folder.

3 In the file list, double-click the 03Lesson file to open it.

This file is a draft of a letter that provides additional conference information to the motivational speaker hired to deliver the opening remarks.

4 On the File menu, click Save As.

The Save As dialog box appears.

5 Click the Look In Favorites button, and then double-click the 6in1 Word folder.

6 Be sure Word Document is in the Save As Type box. Select and delete any text in the File Name box, and then type **Speaker Letter03**

7 Click Save, or press ENTER.

If you share your computer, the screen display might have changed since your last lesson. If your screen does not look similar to the illustrations as you work through this lesson, see the Appendix, "Matching the Exercises."

Applying Character and Paragraph Formatting

When you change the appearance of text—by centering it or by making it bold or italic, for example—you are *formatting* the text. Character formatting and paragraph formatting are two examples of formatting you can use to change the appearance of text. Character formatting, such as bold, italic, underlining, and highlighting, affects only selected text. Paragraph formatting, such as center alignment or indentation, affects entire paragraphs. The Formatting toolbar gives you quick access to the formatting options you are likely to use most often. Additional character formatting options are available by using the Font command, and additional paragraph formatting options are available by using the Paragraph command.

 TROUBLESHOOTING The AutoFormat feature might be affecting your formatting. To turn AutoFormatting off, on the Format menu, click AutoFormat, and then click Options. On the AutoFormat As You Type tab, clear the Define Styles Based On Your Formatting check box, click OK, and then click Close in the AutoFormat dialog box.

Changing Character Formatting

On the Formatting toolbar, you can click a button to apply bold, italic, underlining, and highlighting to selected text. For example, you select text and then

168

click the Bold button to apply bold formatting. If you click the Bold button again, you remove the bold formatting from the selected text. The Formatting toolbar also contains Font and Font Size boxes for changing the type face and the type size of selected text. Additional character formatting options—such as small caps—are available in the Font dialog box.

NOTE Your printer might not be able to print combinations of formatting applied to the same word. Check your printer documentation for any limitations.

Apply bold formatting

As the conference coordinator for the West Coast Sales national sales conference, you want to add the finishing touches to a letter to the keynote speaker. In this exercise, you will apply bold and italic formatting to the company name in the signature block. You begin by selecting the text you want to format.

1   Press CTRL+END to move to the end of the document.

2   Position the mouse pointer in the invisible selection bar to the left of the company name "West Coast Sales."

    When the mouse pointer is in the selection bar, the pointer changes to a right-pointing arrow.

3   Click to select the line.

4   On the Formatting toolbar, click the Bold and Italic buttons.

    Click anywhere to deselect the text. The formatted text should look like the following illustration.

Bold

Italic

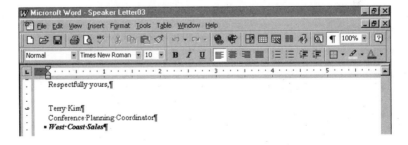

TIP To apply character formatting to a single word, you do not need to select the word. When no text is selected, Microsoft Word applies character formatting to the current word (the one containing the insertion point).

Change the design and size of text

Microsoft Word displays your text in the font and font size in which it will print. The *font* is the design of the text characters (letters, punctuation, and numbers), and the *font size*, which is measured in points, is how large the characters are. A point is a standard measurement in the publishing industry. There are 72 points in an inch. The larger the number of points, the larger the text. You can change the font and font size for selected text by selecting from the Font and Font Size lists on the Formatting toolbar.

1   Click in the selection bar next to the company name to select the line "West Coast Sales."

2   To display the list of fonts, click the Font down arrow.

    The font names in your list might be different from those shown in this illustration.

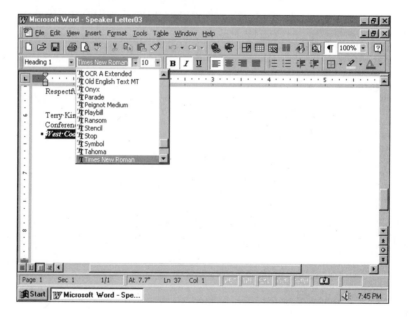

3   On the list of fonts, click Arial.

    You might have to scroll up to Arial. The selected text changes to Arial.

4   To display a list of font sizes for the font you've selected, click the Font Size down arrow.

5   On the list of font sizes, click 9.

Copy formatting to text

If you plan to use the same formatting in different places in your document, you can save time by copying the formatting with the Format Painter. Double-click the Format Painter button if you're going to copy formatting to several locations, or just click the button if you're going to copy formatting only once.

Format Painter

1 In the signature block, verify that the line "West Coast Sales" is selected.

2 On the Standard toolbar, double-click the Format Painter button to store formatting information.

The mouse pointer now has a paint brush icon next to it. You are going to copy the formatting of the signature line.

3 Press CTRL+HOME to move to the beginning of the document.

4 Drag the pointer across the text "West Coast Sales" in the first body paragraph.

The formatting from the signature block text is applied to this text.

5 Drag the pointer across the text "West Coast Sales" in the "Corporate strategies" paragraph to apply the formatting from the signature block line to this text.

6 Click the Format Painter button to turn off the copy formatting feature.

Apply additional formatting to text

1 In the "Corporate strategies" paragraph, place the insertion point in the word "both."

To change the formatting of a single word, you do not need to select the word first.

Underline

2 On the Formatting toolbar, click the Underline button.

The word "both" is underlined.

3 In the paragraph that begins with the text "Note," select the text "imme-diately after the dinner."

4 On the Formatting toolbar, click the Italic button.

The text "immediately after the dinner" is italic. Click anywhere to dese-lect the text.

Italic

Using Additional Formatting Options

In the Font dialog box, there are additional character formatting options you can choose beyond what is available on the Formatting toolbar.

When you click the Format menu and then click Font, you can choose from the character formatting options on the Font tab. These options are described in the following table.

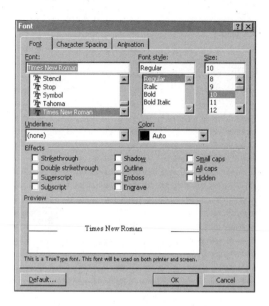

Option	Description
Font	Allows you to choose a font from the Font list. This option is the same as clicking the Font arrow on the Formatting toolbar.
Font Style	Allows you to choose a style from the Font Style list.
Size	Allows you to choose or type a point size. This option is the same as clicking the Font Size arrow on the Formatting toolbar.
Underline	Allows you to choose an underline style from the Underline list by clicking the down arrow. Examples of underlining options include:

Single applies a single, continuous underline to the selected text.

Words Only applies a single underline to each word and punctuation.

Double applies a double, continuous underline.

Dotted applies a dotted single continuous underline

Thick applies a thick single continuous underline.

Dash applies a dashed single continuous underline.

Dot Dash applies a single continuous underline composed of dots and dashes.

Dot Dot Dash applies a single continuous repeating underline of two dots and a dash.

Wave applies a single continuous wavy underline to the selected text.

Option	Description
Color	Allows you to choose a text color by clicking the Color down arrow and selecting a color.
Effects	Allows you to choose a font effect. Examples of effects options include:

> **Strikethrough** ~~looks like this~~
> **Double strikethrough** ~~looks like this~~
> **Superscript** looks like this
> **Subscript** looks like this
> **Shadow looks like this**
> **Outline** looks like this
> **Emboss** looks like this
> **Engrave** looks like this
> **Small caps** LOOKS LIKE THIS
> **All caps** LOOKS LIKE THIS
> **Hidden** looks like this

When you click the Character Spacing tab in the Font dialog box, you can choose from the following character spacing options.

Option	Description
Scaling	In the Scale box, type the value by which you want to increase the width of characters.
Spacing	In the Spacing box, choose Normal, Condensed, or Expanded to adjust the amount of space between characters. In the By box, you can select the exact amount of space (measured in points) to use.
Position	In the Position box, choose Normal, Raised, or Lowered positioning to adjust the height of the characters above or below the line. In the By box, you can select the exact amount of space (measured in points) to use above or below the line.
Kerning	Click the Kerning For Fonts check box to specify whether you want the space between pairs of certain characters to be automatically adjusted for you based on the size of the font.

When you apply an animation effect, your text actually moves, flashes, or twinkles, depending on the effect you've applied. When you click the Animation tab in the Font dialog box, you can choose from the following animation options.

Option	Description
Blinking Background	Background around the text flashes on and off.
Las Vegas Lights	Small shapes of various colors flash and move around the text.
Marching Black Ants	A black dashed line flashes as it moves around the text.
Marching Red Ants	A red dashed line flashes as it moves around the text.
Shimmer	Text shimmers as if reflected in water.
Sparkle Text	Confetti-like colored shapes flash and move randomly around the text.

Displaying More of the Document at Once

When your work in a document focuses heavily on paragraph formatting, it is often useful to see more of the document at one time. By viewing several paragraphs (or even the entire document) at once, you can check the alignment, indentation, and spacing of the paragraphs and make additional adjustments as required. In the Zoom list, there are preset zoom settings you can use to magnify or reduce the document in the document window. You can also type in a value to change the magnification settings to whatever setting you prefer.

Change the magnification

You can adjust the magnification to get an overall view of the page width.

Zoom

1 Click the Zoom down arrow, and then click Page Width.

2 Click the Page Layout View button to the left of the horizontal scroll bar.

Your document should look like the following illustration. The actual font size does not change; only the appearance of the characters on the screen is altered.

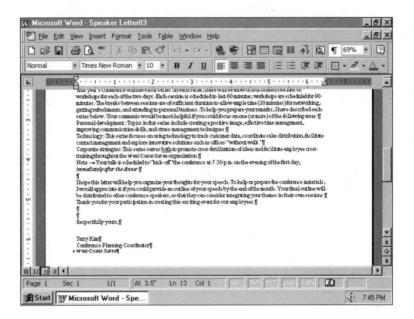

Changing Paragraph Alignment

On the Formatting toolbar, you can click a button to change the alignment or indentation of paragraphs. Using the ruler, you can customize indentation of both the left and right sides of a paragraph. Additional paragraph formatting options, such as adjusting line spacing and the space between paragraphs, are available in the Paragraph dialog box.

 TIP To apply paragraph formatting to a single paragraph, you do not need to select the entire paragraph first. When no text is selected, Microsoft Word applies paragraph formatting to the current paragraph (the one containing the insertion point).

When you change the position of a paragraph between the left and right edges of the page, you are changing the alignment of the text. Text can be left-aligned (which is the default alignment), centered, right-aligned, or justified.

Left-aligned means that all the lines in that paragraph begin at the same point on the left side of the page, and break at different points on the right side, depending on how the lines fit ("ragged right"). Left-aligned text is often used in the body of a business letter, or a book such as this one. *Right-aligned* means that all the lines in that paragraph end at the same point on the right, and begin at different points on the left, according to how the lines fit ("ragged left"). Return addresses and dates are often right-aligned at the top of a letter. *Centered* text extends in both directions from the center of the line, as seen in announcements and invitations, and is ragged both on the right and on the left. *Justified* text starts at the same point on the left for each line in the paragraph, and ends at the same point on the right; Microsoft Word adjusts the amount of space between each word to ensure a uniform edge on both sides of the paragraph.

Right align today's date

In this exercise, you will align the date with the right edge of the page.

1   Press CTRL+HOME to place the insertion point at the top of the document.

2   Place the insertion point anywhere in the date line.

3   On the Formatting toolbar, click the Align Right button.

Align Right

The date is now aligned at the right margin of the page.

Setting Indents

You can quickly indent the left edge of a line or paragraph by using the TAB key or by clicking a button on the Formatting toolbar.

Using the TAB Key to Indent Text

An easy way to indent a single line of text is with the TAB key. You can insert a tab in front of the first character you want to indent. The TAB indents only the line that contains the insertion point. To indent multiple paragraphs at one time, using the Increase Indent and Decrease Indent buttons is usually a better choice.

Use a tab to indent a line

In this exercise, you use TAB to indent a line.

1   Move the insertion point in front of the word "Thank" in the first body paragraph.

2   Press TAB.

Using the Formatting Toolbar to Set Indents

Using the buttons on the Formatting toolbar, you can quickly indent one or more paragraphs. Each time you click the Increase Indent button, Microsoft Word indents all lines of the selected paragraph (or the paragraph containing the insertion point) a half inch. Microsoft Word has preset, or *default,* tab stops every half inch, so you are actually indenting to the next tab stop. The Formatting toolbar also has a Decrease Indent button that decreases the indent of all the lines of a selected paragraph a half inch.

Use the indent buttons

Increase Indent

If you cannot see the Formatting toolbar, use the right mouse button to click an open area on the Standard toolbar, and then on the shortcut menu, click Formatting.

1 Verify that the insertion point is still in the first body paragraph.

2 On the Formatting toolbar, click the Increase Indent button.

Your indented paragraph should look like the following illustration.

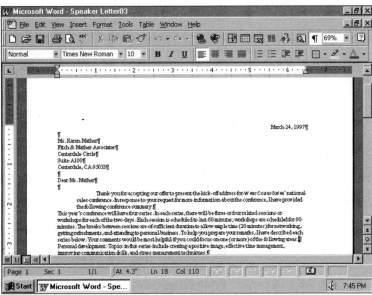

3 Click the Increase Indent button two more times.

Each time you click the button, the paragraph indents a half inch. The wordwrap feature rearranges the text to adjust to the new shorter line length.

4 On the Formatting toolbar, click the Decrease Indent button to move the paragraph left a half inch. Continue clicking the Decrease Indent button until the paragraph reaches the left margin.

Decrease Indent

5 Click the Decrease Indent button again.

The text will not move past the left margin.

Indent several paragraphs

1 Select four paragraphs starting with the paragraph that begins "Personal development" and ending with the paragraph that begins "Note."

2 On the Formatting toolbar, click the Increase Indent button to indent the selected paragraphs a half inch.

3 Click anywhere to deselect the text.

Creating Bulleted and Numbered Lists

Bulleted and numbered lists are common elements in many documents. Bullets clearly separate list items from one another, emphasizing each point; numbers show sequence. The AutoFormat As You Type feature inserts a bullet and a tab whenever you type an o and two spaces (or press TAB) at the beginning of a line. To format existing text with bullets, you can click the Bullets button on the Formatting toolbar. You can also use the Numbering button to create a numbered list when you are typing new text or when you want to format existing text.

Create a numbered list

To draw attention to the paragraphs that identify the different topics covered at the conference, in this exercise, you will change three paragraphs of your document into a numbered list.

1 Select the first three indented paragraphs, starting with the "Personal development" paragraph and ending with the "Corporate strategies" paragraph.

Numbering

2 On the Formatting toolbar, click the Numbering button.

A number appears in front of each selected paragraph, and the indents adjust to separate the text from the numbers.

3 Click anywhere to deselect the text.

When the paragraph is longer than one line, the second line of text aligns with the line of text above, not with the number, as is shown in the following illustration. This paragraph formatting is called a *hanging indent.*

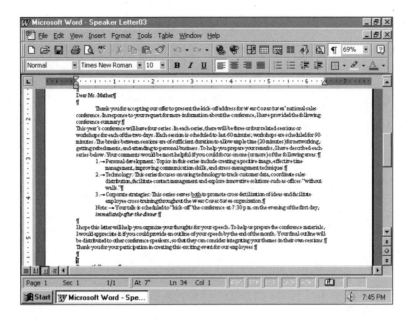

Insert another numbered paragraph

After realizing that you omitted an important item in the list, you decide to insert a new numbered paragraph within the existing numbered list.

1 With the insertion point in the last line of the first numbered paragraph, press END.

2 Press ENTER.

A new blank numbered line is inserted. Notice that the remaining paragraphs are renumbered to reflect the addition of a new item in the list.

3 Type the following text: **Sales excellence: Topics in this series include prospecting, assessing customer requirements, delivering proposals, and closing the deal.**

TIP Although using the Formatting toolbar buttons is the quickest way to create a numbered list, many more options are available through the Bullets And Numbering command on the Format menu. Use this command to change the number formatting.

Change the numbers to bullets

Because these items do not have to be presented in any particular order, you decide to list them with bullets rather than with numbers.

1 Select the numbered paragraphs.

2 On the Formatting toolbar, click the Bullets button.

The numbers are replaced with bullets.

Bullets

Create a new bullet character

The default bullet character is a simple round dot, but you can change the bullet character if you like. On the Bulleted tab in the Bullets And Numbering dialog box you can choose a new bullet character. If the bullet you want to use is not in the dialog box, you can choose from additional bullet characters. In this exercise, you change the bullet character for your bulleted list.

1 Select all the bulleted paragraphs, and with the mouse pointer over the selected paragraphs, click the right mouse button.

2 Click Bullets And Numbering.

3 Click the Bulleted tab, if it is not already in front.

4 Click the first box in the second row.

If you want to use a bullet character not displayed in the dialog box, you can click Customize to choose from other bullet characters.

5 Click OK.

6 On the Formatting toolbar, click the Increase Indent button.

Increase Indent

The bullets appear as shown in the following illustration.

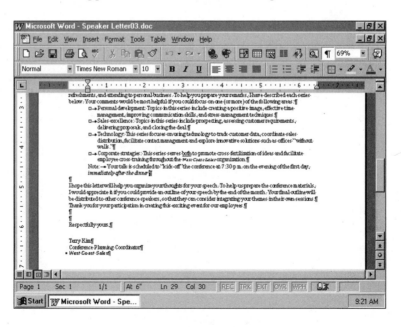

Remove bullets

You can remove the bullet in front of a line simply by clicking the Bullets button again. In this exercise, you type a new line of text and remove the bullet that Word applied.

1 With the insertion point at the end of the first bulleted paragraph, press ENTER, and type **This is our most popular series. Be sure to sign up early!**

2 On the Formatting toolbar, click the Bullets button.

The bullet is removed from the start of the line, and the text moves to the left margin.

3 On the Formatting toolbar, click the Increase Indent button twice to align the start of this line with the text above it.

Setting Custom Indents by Using the Ruler

For a demonstration of how to set custom indents by using the ruler, double-click the Camcorder file named Setting Custom Indents in the Part2 Word Camcorder Files folder. See "Installing and Using the Practice and Camcorder Files," earlier in this book for more information.

Clicking the Increase Indent and Decrease Indent buttons is the fastest way to adjust a left indent in half-inch increments. Sometimes, however, you might want to use different indent settings. Using the ruler at the top of the document window, you can set custom indents.

The markers on the ruler control the indents of the current paragraph. The left side of the ruler has three markers. The top triangle, called the *first-line indent marker*, controls where the first line of the paragraph begins; the bottom triangle, called the *hanging indent marker*, controls where the remaining lines of the paragraph begin. The small square under the bottom triangle, called the *left indent marker*, allows you to move the first-line indent marker and the left indent marker simultaneously. When you move the left indent marker, the distance between the hanging indent and the first line indent remains the same. The triangle on the right side of the ruler, called the *right indent marker*, controls where the right edge of the paragraph ends.

First-line indent marker

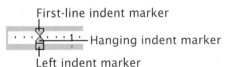

Hanging indent marker

Left indent marker

TIP You can use the ScreenTip feature to identify the correct indent markers on the ruler.

Set a custom left indent

If your ruler is not already displayed, open the View menu, and click Ruler.

In this exercise, you will drag the left indent marker to adjust the entire left edge of the signature block, which will customize the indent settings for the paragraphs of the signature block in the letter.

1 Select the signature block at the end of the document, starting with "Respectfully yours."

The four lines are highlighted.

If only one marker moves, it means you dragged a triangle instead of the square. On the Standard toolbar, click the Undo button, point to the square, and try again.

2 Drag the left indent marker to the 4-inch mark on the ruler, and then release the mouse button.

Both the top and bottom triangles move. Use the dotted line to see where the new indent will be. When you release the mouse button, the text moves to align with the paragraph indent marker. Click anywhere to deselect the text.

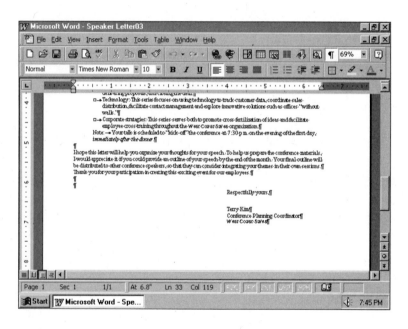

Set a right indent

1 Select the four bulleted items and the paragraph starting with the word "Note."

2 Drag the right indent marker to the 5.5-inch mark.

If you need to scroll to the right to see the right indent marker, scroll back to the left edge when you are done. Click anywhere to deselect the text.

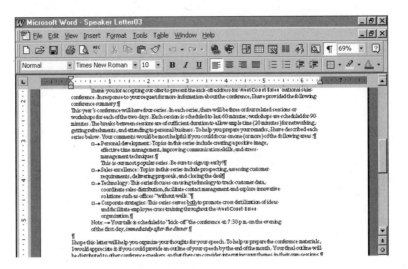

Set a hanging indent

The top triangle on the left of the ruler, the first-line indent marker, controls the start of the first line of a paragraph. To make the "Note" paragraph more distinctive, you decide to format that paragraph with a hanging indent by dragging the first-line indent marker, so that the first line of text extends to the left of the paragraph, with the rest of the paragraph "hanging" below it.

Only the top, or first-line indent, marker should move. If both markers move, it means you dragged the square instead of the top triangle. On the Standard toolbar, click the Undo button. Then point to the top triangle, and try again.

1 With the insertion point positioned in the "Note" paragraph, drag the first-line indent marker left to the .25-inch mark on the ruler.

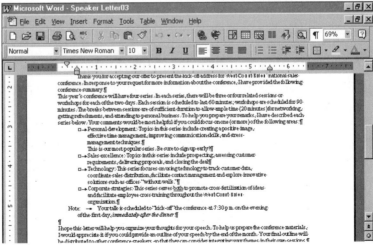

2   Drag the hanging indent marker (the bottom triangle) to the .75-inch mark on the ruler.

Make sure you click only the bottom triangle, and not the square. The first line does not move, but the "hanging" text is now aligned with the items in the bulleted list. Your screen should look like the following illustration.

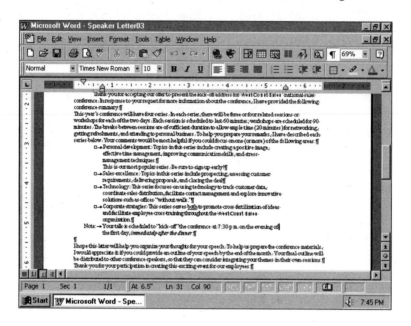

If you know the exact measurements that you need for indents you can also use the Paragraph command on the Format menu.

Indent the first line

1   Click in the paragraph starting "This year's conference."

2   Drag the first-line indent marker (the top triangle) to the .5-inch mark.

3   Repeat step 2 and indent the first line of all the remaining body paragraphs in the letter *except* the ones highlighted with bullets or the "Note" paragraph.

Aligning Text by Using Tabs

When you press TAB, the insertion point (and any text after it) moves to the first tab stop, located every half inch on the ruler. If you press TAB again, your text moves to the next tab stop. Because you can format the alignment of the tab stops to left-align, center, or right-align, you can use tabs to align text in columns. You can also format tabs to align a column of numbers on their decimal point. This feature makes using TAB an easy way to, for example, create a simple table for a price list.

For a demonstration of how to create tabs on the ruler, double-click the Camcorder file named Creating Tab Stops in the Part2 Word Camcorder Files folder. See "Installing and Using the Practice and Camcorder Files," earlier in this book for more information.

Align text with tabs

To help your speaker plan an extended stay in your area after the conference, you decide to add a price list of nearby hotels to your letter. In this exercise, you will enter column headings separated by tabs.

1   Press CTRL+END to move quickly to the end of the document, and then press ENTER to create a new line at the end of the document.

2   Press BACKSPACE to left align the insertion point.

3   Type **Here is the hotel information you requested. If you would like us to make arrangements for you, please let me know.**

4   Press ENTER.

5   Press TAB, and then type **Hotel**

    Left-aligned is the default formatting for a tab stop, so the left edge of your text is aligned with the first tab stop.

6   Press TAB, and then type **Description**

7   Press TAB, and then type **Rate per Night**

Create new tab stops

The defaults tab stops are located at every half-inch increment on the ruler, but you can create your own tab stops at specific locations. When you create a new tab stop, you can also specify its alignment, so that text you align with a tab is aligned the way you want. In this exercise, you want to adjust the amount of space between each column in the price list, so you create new tab stops.

Right Tab

1   Click the tab icon at the left end of the ruler until it looks like the Right Tab icon.

    With this tab alignment selected, you place a right-aligned tab stop.

2   On the ruler, click the 1-inch mark.

    A tab marker appears in the ruler, indicating the location of the first stop. The word "Hotel" is right-aligned on this new tab stop.

Center Tab

3   Click the tab icon at the left end of the ruler until it looks like the Center Tab icon.

    With this tab alignment selected, you place a center tab stop.

4   On the ruler, click the 3-inch mark.

    A tab marker appears in the ruler, indicating the location of the next stop. The word "Description" is centered on this new tab stop.

Decimal Tab

5   Click the tab icon at the left end of the ruler until it looks like the Decimal Tab icon.

    With this tab alignment selected, you place a decimal tab stop.

6   On the ruler, click the 4.5-inch mark.

A tab marker appears in the ruler, indicating the location of the next stop. The text "Rate per Night" is right-aligned on this new tab stop. When you align text with the decimal tab, the text is right-aligned. Numbers will be aligned on the decimal point, starting from the right.

TIP   In this exercise, you do not need to be concerned if you do not place the tab stops in the exact location. Simply drag the marker to the location you want. To remove the tab marker, you can drag the marker from the ruler. You can also use the Tab command on the Format menu to place tab stops more precisely.

Type text in the price list

With the tab stops established in the current paragraph, you can type the remaining lines of text in the price list. Each line will be aligned according to the tab stops you created.

1   Press ENTER to create a new line.

Like other paragraph formatting, the tab stops you've created are carried forward to the next paragraph when you press ENTER.

2   Press TAB, and then type **Plaza Arms**

3   Press TAB, and then type **200, 4-star restaurant**

4   Press TAB, and then type **275.50**

5   Press ENTER to create a new line.

6   Complete the remainder of the price list with the following information. Remember to press ENTER at the end of each line and to press TAB to move to the next tab stop.

For a demonstration of how to add leaders, double-click the Camcorder file named Adding Leaders in the Part2 Word Camcorder Files folder. See "Installing and Using the Practice and Camcorder Files," earlier in this book for more information.

City Suites	large, studio-style rooms	171.15
Country Views	quiet rooms, golf course, pool	199.79
Anna's Inn	bed and breakfast, in-room whirlpools	179.25

Add leaders to the price list

To make your text easier to follow, you can insert leaders in the price list.

1   Select all the columns in the price list.

2   On the Format menu, click Tabs to open the Tab dialog box.

3   In the Tab Stop Position list, click 1". In the Leader area, be sure the None option is selected.

You don't want leaders to precede the first column.

4   Click Set.

5   In the Tab Stop Position list, click 3". In the Leader area, select the 2 option, and then click Set.

6   In the Tab Stop Position list, click 4.5". In the Leader area, select the 2 option, and then click Set.

7   Click OK.

The Tab dialog box closes. Leaders are inserted between the first and second columns and the second and third columns.

NOTE Decimal tab alignment is especially useful when you are aligning numbers formatted with a proportional spaced font. A *proportional spaced font* means that some characters take up more space than others. For example, a 9 takes up more space than a 1. Most of the fonts on your computer are proportional fonts, so you should use a decimal tab whenever you are aligning numbers with tabs.

Adding Borders to a Paragraph

To create a line above, below, around, or on each side of a paragraph, you can use the Outside Border button. By using the Outside Border button, you can choose the parts of the paragraph to which you want to add a border.

Add an outside border to a paragraph

To draw even more attention to the "Note" text, you can add a box border around the paragraph.

Outside Border

➤ With the insertion point in the "Note" paragraph, click the Outside Border button.

The "Note" paragraph is surrounded by a thin black border, as shown in the following illustration.

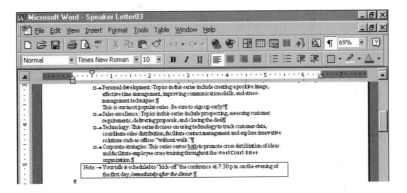

*Tables And
Borders*

 NOTE   Additional border options (such as line style and weight) are available on the Tables And Borders toolbar. You can display this toolbar by clicking the Tables And Borders button on the Standard toolbar. You can use the Borders And Shading command on the Format menu to apply a variety of preset border options. From the Borders And Shading dialog box, you also have the option to display the Tables And Borders toolbar.

Changing Paragraph Spacing

Often a document is easier to read if there is additional space between lines and between paragraphs. By using the Paragraph command, you can change the line spacing of a paragraph and the space between paragraphs, as well as other paragraph formatting options.

Instead of pressing ENTER to add blank lines before and after text, you can specify the exact spacing between paragraphs. This method gives you more flexibility and precision, because you can increase spacing by a fraction of a line—for example, by .5 or 1.75 lines—instead of by whole lines.

Add spacing after a paragraph

To set off the second body paragraph from the bulleted list, you can increase the space after the paragraph.

1   Place the insertion point in the second body paragraph.

2   On the Format menu, click Paragraph.

3   In the Spacing area, click the After up arrow twice so that 12 pt appears.

In the Preview box, you can view the formatting before you apply it.

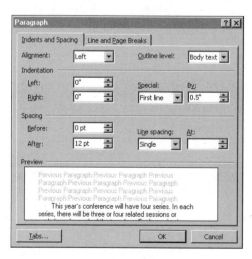

4   Click OK.

188

5 Place the insertion point in the last body paragraph, which starts with "I hope."

6 On the Edit menu, click Repeat Paragraph Formatting to repeat your last editing command.

Add spacing before and after paragraphs

You can increase the spacing before and after each paragraph in the bulleted list to better identify each item.

1 Select the four bulleted items and the "Note" paragraph.

2 On the Format menu, click Paragraph.

3 In the Spacing area, click the Before up arrow once so that 6 pt appears.

4 Press TAB and, in the After box, type **3**

These settings will insert 6 points of space before and 3 points of space after each selected paragraph.

5 Click OK.

Change the line spacing within a paragraph

By default, Microsoft Word creates single-spaced lines. If you want to provide more space between lines (for easier reading or to leave room for written notes), you can change the line spacing.

1 Place the insertion point anywhere in the first body paragraph, and then on the Format menu, click Paragraph.

2 Click the the Line Spacing down arrow to display the spacing options.

3 Select 1.5 Lines.

4 Click OK.

Your paragraph should look like the following illustration.

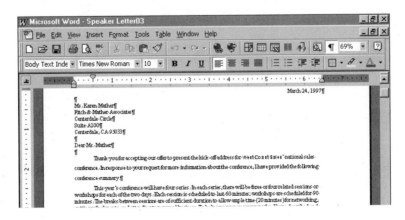

5 Repeat steps 1 through 4 for all body paragraphs, except the bulleted items and "Note" paragraphs.

6 On the Standard toolbar, click the Save button.

Save

 NOTE If you'd like to build on the skills that you learned in this lesson, you can do the One Step Further. Otherwise, skip to "Finish the lesson."

One Step Further: Creating an Instant Resume by Using the Resume Wizard

The Resume Wizard guides you through the process of creating an attractively formatted resume. Using this wizard, you can choose the style of resume you want and select other options. After you have established the basics of the document, you can type the text and edit the document as you wish. As you edit the resume document, examine the different kinds of paragraph and character formatting used throughout the document.

Start the Resume Wizard

In your role as a conference planner, you have asked potential speakers to provide resumes so you can include their profiles in the conference program. Use the Resume Wizard to create a resume of your own that the speakers can use as a model.

1 On the File menu, click New.

2 Click the Other Documents tab, and then double-click the Resume Wizard icon.

3 Answer the questions in the wizard dialog boxes to create a resume (of any type you prefer).

Save the resume

1 On the File menu, click Save.

The Save As dialog box appears.

2 Click the Look In Favorites button, and then double-click 6in1 Word.

3 Drag to select all the text in the File Name box, and then type
Model Resume03

*Look In
Favorites*

4 Click Save, or press ENTER, to close the dialog box and save the file.

Your file is saved with the name Model Resume03 in the 6in1 Word folder.

Finish the lesson

1   To continue to the next lesson, on the File menu, click Close for each document you have open.

2   If you are finished using Microsoft Word for now, on the File menu, click Exit.

Lesson Summary

To	Do this	Button
Set indents	Select the paragraphs to format, and click the Increase Indent button or the Decrease Indent button.	
Create bulleted lists	Select the paragraphs to format, and then click the Bullets button.	
Create numbered lists	Select the paragraphs to format, and then click the Numbering button.	
Set custom indents	Click in the paragraph to be indented, and then drag the triangular indent markers on the ruler to set the first line, left, and right indents.	
Add a border to a paragraph	Click in the paragraph, and then click the Outside Border button on the Formatting toolbar.	
Adjust spacing between paragraphs	On the Format menu, click Paragraph. Select the spacing you want in the Spacing area.	
Adjust line spacing within a paragraph	On the Format menu, click Paragraph. Select the line spacing you want from the Line Spacing list.	
View the entire page width	Click the Zoom down arrow, and then click Page Width.	100%

For online information about	Use the Office Assistant to search for
Adding borders	**Borders,** and then click Add A Border
Setting indents	**Setting indents,** and then click Indent Paragraphs
Creating bulleted or numbered lists	**Bullets and numbering,** and then click Add Bullets Or Numbers To Lists

Printing Your Document

Estimated time
35 min.

In this lesson you will learn how to:

- Examine a document in the Print Preview window.
- View multiple pages in the Print Preview window.
- Edit text in the Print Preview window.
- Insert page breaks.
- Print an entire document.
- Print individual pages and multiple copies of a document.
- Print an envelope.

After you create a document and get it to look the way you want, you frequently want to print the results of your efforts. In this lesson, you'll examine the layout of a document before printing the document. After you edit text and change the flow of text across pages, you'll print your document. You'll also learn how to print only the pages you want and how to print multiple copies. In addition, you'll learn how to print envelopes.

If you don't have a printer, you can still complete all the exercises in this lesson, except those that involve the actual printing.

Start the lesson

Do the following steps to open the 04Lesson practice file, and then save it with the new name Speaker Letter04.

Open

1 On the Standard toolbar, click the Open button.

Be sure that the Part2 Word Practice folder is in the Look In box. If not, click the Look In Favorites button, and then double-click the folder.

2 In the file list, double-click the file named 04Lesson to open it.

3 On the File menu, click Save As.

The Save As dialog box appears.

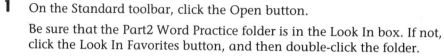

Look In Favorites

4 Click the Look In Favorites button, and then double-click the 6in1 Word folder.

5 In the File Name box, type **Speaker Letter04**

6 Click Save, or press ENTER.

If you share your computer with others, the screen display might have changed since your last lesson. If your screen does not look similar to the illustrations as you work through this lesson, see the Appendix, "Matching the Exercises."

Speaker Letter04 is similar to the document used in the previous lesson. It contains some additional text and formatting revisions to better illustrate the features covered in the exercises in this lesson.

Previewing Your Document

To get a better idea of how your document will look when you print it, you can use the Print Preview window. In the Print Preview window, you can see the overall appearance of one page, or you can see all the pages. You can see where text falls on a page and where it continues on the next page. After examining your document, you can make additional revisions to get everything just right. Previewing the document can save you time and paper, because it reduces the number of times you print the document before it looks exactly the way you want.

Preview the document

You want to get an idea of what the letter to the keynote speaker for next year's conference looks like before you print it, so you preview the document.

Print Preview

➤ On the Standard toolbar, click the Print Preview button.

Your document in the Print Preview window should look like the following illustration.

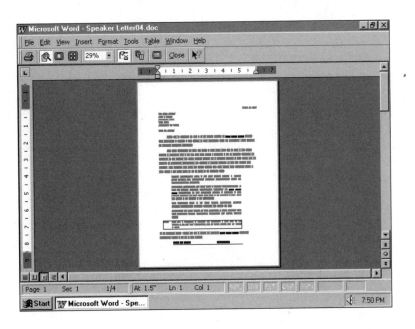

One Page

NOTE If your screen does not match this illustration, on the View menu, choose Ruler to display the ruler in Print Preview. Click the One Page button if you see more than one page of the document.

The current page of your document is displayed in the Print Preview window. The Print Preview toolbar contains the buttons you use to preview the document; the menu bar still contains the same Microsoft Word menu items.

View other pages

Multiple Pages

➤ On the Print Preview toolbar, click the Multiple Pages button, move the pointer across the first two boxes in the second row to select four boxes, and then click the mouse button.

Now you can see all four pages of your document at once, as shown in the following illustration.

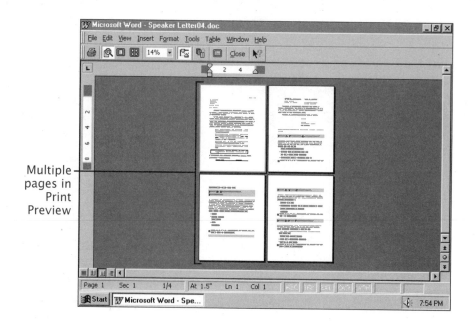

Multiple pages in Print Preview

Editing Text While Previewing

When you're in Print Preview and discover you need to make changes to your document, such as inserting, deleting, or formatting text, you do not need to return to the document window. You can make simple changes to the text directly in the Print Preview window. However, because nonprinting characters are not displayed in the Print Preview window, you should use Normal view, Online Layout view, or Page Layout view to complete more extensive editing or formatting tasks.

Edit text in Print Preview

You decide to add a brief comment to the beginning of the letter, so you zoom in on this part of the page. You do this by clicking the pointer near the text you want to magnify. Notice that the pointer changes shape to look like a magnifying glass as you move the pointer over the currently selected page.

1   Use the magnifier pointer to click near the first body paragraph on page 1 to get a magnified view of the page.

Your screen should look similar to the following illustration.

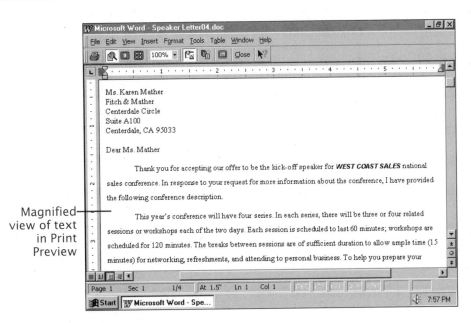

Magnified—
view of text
in Print
Preview

Magnifier

2 On the Print Preview toolbar, click the Magnifier button to change the magnifier pointer to the insertion bar.

3 To position the insertion bar, click immediately in front of the sentence that begins "In response to your request."

4 Type **After hearing your comments on a recent radio broadcast, I am looking forward to hearing your address at next year's conference.**

5 Press the SPACEBAR.

Inserting Page Breaks

For a demonstration of how to insert page breaks, double-click the file named Inserting Page Breaks in the Part2 Word Camcorder Files folder. See "Installing and Using the Practice and Camcorder Files," earlier in this book for details.

Word inserts a *soft page break* automatically when you've typed as much text as will fit on a page. If you add or delete text somewhere on the page, the placement of the soft page break changes. Soft page breaks are indicated in Normal view by a dotted line across the screen. You cannot select or delete soft page breaks. If you are satisfied with the way Microsoft Word has arranged your text flow across pages, you can leave the soft page breaks as they stand. However, if you want to improve the balance of text across pages, or if you want to make sure that the page break remains exactly at the same point, even when you change computers or printers, you can insert manual page breaks (also called *hard page breaks*), either in the document window or in the Print Preview window. After you insert a hard page break, Microsoft Word repaginates the docu-

You can delete hard page breaks, but not soft page breaks.

ment and changes any soft page breaks in the document as necessary. You can use hard page breaks anywhere in your document. If your document needs extensive editing or rewriting, you should not insert hard page breaks until the text is relatively final to avoid removing and reinserting page breaks as your text changes.

You can also control the flow of text across pages by using the Text Flow options available as part of the Paragraph command. You use Text Flow options to determine the flow of text for individual paragraphs. For example, you can format an individual paragraph so that it always appears on the same page as the next paragraph. You can also specify that the lines of a paragraph should appear together. These options are especially useful when you are writing text that you do not want separated by a page break.

Insert a page break

In this exercise, you will insert a page break to separate the letter part of the document from the conference program material.

Zoom

1 On the Print Preview toolbar, click the Zoom down arrow, and then click Page Width.

2 Scroll to about the middle of the second page, and then click to place the insertion point immediately after the period in the postscript at the end of the letter.

3 Press CTRL+ENTER.

   This inserts a hard page break, and the following text moves to the next page.

Multiple Pages

4 On the Print Preview toolbar, click the Multiple Pages button, move the pointer across the first two boxes in the first row to select them, and then click the mouse button.

5 On the Print Preview toolbar, click the Close button.

6 Scroll down to see the new page break at the bottom of page 2.

   The hard page break is represented by a dotted line labeled "Page Break." Neither the line nor the label appears in a printed document. Your screen should look similar to the following illustration.

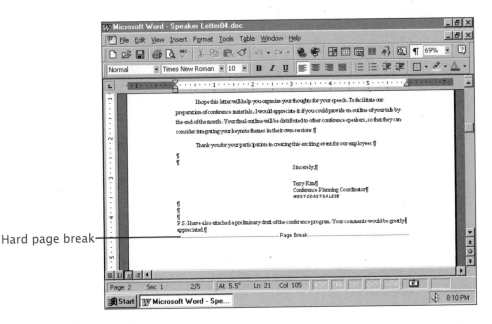

Hard page break

7 Save the document.

Controlling Text Flow

Depending on your printer, the way text flows across pages might be different. To make sure that the text you want to keep together on the same page or the text you want to separate on different pages always flows as you want it to, even on different equipment, you can apply specific text flow formatting to individual paragraphs.

Keep lines within a paragraph together

To ensure that all the lines within each paragraph in the table of names are never separated by a soft page break, you can use the Keep Lines Together option. For example, you want to make sure that the text "Duncan Mann" is never separated from the line *"West Coast Sales Award of Excellence."*

1 Select all the lines in the Name and Award table, except the table heading.

2 On the Format menu, click Paragraph.

3 Click the Line And Page Breaks tab.

4 Click the Keep Lines Together check box to select it, and click OK.

A small square icon to the left of each line of the paragraph indicates that text flow formatting is applied to the text. The paragraph moves to the next page if necessary to keep the designated lines together.

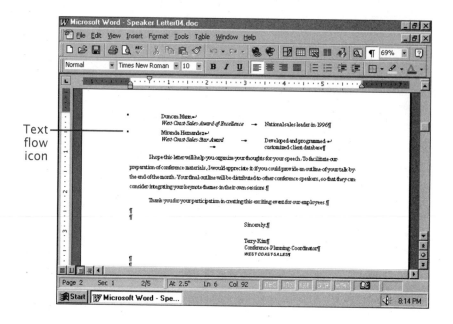

Text flow icon

Display paragraphs together

So that the paragraph that precedes the table never appears at the bottom of the page without the table, you can format the paragraph so that it is always on the same page as the table. To ensure that the paragraphs remain together and are never separated by a soft page break, you can use the Keep With Next option.

1 Select the table heading paragraph and the one that precedes it.

2 On the Format menu, click Paragraph.

The Paragraph dialog box appears.

3 On the Line And Page Breaks tab, select the Keep With Next check box, and click OK.

The paragraphs move to the next page to keep these paragraphs together.

NOTE An orphan line occurs when the first line of a paragraph appears at the bottom of a page and the remaining lines appear on the next page. A widow line occurs when the last line of a paragraph appears at the top of a page by itself. By default, Word prevents widows and orphans from occurring in your documents. If you prefer to control widows and orphans yourself, you can turn off the Widow/Orphan option on the Line And Page Break tab in the Paragraph dialog box.

Printing Your Document

Now that you have finished making changes, you are ready to print your document. You can click the Print button on the Standard toolbar to print the entire document using default settings, or you can use the Print command to select different printing options.

If you don't have a printer connected to your computer, you can skip to the end of this lesson.

> ## Printing While You Work
>
> Because Windows 95 and Windows NT are multitasking operating systems, there is no need to wait idly for your document to print. You can continue to work in Word or in other programs while your document is printing.

Print the entire document

Now that you are satisfied with the appearance of your letter, you are ready to print it. The Print button prints all pages of the currently active document on the default printer connected to your computer.

1   Be sure the printer is on.

2   On the Standard toolbar, click the Print button.

Print

The status bar displays an icon that indicates the pages are being "spooled" (sent) to the printer. The document prints on the printer connected to your computer.

Print two copies of the current page

Occasionally, you might want to print just a page or two from a long document, instead of printing all the pages. When you use the Print command, you have the option of printing only the page that currently contains the insertion point.

You can also print a document directly from the Print Preview window by using the Print button on the Print Preview toolbar or by clicking Print on the File menu.

1   Be sure the printer is on.

2   Double-click anywhere in the page number display on the left side of the status bar.

The Find And Replace dialog box appears.

3   On the Go To tab, be sure that Page is selected in the Go To What list, and then type **1** in the Enter Page Numbers box.

4   Click Go To to move to page 1 of your document, and then click Close.

5   On the File menu, click Print.

The Print dialog box appears.

Select the printer.

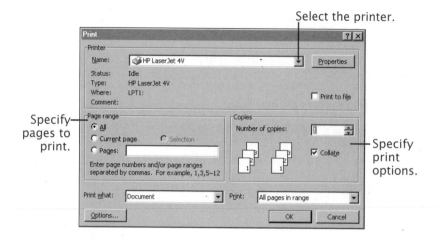

Specify
pages to
print.

Specify
print
options.

5 In the Page Range area, select the Current Page option.

6 In the Number Of Copies box, type **2**

7 Click OK to begin printing.

Printing an Envelope

If your printer can print envelopes, Microsoft Word makes it easy to address
and print an envelope based on the information in an open letter. When you
use the Envelope And Labels command on the Tools menu, you can specify the
size of envelope or brand of label you want to print.

Print an envelope

1 Select the address block in your letter.

2 Place an envelope in your printer.

3 On the Tools menu, click Envelopes And Labels.

The Envelopes And Labels dialog box appears.

 NOTE The default envelope size is for a standard #10 business
envelope. Click the Options button to select other sizes of
envelopes.

4 On the Envelopes tab in the dialog box, be sure that both the delivery
address and the return address (based on the user information you entered when you installed the software) are correct. If necessary, use the
dialog box to make corrections to either entry.

TIP So that you don't need to edit the return address each time, on the Tools menu, click Options. On the User Information tab, type the name and address information that you always want to use as your return address.

5 Click the Print button.

The envelope prints on your printer.

 NOTE If you'd like to build on the skills that you learned in this lesson, you can do the One Step Further. Otherwise, skip to "Finish the lesson."

One Step Further: Shrinking a Document to Fit

Occasionally, you may have a multiple-page document that has only a small amount of text on the last page. In Print Preview, you can use the Shrink To Fit feature to reduce the number of pages by one. Microsoft Word accomplishes this by reducing the document font sizes proportionately.

Reduce the number of pages by one

Print Preview

1 On the Standard toolbar, click the Print Preview button.

2 Click the Multiple Pages button, and drag to select all six boxes to display all five pages in the Print Preview window.

3 On the Print Preview toolbar, click the Shrink To Fit button.

The document now fits on one less page.

Multiple Pages

4 Click the Close button to return to Page Layout view.

Scroll through the document to view the changes.

5 Save the document.

Shrink To Fit

Finish the lesson

1 To continue to the next lesson, on the File menu, click Close.

2 If you are finished using Microsoft Word for now, on the File menu, click Exit.

Lesson Summary

To	Do this	Button
Display a document in Print Preview	On the Standard toolbar, click the Print Preview button.	
View multiple pages of the document at one time	On the Print Preview toolbar, click the Multiple Pages button. Drag across the number of pages you want to see at one time within the window.	
Display a document close up in Print Preview	Position the pointer on the document. When the mouse pointer changes to a magnifying glass, click the area of the document you want to view close up.	
Edit text in print preview	On the Print Preview toolbar, click the Magnifier button to change the pointer to the insertion bar.	
Insert a page break	Place the insertion point where you want the page break. Press CTRL+ENTER.	
Print all pages of a document to the default printer	Click the Print button on the Standard toolbar or on the Print Preview toolbar.	
Print a document using dialog box options	On the File menu, click Print. Select the options you want in the Print dialog box.	

For online information about	Use the Office Assistant to search for
Previewing text	**Print preview,** and then click Preview A Document Before Printing
Printing documents	**Printing documents,** and then click Print A Document

Increasing Editing Productivity

Estimated time
50 min.

In this lesson you will learn how to:

- Identify and replace text.
- Find and replace word forms.
- Store and insert frequently used text.
- Check grammar and spelling.
- Locate objects in a document.
- Look up alternative words.

After you finish drafting a document, you might want to refine the existing text. With the Microsoft Word Find feature and the Replace feature, you can search for and replace both text and formatting. You can search for a onetime occurrence of a word, or you can search globally, which means for all occurrences of the word in the document. If you often repeat the same phrases in your document, you can work more productively by using the AutoText feature to store and insert frequently used text. In addition, every document draft can be checked for spelling and grammatical or stylistic errors. By using the Spelling and Grammar features, you can be sure your documents are letter perfect. And by using the built-in Thesaurus, you can get help choosing the exact words to convey precisely what you mean in your document.

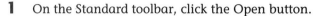

Start the lesson

Follow the steps below to open the practice file called 05Lesson, and then save it with the new name Program Highlights05.

Open

Look In Favorites

1   On the Standard toolbar, click the Open button.

2   Be sure the Part2 Word Practice folder is in the Look In box. If not, click the Look In Favorites button, and then double-click the folder.

3   In the file list, double-click the file named 05Lesson to open it.

4   On the File menu, click Save As to open the Save As dialog box.

5   Click the Look In Favorites button, and then double-click the 6in1 Word folder.

6   Select the text in the File Name box, and then type **Program High-lights05**

7   Click Save, or press ENTER.

Program Highlights05 is similar to the document used in the previous lesson. Some text and formatting changes have been made to better illustrate the features covered in the exercises in this lesson.

Display nonprinting characters

To make it easier to see exactly where you are moving text in your document, you can display nonprinting characters.

Show/Hide ¶

➤   If paragraph marks are not already displayed, click the Show/Hide ¶ button on the Standard toolbar.

If you share your computer, the screen display might have changed since your last lesson. If your screen does not look similar to the illustrations as you work through this lesson, see the Appendix, "Matching the Exercises."

IMPORTANT   To hide any red, wavy lines which identify misspelled or unknown words, click Options on the Tools menu, and then click the Spelling & Grammar tab. Click the Hide Spelling Errors In This Document check box to select it. You can hide any green, wavy lines, which identify grammatical and punctuation errors, by selecting the Hide Grammatical Errors In This Document check box.

Identifying and Replacing Text

In your role as the conference coordinator for the upcoming West Coast Sales conference, you are continuing your efforts to perfect the conference program. You can use the Find and Replace features to quickly find—and, if necessary, replace—all occurrences of a certain word or phrase. For example, you might want to find every instance of an outdated company name in a brochure and substitute the new name. You can make all the changes at once, or you can accept or reject each change individually. Either method ensures that the change is made consistently throughout the document.

Identify text to find and replace

The program document you opened refers to "series" for each set of sessions and workshops at the conference. However, each set should be called a "program" instead. In this exercise, you'll use the Replace command to locate the word "series" and replace it with the word "program." Before you begin replacing text, you'll make sure that no other options are in effect.

1 On the Edit menu, click Replace.

The Find And Replace dialog box appears with the Replace tab in front. For a simple replace, you can use the options available in this basic dialog box. However, for more advanced options, you can click the More button.

2 In the Find What box, type **series**

3 In the Replace With box, type **program**

If text is already in the Replace With box, select the text, and then type **program**

4 Click the More button.

The Find And Replace dialog box expands to show additional options.

5 Be sure that All is in the Search box.

If not, click the Search down arrow, and then select All. Word will search the entire document, rather than just up or just down in the document. Your completed dialog box should look like the following illustration.

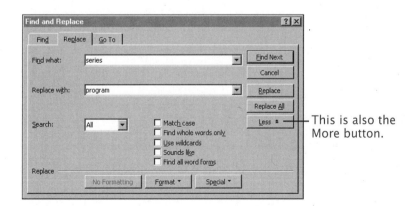

This is also the More button.

6 To replace all occurrences of the word "series," click Replace All.

The changes are made, and a message indicates the number of changes.

7   Click OK to return to the Find And Replace dialog box.

8   In the Find And Replace dialog box, click the Close button to return to your document and view the changes.

Scroll through the document. The word "program" has replaced the word "series" throughout the document.

 NOTE   If you want to selectively decide when to replace a word, you click the Replace button to locate the first occurrence, and then click the Replace button (rather than the Replace All button) to make the specific change, *or* you click the Find Next button to skip the current selection and find the next occurrence of the word.

Finding and Replacing Formatting

On the Find and Replace tabs of the Find And Replace dialog box, you can also type the key combination for the formatting you want to find, such as pressing CTRL+SHIFT+H to search for hidden formatting.

You can locate text that has a specific format, such as bold or underline, and change the formatting as well as the text. You can also search for and change only the formatting without changing the text. For example, suppose you underlined division names in your document but now you want to make them italic and bold instead. With the Replace command, you can quickly find any underlined text and change the underline to italic and bold.

If the formatting you want to use is available on the Formatting toolbar, while you are on the Find or Replace tabs of the Find And Replace dialog box, you can make your formatting selections by clicking the buttons on the toolbar. If the formatting you want to search for or replace is not available on the Formatting toolbar (such as Small Caps), you can click Format at the bottom of the Find or Replace tab of the Find And Replace dialog box, and select the type of formatting you want to locate or replace.

 NOTE   Some of the dialog boxes displayed when you click Format and then select the type of formatting contain check boxes that are dimmed by default. This means that Word won't search for the presence or the absence of this formatting. Each time you click such a check box, it toggles among the three options of not selected, selected, and selected but dim.

Finding and Changing Tenses of a Word

When you want to change a verb in your document, it is easy to forget to change other tenses of the same word. For example, if you want to change every "deliver" in your document to "bring," you also need to change "delivered" to "brought." Using the Find All Word Forms option on the Find or Replace tabs of the Find And Replace dialog box, you can use Microsoft Word to look for and correctly replace all forms and tenses of a word.

IMPORTANT The Setup program you use to install Microsoft Word gives you the option to install or not install the Find All Word Forms option. You need to have this feature installed to see it in the Replace dialog box. If this option does not appear in the Replace dialog box, you can run the Microsoft Office Setup program again and specify that you want to install the Find All Word Forms feature only, which is an option available for the Office Tools item.

Change all tenses of a verb

In the conference program document, you want to replace "talk" or "talked" with the proper form of the word "speak." In this exercise, you will again use the Replace command, but this time you will also enable the Find All Word Forms option. When you use this option, you should not use the Replace All feature. Instead, you use the Replace command so that you can locate and examine each occurrence individually.

1 Press CTRL+HOME to move the insertion point to the start of the document.

2 On the Edit menu, click Replace. If the No Formatting button does not appear in the dialog box, click the More button.

3 In the Find What box, select the text and type **talk**

4 In the Replace With box, select the text and type **speak**

5 Be sure that All is in the Search box.

 If not, click the Search down arrow, and select All.

6 Select the Find All Word Forms check box.

 Your dialog box should look like the following illustration.

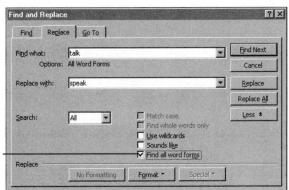

Click to search for all tenses of a word.

TIP   If you are working on several documents in which you want to replace the same text, you can click the Find What down arrow and Replace With down arrow to select any text you searched for or replaced during the current Word session.

7   To locate the first occurrence, click the Find Next button.

Word finds the first occurrence of the word and displays a list of possible word forms.

8   Click the Replace button to make the change to the default word form and to locate the next occurrence. Repeat this step for each occurrence in the document.

9   Click the Close button to return to the document and view the changes.

TIP   You can specify the direction in which you want Word to search for and replace text or formatting. For example, if the insertion point is at the end of the document, you can click the Search down arrow and choose Up to search and replace back through the document, from the end to the beginning.

Storing and Inserting AutoText Entries

You can use the AutoText feature to insert frequently used text. In addition to the common words and phrases Word provides as AutoText entries, you can also create your own AutoText entries, such as your company name or logo. When you create an AutoText entry, you have the option of assigning it to a menu or you can assign it an AutoText name, which allows you to type a few characters and then insert the entry by pressing F3. Because you can include symbols, graphics, numbers, and formatting, AutoText entries are particularly useful when entering serial numbers or text that requires complicated formatting.

Creating an AutoText Entry

You can begin creating an AutoText entry by selecting the text you want to store. Then, with the AutoText command on the Insert menu (you can also press ALT+F3), you can assign it an AutoText entry name. To minimize the amount of typing you need to do, use short names when naming AutoText entries.

Create an AutoText entry

As a special incentive to encourage employees to focus on specific programs at the conference, West Coast Sales is offering a "Bonus Bucks" promotion. Because Bonus Bucks is a term you expect to use frequently as you develop conference documents, you decide to create an AutoText entry.

1   In the paragraph below the first bulleted list, select the text "Bonus Bucks" (include the space after the text in your selection).

2   On the Insert menu, point to AutoText, and then click New.

    The Create AutoText dialog box appears.

3   Replace the existing text by typing **bb**

4   Click OK.

Inserting an AutoText Entry

If you prefer to insert AutoText entries from a toolbar, you can display the AutoText toolbar by clicking any toolbar with the right mouse button and then clicking AutoText.

You can insert an AutoText entry from the AutoText menu (on the Insert menu). You can also type the AutoText entry name and press F3, and Microsoft Word inserts the rest.

 TIP   You can create a toolbar of AutoText entries by "tearing off" the command from the Insert menu. Point to AutoText, click the gray bar at the top of the cascaded menu, and then drag the bar to the location you want.

Use AutoText to insert text

In this exercise, you will type new text in the document and insert your new AutoText entry "Bonus Bucks."

1   Place the insertion point at the end of the paragraph under the bulleted list, type **For about 1000** and then press the SPACEBAR.

2   Type **bb**

3   Press F3.

    Word inserts the text "Bonus Bucks" as shown in the following illustration.

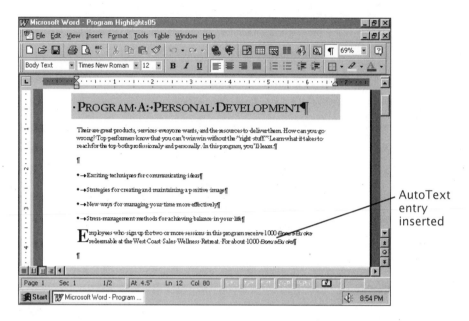

AutoText entry inserted

4 Type **you can enjoy a half-day stay at the retreat.**

5 Place the insertion point at the end of the paragraph under the next bulleted list, and type **For about 4000** and a space.

6 Type **bb**

7 Press F3.

8 Type **you can buy a laptop computer.**

9 Save the document.

Checking Spelling and Grammar

When you click Options in the Spelling And Grammar dialog box, you can specify that you want Word to ignore certain types of words, including words in uppercase, words with numbers, and Internet and file addresses.

The Spelling And Grammar command identifies misspelled words or unknown words (that is, words that are not in Word's dictionary) and sentences that have possible grammatical errors or a nonstandard writing style. For many types of errors, the Grammar feature suggests ways to correct the sentence. You can choose the correction you want to make, or you can make your own changes directly in the document.

Although the Spelling And Grammar command provides a quick and convenient way to find many common spelling and grammatical errors, remember that no proofing tool can replace reading a document carefully.

Start the Spelling and Grammar tools

Microsoft Word normally checks the entire document, beginning at the insertion point. Although you can start proofing from any point in a document, in this exercise, you will position the insertion point at the top of your document.

IMPORTANT The Setup program you use to install Microsoft Word gives you the option to install or not install the Microsoft Word proofing tools, which include the Thesaurus and the Spelling And Grammar tool. You must have installed these components for them to appear on the Tools menu. If these components do not appear on your Tools menu, you can run the Microsoft Office Setup program again and specify that you want to install the Proofing Tools only, which is an option available for the Microsoft Word item.

1 Press CTRL+HOME to move the insertion point to the beginning of the document.

Spelling And Grammar

2 On the Standard toolbar, click the Spelling And Grammar button.

This button starts the Word spelling and grammar tools. The first highlighted error is a grammatical error: the use of "their" instead of "there." Microsoft Word suggests considering "there" instead of "their."

Respond to the grammar and spelling errors

Microsoft Word provides explanations for the suggestions that it makes. In this exercise, you learn about a grammar rule, delete repeated words, and check spelling.

Office Assistant

1 With the suggested grammar replacement still displayed in the dialog box, click the Microsoft Office Assistant button.

The Office Assistant displays an explanation of the grammatical rule concerning the usage of commonly confused words.

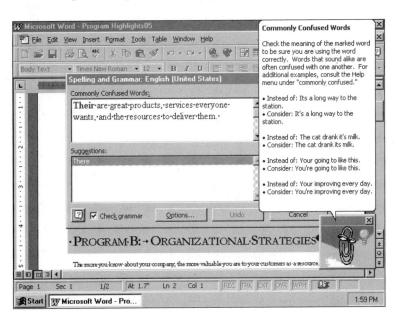

2 Click the Close button on the Office Assistant to close the explanation and hide the Office Assistant.

3 Click Change to insert the correct word.

The word is corrected, and the grammar checker identifies a repeated word.

 NOTE Each time the grammar checker finds a sentence with a possible error, you can click the Ignore button if you don't want to change anything. If you click Ignore, Microsoft Word ignores this occurrence of the "error" and continues checking the sentence. Click the Options button to display the Spelling & Grammar dialog box, where you can specify spelling and grammar options. Click Settings in the Spelling & Grammar dialog box to select writing style and grammar and style options you want to apply to your document.

---

4 Click Delete.

The next error is a misspelled word, "professionaly."

5 Click Change to insert the first suggested spelling.

6 For each possible error Word finds, do the following:

The problem	The solution
Whether to use "a" or "an"	Click the Office Assistant button, and review the explanation. Then, click Change to correct the error.
The word "companys" is misspelled	Select the word "company's" in the Suggestions box, and then click Change.
The word "youcan" is not in the dictionary	In the document, insert a space after the u, and then click Change.
The word "ByteComp" is misspelled	Click Add to add this word to the dictionary.

Locating Specific Parts of a Document

The Select Browse Object button near the bottom of the vertical scroll bar helps you locate a specific item or part of your document. After you click this button you choose the part of the document you want to locate. After Word finds the object you selected, you can move from occurrence to occurrence by clicking the Next Page and Previous Page buttons on the vertical scroll bar. For example, you can click the Select Browse Object button to specify that you want to move among the document headings, pages, sections, tables, or other objects in your document. Other options available when you click the Select Browse Object button include displaying the Go To and Find dialog boxes.

Find text

In the Program Highlights document, you want to find the word "environment" so you can further examine how it is used to describe the dynamic and turbulent sales industry.

Select Browse Object

1 Near the bottom of the vertical scroll bar, click the Select Browse Object button.

Select Browse Object pop-up menu

Find

2 Click the Find button.

The Find And Replace dialog box appears. This is the same dialog box you see when you click the Find command on the Edit menu.

3 In the Find What box, type **environment**

4 Click Find Next to locate this word.

Word selects the word in the document.

5 Click Cancel to return to the document.

Replacing a Word by Using the Thesaurus

You can use the Thesaurus to add variety and accuracy to your choice of words in a document. In the Thesaurus, you can look up alternative words for a selected word or expression. You can also locate antonyms to find words with the opposite meaning.

Look up an alternative word

The selected word "environment" does not have the exact meaning you want in your document. In this exercise, you will use the Thesaurus feature to look up an alternative word.

1 With the word "environment" still selected, on the Tools menu, point to Language, and then click Thesaurus.

The Thesaurus dialog box appears.

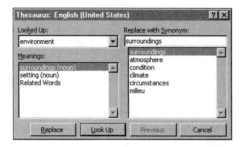

2   In the Replace With Synonym list, click milieu.

3   Click Replace.

The word "milieu" replaces the word you selected.

NOTE   If you'd like to build on the skills that you learned in this lesson, you can do the One Step Further. Otherwise, skip to "Finish the lesson."

One Step Further: Finding and Replacing Special Characters

You can use the Find And Replace feature to help you replace special characters, such as paragraph marks, tab characters, and manual page breaks in your document. For example, if you want to remove extra spacing between paragraphs in your document, you can use the Special button to locate two paragraph marks in a row and replace them with one paragraph mark.

Find and replace the paragraph marks

1   On the Edit menu, click Replace.

2   Click More if you do not see all the Replace options.

If the Special button is not available, clear the Find All Word Forms check box.

3   With the insertion point in the Find What box, click the Special button, and select Paragraph Mark.

Microsoft Word inserts a code that represents a paragraph mark.

4   Click the Special button, and select Paragraph Mark again.

5   If available, click the No Formatting button to clear any formatting specified from a previous search.

6   With the insertion point in the Replace With box, click the Special button, and select Paragraph Mark.

7   Click the No Formatting button to clear any formatting specified from a previous search.

8 Be sure that All is in the Search box. If not, click the Search down arrow, and then select All.

9 To replace all occurrences of double paragraph marks, click the Replace All button.

A message indicates how many changes were made.

10 Click OK to return to the Find And Replace dialog box.

11 Click the Close button to return to the document and view the changes.

12 On the Standard toolbar, click the Save button.

Save

Finish the lesson

1 To continue to the next lesson, on the File menu, click Close.

2 If you are finished using Microsoft Word for now, on the File menu, click Exit.

3 If you see a message asking whether you want to save changes to Normal and you share your computer with others, click No. Your AutoText entries will not be saved.

Click Yes if you are the only one who uses your computer and you want to save the AutoText entries you created in this lesson.

NOTE When you create AutoText entries, they are stored in a template document called Normal. This document contains information about the default settings in effect when you work in Microsoft Word. The options you enable (or disable) and your AutoText and AutoCorrect entries are saved in this template as well. This means that the entries you create in this document will be available in all your documents.

Lesson Summary

To	Do this
Find and replace text	On the Edit menu, click Replace. Type the text you want to find and the replacement text. Click Replace to move to the first word you want to change, and click Replace to replace each occurrence and move to the next. *or* Click Replace All to change all the words at once.

To	Do this	Button
Find and replace formatting	On the Edit menu, click Replace. Type the text you want to find and the replacement text. Use the buttons and options available in the Find And Replace dialog box to specify the kind of formatting to find and the replacement formatting to apply.	
Create an AutoText entry	Select the text for the entry. On the Insert menu, point to Auto-Text and click New. Type a name for the entry. Click OK to return to the document.	
Insert an AutoText entry	Type the name of the entry, and press F3.	
Check spelling and grammar in a document	On the Standard toolbar, click the Spelling And Grammar button. When Word highlights possible grammar or spelling errors, make the suggested changes or ignore them.	ABC ✓
Clarify a grammar rule	In the Spelling And Grammar dialog box, click the Microsoft Office Assistant button.	?

For online information about	Use the Office Assistant to search for
Finding and replacing text	**Find and replace,** and then click Find And Replace
Finding and replacing formatting	**Find and replace,** and then click Find And Replace
Inserting frequently used text	**AutoText entry,** and then click Insert An AutoText Entry.
Checking spelling and grammar	**Spelling and grammar,** and then click Correct Spelling And Grammar

Establishing the Look of a Page

Estimated time
45 min.

In this lesson you will learn how to:

- Set up margins for the entire document.
- Establish the paper size and orientation for a page.
- Create a header or footer that prints on every page.
- Work with alternating headers and footers.
- Specify a unique header or footer for each part of the document.
- Add footnotes to a document.

When you create multiple-page documents in Microsoft Word, it is easy to give all the pages of your document a consistent and polished appearance. In this lesson, you will first learn how to set the margins for the entire document. You'll change the orientation of a page in one section of the document. Finally, you will learn how to print additional information on every page in headers and footers and adjust the footers for different parts of the document.

Start the lesson

Follow the steps below to open the 06Lesson practice file, and then save the file as Program Highlights06.

Open

1 On the Standard toolbar, click the Open button.

2 Be sure that the Part2 Word Practice folder is in the Look In box. If not, click the Look In Favorites button and then double-click the folder.

3 In the file list, double-click the file named 06Lesson to open it.

4 On the File menu, click Save As.

The Save As dialog box opens.

Look In Favorites

5 Click the Look In Favorites button and then double-click the 6in1 Word folder.

6 Select and delete any text in the File Name box, and then type **Program Highlights06**

7 Click Save, or press ENTER.

Program Highlights06 is similar to the document used in Lesson 5. Some text and formatting changes have been made to better illustrate the features covered in the exercises in this lesson.

Display paragraph marks

Show/Hide ¶

➤ If you cannot see the paragraph marks, click the Show/Hide ¶ button on the Standard toolbar.

If you share your computer with others, the screen display might have changed since your last lesson. If your screen does not look similar to the illustrations as you work through this lesson, see the Appendix, "Matching the Exercises."

Setting Up Document Pages

By using the Page Setup command on the File menu, you can define your margins, select your paper size, establish your paper source, and choose an orientation for your document. You also have the option of changing these settings for selected text, for the entire document, or from the current position of the insertion point to the end of the document.

Set document margins

The current version of the West Coast Sales conference program uses the default margins settings. To allow extra *white space* (a blank area) for graphics and other dramatic text effects that you plan to add later, you can increase the margins for the entire document.

1 On the File menu, click Page Setup.

The Page Setup dialog box appears.

2   Be sure the Margins tab is displayed.

3   In the Top box, click up arrow until 1.5" appears in the box.

This setting increases the distance between the top edge of the paper and the top edge of the document text, as shown in the Preview box.

4   In the Left box, increase the left margin to 2".

5   In the Right box, decrease the right margin to 1".

6   Click OK to return to the document.

 TIP   You can also adjust the left and right document margins by using the ruler in Page Layout view. Position the mouse pointer near the gray edge of the ruler and when the mouse pointer changes to a double-headed arrow, drag to change the margins. To see the measurements for the margins, hold down the ALT key as you drag.

Preview the document

Print Preview

Multiple Pages

1   On the Standard toolbar, click the Print Preview button.

2   Click the Multiple Pages button, and then drag across all six boxes.

Selecting all the boxes displays all the pages of the document. When you are previewing multiple pages, the number of boxes you select corresponds to the number of pages shown in the preview.

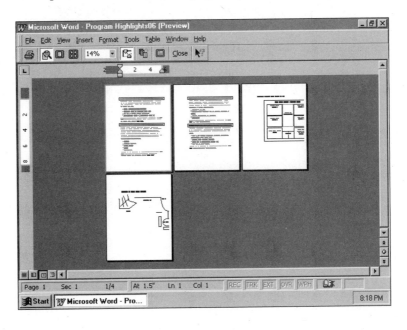

3   On the toolbar, click the Close button to return to Page Layout view.

Change the orientation of specific pages

The maps on pages 3 and 4 no longer fit properly within the new document margins you set. Although you can adjust the margins for just these pages, another solution is to change the setup of these pages so that the pages are displayed in *landscape orientation* (wider than they are tall) rather than the default *portrait orientation* (taller than they are wide). You can change the orientation on the Paper Size tab in the Page Setup dialog box.

1   Place the insertion point in front of the text "Getting Where You Want to Be" on the third page.

2   On the File menu, click Page Setup.

3   Click the Paper Size tab.

4   In the Orientation area, click Landscape.

You can see the results of your change in the Preview box.

5   Click the Apply To down arrow, and choose This Point Forward.

6   Click OK to return to Page Layout view.

7   On the Standard toolbar, click the Save button.

Microsoft Word saves the changes you made in this document.

Save

Delete the extra page break

Whenever you choose different page setup settings in different parts of a document—as, for example, when you choose This Point Forward in the Apply To list—Word inserts a section break between the two parts. This separation allows you to format each document section individually. When you change an option on the Paper Size, Paper Source, or Layout tabs, by default Word inserts a section break that begins on the next page.

This break is indicated by a dotted line labeled "Section Break (Next Page)." As a result, the existing hard page break (indicated by a dotted line labeled "Page Break") in the conference program is no longer needed.

Normal View

1   Click the Normal View button to switch to Normal view.

2   Scroll down to the heading "Getting Where You Want to Be" to view the hard page break and the section break.

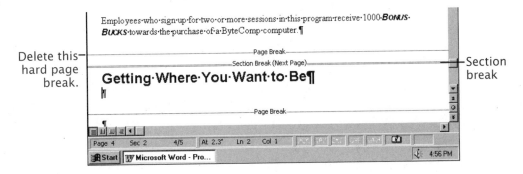

Delete this hard page break.

Section break

The graphics on the last two pages of the document are not visible at the moment.

3 Select the hard page break, and press DELETE.

Adjust the margins for a single page

Now that you have changed the orientation of pages 3 and 4 to landscape, you can adjust the margins for these pages as well.

1 Click the top of the third page, and make sure the insertion point is in section 2.

The status bar should indicate Page 3 Section 2

Page Layout View

2 Click the Page Layout View button to switch to Page Layout view.

3 On the File menu, click Page Setup.

4 Click the Margins tab.

5 In the Top box, change the top margin to 1.5".

6 In the Left box, change the left margin to 2".

7 In the Right box, change the right margin to 1".

Be sure This Section appears in the Apply To box. If not, click the Apply To down arrow, and then choose This Section from the list.

8 Click OK to return to the document.

Preview the document

Print Preview

Multiple Pages

1 On the Standard toolbar, click the Print Preview button.

2 Click the Multiple Pages button, and then drag across four boxes to display all the pages of the document.

3 If you don't see all four pages at one time, put your cursor in the Zoom box and change the percentage to a smaller value, such as 12, and then press ENTER.

Your document looks similar to the following illustration.

Section 1 in portrait orientation

Section 2 in landscape orientation

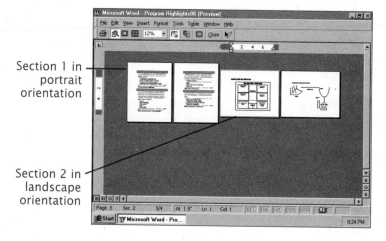

4 On the toolbar, click the Close button to return to Page Layout view.

5 Press CTRL+HOME to move the insertion point to the beginning of your document.

Creating Headers and Footers

In Microsoft Word, you can specify the information you want to appear on every page in the headers and footers. Text appearing at the top of every page is called the *header;* text appearing at the bottom of every page is called the *footer.* Headers and footers can contain whatever text you want, but you usually see information such as the date, the page number, or the document name.

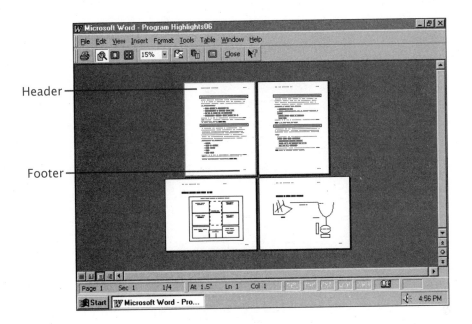

Header

Footer

Viewing Headers and Footers

In Normal view, you cannot see headers or footers; in Page Layout view, the text in the header and footer areas appears in light gray. To create or edit headers and footers, you need to display the header or footer area by clicking the Header And Footer command on the View menu. You use the Header And Footer toolbar to help you add and modify headers and footers quickly.

When you view headers and footers, the header and footer areas are enclosed in a dotted box, and the body text is dimmed on the page. As a result, you cannot edit the body text while you are viewing and editing the headers or footers. You can use buttons on the Header And Footer toolbar to switch between the header area and the footer area, and insert the date, time, and page number. There is also a button that hides the dimmed text if you find it distracting. If you want to modify the page setup, you can click the Page Setup button for quick access to the Page Setup dialog box.

View header and footer information

If you have a header or a footer and you are in Page Layout view, you can double-click the header or the footer to display it.

1 On the View menu, click Header And Footer.

Your document looks like the illustration on the next page.

225

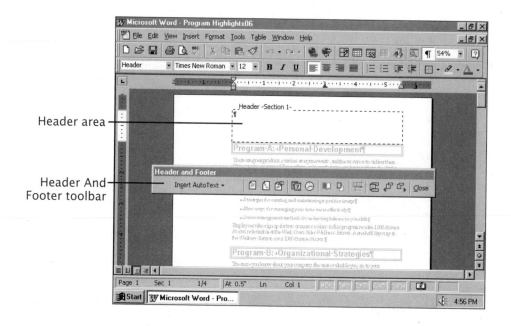

Header area

Header And
Footer toolbar

 TIP   If the Header And Footer toolbar obscures part of the
document window, drag the title bar of the toolbar to dock (position) the toolbar anywhere in the document window. You can
also double-click a gray area in the Header And Footer toolbar
to dock the toolbar above the top ruler.

2   On the Header And Footer toolbar, click the Close button to return to the
Page Layout View.

Creating Simple Alternating Footers

There are two ways to create headers or footers in a document. When you
want to insert a page number on every page, you can use the Page Numbers
command on the Insert menu. This command includes options to hide the
number on the first page, and create alternating headers or footers. This means
that all the odd-numbered pages have the same header or footer, while all the
even-numbered pages have headers or footers that are different from the odd-
numbered pages. When you want additional information to be included in the
header or footer, you can work directly in the header or footer area and use the
Headers And Footers toolbar to create customized headers and footers.

Insert page numbers

1   On the Insert menu, click Page Numbers.

The Page Numbers dialog box appears.

226

2 Click the Position down arrow and choose Bottom Of Page (Footer).

3 Click the Alignment down arrow and choose Center.

4 Clear the Show Number On First Page check box.

5 Click OK.

6 Scroll to the bottom of each page and notice that no page number appears on the first page, but the page number does appear centered on the bottom of subsequent pages.

Create an alternating footer

In this exercise you will create footers that show the page number on the right side of odd-numbered pages and on the left side of even-numbered pages.

1 On the File menu, click Page Setup.

2 Click the Layout tab.

3 Click the Different Odd And Even check box.

4 Be sure that the Different First Page check box is checked.

5 Click the Apply To down arrow, and choose Whole Document from the list.

6 Click OK.

7 On the Insert menu, click Page Numbers.

8 Click the Alignment down arrow, and then choose Outside.

9 Click OK.

10 Scroll to the bottom of each page and notice that no page number appears on the first page, but the page number does appear on the outside edge on the subsequent pages.

Preparing for the Next Part of the Lesson

To insert additional information in a header or footer, it is best to remove the page numbers you created with the Page Number command. Because you will not be creating alternating headers and footers in the next part of the lesson, you can also disable this feature in the Page Setup dialog box.

Remove the alternating footer option

1 On the File menu, click Page Setup.

2 Click the Layout tab.

3 Clear the Different Odd And Even check box.

4 Clear the Different First Page check box.

5 Click OK.

Remove the existing page numbers

1 Double-click the page number at the bottom of page 2.

The Header And Footer toolbar appears, and the footer area is active.

2 Select the page number.

Shading appears over the number.

3 Click the edge of the shading.

Sizing handles appear on the shading.

4 Press DELETE.

5 Click the Close button on the Header And Footer toolbar.

The page numbers are removed.

Creating Customized Headers and Footers

By using the Header And Footer command, you can insert a page number as well as a date, time, text, and fields that contain document information. *Fields* are special instructions you insert in a document that tell Microsoft Word to supply specific information about the document or computer system. You can use the Page Numbers command to specify the starting page number and select a format for the numbers, such as uppercase and lowercase Roman numerals.

Enter text in the header

In this exercise, you will insert text and a date in the header.

If the insertion point is not in the header area, click the Switch Between Header And Footer button on the Header And Footer toolbar.

IMPORTANT If the page number appears in the document as {PAGE}, press ALT+F9 to turn off the display of field codes.

1 On the View menu, click Header And Footer.

2 Make sure the insertion point is in the header area, and then type **West Coast Sales National Expo**

3 Press TAB twice to move the insertion point to the right margin.

4 On the Header And Footer toolbar, click the Insert Date button.

In the header area, the right-aligned tab marker is set to the right margin.

Insert Date

5 Drag the right-aligned tab marker in the ruler so that it is aligned with the 5.5-inch mark.

The header looks like the following illustration.

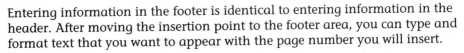

Enter text in the footer

Switch Between Header And Footer

Entering information in the footer is identical to entering information in the header. After moving the insertion point to the footer area, you can type and format text that you want to appear with the page number you will insert.

1 On the Header And Footer toolbar, click the Switch Between Header And Footer button.

2 Type **Page** and press the SPACEBAR.

Insert Page Number

3 On the Header And Footer toolbar, click the Insert Page Number button.

The page number appears next to the word "Page."

4 On the Formatting toolbar, click the Align Right button.

5 On the Header And Footer toolbar, click the Close button to return to Page Layout view.

Align Right

You can also double-click the gray document text when viewing the header or footer to exit the header or footer area.

TIP The Header And Footer toolbar includes an Insert AutoText button. Click this button to insert common expressions and information in your headers or footers. See the One Step Further exercise at the end of this lesson to practice using the Insert AutoText button on the Header And Footer toolbar.

229

Preview the document

Print Preview

1 On the Standard toolbar, click the Print Preview button.
Your document looks like the following illustration.

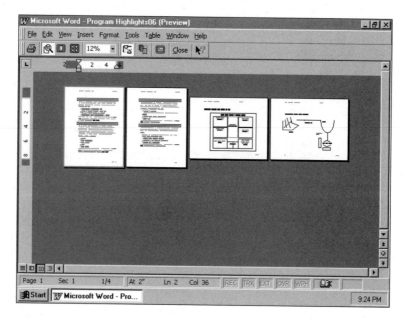

2 On the toolbar, click the Close button to return to the document in Page Layout view.

3 Save the document.

Numbering Different Parts of a Document

In longer documents, it is common to see different parts of the document numbered differently. For example, the table of contents pages might be numbered i, ii, iii, and so on. The second section would have a different numbering pattern and might be numbered as "Page 1-1, Page 1-2," and so on. To number parts of the same document differently, you first separate the document into sections by inserting section breaks for the different parts. Then, you can format the numbering in each section independently.

Break the link between sections

When you divide a document into sections, the header and footer information carries over from the previous section by default. To create unique headers and footers or page numbering for each section, you must break the connection between sections before you adjust the headers and footers. You break the connection between sections by clicking the Same As Previous button, which is depressed by default on the Header And Footer toolbar.

In this exercise, you will change the footer and page numbering of the second section, the pages containing the maps. Your document is already divided into sections for the pages you want to number differently, so you can proceed by breaking the link between sections.

Switch Between Header And Footer

1   Click to position the insertion point on page 3 (the first page of the second section of the document), and on the View menu, click Header And Footer.

2   On the Header And Footer toolbar, click the Switch Between Header And Footer button to move the insertion point to the footer area for this section.

In this example, the header remains the same in both sections.

Same As Previous

3   On the Header And Footer toolbar, click the Same As Previous button.

The button is no longer depressed. This means that the current section can have a different footer from that in the previous section.

Number the second section

Now that the document is separated into sections and the connection between footers is broken, you can format the page numbering of each section. You can also create unique headers or footers in each section. For the last two pages of the document, you will use the Roman numeral page number format.

Format Page Number

1   On the Header And Footer toolbar, click the Format Page Number button.

The Page Number Format dialog box appears.

2   In the Page Number Format dialog box, click the Number Format down arrow, and choose I, II, III.

3   In the Page Numbering area, click the Start At option button.

The numbering in this section is set to start at I.

4   Click OK to return to the Header And Footer toolbar.

The page number on the first page of this section is I, even though it is the third page of the document.

Modify the text in the footer

To make the footer in section two even more distinct from the footer in section one, you can modify the text next to the page number.

1   Position the insertion point in front of the word "Page" in the footer, type **Maps** and press the SPACEBAR.

2   On the Header And Footer toolbar, click the Close button to return to Page Layout view.

Preview your footers

Print Preview

Multiple Pages

1 Press CTRL+HOME to go to the top of document.

2 On the Standard toolbar, click the Print Preview button.

3 Click the Multiple Pages button, and drag horizontally across two boxes if two pages are not displayed.

4 Double-click near the bottom of page 2 in the second section to get a magnified view of the footer; scroll through the document to examine each of the footers on each page.

5 Click the Close button to close the Print Preview window.

6 Save the document.

Inserting Footnotes

In addition to footers, *footnotes* are another kind of text that can appear at the bottom of a page. When you want to make a reference to additional information in a document, you insert a footnote reference mark (or you can have Microsoft Word assign a number), and then you enter the text. If you add or delete a footnote, Microsoft Word renumbers the footnotes. Although you don't see the footnotes in Normal view, you can see them in Page Layout view and Print Preview, as well as when you print the document.

 TIP To edit a footnote in Normal view, double-click the footnote marker in the document. To edit a footnote in Page Layout view, double-click the footnotes pane of the document.

Insert a footnote

Normal View

To create an endnote, in the Footnotes dialog box, click the Endnote option button. An endnote is placed at the end of a docu-ment instead of at the bottom of a page.

1 Click the Normal View button at the lower left of the window.

2 Move the insertion point to the end of the fourth bulleted item on page 2.

3 On the Insert menu, click Footnote.

4 Click OK.

5 In the footnotes pane, type **The Personal Effectiveness Hospitality room is available on both days of the conference.**

Your text in the footnotes pane looks like the following illustration.

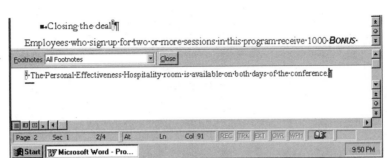

6   On the footnotes pane, click Close.

7   Click the Page Layout View button, and scroll down to see the footnote.

8   Save the document.

Page Layout View

> **NOTE**   If you'd like to build on the skills that you learned in this lesson, you can do the One Step Further. Otherwise, skip to "Finish the lesson."

One Step Further: Inserting AutoText Entries by Using the Header And Footer Toolbar

The Header And Footer toolbar includes AutoText entries that make it easier for you to create your document. These entries insert common expressions and information you frequently see in document headers and footers, such as the name of the author, the date the document was printed, the word "Confidential," and the filename.

Display the header and footer for the first section

In the Program Highlights document, you decide to include the author's name and the document filename to help you locate the document on your computer when you need to edit it in the future. You will add this information only to the first section of the document.

1   Press CTRL+HOME to move the insertion point to the beginning of your document.

2   Double-click the footer area on the first page.

The footer area opens for the first section of the document.

233

Insert AutoText in the footer for the first section

1 On the Header And Footer toolbar, click the Insert AutoText button.

A list of header and footer AutoText entries is displayed.

2 Click Filename, and press the SPACEBAR.

The filename of the document appears in the footer. Word inserts a space following the filename.

3 On the Header And Footer toolbar, click the Insert AutoText button, click Created by, and then press the SPACEBAR.

The text "Created by" followed by the author's name appears after the filename.

4 Click the Close button to return to the document text.

5 Save the document.

Finish the lesson

➤ If you are finished using Microsoft Word for now, on the File menu, click Exit.

Lesson Summary

To	Do this	Button
Establish margins in a document	On the File menu, click Page Setup. On the Margins tab, set the desired margins.	
Create a header or footer	On the View menu, click Header And Footer. In the Header Or Footer area, type the text or click the buttons for the data you want.	
View page numbers and headers or footers	On the View menu, click Page Layout.	
Break a link between sections	On the Header And Footer toolbar, click the Same As Previous button to deselect it.	
Insert a footnote	Click to position the insertion point where you want the footnote reference to be. On the Insert menu, click Footnote. Select the footnote option, and click OK. In the footnotes pane, type the text of your footnote, and then click the Close button.	

To	Do this	Button
Insert a date in a header or footer	On the Header And Footer toolbar, click the Date button.	
Insert a page number in a header or footer	On the Header And Footer toolbar, click the Page Number button.	
Insert page numbers	On the Insert menu, click Page Numbers. Click OK.	
Create an alternating header or footer of page numbers	On the File menu, click Page Setup. On the Layout tab, in the Headers And Footers area, click the Different Odd And Even check box. On the Insert menu, click Page Numbers. Click the Alignment down arrow, and then click Outside. Click OK.	

For online information about	Use the Office Assistant to search for
Adjusting document margins	**Margins,** and then click Page Margins
Inserting and formatting page numbers	**Page numbers,** and then click Add Page Numbers
Creating headers and footers Create	**Headers and footers,** and then click Headers And Footers

Part 3

Microsoft Excel 97

Working in the Excel Environment

Lesson

1

In this lesson you will learn how to:

Estimated time
45 min.

- Open and save a workbook file.
- Navigate through a workbook and a worksheet.
- Enter, edit, and delete data.
- Use AutoComplete and AutoCorrect to speed data entry.
- Move and copy cells and sheets.
- Write and edit simple formulas.

The basic working environment in Microsoft Excel is a workbook file that can contain one or more worksheets. A worksheet is similar to an accountant's ledger, with numbers, text, and calculations lined up in columns and rows. But, unlike in an accountant's ledger, when you type the numbers in Microsoft Excel, the program performs the calculations for you.

With Microsoft Excel, it's easy to enter information into a worksheet, and then change, delete, or add to the information. You don't need to worry about entering your data perfectly or completely the first time; you can always edit it later. You can arrange multiple worksheets within a workbook (for example, you might place all the worksheets for a single client or a single project into one workbook), and then name them so that you can locate the information you need quickly.

In this lesson, you'll learn how to work with worksheets and workbooks; open, save, and close a workbook; and enter and edit data in a worksheet. You'll also

239

learn how to work more efficiently by using features like AutoComplete and AutoCorrect to do some of your work for you, and by writing simple formulas.

Starting the Lesson

If you have not installed the Part3 Excel Practice files, refer to "Installing and Using the Practice and Camcorder Files," earlier in this book.

In the following exercises, you'll open the practice file called Customer List, and then save the file with a different name, Lesson 01. This process creates a duplicate of the practice file, which you can work on and modify during the lesson. The original file, Customer List, will remain unchanged and will be used again later in this book.

Open a workbook

Open

1   On the Standard toolbar, click the Open button.

The Open dialog box appears. In this dialog box, you select the folder and the document you want to open. The box labeled Look In shows the folder that is currently selected.

Look In Favorites

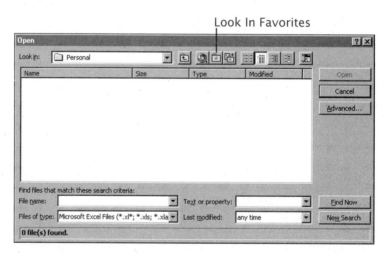

2   Click the Look In Favorites button.

The names of all folders and files that are contained within the Favorites folder are listed.

3   Double-click the folder named Part3 Excel Practice.

The list of practice files appears.

4   In the file list, double-click the Customer List file.

The Open dialog box closes, and the Customer List file appears in the document window.

Save the practice file with a new name

When you save a practice file, you give it a name and specify where you want to store it. For each file you use in Part 3 of this book, you'll usually save it in the Part3 Excel Practice folder with a new name so that the original practice file will remain unchanged.

 IMPORTANT For the purposes of Part 3 of this book we have elected to show the file extensions. To match the illustrations in Part 3, click the Start button, point to Programs, and then click Windows Explorer or Windows NT Explorer. On the View menu, click Options. On the View tab for Windows 95, clear the Hide MS-DOS File Extension For File Types That Are Registered check box. On the View tab for Windows NT, clear the Hide File Extensions For Known File Types check box. Click OK.

---

1 On the File menu, click Save As.

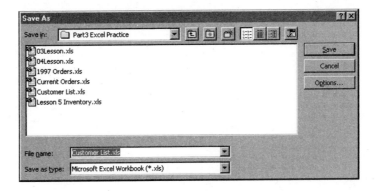

2 Be sure that Part3 Excel Practice appears in the Save In box.

If the Part3 Excel Practice folder does not appear, repeat steps 2 through 4 of the previous exercise to select the folder.

3 In the File Name box, type **Lesson 01**

4 Click the Save button or press ENTER to close the dialog box and save the file.

Getting Around in a Workbook

In Microsoft Excel, files are called *workbooks*. Workbooks can contain multiple worksheets, as well as chart sheets. You'll learn more about charts and chart sheets in Lesson 6, "Charting to Assess Trends and Relationships." In this lesson, you'll learn about moving around in a worksheet as well as in a workbook that contains worksheets.

Moving Around in a Workbook

The practice file you opened in the previous exercise contains customer information for the Island Tea & Coffee Company. The first worksheet, as shown in the following illustration, contains a list of customer names and addresses, and the remainder of the worksheets are blank. You can select different sheets in a workbook by clicking the Sheet tabs (also called "tabs") that are located at the bottom of each sheet. You can use the Sheet tab scroll buttons to bring hidden sheet tabs into view so that you can select them. The selected sheet is called the *active* sheet.

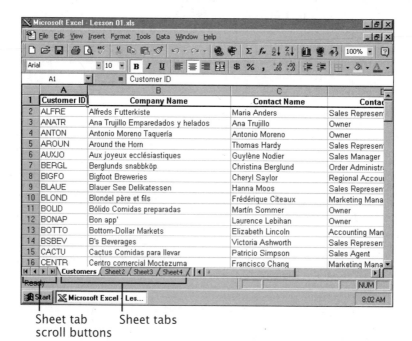

Sheet tab
scroll buttons

Sheet tabs

Additionally, you can select several sheets at a time, even if they are non-adjacent sheets, and enter the same data on all the active sheets at once. This is particularly useful if you need to set up several worksheets that are identical in some respect (for example, adding common labels to a monthly report).

Select worksheets in a workbook

In this exercise, you select different sheets in the workbook.

1 Click the Sheet tab labeled Sheet2.

Sheet2 becomes the active sheet.

2 Click the tab labeled Customers.

Last Tab Scroll

3 Click the Last Tab Scroll button.

The sheet tabs scroll so that you can see the last tab in the workbook, which is Sheet10. The Customers sheet is still the active sheet.

4 Click the tab labeled Sheet10.

Sheet10 becomes the active sheet.

5 Use the right mouse button to click a Sheet tab scroll button.

A shortcut menu appears, listing the names of all the sheets contained in the workbook.

6 On the shortcut menu, click Customers.

The Customers sheet becomes the active sheet.

Select several worksheets at once

In this exercise, you select several sheets at the same time. All the selected sheets become active and, if you enter data in one of the sheets, the data is automatically entered in all of the other active sheets.

To select a group of non-adjacent sheets, hold down CTRL while you click the Sheet tabs.

1 Click the tab for Sheet2.

2 Hold down SHIFT and click the Sheet4 tab.

Sheet2, Sheet3, and Sheet4 are all selected and active. The word [Group] appears in the title bar next to the filename.

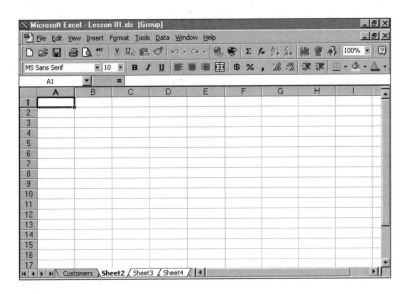

3 Use the right mouse button to click the Sheet2 tab.

4 On the shortcut menu, click Ungroup Sheets.

Only Sheet2 remains active.

Ask the Office Assistant for help

If you want to know more about moving around in worksheets, you can enlist help from the Office Assistant.

An Introduction to the Office Assistant

While you are working with Microsoft Office 97, an animated character called the *Office Assistant* pops up on your screen to help you work productively. As you work, you can ask the Office Assistant questions by typing your question, and then clicking Search. The Office Assistant then shows you the answer to your question.

You will sometimes see a light bulb next to the Office Assistant—clicking the light bulb displays a tip about the action you are currently performing. You can view more tips by clicking Tips in the Office Assistant balloon. In addition, the Office Assistant is tailored to how you work—after you master a particular skill, the Office Assistant stops offering tips.

You can close any Office Assistant tip or message by pressing ESC.

Clippit, an Office Assistant, in action

The Office Assistant appears in the following situations:

Office Assistant

- When you click the Office Assistant button on the Standard toolbar.
- When you choose Microsoft Excel Help on the Help menu or press F1.
- When you type certain phrases.

The Office Assistant is a shared application—any settings that you change will affect the Office Assistant in other Office 97 programs.
You can customize the Office Assistant in two ways. You can:

Determine under what circumstances you want to see the Office Assistant

You can use the right mouse button to click the Office Assistant and click Options to open the Office Assistant dialog box. You can then define when you want the Office Assistant to appear, and what kind of help you want it to offer.

Change your Office Assistant character

You can use the right mouse button to click the Office Assistant and click Options to open the Office Assistant dialog box. Click the Gallery tab.

IMPORTANT If the Office Assistant appears, click the Start Using Microsoft Program option. If the User Name dialog box appears, fill in your name and initials, and then click OK. In the Office Assistant, click the Close button.

For the purposes of this book, the Office Assistant will not appear in the illustrations. If you want to match the illustrations, any time the Office Assistant appears, use the right mouse button to click the Office Assistant, and then click Hide Assistant. If you want to leave the Office Assistant on top to help guide you, but it is in your way, simply drag it to another area on the screen.

1 Click the Office Assistant button.

2 In the What Would You Like To Do area, type **Learn about moving around in a worksheet**, and then click Search.

3 Click See More, and then click the Change Options For Entering And Editing Data topic.

4 Read the Help topic, and then click the Close button in the Help window.

Close

Moving Around in a Worksheet

Column headers are also referred to as column letters. Row headers are also referred to as row numbers.

A worksheet consists of *columns* and *rows*. Columns run vertically and are identified by letters, called *column headers*, which run across the top of a worksheet. Rows run horizontally and are identified by numbers, called *row headers*, which run down the left side of a worksheet. The intersection of a row and a column is called a *cell*. Cells are identified according to their positions in the rows and columns. The combination of the column letter and row number for a cell is called the *cell reference*. For example, the cell reference for the cell located in column A and row 1 is A1.

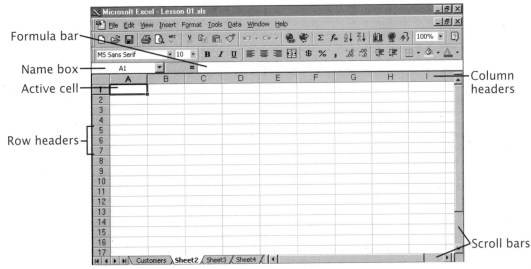

245

When you select a cell by clicking it, that cell becomes the *active cell* and you can enter data in it. The active cell is surrounded by a heavy border. The cell reference for the active cell appears in the Name box, on the left side of the formula bar, and the corresponding row and column headers become bold and raised. You can also change the active cell by pressing the ENTER key, the TAB key, or the arrow keys.

Scroll bars appear on the right and bottom side of the worksheet, and are used to view different parts of a worksheet quickly when it contains more information than can be displayed on one screen. When you change the view of a worksheet using the scroll bars, the active cell does not change; only your view of the worksheet changes. You can only see a small portion of your worksheet in the Microsoft Excel window (an entire worksheet is 256 columns by 65536 rows), but the scroll bars help you to move around quickly to view any part of the worksheet.

In the following exercises, you'll learn how to select cells and view worksheets.

Select cells on a worksheet

In this exercise, you practice moving around in a worksheet and selecting data.

1 Click the Customers sheet tab to select it.

2 Click the cell at the intersection of column B and row 2.

Cell B2 is selected.

B2	▼	=	Alfreds Futterkiste	
	A	B	C	D
1	Customer ID	Company Name	Contact Name	Contac
2	ALFRE	Alfreds Futterkiste	Maria Anders	Sales Represen
3	ANATR	Ana Trujillo Emparedados y helados	Ana Trujillo	Owner
4	ANTON	Antonio Moreno Taquería	Antonio Moreno	Owner

Because it is the active cell, B2 is surrounded by a heavy border. The cell reference, B2, appears in the Name box, and the headers for column B and row 2 are bold and raised. The contents of the cell appear in the formula bar.

3 Press the down arrow key.

The active cell is now B3.

4 Press CTRL+HOME.

The active cell moves to the beginning of the worksheet, cell A1.

5 Drag from cell A1 to cell C3.

A rectangular *range* of cells is selected.

To drag, point to the first cell, hold down the mouse button as you move the pointer, and release when the pointer is over the last cell.

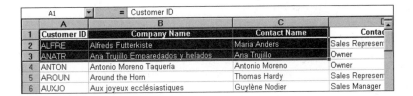

Cell A1 is the active cell within the selected range, and the headers for the range (columns A through C and rows 1 through 3) are highlighted.

6 Press ENTER repeatedly.

The active cell moves around within the selected range.

Pressing the TAB key will also move the active cell around within a selected range, from left to right instead of top to bottom.

7 Click cell A5.

Cell A5 becomes the active cell and the range A1 to cell C3 is no longer highlighted.

8 Move the mouse over the bottom border of the cell until the pointer becomes a white arrow, and then double-click the bottom border of the cell.

Double-click this border.

The active cell moves to the bottom of the list of data (cell A119 is selected).

9 Double-click the top border of the active cell.

The active cell moves to the top of the list (cell A1 is selected).

View different areas of the worksheet

You can use the scroll bars to see different areas of your worksheet. In this exercise, you move around your worksheet to familiarize yourself with its different areas.

1 Move the mouse pointer over the vertical scroll box (the box that moves within the vertical scroll bar), and press and hold down the mouse button.

A ScrollTip appears that contains the number of the row at the top of your worksheet window (Row: 1).

247

2 Drag the scroll box downward as far as it will go.

The ScrollTip displays the number of the row that will be visible at the top of your worksheet window when you release the mouse button.

3 Release the mouse button.

You can now see the data at the end of the list.

4 Drag the horizontal scroll box until the ScrollTip reads Column: D, and then release the mouse button.

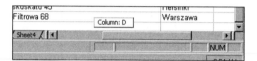

Column D is the leftmost visible column in the worksheet.

5 Press CTRL+HOME to return to cell A1, the first cell of the worksheet.

Display helpful tips

In addition to ScrollTips, there are ScreenTips to help you identify buttons on the toolbars, and comments to add extra information to your worksheet. You'll learn how to add comments to cells in your worksheet in Lesson 2, "Setting Up a Worksheet."

If the ScreenTips do not appear, use the right mouse button to click a toolbar, and then click Customize. Click the Options tab, and then select the Show ScreenTips On Toolbars check box.

1 Move the pointer over any tool on a toolbar.

A ScreenTip will appear below the pointer and will display the name of the button.

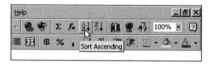

If comment indicators do not appear, on the Tools menu, click Options. On the View tab, click the Comment Indicator Only option button.

2 Move the pointer over cell A1.

A comment appears and displays information entered by the workbook's author. A cell containing a comment is identified by a small red triangle in its upper right corner.

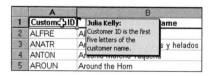

248

Entering and Editing Data

You can enter text, numbers, and formulas into any cell on a worksheet. When you enter data, Microsoft Excel recognizes it as either text, a date, a number that can be calculated, or a formula. You can also edit or delete anything that you have entered. Whatever you type appears in both the active cell and the formula bar, and can be edited in either location.

Entering Data

Entering data is simple. You first select the cell in which you want the information to appear, type the text or numbers you want, and then press ENTER or TAB to enter what you typed. You can also press an arrow key or click another cell to enter typed information.

You can cancel an entry before you enter it (for example, if you entered it in the wrong cell or misspelled it) by pressing ESC. If you make a mistake while typing, you can use the BACKSPACE key to undo the mistake.

When you first create a worksheet, you'll start by typing in your data. After a while, your worksheet will start to fill up with information, and you might not be able to see all your data on your screen. When you are revising a large worksheet, you can make your editing tasks easier by controlling what you can see on the worksheet.

For example, the customers list is too long to see in one window, so when you enter data at the bottom of the list, you can't see the column headings at the top of the list. You can *freeze* the first row (the row with the column headings) so that it remains visible regardless of where you are working in the list.

Another way to make your editing tasks easier and speed up data entry is by using AutoComplete to type recurring entries in a column. For example, in the customers list, contact titles are repeated for many customers. AutoComplete can save you time by entering these repeated entries for you.

Freeze panes to keep column headings visible

In this exercise, you freeze row 1 so that the column labels will remain visible while you enter new data at the bottom of the list.

If you select cell B2, both row 1 and column A will be frozen.

1 On the Customers sheet, click cell A2.

2 On the Window menu, click Freeze Panes.

The top row, row 1, is frozen. You can scroll down the worksheet, and row 1 will remain in view.

Enter text

A new customer of the Island Tea & Coffee Company needs to be added to the customers list. In this exercise, you enter the Company Name, Contact Name, and Contact Title of the new customer. Microsoft Excel recognizes text entries as text, and aligns them automatically on the left side of the cell.

1 Click cell B1.

2 Double-click the bottom border of cell B1 to move quickly to the last entry in the column.

The cell containing the last entry in the Company Name column is selected.

3 Click cell B120.

4 Type **Hanari Carnes**, and then press TAB.

The new company name is entered, and the next cell on the right is selected.

5 Type **Mario Pontes**, and then press TAB.

The new contact name is entered, and the next cell on the right is selected.

6 Type **Ac**

AutoComplete has guessed, based on the closest match to previous entries in the D column, that you want to enter Accounting Manager and has inserted it for you.

118	Matti Karttunen	Owner/Marketing Assistant	Keskuskat
119	Zbyszek Piestrzeniewicz	Owner	ul. Filtrowa
120	Mario Pontes	Accounting Manager	
121			
122			

7 Press ENTER to complete the entry.

A feature called AutoReturn returns the active cell to the next cell in which you have started to type—in this case cell B121, the next company name.

 TIP In a column of repeated entries, such as the Contact Title column, you can use the right mouse button to click the cell, and then click the Pick From List command on the shortcut menu. A list of all entries available in the column will appear. You can then click the entry you want to enter in the cell.

Enter numbers

In this exercise, you practice entering numbers on a blank worksheet. You enter numbers the same way you enter text: type the number, and then press ENTER. Microsoft Excel recognizes numbers and aligns them automatically on the right side of the cell.

1   Click the tab for Sheet2.

Sheet2, a blank worksheet, is the active sheet.

2   In cell B2, type **12**, and then press ENTER.

The value 12 is entered in cell B2, and B3 becomes the active cell.

3   In cell B3, type **100**, and then press ENTER.

The value 100 is entered in cell B3, and B4 becomes the active cell. Your screen should look similar to the following illustration.

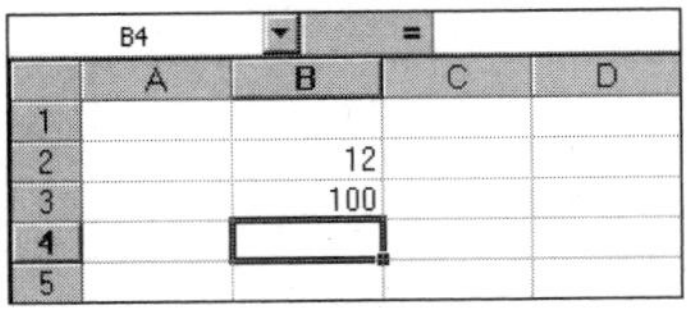

Making Changes

You can change or edit data in a worksheet by deleting the data, typing a new entry over an existing entry, or changing a few characters in an entry. In the following exercises, you will change data, and then practice undoing and redo-ing deletions and entries.

Delete data

To delete an entry and leave the cell blank, click the cell, and then press DELETE.

1   Click cell B3, type **200**, and then press ENTER.

Your new entry replaces your previous entry.

2   Double-click cell B2.

The data contained in cell B2 is ready to be edited.

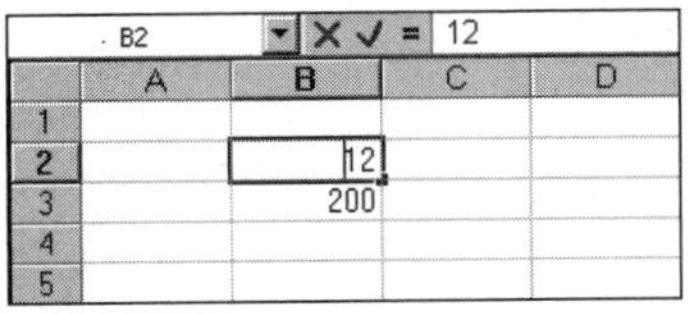

3   Click between the 1 and the 2 to place the insertion point there, and then press BACKSPACE to erase the 1.

4   Type **5**, and then press ENTER.

Cell B2 now contains the number 52.

Undo a previous action

➤ Click the Undo button on the Standard toolbar.

The change you just made to cell B2 is undone, and the value is 12 again.

Undo several previous actions

Undo

1 Point to the Undo button on the Standard toolbar, and then click the down arrow that appears on the right side of the button.

A list of recent actions appears.

2 Click the third action in the list.

Your last three actions are undone. All the numbers you entered in Sheet2 are deleted.

Redo previous actions

Redo

1 Point to the Redo button on the Standard toolbar, and then click the down arrow that appears on the right side of the button.

A list of recently undone actions appears.

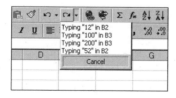

2 Click the fourth action in the list.

All of the actions you had undone in the previous exercise are redone. The number in cell B2 is 52, and the number in B3 is 200.

Making Corrections Using AutoCorrect

To turn off AutoCorrect, on the Tools menu, click AutoCorrect, and then clear the Replace Text As You Type check box.

To undo an AutoCorrect change without turning off AutoCorrect, click the Undo button as soon as the AutoCorrect change is made.

AutoCorrect corrects typing mistakes for you as you type. You don't have to do anything extra, and you might not even be aware that you made a mistake and that it was corrected. AutoCorrect includes an extensive list of commonly misspelled words, but you can customize it by adding your own words to the list. You can also customize AutoCorrect to insert long words or phrases when you type a short abbreviation or acronym.

In the following exercises, you will see how AutoCorrect works, and then customize AutoCorrect to insert the company name, Island Tea & Coffee, when you type the acronym "itc."

Correct commonly misspelled words

1 Click cell B14.

2 Type **teh** followed by a space, type **adn**, and then press ENTER.

When you press SPACEBAR or ENTER, the spelling of the word you just typed is corrected.

Customize AutoCorrect to type long words

1 On the Tools menu, click AutoCorrect.

The AutoCorrect dialog box appears.

2 In the Replace box, type **itc**

3 In the With box, type **Island Tea & Coffee**

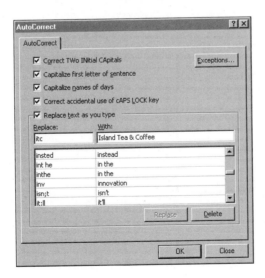

If you have more words to add to the list, click Add, add the desired acronyms and terms, and then click OK to close the dialog box when you are finished.

4   Click OK.

5   Click cell B14.

6   Type **itc**, and then press ENTER.

Island Tea & Coffee is entered in the cell.

Rearranging a Worksheet by Moving and Copying Cells

Sometimes you might enter information in the wrong cells, or you might want to enter the same information in three different places in a workbook. Instead of deleting and re-entering the information, or entering the same information several times, you can move or copy it easily. In the following exercise, you will practice moving and then copying cells.

NOTE Although what you will be doing in the following exercises is commonly referred to as "moving" and "copying" cells, you are actually moving and copying the entries in cells, rather than the cells themselves.

Move cells to a new location on the same worksheet

In this exercise, you move cells by dragging them to another location on your worksheet.

1   On Sheet2, select the B2:B3 range.

2   Point to a border of the selection, and then hold down the mouse button while you drag the selected range to cells D2:D3.

While you drag the selected cells, a tip appears next to the pointer to tell you what range of cells your selection is in.

	A	B	C	D	E	F
1						
2		52				
3		200				
4						
5				D2:D3		

3   When the D2:D3 range is selected, release the mouse button.

The cells are moved to the D2:D3 range.

Move cells to a different worksheet

Dragging cells to move them works well when you are moving the cells short distances on the same worksheet, but if you want to move cells to a different area of the worksheet or to another worksheet, using the toolbar buttons is easier.

Cut

Paste

1   On Sheet2, verify that the D2:D3 range is still selected.

2   On the Standard toolbar, click the Cut button.

   A moving border appears around the cut selection.

3   Select Sheet3.

4   On Sheet3, select cell B2, and then click the Paste button.

   The cut cells are pasted onto Sheet3. The upper-left corner of the cut selection is pasted into the cell you selected on the new sheet.

Copy cells to another location on the same worksheet

There are many ways to copy cells. In this exercise, you practice two of the easiest methods.

1   On Sheet3, verify that the B2:B3 range is selected.

2   Point to a selection border, and then hold down CTRL while you drag the selection to the F2:F3 range.

   While you are dragging the selection, a small plus sign (+) appears next to the pointer to tell you that you are dragging a copy of the selection.

	A	B	C	D	E	F	G	H
1								
2		52						
3		200						
4						F2:F3		
5								

3   Release the mouse button, and then release CTRL.

   The cells are copied to a new location.

4   Select the B2:B3 range.

5   Point to a selection border, and then use the right mouse button to drag the selection to the C7:C8 range.

   A shortcut menu appears after you release the right mouse button.

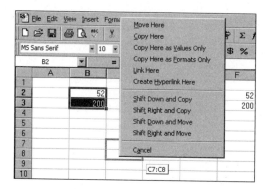

6   On the shortcut menu, click Copy Here.

The cells are copied to the new location.

Move cells to a different worksheet

As with moving cells, dragging cells to copy them works well when you copy the cells across short distances on the same worksheet, but if you want to copy cells to another area of the worksheet or to another worksheet, using the toolbar buttons is easier.

1   On Sheet3, select the range F2:F3.

2   On the Standard toolbar, click the Copy button.

A moving border appears around the copied selection.

Copy

3   Select Sheet2.

4   On Sheet2, select cell C4, and then click the Paste button.

Paste

The copied cells are pasted onto Sheet2. The upper-left corner of the copied selection is pasted into the cell you selected on the new sheet.

Rearranging a Workbook by Moving and Copying Sheets

Now you know how to move and copy cells in a workbook, but suppose you want to rearrange your workbook by moving or copying an entire sheet. This is even simpler than moving and copying cells. In the following exercises, you re-arrange your workbook by moving a worksheet, and then copying it.

Move a sheet to a new location in the same workbook

In this exercise, you move Sheet2 behind Sheet3.

1   Click the Sheet2 tab.

2 Drag the Sheet2 tab to the right, until the small triangle appears on the right of the Sheet3 tab. Your screen should look similar to the following illustration.

3 Release the mouse button.

Sheet2 is now behind Sheet3 in the workbook.

Copy a sheet in the same workbook

Suppose you have spent time creating a worksheet, and would like to re-use it as a starting point for another worksheet. Instead of recreating the worksheet, you can just make a copy of it. In this exercise, you create a copy of Sheet2.

1 Click the Sheet2 tab.

2 Hold down CTRL while you drag the Sheet2 tab to the right.

3 When the small triangle appears on the right of the Sheet2 tab, release the mouse button, and then release CTRL.

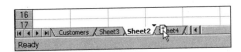

Sheet2 is now copied, and the copy is named Sheet2 (2).

Writing Simple Formulas

Microsoft Excel was specifically created to calculate numbers. You can place raw data (numbers) in a worksheet, and then tell Microsoft Excel how to calculate the numbers to give you the results you want. You tell Microsoft Excel how you want the numbers calculated by writing a formula. In its simplest form, a formula might be used to add two numbers together. One of the main advantages of using a powerful spreadsheet program like Microsoft Excel is that you can insert a formula in a cell and have it perform a calculation on values that are in other cells. For example, you can enter a formula in a cell to total the values in another range of cells, such as the cells above the formula. Regardless of what numbers you place in the specified range, the correct total will appear in the cell containing the formula.

You can perform calculations with your data using arithmetic operators (such as +, -, and *) and with *functions*, which are built-in formulas. Microsoft Excel comes with hundreds of functions that you can use in formulas to save you

You'll learn more about the Formula Palette in Lesson 3, "Writing Formulas."

time. For example, there are functions that calculate the periodic payment on a loan or annuity (the PMT function), the standard deviation based on a sample (the STDEV function), and the square root of a number (the SQRT function). The Formula Palette makes it easy to write formulas that use these and other functions.

In Microsoft Excel, all formulas begin with an equal sign (=). After the equal sign, you type the formula, and then press ENTER. After the formula has been entered, the cell will display the results of the calculation. You can easily edit the formula to change any part of it.

In the following exercises, you will practice writing and editing simple formulas.

Write a simple formula

In this exercise, you write a formula to add two numbers.

1   On Sheet2, select cell E4.

2   Type **=52+200**, and then press ENTER.

The formula is entered in the cell, and the result of the addition appears.

3   Select cell E4.

The formula appears in the formula bar, and the result appears in the cell.

E4			=	=52+200		
	A	B	C	D	E	F
1						
2						
3						
4			52		252	
5			200			

4   Select cell E5.

5   Type **=**, and then click cell C4.

The cell reference is entered in the formula.

SUM		X ✓	=	=C4		
	A	B	C	D	E	F
1						
2						
3						
4			52		252	
5			200		=C4	
6						

6   Type **+**, click cell C5, and then press ENTER.

The formula, which adds the contents of cells C4 and C5, is entered in the cell. The result of the addition appears in the cell.

7 Click cell C4, type **100**, and then press ENTER.

The formula in cell E5 displays the result of the addition.

 NOTE You can also write formulas that use a combination of cell references and numbers. For example, you can write a formula that calculates a sales tax of 7% on a price by multiplying .07 times a cell reference.

Edit an existing formula

You can edit a formula by selecting the cell that contains it and then making changes in the formula bar. You can also double-click the cell and then make changes to the formula directly in the cell. In this exercise, you change the operator, and then modify a reference in the formula.

1 Double-click cell E5.

Cell E5 is opened for editing. The cell references in the formula and the cells that are referred to are color-coded to help you see which cells the formula refers to.

2 Select the plus sign (+) by dragging the insertion point over it, type an asterisk (*), and then press ENTER.

The formula multiplies the two cells and displays the result of the multiplication.

3 Double-click cell E5, and then double-click the reference to cell C5 in the formula.

The reference to cell C5 is selected.

SUM	▼	X ✓ =	=C4*C5		
A	B	C	D	E	F
1					
2					
3					
4		100		252	
5		200		=C4*C5	
6					

4 Click cell E4, and then press ENTER.

The formula now multiplies the value in cell C4 by the value in cell E4. The result is 25200.

 NOTE If you'd like to build up on the skills you learned in this lesson, you can do the One Step Further. Otherwise, skip to "Finish the Lesson."

One Step Further: Creating a Form to Enter Data Easily

In this lesson, you entered data in the Customers sheet by typing text directly in the cells, but it can be time-consuming to move from cell to cell in a worksheet, and you might enter data in the wrong cells. Sometimes it's easier to enter data in a form because you don't have to scroll around in the worksheet or move from cell to cell. By using a form, you can make certain that you're entering the right data in the right place. You can create a data form quickly for any worksheet.

1   Select the Customers sheet, and be sure that a cell within the customer list table is selected.

2   On the Data menu, click Form.

A data entry form is created for the Customers sheet. The column headings in the worksheet become field names on the left side of the form. The form opens with the first record in the worksheet showing.

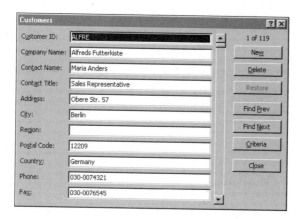

3   On the data form, click New.

The form displays a new blank record, and you can enter data for a new customer. You can move from box to box in the data form by pressing TAB.

4   When you are finished using the data form, click Close.

Finish the lesson

1   On the File menu, click Save.

2   To continue to the next lesson, on the File menu, click Close.

3   If you are finished using Microsoft Excel for now, on the File menu, click Exit.

Lesson Summary

To	Do this	Button
Open a file	On the Standard toolbar, click the Open button. Locate the folder that contains the file you want to open, and then double-click the filename.	
Save a file with another name	On the File menu, click Save As. Open the folder in which you want to save the file, type the new name in the File Name box, and then click Save.	
Select a worksheet	Click the sheet tab.	
Select multiple worksheets	Click the sheet tab for the first worksheet you want to select, hold down SHIFT, and then click the sheet tab for the last worksheet you want to include (hold down CTRL to select non-adjacent sheets).	
Select a cell	Click the cell.	
Select a range of cells	Hold down the mouse button and drag from one corner to the opposite diagonal corner of the range you want.	
Enter data	Select a cell. Type the data, and then press ENTER or select another cell.	
Freeze panes	Select a cell immediately below or to the right of the row or column, and then, on the Window menu, click Freeze Panes.	
Change data	Select the cell containing the data you want to change. Type the new data, and then press ENTER or select another cell.	
Delete data	Select the cell (or range of cells) containing the data you want to delete, and then press DELETE.	

To	Do this	Button
Undo an action	On the Standard toolbar, click the Undo button. To undo several actions, click the Undo down arrow, and then select the actions you want to undo.	
Redo an undone action	On the Standard toolbar, click the Redo button. To redo several undone actions, click the Redo down arrow, and then select the actions you want to redo.	
Customize AutoCorrect	On the Tools menu, click AutoCorrect. Type the misspelled word or the acronym in the Replace box, type the correct spelling or long phrase in the With box, and then click OK.	
Move cells	Drag a cell or range of cells by its border.	
Copy cells	Hold down CTRL while you drag a cell or range of cells by its border.	
Move a worksheet	Drag the sheet tab.	
Copy a worksheet	Hold down CTRL while you drag the sheet tab.	
Write a formula	Type =, type the rest of the formula, and then press ENTER.	
Edit a formula	Double-click the cell containing the formula. Select the part of the formula you want to change, type your changes, and then press ENTER.	

For online information about	Use the Office Assistant to search for
Opening files	**Opening files,** then click Troubleshoot Finding And Opening Files
Saving files	**Saving files,** then click Troubleshoot Saving And Closing Files
About workbooks and worksheets	**Workbooks and worksheets,** then click About Workbooks And Worksheets
Selecting cells	**Selecting cells,** then click Select Cells On A Worskheet
Moving or copying cells	**Move or copy cells,** then click Move Or Copy Cell Data
Editing cell data	**Editing data,** click See More, then click Troubleshoot Editing Data
Entering formulas	**Entering formulas,** then click Enter A Forumla To Calculate A Value
Data forms	**Data forms,** then click Enter Data In A Microsoft Excel List By Using A Form

Setting Up a Worksheet

In this lesson you will learn how to:

**Estimated time
30 min.**

- Add a keyword to a file to quickly find it later.
- Name a worksheet.
- Delete worksheets.
- Set column widths.
- Add comments to a worksheet to document it.
- Control data entry with Data Validation.
- Print a worksheet.

In the next few lessons, you'll learn how to perform many basic Microsoft Excel tasks while creating a template. Templates are great time-savers. When you open a copy of a template, such as the invoice template you are about to create, all the labels, formulas, and formatting are in place and ready for you to build upon. You simply enter your new data and change any formatting that you want, and you're finished.

To find the templates supplied with Microsoft Excel, on the File menu, click New, and then click the Spreadsheet Solutions tab.

To create a template, you can use any workbook that contains formatting and data that you use repeatedly, such as a time sheet, a weekly task list, an inventory form, an order form, or a tax-estimation worksheet, and then simply save your workbook as a template, as you'll do later in Lesson 4.

In this lesson, you'll create a new workbook and build the structure of the Island Tea & Coffee Company invoice. You'll add and position text entries, add instructions for users, set data validation rules so that only the appropriate data can be entered in specific cells, and then you'll preview and print a copy of the new (unfinished) invoice. This invoice, which you'll continue to build in Lessons 3 and 4, will be the basis for the template that you'll create in Lesson 4.

 NOTE Although you are starting to build your template in this lesson, you won't save your workbook as a template until the end of Lesson 4, when the template has been completed with formulas and formatting. Until then, the file you work on will be a workbook file like any other.

Setting Up a New Workbook

The first task in setting up a workbook is to open a new workbook and save it with a name that makes sense to you and that will remind you of its contents. Next, you can add a keyword to the file properties (file properties include such things as the title, author, subject, date saved, and so on) so that, in the future, you can find the file quickly by searching for the keyword.

The invoice template that you will be creating will only require one worksheet. In the following exercises, you will open and save a new workbook, name the worksheet that will become the invoice, and then delete all the remaining worksheets in the workbook.

Open a new workbook

Microsoft Excel opens with a new, unsaved workbook ready for you to start using. If you have already been working in Microsoft Excel, however, you might need to open a new workbook to use in this lesson.

If you need to open a new workbook, follow this exercise. If you have just started Microsoft Excel and a new, blank workbook is already open, skip to the next exercise, "Save a new workbook."

New

 On the Standard toolbar, click the New button.

A new workbook appears. It will display an unsaved workbook name, such as Book1 or Book2, in the title bar.

Save a new workbook

You are ready to start working on your invoice template. The first step is to save your workbook under a name that describes its contents. In this exercise, you name the new workbook "ITC Invoice" and save it in the Part3 Excel Practice folder.

Save

1   On the Standard toolbar, click the Save button.

The Save As dialog box appears.

2   In the Save As dialog box, click the Look In Favorites button.

The Favorites folder appears in the Save In box. The Part3 Excel Practice folder appears in the list of folders and files.

3   Double-click the Part3 Excel Practice folder.

Part3 Excel Practice appears in the Save In box, and the names of the practice files appear in the file list.

4   In the File Name box, drag over the default book name to select it, and then type **ITC Invoice**

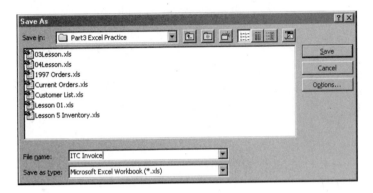

5   Click Save.

The file is saved with the name ITC Invoice in the Part3 Excel Practice folder. The new file name, ITC Invoice, appears in the title bar.

Add a keyword to easily find the file later

The Island Tea & Coffee Company creates many files in the course of conducting business, and it can be tedious to find the specific file or files you need among hundreds of filenames in a list. Microsoft Excel speeds up the process by letting you search for specific files based on *file properties*.

You can add as many file properties as you want.

There are many file properties you can base your search on, including title, author, date last saved, or subject. Some properties, such as date last saved and author, are automatically recorded as file properties, but others, like subject and keyword, must be specifically entered before you can use them in a file search. For example, if you create monthly budget workbooks, you can add the keyword "budget" to each of those files. Later, you can search for the keyword "budget," and Microsoft Excel will find all the files that have that keyword as a file property.

In this exercise, you add the keyword "invoice" to your invoice worksheet. When you create a template from this worksheet, all copies of the template will contain this keyword.

1   On the File menu, click Properties.

The Properties dialog box appears.

2   On the Summary tab, click in the Keywords box, type **invoice**, and then click OK.

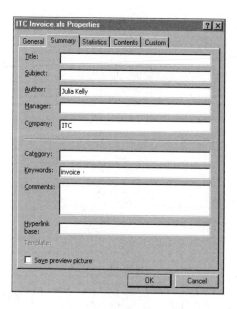

Save

3   On the Standard toolbar, click the Save button.

The new keyword is saved with the file.

Name a worksheet

If a workbook contains several sheets, the sheet names (on the sheet tabs) are important for identification purposes. Even if, as in this case, there will only be one sheet in the workbook, the sheet name is important because it might be used in formulas and it provides the default header for the printed page.

You can easily give your worksheets names that make more sense than "Sheet1." In this exercise, you name the invoice worksheet "Invoice."

1   Double-click the Sheet1 tab.

The sheet name is highlighted.

268

2 Type **Invoice**, and then press ENTER.

The sheet is renamed "Invoice."

Delete unnecessary sheets to streamline your workbook

By default, new workbooks contain three worksheets. If you don't need the extra sheets, you can streamline your workbook by deleting them—you can always add worksheets later if you need them. In this exercise, you delete the two extra worksheets you won't be needing.

1 Click the Sheet2 tab, hold down SHIFT, and then click the Sheet3 tab.

Sheet2 and Sheet3 are selected.

2 Use the right mouse button to click one of the selected tabs.

A shortcut menu appears.

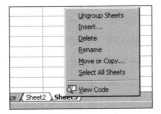

3 Click Delete.

A message box appears, prompting you to confirm the deletion of the worksheets.

4 Click OK.

The extra sheets are deleted.

 TIP If you need to insert a worksheet, use the right mouse button to click a sheet tab, click Insert on the shortcut menu, and then double-click the Worksheet icon on the General tab.

Building a Template

Your invoice template will be a standard form that the Island Tea & Coffee Company sales staff can fill out, print, and then mail or fax to customers along with their orders.

You will create the invoice template in stages. First, you'll build the structure of the invoice by entering labels on the worksheet and arranging them to create a useful layout on the invoice printed page. Then, you'll add formulas to the template so that calculations are automatic, and finally, you'll apply formatting to the template for a professional appearance.

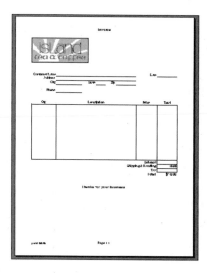

Entering Data to Build the Invoice

In the following exercises, you'll enter text labels that will identify the cells where the sales staff will enter data.

Enter labels for the customer information cells

In this exercise, you enter labels for the customer information cells.

1   In cell A1, type **Customer Name**, and then press ENTER.
2   In cell I1, type **Date**, and then press ENTER.
3   In cell A2, type **Address**, and then press ENTER.
4   In cell A3, type **City**, and then press ENTER.
5   In cell D3, type **State**, and then press ENTER.
6   In cell G3, type **Zip**, and then press ENTER.
7   In cell A5, type **Phone**, and then press ENTER.

Enter labels for the order information area

In this exercise, you enter labels for the order information area.

1   In cell A8, type **Qty**, and then press ENTER.

2   In cell B8, type **Description**, and then press ENTER.

3   In cell I8, type **Price**, and then press ENTER.

4   In cell J8, type **Total**, and then press ENTER.

Your worksheet should look similar to the following illustration.

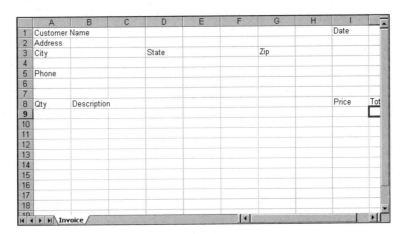

Enter labels for the subtotal and total area

In this exercise, you enter labels for the subtotal/total area.

1   In cell I23, type **Subtotal**, and then press ENTER.

2   In cell I24, type **Shipping & Handling**, and then press ENTER.

3   In cell I25, type **Tax**, and then press ENTER.

4   In cell I26, type **Total**, and then press ENTER.

Enter a farewell note at the bottom of the invoice

In this exercise, you enter a cheerful closing sentence.

➤   In cell A29, type **Thanks for your business!**, and then press ENTER.

Your worksheet should look similar to the following illustration.

Arranging the Labels

In the following exercises, you will align the labels and set column widths so that the invoice layout makes the best use of the printed page space.

Align text entries for effective use of available space

By default, Microsoft Excel aligns text entries on the left side of the cell. However, you can modify the alignment. In this exercise, you change label alignment to create a better page layout.

Align Right

1 Select cells A1 through A5, and then click the Align Right button on the Formatting toolbar.

The entries in cells A1 through A5 are aligned to the right.

	A	B	C	D
1	mer Name			
2	Address			
3	City			State
4				
5	Phone			
6				

2 Select cells I23 through I26, and then click the Align Right button on the Formatting toolbar.

The entries in cells I23 through I26 are aligned to the right.

3 Select cell D3, hold down CTRL and select cells G3 and I1, and then click the Align Right button on the Formatting toolbar.

The entries in cells D3, G3, and I1 are aligned to the right.

	A	B	C	D	E	F	G	H	I	
1	mer Name								Date	
2	Address									
3	City			State			Zip			
4										
5	Phone									
6										

Center

4 Select cell A8, hold down CTRL and select cells I8 and J8, and then click the Center button on the Formatting toolbar.

The entries in cells A8, I8, and J8 are centered.

Merge And Center

5 Select cells B8 through H8, and then click the Merge And Center button on the Formatting toolbar.

The entry in cell B8 is centered across all the selected cells.

	A						
6							
7							
8	Qty		Description			Price	
9							
10							

TIP To indent text from the left without aligning it on the right of the cell, use the right mouse button to select the cell, and then click Format Cells. On the Alignment tab, under Horizontal, select Left (Indent). Under Indent, select a number of character widths to indent by, and then click OK.

Set column widths to space entries

In this exercise, you set column widths to make the best use of space on the invoice page.

As you drag, a tip appears indicating the column width.

1 Drag the right border of the column A header until the entry in cell A1 fits within the cell.

B8	Width: 14.57	Desc
	A	B
1	mer Name	
2	Address	

You can set multiple columns to the same width by selecting multiple columns before setting the column width. (Use CTRL to select non-adjacent columns.)

2 Drag the right column border to manually change the column width based on the following table.

Column	Width
B	16
C	2
D	5
E	5
F	2
G	3
H	12

3 Use the right mouse button to click column I.

Column I is selected, and a shortcut menu appears.

Column width is the number of characters (in the default font) that fit in a cell in the column.

4 Click Column Width.

The Column Width dialog box appears.

5 Type 12, and then click OK.

Column I width is set to a width of 12.

6 Repeat steps 3 through 5 to change the width for column J.

Your worksheet should look similar to the following illustration.

	A	B	C	D	E	F	G	H	I	J
1	Customer Name								Date	
2	Address									
3	City			State			Zip			
4										
5	Phone									
6										
7										
8	Qty			Description					Price	Tota
9										
10										
11										

Save

7   On the Standard toolbar, click Save.

   NOTE   If you want to delete a column or a row, use the right mouse button to click the column header, and then, on the shortcut menu, click Delete. If you want to insert a column or a row, use the right mouse button to click the column to the right of which you want to insert the new column or the row under which you want to insert the new row, and then, on the shortcut menu, click Insert.

Documenting the Template for Other Users

Your invoice will be used by several sales people at Island Tea & Coffee Company. You can ensure that it is used correctly by adding helpful instructions and data validation to the worksheet. Data validation can prevent the entry of inaccurate data (for example, entering text in a cell that should contain a number value), or allow the entry of any type of data but display an error message if an inappropriate data type is entered. This allows you to maintain control over the usefulness of the data.

Add an instruction in a comment

A simple way to insert the current date in a cell is to press CTRL+; and then press ENTER. You can help your co-workers by sharing this tip with them in a comment. In this exercise, you add a comment to the date cell.

1   Select cell J1.

2   On the Insert menu, click Comment.

A comment box, surrounded by a hatched border and containing your user name, appears on the worksheet.

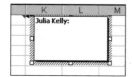

3   Type the instruction **Enter CTRL+; to insert the current date**, and then click outside the comment box.

The comment is entered in the cell. You can read the new comment by holding the mouse pointer over the cell.

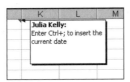

Control data entry with data validation

Sometimes it's critical that the correct type of data is entered in a cell. For example, at Island Tea & Coffee Company, products are sold by the pound, with a 10-pound minimum order per item. You can ensure that quantities in an invoice meet these requirements by adding data validation to the cells in the Qty column. In this exercise, you add data validation to the Qty cells.

1   Select cells A9 through A22.

2   On the Data menu, click Validation.

The Data Validation dialog box appears.

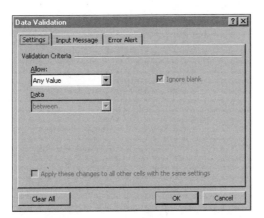

3   Click the Allow down arrow, and then click Whole Number.

4   Click the Data down arrow, and then select Greater Than Or Equal To.

5   In the Minimum box, type **10**

6   Click the Error Alert tab, and then verify that the Style box reads Stop.

7   In the Title box, type **Invalid Entry**, and then, in the Error Message box, type **You must enter a whole number greater than or equal to 10.**

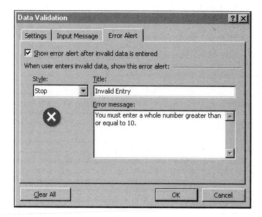

8   Click OK.

9   Select cell A16, type **9**, and then press ENTER.

An error message appears containing the text you entered in the Data Validation dialog box.

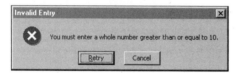

10   Click Retry, type **10**, and then press ENTER.

11   Select cell A16, and then press DELETE to delete the entry.

12   Save your work.

Printing a Copy Quickly

In the following exercises, you will preview your worksheet and print a single copy of it.

Preview the worksheet to see it before you print it

No matter how quickly you need to print a document, it is always a good idea to preview it before you print. Previewing saves time and paper by allowing you to find and fix small errors before sending the worksheet to the printer. It also gives you a clear view of the layout of the printed page.

IMPORTANT   You must have a printer set up and configured to work with Windows 95 or Windows NT before you can use Print Preview.

Print Preview

To print worksheet gridlines, click Page Setup on the File menu, and then select the Gridlines check box on the Sheet tab.

1 On the Standard toolbar, click the Print Preview button.

The Preview window appears, letting you see what the worksheet will look like when you print it. By default, worksheet gridlines are not printed.

2 Move the mouse pointer over the preview page so that the pointer takes the shape of a magnifying glass, and then click.

A close-up of the area you clicked appears.

3 Click the page again.

The full-page preview appears again.

4 Click Close.

Your worksheet reappears.

Print a quick copy

You can use the Print button to quickly print a single copy of the active worksheet, using the default print settings.

Print

➤ On the Standard toolbar, click the Print button.

Your worksheet is sent to the printer.

 NOTE If you'd like to build up on the skills you learned in this lesson, you can do the One Step Further. Otherwise, skip to "Finish the Lesson."

One Step Further: Adding a Graphic to a Worksheet

Considering that the invoice will be sent to customers, it needs to look professional and attractive. One way to improve its appearance is to add the company logo to the invoice.

In this exercise, you first insert the logo picture, and then resize the row in which it was pasted to accommodate the picture.

1 Use the right mouse button to click the row 1 header.

Row 1 is selected and a shortcut menu appears.

2 On the shortcut menu, click Insert.

A new row is inserted at the top of the worksheet, above the selected row.

3 Select cell A1.

4 On the Insert menu, point to Picture, and then click From File.

The Insert Picture dialog box appears.

277

5　In the Look In box, locate the Part3 Excel Practice folder, and then double-click the Logo file.

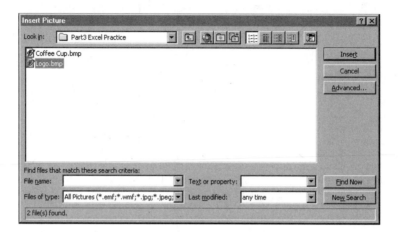

The Island Tea & Coffee Company logo is pasted into the worksheet, with the upper-left corner of the picture in the upper-left corner of the worksheet. The "handles" on the sides and corners of the picture indicate that the picture is selected, and that you can move or resize it.

6　Use the right mouse button to click the graphic, and then, on the short-cut menu, click Format Picture.

7　Click the Properties tab, select the Don't Move Or Size With Cells option button, and then click OK.

8　Move the pointer between the headers for rows 1 and 2 until the pointer becomes a two-headed arrow, and then drag the header border downward until it is taller than the picture (about 110).

Your worksheet should look similar to the following illustration.

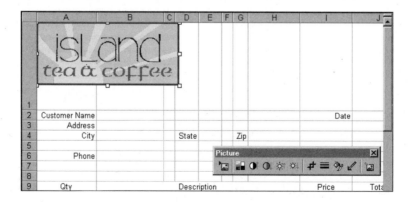

9　Save your work.

Finish the lesson

1   To continue to the next lesson, on the File menu, click Close.

2   If you are finished using Microsoft Excel for now, on the File menu, click Exit.

Lesson Summary

To	Do this	Button
Add a file property	On the File menu, click Properties. On the Summary tab, enter the properties you want, and then click OK.	
Name a worksheet	Double-click the sheet tab, type the new name, and then press ENTER.	
Delete a worksheet	Use the right mouse button to click the appropriate sheet tab, and then, on the shortcut menu, click Delete. Click OK in the message box to confirm the deletion.	
Align cell entries on the right	Select the cells, and then, on the Formatting toolbar, click the Right Align button.	
Center cell entries	Select the cells, and then, on the Formatting toolbar, click the Center button.	
Center a label across columns	Enter the label in the leftmost cell of the selection you want to center across. Select all the cells you want to center across, and then, on the Formatting toolbar, click the Merge And Center button.	
Set column width	Use the right mouse button to click the column header, and then click Column Width. Type a width, and then click OK.	
Add a comment to a cell	On the Insert menu, click Comment. Type your comment text, and then click outside the comment box.	

279

To	Do this	Button
Set data validation	Select the cells to be validated. On the Data menu, click Validation. Select the validation criteria, and then click OK.	
Preview a worksheet	On the Standard toolbar, click the Print Preview button.	
Print a worksheet	On the Standard toolbar, click the Print button.	

For online information about	Use Office Assistant to search for
File properties	**File properties,** then click Use File Properties To Locate Files
Adding comments	**Comments,** then click Add A Comment To A Cell
Validating data	**Data validation,** then click About Defining The Valid Entries For A Cell
Printing	**Printing,** then click Troubleshoot Printing

Writing Formulas

Estimated time
30 min.

In this lesson you will learn how to:

- Find files using a keyword.
- Write formulas to calculate data.
- Name cells.
- Use names and labels in formulas.

As you work through Lessons 2, 3, and 4, you are learning basic and important Microsoft Excel tasks while creating a template. In this lesson, you will learn to write formulas in Microsoft Excel by adding formulas to a partially built invoice that is going to become a template. The advantage of creating and using a template is that the time-consuming work of setting up the worksheet is done only once. To use a template, you open a copy of it, and then enter your current data. There is no need to write formulas to calculate totals because the formulas are already in place in the template worksheet.

If you completed Lesson 2 and the One Step Further exercise, you can continue working with the file you previously saved.

In the following exercises, you will add formulas to the invoice to calculate the item totals, subtotal, sales tax, and grand total automatically. You will also learn how to name cells, and then write formulas using names and labels.

To begin this lesson, you locate and open the 03Lesson.xls file in the Part3 Excel Practice folder.

Finding Files Using File Properties

As time goes by and the number of Island Tea & Coffee Company invoice files increases, it becomes easier to have Microsoft Excel find the invoice files by searching for file properties that they have in common, rather than looking through folders to find them.

Whether you plan on using your own file or use the 03Lesson.xls file, you need to first locate the file.

Search for a file using a keyword

In this exercise, you search for the invoice keyword to find and open the ITC Invoice file.

Open

1   On the Standard toolbar, click the Open button.

2   Click the Look In down arrow, and then select the letter icon for your hard disk (usually C:).

    Microsoft Excel will search the entire hard disk.

3   Click Advanced.

    The Advanced Find dialog box appears.

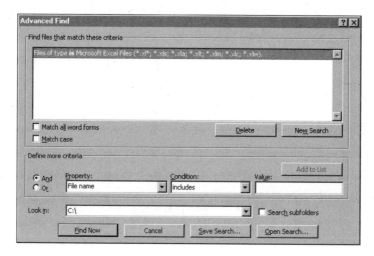

4   In the lower part of the Advanced Find dialog box, click the Property down arrow, and then scroll down and select Keywords.

5   Make sure that Includes Words appears in the Condition box, and then type **invoice** in the Value box.

6   Click Add To List.

    The keyword is added to the Find Files That Match These Criteria list at the top of the dialog box.

7   Select the Search Subfolders check box.

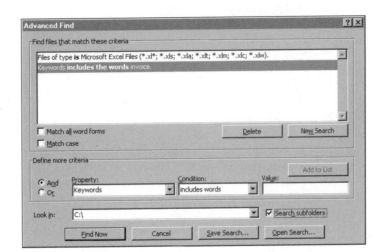

8   Click Find Now.

The results of the search appear in the Open dialog box.

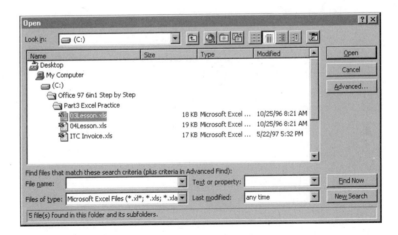

9   Double-click the 03Lesson file. (If you did Lesson 2, you can double-click the ITC Invoice file.)

The file opens.

Save the file with a new name

If you did not do Lesson 2, you need to save the 03Lesson file as ITC Invoice. If you opened the ITC Invoice file in the last exercise, you can skip this exercise.

1 On the File menu, click Save As.

The Save As dialog box opens. Be sure that the Part3 Excel Practice folder appears in the Save In box.

2 In the File Name box, drag over the name to select it, and then type **ITC Invoice**

3 Click Save, or press ENTER.

Adding Calculation Formulas

In the following exercises, you will write formulas to automate the calculations in your invoice. You will first create formulas that compute the total amount for each item in the order, and then add formulas that calculate the order sub-total, sales tax, and grand total.

Add mock data to test the formulas as you write them

When you write a formula, you can tell if it is written correctly by checking the accuracy of the result it displays. In this exercise, you enter a few items of mock data so that you can instantly verify that your formulas were written correctly by checking the results that are immediately displayed.

1 Select cell A10.

2 Type **20**, press TAB, type **Keemun Tea**, and then press ENTER.

When you press ENTER, AutoReturn returns the active cell to the beginning of the next row in your list.

3 Repeat step 2 to enter orders of 30 pounds of Darjeeling Tea and 100 pounds of Kona Coffee.

4 Select cell I10.

5 Type **4.85**, and then press ENTER.

6 Repeat step 5 to enter the price per pound of the Darjeeling Tea (10.15) and the Kona Coffee (5.25).

Your screen should look similar to the following illustration.

	A	B	C	D	E	F	G	H	I	J
2	Customer Name								Date	
3	Address									
4	City			State			Zip			
5										
6	Phone									
7										
8										
9	Qty				Description				Price	Tota
10	20	Keemun tea							4.85	
11	30	Darjeeling tea							10.15	
12	100	Kona coffee							5.25	
13										
14										

Write a formula to compute an item total

In this exercise, you write a formula that calculates an item total by multiply-ing the quantity ordered by the price.

1 Select cell J10.

2 Type =, click cell A10, type *, click cell I10, and then press ENTER.

		J10	▼		=	=A10*I10						
	B		C	D	E	F	G	H		I	J	K
8												
9						Description				Price	Total	
10	Keemun tea									4.85	97	
11	Darjeeling tea									10.15		
12	Kona coffee									5.25		

Copy the formula to other cells using AutoFill

All of the cells in the Total column need to use the formula you just wrote. Copying cells one by one can be tedious, but AutoFill provides an easy and quick alternative. It allows you to copy the formula into a range of adjacent cells and automatically adjust the cell references to new cells, so the results will be accurate in all the new formulas. In this exercise, you use AutoFill to quickly copy the formula you created in the previous exercise into additional cells.

1 Select cell J10.

2 Move the mouse pointer over the small black box, also called *fill handle*, located in the lower right corner of the active cell, until the pointer be-comes a black cross shape.

In Lesson 4, "Formatting Your Worksheet for a Profes-sional Look," you will apply formatting to hide the zeroes.

3 Drag the fill handle down to cell J23, and then release the mouse button.

The formula is copied into cells J11 through J23. Cells J13 through J23 display zeroes because Microsoft Excel will interpret the blank cells from A13 to A23 and I13 to I23 as having a value of zero.

285

Add a SUM formula to calculate the order total

In this exercise, you write a formula that adds up the total price of items ordered. You use AutoSum to write the formula quickly.

1 Select cell J24.

2 On the Standard toolbar, click the AutoSum button.

AutoSum inserts a formula that uses the SUM function, displays a moving border around the range Microsoft Excel anticipates you want to add up, and inserts the range reference in your formula. In this case, the range AutoSum has selected (J10 through J23) is correct.

AutoSum

If the AutoSum range isn't correct, simply drag the correct range before pressing ENTER.

Price	Total
4.85	97
10.15	304.5
5.25	525
	0
	0
	0
	0
	0
	0
	0
	0
	0
	0
	0
Subtotal	=SUM(J10:J23)
& Handling	
Tax	

3 Press ENTER.

The result of the SUM formula, 926.5, appears in the subtotal cell.

Calculate sales tax

The Island Tea & Coffee Company must charge 7% tax on all orders, and you want the invoice to calculate the tax automatically. In this exercise, you write a formula that calculates tax based on the subtotal cell.

1 Select cell J26.

In Lesson 4, "Formatting Your Worksheet for a Professional Look," you'll apply formatting to display the result as dollars and cents, with two decimal places.

2 Type =, click cell J24, type *.07, and then press ENTER.

The tax formula is entered.

=J24*0.07						
D	E	F	G	H	I	J
						0
					Subtotal	926.5
				Shipping & Handling		
				Tax		64.855
				Total		

3 Save your work.

Using Cell Names and Labels to Make Formulas Easier to Understand

All the formulas you've written so far are correct and functional, but when you read them, it's not immediately clear which values are being calculated. You can identify specific cells and ranges more clearly by giving them *names*, and then use those names instead of cell references when you write formulas. For example, the formula: =Price*Qty is instantly understandable, whereas =A16*I16 might not be so clear.

In the following exercises, you will name some of the cells in the invoice, and then write formulas using the new names.

Name cells to use in formulas

In this exercise, you name the Subtotal, Shipping & Handling, and Tax cells.

You can also use row and column labels in your formulas, without having to name the cells first.

1 Select the range I24 through J26.

This range contains the Subtotal, Shipping & Handling, and Tax labels and data cells. Be sure to select both the cells that include labels and the cells that include data.

2 On the Insert menu, point to Name, and then click Create.

The Create Names dialog box appears. The Left Column check box is selected because Microsoft Excel recognizes labels that are located in the left column of the selected range.

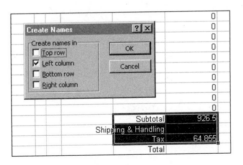

3 Click OK.

Cells J24 through J26 are named with the labels in cells I24 through I26.

4 On the formula bar, click the Name Box down arrow.

The names you created are listed.

5 Click Subtotal.

The cell named Subtotal is selected.

Write a formula using cell names

In this exercise, you write a formula in the Total cell that sums the named cells.

1 Select cell J27, and type =

The Functions list replaces the Name Box list.

2 On the Functions list, click SUM.

The Formula palette appears to help you write the SUM formula. The Number1 box is highlighted.

3 Click cell J24, named Subtotal.

The cell name is inserted in the Number1 box.

4 Press TAB, click cell J25 (named Shipping___Handling), press TAB, and then click cell J26 (named Tax).

The cell names are inserted in the Formula palette.

Spaces and ampersands (&) are not allowed in cell names, so Microsoft Excel changes Shipping & Handling to Shipping ___Handling when it creates the cell name.

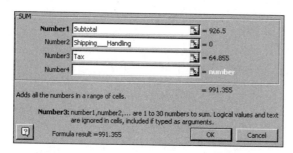

5 Click OK.

The SUM formula is entered in the Total cell. It is now easy to discern which cells are being calculated because you can read their names in the formula.

Use labels in formulas

When cells have identifying labels nearby, you can often write clear formulas using those labels instead of cell references and instead of naming the cells. Using labels is quicker than using names because you don't have to perform the extra steps required to name cells. But there are instances in which using names is more efficient than using labels. For example, if you need to include the label of a range of cells in a formula, you must drag the whole range, but if the range is named you can simply insert its name. Also, you can name a non-contiguous range of cells, but you cannot label it; or, you might set up your worksheet so that the labels are too far away from the data to be recognizable to Microsoft Excel as labels.

In the ITC Invoice worksheet, Microsoft Excel automatically recognizes the labels for the Qty and Price columns. When you type a label into your formula, Microsoft Excel knows which cell to calculate. In this exercise, you rewrite your total price formula using labels.

1 In cell J10, type **=Qty*Price**, and press ENTER.

	J10		=	=Qty*Price						
	B	C	D	E	F	G	H	I	J	K
8										
9				Description				Price	Total	
10	Keemun tea							4.85	97	
11	Darjeeling tea							10.15	304.5	
12	Kona coffee							5.25	525	

Your new formula with labels is clearer than the old formula with cell references. In addition, if you change the label in the worksheet (for example, if you change Qty to Quantity in cell A10), the formula will change automatically to use the new label.

 TROUBLESHOOTING If you get a very large number (in the order of billions) in cell J10 after you enter the forumla, you may have the Analysis ToolPak add-in enabled. PRICE is a function used by the Microsoft Excel Analysis ToolPak add-in. If you have this add-in enabled, rather than recognizing the label for the Price column, Excel will apply the Analysis ToolPak PRICE function to the number in the Qty column, causing an unexpected result to appear in cell J10. To correct this, you can add single quotes around Price, as shown here:

In cell J10, type **=Qty*'Price'**, and press ENTER.

289

2   Use AutoFill to copy the new formula in cells J11 through J23.

3   Save your work.

NOTE   If you'd like to build up on the skills you learned in this lesson, you can do the One Step Further. Otherwise, skip to "Finish the Lesson."

One Step Further: Calculating a Specific Cost

You want to automate the calculation of the shipping charge for an order so that you do not have to look up the charge manually each time you fill out an invoice. In this section, you write a formula that sums the total weight of the order (in the Qty column), and then applies a lower shipping charge for orders under 50 pounds and a higher shipping charge for orders of 50 pounds or more.

In order to write your formula properly, you will have to use an IF function, a *logical* function that evaluates whether a mathematical statement is true or false. If the mathematical statement is true, the IF formula returns one value; if the statement is false, the IF formula returns another value.

An example of an IF formula is =IF(A3<5,100,350). This equation means that if A3 is less than 5, the value returned will be 100; if A3 is 5 or higher than 5, the value returned will be 350.

A function is a calculation tool that a formula can use; a formula is a mathematical equation that begins with an equal sign and returns a calculated value.

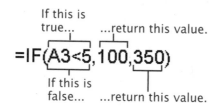

In the following exercises, you will write an IF formula that determines a shipping charge ($10 or $20) based on the order weight (less than 50 pounds, or 50 pounds and up). The IF formula will determine the order weight by using a *nested* SUM function. A nested function is a function within another function; in this case, the SUM function will be contained within the IF function. Microsoft Excel will calculate the SUM function first, and then the IF function will be calculated using the result of the SUM function.

Name the Qty range

In this exercise, you name the range of cells in the Qty column because a name is more efficient than a label when you're summing a range of cells.

1   Select the range A10 through A23.

2 On the formula bar, click in the Name Box.

The cell reference is highlighted.

3 Type **Pounds**, and then press ENTER.

The new name appears in the Name Box. Be sure you press ENTER before you click another cell.

Calculate the shipping cost using a named cell

In this exercise, you write the formula that determines the shipping charge.

1 On the formula bar, click the Name Box down arrow, and then click Shipping___Handling.

The cell named Shipping___Handling becomes the active cell.

2 Type =, and then click the Name Box down arrow, which is now called the Functions down arrow since you've begun to write a formula.

3 In the Functions list, click IF.

The Formula palette opens up to help you write the IF formula. The insertion point is in the Logical_Test box, which is the first of the three *arguments*, or components, required by the IF function.

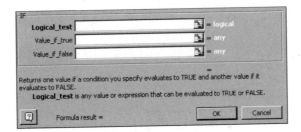

4 Type **sum(Pounds)<50**, and then press TAB.

The sum(Pounds)<50 statement is entered in the Formula palette as well as in the formula, and the insertion point moves to the Value_If_True box. The nested function, SUM(Pounds), has been inserted into the IF formula.

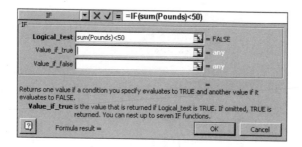

5 In the Value_If_True box, type **10**, and then press TAB.

6 In the Value_If_False box, type **20**, and then click OK.

The IF formula that calculates a shipping & handling charge based on the weight of the order is entered in the Shipping___Handling cell.

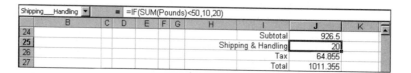

7 Save your work.

 TROUBLESHOOTING When you type a function name, such as SUM, be sure to type it in lowercase. This is a good way to check whether you've typed the function name correctly; if you have spelled it correctly, it will be converted to uppercase when you enter the formula. If you get an error message and the function name is still lowercase, check the spelling.

Finish the lesson

1 To continue to the next lesson, on the File menu, click Close.

2 If you are finished using Microsoft Excel for now, on the File menu, click Exit.

Lesson Summary

To	Do this	Button
Search for a file based on a keyword	Click the Open button, and then select your hard disk or a folder to search. Click the Advanced button, select Keywords in the Property box, and then type the keyword in the Value box. Click Add To List, and then select the Search Sub-folders check box. Click Find Now.	
Copy cells using AutoFill	Drag the fill handle down to the last cell you want to include, and then release the mouse button.	
Sum a range using AutoSum	Click the cell where you want to insert the SUM formula, and then click the AutoSum button. Define the range you want to sum by dragging, and then press ENTER.	Σ
Create cell names using labels in adjacent cells	Select a range that includes the cells to be named and the cells containing the name labels. On the Insert menu, point to Name, and then click Create. Be sure the correct label location is checked, and then click OK.	
Use names in formulas	Click the named cell to insert in the formula.	
Use labels in formulas	Type the data label in the formula.	
Write a formula using the Formula palette	Type =, and then select a function name from the Functions list. Click cells to paste them into the Formula palette boxes, and then click OK when you are finished.	

For online information about	Use the Office Assistant to search for
Finding files	**Finding files,** then click Find Files
AutoFill	**Autofill,** then click Types Of Series That Microsoft Excel Can Fill In For You
Naming cells	**Naming cells,** then click Name Cells In A Workbook
Cell labels (in formulas)	**Labels in formulas,** then click About Labels And Names In Formulas
Formulas	**Formulas,** click See More, and then click How Formulas Calculate Values

Formatting Your Worksheet for a Professional Look

Estimated time
45 min.

In this lesson you will learn how to:

- Format cells.
- Create, apply, and change styles.
- Format numbers.
- Create a custom number format.
- Create custom headers and footers.
- Save a workbook as a template.

Now that you have automated the calculations in your invoice using formulas, you are ready to start formatting the invoice page to make it look professional. Formatting also allows you to make your worksheet easier to read and group data visually, for example. You can format fonts, cell borders, and cell shading, as well as the way numbers are displayed. You can create styles, which are packages of formatting attributes, to save you time in the future when you want to change the formatting of a group of cells. You can also create headers and footers that print on every page, and include codes that automatically print the current date or number of pages in the printed document. After you finish formatting your invoice worksheet, you'll save it as a template so that Island Tea & Coffee Company employees can easily open a copy of the invoice and fill it out.

Open a file and save it with a new name

As you begin this lesson, one of your co-workers has partially formatted your invoice worksheet for you. But he has been called away on other business, and has asked you to complete the invoice formatting.

Open

1   On the Standard toolbar, click the Open button.

2   In the Open dialog box, click the Look In Favorites button.

3   In the file list, double-click the Part3 Excel Practice folder, and then double-click the 04Lesson file.

The Open dialog box closes, and the 04Lesson file appears in the document window.

4   On the File menu, click Save As.

The Save As dialog box opens. Be sure that the Part3 Excel Practice folder appears in the Save In box.

5   In the File Name box, type **ITC Invoice**

6   Click the Save button or press ENTER.

Save

If a dialog box appears asking you confirm that you want to replace the existing file, click Yes.

Formatting Cells

In the following exercises, you will practice formatting with fonts and learn how to use styles to save time when changing cell formatting. You will also practice formatting borders and cell shading, as well as setting page margins so that the invoice fits in the center of a single page.

Format fonts

A co-worker at Island Tea & Coffee Company has formatted part of the invoice worksheet for you, but didn't complete the job. You need to format the remaining labels to make the worksheet look professional enough to be sent out to customers. In this exercise, you change the font for one of the labels, and then apply the new formatting to other labels.

1   Select cell A9.

Font

2   On the Formatting toolbar, click the Font down arrow, and then select Times New Roman.

Font Size

3   On the Formatting toolbar, click the Font Size down arrow, and then select 12.

B

Bold

4 On the Formatting toolbar, click the Bold button.

Your screen should look similar to the following illustration.

A9	▼	=	Qty							
	A		B	C	D	E	F G	H	I	J
8										
9	**Qty**		Description						Price	Tot
10	20	Keemun tea							4.85	
11	30	Darjeeling tea							10.15	
12	100	Kona coffee							5.25	
13										

Format Painter

5 With cell A9 still selected, on the Standard toolbar, double-click the Format Painter button.

The mouse pointer takes the shape of the Format Painter button face. Until you click the Format Painter button again to turn it off, the formatting from cell A9 will be applied to every cell you click.

6 Click cell B9, then cell I9, and then cell J9.

The new formatting is applied to all the selected cells.

7 On the Standard toolbar, click the Format Painter button to turn it off.

Your screen should look similar to the following illustration.

	A		B	C	D	E	F G	H	I	J
8										
9	Qty		**Description**						**Price**	**Tot**
10	20	Keemun tea							4.85	
11	30	Darjeeling tea							10.15	
12	100	Kona coffee							5.25	
13										

Create styles by example

Applying formatting is a simple procedure, but if you have to apply the same formatting to several worksheets it can become quite tedious. Suppose you have several worksheets in a workbook that all have the same types of labels (such as titles and subtitles), and you need to change the formatting of all the labels. You can save a lot of time by applying a *style* instead of reapplying the formatting: you can simply change the style definition instead of reformatting each individual cell.

A style is a collection of formatting attributes such as font, font size, bold, italic, cell shading, or color, and is simple to create, apply, and change. When you apply a style to a cell, all of the formatting attributes contained in the style are applied to the cell. When you change a formatting attribute in a style (for example, you might change the font from Times New Roman to Tahoma), the attribute is automatically changed in all cells to which the style has been applied.

All Island Tea & Coffee Company documentation that will be seen by customers has to be approved by the Marketing manager. Considering that the Marketing manager will most likely request formatting changes, you have decided to set up the invoice formatting using styles to speed up future modifications. If you need to change the formatting later, you can simply redefine the style and the changes will be reflected in all the cells to which that style has been applied. In this exercise, you create a style based on existing cell formatting, and then apply the style to several cells.

1 Select cell A9.

You can remove an attribute from a style definition by clearing the appropriate check box in the Style dialog box.

2 On the Format menu, click Style.

The Style dialog box appears, and the Style Name box is highlighted. The dialog box lists the attributes associated with the style shown in the Style Name box.

3 In the Style Name box, type **Label**, and then click OK.

The formatting applied to cell A9 is now available as a style named Label.

4 Click cell B9, and then hold down CTRL and click cells I9 and J9.

The three remaining information labels are selected.

5 On the Format menu, click Style. Click the Style Name down arrow, select Label, and then click OK.

The Label style is applied to all four information labels.

Merge And Center

6 Select cells B9 through H9, and then click the Merge And Center button.

The Description text is centered, and the Label style continues to be applied.

Change a style definition

You have just received the formatting changes requested by the Marketing manager. In this exercise, you change the font in the labels by simply modifying the Label style definition.

1 Click cell A9.

2 On the Format menu, click Style.

The Style dialog box appears.

3 In the Style dialog box, click Modify.

The Format Cells dialog box appears.

4 Click the Font tab, select Arial in the Font list, and then 10 in the Size list.

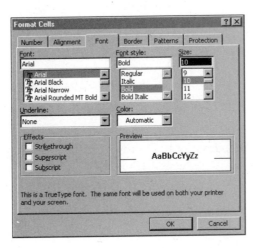

5 Click OK, and then click OK again.

All of the labels on the worksheet are reformatted. Your screen should look similar to the following illustration.

	A	B	C	D	E	F	G	H	I	J
8										
9	Qty				Description				Price	Tot
10	20	Keemun tea							4.85	
11	30	Darjeeling tea							10.15	
12	100	Kona coffee							5.25	
13										

Apply borders

Right now, your invoice is full of information that is not easily identifiable. In order to make the invoice more usable for the other employees of the Island Tea & Coffee Company and more readable for your customers, you decide to break the page into clearly defined areas. In this exercise, you apply borders to visually separate different areas of information.

299

TIP You can quickly select a range of cells by typing the range reference in the Name Box, and then pressing ENTER. For example, if you want to select the range A22 through A35, you can type **A22:A35** in the Name Box, and then press ENTER. The range will be selected.

1 Select cells A10 through A23, and then hold down CTRL and select cells B10 through H23, I10 through I23, and J10 through J23.

The ranges containing order information are selected. You can select each range individually and place a border around it, but you can also save time by selecting all of the individual ranges that you want to place borders around as if they were non-adjacent, using the CTRL key, and placing borders around each of the ranges all at once.

Borders

2 On the Formatting toolbar, click the Borders down arrow.

The Borders palette appears.

3 Click the top border of the Borders palette, and then drag it onto the worksheet.

The Borders palette "floats" on the worksheet, which means it can be placed anywhere that is convenient, rather than being docked at one edge of the document window.

4 Click the Outline border button.

An Outline border is applied to each of the selected ranges.

5 Select cells J24 through J26, and then click the outline-and-inside border button.

6 On the Borders palette, click the Close button.

Your worksheet should look similar to the following illustration.

	B	C	D	E	F	G	H	I	J	K
13									0	
14									0	
15									0	
16									0	
17									0	
18									0	
19									0	
20									0	
21									0	
22									0	
23									0	
24								Subtotal	926.5	
25								Shipping & Handling	20	
26								Tax	64.855	
27								**Total**	**1011.355**	
28										

Apply shading

In order to ensure that your colleagues at the Island Tea & Coffee Company will not be entering information in cells that contain formulas, you decide to format them differently. Considering that one of the company's internal formatting conventions is that information is not entered into shaded cells, you elect to follow this convention. In this exercise, you apply shading to the cells that contain formulas as a visual reminder to users not to enter information in those cells.

1 Select cells J10 through J27.

2 On the Formatting toolbar, click the Fill Color down arrow, and then click the Pale Blue color.

Your screen should look similar to the following illustration.

Fill Color

You can also drag the Fill Color palette onto the worksheet.

	B	C	D	E	F	G	H	I	J	K
9			Description					Price	Total	
10	Keemun tea							4.85	97	
11	Darjeeling tea							10.15	304.5	
12	Kona coffee							5.25	525	
13									0	
14									0	
15									0	
16									0	
17									0	
18									0	
19									0	
20									0	
21									0	
22									0	
23									0	
24								Subtotal	926.5	
25								Shipping & Handling	20	
26								Tax	64.855	

301

Set page margins

Before printing your invoice, you preview it to make sure that it all fits on one page. In this exercise, you change the page margins so that the entire invoice fits on a single page, center the invoice on the printed page, and preview the invoice.

1 On the File menu, click Page Setup.

The Page Setup dialog box appears.

2 Click the Margins tab.

3 Double-click in the Left box, and then type .5

4 Double-click in the Right box, and then type .5

5 In the Center On Page area, select the Horizontally check box, and then click Print Preview.

Your screen should look similar to the following illustration.

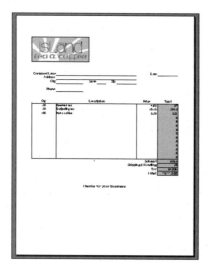

6 Click Close.

7 Save your work.

Formatting Numbers

Number formatting determines the display of number values, and such formatting takes effect only when a cell contains a number. By default, all the cells in a worksheet use the General number format, in which extra zeroes on the right of the decimal point are left out, all calculated decimal places are shown, and numbers are aligned on the right. For example, in column J, the formula results look like "general numbers" rather than dollars and cents.

You are now ready to finalize your invoice by formatting the numbers. In the following exercises, you will format the cells located in the Total column to display numbers as prices, remove the extra zeroes in the Total column, and format the Qty column to display numbers with the suffix "lbs," as in "100 lbs."

Format numbers to look like prices

In order to have the number formatting in the invoice look like product prices, you need to modify the formatting of the Total column. In this exercise, you format numbers in the Total column to have two decimal places and a thousands separator.

1 Select cells I10 through J26.

2 Use the right mouse button to click the selection, and then, on the shortcut menu, click Format Cells.

The Format Cells dialog box appears.

3 Click the Number tab.

4 In the Category list, select Number, verify that the number in the Decimal Places box is 2, and then select the Use 1000 Separator (,) check box.

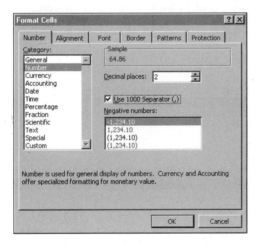

5 Click OK.

All the numbers in the Totals column are rounded to two decimal places, and extra zeroes are displayed to fill out the two decimal places on the right of the decimal point.

6 Select cell I10, and then hold down CTRL and click cells J10, J24, and J27.

7 Use the right mouse button to click any one of the selected cells, and then, on the shortcut menu, click Format Cells.

8 On the Number tab, select the category Currency, and then click OK.

Your screen should look similar to the following illustration.

303

	B	C	D	E	F	G	H	I	J	K
9	Description							Price	Total	
10	Keemun tea							$4.85	$97.00	
11	Darjeeling tea							10.15	304.50	
12	Kona coffee							5.25	525.00	
13									0.00	
14									0.00	
15									0.00	
16									0.00	
17									0.00	
18									0.00	
19									0.00	
20									0.00	
21									0.00	
22									0.00	
23									0.00	
24								Subtotal	$926.50	
25								Shipping & Handling	20.00	
26								Tax	64.86	
27								Total	$1,011.36	
28										

Invoice

Format numbers using a custom number format

You need to include the suffix "lbs" after entries in the Qty column. This is to make sure that the employees of the Island Tea & Coffee Company using the invoice know to enter quantities in pounds in this column, and to make it clear to customers that the amount of each order is measured in pounds. In this exercise, you format the numbers in the Qty column to include the "lbs" text suffix.

1 Select cells A10 through A23, use the right mouse button to click the selection, and then, on the shortcut menu, click Format Cells.

2 In the Category list of the Number tab, click Custom.

3 In the Type box, select the entry, and then type **0 "lbs"**

Be sure you type a zero, not the letter O.

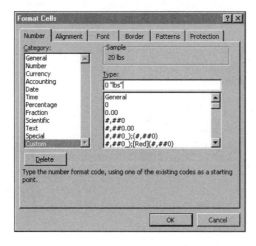

4 Click OK.

The Custom number format is applied, and saved as a Custom format that you can apply again later.

	A	B
9	Qty	
10	20 lbs	Keemun tea
11	30 lbs	Darjeeling tea
12	100 lbs	Kona coffee
13		
14		

 NOTE A custom format is similar to a style. A style encompasses many aspects of a cell's formatting, including the number format; a custom number format is like any other number format. In fact, you can create a style that includes your new custom number format.

Turn off zeroes

The formulas located in the Totals column that don't have data to calculate are displaying values of zero, and that might be confusing to future users and to customers. In this exercise, you turn off the zero values display.

1 On the Tools menu, click Options.

The Options dialog box appears.

2 Click the View tab, clear the Zero Values check box, and then click OK.

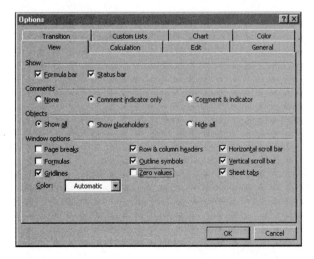

The extraneous zero values on the worksheet are hidden.

305

Creating Custom Headers and Footers

By default, Microsoft Excel creates no headers or footers, but you can easily create and customize the header and/or the footer, if you want.

Create a custom header

After looking at the ITC invoice in the Print Preview window, you decide that it needs a custom header. In this exercise, you create a custom header to match the rest of the invoice.

1 On the File menu, click Page Setup.

The Page Setup dialog box appears.

2 Click the Header/Footer tab.

3 Click Custom Header.

The Header dialog box appears.

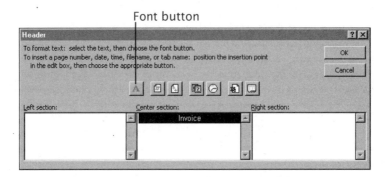

Font button

4 In the Center box, type **Invoice**, double-click the text to select it, and then click the Font button.

The Font dialog box appears

5 In the Font Style box, select Bold, and in the Size box, select 12, and then click OK.

The Font dialog box closes.

6 In the Header dialog box, click OK.

The Header dialog box closes. You can see the changes to your header in the Header/Footer tab.

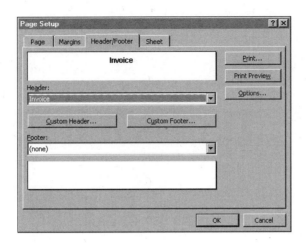

Create a custom footer

In order to track each invoice more easily, you decide to add useful information in the footer. In this exercise, you create a footer that will display the print date as well as the individual page number and number of pages on each invoice page.

1   On the Header/Footer tab, click Custom Footer.

2   In the Left Section box, type **printed**

3   Press SPACEBAR, and then click the Date button.

Date button

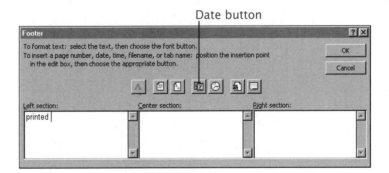

4   Select all the text in the Left Section box, and then click the Font button.

The Font dialog box appears.

5   Select 8 in the Size box, and then click OK.

The Font dialog box closes.

6 In the Center Section, type **Page**, and then press SPACEBAR.

7 Click the Page button, press SPACEBAR, type **of**, and then press SPACEBAR.

8 Click the Pages button, press SPACEBAR, and then type **Pages**

Page button

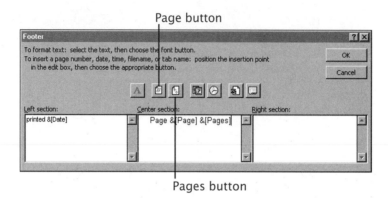

Pages button

The Page and Pages codes will automatically appear and print the individual page number and the total number of pages in the invoice, for example, "Page 1 of 2."

9 Click OK to close the Footer dialog box, and then click OK to close the Page Setup dialog box.

Saving Your Workbook as a Template to Re-Use It Easily

Now that you are finished building the ITC invoice, you are ready to save it as a template. In the following exercises, you will delete the mock data you inserted during the creation of the invoice and save the workbook as a template.

Delete the mock data

➤ Select cells A10 through I12, and then press DELETE.

The mock data is deleted and the formula cells are cleared, but the important formatting work that you've done remains. The Shipping & Handling value remains because the cell contents are based on the result of the formula you created in Lesson 3, "Writing Formulas."

Save a workbook as a template

Your invoice is now ready to be saved as a template. In this exercise, you save the workbook as a template.

1 On the File menu, click Save As.

2   In the Save As Type box, select Template.

The filename automatically changes to ITC Invoice.xlt.

3   In the Save In box, locate the Spreadsheet Solutions folder.

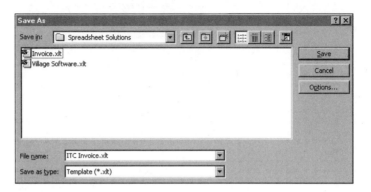

4   Click Save.

The workbook is saved as a template in the Spreadsheet Solutions folder.

5   On the File menu, click Close.

Open a copy of the template

The template is complete and available to any Island Tea & Coffee Company employee who has access to your templates folder. In this exercise, you verify that your invoice opens correctly and looks the way you want.

1   On the File menu, click New.

2   Click the Spreadsheet Solutions tab.

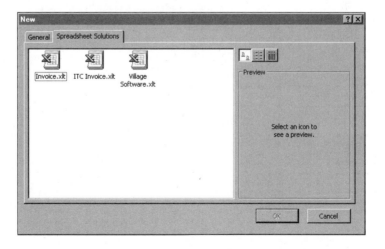

3 Double-click the ITC Invoice icon.

A copy of your invoice, temporarily named ITC Invoice1, opens and is ready to be filled out and saved with a permanent name.

4 Close the ITC Invoice File. If prompted to save, click No.

If You Have Microsoft FrontPage...

If you have Microsoft FrontPage, you can place a link to your template in a Web page on the company intranet. Then, the rest of the Island Tea & Coffee Company employees will be able to open your Web page, click the hotlink you created to the invoice template, and open copies of the template on their computers.

 NOTE If you'd like to build on the skills you learned in this lesson, you can do the One Step Further. Otherwise, skip to "Finish the Lesson."

One Step Further: Editing the Template

During the Marketing manager's final review of the invoice, she suggested that the shading added to the formula cells in column J should not appear on the customer copy. But you still want to keep the shaded cells on the ITC invoice template to help the Island Tea & Coffee Company employees fill out the invoice properly. Fortunately, Microsoft Excel allows you to prevent the shading from being printed.

Open the template

If you need to make changes to your template (for example, add more formulas or modify the formatting), you should open the template itself rather than a copy of the template. In this exercise, you open the template.

1 On the File menu, click Open, and then locate the Spreadsheet Solutions folder.

2 Double-click the ITC Invoice file.

The template opens, rather than a copy. The name in the title bar is ITC Invoice.

Select black and white printing

You don't want the shaded cells to be printed on the copies that you mail or fax to customers. In this exercise, you set the worksheet to print in black and white, with no shades of gray except in the graphic so that your customers will not see the cell shading.

1 On the File menu, click Page Setup.

The Page Setup dialog box appears.

2 Click the Sheet tab.

3 Select the Black And White check box, and then click OK.

4 On the Standard toolbar, click the Print Preview button.

Your worksheet should look similar to the following illustration.

Print Preview

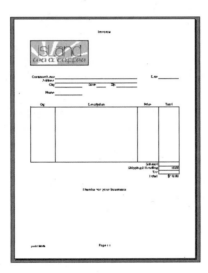

5 Click Close, and then save your work.

Finish the lesson

1 To continue to the next lesson, on the File menu, click Close.

2 If you are finished using Microsoft Excel for now, on the File menu, click Exit.

Lesson Summary

To	Do this	Button
Format font for typeface, size, or formatting (such as bold, italic or underline)	Select cells, and then click the appropriate buttons on the Formatting toolbar.	
Copy formatting	Select a cell that contains the formatting you want to apply to other cells, and then double-click the Format Painter button. Click the cells to which you want to apply the formatting.	
Create a style by example	Select a cell that contains all the formatting attributes you want to include in the style, and then, on the Format menu, click Style. Type a new style name, and then click OK.	
Apply a style	Select cells you want to apply the style to, and then, on the Format menu, click Style. Select the style you want in the Style Name box, and then click OK.	
Change a style definition	On the Format menu, click Style. Select the style to change in the Style Name box, and then click Modify. Change the style attributes as needed, and then click OK twice.	
Apply borders	Select cells to be formatted. On the Formatting toolbar, click the Borders down arrow, and then click the appropriate border button.	
Drag a palette away from the toolbar to make it float on the worksheet	Drag the palette by its top border onto the worksheet.	
Apply shading	Select cells to be formatted. On the Formatting toolbar, click the Fill Color down arrow, and then click a color.	
Set page margins	On the File menu, click Page Setup. Click the Margins tab, and then set the margins.	

To	Do this
Format numbers	Select the cells containing the numbers you want to format, and then use the right mouse button to click one of them. On the shortcut menu, click Format Cells, click the Number tab, select a Category, set the appropriate formatting options for the category, and then click OK.
Hide zero values on the worksheet	On the Tools menu, click Options. On the View tab, clear the Zero Values check box, and then click OK.
Create custom headers and footers	On the File menu, click Page Setup. Click the Header/Footer tab, and then click the Custom Header or Custom Footer button. Type and format headers and footers in the Header and Footer dialog boxes.
Save a workbook as a template	On the File menu, click Save As. In the Save As Type box, select Template, and then click Save.
Open a copy of a template	On the File menu, click New. Click the tab representing the folder where you stored your template, and then double-click the template icon.

For online information about	Use the Office Assistant to search for
Formatting worksheets	**Formatting cells,** then click Basic Worksheet Formatting
Styles	**Styles,** then click Format Cells And Lists Quickly With Styles Or Built-in Table Formats
Headers and footers	**Headers and footers,** then click Create Custom Headers And Footers
Templates	**Templates,** then click Customize The Defaults For A Workbook Or Worksheet By Using A Template

Lesson

5

Filtering to Find Specific Information

Estimated time
30 min.

In this lesson you will learn how to:

- Filter a list to find specific information.
- Find totals and averages quickly using AutoCalculate.
- Calculate sets of filtered records using the SUBTOTAL function.

As the office manager for the Island Tea & Coffee Company, one of your responsibilities is to keep the inventory updated. For that reason, your co-workers often call you when they want to know what's in stock. You can easily answer their questions by using a few simple filtering techniques on your inventory list. Filtering allows you to quickly find and bring up information matching the criteria you set.

Your list is composed of records, or rows, and fields, or columns. All of the records in a list have the same information fields (for example, each record has a Product Name field, a Source Country field, a Warehouse Location field, and so on). Each field in a list provides a specific type of information (for example, the Source Country field contains the source country information for each record).

When you filter a list, you define conditions known as *criteria* that are shared by the subset of records you want to locate. For example, all of the records for products that come from Mexico share the criterion Source Country = Mexico, and all of the records for products that have a per pound price less than $10 share the criterion Price $/lb < 10. You can also filter your list using multiple criteria, such as all products from Mexico with prices less than $10 per pound.

Open an existing file

You have been asked to find out if some specific items are in stock. In order to perform the most accurate search possible, you need to open the current inventory list. In this exercise, you open the most up-to-date inventory file.

Open

1 On the Standard toolbar, click the Open button.
2 In the Open dialog box, click the Look In Favorites button.
3 In the file list, double-click the Part3 Excel Practice folder.
4 Double-click the Lesson 5 Inventory file.

You can also open this file using Microsoft Outlook

You can open Microsoft Excel and the Lesson 5 Inventory file with Microsoft Outlook by using the following procedure.

1 In Microsoft Outlook on the Outlook Bar, click the Other shortcut bar.

The folders in the Other group appear.

2 On the Outlook Bar, click the Favorites icon.

Your Favorites appear in the Information viewer.

3 In the Information viewer, double-click the Part3 Excel Practice folder.

4 In the Information viewer, double-click the Lesson 5 Inventory file.

Save the file with a new name

1 On the File menu, click Save As.

The Save As dialog box opens. Be sure that the Part3 Excel Practice folder appears in the Save In box.

2 In the File Name box, type **Lesson 05**, and then click Save.

Filtering to Display a Set of Related Records

Filtering allows you to display only the records that share specific *criteria*, or field values. With Microsoft Excel, the easiest way to filter records in a list is to use AutoFilter. When you turn on AutoFilter, *filter arrows*, which look like down arrows, will appear next to the column headings in your list. You click an arrow to display a list of the values in that field, and then select a value to use as a criterion or condition for filtering the list. After you have selected a criterion, the filter arrow for that field and the row numbers for the filtered records appear in blue to provide a quick reminder of which field you filtered on.

Find a subset of items quickly using an AutoFilter

One of your co-workers needs to find out if the Island Tea & Coffee Company offers any coffees from Mexico. In this exercise, you filter the inventory list to locate coffees imported from Mexico, and then you remove the filter.

1   Select cell C7.

You could select any cell in your list. Microsoft Excel will then select the entire contiguous range of cells.

2   On the Data menu, point to Filter, and then click AutoFilter.

Filter arrows appear next to your column headers.

Filter arrows

	A	B	C	D	E	F	
1	Product Name ▾	Categoi ▾	Source Country ▾	Cost $/I ▾	Price $/I ▾	Qty In Stocl ▾	Wai
2	Antigua	Coffee	Guatemala	5.25	10.50	500	
3	Blue Mountain	Coffee	Jamaica	28.00	36.00	400	
4	Bourbon Santos	Coffee	Brazil	4.75	9.50	200	
5	Celebes	Coffee	Indonesia	4.75	9.50	800	
6	Chanchamayo	Coffee	Peru	5.25	10.50	600	
7	Coatepec	Coffee	Mexico	5.25	10.50	900	
8	Coban	Coffee	Guatemala	4.75	9.50	800	
9	Costa Rica	Coffee	Costa Rica	5.25	10.50	1000	
10	Ecuador	Coffee	Ecuador	5.25	10.50	500	
11	Haiti	Coffee	Haiti	4.75	9.50	400	

3   Click the Source Country filter arrow column heading (in cell C1).

An alphabetical list of all the source countries appears.

You can copy and paste the filtered records into another worksheet for further reference or manipulation, or into an e-mail message to your co-worker.

You can remove filtering from a list either by removing the specific criterion that you set, or by turning off the AutoFilter.

	A	B	C	D	E	F	
1	Product Name ▾	Categoi ▾	Source Country ▾	Cost $/I ▾	Price $/I ▾	Qty In Stocl ▾	Wai
2	Antigua	Coffee	(All)	5.25	10.50	500	
3	Blue Mountain	Coffee	(Top 10...)	28.00	36.00	400	
4	Bourbon Santos	Coffee	(Custom...)	4.75	9.50	200	
5	Celebes	Coffee	Brazil / China	4.75	9.50	800	
6	Chanchamayo	Coffee	Columbia	5.25	10.50	600	
7	Coatepec	Coffee	Costa Rica / Dominican Republic	5.25	10.50	900	
8	Coban	Coffee	Ecuador	4.75	9.50	800	
9	Costa Rica	Coffee	Ethiopia	5.25	10.50	1000	
10	Ecuador	Coffee	Guatemala / Haiti	5.25	10.50	500	
11	Haiti	Coffee	Hawaii	4.75	9.50	400	
12	Harrar	Coffee	India	4.95	9.90	800	
13	India	Coffee	Indonesia / Jamaica	4.75	9.50	700	
14	Java	Coffee	Japan	5.25	10.50	800	
15	Kenya	Coffee	Kenya	5.40	10.80	900	
16	Kona	Coffee	Mexico	5.25	10.50	1000	
17	Medellin	Coffee	Peru / Columbia	4.75	9.50	1100	

4   Click Mexico.

All the records for products from Mexico remain in view, and all other records are hidden.

5   To remove the filter, click the Source Country filter arrow (in cell C1), and then scroll to the top of the list and click All.

The filter is removed and all the records are displayed.

Find the seven lowest-priced coffees

One of the sales representatives of the Island Tea & Coffee Company wants to know what the seven lowest-priced coffees are, and what quantities of each are available. In this exercise, you filter your inventory list to find the seven lowest-priced coffees.

AutoFilter's Top 10 feature only works in numeric fields.

1   Click the Category filter arrow (in cell B1), and then click Coffee.

All the teas are hidden and only the coffees appear.

2   Click the Price $/lb filter arrow (in cell E1), and then click Top 10.

The Top 10 AutoFilter dialog box appears.

3   In the leftmost list box, select Bottom.

4   In the center list box, select 7, and then click OK.

The seven lowest-priced coffees are filtered. In fact, the filtered list contains nine entries because the nine lowest-priced coffees have the same price.

5   Click the Price $/lb filter arrow, and then click All.

6   Click the Category filter arrow, and then click All.

The filter is removed and all the records are displayed.

Filter data using multiple criteria with a custom AutoFilter

One of your co-workers in the Marketing department is creating a new ad campaign, and he wants to know which products are priced between $10 and $15 per pound. In this exercise, you create and then use a custom filter to quickly bring up the list requested by your colleague.

1   Click the Price $/lb filter arrow (in cell E1), and then click Custom.

The Custom AutoFilter dialog box appears.

2   In the upper-left list box, click Is Greater Than.

3   In the upper-right list box, type **10**

4   Be sure that the And option button is selected.

5   In the lower-left list box, click Is Less Than.

6   In the lower-right list box, type **15**

The dialog box should look similar to the following illustration.

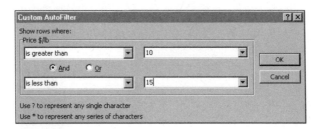

7   Click OK.

Products with prices higher than $10 per lb but lower than $15 per lb are in view, and all other products (those with prices $10/lb or less and those with prices $15/lb or more) are hidden.

Calculating Filtered Sets of Records

After you have filtered the records you need, you might want to manipulate them further. For example, you might have several fields in a list that need to be summed or averaged, and you might need to perform the same calculations on several different filtered subsets of records; or, you might want to average both price and cost for products from different countries. There are specific functions, such as SUBTOTAL, that are very useful when trying to calculate filtered data quickly.

In the following exercises, you will also learn about AutoCalculate, a Microsoft Excel feature that performs calculations without written formulas.

Calculate a total using AutoCalculate

Your list is currently filtered to show the records for products priced between $10 and $15 per pound. Your colleague in Marketing also wants to know what the average price is. In this exercise, you find out what the average price of the coffees in the $10 to $15 range is.

1 Select cells E2 through E38, and then look at the AutoCalculate box on the status bar.

	A	B	C	D	E	F
9	Costa Rica	Coffee	Costa Rica	5.25	10.50	1000
10	Ecuador	Coffee	Ecuador	5.25	10.50	500
14	Java	Coffee	Indonesia	5.25	10.50	800
15	Kenya	Coffee	Kenya	5.40	10.80	900
16	Kona	Coffee	Hawaii	5.25	10.50	1000
18	Merida	Coffee	Venezuela	5.25	10.50	700
19	Mocha	Coffee	Yemen	5.75	11.50	800
21	Pluma	Coffee	Mexico	5.25	10.50	400
23	Sumatra	Coffee	Indonesia	5.75	11.50	600
26	Black Lychee	Tea	China	5.25	10.50	250
27	Ceylon	Tea	Sri Lanka	5.85	11.70	600
31	Lapsang Souchong	Tea	China	5.05	10.10	250
32	Oolong	Tea	Taiwan	10.00	14.40	150
35	Dragonwell	Tea	China	5.35	10.70	500
37	Gyokuru	Tea	Japan	5.60	11.20	150
38	Pi Lo Chun	Tea	China	5.55	11.10	500
39						

Inventory 1-15-97

19 of 37 records found   Sum=208.00   NUM

AutoCalculate box

Your AutoCalculate box might look different from the illustration if a different function was previously selected.

2 Use the right mouse button to click the AutoCalculate box, and then click Average.

The selected cells are averaged. Only the visible records (those not hidden by the filter) are averaged, and the hidden records are ignored.

Calculate filtered sets of records using the SUBTOTAL function

In preparation for an upcoming sales meeting, your manager asks you to compare the average costs and average prices of products from each different country. In this exercise, you filter your inventory to first locate the country of origin for each product, and then average their prices using the SUBTOTAL function.

1 Click the Price $/lb filter arrow (in cell E1), and then click All.

The previous filter is removed.

2 Click the Source Country filter arrow (in cell C1), and then click China.

Your list only shows products from China.

	A	B	C	D	E	F	
1	Product Name ▾	Categor ▾	Source Country ▾	Cost $/l ▾	Price $/l ▾	Qty In Stocl ▾	War
26	Black Lychee	Tea	China	5.25	10.50	250	
29	Jasmine	Tea	China	4.90	9.80	500	
30	Keemun	Tea	China	4.85	9.70	600	
31	Lapsang Souchong	Tea	China	5.05	10.10	250	
34	Chunmee	Tea	China	4.85	9.70	100	
35	Dragonwell	Tea	China	5.35	10.70	500	
36	Gunpowder	Tea	China	4.50	9.00	400	
38	Pi Lo Chun	Tea	China	5.55	11.10	500	
39							

AutoSum

3   Select cell D41.

4   On the Standard toolbar, click the AutoSum button, and then press ENTER.

The SUBTOTAL formula for a sum is entered. If a range is filtered, the AutoSum button enters a SUBTOTAL formula; if the range is not filtered, the AutoSum button enters a SUM formula.

5   Double-click the cell containing the formula.

The formula is ready for editing.

6   Select the first argument in the parentheses to the left of the first comma: the number 9 in this case.

Arguments provide the information that tells the function what data to calculate and what operations to perform. Arguments are contained within parentheses and separated by commas. The first argument in the SUBTOTAL function indicates which function should be used in the subtotal calculation. A "9" represents the SUM function, but you want to use the AVERAGE function, which is represented by a "1." Your formula should look similar to the following illustration.

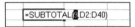

7   Type **1**, and then press ENTER.

Your SUBTOTAL formula calculates an average of the filtered cells in the Country Source field.

> **NOTE**   For your easy reference, the SUBTOTAL function arguments are as follows: 1=AVERAGE, 2=COUNT, 3=COUNTA, 4=MAX, 5=MIN, 6=PRODUCT, 7=STDEV, 8=STDEVP, 9=SUM, 10=VAR, and 11=VARP. To learn more about these functions, you can ask the Office Assistant for help.

8   Select cell D41, and then drag its fill handle to cell E41.

The SUBTOTAL formula is copied to cell E41.

9   Change the filter criterion to India.

The average cost and price of products imported from India appear.

	A	B	C	D	E	F	
1	Product Name ▾	Categoi ▾	Source Country ▾	Cost $/l ▾	Price $/l ▾	Qty In Stocl ▾	War
13	India	Coffee	India	4.75	9.50	700	
25	Assam	Tea	India	4.85	9.70	550	
28	Darjeeling	Tea	India	10.15	20.30	550	
39							
40							
41				6.5833333	13.166667		
42							

321

10   On the Data menu, point to Filter and then click AutoFilter.

The AutoFilter is removed.

11   On the File menu, click Save.

NOTE   If you'd like to build on the skills you learned in this lesson, you can do the One Step Further. Otherwise, skip to "Finish the Lesson."

One Step Further: Summing Up a Set of Records Without Filtering

You can use the SUMIF function to calculate a sum of values for specific records. The SUMIF function sums cells that meet conditions you specify, without having to filter the list first.

Your manager wants to quickly find out the total quantity of tea that is in stock. In this exercise, you write a SUMIF formula to rapidly produce the answer.

Calculate the quantity of tea in stock

1   Select cell I2, and then click the equal sign in the formula bar.

The Formula palette appears, and the Name Box becomes a Formula list.

2   Click the Formula list down arrow, and then click SUMIF.

The Formula palette expands to help you write your SUMIF formula. You might need to drag it out of your way when you select cells on the worksheet.

3   Click in the Range box, and then click the column B header to select the entire column.

"B:B" appears in the Range box.

4   In the Criteria box, type **"tea"** (be sure you include the quotation marks).

5   Click in the Sum_Range box, and then click the column F header to select the entire column.

6   Click OK.

The sum of pounds of tea in stock, 5700, appears in cell I2.

7   Save your work.

Finish the lesson

1   To continue to the next lesson, on the File menu, click Close.

2   If you are finished using Microsoft Excel for now, on the File menu, click Exit.

Lesson Summary

To	Do this
Turn AutoFilter on and off	Select a cell in the table that you want to filter. On the Data menu, point to Filter, and then click AutoFilter.
Select filter criteria	Use the filter arrows to select filtering criteria.
Remove a filter criterion	In the column header, click the filter arrow for the criterion you want to remove, and then click All.
Filter the ten highest or lowest values	In the column header, click Top 10, and then in the Top 10 AutoFilter dialog box, select Top or Bottom.
Filter using multiple criteria	Click any filter arrow, and then click Custom.
Select an AutoCalculate function	Use the right mouse button to click the AutoCalculate box, and then click the function you want.
Calculate filtered records using the SUBTOTAL function	Turn on AutoFilter, and then select a cell at least one row beneath the last cell in the field you want to calculate. On the Standard toolbar, click the AutoSum button, and then edit the first argument as appropriate.

For online information about	Use the Office Assistant to search for
Using AutoFilter	**Autofilter**, and then click Find Data In A List
Filtering records	**Filters**, and then click Ways to Find Values In A List By Using Filters
The SUBTOTAL function	**Subtotal function**, click See More, and then click SUBTOTAL

Charting to Assess Trends and Relationships

Estimated time
30 min.

In this lesson you will learn how to:

- Create a chart.
- Customize a chart.
- Make a chart format re-usable.
- Create a trendline.

A worksheet can help you calculate precise numbers, trends, and changes over time, but it can be difficult to grasp the overall meaning of numbers and trends just by looking at figures. A chart, on the other hand, creates a visual presentation of data and its relationship to other data so that the overall meaning can be grasped very quickly.

You can easily create and customize charts in Microsoft Excel by using the Chart Wizard. You can also save the formatting of the chart you create, and then re-use it in other charts. Charts can be *embedded* on the worksheet next to your data; they can also appear on a *chart sheet*. A chart sheet is a sheet in a workbook that contains only a chart. You can easily make an embedded chart into a chart sheet, or a chart sheet into an embedded chart, depending on what you prefer at any point in time.

Other features, such as trendlines and secondary axes, make charted data even more useful. A trend in a series of data, such as monthly sales for a year, can be calculated and used to forecast sales; you can show that trend and forecast in the chart by using a trendline. Data series that are related but are on different number scales, for example volume sold (in thousands of pounds) and price per pound (in dollars per pound), can be displayed on the same chart by using a secondary axis for the second number scale. This enables you to relate sales volume to sales price in a direct and meaningful manner.

At the Island Tea & Coffee Company, your manager has asked you to generate two documents based on the current sales orders for 1997, which run through June: monthly sales performances for the entire company and for each employee, and a sales forecast for the next six months based on sales since January 1997. The data needed to produce these documents is currently stored in multiple worksheets.

Open an existing file

You keep the current orders data in a workbook named Current Orders. In this exercise, you open the Current Orders file.

Open

1 On the Standard toolbar, click the Open button.
2 In the Open dialog box, click the Look In Favorites button.
3 In the file list, double-click the Part3 Excel Practice folder.
4 Double-click the Current Orders file.

Save the file with a new name

1 On the File menu, click Save As.

The Save As dialog box opens. Be sure the Part3 Excel Practice folder appears in the Save In box.

2 In the File Name box, type **Charting Lesson**, and then click Save.

Presenting Data Graphically with Charts

Your manager at the Island Tea & Coffee Company has asked for a chart of the company's sales by category for each month this year. A table has been created on the Chart Data sheet (based on the 1997 Orders worksheet) to show this data. After you create the chart, you'll customize it by changing the color of the Tea series to a two-color fade, and changing the column markers in the coffee series into picture markers of stacked coffee cups.

Create a chart

Now that you have opened your current orders list, you are ready to start chart-ing it. In this exercise, you create an embedded column chart based on the data in the Chart Data worksheet.

Chart Wizard

1 Select the Chart Data sheet.

2 Select cells A4 through C10.

3 On the Standard toolbar, click the Chart Wizard button.

The Chart Wizard appears.

4 In the Step 1 dialog box, be sure that Column is selected in the Chart Type list, and then click Next.

5 In the Step 2 dialog box, be sure that the Columns option button is se-lected, and then click Next.

6 In the Step 3 dialog box, on the Titles tab, click in the Chart Title box, type **Current Orders by Category**, and then click Next.

7 In the Step 4 dialog box, be sure that the As Object In option button is selected and that the list reads Chart Data, and then click Finish.

The new chart is created in the middle of the worksheet. Your worksheet should look similar to the following illustration.

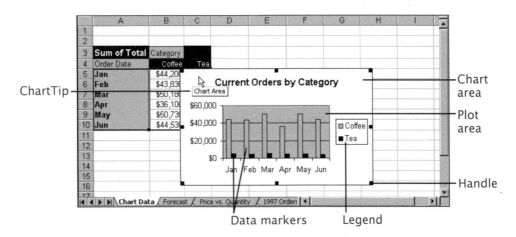

327

Customize a chart to match specific requirements

Now that you have created your embedded chart, you need to format it according to the Island Tea & Coffee Company standard. In this exercise, you customize the formatting of your chart.

For a demonstration of how to customize charts, double-click the Camcorder file named Customize A Chart in the Part3 Excel Camcorder Files folder. See "Installing and Using the Practice and Camcorder Files," earlier in this book for more information.

If you have trouble selecting a chart element, select any element, and then press an arrow key to cycle through all the elements in the chart.

1   If you do not see handles around the edges of your chart, point to an empty area of the chart background, and then, when the ChartTip shows Chart Area, click the chart.

   Handles appear around the edges of the chart showing that it is selected, and the Name box shows Chart Area.

2   Drag the corner handles of the chart until cells B3 through I16 are covered by the chart to make it larger and easier to see.

3   Point to the gray area behind the data markers (the plot area), and when the ChartTip shows Plot Area, double-click.

   The Format Plot Area dialog box appears.

4   Under Area, click the None option button, and then click OK.

   The plot area background color disappears.

5   Double-click one of the data markers in the Tea series.

   The Format Data Series dialog box appears.

6   On the Patterns tab, click the Fill Effects button.

   The Fill Effects dialog box appears.

7   On the Gradient tab, under Colors, click the Preset option button; under Preset Colors, select Daybreak; under Shading Styles, be sure that Horizontal is selected; and under Variants, select the upper-right box.

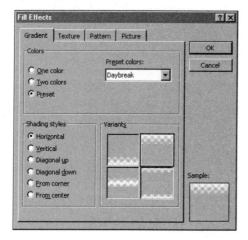

8 Click OK to close the Fill Effects dialog box, and then click OK again to close the Format Data Series dialog box.

Your chart should look similar to the following illustration.

Add picture markers to a series

Before printing your chart, you need to finish bringing it up to the Island Tea & Coffee Company formatting standard. In this exercise, you make the data markers for the coffee series look like stacked coffee cups.

1 Double-click one of the data markers in the Coffee series.

The Format Data Series dialog box appears.

2 On the Patterns tab, click the Fill Effects button.

3 In the Fill Effects dialog box, click the Picture tab, and then click Select Picture.

The Select Picture dialog box appears.

4 In the Part3 Excel Practice folder, double-click the Coffee Cup file.

The clipart picture appears in the Fill Effects dialog box.

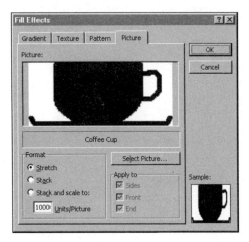

5 Under Format, click the Stack option button, and then click OK.

6 In the Format Data Series dialog box, click OK.

Your completed chart should look similar to the following illustration.

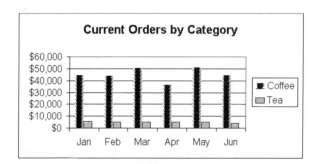

Draw your own markers

Another way to customize a chart is to draw your own markers using Microsoft Excel's drawing tools.

Using the drawing tools, you can draw objects of any shape in both worksheets and charts. You can replace markers in a chart with an object you draw—you can replace an entire series, or just a single marker to make it stand out. You can even draw an object and give it a shadow or a 3-D effect.

Before you print the chart, you decide to experiment with its look—you want to replace the Tea series markers with a drawn object of your own.

1 Use the right mouse button to click a toolbar, and then click Drawing.

The Drawing toolbar appears.

2 On the Drawing toolbar, click the Oval button.

The mouse pointer becomes a crosshair.

Oval

3 Drag the crosshair pointer diagonally on the chart or the worksheet to draw a circular object.

The object can be either circular or oblong.

4 Make the object approximately 1 inch in diameter.

When you release the mouse button, the object is selected and has handles around it.

Fill Color

5 While the object is selected, on the Formatting toolbar, select a red color from the Fill Color button palette.

The drawn object is colored red.

3-D

6 On the Drawing toolbar, click the 3-D button.

A shortcut menu of 3-D shapes appears.

Copy

Paste

To replace a single marker, click the marker twice (do not double-click), and then paste the drawn object.

7   Click the shape in the lower right corner (3-D Style 20).

The drawn object takes on a 3-D shape.

8   While the object is still selected, on the Standard toolbar, click the Copy button.

9   In the chart, click a Tea series marker.

The entire Tea series is selected.

10   On the Standard toolbar, click the Paste button.

The Tea series markers take on the shape of your drawn, 3-D object.

11   Click the object you drew, and then press DELETE.

The drawn object is deleted, and your chart has custom-drawn markers in it.

12   Close the Drawing toolbar.

Undo the changes

You decide that you don't like the drawn-object markers in this particular chart, so you undo the changes you made.

Undo

➤   On the Standard toolbar, click the down arrow next to the Undo button, and undo actions until the Tea series markers are in their original form.

Print the chart

   IMPORTANT   In order to complete this exercise, you'll need to be connected to a printer.

Before distributing the chart for further review, you decide to show it to your manager. In this exercise, you print a copy of the chart.

Print

➤   Click the chart to select it, and then, on the Standard toolbar, click the Print button.

Make an embedded chart into a chart sheet (and vice versa)

In this exercise, you convert the embedded chart into a chart sheet so that it remains functional but is off the worksheet.

1   Use the right mouse button to click in the chart area.

2   On the shortcut menu, click Location.

The Chart Location dialog box appears.

331

3 Click the As New Sheet option button, and then click OK.

The embedded chart is moved onto a separate chart sheet.

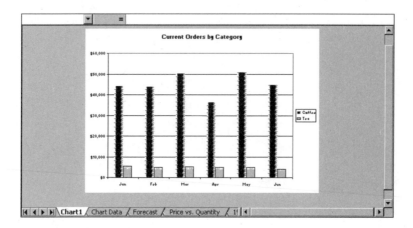

You can rename, move, copy, and delete a chart sheet in the same way that you would a worksheet.

Making a Chart Format Re-Usable

Even though customizing your chart was easy, it would be even easier in the future if you could reapply the Island Tea & Coffee Company custom formatting to any chart without having to perform the individual formatting steps. You can save your chart formatting by making it into a custom chart type, and then simply reapply it whenever you create a new chart.

Create a custom chart type

Because you formatted your chart based on the Island Tea & Coffee Company guidelines, you decide to save the settings for future use. In this exercise, you create a custom chart type and remove the chart title so that it doesn't become part of the custom chart type formatting.

1 Click the chart title, and then press DELETE.

2 On the Chart menu, click Chart Type.

3 Click the Custom Types tab.

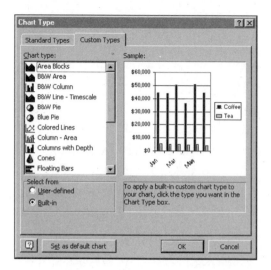

4 Under Select From, click User-Defined, and then click Add.

5 In the Name box, type **ITC Standard**, and in the Description box, type **Company standard chart format**, and then click OK.

The new chart type is added to the Chart Type list. The next time you run the Chart Wizard, you can click the User-Defined option button and then select your custom chart type on the Custom Types tab in the Step 1 dialog box.

6 Click OK.

Forecasting Trends

One of the charts your manager requested is a six-month sales forecast based on the sales data for the first five months. By using one of several mathematical line equations, Microsoft Excel can create a *trendline* for a data series that shows the trend of the existing data. You can extend that trendline into a forecast for as many periods as you want.

Forecast future sales based on current data trends

In preparation for a company-wide sales meeting, your manager asks you to create a chart that will help her forecast the projected company sales for the next six months. In this exercise, you create a chart with a trendline and six-month forecast for total company sales.

Chart Wizard

1   Select the Forecast worksheet.

2   Select cells A1 through B6, and then click the Chart Wizard button.

3   In the Chart Wizard Step 1 dialog box, click Finish.

   A default column chart is created.

4   Use the right mouse button to click any data marker in the chart.

   The entire data series is selected.

5   On the shortcut menu, click Add Trendline.

   The Add Trendline dialog box appears.

6   On the Type tab, click Linear.

7   On the Options tab, under Forecast, in the Forward box, click the up arrow until it shows 6, and then click OK.

   A trendline with a six-month forecast is inserted in the chart. You might want to try different trendlines to decide which type best displays a logical forecast based on your data.

8   Save your work.

NOTE   If you'd like to build on the skills you learned in this lesson, you can do the One Step Further. Otherwise, skip to "Finish the Lesson."

One Step Further: Creating a Chart with a Secondary Axis

After reviewing the six-month forecast you created in the previous exercise, your manager requests a chart of sales volume vs. average price, to see if changing prices affect the volume sold. The two series in your chart, sales volume and price per pound, have very different number scales: the volume will be in thousands, and the average price will be less than 15. This means that when both series are displayed in the same chart using the same value axis, only the volume series will be visible. The solution is to show each series on a different value axis. This way you can see how the volume and price change relative to each other over time, and then estimate how changing the price affects the volume sold.

Use a secondary axis to display data series that have different value scales

To make the chart as useful as possible, you decide to add a second axis to display each data series at the appropriate scale. In this exercise, you create a chart of sales volume vs. average price, and then add a secondary axis so that the average price series can be seen in the chart.

1   Select the Price Vs. Quantity sheet.

2   Select cells A1 through C7, click the Chart Wizard button, and then, in the Step 1 dialog box, click Finish.

A default chart is created on the worksheet.

If the Chart toolbar is not displayed, use the right mouse button to click any toolbar, and then click Chart.

3   On the Chart toolbar, click the Chart Objects down arrow, and then select Series "price."

4   On the Format menu, click Selected Data Series.

The Format Data Series dialog box appears.

5   On the Axis tab, under Plot Series On, click the Secondary Axis option button, and then click OK.

A secondary axis is added to the right side of the chart. The Price data markers are visible because they have an axis that is scaled to their values.

6   Use the right mouse button to click the Price series, and then click Chart Type.

7   In the Chart Type dialog box, click the Standard Types tab, verify that the Apply To Selection check box is selected, click the Line icon, and then click OK.

The Price data is displayed by line markers instead of by column markers, which makes it easier to distinguish.

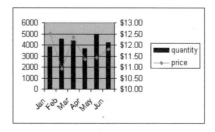

8   Save the workbook.

Finish the lesson

1   To continue to the next lesson, on the File menu, click Close.

2   If you are finished using Microsoft Excel for now, on the File menu, click Exit.

Lesson Summary

To	Do this	Button
Create a chart	Select the data you want to chart, and then click the Chart Wizard button. Follow the steps in the Chart Wizard to create the chart.	
Customize a chart	Double-click the chart element you want to customize, and then select the desired colors, patterns, and effects in the Format dialog box.	
Add picture markers to a series	Double-click a marker in the series you want to add picture markers to, and then, in the Format Data Series dialog box, click Fill Effects. Click the Picture tab, click Select Picture, and then locate a picture you want. Double-click the picture you want, click OK to close the Fill Effects dialog box, and then click OK to close the Format Data Series dialog box.	
Replace series markers with a drawn object	Use the right mouse button to click a toolbar, and then select Drawing. On the Drawing toolbar, click a shape button and draw an object in the worksheet or chart. Select the object, and then, on the Standard toolbar, click the Copy button. Click a marker in the series you want to replace. On the Standard toolbar, click the Paste button. Select the object you drew, and then press DELETE.	
Make a drawn object a 3-D object	Select the drawn object. On the Drawing toolbar, click 3-D, and then select a 3-D shape from the shortcut menu.	

To	Do this	Button
Make an embedded chart into a chart sheet	Use the right mouse button to click in the chart area, and then, on the shortcut menu, click Location. In the Chart Location dialog box, select the As New Sheet option button, and then click OK.	
Create a custom chart type	On the Chart menu, click Chart Type, and then click the Custom Types tab. Click User Defined, and then click Add. Type a name and description for the new custom chart type, and then click OK.	
Create a trendline	Use the right mouse button to select the series you want a trendline for, and then, on the shortcut menu, click Add Trendline. On the Type tab, select a trendline type. If you want a forecast, on the Options tab, select a number of forecast periods, and then click OK.	

For online information about	Use the Office Assistant to search for
Creating charts	**Creating charts**, then click Create A Chart
Formatting charts	**Formatting** charts, then click About Formatting Charts
Trendlines	**Trendlines**, then click Trendlines In Charts

Printing Reports to Distribute Information Offline

Estimated time
30 min.

In this lesson you will learn how to:

- Print a multiple-page worksheet.
- Set print titles to easily identify data on all pages.
- Change the page printing order.
- Print only selected data from a worksheet.
- Define print areas to print the same data repeatedly.
- Fit information onto a specific number of printed pages.
- Print charts with or without a worksheet.

As the office manager for the Island Tea & Coffee Company, you keep a current list of the company's orders. Different members of the sales staff often ask you for a printed copy of this data—sometimes the entire list, sometimes just portions of it.

In this lesson, you will learn a variety of methods for printing worksheet data depending on the requirements.

 IMPORTANT In order to perform the exercises in this lesson, your computer will need to be connected to a printer.

Open an existing file

You keep the current orders in a workbook named 1997 Orders. In this exercise, you open the 1997 Orders workbook.

Open

1 On the Standard toolbar, click the Open button.

2 In the Open dialog box, click the Look In Favorites button.

3 In the file list, double-click the Part3 Excel Practice folder.

4 Double-click the 1997 Orders file.

Save the file with a new name

In this exercise, you save the 1997 Orders file as Printing Lesson.

1 On the File menu, click Save As.

The Save As dialog box opens. Be sure the Part3 Excel Practice folder appears in the Save In box.

2 In the File Name box, type **Printing Lesson**, and then click Save.

Printing an Entire Worksheet

The 1997 Orders list is a very large worksheet that will extend over several pages when printed. A common problem encountered while printing large worksheets is that each identifying column or row label is printed only on the first page. Another common problem relates to the default layout of the printed pages. For example, the default layout may print six columns on one page and a single column on the next page; or it may print the left side of a long worksheet followed by the right side, when you would rather print the top of the worksheet followed by the bottom. You can remedy these problems easily by changing some print settings for the worksheet.

First, you will preview the worksheet using two different preview methods, and then you will change print settings so that the 1997 Orders list prints out the way you want it to.

Preview the worksheet

You usually preview a worksheet before printing it so that you can determine the optimal way to lay out the printed pages. In this exercise, you use two different methods of previewing: Print Preview and Page Break Preview. Print Preview shows you what the printed page will look like, page by page; Page Break Preview shows you how the worksheet is broken up into pages, and allows you to easily alter the page layout.

Print Preview

1 Be sure that the Orders worksheet is active, and then, on the Standard toolbar, click the Print Preview button.

Page 1 appears in Print Preview mode. Only four columns are printed on page 1, and the status bar message tells you that there are 16 pages in the worksheet.

2 On the button bar, click Page Break Preview.

3 If you see a Welcome To Page Break Preview dialog box, select the Do Not Show This Dialog Again check box, and then click OK.

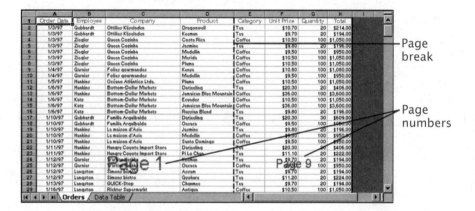

Page break

Page numbers

Page Break Preview shows you how the entire worksheet is broken into pages. The dotted lines show where the page breaks are, and the page numbers show the order in which the worksheet will be printed (in this case, the pages on the left side of the worksheet will be printed first, from the top down, and then the right side will be printed from the top down). This printing order is called *Down, Then Over*.

4 Point to the vertical page break line, and then, when the mouse pointer becomes a two-headed arrow, drag the line to the left by one column.

The vertical page break is reset so that only three columns print on the first eight pages. The page break line becomes a solid line after you move it to indicate that it is now a manual page break instead of an automatic page break.

5 On the Standard toolbar, click the Print Preview button.

6 On the button bar, click Next, and then click near the top of the page.

		Orders
1/27/97	Hankins	Split Rail Beer & Ale
1/30/97	Hankins	Folk och fä HB
1/30/97	Hankins	Folk och fä HB
1/30/97	Hankins	Princesa Isabel Vinhos
1/31/97	Garnier	Consolidated Holdings
1/31/97	Garnier	Consolidated Holdings

341

Page 2 is magnified, and there are no labels at the top of the page to identify the data in the columns. In the next exercise, you will fix this by adding
print titles, labels that are automatically printed at the top of each page.

7   On the button bar, click Close.

Set print titles

While previewing the worksheet you saw that the identifying column labels appear only on pages 1 and 9, and the identifying order dates appear only on
pages 1 through 8, so the data on every page except page 1 is not adequately
identified. In this exercise, you set print titles so that no matter where the page
breaks are, the order dates and column labels will be printed on each page.

1   On the File menu, click Page Setup.

2   In the Page Setup dialog box, click the Sheet tab.

3   Under Print Titles, click in the Rows To Repeat At Top box, and then click
a cell in row 1. You might have to drag the dialog box out of the way to
click in row 1.

The row reference $1:$1 is entered in the Rows To Repeat At Top box.

4   Click in the Columns To Repeat At Left box, and then click a cell in
column A.

The column reference $A:$A is entered in the Columns To Repeat At Left box.

5   Click OK.

6   On the Standard toolbar, click the Print Preview button, and then, on the
button bar, click Next until you can see page 10.

Print Preview

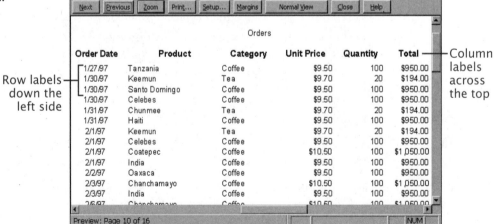

Column labels and order dates now appear on every page. Magnify the
page to read the headings, if necessary.

7   On the button bar, click Close.

Change the page layout

Your list of current 1997 orders is wide as well as long, and you need to define whether to print the pages "Over, Then Down" or "Down, Then Over." In this exercise, you look at page printing order layouts to determine which is most effective.

1   If you are not in Page Break Preview, on the View menu, click Page Break Preview.

The default page layout is "Down, Then Over."

2   On the File menu, click Page Setup.

The Page Setup dialog box appears.

3   On the Sheet tab, click the "Over, Then Down" option button under Page Order, and then click OK.

Page 2 now appears on the right of page 1, which means that the pages will print from left to right instead of top to bottom.

Print

4   On the View menu, click Normal.

Page Break Preview is replaced by the worksheet view.

5   On the Standard toolbar, click the Print button.

Printing Selected Areas on a Worksheet

As keeper of the Island Tea & Coffee Company list of current orders, you receive many requests for printouts of different kinds: selected data for a specific month; a segment of data that needs to fit on a single page; or a summary report for a management meeting.

Print only selected data

In addition to a printout of the entire list of 1997 orders, your manager would like a printout of the orders data for March 1997. Because you have already set print titles, all you have to do is select the month's data; the column labels will be included automatically. In this exercise, you print the March orders data.

1 Select cells A121 through H182 (the March data).

2 On the File menu, click Print.

3 In the Print dialog box, under Print What, click the Selection option button.

4 In the Print dialog box, click Preview.

The pages for your selected data are previewed. Because of the settings you defined in earlier exercises, the pages will print "Over, Then Down," and correct column and row labels will print on every page.

5 On the button bar, click Print.

The worksheet is printed and Microsoft Excel returns to the worksheet view.

Define a print area

Co-workers regularly ask you for printouts of the list of orders for previous completed months, not including the orders for the current month. Since you do this several times each month, you can save time by defining a *print area*, an area of the worksheet that will be printed automatically when you click the Print button on the Standard toolbar. In this exercise, you define a print area that includes data for completed months only.

To set a print area from the worksheet view, select the print range, and then, on the File menu, point to Print Area and click Set Print Area.

1 On the View menu, click Page Break Preview.

2 In Page Break Preview, select the cells A1 through H356 (the records for January through June).

3 Use the right mouse button to click the selected range, and then click Set Print Area.

4 On the View menu, click Normal to return to worksheet view.

Now that you have set a print area, only that area of the worksheet will be printed when you click the Print button on the Standard toolbar.

Print a worksheet on a specific number of pages

In preparation for a meeting, your manager has asked you to reduce the size of the completed months' data so that it will fit on a single page width and won't be longer than 5 pages. In this exercise, you make the print area 1 page in width by 5 pages in length.

1   On the File menu, click Page Setup.

2   On the Page tab, under Scaling, click the Fit To option button, and set the spinner boxes to show 1 Page(s) Wide By 5 Tall.

3   Click Print Preview.

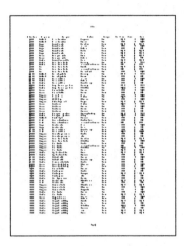

The status bar message indicates that the data fits on 5 pages, and you can see that it has been reduced in width so that all columns fit on a single page.

4   On the button bar, click Print.

The Print dialog box appears.

5   Click OK.

Center data on the printed page

The data on the printed page is left-aligned, but your manager wants it centered on the page. In this exercise, you center the data horizontally on the pages.

Print Preview

You can drag margin lines and column breaks to change margins and column widths.

1   On the Standard toolbar, click the Print Preview button, and then click the page to zoom out if you need to so that you can see the whole page.

2   On the button bar, click Margins.

Margin lines appear around the edges of the page, and column breaks appear across the top of the page. The margin lines help you see whether the data looks centered.

3   On the button bar, click Setup.

4   In the Page Setup dialog box, click the Margins tab.

345

5 Under Center On Page, select the Horizontally check box, and then click OK.

The data on every page is centered horizontally.

6 On the button bar, click Print.

The Print dialog box appears.

7 Click OK.

8 Save your workbook.

Printing Charts

As the office manager, you keep the Island Tea & Coffee Company workbooks arranged so that you can get to any type of data you want as quickly and efficiently as possible. This usually means that the worksheets and charts aren't arranged for instant printing. For example, you keep your charts embedded in worksheets because it's often more convenient to use an embedded chart than to flip back and forth between a worksheet and a chart; however, you sometimes need to print the worksheet without its embedded chart, or the chart without its source worksheet. You can easily do both without changing your workbook setup.

When you print a chart separately from its worksheet, you might notice that the chart's proportions are changed so that the printed chart is not in *scale* (not the same relative height and width) with the chart you created on the worksheet. If this presents a problem, you can easily re-scale the printed chart so that it retains the same relative proportions as the embedded chart.

Print a worksheet without printing the embedded chart

You can use the procedure in this exercise to prevent any graphical object on a worksheet from being printed with the worksheet.

Sometimes a chart covers up the data it is based on—for example, a large table of data might be covered by its embedded chart—and you need to print the data but don't want to print the chart. In this exercise, you print a worksheet without printing its embedded chart.

1 On the Data Table sheet, point to an empty part of the chart background so that the ChartTip reads Chart Area, and then click with the right mouse button.

2 On the shortcut menu, click Format Chart Area.

3 In the Format Chart Area dialog box, click the Properties tab.

4 Clear the Print Object check box, and then click OK.

5 Click a cell in the worksheet, and then click Print Preview.

The Print Preview window appears showing you that the worksheet will be printed without the embedded chart.

Print Preview

6 On the button bar, click Close.

Print an embedded chart without printing the worksheet

Your manager has asked you to present your charted data at a company meeting. In order to create a clear overhead slide, you want to print the chart without the extra clutter of the worksheet data. In this exercise, you print an embedded chart without printing its source worksheet.

1 Click anywhere on the chart, and then click the Print Preview button.

The Print Preview window opens, showing you that the chart will be printed separately.

2 On the button bar, click Print.

The Print dialog box appears.

3 Click OK.

Re-scale a printed chart

When you print a chart on its own page, by default the chart is scaled (its proportions are changed) to fill up the entire page. Your Data Table chart is a short, wide rectangle, but when you print it, its scale changes so that it is taller and narrower. In this exercise, you re-scale the chart to print it with its original proportions.

1 Click anywhere on the chart.

2 On the File menu, click Page Setup, and then click the Chart tab.

3 On the Chart tab, click the Scale To Fit Page option button, and then click Print Preview.

The Print Preview window appears showing you that the chart will be printed with the proportions it has in the worksheet.

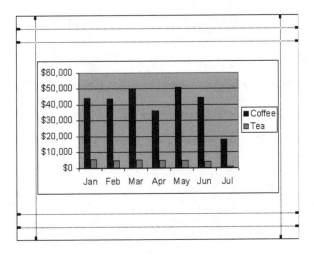

347

4   On the button bar, click Print.

The Print dialog box appears.

5   Click OK.

6   On the File menu, click Save.

 NOTE   This lesson has covered various ways to print data in a single worksheet, but you can also print all the worksheets in a workbook with one step. Be sure that a worksheet cell (not a chart) is selected, and then on the File menu, click Print; under Print What, click the Entire Workbook option button, and then click OK.

 NOTE   If you'd like to build on the skills you learned in this lesson, you can do the One Step Further. Otherwise, skip to "Finish the Lesson."

One Step Further: Setting Multiple Print Areas in a Worksheet

One of the Island Tea & Coffee Company's sales people has asked for printouts of March and June data. In this exercise, you set two print areas in one worksheet.

1   Select the Orders sheet, and then, on the View menu, click Page Break Preview.

2   Select cells A121 through H182 (the March records), and then hold down CTRL and select cells A302 through H356 (the June records).

3   Use the right mouse button to click in one of the selected ranges, and then, on the shortcut menu, click Set Print Area.

Two print areas are set.

Print Preview

4   On the Standard toolbar, click the Print Preview button.

Each print area prints on its own page, and since your settings from previous exercises are still in place, each print area is centered on a single page.

5   On the button bar, click Print.

The Print dialog box appears.

6   Click OK.

7   On the File menu, click Save.

Finish the lesson

> If you are finished using Microsoft Excel for now, on the File menu, click Exit.

Lesson Summary

To	Do this	Button
See a preview of printed pages	On the Standard toolbar, click the Print Preview button.	
See a preview of the page layout	On the View menu, click Page Break Preview.	
Change page breaks	On the View menu, click Page Break Preview. Drag page break lines to reposition page breaks.	
Set print titles	On the File menu, click Page Setup, and then click the Sheet tab. Click in the Rows To Repeat At Top box, and then click a cell in the row you want to appear at the top of each page. Click in the Columns To Repeat At Left box, and then click a cell in the column you want to appear down the left side of each page. Click OK.	
Change the page printing order	On the File menu, click Page Setup, and then click the Sheet tab. Under Page Order, click the "Over, Then Down" option button or the "Down, Then Over" option button, and then click OK.	
Print only selected data on a worksheet	Select the range to print, and then, on the File menu, click Print. Under Print What, click the Selection option button, and then click OK.	
Define a print area	On the View menu, click Page Break Preview. Select the range you want to set as a print area, and then use the right mouse button to click the selection. On the shortcut menu, click Set Print Area.	

To	Do this	Button
Print a worksheet on a specific number of pages	On the File menu, click Page Setup, and then click the Page tab. Under Scaling, click the Fit To option button, set the number of pages wide by number of pages tall, and then click OK.	
Center data on a printed page	On the File menu, click Page Setup, and then click the Margins tab. Under Center On Page, select the Horizontally or Vertically check box, or both, and then click OK.	
Print a worksheet with an embedded chart	On the Standard toolbar, click the Print button.	
Print a worksheet without its embedded chart	Use the right mouse button to click an empty part of the chart, and then, on the shortcut menu, click Format Chart Area. Click the Properties tab, clear the Print Object check box, and then click OK. Click a cell in the worksheet, and then, on the Standard toolbar, click the Print button.	
Print an embedded chart without its worksheet	Select any part of the chart, and then, on the Standard toolbar, click the Print button.	
Print a chart sheet	Select the chart sheet, and then, on the Standard toolbar, click the Print button.	
Re-scale a printed chart	Select the chart, and then, on the File menu, click Page Setup. Click the Chart tab, select the Scale To Fit Page option button, and then click OK.	

For online information about	Use the Office Assistant to search for
Print Preview	**Print preview,** then click About The Print Preview Window
Printing problems	**Printing problems,** then click Troubleshoot Printing

Microsoft PowerPoint 97

Part **4**

Creating a Presentation

In this lesson you will learn how to:

Estimated time
35 min.

- Start PowerPoint.
- Use the AutoContent Wizard.
- Move around in a presentation.
- Change text in Outline view.
- Understand and change presentation views.
- Move from slide to slide.
- Change and add text in Slide view.
- Preview slides in Slide Sorter view.
- Save a presentation.

With Microsoft PowerPoint you can create overhead slides, speaker's notes, audience handouts, and an outline, all in a single presentation file. PowerPoint offers powerful wizards to help you create and organize your presentation step by step.

As the Director of Communications for Ferguson & Bardell, you're responsible for managing the development of an investment seminar series. For your manager, you need to present a progress report for the seminar series.

In this lesson, you'll learn to start PowerPoint, use the AutoContent Wizard to create a presentation, and change and insert text. You'll edit title and bulleted text, move around in your presentation, look at your content in different views, and save your work.

353

Starting PowerPoint

The quickest way to start PowerPoint and all your other applications is by using the Start button on the taskbar.

Start Microsoft PowerPoint

1 On the taskbar, click the Start button.

2 On the Start menu, point to Programs, and then click Microsoft PowerPoint.

The PowerPoint Startup dialog box appears. This dialog box gives four options for beginning your PowerPoint session.

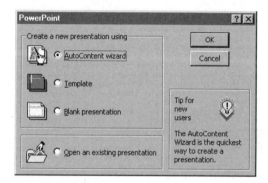

 IMPORTANT If the Office Assistant appears, click the Start Using Microsoft PowerPoint option.

For the purposes of this book, the Office Assistant will not appear in the illustrations. If you want to match the illustrations, any time the Office Assistant appears, use the right mouse button to click the Office Assistant, and then click Hide Assistant. If you want to leave the Office Assistant on top to help guide you, but it is in your way, simply drag it to another area on the screen.

An Introduction to the Office Assistant

While you are working with Microsoft Office 97, an animated character called the Office Assistant pops up on your screen to help you work productively. The Office Assistant offers helpful messages as you work. You can ask the Office Assistant questions by typing your question and then clicking Search. The Office Assistant then shows you the answer to your question.

You can close any Office Assistant tip or message by pressing ESC.

You will sometimes see a lightbulb next to the Office Assistant—clicking the lightbulb displays a tip about the action you are currently performing. You can view more tips by clicking Tips in the Office Assistant balloon when the Office Assistant appears. In addition, the Office Assistant is tailored to how you work—after you master a particular skill, the Office Assistant stops offering tips.

Clippit, an Office Assistant, in action

Office Assistant

The Office Assistant appears in the following situations:

- When you click the Office Assistant button on the Standard toolbar.
- When you choose Microsoft PowerPoint Help on the Help menu or when you press F1.
- Whenever you click certain commands or try new tasks, for example, when you use Open for the first time.

The Office Assistant is a shared application—any settings that you change will affect the Office Assistant in other Office 97 programs. You can customize the Office Assistant in two ways. You can:

Determine when you want to see the Office Assistant

Use the right mouse button to click the Office Assistant and click Options to open the Office Assistant dialog box. You can then define when you want the Office Assistant to appear, and what kind of help you want it to offer.

Change your Office Assistant character

Use the right mouse button to click the Office Assistant and click Options to open the Office Assistant dialog box. Click the Gallery tab.

To begin your PowerPoint session, in the PowerPoint Startup dialog box, choose from one of four options to create a new presentation or open an existing one. The following table describes the available options:

	Select	To
	AutoContent Wizard	Create a new presentation using the AutoContent Wizard, which prompts you for a presentation title and information about your topic. Click a presentation type and style, and then PowerPoint provides a basic outline to help guide you in organizing your content into a professional presentation.
	Template	Create a new presentation based on a design template, which is a presentation with predefined slide colors and text styles. The New Presentation dialog box appears, where you can choose a template.
	Blank Presentation	Create a new blank presentation. The New Slide dialog box appears with 24 predesigned slide layouts you can choose from to help you create a new slide.
	Open An Existing	Open an existing PowerPoint Presentation presentation. The Open dialog box appears. Select a presentation file.

Using the AutoContent Wizard

If you have trouble thinking of what you want to present in your presentation, let PowerPoint help you get started with the AutoContent Wizard. Creating a presentation can be much easier with the AutoContent Wizard, because it helps you organize your presentation in minutes.

Select the AutoContent Wizard

The AutoContent Wizard helps to get you started with ideas and an organization for your presentation in an easy, step-by-step process.

1   Click the AutoContent Wizard option button.
2   Click the OK button.

Read the AutoContent Wizard Introduction

The *AutoContent Wizard* displays a Start dialog box and then leads you through choosing a presentation type and entering title slide information.

➤   After reading the introduction, click the Next button.

Choose a presentation type

First, the AutoContent Wizard prompts you to select a presentation type. To help you identify presentation types quickly, the wizard organizes presentations by category.

1   Click the General button.

2   In the presentation type box, click Reporting Progress.

If Reporting Progress is not listed, this template might not be installed. To install it, run the Office 97 Professional Setup program and add the PowerPoint Additional Content Templates option.

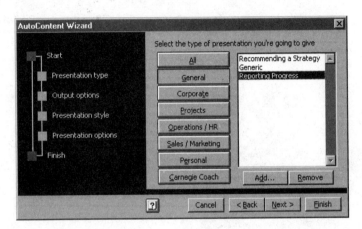

3   Click the Next button.

Choose output options

The AutoContent Wizard now prompts you to select the way you want to use the presentation.

1   Click the Presentation, Informal Meetings, Handouts option button.

2   Click the Next button.

Choose a presentation style

The AutoContent Wizard now prompts you to select the media type for your presentation.

1   In the What Type Of Output Will You Use area, click the Color Overheads option button to select a presentation type.

2   Click the Yes option to print handouts, if necessary.

3   Click the Next button.

Enter presentation title slide information

The AutoContent Wizard now prompts you to enter information for the *title slide*, the first slide in your presentation. Type in some title slide information. If you make a mistake as you type, press the BACKSPACE key to delete the mistake, and then type the correct text.

1 In the Presentation Title box, type **Investment Seminar Series** and press TAB.

2 If your name appears correctly in the Your Name box, press TAB to continue. Otherwise, type *Your Name* and then press TAB.

3 In the Additional Information box, type **Ferguson & Bardell**

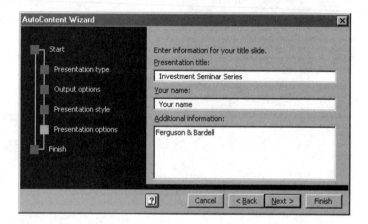

4 Click the Next button.

Finish the AutoContent Wizard

If you want to make any changes to the information before the AutoContent Wizard creates your presentation, you can click the Back button.

➤ Click the Finish button.

Upon completion, the PowerPoint presentation window appears with content provided by the AutoContent Wizard in outline form.

Moving Around in a Presentation

The *presentation window* is the canvas on which you type text, draw shapes, create graphs, add color, and insert objects. Along the top of the presentation window are the menus and buttons you'll use to do most common presentation tasks. The buttons you see are organized on *toolbars*. Toolbar buttons are shortcuts to commonly used menu commands and formatting tools. Simply click a button on a toolbar for one-step access to tasks such as formatting text and saving your presentation. At the bottom of the presentation window are view buttons that allow you to look at your presentation in different ways—in Slide, Outline, Slide Sorter, Notes Pages, and Slide Show views. At the left of the presentation window are the tools you'll use to rearrange title and paragraph text in Outline view. In Outline view, a slide icon appears to the left of each slide's title. The paragraph text underneath each title appears indented with bullets. The title, your name, and the company name you entered appear selected on the first slide along with a miniature of the presentation slide to the right, as shown in the following illustration:

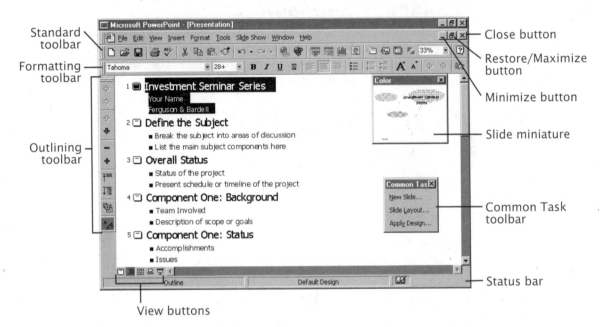

As with any Windows program, you can adjust the size of the PowerPoint and presentation windows with the Minimize and Restore/Maximize buttons or close Microsoft PowerPoint or the presentation window with the Close button.

NOTE Your screen might look different than the previous illustration if your presentation window is minimized or resized. In this book, all illustrations of the presentation window are shown maximized.

ScreenTips and the Status bar

Save

ScreenTip

To find out about different items on the screen, you can display a *ScreenTip*. When you place your mouse pointer over a toolbar button a yellow box appears telling you the name of the button, as shown in the margin. You can turn ScreenTips on and off in the following way: On the View menu, point to

Toolbars, and then click Customize. On the Options tab of the Customize dialog box, clear the Show ScreenTips On Toolbars check box, and then click Close. To find out more information about an item, click the What's This? command on the Help menu and click the item about which you want to show information. A yellow box appears telling you more information about the item.

Messages appear at the bottom of the window in an area called the *status bar*. These messages describe what you are seeing and doing in the PowerPoint window as you work.

Scrolling in a Window

The presentation outline you're working on contains more text than you can see on the screen at one time. To see the rest of the text, you need to scroll through the outline. You can click the scroll arrows or drag the scroll box located on the vertical and horizontal scroll bars to move through the window.

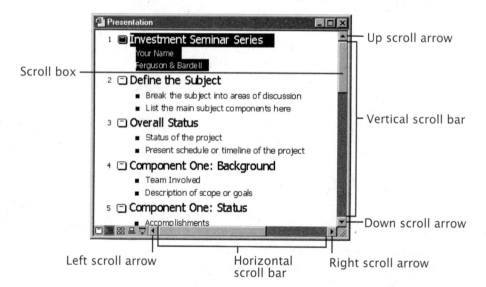

Scroll in a window

You can use one of three methods for scrolling in PowerPoint, depending on how quickly you want to move through a window. You can scroll line by line, scroll window by window, or jump immediately to the beginning, middle, or end of a window.

1 Click the down scroll arrow a few times to see the text below the current window.

Each time you click a scroll arrow, PowerPoint changes the screen to show you one more line.

2 Click below the scroll box in the scroll bar.

The bottom of the outline appears. When you click below or above the scroll box, PowerPoint scrolls window by window. You can also press the PAGE UP key or the PAGE DOWN key to scroll window by window.

3 Drag the scroll box to the top of the scroll bar—you cannot drag it off the scroll bar.

The top of the outline appears. With this method, you can quickly jump to the beginning, middle, or end of an outline, or anywhere in between.

Changing Text in Outline View

The AutoContent Wizard helps you get started with a suggested presentation outline. Now, your job is to modify and add the outline text to meet your specific needs.

Edit text in Outline view

1 Position the I-beam cursor to the left of the text "Define the Subject" in slide 2 and drag to select the title text.

PowerPoint selects the text so that it is highlighted. Once you've selected text, the subsequent text you type—regardless of its length—replaces the selection.

2 Type **Investment Seminar Development**

3 Position the I-beam cursor (which changes to a four-headed arrow) over the bullet next to the text "Break the subject into areas of discussion" in slide 2 and click. The text is highlighted.

Four-headed Arrow

4 Type **Basic Investment Strategies**

5 In slide 2, click the bullet next to the text "List the main subject components here." The text is highlighted.

6 Type **Tax Free Investment Strategies**

You can add a new bullet by pressing the ENTER key.

7 Press the ENTER key.

A new bullet appears underneath the previous line of text.

8 Type **Retirement Investment Strategies**

Your presentation window should look like the following illustration:

Change your mind

A handy feature in PowerPoint is the Undo command on the Standard toolbar or Edit menu, which reverses up to your last 20 actions. For example, choosing the Undo command now will remove the paragraph text you just entered. Whenever something happens that is not what you intended, click Undo to reverse previous actions. If you decide that the undo action is not exactly what you wanted, you can click the Redo button to restore the undo action.

Undo

1 On the Standard toolbar, click the Undo button to reverse your last action.

To undo a number of actions at the same time, you can use the Undo drop-down menu.

2 On the Standard toolbar, click the Arrow next to the Undo button.

The Undo drop-down menu appears.

3 Drag down to select the top two items in the list and click.

The last two entires in the outline have been reversed.

Redo

4 On the Standard toolbar, click the Redo button.

5 On the Standard toolbar, click the Redo button drop-down arrow, drag to select the top two items, and click to restore the text.

Understanding PowerPoint Views

For a demonstration of how to work in PowerPoint views, double-click the Camcorder file named "PowerPoint Views in the Part4 PowerPoint Camcorder Files folder. See "Installing and Using the Practice and Camcorder Files," earlier in this book for more information.

PowerPoint has five views to help you create, organize, and show your presentation. *Slide view* allows you to work on individual slides. *Outline view* allows you to work on the title and body text of your presentation. *Slide Sorter view* allows you to organize the order and status of the slides in your presentation. *Notes Pages view* allows you to create speaker's notes. *Slide Show view* allows you to see your slides as an electronic presentation on your computer. Slide Show view displays your slides as you would see them in Slide view using the entire screen. You can switch among views using the view buttons at the bottom of the presentation window. Illustrations of Slide view, Outline view, Notes Pages view, and Slide Sorter view are shown below.

Click this button for Slide view

Click this button for Outline view

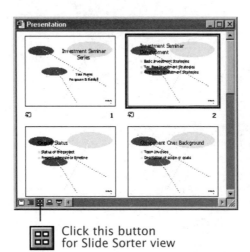

Click this button for Slide Sorter view

Click this button for Notes Pages view

Changing Presentation Views

The view buttons at the bottom of the presentation window let you view or work on your presentation in different ways—in Slide view, Outline view, Slide Sorter view, and Notes Pages view. These view commands are also available on the View menu.

Change to Slide view

You can change to Slide view and look at the slide you just changed in your outline. In Slide view, you can see how the title and paragraph text appear on the slide. PowerPoint changes the view of the current slide when you click one of the view buttons.

Slide View

➤ Click the Slide View button.

 TIP Double-clicking the slide number or slide icon in Outline view also takes you to the selected slide in Slide view.

Your presentation window should look like the following illustration:

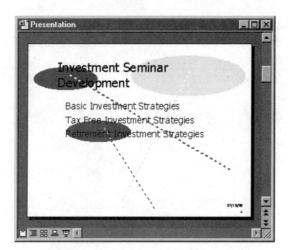

Changes to the text that you make in Outline view appear in Slide view. You change text in Slide view the same way you change text in Outline view.

Moving from Slide to Slide

To move from one slide to another in Slide view or Notes Pages view, click the Next Slide and Previous Slide buttons located in the lower-right corner of the presentation window to move one slide at a time. To move more than one slide at a time, drag the scroll box in the vertical scroll bar. As you drag the scroll box, a slide indicator box appears showing you the number of the slide you're about to display.

Move from slide to slide

Previous Slide

1 Click the Previous Slide button.

Slide 1 appears in Slide view. Use the Next Slide button to look at the slides in your presentation.

Next Slide

2 Click the Next Slide button until you reach the end of the presentation.

As you can see, each slide contains suggestions for how you might develop and organize your presentation.

3 Drag the scroll box up the vertical scroll bar to view slide 3, but don't release the mouse button.

Your presentation window should look like the following illustration:

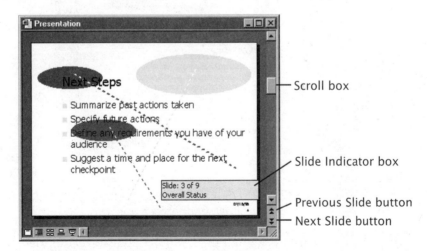

A slide indicator box appears, telling you which slide is selected. The scroll box displays the slide number and title, and indicates the relative position of the slide in the presentation on the scroll bar.

4 Release the mouse button.

The status bar changes from "Slide 9 of 9" to "Slide 3 of 9."

> **TIP** In Slide view or Notes Pages view, you can press the PAGE UP key or click above the scroll box to view the previous slide, or press the PAGE DOWN key or click below the scroll box to view the next slide.

Changing and Adding Text in Slide View

You can work with your presentation's text in Slide or Outline view. In Slide view you work with one slide at a time, while in Outline view you can view and edit text for all your slides at once.

Change text in Slide view

I

I-beam Cursor

1 Position your pointer (which changes to an I-beam) over the title text in slide 3 and click to let PowerPoint know that you want to change text.

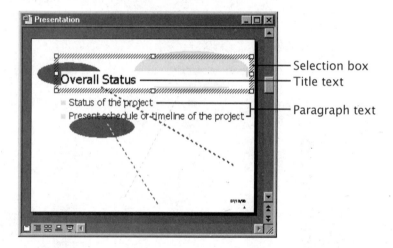

The text is surrounded by a rectangle of gray slanted lines called a *selection box* with the I-beam cursor placed in the text. The selection box lets PowerPoint know what object you want to change on the slide. An object containing slide text is called a *text object*. A typical slide contains a title, called *title text*, and the major points beneath the title, called *paragraph* or *bullet* text.

2 Drag to select the title text "Overall Status."

3 Type **Seminar Development Status**

4 Position your pointer (which changes to an I-beam) over any of the bulleted text in slide 3 and click.

5 Drag to select the text "Status of the project."

6 Type **Content Development Stage**

7 Drag to select the text "Present schedule or timeline of the project."

8 Type **Final Content Scheduled for Q2**

Add text in Slide view

To add more bulleted text to the text object, you place the insertion point at the end of a line of text and press ENTER. With the insertion point at the end of the text, add another line of text.

1 Press ENTER to create a new bullet.

A new bullet automatically appears in the outline.

2 Type **Seminar Rollout Scheduled for Q4**

3 Click outside of the selection box to deselect the text object.

Your presentation window should look like the following illustration:

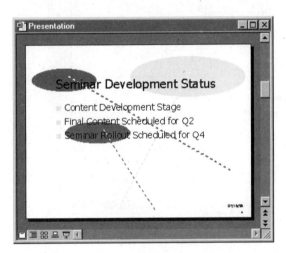

Previewing Slides in Slide Sorter View

Another way to view your presentation is to use Slide Sorter view. Slide Sorter view allows you to preview your entire presentation as if you were looking at slides on a light board. In this view—as well as in Outline view—you can easily rearrange the order of the slides in your presentation, which you'll learn in Lesson 2, "Working with a Presentation."

367

Change to Slide Sorter view and preview slides

Slide Sorter View

1   Click the Slide Sorter View button.

All the slides now appear in miniature on the screen, and the slide you were viewing (the one with the insertion point) in Slide view is surrounded by a black box indicating that the slide is selected. Just as you scrolled through Outline view to see all the slides in your presentation, you can do the same in Slide Sorter view.

2   Click below the scroll box in the scroll bar to see the slides at the end of the presentation.

3   Click above the scroll box.

The top of Slide Sorter view appears.

Your presentation window should look like the following illustration:

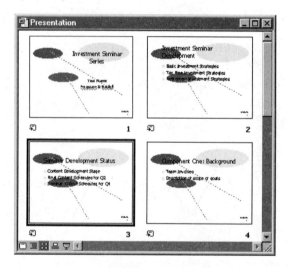

When slides are formatted in Slide Sorter view, titles might be hard to read. PowerPoint allows you to suppress the slide formatting to read the slide titles.

4   Hold down the ALT key and click and hold the mouse button on an individual slide.

The formatting for the slide disappears and the title appears clearly. When you release the mouse button, the display format reappears.

Change to a specific slide in Slide view

In Slide Sorter view, you can double-click a slide miniature to switch to Slide view for a specific slide. Try switching to slide 1 in Slide view.

   Double-click slide 1.

The presentation view changes to Slide view showing slide 1.

Saving a Presentation

The work you've done is currently stored only in the computer's memory. To save the work for further use, you must give the presentation a name and store it on your hard drive.

Save

Look In Favorites

If you have not installed the Part4 Power-Point Practice files, refer to "Installing and Using the Prac-tice and Cam-corder Files," earlier in this book.

1   On the Standard toolbar, click the Save button.

The Save dialog box appears.

2   In the Save dialog box, click the Look In Favorites button.

The Favorites folder appears in the Save In box. The Part4 PowerPoint Practice folder appears in the list of folders and files.

3   Double-click the Part4 PowerPoint Practice folder.

Part4 PowerPoint Practice appears in the Save In box, and the names of the practice files appear in the files list.

4   In the File Name box, type **F&B Report Pres 01**

The Word "Pres" in the file name is an abbreviation for Presentation.

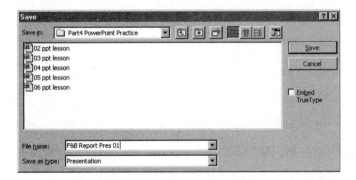

 TIP   You can save a slide as an overhead picture to use in other programs. Display or select the slide that you want to save and click Save As on the File menu. In the Save As Type box, click Windows Metafile and click the Save button.

5   Click the Save button or press ENTER to save the presentation.

The Title bar name changes from "Presentation" to "F&B Report Pres 01."

One Step Further

In this lesson, you have learned how to start PowerPoint and use the AutoContent Wizard to enter your ideas into a PowerPoint presentation. In addition, you have learned how to enter and change text in Slide and Outline views, how to switch between views, how to move from slide to slide, and how to preview and save your presentation.

Add presentation properties

With PowerPoint's Presentation Properties dialog box, you can enter information about your presentation that will help you find the file if you forget its name or location. You can use the property information to search for your presentation by its contents, a keyword, or a date.

1   On the File menu, click Properties.

The Presentation Properties dialog box appears displaying summary information. Generally, you should enter keywords that might help you identify the file later.

2   In the Category text box on the Summary tab, type **Progress Report**

3   In the Keywords text box, type **Investment Seminars**

You can click other tabs in the Presentation Properties dialog to display other information about your presentation.

4   Click the OK button.

If you want to continue to the next lesson

1   On the File menu, click Close (CTRL+W).

2   If a dialog box appears asking whether you want to save the changes to your presentation, click the Yes button.

If you want to quit PowerPoint for now

1   On the File menu, click Exit (CTRL+Q).

2   If a dialog box appears asking whether you want to save the changes to your presentation, click the Yes button.

Lesson Summary

To	Do this	Button
Create a presentation using the AutoContent Wizard	In the PowerPoint Startup dialog box, click the AutoContent Wizard option button.	
Scroll in a window	Click a scroll arrow on the vertical or horizontal scroll bars.	
Change text in Outline view or Slide view	Select the text and then make the changes you want.	
Reverse an action	On the Edit menu, click Undo or click the Undo toolbar button.	
Redo an undo action	On the Edit menu, click Redo or click the Redo toolbar button.	
Change presentation views	Click any of the view buttons: Slide, Outline, Slide Sorter, Notes Pages, or Slide Show.	
Move from slide to slide	Click the Next Slide button or click the Previous Slide button.	
Preview slide miniatures	Click the Slide Sorter View button.	
Save a new presentation	On the File menu, click Save or click the Save toolbar button.	
Enter presentation properties	On the File menu, click Properties and type text in the appropriate text box.	
End a PowerPoint session	On the File menu, click Exit.	

For online information about	Use the Office Assistant to search for
Creating a presentation	**Create a presentation**, and then click Create A New Presentation
Using Slide or Slide Sorter views	**Slide view** or **Slide Sorter view**, and then click PowerPoint Views

Lesson
2

Working with a Presentation

In this lesson you will learn how to:

Estimated time
40 min.

- Start a new presentation.
- Enter text in a slide.
- Create new slides.
- Enter text in an outline.
- Insert slides from other presentations.
- Rearrange slides.
- Create speaker's notes pages.
- Show your slides in Slide Show view.

To work efficiently with PowerPoint, you need to become familiar with the important features of the product. In the previous lesson, you learned how to create a presentation using the AutoContent Wizard, change title and paragraph text, change views, move from slide to slide, and preview slides.

After quickly and easily creating a progress report presentation for the investment seminar series, you decide to use PowerPoint to develop the seminar content. The next step is to start a new presentation and develop the content for the first investment seminar, "Basic Investment Strategies."

In this lesson, you'll learn how to start a new presentation with a presentation design, enter slide text, create new slides, insert slides from other presentations, rearrange slides in Slide Sorter view, enter text in Notes Pages view, and show your slides in Slide Show view.

373

Starting a New Presentation

In addition to starting a presentation with sample text from the AutoContent Wizard, as you did in Lesson 1, you can also start a new presentation without any text, with a pre-formatted or blank design. To start a new presentation, use the New command on the File menu.

Start a new presentation with a presentation design

If you quit PowerPoint at the end of the last lesson, restart PowerPoint now.

1 If you have just restarted PowerPoint, in the PowerPoint Startup dialog box, click the Template option button, and then click the OK button.

or

If you are continuing from the previous lesson, click the File menu and then click New.

The New Presentation dialog box appears.

2 Click the Presentation Designs tab.

A list of different presentation designs appears.

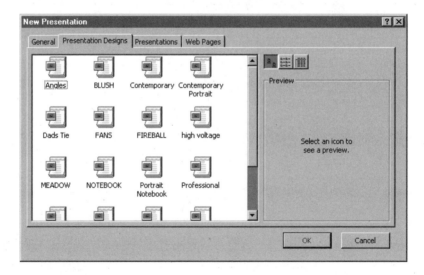

From the New Presentation dialog box, you can also start a blank presentation from the General tab, start an AutoContent Wizard from the Presentations tab, or create Internet pages from the Web Pages tab.

3 Click the Contemporary icon.

A sample slide appears in the Preview box.

4 Click the OK button.

The New Slide dialog box appears. You can choose a different layout for each slide to create a specific design look, such as a slide with a graph. Choose a layout by clicking it in the AutoLayout gallery list. You can scroll down to see more layouts. The layout title for the selected slide type appears to the right of the gallery list.

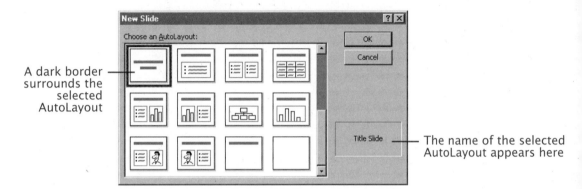

A dark border surrounds the selected AutoLayout

The name of the selected AutoLayout appears here

5 Click the OK button to use the default Title Slide.

The title slide appears in the presentation window.

Entering Text in Slide View

The new presentation window includes an empty slide with two text boxes called *text placeholders*. The box at the top is a placeholder for the slide's title text. The lower box is a placeholder for the slide's subtitle text. After you enter text into a placeholder, the placeholder becomes a *text object*.

Type title and subtitle text in Slide view

To give your slide a title, you can click the title placeholder and start typing.

1 Click the text "Click to add title."

The placeholder is surrounded by a rectangle of gray slanted lines called a *selection box* to indicate that the placeholder is ready to enter or edit text. A blinking insertion point appears.

2 Type **Basic Investment Strategies**

3 Click the text "Click to add sub-title."

The title object is deselected, and the subtitle object is selected.

4 Type *Your Name* and press ENTER.

5 Type **Ferguson & Bardell**

Your presentation window should look like the following illustration:

Title text ——

Subtitle text ——

Selection box

> **TIP** PowerPoint may display a wavy-red line under words that are misspelled or not recognized by the dictionary. For more information, see Lesson 4, "Adding and Modifying Text."

Creating a New Slide in Slide View

You can create a new slide in your presentation using the New Slide button on the Standard toolbar, or the New Slide command on the Insert menu.

Create a new slide

New Slide

1. On the Standard toolbar, click the New Slide button.

   The New Slide dialog box appears.

2. Click the OK button to use the default Bulleted List.

   A new empty slide is added after the current slide in Slide view. The Status bar displays "Slide 2 of 2."

> **TIP** You can hold down SHIFT and click the New Slide button to add a new slide that has the same layout as the current slide without having to select the layout from the New Slide dialog box.

Enter text in a new slide

If you start typing on an empty slide with nothing selected, PowerPoint enters the text into the title object.

> Type **Develop An Investment Plan**

PowerPoint lets you work directly in Slide view or Outline view to enter your ideas. Let's change views and complete this slide in Outline view.

Change to Outline view

Outline view shows your presentation text in outline form just as if you had typed the text in Microsoft Word. From Slide view, switch to Outline view.

Outline View

> Click the Outline View button.

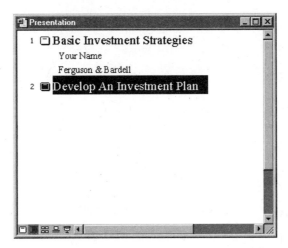

Slide Icon

A slide icon appears to the left of each slide's title. Body text underneath each title appears indented one level. The title from slide 2 is selected, as shown in the following illustration:

Entering Text in Outline View

To enter text in Outline view, position the insertion point where you want the text to start or click New Slide on the Standard toolbar, and begin typing. Adding a new slide in Outline view creates a new slide icon.

Enter paragraph text

In this section, you'll change a paragraph text indent level and type in paragraph text to complete slide 2. If you make a mistake as you type, press the BACKSPACE key to delete the mistake and then type the correct text.

1 Click to the right of the title in slide 2.

A blinking insertion point appears.

2 Press ENTER.

PowerPoint adds a new slide. To add paragraph text to slide 2 instead of starting a new slide, change the outline level from slide title to a bullet.

Demote

3 On the Outlining toolbar, click the Demote button or press the TAB key.

The Demote button indents your text to the right one level and moves the text from slide 3 to slide 2. The slide icon changes to a small bullet on slide 2.

4 Type **Diversity** and press ENTER.

A new bullet is added at the same indent level.

5 Type **Invest for Your Goals and Objectives** and press ENTER.

6 Type **Re-Evaluate Your Portfolio Regularly**

Create a new slide and enter text

With the insertion point after the word "Regularly," create a new slide from an indented outline level using a toolbar button and a keyboard command.

1 Press ENTER.

Promote

2 On the Outlining toolbar, click the Promote button.

A new slide is created with the insertion point to the right of the slide icon. Type title and paragraph text.

3 Type **Focus on Your Objectives** and press ENTER.

4 Press TAB.

A new indent level is created for slide 3. Now enter three bullet points under slide 3 at the same indent level to finish the slide.

5 Type **Retirement** and press ENTER.

6 Type **Education** and press ENTER.

7 Type **Tax Free**

8 Hold down the CTRL key and press ENTER.

A new slide is created using a keyboard command.

9 Type **Summary**, press ENTER, and then press TAB.

A new indent level is created for slide 4.

10 Type **Develop an Investment Plan Tailored to Your Objectives** and press ENTER.

11 Type **Begin Your Investment Program as Early as Possible** and press ENTER.

12 Type **Diversify Your Investment Portfolio**

Insert new text

You can easily insert new text anywhere in Outline view and in Slide view.

1   Position the I-beam cursor just after the word "Regularly" and click.

This places the blinking insertion point where you are to begin typing, as shown in the following illustration:

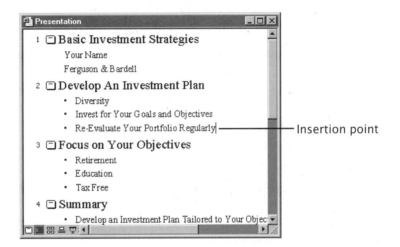

Insertion point

TROUBLESHOOTING   If the insertion point is not where you want it, reposition the I-beam cursor and click again to place the insertion point in the desired location.

---

2   Press the SPACEBAR and type **and Make Adjustments as Needed**

PowerPoint makes room in the outline for the new text.

Select and replace text

You can select individual characters, sentences, paragraph text, or title text in either Outline or Slide view. Selecting text in PowerPoint works just as it does in Microsoft Word 97 for Windows.

1   Position the I-beam cursor over any part of the word "Free" in the third bullet point of slide 3.

2   Double-click to select the word.

To select one or more words or characters, you can also drag.

Your presentation window should look like the following illustration:

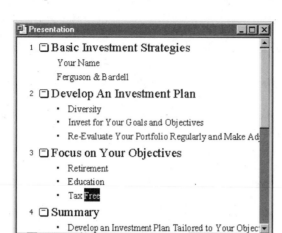

The text is now highlighted, indicating it has been selected. When you double-click a word, PowerPoint also selects the space that follows. This maintains correct spacing if you delete a word. Once you've selected text, the next text you type—regardless of its length—replaces the selection.

3 Type **Reduction**

The new word replaces the text in the outline.

Select and rearrange text

You can easily select and rearrange title and paragraph text in Outline and Slide views. In Outline view, you can select and rearrange text, a range of text, an individual slide, or a group of slides. To select paragraph text or an individual slide, click the associated bullet or slide icon to its left.

Four-headed Arrow

Move Up

1 Move your pointer over the bullet titled "Tax Reduction" in slide 3.

The pointer changes to a four-headed arrow.

2 Click the bullet to select the entire line.

3 On the Outlining toolbar, click the Move Up button.

The entire line moves up one level.

4 Double-click slide 3 to display the slide in Slide view.

Inserting Slides from Other Presentations

You can save time creating a presentation by using work that has already been done by you or a co-worker. When you insert slides from another presentation, the new slides conform to the color and design of your presentation, so you don't have to make many changes.

Insert slides into your presentation

1 On the Insert menu, click Slides From Files.

The Slide Finder dialog box appears.

2 Click the Browse button.

The Insert Slides From Files dialog box appears.

3 Click the Look In Favorites button.

*Look In
Favorites*

The Part4 PowerPoint Practice folder appears in the list of folders and files.

4 Double-click the Part4 PowerPoint Practice folder.

5 In the list of file names, click 02 PPT Lesson and then click the Open button.

The Slide Finder dialog box appears.

6 Click the Display button.

For a demonstration of how to insert slides, double-click the Camcorder file named Inserting Slides in the Part4 Power-Point Camcorder Files folder. Seè "Installing and Using the Practice and Camcorder Files," earlier in this book for more information.

7 Click slide 2, click slide 3, click the right scroll arrow, and then click slide 4 to select the slides you want to insert.

Your Slide Finder dialog box should look like the following illustration:

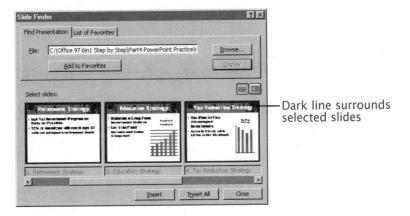

Dark line surrounds selected slides

8 Click the Insert button.

PowerPoint inserts the slides into your presentation after the current slide.

9 Click the Close button.

The last inserted slide appears in Slide view.

Rearranging Slides in Slide Sorter View

After copying slides from your other presentation into your new one, you'll want to rearrange the slides into the order that most effectively communicates your message.

Move a slide in Slide Sorter view

In Slide Sorter view, you can drag one or more slides from one location to another.

Slide Sorter View

Insert Pointer

1 Click the Slide Sorter View button.

2 Click slide 6.

3 Drag the slide between slide 4 and slide 5.

You'll notice the mouse pointer changes to an insert pointer when you begin to drag. When you release the mouse button, slide 5 and slide 6 move to their new positions and the other slides in the presentation are repositioned and renumbered.

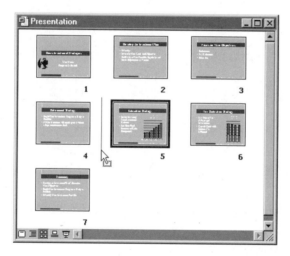

4 Click the scroll up arrow and click slide 2.

5 On the Standard toolbar, click the Zoom Control drop-down arrow and click 50%.

Zoom Control

TIP In Slide Sorter view, you can also move slides between two or more open presentations. Open each presentation, switch to Slide Sorter view, and click Arrange All on the Window menu. Drag the slides from one presentation window to the other.

Entering Text in Notes Pages View

In Notes Pages view, you can create speaker's notes for your presentation. Each slide in your presentation has a corresponding notes page. At the top of each notes page is a reduced image of the slide. To enter speaker's notes, on a notes page, change to Notes Pages view, select the Notes placeholder, and begin typing. Entering and changing text in Notes Pages view works the same as it does in Slide view. You can also enter speaker notes from other views by clicking Speaker Notes on the View menu.

Notes Pages View

1 Click the Notes Pages View button.

Notes Pages view appears at 33% view for most screens to display the entire page. Your view scale might be different depending on the size of your monitor.

Your presentation window should look like the following illustration:

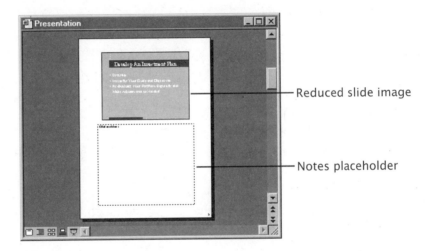

Reduced slide image

Notes placeholder

2 Click the Notes placeholder to select it.

Zoom Control

3 On the Standard toolbar, click the Zoom Control drop-down arrow and click 75%.

The view scale size increases to 75%, and displays the selected Notes placeholder for the notes page.

4 Type the paragraph below without pressing the ENTER key. If you make a mistake as you type, press the BACKSPACE key to delete the mistake, and type the correct text.

While no investment portfolio is right for everyone, there are a few elements to keep in mind as you plan your investment strategy.

Move from notes page to notes page

In Notes Pages view, you can move from notes page to notes page in the same way as in Slide view.

Next Slide

1 Click the Next Slide button.

2 Click the Notes placeholder to select it.

3 Type **Many investors believe these three investment objectives are important elements in their investment plans. As you plan, define your goals and the time you need to obtain them.**

4 On the Standard toolbar, click the Zoom Control drop-down arrow and click Fit.

Slide View

5 Click the Slide View button.

Switching to Slide view saves your presentation in Slide view instead of Notes Pages view.

Save the presentation

Save

1 On the Standard toolbar, click the Save button.

PowerPoint displays the Save dialog box.

2 Click the Look In Favorites button.

Look In Favorites

3 Double-click the Part4 PowerPoint Practice folder.

4 In the File Name box, type **F&B Training Pres 02**

For information about saving a presentation, see Lesson 1, "Creating a Presentation."

The "02" at the end of the presentation file name matches the lesson number.

5 Click the Save button.

PowerPoint saves the presentation with the new name F&B Training Pres 02, which appears in the title bar.

Showing Your Slides in Slide Show View

For information about using slide show, see Lesson 6, "Producing a Slide Show."

Now that you have saved your presentation, review the slides for accuracy and flow. You can review your slides easily in Slide Show view. Slide Show view displays your slides using the entire screen as an on-screen presentation on your computer.

1 Drag the scroll box to slide 1.

2 Click the Slide Show button.

Slide Show

PowerPoint displays the first slide in the presentation.

3 Click to advance to the next slide.

4 Click once for each slide to advance through the presentation.

After the last slide in the presentation, PowerPoint returns to the current view.

One Step Further

You have learned how to open a presentation, insert and rearrange text, insert new slides, insert slides from other presentations, and rearrange slides in Slide Sorter view. You can open recently used files by accessing them on the File menu. With the Options command, you can change the number of recently used files that appear on the File menu.

Change PowerPoint options

1 On the Tools menu, click Options, and then click the General tab.

2 Click the Recently Used File List up arrow twice to reach 6 entries, as shown in the following illustration:

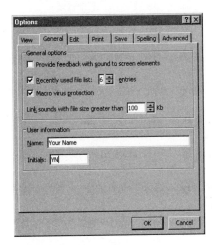

3 Click the OK button.

4 Click the File menu to see the expanded list of recently used files, and then press the ESC key to cancel the menu.

If you want to continue to the next lesson

1 On the File menu, click Close (CTRL+W).

2 If a dialog box appears asking whether you want to save the changes to your presentation, click the Yes button.

If you want to quit PowerPoint for now

1 On the File menu, click Exit (CTRL+Q).

2 If a dialog box appears asking whether you want to save the changes to your presentation, click the Yes button.

Lesson Summary

To	Do this	Button
Start a new presentation using a presentation design	On the File menu, click New, and then click a tab for the presentation type. Double-click a presentation icon.	
Type title or subtitle text on a slide	Click the title object or subtitle text object and begin typing.	
Create a new slide	Click the Insert New Slide button on the Standard toolbar or click New Slide on the Insert menu.	![button]
Insert slides from a presentation file	On the Insert menu, click Slides From Files. Click Browse to select a file. Click Display and click the slides you want to insert. Click Insert and click Close.	
Rearrange slides in Slide Sorter view	Select slides in Slide Sorter view. Drag the slides to the new location.	![button]
Enter text in Notes Pages view	Click the Notes Pages View button. Click the placeholder and type.	![button]
Show your slides in Slide Show	Click the Slide Show button. Click each slide.	![button]
Change PowerPoint options	On the Tools menu, click Options.	

For online information about	Use the Office Assistant to search for
Using a presentation template	**Design template**, and then click Create A New Presentation
Making a new slide	**New slide**, and then click Make A New Slide
Creating speaker's notes pages	**Notes pages**, and then click Create Speaker Notes And Handouts

Printing a Presentation

In this lesson you will learn how to:

Estimated time
20 min.

- Open an existing presention.
- Preview slides in black and white.
- Add a header and footer.
- Change a presentation slide setup.
- Choose a printer.
- Print presentation slides, audience handouts, and speaker's notes.

PowerPoint gives you great flexibility for printing both the slides of the presentation and any additional supplements. For example, you can preview your presentation in black and white to see how color slides will look after printing, add headers and footers, and print your presentation slides, speaker's notes, audience handouts, and outlines. You can easily customize the printing process by selecting paper size, page orientation, print range, and printer type to meet your needs.

As the Director of Communications for Ferguson & Bardell, you want to create a series of investment seminars. In the previous lesson you created a Basic Investment Seminar presentation, and now you'd like to open and print the presentation and accompanying speaker's notes pages.

In this lesson, you'll learn how to open an existing presentation, preview slides in black and white, add a footer and header, choose a printer, print slides, speaker's notes, and audience handouts, and change a slide size.

Opening an Existing Presentation

You can open an existing presentation—one that you or a co-worker have already created—and work on it in the same way you would a new presentation. To open an existing presentation, you must first tell PowerPoint the name of the presentation and where it's located. You do this by using the Open command on the File menu.

Open a presentation

Open

Look In Favorites

1 On the Standard toolbar click the Open button, or click the File menu and then click Open to display a list of presentations.

PowerPoint displays the Open dialog box.

2 Click the Look In Favorites button.

3 Double-click the Part4 PowerPoint Practice folder.

If you don't remember the name of a presentation file but you know some of the presentation contents, you can search for the presentation.

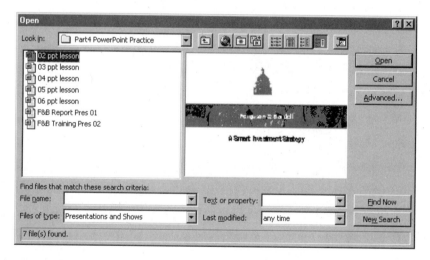

4 Click the Text Or Property text box to place the insertion point.

5 Type **Basic Investment**

The next time you would like to find presentations with Basic Investments in it, you can click the Text Or Property drop-down arrow and click Basic Investment in the list. PowerPoint remembers what you enter.

6   Click the Find Now button.

The Find Now button changes to Stop as PowerPoint searches through your presentation and then changes back to Find Now when the search is complete. The presentations that meet the search criteria in the current folder are displayed in the list of file and folder names.

7   In the list of file names, click 03 PPT Lesson, if it's not already selected.

TIP   You can also click the Advanced button to search for files on your hard drive by property and text criteria. In the Advanced dialog box, select and type your search information, add the criteria to the match list, and then click the Find Now button.

---

8   Click the Open button.

PowerPoint displays the presentation 03 PPT Lesson.

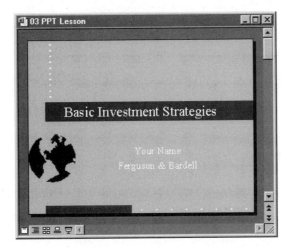

TIP   PowerPoint makes it easy to open recently used files by adding your most recently opened presentation names to the bottom of the File menu. You can open one of these presentations by clicking the file name.

Previewing Slides in Black and White

If you are printing a color presentation on a black and white printer, you need to be sure it will be legible on paper. For example, dark red text against a shaded background shows up in color, but when seen in black and white or shades of gray, the text might be indistinguishable from the background. To prevent this, you can preview your color slides in black and white to see how they will look when printed on a black and white or grayscale printer.

Change to black and white view

Black And White View

1 On the Standard toolbar, click the Black And White View button.

Your slide switches from color to black and white and a slide miniature window appears showing the slide in color. The slide miniature window shows your slide in the opposite color view, making it easier to compare how your slide looks in both color and black and white.

Next Slide

2 Click the Next Slide button.

The next slide also appears in black and white and the slide miniature in color.

Slide Sorter View

3 Click the Slide Sorter View button.

All the slides in the Slide Sorter view also appear in black and white.

4 Double-click slide 2.

Black And White View

5 On the Standard toolbar, click the Black And White View button.

Your slide switches back to color and the slide miniature window closes.

View a slide miniature in black and white

Instead of clicking the Black And White View button back and forth to see how your presentation looks in color and in black and white, you can simply click the slide miniature window.

1 On the View menu, click Slide Miniature.

The slide miniature window appears with the slide in black and white.

2 Right-click the Slide Miniature window and then click Color View.

The display changes from black and white to color.

3 Click the Slide Miniature window Close button.

Adding a Header and Footer

Before you print your work, consider adding a header or footer that can appear on every page, such as your company name or product name. You can add a header and footer to your slides, speaker's notes, and audience handouts quickly and easily with the Header And Footer command on the View menu. This command also allows you to add and customize the slide number and date.

Add a header and footer to your presentation

1   On the View menu, click Header And Footer.

The Header and Footer dialog box appears.

2   Click the Footer check box and type **Ferguson & Bardell**

In the Preview box, a black rectangle highlights the placement of the footer.

Your dialog box should look like the following illustration:

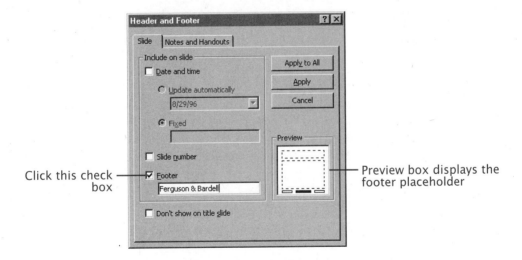

Click this check box ——— (points to Footer check box)

——— Preview box displays the footer placeholder

3   Click the Notes And Handouts tab.

The header and footer settings for the Notes and Handout pages appear.

4   Click the Page Number check box.

5   Click the Header check box and type **F&B Investments**

6   Click the Apply To All button.

The header and footer information is applied to your slides, notes pages, and handouts pages. Notice that the current slide appears with the footer in place.

Changing the Page Setup

The page setup determines the size and orientation of your slides, notes pages, handouts, and outline on the printed page. For a new presentation, PowerPoint opens with default slide format settings: on-screen show, landscape orientation, and slide numbers starting at one, which you can change at any time.

Change the slide size

Change the slide size setting from On-screen Show to Letter Paper.

1   On the File menu, click Page Setup.

   The Page Setup dialog box appears.

2   Click the Slides Sized For drop-down arrow.

   Your dialog box should look like the following illustration:

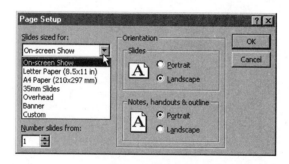

PowerPoint has seven slide size formats to choose from:

On-screen Show   Use this setting when designing an on-screen slide show. The slide size for the screen is smaller than the Letter Paper size.

Letter Paper (8.5 x 11 in)   Use this setting when printing a presentation on U.S. letter-size paper (8.5 x 11 in).

A4 Paper (210 x 297 mm)   Use this setting when printing on international A4 paper (210 x 297 mm or 10.83 x 7.5 in).

35mm Slides   Use this setting when designing a presentation for 35mm slides. The slide size is slightly reduced to produce the slides.

Overhead   Use this setting when printing overhead transparencies on U.S. letter-size paper (8.5 x 11 in).

Banner   Use this setting when designing a banner (8 x 1 in).

Custom   Use this setting to design a presentation with a special size. Change the width and height settings to create a custom size.

3   Click Letter Paper (8.5 x 11 in).

4   Click the OK button.

Choosing a Printer

PowerPoint prints presentations on the default Windows printer unless you select a different printer. Your default printer is set up in the Windows 95 or Windows NT print settings. You can select another printer in PowerPoint's Print dialog box.

1   Make sure your printer is turned on and connected to your computer.

2   On the File menu, click Print.

The Print dialog box appears.

3   In the Printer area, click the Name drop-down arrow.

A drop-down list appears with the installed printers on your computer. Your list of installed printers might look different than the following illustration:

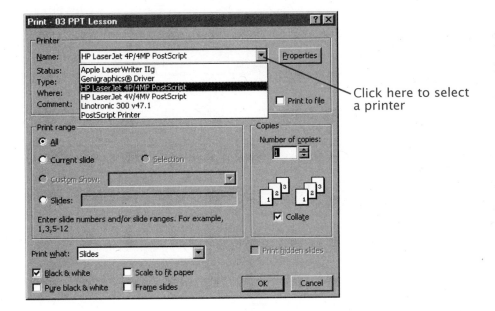

Click here to select a printer

4   Click a printer.

After choosing a printer, you can customize your printer settings.

5   Click the Properties button.

The Properties dialog box appears, showing current printer settings. The Properties dialog settings differ depending on your specific printer.

6   Click the OK button.

The Properties dialog closes to display the Print dialog box.

Printing in PowerPoint

PowerPoint allows you to print your presentation in four different ways: You can print slides, speaker's notes, audience handouts, and the outline. A sample of each printing type is shown in the following illustrations:

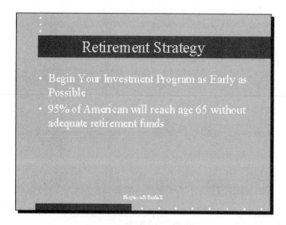

Slide (landscape)

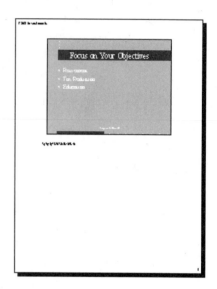

Notes Page

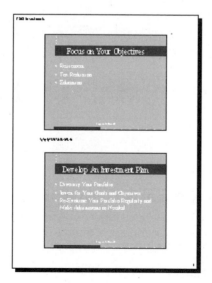

Handout Page

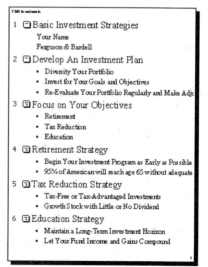

Outline

Printing Slides, Handouts, and Notes

PowerPoint makes it easy to print your slides, audience handouts, and speaker's notes with the Print command. When you use the Print command to print your slides or presentation supplements, PowerPoint automatically detects the type of printer chosen and prints the appropriate color or black and white version of the slides.

Print presentation slides

Print

PowerPoint prints your slides based on the settings in the Print dialog box. If you know the current Print dialog box settings, you can click the Print button on the Standard toolbar to print directly. Otherwise, choose the Print command on the File menu to print with new settings.

1   On the File menu, click Print, if the Print dialog box is not already displayed.

The Print dialog box appears.

2   Click the Print What drop-down arrow.

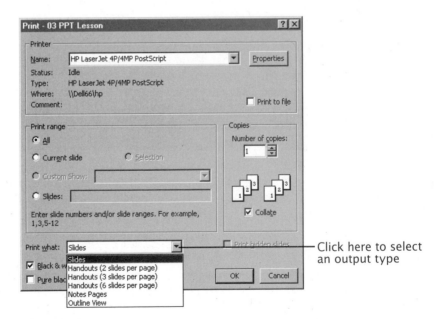

Click here to select an output type

Six print options are available.

Slides   Prints your slides as they appear on the screen, one per page.

Handouts (2 slides per page)   Prints two slides per page.

Handouts (3 slides per page)   Prints three slides per page.

Handouts (6 slides per page)   Prints six slides per page.

Notes Pages   Prints the speaker's notes pages that correspond to the slide numbers selected in the Print Range.

Outline View   Prints your outline according to the current view setting. What you see in Outline view is what you get on the printout.

3   In the Print What drop-down list, click Slides.

4   In the Print Range area, click the Current Slide option button.

5   Click the OK button.

When you click the OK button, PowerPoint prints the current slide in your presentation. A small print icon appears in the status bar, giving your printing status.

NOTE   In PowerPoint, your presentation slides automatically size to the printer you have chosen. Using scalable fonts such as TrueType fonts allows you to print your presentation on different printers with the same great results.

Print audience handouts

You can print audience handouts in three different formats: 2 slides per page, 3 slides per page, and 6 slides per page. When printing the audience handouts, you'll add a frame around the slides.

1   On the File menu, click Print.

The Print dialog box appears.

2   Click the Print What drop-down arrow and click Handouts (2 slides per page).

To enhance the look of your audience handouts, you click the Frame Slides check box at the bottom of the Print dialog box, which adds a black frame or border around the slides.

3   Click the Frame Slides check box, if it is not already checked.

The print options available in the Print dialog box include the following:

Print to File   Use this option to print slides to a presentation file that you can send to a Genigraphics service center. See "One Step Further" later in this lesson for more information.

Collate   Use this option to print multiple copies of your presentation. This option is usually available for laser printers only.

Print Hidden Slides   Use this option to print all hidden slides.

Scale to Fit Paper   Use this only if the paper in the printer does not correspond to the slide size and orientation settings. This option scales slides automatically to fit the paper size in the printer.

Black & White   Use this option to turn all fills to white (or black and white, if patterned). Unbordered objects that have no text appear with a thin black frame.

Pure Black & White   Use this option when printing draft copies of your presentation on a color printer. This option turns all color fills to white, turns all text and lines to black, adds outlines or borders to all filled objects, and renders pictures in grayscale.

Frame Slides   Prints a frame around the presentation slides.

4   Click the OK button.

A small print icon appears in the status bar, giving your printing status.

Print speaker's notes

You can print speaker's notes in the same way you print presentation slides. A reduced image of the presentation slide prints on each notes page. Before you print the speaker's notes, you'll want to turn off the Frame Slides option in the Print dialog box.

1   On the File menu, click Print.

The Print dialog box appears.

2   Click the Print What drop-down arrow, scroll down, and click Notes Pages.

3   In the Print Range area, click the Slides option button.

The insertion point appears in the range box.

4   Type **1-3,5**

The numbers 1-3 appear in the slide range. PowerPoint will print notes pages 1 through 3 and page 5. You can print notes pages or slides in any order by entering slide numbers and ranges separated by commas.

5   Click the Frame Slides check box, if it is checked.

6   Click the OK button.

A print message box appears, giving your printing status.

Save the presentation

1   On the File menu, click Save As.

The Save As dialog box opens. Be sure the Part4 PowerPoint Practice folder appears in the Save In box.

2   In the File Name box, type **F&B Training Pres 03**

3   Click the Save button.

The presentation is saved and the title bar changes to the new name.

One Step Further

In this lesson, you have learned to preview slides in black and white, add headers and footers to slides, notes pages, and handouts, set your slide format, and print your presentation in different ways. You can also send your presentation to a Genigraphics Service Center that will create 35mm color slides directly from your PowerPoint slides.

Order 35mm slides from Genigraphics

If Genigraphics is grayed out, this wizard might not be installed. To install it, run the Office 97 Professional Setup program and add the PowerPoint Genigraphics Wizard & GraphicsLink option.

1   On the File menu, point to Send To, and then click Genigraphics.

The Genigraphics Wizard displays an introduction dialog box. Read the instructions carefully before you continue.

2   Click the Next button.

The Genigraphics Wizard asks you what output products and services you would like to order.

3   Click the 35mm check box to select the option, if necessary.

4   Click the Next button.

The Genigraphics Wizard asks you what presentation file you would like to send. Your active presentation file is selected by default.

5   If you have a modem installed, click the Send Via Direct Dial Modem option button; if you have an Internet connection, click the Send Via Internet Connection; otherwise click the Send On Disk option button.

6   Click the Next button and follow the instructions until the wizard indicates that your order is ready to send on disk or to transmit.

The Genigraphics Wizard asks you to choose slide mounts and to provide information about processing your order, shipping, and billing.

7   Click the Finish button.

The Genigraphics Wizard transmits your presentation file to a Genigraphics Service Center or saves it on disk.

If you selected the Send File Via Modem option, the Genigraphics Wizard transmits your presentation file using GraphicsLink (Graflink). A Send Status dialog appears, showing you the progress of your transmission. After your transmission is final, a transmission summary appears, telling you the results of your transmission.

Graflink

GraphicsLink is an application that allows you to send your presentation file to a Genigraphics Service Center and to keep track of all presentation files, their job descriptions, and their billing information. You can also use the GraphicsLink application independently of the wizard by starting Windows Explorer or Windows NT Explorer and then double-clicking the GraphicsLink icon located in the Microsoft Office folder.

If you want to continue to the next lesson

1   On the File menu, click Close (CTRL+W).

2   If a dialog box appears asking whether you want to save the changes to your presentation, click the No button.

If you want to quit PowerPoint for now

1   On the File menu, click Exit (CTRL+Q).

2   If a dialog box appears asking whether you want to save the changes to your presentation, click the No button.

Lesson Summary

To	Do this	Button
Open a presentation	Click the File menu, and then click Open. Click the file you want to open and click the Open button.	
Preview a slide in black and white	On the Standard toolbar, click the Black and White View button.	
Add a header and footer	On the View menu, click Header And Footer. Click the appropriate check boxes and type your text.	
Change the slide format	On the File menu, click Page Setup and then select a slide format.	
Choose a printer	On the File menu, click Print. Click the Name drop-down arrow and click a printer.	
Print slides	On the File menu, click Print. Click the Print What drop-down arrow and click Slides.	
Print with the current Print dialog box settings	On the Standard toolbar, click the Print button (no dialog box appears).	
Print audience handouts	On the File menu, click Print. Click the Print What drop-down arrow and click Handouts (2, 3, or 6 slides).	
Print notes pages	On the File menu, click Print. Click the Print What drop-down arrow and click Notes Pages.	
Create 35mm slides	On the File menu, point to Send To, and then click Genigraphics.	

For online information about	Use the Office Assistant to search for
Viewing in black and white	**Black and white view**, and then click Change The View To Black And White
Adding headers and footers	**Header or footer**, and then click Add Or change The Date, Time, Slide Number, Or Footer Text
Printing a presentation	**Print slides**, and then click Print Slides, Notes, Handouts, And Outlines

Adding and Modifying Text

Estimated time
35 min.

In this lesson you will learn how to:

- Select and deselect objects.
- Correct text as you type.
- Add text to slides.
- Adjust and format text.
- Find and replace text and fonts.
- Check spelling.
- Check presentation styles.
- Look up information in Microsoft Bookshelf.

In PowerPoint, adding and modifying text is simple. PowerPoint offers several alternatives for placing text on your slides; you can use text placeholders for entering your slide titles and subtitles, text labels for short notes and phrases, text boxes for longer supporting text, and finally, you can place text inside shaped objects.

As Director of Communications at Ferguson & Bardell, you have been working on a company presentation. After working with your presentation outline in the previous lesson, you're ready to fine-tune your message.

In this lesson, you'll learn how to let PowerPoint automatically correct text while you type, create several kinds of text objects, edit text, change the appearance of text, find and replace text, replace fonts, check spelling, check presentation style, and look up information in Microsoft Bookshelf.

Start the lesson

Follow the steps below to open the practice file called 04 PPT Lesson, and then save it with the new name F&B Company Pres 04. If you haven't already started PowerPoint, do so now.

Open

1   On the Standard toolbar, click the Open button or click the Open An Existing Presentation option button on the Start-up dialog box and click OK.

2   Click the Look In Favorites button.

Look In Favorites

3   Double-click the Part4 PowerPoint Practice folder.

4   In the file list box, double-click the file named 04 PPT Lesson to open it.

5   On the File menu, click Save As.

For information about opening a presentation, see Lesson 3, "Printing a Presentation."

The Save As dialog box opens. Be sure that the Part4 PowerPoint Practice folder appears in the Save In box.

6   In the File Name box, type **F&B Company Pres 04**

7   Click the Save button.

The presentation is saved and the title bar changes to the new name.

Selecting and Deselecting Objects

To make formatting changes to all of the text in a text object, you need to select the object. To select an object, click a part of the object using the Select Objects tool or "pointer." To deselect an object, move your pointer off the object into a blank area of the slide and click.

Select and deselect a text object

Selection Cursor

1   Position the pointer near the edge of the bulleted text box until it changes to the selection cursor shown in the margin, as shown in the following illustration:

Ferguson & Bardell

Your Personal Investment Managers

2   Click the mouse button to select the text box.

The text object is surrounded by a fuzzy outline called a *dotted selection box*, indicating that it's selected and ready to be edited as an object. The white squares at each corner of the object are resize handles, which are used to adjust and resize objects.

3   Click outside the selection box to deselect the text box.

The text box is deselected.

AutoCorrecting Text While Typing

With AutoCorrect, PowerPoint automatically replaces common misspellings with the correct spelling as you type. For example, if you always type "tehm" instead of "them," you can create an AutoCorrect entry named "tehm." Whenever you type **tehm** followed by a space or punctuation mark, Power-Point replaces it with "them." Before beginning your work on the company presentation, you decide to use AutoCorrect to prevent errors in spelling the company name.

Add an AutoCorrect entry

1   On the Tools menu, click AutoCorrect.

The AutoCorrect dialog box appears.

2   In the Replace box, type **Fergusen**

Ferguson is commonly misspelled as Fergusen.

3   Press TAB.

4   In the With box, type **Ferguson**

Your AutoCorrect dialog box should look like the following illustration:

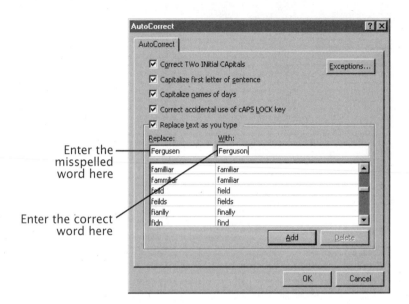

Enter the
misspelled
word here

Enter the correct
word here

Now, whenever you type Fergusen, PowerPoint will automatically re-place it with Ferguson. In the next section, you'll see this in practice.

5   Click the OK button.

Change to another slide

➤   Drag the scroll box to advance to slide 3.

Adding Text to Your Slide

Usually, slides contain a title placeholder and a main text placeholder in which to enter your main ideas, as you saw in Lesson 1. With PowerPoint, you can also place other text objects on your slide with the Text Box tool.

There are two primary types of text objects: a *text label*, which refers to text that does not word-wrap within a defined box, and a *word processing box*, which re-fers to text that word-wraps inside the boundaries of an object. You usually use a text label to enter short notes or phrases, while for longer sentences you use a word processing box.

Add text in a text object

You can add text in any PowerPoint text object by placing the insertion point where you want and typing your new text.

I-Beam Cursor

1 Click the I-beam cursor just to the right of the word "Provide" in the bulleted list to place the insertion point.

A blinking insertion point appears where you clicked the I-beam cursor.

2 Press the SPACEBAR and type **comprehensive**

The paragraph automatically wraps in the text object.

Your presentation window should look like the following illustration:

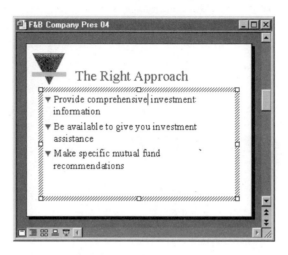

3 Click outside the slanted-line selection box to deselect the text object.

Create a text label

To create a text label on your slide, use the Text Box tool to select a place on the slide for your text, and start typing. Text created on a slide with the Text Box tool doesn't appear in Outline view. Only text entered in a title place-holder and a main text placeholder appears in Outline view.

Text Box

1 On the Drawing toolbar, click the Text Box button.

If the Drawing toolbar is not displayed, on the View menu, point to Toolbars, and then click Drawing.

2 Position your pointer at the bottom of the slide directly below the last bullet.

3 Click to create a text label.

Empty Text Box

An empty text box with a slanted-line selection appears. The slanted-line selection box lets you know you're ready to enter or edit the text within a text object. When a text box is empty, you can enter text simply by typing.

4 Type **Mutual funds are not insured by the FDIC**

405

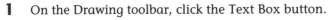

Your presentation window should look like the following illustration:

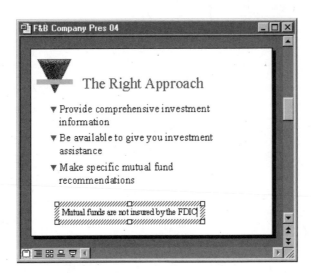

5 Click outside the slanted-line selection box to deselect the text label.

The text label is deselected.

Change to the next slide

Next Slide

➤ Click the Next Slide button to advance to slide 4.

Create a word processing box

To create a word processing box, use the Text Box tool just as you did for the text label, but instead of clicking, drag the box to the width you want and start typing.

Text Box

Cross Hairs Cursor

1 On the Drawing toolbar, click the Text Box button.

2 Position your pointer below the last bullet.

3 Drag to create a box approximately 5 inches long.

As you drag, the pointer changes to the cross hairs cursor shown to the left. When you release the mouse button, a slanted-line selection box appears. PowerPoint is ready for you to enter your text.

4 Type **Fergusen & Bardell is committed to helping you achieve your financial goals.**

As you enter your text, the misspelled word, "Fergusen," is automatically corrected with the AutoCorrect feature. The width of the box stays the same, the words wrap, and the box height increases to accommodate the complete entry.

Your presentation window should look like the following illustration:

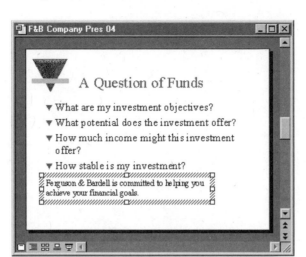

TIP You can convert a word processing box to a text label by selecting the word processing box, clicking Text Box on the Format menu, and then clicking the Text Box tab and clearing the Word-wrap Text In Autoshape check box. To convert a text label to a word processing box, add a check mark to the Word-wrap Text In Autoshape check box.

Adjusting Text

You have complete control over the placement and position of your text in PowerPoint. You can adjust the arrangement, alignment, and line spacing of text in an object to achieve the best look.

Adjust text in an object

You can adjust text in an object by setting the word-wrap option and the fit text option in the Format AutoShape dialog box. Turning on the word-wrap setting changes a text attribute from a text label to a word processing box. Turning on the fit text setting adjusts a text object to the size of the text.

Selection Cursor

1 Position the pointer near the edge of the bulleted text (which changes to the selection cursor) and click to select it.

Notice that the dotted selection box is larger than it needs to be.

2 On the Format menu, click AutoShape.

The Format AutoShape dialog box appears.

3 Click the Text Box tab.

407

4   Click the Resize Autoshape To Fit Text check box.

Click here to add
the check box

5   Click the OK button.

The object adjusts to fit the size of the text.

Change spacing between lines of text

Using PowerPoint's Line Spacing command, you can easily adjust the vertical
space between selected lines and paragraphs to achieve a certain look.

1   On the Formatting toolbar, click the Decrease Paragraph Spacing
button.

*Decrease
Paragraph
Spacing*

The paragraph spacing in the text box decreases by 0.1 from 1.0 to 0.9.
To make other line spacing changes, use the Line Spacing command.

2   On the Format menu, click Line Spacing.

The Line Spacing dialog box appears.

3   Click the Before Paragraph down arrow until 0.1 appears.

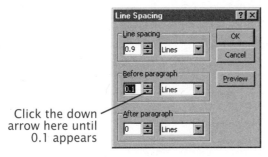

Click the down
arrow here until
0.1 appears

408

The paragraph spacing before each paragraph decreases by 0.1.

4 Click the OK button.

Your presentation window should look like the following illustration:

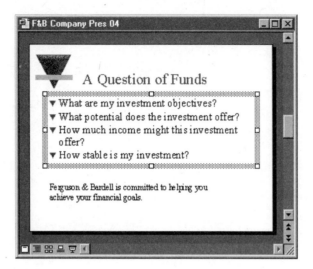

Formatting Text

After you have finished adjusting your text, you can change text formatting, such as bullets, font size, italic, bold, underline, or shadow, by selecting the text object and clicking one or more formatting buttons on the PowerPoint Formatting toolbar.

Remove text bullets and decrease font size

Bullets

1 Ensure that the bulleted text box is still selected.

2 On the Formatting toolbar, click the Bullets button.

The bullets for the four bulleted lines disappear.

Decrease Font Size

3 On the Formatting toolbar, click the Decrease Font Size button to reduce the font size setting to 28.

Format text in a text object

Selection Cursor

1 Position the pointer near the left edge of the text "Ferguson & Bardell . . ." (which changes to the selection cursor) and click to select it.

A dotted selection box appears around the text object indicating that it's selected.

Italic

2 On the Formatting toolbar, click the Italic button.

The text in the object changes to italic.

Font Color

3   On the Drawing toolbar, click the Font Color drop-down arrow button.

A text color menu of the current color scheme appears.

4   Click the purple color as indicated in the following illustration:

The font color changes to purple. The line on the Font Color button also changes to purple, indicating the currently selected font color.

Change text alignment

To align text in an object, first select the object and then point to Alignment on the Format menu. A submenu opens, giving you four options: Left, Center, Right, and Justify.

Center Alignment

➤   On the Formatting toolbar, click the Center Alignment button.

The text in the text object aligns to the center.

Move a text object

You can move a text object to any place on a slide to give your presentation the best look. To move a text object, drag the edge of the text object's selection box.

➤   Drag the edge of the selection box to center the text object between the bottom of the slide and the bulleted text box.

Your presentation window should look like the following illustration:

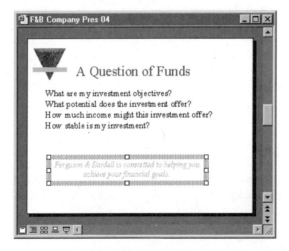

Finding and Replacing Text and Fonts

The Find and Replace commands allow you to locate and change specific text in your presentation. Find helps you locate a specific word, while Replace locates all occurrences of a word and replaces them with a different one.

Replace text

Use the Replace command to find the word "Exchange" and replace it with the word "Transfer" for the company presentation.

1   On the Edit menu, click Replace (CTRL+H).

The Replace dialog box appears.

2   In the Find What box, type **Exchange**

3   Press TAB or click the I-beam cursor in the Replace With box.

4   Type **Transfer**

Type Exchange here ——→

Type Transfer here ——→

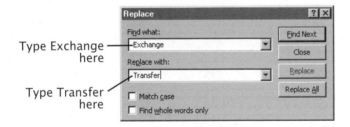

5   Click the Find Next button.

PowerPoint finds the word "Exchange" on slide 7. If you can't see the selected text, drag the Replace dialog box title bar up so you can see the text.

6   Click the Replace button.

A dialog box appears telling you PowerPoint is finished searching the presentation.

7   Click the OK button.

8   Click the Close button in the Replace dialog box.

The Replace dialog box closes.

Replace fonts

With the Replace Fonts command, you can replace a current font style you have been using with another style throughout your entire presentation. Try changing Times New Roman to Arial.

1   On the Format menu, click Replace Fonts.

The Replace Font dialog box appears.

411

2 Click the Replace drop-down arrow.

3 Click Times New Roman.

4 Click the With drop-down arrow.

5 Scroll if necessary and click Arial.

6 Click the Replace button.

Throughout your presentation, the text formatted with the Times New Roman font changes to the Arial font.

7 Click the Close button.

Checking Spelling

The spelling checker checks the spelling of the entire presentation, including all slides, outlines, notes pages, and handout pages. To help you identify misspelled words, PowerPoint underlines them with a wavy red line. To turn off this feature, click Options on the Tools menu, click the spelling tab, and then click the Hide Spelling Errors check box. PowerPoint uses different built-in dictionaries to check your presentation in more than one language. You can also create custom dictionaries in PowerPoint to check spelling for unique words or use custom dictionaries from other Microsoft applications.

Select another language to check in your presentation

1 Double-click the Spanish word "Español" in the bulleted text box.

The word "Español" appears with a red underline, indicating that it is misspelled or not recognized by the dictionary.

2 On the Tools menu, click Language.

The Language dialog box appears.

3 Scroll down and click Spanish (Mexican).

PowerPoint marks the selected word as a Mexican Spanish word for the spell checker.

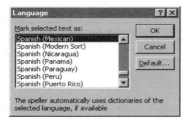

4 Click the OK button.

You'll notice the red line under the word doesn't appear, indicating that the word is recognized by the dictionary. You can also correct the spelling of a word by right-clicking the misspelled word and clicking the correct spelling of the word from the list in the shortcut menu.

Correct the spelling of a word

➤ Right-click the word "Guidence," and then click Guidance.

The misspelled word is replaced with the correct spelling.

Check the spelling in your presentation

Spelling

1 On the Standard toolbar, click the Spelling button.

PowerPoint begins checking the spelling on the current slide. The spelling checker stops and highlights the proper name "Bardell."

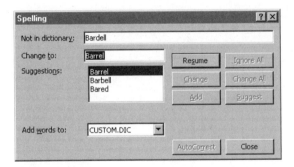

2 Click the Ignore All button.

All appearances of the word "Bardell" are ignored by the spelling checker. The spelling checker stops and highlights the misspelled word "portfolioes." A list appears, showing possible correct spellings of the misspelled word. The correct word spelling, "portfolios," appears selected.

TIP You can click the AutoCorrect button to add the misspelled and correct spelling of the word to the AutoCorrect table of entries to avoid the misspelling in the first place.

3 Click the Change button to correct the spelling.

The spelling checker continues to check your presentation for misspelled words or words not found in the dictionary. A dialog box appears, indicating that PowerPoint finished spell checking.

4 Click the OK button.

Checking Presentation Styles

Use PowerPoint's Style Checker to help you correct common presentation style design mistakes so your audience focuses on you and not your mistakes. The Style Checker reviews your presentation for typical mistakes like font size, number of fonts, number of words, punctuation, and other readability problems and then suggests ways to improve your presentation.

Check the style of your presentation

1 On the Tools menu, click Style Checker.

The Style Checker dialog box appears.

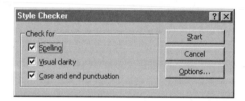

Since you already checked the spelling of the presentation, turn off the spelling option.

2 Click the Spelling check box to uncheck the option.

3 Click the Options button.

The Style Checker Options dialog box appears, displaying tabs for Case And End Punctuation and Visual Clarity.

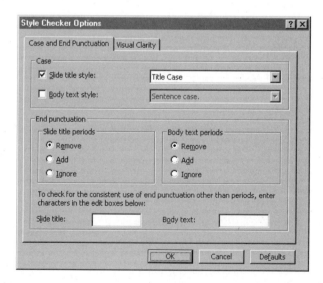

4   In the Case area, be sure the Body Text Style check box is checked.

The Style Checker disregards the case of body text style in the presentation. You'll see another way to change text case in the "One Step Further" at the end of this lesson.

5   Click the OK button.

The Style Checker dialog box appears.

6   Click the Start button.

The Style Checker dialog box reappears to warn you of an inconsistency. Paragraph 1 of placeholder 2 of slide 5 has end punctuation.

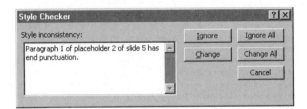

7   Click the Change button.

The Style Checker Summary dialog box appears.

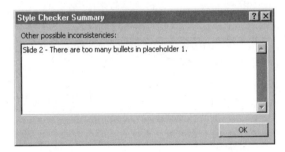

The Style Checker found other possible style inconsistencies. Based on the current Style Checker settings, slide 2 contains too many bullets in placeholder 1.

8   Click the OK button.

Looking Up Information in Microsoft Bookshelf

When Microsoft Bookshelf 97 or Microsoft Bookshelf Basics, a multimedia reference collection with online books, is installed with Microsoft Office 97, a special command, Look Up Reference, is added to PowerPoint so that you can look up information in Bookshelf without leaving your presentation. In addition, you can also right-click a word in your presentation and then click Define on the shortcut menu to quickly find a definition from information provided on the Bookshelf 97 or Bookshelf Basics CD-ROMs.

415

Look up information in Microsoft Bookshelf

1   Insert the Bookshelf CD into your CD-ROM drive.

2   On the Tools menu, click Look Up Reference.

The Look Up Reference dialog box appears.

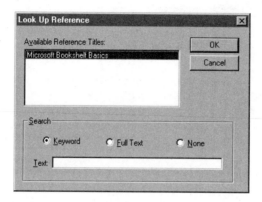

3   In the Available Reference Titles area, click Microsoft Bookshelf Basics.

4   Click OK.

Bookshelf Basics opens.

For information about using Bookshelf Basics, use the Office Assistant to search for "Bookshelf Basics."

5   Select information from the Bookshelf Basics CD-ROM.

6   On the Bookshelf Basics Edit menu, click Copy To PowerPoint.

7   Choose the locaton where you want the information, and then click Paste.

The information from Bookshelf Basics appears on your slide.

Save the presentation

Save

➤   On the Standard toolbar, click the Save button.

No dialog box appears because the presentation already has a name. The current information in your presentation is saved with the same name.

One Step Further

You have learned to create and edit a text object, format text using the toolbar, adjust text alignment and line spacing, find and replace text, check spelling, and check presentation style. As part of the style checking process, PowerPoint checks case, but you can independently change text case for sentences with a command from the Format menu.

Change the case of text

1 Drag the scroll box to slide 7, if necessary.

2 Position the pointer near the bulleted text box (which changes to the selection cursor) and click to select it.

3 On the Format menu, click Change Case.

    The Change Case dialog box appears with the Sentence Case option button set as the default.

4 Click the OK button.

    The paragraph text changes to sentence case.

If you want to continue to the next lesson

1 On the File menu, click Close (CTRL+W).

2 If a dialog box appears asking whether you want to save the changes to your presentation, click the Yes button.

If you want to quit PowerPoint for now

1 On the File menu, click Exit (CTRL+Q).

2 If a dialog box appears asking whether you want to save the changes to your presentation, click the Yes button.

Lesson Summary

To	Do this	Button
Select a text object	Click a text box with the selection cursor.	⊹
Deselect a text object	Click a blank area on the slide.	
Add AutoCorrect text	On the Tools menu, click AutoCorrect and type in an entry.	
Create a text label	On the Drawing toolbar, click the Text Box button. Click the slide and type your text.	🄰
Create a word processing box	On the Drawing toolbar, click the Text Box button. Drag to create a text box, and then type your text.	🄰
Change line spacing	Select a text object. On the Format menu, click Line Spacing and set the line spacing, or click one of the paragraph spacing buttons on the Formatting toolbar.	

417

To	Do this	Button
Remove a bullet	Select the bulleted text. On the Formatting toolbar, click the Bullets button.	
Change text alignment	Select the text. On the Formatting toolbar, click the alignment buttons.	
Replace fonts	On the Format menu, click Replace Fonts.	
Find or replace text	On the Edit menu, click Find or Replace.	
Check spelling	On the Standard toolbar, click the Spelling button.	
Check style	On the Tools menu, click Style Checker.	
Look up information in Bookshelf	On the Tools menu, click Look Up Reference and select a reference.	

For online information about	Use the Office Assistant to search for
Working with text	**Add text,** and then click Add Text
Selecting and editing text	**Select text,** and then click Select Text
Formatting text	**Format text,** and then click Change The Way Text Looks
Finding and replacing text	**Find text,** and then click Find Text or Replace Text

Applying and Modifying Templates

In this lesson you will learn how to:

Estimated time
25 min.

- Understand and apply a template.
- Understand and view a master.
- Change the display using master objects.
- Modify and format master text.
- Adjust master text indents.
- Reapply a layout from the master.
- Save a presentation as a template.

A *template* is a presentation file that has a predefined set of color and text characteristics. You can create a presentation from a template or you can apply a template to an existing presentation. When you apply a template to a presentation, the slides in the presentation take on the characteristics of the template, so you can maintain a uniform design. To make maintaining a uniform design even easier, PowerPoint uses *masters* that control the look of the individual parts of the presentation, including formatting, color, graphics, and text placement. Every presentation has a set of masters, one for each view.

As Director of Communications at Ferguson & Bardell, you have been working on a company presentation. After adding and modifying your text in the previous lesson, you're ready to apply a presentation design template.

In this lesson, you'll learn how to apply a PowerPoint template, change the display for master objects, modify and format the master text, reapply a layout from the master, and save a presentation as a template.

Start the lesson

Follow the steps below to open the practice file called 05 PPT Lesson, and then save it with the new name F&B Company Pres 05. If you haven't already started PowerPoint, do so now.

Open

1 On the Standard toolbar, click the Open button or click the Open An Existing Presentation option button on the Start-up dialog box and click OK.

2 Click the Look In Favorites button.

Look In Favorites

3 Double-click the Part4 PowerPoint Practice folder.

4 In the file list box, double-click the file named 05 PPT Lesson to open it.

5 On the File menu, click Save As.

For information about opening a presentation, see Lesson 3, "Printing a Presentation."

The Save As dialog box opens. Be sure the Part4 PowerPoint Practice folder appears in the Save In box.

6 In the File Name box, type **F&B Company Pres 05**

7 Click the Save button.

The presentation is saved and the title bar changes to the new name.

Understanding and Applying Templates

PowerPoint comes with a wide variety of templates that are professionally designed to help you achieve the look you want. When you apply a template to your presentation, PowerPoint copies the information from each master in the template to the corresponding masters in your presentation. All slides in your presentation then acquire the look of the template. You can use the templates that come with PowerPoint, or you can create your own from existing presentations. Moreover, you can apply any number of templates to your presentation at any point during the development process until you find the look you like best.

Apply a template

To apply a template to an existing presentation, you can open the presentation and then use the Apply Design dialog box to locate and select the template you want. For the Ferguson & Bardell presentation, you'll apply a company template one of your employees in the Communications department created.

Apply Design

1 On the Standard toolbar, click the Apply Design button.

The Apply Design dialog box appears.

*Look In
Favorites*

2 Click the Look In Favorites button.

3 Double-click the Part4 PowerPoint Practice folder.

4 In the list of file and folder names, click 05 PPT Template.

Make sure the
Practice folder
appears here

Click the
template here

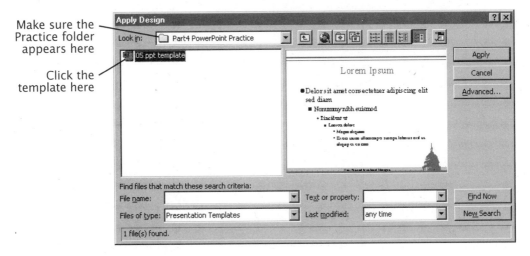

5 Click the Apply button.

The information from the template file, 05 PPT Template, is applied, or copied, to the masters in your presentation. The text style and format, slide colors, and background objects change to match the template. Your content remains the same.

Your presentation window should look like the following illustration:

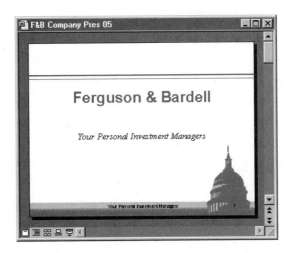

421

Understanding PowerPoint Masters

PowerPoint comes with a special slide called the *Slide Master*. The Slide Master controls the properties of every slide in the presentation. All the characteristics (background color, text color, font, and font size) of the Slide Master appear on every slide in the presentation. When you make a change on the Slide Master, the change affects every slide. For example, if you want your company's logo or the date to appear on every slide, you can place it on the Slide Master. Note that the Slide Master controls all slides except for the title slide, which has its own master, the Title Master.

View the Slide Master

Your company presentation has a new look now that you've applied a different template, but you'd like to make some changes to the Slide Master.

➤ On the View menu, point to Master, and then click Slide Master.

The Slide Master contains master placeholders for title text, paragraph text, the date and time, footer information, and slide number. The master title and text placeholders control the text format for your slide presentation. For example, when you change the master title text format to italic, the title on each slide changes to italic to follow the master. If for some reason you don't want to follow the Slide Master on a particular slide, you can easily override it.

Your presentation master should look like the following illustration:

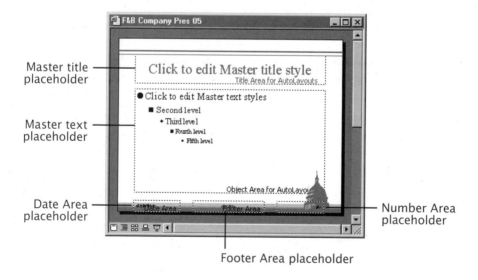

Master title placeholder

Master text placeholder

Date Area placeholder

Number Area placeholder

Footer Area placeholder

View the Title Master

The Title Master contains placeholders similar to the Slide Master. The main difference between the two Slide view masters is the Title Master's use of a master subtitle style instead of the master text style.

➤ On the View menu, point to Master and then click Title Master.

The Title Master slide appears, as shown in the following illustration:

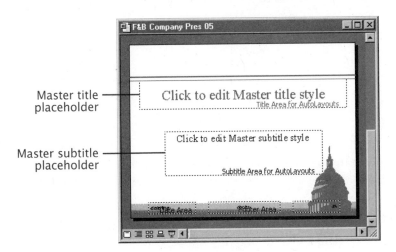

Master title placeholder

Master subtitle placeholder

TROUBLESHOOTING   If you don't have a Title Master, you can create one by switching to the Slide Master and clicking the New Title Master button on the standard toolbar.

Switch between the Title Master and the Slide Master

➤ In Title Master view, drag the scroll box on the scroll bar up.

The Slide Master appears.

Switch to Handout Master and Notes Master

PowerPoint also comes with a handout master and a notes pages master, where you can add items that you want to appear on each page.

1 On the View menu, point to Master, and click Handout Master.

The Handout Master view and Handout Master toolbar appear. With the Handout Master toolbar you can show the positioning of 2, 3, or 6 handouts per page and outline view.

2 On the Handout Master toolbar, click the Show Positioning Of 3-Per-Page Handouts button.

3 On the View menu, point to Master, and then click Notes Master.

The Notes Master view appears, showing the slide and speaker note text positioning for the notes pages.

4 On the Master toolbar, click the Close button.

PowerPoint returns you to the first slide in your presentation.

Changing the Display Using the Master

Each master contains placeholders where you can add background objects, such as text and graphics, that can appear on every page. Some examples are your company name, logo, or product name. With PowerPoint you can determine what appears on your slides.

Remove footer display from the Title Slide

The footer information on the title slide for the F&B presentation already appears in the subtitle of the slide, so remove the duplicate information from the title slide.

1 On the View menu, click Header And Footer.

The Header And Footer dialog box appears.

2 Click the Don't Show On Title Slide check box.

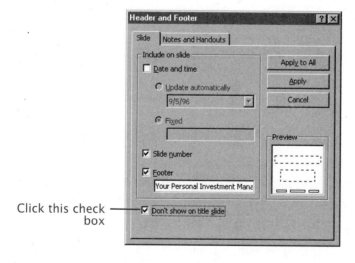

Click this check box

424

3   Click the Apply To All button.

The slide footer information disappears from the title slide.

Next Slide

4   Click the Next Slide button to view slide 2.

The slide footer information remains on the rest of the slides in the presentation.

Modifying Master Placeholders

You can modify and arrange placeholders for the date and time, footers, and slide numbers on all of the master views.

Edit master placeholders

The footer, date and time, and slide number appear on the Slide Master in the default position. For the F&B company presentation, customize the position of the placeholders.

Slide View

1   Hold down the SHIFT key and click the Slide View button.

The Slide Master view appears. Holding down the SHIFT key and clicking a view button switches you to the corresponding master view. With the title slide displayed, the Slide View button becomes the Title Master button. With any of the other slides displayed, the Slide View button becomes the Slide Master button.

2   Select the Date Area placeholder (bottom left corner).

Be sure you click the placeholder border so the resize handles appear.

3   Press the DELETE key.

TIP   If you delete a placeholder by mistake, you can click Master Layout on the Format menu, click the appropriate placeholder check box, and click the OK button to reapply the placeholder.

---

4   Click the dotted edge of the Footer Area placeholder to select it.

Be sure the resize handles appear around the placeholder.

5   Hold down the SHIFT key and drag the Footer Area placeholder to the left until the edge of the placeholder matches the edge of the master text placeholder.

Holding down the SHIFT key while you drag a PowerPoint object constrains the movement of the object horizontally or vertically.

6   Click a blank area of the slide to deselect the placeholder.

Formatting Master Text

Formatting the placeholders in Slide Master view provides consistency to your presentation. The master placeholders for the title, bulleted text, date and time, slide number, and footer determine the style and placement of those objects.

Format master text attributes

To format master text, you select the text placeholder and change the format until it looks the way you want. Format the text in the Footer and Number Area placeholders for the F&B company presentation.

Font Size

Italic

Slide View

1   Hold down the SHIFT key, click the Footer Area placeholder, and click the Number Area placeholder to select both objects.

2   On the Formatting toolbar, click the Font Size drop-down arrow, and click 20.

3   Hold down the SHIFT key and click the Footer Area placeholder.

The Footer Area placeholder is deselected.

4   On the Formatting toolbar, click the Italic button.

The Number Area placeholder becomes italic.

5   Click the Slide View button.

Your presentation window should look like the following illustration:

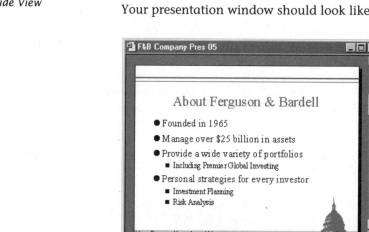

Format master title and bulleted text

To format bulleted text, you have to place the insertion point in the line of the bulleted text you want to change.

Slide View

1 Hold down the SHIFT key and click the Slide View button.

2 In the master text placeholder, position the I-beam cursor to the right of the text "Second level."

Italic

3 On the Formatting toolbar, click the Italic button.

4 Click outside the master text placeholder in a blank area to deselect it.

Your Slide Master should look like the following illustration:

Format master bullets

PowerPoint allows you to customize the bullets in your presentation for individual paragraphs or entire objects.

1 Click the first line of text titled "Click to edit Master text styles" in the master text placeholder.

The insertion point is placed in the text.

2 On the Format menu, click Bullet.

The Bullet dialog box appears, with the current bullet symbol selected. You can change the symbol font in the Bullets From drop-down list, click a different bullet color in the Color drop-down list, or adjust the font size percentage in the Size box.

427

3   In the Bullet dialog box, click the diamond bullet, as shown in the following illustration:

Click the diamond bullet here

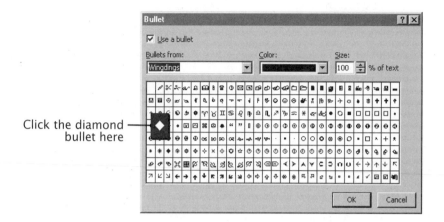

4   Click the Color drop-down arrow and click the blue color.

5   Click the Size down arrow until 85% appears.

The new bullet size will be 85% of the text on the slide.

6   Click the OK button.

The bullet appears in the first line of text.

7   Click the Slide View button.

PowerPoint returns to slide 2 and shows the font and bullet changes as shown in the following illustration:

New diamond bullet

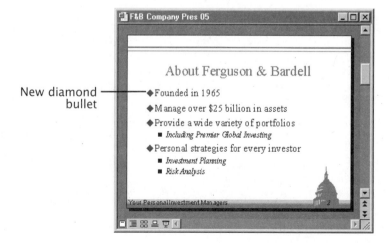

Adjusting Master Text Indents

PowerPoint uses indent markers to control the distance between bullets and text levels. To work with indented text and bullets, select a text object and show its ruler to make adjustments. Adjusting indents in PowerPoint works the same way it does in Microsoft Word for Windows.

Display the ruler

To change the distance between a bullet and its corresponding text, you first display the ruler, which shows the current bullet and text placement.

Slide View

1 Hold down the SHIFT key and click the Slide View button.

The Slide Master appears.

2 Click the first line of text titled "Click to edit Master title style" in the master text placeholder.

3 On the View menu, click Ruler.

Your presentation window should look like the following illustration:

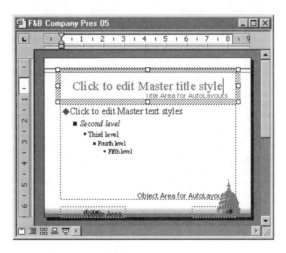

Setting Indent Markers

Indent Markers

Margin Marker

The indent markers on the ruler control the indent levels of the master text object. Each indent level consists of two triangles, called *indent markers*, and a small box, called a *margin marker*. The upper indent marker controls the first line of the paragraph; the lower indent marker controls the left edge of the paragraph. Each indent level is set so that the first line extends to the left of the paragraph, with the rest of the paragraph "hanging" below it. This indent setting is called a *hanging indent*.

429

Adjust indent markers

To adjust an indent marker, you move the triangle on the ruler to a new position. In the F&B company presentation, the diamond bullet in the first indent level appears too close to the text. Adjust the indent markers of the first indent level to put more space between the bullet and the text to create a hanging indent.

1 Click the line of text titled "Click to edit Master text styles" in the master text placeholder.

The ruler adds indent markers for each level of text represented in the bulleted list. Five indent markers appear.

2 Drag the lower indent marker of the first indent level to the left margin of the ruler, as shown in the following illustration:

Move the lower
indent marker
to here

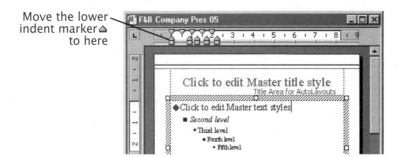

When you release the mouse button, the text for the first indent level moves next to the bullet on the left margin.

Adjust the margin level

You can move the entire level, including bullet and text, using the margin marker.

1 Slowly drag the margin marker of the first indent level to the 0.5 inch mark on the ruler.

NOTE If you drag an indent level or margin marker into another indent level, the first indent level (or marker) pushes the second indent level until you release the mouse button. To move an indent marker back to its original position, drag the indent level's margin marker or click the Undo button.

Your presentation window should look like the following illustration:

Move the margin
marker to here

Moving the first indent marker repositions the left margin of the master text object to the 0.5 inch mark. (Notice the first text level in the master text object.)

 TROUBLESHOOTING   If the ruler on your screen looks different from the one in the previous illustration, you might not have moved the margin marker.

---

2   Drag the upper indent marker of the first indent level to the left edge of the ruler.

The first indent level of your ruler is formatted again as a hanging indent.

Your presentation window should look like the following illustration:

Move the upper
indent marker
to here

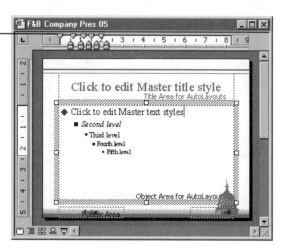

3 In a blank area of the Slide Master, click the right mouse button and then click Ruler.

The ruler closes.

4 On the View menu, click Slide.

PowerPoint returns you to slide 2.

Reapplying a Slide Layout

If you make changes to items on a slide and then decide that you want the original slide layout back, you can reapply the slide layout to that slide using the Slide Layout command. You can also change the current layout of a slide by selecting a new layout from the Slide Layout dialog box.

Apply a slide layout

1 Drag the title object to the right edge of the slide.

Your presentation window should look like the following illustration:

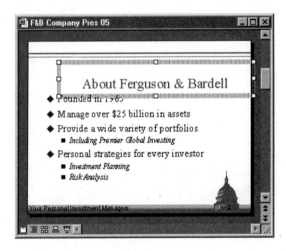

Slide Layout

2 On the Standard toolbar, click the Slide Layout button.

The Slide Layout dialog box appears with the current slide layout style selected.

3 Click the Reapply button.

PowerPoint uses the slide layout to reposition the title object to its original position on the slide.

Save the presentation

Save

➤ On the Standard toolbar, click the Save button.

No dialog box appears because the presentation already has a name. The current information in your presentation is saved with the same name.

Saving a Presentation as a Template

After changing the masters in your presentation the way you want, you can save the presentation as a template, which you can apply to other presentations in the future. You can create specialized templates for different types of presentations.

1 On the File menu, click Save As.

The Save As dialog box appears. F&B Company Pres 05 appears in the File Name box.

2 In the File Name box, type **F&B Company Template**

3 Click the Save As Type drop-down arrow and click Presentation Template.

PowerPoint displays the Templates folder. To include your new template with the others that come with PowerPoint, you need to save the template in one of the corresponding folders. A new template icon will appear in the New Presentation dialog box. For the purposes of this lesson, save this template with the rest of your practice files.

Look In Favorites

4 Click the Look In Favorites button.

5 Double-click the Part4 PowerPoint Practice folder.

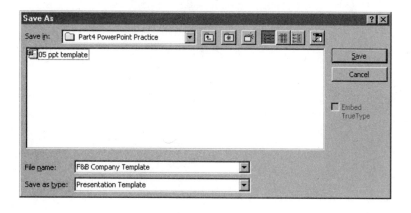

6   Click the Save button.

The template is saved in the Practice folder.

One Step Further

You have learned how to apply a template, view and switch to a master, change the master title and master text of your presentation, change bullets, adjust margin indents, reapply a slide layout, and save a presentation as a template.

For individual slides, you might want to hide background objects, such as date and time, header and footer, and slide number placeholders, graphics, shapes, and lines, so that they do not appear on the screen. Try hiding the master objects from slide 3.

Hide objects from the Master

Next Slide

1   Click the Next Slide button.

2   In a blank area of the slide, click the right mouse button, and click Background.

3   Click the Omit Background Graphics From Master check box.

The Omit Background Graphics From Master option is turned on.

4   Click the Apply button.

The background objects are omitted from the slide.

If you want to continue to the next lesson

1   On the File menu, click Close (CTRL+W).

2   If a dialog box appears asking whether you want to save the changes to your presentation, click the No button.

If you want to quit PowerPoint for now

1   On the File menu, click Exit (CTRL+Q).

2   If a dialog box appears asking whether you want to save the changes to your presentation, click the No button.

Lesson Summary

To	Do this	Button
Apply a template	On the Standard toolbar, click the Apply Design button. Select the folder that contains the template you want to use, and select the template file. Click the Apply button.	
Switch to master views	On the View menu, point to Master, and then click the view you want from the menu or hold down the SHIFT key and click the View button you want.	
Format the master text	Select the master text or text object and click the formatting effects you want on the Formatting toolbar.	
Change the bullet format	Click a line of text and on the Format menu, click Bullet. Click a bullet.	
Display the text object ruler	On the View menu, click Ruler or click the right mouse button and click Ruler on the Shortcut menu.	
Set the indent marker for the first line of text	On the View menu, click Ruler. Place the cursor in text. Drag the upper triangle.	
Set the indent marker for a paragraph other than the first line of text	On the View menu, click Ruler. Place the cursor in text. Drag the lower indent marker.	
Adjust a paragraph margin	On the View menu, click Ruler. Place the cursor in text. Drag the indent margin marker.	
Create a hanging indent	On the View menu, click Ruler. Place the cursor in text. Move the upper triangle to the left of the lower indent marker.	
Reapply a slide layout	Move to the slide. Click the Slide Layout button on the Standard toolbar, select a layout, and click the Reapply button.	
Save as a template	On the File menu, click Save As. Click the Save As Type drop-down arrow, click Presentation Templates and click the Save button.	

435

For online information about	Use the Office Assistant to search for
Applying a template	**Apply template**, and then click Apply A Different Design To A Presentation
Working with the slide or title master	**Master**, and then click Go To Where I Can Work On The Slide Master
Changing master text	**Indents**, and then click Display Tab And Indent Settings, or Set Paragraph Indentations
Formatting master bullets	**Bullet**, and then click Add, Change, Or Remove A Bullet
Reapplying a layout	**Slide layout**, and then click Change The Layout Of A Slide

Producing a Slide Show

Estimated time
25 min.

In this lesson you will learn how to:

■ Navigate in slide show.

■ Draw freehand in a slide show.

■ Set slide transitions.

■ Animate slide text.

■ Animate slide objects.

■ Hide a slide during a slide show.

■ Create and edit a custom show.

In PowerPoint you can display your presentations on your computer monitor using slide show. The Slide Show feature turns your computer into a projector that displays your presentation on your monitor's full screen or, using special hardware, on an overhead screen. A slide show can also operate continuously, unattended, to show a presentation.

As Director of Communications at Ferguson & Bardell, you have been working on a company presentation. With your slides in place, you are ready to set up your slide show for Ferguson, one of the partners, who plans to give the presentation at next month's stockholders' meeting.

In this lesson, you'll learn how to give a slide show, draw on a slide during a slide show, add slide transitions, add text and object slide animation, hide a slide during a slide show, and create and edit a custom slide show.

Start the lesson

Follow the steps below to open the practice file called 06 PPT Lesson, and then save it with the new name F&B Company Pres 06. If you haven't already started PowerPoint, do so now.

Open

Look In Favorites

For information about opening a presentation, see Lesson 3, "Printing a Presentation."

1 On the Standard toolbar, click the Open button or click the Open An Existing Presentation option button on the Start-up dialog box and click OK.

2 Click the Look In Favorites button.

3 Double-click the Part4 PowerPoint Practice folder.

4 In the file list box, double-click the file named 06 PPT Lesson to open it.

5 On the File menu, click Save As.

The Save As dialog box opens. Be sure the Part4 PowerPoint Practice folder appears in the Save In box.

6 In the File Name box, type **F&B Company Pres 06**

7 Click the Save button.

The presentation is saved and the title bar changes to the new name.

Navigating in Slide Show

In earlier lessons, you learned to click the mouse button to advance to the next slide in slide show. Besides clicking the mouse to advance to each slide, PowerPoint gives you several different ways to navigate through your slide show presentation. You can press keys on the keyboard or use commands on the Show Popup menu in Slide Show view to move from slide to slide. With the Slide Navigator, you can jump to slides out of sequence.

Navigate through your slide show presentation

Use the Slide Navigator on the Show Popup menu to navigate through your presentation in slide show.

Slide Show

Show Popup Menu

1 Click the Slide Show button.

PowerPoint displays the first slide in the presentation.

2 Move the mouse to display the pointer.

The Show Popup menu button appears in the lower left corner of the screen, as shown in the margin.

3 Click the Show Popup menu button.

The Show Popup menu appears, showing different slide show navigation controls.

438

4   On the Show Popup menu, click Next.

Slide 2 appears in Slide Show view. You can also press the N key to advance to the next slide.

5   Move the mouse pointer, click the Show Popup menu button, and then click Previous.

Slide 1 appears in Slide Show view. You can also press the P key to return to the previous slide. Besides clicking the Show Popup menu button to access the menu, you can also click the right mouse button to display the menu.

   TIP   You can press the RIGHT ARROW key or the PAGE DOWN key to advance to the next slide and you can press the LEFT ARROW key or the PAGE UP key to return to the previous slide.

---

6   Click the right mouse button, point to Go, and then click Slide Navigator.

The Slide Navigator dialog box appears, showing a list of slides in your presentation with the current slide selected.

7   In the list of slide names, click slide 9.

The Slide Navigator dialog box should look like the following illustration:

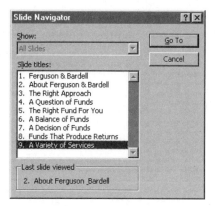

8   Click the Go To button.

Slide 9 appears in Slide Show view.

9   Click the mouse button to advance to the next slide.

Advancing to the next slide when you are viewing the last slide in your presentation exits slide show or displays a black slide, depending on your slide show setting in the Options dialog box.

Slide 1 appears in Slide view.

Drawing Freehand in a Slide Show

During a slide show presentation, you can draw freehand lines, circles, and arrows to emphasize your message. You simply move the mouse to display the pointer, select the pen tool, and then draw. When you finish drawing, you can continue the presentation.

Draw a freehand line

Try underlining your slide title during a slide show using the Pen tool.

Slide Show

1   Click the Slide Show button.

PowerPoint displays the current slide in the presentation.

2   Click the right mouse button and click Pen (CTRL+P).

The pointer changes to the pen cursor. Now you are ready to draw on the slide.

Pen Cursor

 NOTE   When the cursor changes from the pointer to the pen in Slide Show view, clicking the mouse button doesn't advance to the next slide. You need to change the pen cursor back to the pointer to advance using the mouse button.

---

3   Draw a line under the phrase "Your Personal Investment Managers."

Now erase the line.

4   Click the right mouse button, point to Screen, and then click Erase Pen.

The annotation erases so you can drawing something else. You can also press the E key to erase the annotation drawing.

Change the pen color

You can change the freehand drawing pen color at any time during the presentation by choosing a new color from the Show Popup menu.

1   Click the Show Popup menu button, point to Pointer Options, and then point to Pen Color.

The Pen Color menu appears, showing a selection of different colors.

2   On the Pen Color menu, click Magenta.

3   Draw a line under the phrase "Ferguson & Bardell."

4   Press the E key to erase the annotation drawing.

5   Click the right mouse button and click Arrow (CTRL+A).

The pen cursor changes back to the pointer. With the pointer, you can click the mouse button to advance to the next slide.

Exit Slide Show

You can exit slide show at any time by clicking the End Show command on the Show Popup menu or by pressing the ESC key.

➤ Click the right mouse button and click End Show.

The current slide in slide show appears in Slide view.

Setting Slide Transitions

A slide transition is the visual effect given to a slide as it moves on and off the screen during a slide show. Slide transitions include such effects as Checkerboard Across, Cover Down, Cut, and Split Vertical Out; there are a total of 41 slide transition effects. You can set a transition for one slide or a group of slides by selecting the slides in Slide Sorter view and applying the transition.

Apply a slide transition effect

Slide Sorter View

1 Click the Slide Sorter View button and then click slide 1 to select it.

2 On the Slide Sorter toolbar, click the Slide Transition Effects drop-down arrow, click the down scroll arrow several times, and click Dissolve.

PowerPoint places a transition symbol below the lower left corner of slide 1. This tells you a slide transition effect has been applied to this slide.

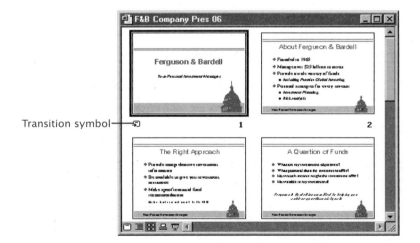

Transition symbol

1

2

TIP   You can click the transition symbol below the slide to display the slide transition in the slide miniature.

Slide Show

3 Click the Slide Show button.

Slide Show displays slide 1 with the Dissolve transition effect.

4 Press the ESC key to stop the slide show.

Apply multiple transitions and change transition speed

The Slide Transition button on the toolbar is the fastest and easiest way to apply a slide transition effect. To apply other transition effects to a slide, you need to use the Slide Transition dialog box. Try applying a transition effect to the rest of the slides and then changing the transition speed.

1 On the Edit menu, click Select All (CTRL+A).

All the slides in the presentation appear selected. Deselect slide 1 because it already has a slide transition.

2 Hold down the SHIFT key and click slide 1 to deselect the slide.

Slide Transition

3 On the Slide Sorter toolbar, click the Slide Transition button or on the Tools menu, click Slide Transition.

The Slide Transition dialog box appears.

4 Click the Effect drop-down arrow, click the down scroll arrow, and then click Random Bars Horizontal.

The preview box demonstrates the transition effect.

5 Click the Medium option button to set the transition speed.

The Slide Transition dialog box should look like the following illustration:

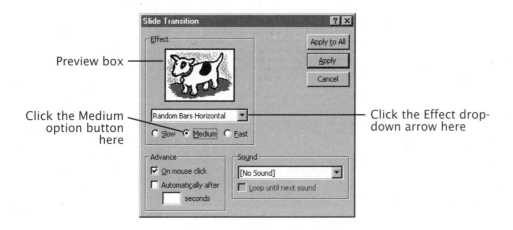

6 Click the Apply button.

The transition effect is applied to the selected slides. Notice that all the slides now have a transition symbol below their left corners.

Slide Show

7 Click the Slide Show button.

Slide Show displays slide 2 with the Random Bars Horizontal effect.

8 Click the mouse button several times to advance through the slides, watch the transition effect, and then press the ESC key to end the slide show.

PowerPoint returns you to Slide Sorter view with the last slide presented in slide show selected.

Animating Slide Text

In a slide show, you can have slide text appear one paragraph, word, or letter at a time on the screen. A slide with text that you set to appear incrementally (a paragraph at a time in slide show) is called a text animation slide. You can apply the Animation feature, which offers over 40 different transition effects, in Slide Sorter view and in Slide view.

View the Animation Effects toolbar

With the Animation Effects toolbar, you can apply preset animation effects to your presentation slides.

➤ Right-click any toolbar, and click Animation Effects.

The Animation Effects toolbar appears below the Slide Sorter toolbar. The special effects toolbar contains several predefined effects, such as Drive-In, Flying, Camera, and Flash Once, that you can use with your presentation objects.

Animate title slide text

You can animate slides with special effects using the Animation Effects toolbar.

1 Drag the vertical scroll bar scroll box to the top, and then click slide 1.

2 On the Animation Effects toolbar, click the Animate Title button.

Animate Title

The Animate Title button applies the Drop-In animation effect to the title of the slide. The Drop-In animation effect is the default setting for the Animate Title button.

Camera

3 On the Animation Effects toolbar, click the Camera button.

The Animate Slide Text button on the Animation Effect toolbar is now pushed in. The Text Preset Animation list on the Slide Sorter toolbar changes to Box Out.

Slide Show

4 Click the Slide Show button.

The title slide appears with a Dissolve transition and then the title flies down from the top.

443

5 Click the mouse button.

The subtitle text animation appears.

6 Press the ESC key to end the slide show.

Animate text for multiple slides

Instead of changing text animation slide by slide, you can animate text for more than one slide by selecting multiple slides in Slide Sorter view and applying an animation effect. Besides the preset animations effects found on the Animation Effects toolbar, PowerPoint also provides animation effects in the Text Preset Animation list on the Slide Sorter toolbar.

1 Click slide 2, hold down the SHIFT key, and then click slide 3 and slide 4.

Slides 2, 3, and 4 are selected.

Text Preset Animation

2 On the Slide Sorter toolbar, click the Text Preset Animation drop-down arrow, and then click Fly From Left.

The Text Preset Animation list on the Slide Sorter toolbar changes to Fly From Left.

Slide Show

3 Click the Slide Show button.

Slide 2 appears with a Random Bars Horizontal transition and without the bulleted text.

4 Click the mouse button four times to display the animations.

The bulleted text flies across the screen from the left one at a time.

5 Press the ESC key to end the slide show.

6 Double-click slide 1.

Change text animation slide settings

Instead of animating the entire subtitle text all at once on the first slide, you can animate the text one word at a time. To change this setting, you need to open the Custom Animation dialog box.

Custom Animation

1 On the Animation Effects toolbar, click the Custom Animation button, or on the Slide Show menu, click Custom Animation.

The Custom Animation dialog box appears with current animation settings and a preview of the current slide.

2 Click the Effects tab.

The Effects settings appear.

3 In the Animation Order box, click the text "2. Text 2"

The subtitle text object appears selected in the preview box.

The Custom Animation dialog box should look like the following illustration:

4   In the Introduce Text area, click the top drop-down arrow, and then click By Word.

The option sets the text to animate one word at a time.

5   Click the OK button.

Start the slide show to demonstrate the new animation effect.

Slide Show

6   Click the Slide Show button.

The animation effect displays automatically after the transition effect.

7   Click the mouse button to display the effect, and then press the ESC key.

Next Slide

8   Click the Next Slide button to advance to slide 2.

Change text animation levels for a slide

You can determine what text indent levels you want to animate. For example, in slide 2 there are two levels of bulleted text. When the Grouped By 1st Level Paragraphs option is selected, 2nd level paragraph text animates along with the 1st level paragraph text. When the By 2nd Level Paragraph option is selected, the 1st and 2nd level paragraph text animate separately.

Custom Animation

1   On the Animation Effects toolbar, click the Custom Animation button.

The Custom Animation dialog box appears with current animation settings and a preview of the current slide.

2   Click the Effects tab.

3   In the Animation Order box, click the text "1. Text 2"

The bulleted text object appears selected in the preview box. In the Introduce Text area, the Grouped By 1st Level Paragraphs animation setting is selected.

4   In the Introduce Text area, click the Group By drop-down arrow, and then click 2nd.

The option sets the text to animate 1st and 2nd level paragraph text separately.

5   Click the OK button.

Start the slide show to demonstrate the new animation effect.

Slide Show

6   Click the Slide Show button.

7   Click the mouse button seven times to display the animation effects.

The bulleted text flies across the screen from the left one at a time.

8   Press the ESC key to end the slide show.

Animating Slide Objects

In a slide show, you can also have slide objects transition one at a time on the screen just like you did with text. To animate objects on a slide, select the objects you want to animate in Slide view. For objects with text, you can either animate the text in the object or animate the text and object together.

Animate slide object text

When you animate an object and its text, the object and text animate all at the same time by default. However, you can animate only the text in an object, while the object remains unaffected, by clearing the Animate Attached Shape check box in the Custom Animation dialog box.

1   Drag the scroll box to slide 5.

Slide 5 appears in Slide view.

2   Drag to select the shapes and connectors at the bottom of the slide.

3   On the Animation Effects toolbar, click the Custom Animation button.

Custom Animation

The Custom Animation dialog box appears with all the objects selected in the preview box and in the Animation Order box.

4   In the Entry Animation And Sound area, click the top drop-down arrow, scroll down, and then click Peek From Bottom.

5   Click the Preview button.

The multidocument objects appear one at a time and then the connector objects appear one at a time.

6   Click the OK button.

NOTE   If you print a presentation that contains slides with animation, the Print What option changes to Slides (with Animations) and Slides (without Animations). The Slides (with Animations) option prints each bullet point on a separate page. The Slides (without Animations) option prints the complete slide on one page.

Change the animation order

To customize object animation on a slide, you can change the order of appearance for text or shapes on the screen during a slide show.

Custom Animation

1   On the Animation Effects toolbar, click the Custom Animation button.

The Custom Animation dialog box appears.

2   In the Animation Order box, click "4. Curved connector 6"

The left connector appears selected in the preview box.

3   Click the Up Arrow button.

The left connector animation order changes from fourth to third.

For a demonstration of how to animate objects, double-click the Camcorder file named Animate Objects in the Part4 Power-Point Camcorder Files folder. See "Installing and Using the Practice and Camcorder Files," earlier in this book for more information.

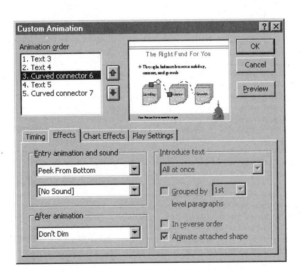

4   Click the Preview button.

The left and center objects appear, and then the connector appears.

5   Click the OK button.

Now start slide show to see the order changes.

Slide Show

6   Click the Slide Show button.

7   Click the mouse button five times to display the animation effects.

8   Press the ESC key to end the slide show.

Hiding a Slide During a Slide Show

You might want to customize an on-screen presentation for a specific audience. With PowerPoint, you can hide the slides you don't want to use during a slide show by using the Hide Slide command.

Hide a slide during a slide show

Slide Sorter View

Hide Slide

1   Click the Slide Sorter View button.

2   Drag the scroll box down and click slide 8 to select it.

3   On the Slide Sorter toolbar, click the Hide Slide button.

A hide symbol appears over the slide number, as shown in the following illustration:

Hide symbol

4   Click slide 7 to select it.

5   Click the Slide Show button and then click the mouse button.

Slide Show

The slide show hides slide 8 and displays slide 9.

6   Press P to go back to slide 7.

7   Click the right mouse button, point to Go, and click Hidden Slide or press the H key to show the hidden slide.

The hidden slide appears in Slide Show view.

8   Click the mouse button twice to complete the slide show.

Switch to Slide view so PowerPoint can save your presentation in Slide view instead of Slide Sorter view.

Slide View

9   Click the Slide View button.

Creating and Editing a Custom Show

With PowerPoint you can create a presentation within a presentation. Instead of creating multiple, nearly identical presentations for different audiences, you can group together and name the slides that differ and then jump to these slides during your presentation.

Create a custom show

1   On the Slide Show menu, click Custom Shows.

The Custom Shows dialog box appears.

2   Click the New button.

The Define Custom Show dialog box appears.

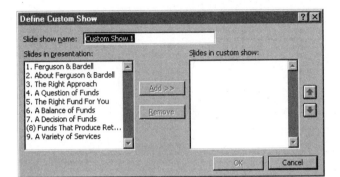

The default custom show name appears selected in the Slide Show Name box. To give the custom show a name, you can type a name.

3   In the Slide Show Name box, type **F&B Custom Show 06**

4   In the Slides In Presentation box, click Slide 1, and then click the Add button.

Slide 1 appears in the Slides In Custom Show box to the right.

5   Select and add slides 2, 3, 4, 7, 8, and 9 to the custom slide show to match to the following illustration:

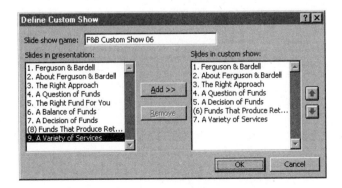

6 Click the OK button.

The Custom Shows dialog box appears.

7 Click the Show button.

8 Click the mouse button multiple times to view the slide show.

9 Press the ESC key to end the slide show.

The Custom Shows dialog box appears.

10 Click the Close button.

Edit a custom show

1 On the Slide Show menu, click Custom Shows.

The Custom Shows dialog box appears.

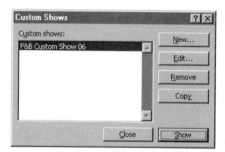

2 Click F&B Custom Show 06 and then click the Edit button.

The Define Custom Show dialog box appears.

3 In the Slides In Custom Show box, click Slide 6.

The Up Arrow button, Down Arrow button, and Remove button appear for use. To change the order of the selected slide, you click the Up Arrow button or the Down Arrow button. To remove the selected slide, you click the Remove button.

4 Click the Remove button.

Slide 6 is removed from the custom show.

5 Click the OK button.

The Custom Shows dialog box appears.

6 Click the Close button.

Save the presentation

Save

➤ On the Standard toolbar, click the Save button.

No dialog box appears because the presentation already has a name. The current information in your presentation is saved with the same name.

450

One Step Further

You have learned to produce and present a slide show in PowerPoint using Slide Navigator, transitions, and text and object animations. You also learned to hide a slide and create and edit a custom slide show.

You practiced using several animation slide settings, including animating 1st level paragraph text, 2nd level paragraph text, and individual words. You can also dim out or hide animation text after displaying it.

Dim out animated text

PowerPoint dims out animation text by changing its color. For the company presentation, set your animation text so that each animated text paragraph dims out once you've shown it.

Custom Animation

1   Ensure slide 9 appears in Slide view.

2   Click a word in the bulleted text to place the insertion point.

3   On the Animation Effects toolbar, click the Custom Animation button.

      The Custom Animation dialog box appears.

4   On the Effects tab in the Entry Animation And Sound area, click the top drop-down arrow and click Fly From Left.

5   Click the After Animation drop-down arrow and click the dark gray color.

      After an animated text paragraph transition, the previous animated text is grayed out.

6   Click the OK button.

      Start the slide show to demonstrate the animation effect.

Slide Show

7   Click the Slide Show button.

8   Click the mouse button five times to display the animation effect.

9   Press the ESC key to end the slide show.

If you want to quit PowerPoint for now

1   On the File menu, click Exit (CTRL+Q).

2   If a dialog box appears asking whether you want to save the changes to your presentation, click the Yes button.

Lesson Summary

To	Do this	Button
Run a slide show	Click the Slide Show button.	
Stop a slide show	Press the ESC key.	
Navigate in a slide show using the Slide Navigator	Click the Slide Show button. Right-click the screen, point to Go, and then click Slide Navigator.	
Draw freehand in a slide show	Click the Slide Show button. Right-click the screen, click Pen, and then draw. Right-click the screen and click Arrow to stop.	
Set slide transitions	Select the slides in Slide Sorter view. On the Slide Sorter toolbar, click the Slide Transition button.	
Apply text animations to slides	In Slide view, click the Custom Animation button on the Animation Effects toolbar.	
Apply object animations to slides	On the Animation Effects toolbar, click the Custom Animation button.	
Hide a slide	In Slide Sorter view, select one or more slides. On the Slide Sorter toolbar, click the Hide Slide button.	
Create a new custom slide show	On the Slide Show menu, click Custom Shows, and then click the New button.	

For online information about	Use the Office Assistant to search for
Freehand drawing	**Annotate**, and then click Write Or Draw (Annotate) On Slides During A Slide Show
Adding a slide transition	**Transition**, and then click Add Transitions To A Slide Show
Animating a slide	**Animate**, and then click Create Animated Slides

Part
5

Microsoft
Access 97

Viewing, Entering, and Customizing Data

Estimated time
45 min.

In this lesson you will learn how to:

- Open a database.
- Enter and modify data using a form.
- Select an option or a check box.
- Navigate between records.
- Switch between Form and Database views.
- Use editing tools.
- Select values from a list.

When you run a business, manage an office, or even just keep track of day-to-day tasks, there are hundreds of pieces of information that you use. The most convenient place to keep that information is right at your desk. For a while you might stack paper forms in a file folder next to the phone, as long as the stack doesn't get too big. But you'll have a problem if you try to keep all the information you need at your desk—pretty soon you won't be able to find the desk!

You can use Microsoft Access to organize and store all kinds and all quantities of information and have the data you need available with only a few clicks of your mouse. In this lesson, you'll find out how to open a Microsoft Access database, use a form to add new data, and move from record to record.

Data and Databases

Data is anything you want to store and refer to again. In Microsoft Access, data can be text, numbers, dates, pictures, files, and many other types of material. For example, if you sell boxes of bonbons, you can store the names, pictures, and recipes of your bonbons, the prices and quantities of boxes, and the dates of sales, to name just a few.

A *database* is an integrated collection of data that shares some common characteristic. For example, many businesses view all the data that relates to running that business as a corporate database. Databases also assist consumer groups, educational facilities, and government organizations in managing information. Even individuals or families have uses for databases. Databases are really just a way of organizing data so that it is more useful.

In most cases, the easiest way to enter data is by using a *form*. Forms used to enter data in Microsoft Access resemble the paper forms we see in offices. You type the data in the form, and then Microsoft Access stores it in a table.

A database *table* is a collection of data about the same subject or topic stored in records (rows) and fields (columns). A *record* is a set of information that belongs together, such as all the information about a magazine subscription card or a listing in a phone book. Records are made up of individual *fields*. Each field contains a discrete piece of data. For example, a magazine subscription table would contain one field for the subscriber name, another for the address, and as many other fields as the database designer believes are necessary to completely describe a subscriber.

Setting the Scene

To attract new customers, Sweet Lil's Chocolates, Inc., a fast-growing gourmet chocolate company, started a monthly newsletter called *The Chocolate Gourmet*. The newsletter has generated so many sales that Sweet Lil's decided to switch to Microsoft Access to store data about its product lines and sales. After seeing how much time using the database has saved other departments and how many errors have been prevented, the Marketing Department wants to keep subscription information in the database as well.

You have been recruited to enter data using a new form called "Subscriptions." The Sweet Lil's database contains the form you need. You'll open the database, open the Subscription form, and enter subscription data. The records you enter will be stored in the Customers table.

Opening a Database

First, you'll start Microsoft Access and open a database.

 TIP After you have opened a database, the next time you start Microsoft Access you'll see the database name listed in the Microsoft Access dialog box. When the database name appears in the Microsoft Access dialog box, you can double-click the name to open the database.

Start Microsoft Access from Microsoft Windows 95 or Windows NT

1 On the taskbar, click the Start button.

2 Point to Programs, and then click Microsoft Access.

The Microsoft Access dialog box appears as shown in the following illustration. From here, you can create a new database, open an existing database, or start the Database Wizard, which will help you create a new database.

An Introduction to the Office Assistant

While you are working with Microsoft Office 97, an animated character called the *Office Assistant* pops up on your screen to help you work productively. The Office Assistant offers help messages as you work. You can ask the Office Assistant questions by typing your question, and then clicking Search. The Office Assistant then shows you the answer to your question.

You can close any Office Assistant tip or message by pressing ESC.

You will sometimes see a light bulb graphic next to the Office Assistant—clicking the light bulb displays a tip about the action you are currently performing. You can view more tips by clicking Tips in the Office Assistant balloon when the Office Assistant appears. These tips are tailored to how you work—when you master a particular skill, the Office Assistant stops offering help.

Clippit, an Office
Assistant, in action

The Office Assistant appears in the following situations:

■ When you click the Office Assistant button on the Standard toolbar.

■ When you choose Microsoft Access Help on the Help menu, or when you press F1.

■ Whenever you click certain commands or try new tasks, for example, when you use Open for the first time.

Office Assistant

You can customize the Office Assistant. Use the right mouse button to click the Office Assistant, and then click Options to open the Office Assistant dialog box. You can then define when you want the Office Assistant to appear, and what kind of help you want it to offer. You can even change your Office Assistant character by clicking the Gallery tab. The Office Assistant is a shared application—any settings that you change in Microsoft Access will affect the Office Assistant in other Office 97 programs.

IMPORTANT If the Office Assistant appears, click the Start Using Microsoft Access option. If the User Name dialog box appears, fill in your name and initials, and then click OK. On the Office Assistant, click the Close button.

For the purposes of this book, the Office Assistant will not appear in the illustrations. If you want to match the illustrations, any time the Office Assistant appears, use the right mouse button to click the Office Assistant, and then click Hide Assistant. If you want to leave the Office Assistant on top to help guide you, but it is in your way, simply drag it to another area on the screen.

If you have not installed the Part5 Access Practice files, refer to "Installing and Using the Practice and Camcorder Files," earlier in this book.

Open a database

In this exercise, you open the Sweet Lil's database.

1   In the Microsoft Access dialog box, be sure that the Open An Existing Database option is selected, and then click OK.

The Open dialog box appears.

2   In the Open dialog box, click the Look In Favorites button.

Look in Favorites

The names of all folders and files in the Favorites folder are displayed in the file list. Your dialog box should look similar to the following illustration.

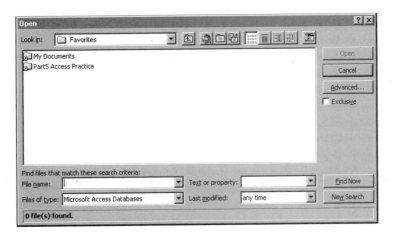

3   Double-click the Part5 Access Practice folder.

4 Double-click the Sweet Lil's filename.

The Database window for the Sweet Lil's database opens. The Database window has tabs—the Tables tab lists the tables that store data about Sweet Lil's business; the Forms tab lists the forms that were created for the Sweet Lil's database; and so forth. From the Database window, you can open and work with any object in the database. The Sweet Lil's Database window looks like the following illustration.

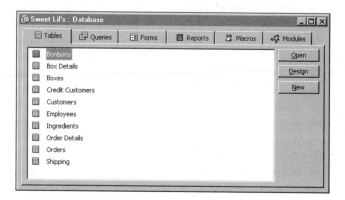

Entering and Viewing Data by Using Forms

Now that you're in the Sweet Lil's database, you can open the Subscription form to enter the subscription information for a new customer. The Subscription form contains blank boxes—*fields*—where you type the information from the paper form. A field is an area on a form where you enter data, such as a last name or an address.

The *insertion point*, the blinking vertical bar on your screen, indicates where the information appears when you type. You can move the insertion point by clicking a different field or by pressing the TAB key. In general, forms are set up so that when you press TAB, the insertion point moves through the fields from left to right or from top to bottom.

Microsoft Access fills in the current date in the Date Received field automatically so that you don't have to type the date.

Open a form

In this exercise, you open a form.

1 In the Sweet Lil's Database window, click the Forms tab.

A list of the forms in the Sweet Lil's database is displayed.

2 Double-click the Subscription form.

The Subscription form appears.

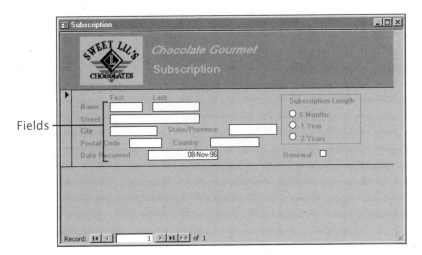

Updating the Database by Using a Form

You'll use the blank Subscription form on your screen to enter the subscription for a fan of *The Chocolate Gourmet* from Ohio. Here's what his paper subscription form looks like.

Subscribe or Renew

SWEET LIL'S
CHOCOLATES *The Chocolate Gourmet*

Name: ___Earl Lee_____

Street: ___28 Dorothy St._____

City: ___Fairborn_____ State/Province: ___OH_____

Postal Code: ___45324_____ Country: ___USA_____

○ *6 Months $9.97 (6 issues)*   ☒ *Renewal*
○ *1 Year $18.95 (12 issues)*
☒ *2 Years $26.95 (24 issues)*

Add a name

If you make a mistake, just press the BACK-SPACE key and then retype.

1 Type **Earl** in the First Name field.

As soon as you start typing, a new blank form appears below the one you're working in.

2 Press TAB to move the insertion point to the Last Name field.

You can also click anywhere in the Last Name field.

When your hands are already on the keyboard, you press TAB to move to the next field and press SHIFT+TAB to move to the previous field.

3 Type **Lee** in the Last Name field.

Add an address

➤ Type the following address information, pressing TAB to move from field to field.

Street:	**28 Dorothy**
City:	**Fairborn**
State/Province:	**OH**
Postal Code:	**45324**
Country:	**USA**

Selecting an Option or a Check Box

When you press TAB after typing "USA" in the Country field, Microsoft Access draws a dotted line around "6 Months" in the Subscription Length field instead of displaying the insertion point.

Subscription Length is an *option group*. Because an option group presents a set of options to select from, you don't have to type the data yourself—you just select an option. In this case, Earl Lee wants a 2-year subscription.

Option group

Check box

Select an option

If you press TAB in this step, be sure the insertion point is in the Country field.

 Click the circle next to 2 Years. You can also press TAB, and then press the DOWN ARROW key twice.

A dot appears in the button next to 2 Years, indicating that the option is selected. Next, you'll fill out the Renewal field.

Select a check box

The subscription for Earl Lee is a renewal. The Renewal field contains a check box. When this kind of field is selected, you see a check mark in the box.

 Click the Renewal check box.

A check mark appears in the box.

 TIP To clear a selected check box, click it again. If you prefer to use the keyboard, you can press the SPACEBAR to select or clear a check box.

Navigating Between Records

All the information in Earl Lee's subscription makes up one complete record. Now that you've entered Earl Lee's subscription, you're ready to move to the next record.

 TIP You can move to a field by pressing TAB. If you do, Microsoft Access selects the entire value in the field. To cancel the selection and place the insertion point at the end of the field, press F2.

To move to the next record, you can also press TAB in the Renewal field of the current record.

You might be able to see more than one record at a time while you are entering data. If you can see the next record, you can move to that record by clicking in it. Whether you can see the next record or not, you can move to the next record by pressing TAB when your insertion point is in the last field in the current record (the record you're in now).

Save the record and move to the next record

▶ Click in the First Name field of the next record.

The subscription information for Earl Lee is saved automatically when you go to a new record.

Return to the previous record

Looking over your first entry, you notice that you didn't type "St." in Earl Lee's street address. You'll return to the previous record to make the change.

You can also use the PAGE UP key to go to the first field in the first record. Then, press TAB to move to the Street field.

1 In the Street field of Earl Lee's record, click after the "y" in "Dorothy" to return to the record.

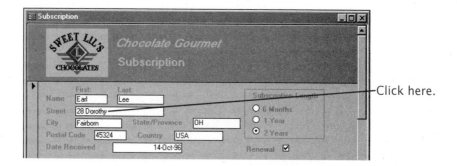

Click here.

2 Press the SPACEBAR to insert a space after "Dorothy," and then type **St.**

You can also click Save on the File menu to save changes to the current record.

3 Click in the First Name field of the next record.

The change is saved.

While you were editing Earl Lee's record, a pencil symbol appeared in the area on the left side of the form. The pencil symbol indicates that you've changed data in the current record but that your changes aren't saved yet. If you haven't changed data in the current record, a triangle appears instead of a pencil. You can see how this works while you add the next record.

Add the second record

1 Type **Becky** in the First Name field.

2 Type the following data, pressing TAB to move from field to field.

Last name:	**Sawyer**
Street Address:	**260 Kent Street Station 1551**
City:	**Ottawa**
State/Province:	**Ontario**
Postal Code:	**K1A 0E6**
Country:	**Canada**

Subscription Length: **6 Months**
Renewal: **No**

Proofread your entries. When you're finished, you will close the Subscription form.

Close the form

You can also click Close on the File menu.

➤ On the Subscription window, click the Close button.

Be sure that you click the Close button on the form, not the Close button on the Microsoft Access window. When you close the form, your new entry is saved.

Click here

Opening a Table to View the Data

Just as a record is used to group similar pieces of information together, a table is used to group records together. A table organizes data into rows and columns. Each column describes some characteristic of the data (a field), and each row contains an item of the data (a record). For example, a field might contain the subscriber's last name, while a record would completely describe one person's subscription.

The records you just added using the Subscription form were saved in the Customers table in the Sweet Lil's database. In the next exercise, you look at the new records in the Customers table.

Open the Customers table

1 In the Database window, click the Tables tab.

The list of tables in the Sweet Lil's database is displayed.

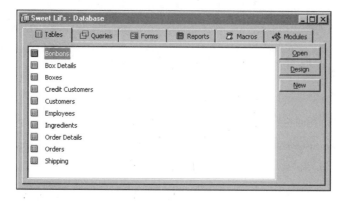

2   Double-click the Customers table.

The Customers table opens, and its records are displayed.

The two records you added are at the end of the list of customers. You can use the navigation buttons at the bottom of the Customers Table window to move directly to the first, previous, next, or last record.

Move to the last record

1   In the lower-left corner of the window, click the navigation button for the last record.

The last few records in the table appear. The last two records are the ones you just added for Earl Lee and Becky Sawyer. This table was set up to automatically assign customer ID numbers to all new records. Lesson 4, "Controlling Database Growth," discusses how to set up a table that assigns ID numbers.

2   To return to the Database window, click the Close button.

TIP You can use the keyboard or the vertical scroll bar to move between records, but the fastest way to move around in a large database is by using the navigation buttons and the mouse.

Understanding Views

A paper form shows one arrangement of your data. To see another arrangement, you have to look at a different paper form. A Microsoft Access form, however, provides the flexibility of two *views*, or arrangements, of your data: Form view and Datasheet view. In Form view, the fields are arranged to show each individual record to its best advantage. Datasheet view shows the same data arranged in rows and columns, like a spreadsheet, so that you can see multiple records at the same time.

Switching Between Views of a Form

You've just been put in charge of Sweet Lil's new Fudge Mocha line. You'll use the Bonbons form to update existing records for Fudge Mocha bonbons and to add records for several new bonbons.

Open a form

1   In the Database window, click the Forms tab.

A list of the forms in the Sweet Lil's database is displayed.

2   Double-click the Bonbons form.

The Bonbons form appears, and the record for Candlelight Ecstasy is displayed.

In Form view, the fields on the Bonbons form are arranged so that you can see all the information about an individual bonbon at a glance. For your current task, a row-and-column format would make it easier to compare fields from different Fudge Mochas.

Switch to Datasheet view

View

➤   On the toolbar, click the View down arrow, and then click Datasheet View.

The records in the Bonbons form appear in a table layout (that is, a layout that has rows and columns). The triangle next to the Candlelight Ecstasy record indicates that Candlelight Ecstasy is the current record.

Record indicator   Field selector

Bonbon Name:	Bonbon ID:	Description:	Chocolate Type:	Filling Type:
Candlelight Ecstasy	B01	Cashew in mocha c	Bittersweet	Mocha cream
Bittersweet Blueberry	B02	Cascade Mountain	Bittersweet	Blueberry
Marzipan Oakleaf	B03	Marzipan shaped ir	Bittersweet	Marzipan
Bittersweet Strawberry	B04	Olympic Wilderness	Bittersweet	Strawberry
Bittersweet Raspberry	B05	Orcas Island raspbe	Bittersweet	Raspberry
Bittersweet Marmalade	B06	Marmalade covered	Bittersweet	Marmalade

Record selector

You can see that two of the bonbons in the new Fudge Mocha line—Walnut Fudge Mocha and Pistachio Fudge Mocha—are already in the database (Bonbon IDs F01 and F02). These are the records you want.

Move to a different record

> Click anywhere in the row for Walnut Fudge Mocha.

Now the record for Walnut Fudge Mocha is the current record. The triangle at the left edge of the datasheet is now pointing to the Walnut Fudge Mocha record. If you switch back to Form view, Walnut Fudge Mocha is the record you'll see on the form.

Switch views

1   On the toolbar, click the View down arrow, and then click Form View.

The record for Walnut Fudge Mocha is displayed in Form view.

2   Click the View down arrow, and then click Datasheet View.

The form appears in Datasheet view. Walnut Fudge Mocha is still the current record.

Changing the Appearance of a Datasheet

The Bonbon Description field describes each bonbon in a sentence or two. You are going to include these descriptions in Sweet Lil's catalog, so you want to make sure that the text is just right. With the datasheet laid out as it is now, you can see only part of each bonbon's description. To read an entire description, you'd have to use the arrow keys and the HOME and END keys to scroll through the text.

Rather than doing a lot of scrolling, you decide to change the datasheet layout so that you can read the entire description at once. To change the height of a row in a datasheet, you use the *record selector* on the left side of the record. You use the *field selector* at the top of a column to change the column width.

You'll start by maximizing the Form window and then changing the row height so that you can see the entire description of a bonbon.

Change the row height

You can double-click the Form window title bar to maximize the window.

1 Maximize the Form window.

It is easier to work in a maximized window.

2 Position the mouse pointer on the lower border of any record selector.

Bonbon Name:	Bonbon ID:	Description:	Chocolate Type:	Filling Type:	Nut Type:
Candlelight Ecstasy	B01	Cashew in mocha c	Bittersweet	Mocha cream	Cashew
Bittersweet Blueberry	B02	Cascade Mountain	Bittersweet	Blueberry	None
Marzipan Oakleaf	B03	Marzipan shaped ir	Bittersweet	Marzipan	None
Bittersweet Strawberry	B04	Olympic Wilderness	Bittersweet	Strawberry	None
Bittersweet Raspberry	B05	Orcas Island raspbe	Bittersweet	Raspberry	None

To resize a record, position the mouse pointer here.

3 Drag the border down to make the row higher.

Microsoft Access resizes all the rows. (One row cannot be sized differently from the other rows in the table.)

4 Adjust the height of the rows until you can read the complete description for Bittersweet Blueberry (Bonbon ID B02).

Change the column width

Now that you've resized the rows, you'll adjust the width of some of the columns. The Bonbon ID field and the Cost field are wider than necessary. If you make these columns narrower, you'll be able to see more of the other fields in the datasheet.

1 Position the mouse pointer on the right border of the field selector for the Bonbon ID field.

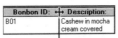

Bonbon ID:	Description:
B01	Cashew in mocha cream covered

Position the mouse pointer here.

2 Double-click the right edge of the field selector.

The column is sized to fit the widest entry in the field, including the complete field name at the top of the column.

3 At the bottom of the Datasheet window, click in the scroll bar to scroll to the right to see the rest of the fields.

Click here to scroll in large increments.

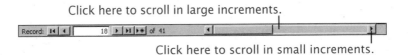

Record: [◄◄] [◄] 18 [►] [►I] [►*] of 41   [◄]   [►]

Click here to scroll in small increments.

4 Make the column for the Cost field narrower by double-clicking the right border of the field selector.

 TIP You can click the arrows at either end of the scroll bar to scroll one field (one column) at a time.

Save the datasheet layout

Records are automatically saved as you move from record to record, but changes to the layout of a form or table must be saved by using the Save command.

You can save this convenient layout so that your datasheet appears this way every time you use it.

➤ On the File menu, click Save.

Scroll through the records

You're ready to work with the records in the Fudge Mocha line. But now that you've increased the height of your datasheet rows, the records you want aren't visible. You can use either the vertical scroll bar or the PAGE DOWN key to scroll through the records.

1 In the vertical scroll bar, click below the scroll box. Or, press PAGE DOWN.

Microsoft Access scrolls down one page (window).

2 Continue to click below the scroll box until you see Walnut Fudge Mocha in the list.

To scroll up or down one record at a time, click the arrows at the top or bottom of the scroll bar.

Each time you click below the scroll box, the box moves down the scroll bar to show your relative position in the records.

 TIP If you hold down the left mouse button while moving the scroll box, a ScrollTip (a small box that displays information) indicates the record number that will be at the top of your display when you release the mouse and the total number of records (for example, Record: 187 of 322). If you know the relative position of the records you're looking for, you can move to them very quickly by dragging the scroll box. For example, if you're looking for a record in the middle of the list, drag the scroll box to the middle of the vertical scroll bar. You can see the records change as you drag the scroll box.

Speeding Up Data Entry by Using Editing Tools

You keep a database current and accurate by updating data in fields. Microsoft Access has convenient editing features that help you edit, move, copy, and delete data in fields. You'll find most of the editing features on the Edit menu and on the toolbar.

When you edit in Microsoft Access, keep in mind a principle called *select, then do.* If you want to copy, delete, or change something, you first *select* it, and *then* you *do* it by clicking the command you want on a menu or by clicking the appropriate button on the toolbar. Many menu commands show a toolbar button image to the left of the command to indicate which button corresponds to that command. Using the toolbar buttons is usually faster than clicking menu commands. Convenient keyboard shortcuts are also listed to the right of many menu commands. If you do a lot of typing, you might want to memorize the keyboard shortcuts for the commands you use frequently. Find the command method that works best for you—for example, if you want to delete text, first you drag to select the text, and then you can click Cut on the Edit menu, press the shortcut keys CTRL+X, or click the Cut button on the toolbar.

When you cut or copy text or an object, the object is placed in the Windows storage area called the *Clipboard.* When you paste, Microsoft Access pastes whatever is on the Clipboard to the current location of the insertion point. You can copy text from one field and then paste it into another field or into as many other fields as you need. That's because Windows keeps the Clipboard contents until you copy or cut something else or until you exit Windows.

Add text to a field

Market research indicates that chocolate fudge is a key ingredient for the success of your new line. You'll add the phrase "smothered in fudge" to the end of each bonbon description.

1   In the Description field for the Walnut Fudge Mocha bonbon, click between the t in "walnut" and the period.

The insertion point appears where you click.

2   Press the SPACEBAR to insert a space, and then type **smothered in fudge**

Copy text from one field to another

Rather than type the phrase again, you can copy it to the Description field for the Pistachio Fudge Mocha bonbon.

1   Select the phrase "smothered in fudge," including the space in front of "smothered" but not the period at the end.

Hint: Click in the space after the t in "walnut." Drag to select the text you want.

Copy

You can also click Copy on the Edit menu.

2   On the toolbar, click the Copy button.

Microsoft Access places a copy of the selected text on the Clipboard.

Paste

You can also click Paste on the Edit menu.

Cut

3 In the Description field for the Pistachio Fudge Mocha bonbon, position the insertion point between the o in "pistachio" and the period.

4 On the toolbar, click the Paste button.

The text is pasted from the Clipboard.

 NOTE You use the same steps to move text, except you click Cut instead of Copy on the Edit menu (or click the Cut button, which is to the left of the Copy button on the toolbar). The highlighted copy is removed from the text and placed on the Clipboard. Then, you can paste the text where you want it.

Add new records

Next, you'll enter records for Sweet Lil's three new Fudge Mochas—Pecan, Cashew, and Almond. You can add new records in either Datasheet view or Form view, but it's easier in Form view because you can see all the fields in a record at once.

1 On the toolbar, click the View down arrow, and then click Form View.

The Bonbons form appears in Form view.

2 Click the New Record navigation button.

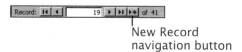

New Record
navigation button

The new record is displayed following the last record in the set.

3 Type this data in the first two fields:

Bonbon Name: **Pecan Fudge Mocha**

Bonbon ID: **F03**

4 In the Description field, type **Creamy sweet mocha and nutty pecan**.

The next part of the description, "smothered in fudge," is still on the Clipboard. Instead of typing the description, you can paste it again.

You can also click the right mouse button, and select Paste.

5 On the toolbar, click the Paste button.

6 Type a period at the end of the description.

Edit text

"Nutty" is redundant as an adjective for "pecan," so you'll delete it. To match the other Fudge Mocha descriptions, you want this description to start with

"Sweet creamy" rather than "Creamy sweet." You can replace the old text at the same time that you type the new text; you don't have to delete the old text first.

1 In the Description field, select the word "nutty" and the space after it, and then press DELETE.

2 Select "Creamy sweet."

3 Type **Sweet creamy**

The text you type replaces the selected text. Now your description is correct.

Selecting Data Entry Values from a List

A *value* is an individual piece of data, such as a last name, an address, or an ID number. Sometimes a database designer will add a list of correct values to some fields. If the person entering the data doesn't know or can't remember what to enter, he or she can select the appropriate value from the list. Selecting a value from a list is often quicker than typing the value yourself. But using lists has another advantage besides speed—your data is more accurate. When you select a value from a list, you know that it's spelled consistently and that it's a valid entry.

The Chocolate Type field on the Bonbons form is a special kind of field called a *list box.* List boxes display a list of values to select from. You can use either the mouse or the keyboard to select a value from the list.

The Nut Type and Filling Type fields are both *combo boxes,* which are combinations of text entry and list boxes. In a combo box, you can either type the value yourself or select it from the list.

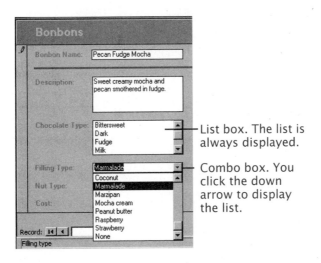

List box. The list is always displayed.

Combo box. You click the down arrow to display the list.

473

Select a value from a list

You can also press TAB to move to the Chocolate Type field.

▶ In the Chocolate Type field, click "Fudge" to select it.

Fudge is the only value in the Chocolate Type list that starts with f, so you can select Fudge by typing the first letter of the word. If the list has more than one f value, you can type f to go to the first one and then use the DOWN ARROW key to move down the list.

Select a value in a combo box

You can either type the value you want in the Filling Type combo box, or you can select a value from the list. Often, it's easier and more accurate to select a value.

You can also press TAB to move to the Filling Type field, and then press F4 to display the drop-down list.

1   Click the down arrow in the Filling Type field to display the list.

This list shows you the fillings that Sweet Lil's uses.

2   Select Mocha Cream from the list.

To select the value without using the mouse, type **mo**, the first two letters in Mocha. Because Mocha Cream is the only value that starts with those two letters, Microsoft Access selects it. If you wanted to select Marmalade instead of Marzipan, you'd type **marm**

3   Type **Pecan** in the Nut Type field, or select it from the list.

Enter the bonbon cost

▶ Type **.25** in the Bonbon Cost field, and then press TAB to move to the last field on the form.

When you exit the Bonbon Cost field, the value is automatically formatted as a currency value.

NOTE   If you'd like to build on the skills that you learned in this lesson, you can do the One Step Further. Otherwise, skip to "Finish the lesson."

One Step Further: Manipulating Datasheet Views

Datasheets display all the fields and records of a table. If the table has a large number of fields, Datasheet view might be difficult because you can't see all the fields on a single screen. Two techniques that make large datasheets easier to work with are freezing and hiding columns.

Freeze a column

When you scroll to the fields on the far right of the Bonbon Table datasheet, you can no longer see the Bonbon Name field, so you can't tell which bonbon records you're viewing. It would be much easier to scroll through the data fields to the right while the Bonbon Name field remains anchored, or frozen, on the left. You can do that by freezing the column.

1   On the toolbar, click the View down arrow, and then click Datasheet.

2   Scroll back to the left side of the datasheet.

If your screen resolution is more than 640 x 480 pixels, you might not need to scroll and you will not see the scroll bars.

Click here to scroll to the left.

3   Click in any record in the Bonbon Name column.

4   On the Format menu, choose Freeze Columns.

Microsoft Access displays a bold line on the right border of the Bonbon Name column. Now the column is frozen.

5   Scroll horizontally to see the fields on the right side of the record, and then scroll to the left side of the form.

This column doesn't scroll. All other columns scroll.

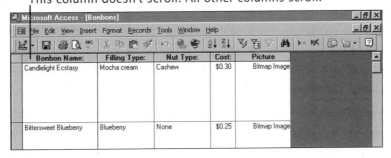

Hide a column

In Datasheet view, the bonbon pictures cannot be seen. Because the pictures aren't visible anyway, you can hide the Picture column.

The Format menu also contains a Hide Columns command. When you choose the command, it hides the column that contains the insertion point.

▶   Click the right border of the Picture column at the column heading, and drag the right border past the left border.

Microsoft Access hides the column.

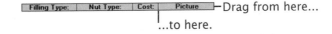
Drag from here...

...to here.

Restore hidden columns

1   On the Format menu, click Unhide Columns.

If the Unhide Columns dialog box indicates that the Picture column is already showing, the column might not be completely hidden. Make sure that you dragged the column's right border *all the way* to its left border.

2   Select the Picture field check box, and then click Close.

Finish the lesson

1   To continue to the next lesson, on the File menu, click Close.

2   If you are finished using Microsoft Access for now, on the File menu, click Exit.

Lesson Summary

To	Do this
Open a database	In the Microsoft Access dialog box, double-click the database you want to open. *or* In the Microsoft Access dialog box, double-click More Files. In the Open dialog box, select the folder where the database file is stored, and double-click the database filename.
Open a form	In the Database window, click the Forms tab, and then double-click the form you want to open.
Select an option in an option group	Click the option. *or* Press an arrow key until the option is selected.
Select or clear a check box	Click the check box. *or* Press TAB to move to the check box, and then press the SPACEBAR.

To	Do this	Button
Move to the next record on a form	Click the Next Record button at the bottom of the form. *or* With the insertion point in the last field, press TAB.	
Move from field to field	Click the field you want to move to. *or* Press TAB to move to the next field, and press SHIFT+TAB to move to the previous field.	
Move to the previous record in a form	Press the PAGE UP key. *or* Click the Previous Record navigation button at the bottom of the form.	
Save data	Microsoft Access automatically saves your data when you move to another record or window, close the form, or exit the program. *or* If you want to save your data at any other time, click Save on the File menu or click the Save button.	
Open a table	In the Database window, click the Tables tab, and then double-click the table you want to open.	
Switch between Form view and Datasheet view	Click the View down arrow, and then click Datasheet View or Form View.	
Change the height of rows or the width of a column in a datasheet	To resize rows, drag the lower border of any record. To resize a column, drag the right border of the column's field selector.	
Copy text from one field to another	Select the text. On the toolbar, click the Copy button. Place the insertion point where you want the text to appear. On the toolbar, click the Paste button.	

To	Do this	Button
Move text from one field to another	Select the text. On the toolbar, click the Cut button. Place the insertion point where you want the text to appear. On the toolbar, click the Paste button.	
Freeze columns	Click any record in the column you want to freeze, and then click Freeze Columns on the Format menu.	

For online information about	Use the Office Assistant to search for
Opening databases	**Opening databases,** and then click Open A Database
Moving between records	**Moving between records,** and then click Moving Between Records Using Navigation Buttons In Datasheet Or Form View
Saving a record	**Saving a record,** and then click Save A Record
Opening tables	**Opening tables,** and then click Open A Table
Changing column widths	**Resizing columns,** and then click Resize A Column In Datasheet View
Hiding a column	**Hiding a column,** and then click Hide Columns In Datasheet View
Freezing columns	**Freezing columns,** and then click Freeze And Unfreeze Columns In Datasheet View
Copying or moving text from one field to another	**Copying or moving data,** and then click Copy Or Move Data

Increasing Efficiency by Using Subforms

Estimated time
40 min.

In this lesson you will learn how to:

- Use a subform.
- Use a validation message to help you enter the right data.
- Undo your edits.
- Simplify tasks by using command buttons.
- Find records.
- Delete a record.

When you fill out a form, it's easy to make a small mistake that can turn into a big problem. A simple subtraction error can result in a frustrating check of the numbers; a search for a forgotten bit of information can eat up time; and there's always the possibility of writing the right information in the wrong box. What you need is a form that does calculations for you, looks up missing information, and warns you when the data you enter doesn't make sense.

Microsoft Access forms can do all this for you. In this lesson, you'll find out how to use forms that help you start and stay with the right data.

Understanding Forms That Have Subforms

In this lesson, you will use a form that has been named Boxes. The Boxes form is more complex than either the Subscription form or the Bonbons form used in Lesson 1. But when you use Microsoft Access forms, "more complex" doesn't necessarily mean "harder."

The Boxes form contains a *subform*, which is a form within a form. Because the Boxes form has a subform, you can look at all the information about the box (number of boxes in stock, total cost of the box, and so on) on the main form at the same time you look at detailed information on the subform about the candies that are in the box (what type of bonbons are in the box, how many are in the box, type of filling, individual cost of each bonbon, and so on). You can scroll through the records in the subform, adding and deleting types of bonbons, until the box contains the candies that you want.

Box Details subform

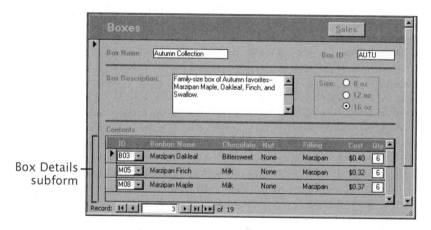

The advantage of using a form that has a subform is that you can work with data from two different tables at the same time. This approach not only simplifies using Microsoft Access, it increases the reliability of the data in the tables.

When you use the Boxes form, data you enter on the main form is stored in the Boxes table. Data you enter on the subform is stored in the Box Details table. You'll learn more about why the data is stored in separate tables in Lesson 4, "Controlling Database Growth."

Start the lesson

➤ If Microsoft Access isn't started yet, start it. Open the Sweet Lil's Lesson02 database. If the Microsoft Access window doesn't fill your screen, maximize the window.

If you need help opening the database, see Lesson 1, "Viewing, Entering, and Customizing Data."

480

Focusing on Specific Data by Using a Subform

Microsoft Access forms are very versatile tools. A well-designed form can accomplish several tasks simultaneously. For example, a single form can be used to update two or more tables at once. When a form uses information from more than one table, you should create a subform. The main form is based on the data from one table, and the subform is based on the data from the second table. Using the subform structure increases the control you have over your tables and makes your database easier to maintain.

You'll use the Boxes form to add a new box of bonbons called Winter Collection to Sweet Lil's line of products. The Boxes form contains the Boxes subform. The Boxes subform can be thought of as a "window" into another set of data, which is stored in a separate table. The Boxes table stores data about all the boxes. The Boxes form draws its data from the Boxes table. The details of what makes up a particular box are stored in a table called Box Details. The Boxes subform draws its data from the Box Details table. In Microsoft Access, viewing a form and a subform together has several advantages. It is more convenient, and it makes working with the database easier.

 NOTE The reasons for storing the external and internal box details in separate tables are discussed in Lesson 4, "Controlling Database Growth." In general, however, this type of storage structure helps ensure the integrity of the data and simplifies database maintenance.

Open a form, and go to the new record

You can also select the Boxes form, and click the Open button in the Database window.

1 Double-click the Boxes form.

The record for the All Seasons—the first box in the Boxes table—appears in the main form, and the contents of the All Seasons box are displayed in the subform.

2 At the bottom of the form, click the New Record navigation button.

The new blank record appears at the end of the existing records.

New Record

Enter data in the main form

1 Type the following data in the fields on the main form:

Box Name   **Winter Collection**

Box ID   **WINT**

Box Description   **Nuts and berries coated with chocolate and fudge for those long winter evenings by the fire.**

2 In the Size option area, select 12 oz.

3 Press TAB to move to the subform.

The insertion point moves to the first field in the subform.

Locate data and enter a record in the subform

The first field in the subform will contain the Bonbon ID for the first candy in the Winter Collection box. The bonbon you want is Bittersweet Blueberry, but you're not sure of its ID number. You'll use the ID combo box to find the ID you want. A *combo box* is a control area, similar to a list box or text box, in which you can either type a value or select a value from a list.

1 Click the ID down arrow to display the ID combo box list.

The list has two columns: IDs are in the first column, and the corresponding bonbon names are in the second column. When you select a row, only the ID is stored in the field. The names are there to help you make the right selection.

Box list —
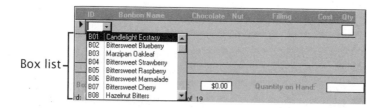

2 Select Bittersweet Blueberry.

The Bonbon ID B02 appears in the ID field; and the Bonbon Name, Chocolate, Nut, Filling, and Cost fields are filled in. The fields for which you supply information have a white background; all the other fields have a gray background.

3 Press TAB to move to the next empty field.

The insertion point skips fields that are already filled in and moves to the Qty field.

4 Type **3** in the Qty field, and then press TAB.

Microsoft Access saves the first record in the subform and moves the insertion point to the first field in the second record.

Enter more subform records

As you add the remaining bonbons to the subform in this exercise, the Box Cost field in the lower left of the main form will change for each new record because how much a box costs depends on which bonbons are in the box.

NOTE Look at the vertical scroll bar on the right side of the subform. The presence of the scroll bar means that the subform contains more records, and you can scroll through the records to view them.

1 Add the following two bonbons to the Winter Collection:

ID		Qty
B05	Bittersweet Raspberry	3
D03	Cashew Supreme	3

2 Press TAB to move to the next record in the subform.

A new, blank record appears.

3 Add the following three bonbons to the Winter Collection:

ID		Qty
D07	Classic Cherry	3
F01	Walnut Fudge Mocha	3
F02	Pistachio Fudge Mocha	3

4 Scroll through the subform to check your work. Be sure that each record is correct before continuing.

Exit the subform

Now that you've added all the bonbons to the new box, you're ready to fill in the two fields in the lower portion of the main form—Box Price and Quantity On Hand.

 Press CTRL+TAB to move to the next field on the main form.

The insertion point moves from the subform to the Box Price field on the main form. You can also move to the Box Price field by clicking that field, but when you're entering new records, it's easier to keep your hands on the keyboard than to switch between the mouse and the keyboard.

 TIP When you're using a form that has a subform, you can think of the CTRL key as the "switch form" key. Just as pressing TAB moves you to the next field in a form, pressing CTRL+TAB moves you from the subform to the next field in the main form. And just as pressing SHIFT+TAB moves you to the previous field in a subform or main form, pressing CTRL+SHIFT+TAB moves you from the subform to the previous field in the main form.

Validating Your Data

You will learn more about validation rules and how to create forms for automatic data entry in Lesson 5, "Keeping Database Information Reliable."

You've already seen a number of ways that using a Microsoft Access form can help you enter the correct data. For example, the ID combo box in the subform helps you pick the right ID by showing you bonbon names as well as IDs. After you pick a bonbon, Microsoft Access fills in fields, such as the Bonbon Name and Chocolate fields, saving you time and eliminating the possibility of data entry errors in those fields. As you're adding bonbons to the box, the cost of the box is automatically calculated and is displayed in the Box Cost field.

A form can be of even more help when you're entering data. Microsoft Access displays a message when you enter incorrect information in a form. The value you enter in a field is checked against a validation rule that was established when the table was created. If the value you attempt to enter breaks the rule, a message appears. You can't exit the field until you correct the invalid data.

Correct the data

The note you have from Sweet Lil's Marketing Department says to give the new box the special introductory price of $7.50.

1   Type **7.50** in the Box Price field, and then press TAB.

A validation message tells you the value you entered is incorrect, and gives you information about how to correct the problem.

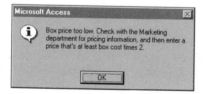

   NOTE If the message doesn't appear, you might have incorrect data in the Box Cost field. The validation rule for the Box Price field allows those values that are at least twice as much as the value in the Box Cost field. An error message is displayed if the price is less than twice the cost. The Box Cost field is calculated automatically from the records entered in the subform.

---

2   Click OK.

At this point, you double-check with the Marketing Department and discover that the introductory price of the new box should be $17.50.

3   Type a **1** before the 7 in the Box Price field, and then press TAB.

Microsoft Access accepts this price, adds a dollar sign, and moves the insertion point to the Quantity On Hand field.

4 Type **0** (zero) in the Quantity On Hand field.

This is a new box type, so you don't have any in stock yet.

Undoing Your Edits

In Microsoft Access, you can use the Undo button to reverse changes you make to the current field or record. Because there are different types of actions that you might want to undo, the ScreenTip for the Undo button changes to reflect the most recent reversible action. For example, if your most recent action was to enter data, the Undo button is labeled the Undo Typing button. If your most recent action was to delete a field, the available Undo action will be Undo Delete.

Undo your most recent action

1 Select "Nuts and berries" at the beginning of the Box Description field for the Winter Collection, and then type **Berries and nuts**

2 Place the insertion point in front of the word "fire," type **roaring** and then press the SPACEBAR.

3 On the toolbar, click the Undo button.

The word "roaring," your most recent change, is deleted.

Undo

You can also choose Undo on the Edit menu.

Undo all edits in the current field

After making numerous changes to the text in a field, you might decide that you prefer the original text. Rather than restore the original text one change at a time, you can undo all the changes to that field at once.

➤ On the Edit menu, click Undo Current Field/Record.

All the edits you made to the Box Description field since moving the insertion point into the field are undone. The Undo button becomes the Undo The Current Field button.

Using a Command Button

Sometimes one task turns into many related tasks. For example, you might be looking at information about the contents of a product on one form and realize that you also want to see sales information for the product. So you open a sales form and find the appropriate sales information. These related tasks can require a number of steps, and you might need to repeat these actions many times.

A *command button* (a button that initiates a series of commands) condenses related tasks into a single step. A command button can be used to perform one action or to perform a series of actions, depending on how you define the button. Command buttons can be used to either execute macros or run programs written in Visual Basic for Applications, which is a special programming language. A *macro* is a recording of a list of tasks or a set of keystrokes. When a macro is played, Microsoft Access performs the prescribed actions very quickly, thus improving productivity.

Use a command button to go to a specific record

The Sales command button on this form executes a macro called Show Box Sales. The Sales command button was added to the form when the form was created, and the Show Box Sales macro was assigned to the Sales command button. In this exercise, you'll use the Sales command button to check the sales of one of Sweet Lil's best sellers: the Autumn Collection. The Autumn Collection is the third record in the Boxes form.

1   To the right of the word "Record," in the lower-left corner of the window, select the current record number, and then type **3**

Record indicator

2   Press ENTER.

The record for the Autumn Collection is displayed.

3   At the top of the Boxes form, click the Sales command button.

Sales command button

The Box Sales form appears. Just as the Boxes form has a subform, the Box Sales form has a subform called Daily Sales. The main form shows the name of the box at the top and the total sales for the box at the bottom of the form. The subform shows daily sales for the box.

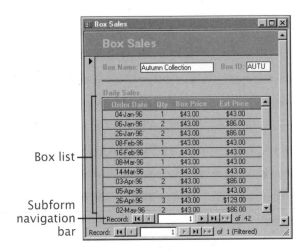

Box list

Subform
navigation
bar

You can also
click Close on
the File menu.

4 Scroll through the records in the Daily Sales subform to see all the sales.

5 To close the Box Sales form, click the Close button.

6 To close the Boxes form, click the Close button.

Maintaining Your Database by Entering Data in Forms

In most databases, the only real constant is that data is constantly changing. You add records when you have to keep track of new people or things. You change records when the data changes. And you delete records when you no longer need to track the people or things represented by the records. Most data entry should be accomplished through forms. When designing a database, it is a good idea to use forms for entering data, rather than directly changing the tables. This method allows you, as the database designer, to build in controls to increase security.

In the following exercises you find and delete records. Sweet Lil's receives this note in the morning's mail:

Dear Sweet Lil's:

My son buys your chocolates frequently and loves them. In fact, he told me that he recently gave you my name to add to your customer list. I'm trying to lose some weight, so please don't add me to your list. No need to waste the catalog.

Thank you,

Francois Marcus

Find the record you want to delete

In this exercise, you find Francois Marcus in the Customers table.

1 Open the View Customers form.

2 Click in the Last Name field

Find

3 On the toolbar, click the Find button.

The Find In Field dialog box appears. The title bar of the Find In Field dialog box shows the name of the field you're searching: Last Name.

4 In the Find What box, type **Marcus**

You have the option of searching in all the fields for Marcus. Because you know the value is in the Last Name field (the current field), you can make the search go faster by searching only in that field. The dialog box should look like the following illustration.

5 Click Find First.

The record for a Francois Marcus is displayed. This appears to be the record for the customer you need to call, but you must make sure there's not another customer who has the same name.

6 Click Find Next.

Microsoft Access displays a message indicating that it cannot find another Marcus.

7 Click OK and then close the Find In Field dialog box.

Delete a record

1 On the toolbar, click the Delete Record button.

Delete Record

2 When a message appears asking you to confirm the deletion, click Yes.

The record is deleted.

You can also choose Delete Record on the Edit menu.

3 Close the View Customers form.

Find a record when you are missing details

As soon as you delete the record for Francois Marcus, you get a call from a clerk in Sweet Lil's Shipping Department. He's having trouble reading the address on a shipping label. All he can make out is part of the street name, which starts

with "Stew." He asks whether you can use this information to find the name and address of the customer.

1 Open the Customer Review form.

2 In the Customer Review form, click in the field that contains the street address (the first line in the address).

You don't have to go back to the first record in the table—you can use the Find button when you are in any record.

3 On the toolbar, click the Find button.

The Find In Field dialog box appears. The Find What box still contains your last entry, Marcus.

4 In the Find What box, type **Stew**

5 Click the Match down arrow, and select Any Part Of Field.

Because Stew is only part of the street name, you want to search for Stew no matter where it occurs in the field.

6 Click Find First.

Microsoft Access finds an address that has "Stewart" in the street address.

You can make a search case-sensitive (find only text that has the same uppercase and lowercase letters) by selecting the Match Case check box. For example, if you want to find McDaniel and not Mcdaniel, use the Match Case check box.

7 Click Find Next.

Microsoft Access finds a second record that has "Stew" in the address.

8 Click Find Next again.

Microsoft Access doesn't find another "Stew," so you have two possible customers for the Shipping Department.

9 Click OK and then click Close to close the Find In Field dialog box.

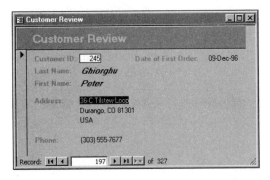

10 Close the Customer Review form.

 NOTE If you'd like to build on the skills that you learned in this lesson, you can do the One Step Further. Otherwise, skip to "Finish the lesson."

One Step Further: Replacing Data

In many instances, you will not only want to find data, you will want to replace the data with more up-to-date information. In addition to finding data, Microsoft Access can assist you with quickly replacing data that meets certain criteria. For example, if you know that a customer address has changed, you can combine the process of finding and replacing the data into one step.

Replace data meeting known criteria

Sweet Lil's has merged its Marketing and Acquisitions Departments. All employees are now members of the Marketing Department. You need to replace all Acquisitions entries in the Department Name field of the Employees table with the word "Marketing."

1   Make sure the Tables tab is selected in the Database window, and then double-click the Employees table.

2   Click anywhere in the Department Name field, and then click the Replace command on the Edit menu.

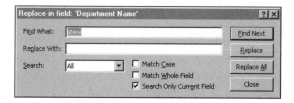

3   Type **Acquisitions** in the Find What field and **Marketing** in the Replace With field.

4   Click Replace All.

All instances of Acquisitions in the Employees table will be replaced with Marketing. A message appears, indicating that the Replace operation cannot be undone.

5   Click Yes to continue.

6   Close the Replace In Field Department Name dialog box.

7   Close the Employees table.

Find and replace data simultaneously

You have already seen how Microsoft Access can help you to quickly locate data. In some cases, you might not know exactly which records you need to replace. For example, if some characters of the field are missing, you might need to use wildcard characters to find the data. *Wildcard characters* are special symbols that can be used to substitute for unknown characters. For example, if you

are searching for a record that contains the letters "man" as the last three characters, but you are not sure whether the name is Freeman or Friedman, you can search with the * wildcard character. The * character replaces a group of characters, so searching for F*man find records that contain either spelling.

This morning, the Sweet Lil's Marketing Department received a call from a customer, V.J. Bernstein. She said she was recently married, and her last name is now Grable. The customer hung up before the clerk could find out how the customer spelled Bernstein. The Marketing Department has asked you to help find and replace the record.

1   Double click the Customers table to open it in Datasheet view.

2   Click anywhere in the Last Name field.

3   On the Edit menu, click Replace.

4   Type ***stein** in the Find What field, and then type **Grable** in the Replace With field.

5   Click the Find Next button.

    The record for V.J. Bernstein is located. The customer address is the same.

6   Click the Replace button.

    The last name is changed to Grable.

7   Close the Replace in Field Last Name dialog box.

8   Close the Customers table.

Finish the lesson

1   To continue to the next lesson, on the File menu, click Close.

2   If you are finished using Microsoft Access for now, on the File menu, click Exit.

Lesson Summary

To	Do this	Button
Add a record	Click the New Record navigation button at the bottom of the form.	▶＊
Move from a main form to a field on a subform	Click the field in the subform. *or* In the last field on the main form before the subform, press TAB.	
Move from a subform to the next field on a main form	Click the field in the main form. *or* Press CTRL+TAB.	

To	Do this	Button
Move from a subform to the previous field on a main form	Press CTRL+SHIFT+TAB.	
Undo your most recent changes	On the toolbar, click the Undo button. *or* On the Edit menu, click Undo.	
Undo all edits in the current field	On the Edit menu, click Undo Current Field/Record.	
Go directly to a specific record	Type the record number in the Record Number box at the bottom of the form, and then press ENTER.	
Delete a record	Click in any field in the record to select it. Then click the Delete Record button.	
Find a record	On the toolbar, click the Find button, and fill in the dialog box.	

For online information about	Use the Office Assistant to search for
Adding records to a form	**Adding records,** and then click Add New Data In Datasheet Or Form View
Undoing changes	**Undo,** and then click Undo Changes When Adding Or Editing Records
Deleting records	**Deleting records,** and then click Delete A Group Of Records With A Query
Finding records	**Finding records,** and then click Find Data

Viewing Only the Information You Need

Estimated time
45 min.

In this lesson you will learn how to:

- Sort records.
- Specify a set of related records by using a filter.
- Report only the information you need.
- Preview and zoom in on report details.
- Print a report.
- Create mailing labels.

Databases can be very large and describe a wide variety of details. However, when you consult a database, you don't want all the available information at once. When you're interested in milk chocolate, you don't want to look at data about bittersweet chocolate. When you're interested in your Canadian customers, you don't want to see data about customers in the United States. As a user of the database, you will ask questions to narrow your search to the information you want; Microsoft Access will provide the answers.

While you're viewing data in forms, you can focus on the information you're interested in without wading through irrelevant data. In this lesson, you'll learn how to make sure that Microsoft Access displays only the data you want to see.

Organizing Your Data

Microsoft Access is more helpful than a filing cabinet or a pile of paper, because when you use Microsoft Access, you can find just the records you need, and you can *sort* (rearrange in a specified order) them the way you want them. Whether your database contains hundreds, thousands, or even millions of records, Microsoft Access finds exactly what you ask for and sorts the data to meet your requirements.

For quick searches, when you're looking for only one record, you use the Find button on the toolbar. When you want to see a particular group of records, such as all the employees hired after a certain date, you create a *filter* to tell Microsoft Access which records you want. When you create a filter, you give Microsoft Access a set of *criteria* or characteristics that describe the records you want to see. Microsoft Access then displays the records in a form or in a form datasheet.

You can sort records alphabetically, numerically, chronologically, or by a specified characteristic. For example, you could sort your customers alphabetically by last name.

Start the lesson

➤ If Microsoft Access isn't started yet, start it. Open the Sweet Lil's Lesson03 database. If the Microsoft Access window doesn't fill your screen, maximize the window.

If you need help opening the database, see Lesson 1.

Putting Records in Order by Using the Sort Button

In addition to using Microsoft Access to keep track of candy orders, Sweet Lil's maintains employee records in a table called Employees. You use the Employees table to conduct annual employee performance reviews. You'll find it easiest to keep your view of the Employees table sorted into departments so you can review the employees a department at a time.

To see the Employee table grouped by department, you sort the table by the Department field.

Sort on the Department field

1 Make sure the Tables tab is in front, and then double-click the Employees table.

2 Click in the Department Name field.

Sort Ascending

3   On the toolbar, click the Sort Ascending button.

The records are sorted by department, in ascending alphabetical order, from A to Z.

First Name	Last Name	Title	Extension	Department Na	Birthda
Ursula	Halliday	Buyer	677	Acquisitions	7/
Donna	Petri	Buyer	678	Acquisitions	5/
Rowen	Gilbert	VP Planning	679	Acquisitions	8/1
Mary	Culvert	VP Marketing	134	Marketing	12/1
Jerome	Woods	Marketing Agen	135	Marketing	3/
Nora	Bromsler	Marketing Agen	136	Marketing	5/
Dale	Wilson	Designer	137	Marketing	9/3
Hans	Orlon	VP Operations	787	Operations	5/
Charles	Beatty	Administrative A	788	Operations	10/
Elizabeth	Yarrow	Administrative A	777	Operations	9/
Frederick	Mallon	Shipping Coordi	546	Shipping	7/
Adrienne	Snyder	Shipping clerk	547	Shipping	12/
Henry	Czynski	Shipping clerk	548	Shipping	6/1
Robin	Saito	Shipping clerk	549	Shipping	3/1

Employees : Table

Record: 1 of 14

Narrowing Your View by Using Filters

For a demonstration of how to create and use filters, double-click the Camcorder file named Using Filters in the Part5 Access Camcorder Files folder. See "Installing and Using the Practice and Camcorder Files," earlier in this book for more information.

In Microsoft Access, you can limit the number of records you see by using a filter. A *filter* is a set of criteria you apply to records to sort them. Filters do not change your data. Instead, they adjust your view of the data, so that only the information you need is visible. Filters are not saved when the table or form is closed. If you want to save a particular view of your data, you use a query, which is like a saved filter that you can use again and again. Queries are covered in Lesson 7, "Getting Answers to Questions About Your Data."

View only employees in the Marketing Department

Mary Culvert, Sweet Lil's vice-president of Marketing, has decided to call a meeting of the Marketing Department managers. She wants you to use Microsoft Access to quickly send them all a meeting notice. In this exercise, you use a filter to identify the Marketing Department managers.

1   Be sure you are in the Department Name field.

2   Click the Find button to locate a record containing Marketing in the Department Name field.

3   In the Find What box, type **Marketing**, and make sure the Search Only Current Field check box is selected.

4   Click Find First, and then click Close.

Find

*Filter By
Selection*

5 On the toolbar, click the Filter By Selection button.

Because you selected Marketing in the Department Name field, the filter locates all employees in the Marketing Department. The navigation area at the bottom of the window indicates that you are viewing filtered data.

	First Name	Last Name	Title	Extension	Department Na	Birthda
▶	Mary	Culvert	VP Marketing	134	Marketing	12/17/96
	Jerome	Woods	Marketing Agen	135	Marketing	3/4/62
	Nora	Bromsler	Marketing Agen	136	Marketing	5/6/63
	Dale	Wilson	Designer	137	Marketing	9/30/59
*						

Record: 14 ◀ 1 ▶ ▶I ▶* of 4 (Filtered)

Add another criteria

The Marketing staff at Sweet Lil's are classified as either managers or sales personnel. Now that you have filtered the Employees table for the department, you also need to see whether the employee is a manager. To add another criteria to the filter, you use the Filter By Form button. The Filter By Selection button works only for simple filters. When building filters that have more than one criteria, it is necessary to use the Filter By Form feature.

Filter By Form

1 On the toolbar, click the Filter By Form button.

A blank row that has a column for each field is displayed; the word "Marketing" is highlighted in the Department Name column.

2 Scroll to view Classification data.

3 Click in the Classification column.

A down arrow appears, which indicates that the column has a drop-down list.

4 Click the Classification down arrow, and then select Manager.

5 On the toolbar, click the Apply Filter button.

Apply Filter

	Employee ID	First Name	Last Name	Title	Extension	Departmer
▶	3	Dale	Wilson	Designer	137	Marketing
	1	Mary	Culvert	VP Marketing	134	Marketing
*	(AutoNumber)					

6 Scroll to view the Classification column.

7 On the Employees table, click the Close button, and then click No to close the table without saving your changes.

Communicating Through Reports

After you have organized your data, you might want to share the data with others or make a paper record of the results. Sharing data in this way is done through reports. Reports are similar to forms in that they draw data together from tables or queries. You can create reports yourself by using the Design window, or you can use one of the predefined report types available in the Report Wizard.

View data in report

You must set a default printer before you can print or preview reports. See Access Help for more information.

The Sales manager has created a report to show sales for the month of November 1996. You will now view this report.

1 In the Database window, click the Reports tab.

2 Double-click the Sales By Box report.

A message appears asking you to enter the dates for the period you want the report to cover.

3 Type **1-Nov-96** as a starting date, and then press ENTER.

Microsoft Access recognizes a number of ways to enter dates. For example, you could have used 11/1/96, another United States format. The Canadian (English) format is 1/11/96.

To find out which country your computer is set for, open the Windows Control Panel, and double-click the Regional Settings icon.

4 In the next dialog box, type **30-Nov-96** as an ending date, and then press ENTER.

Microsoft Access collects the appropriate data and opens the report in Print Preview. Your toolbar has changed.

Look at a whole page at once

The report is magnified in Print Preview so that you can clearly read the data. In Print Preview you can switch to a detailed view by using the magnifying-glass pointer. You use the pointer to zoom out when you want to see how the data is laid out on the whole page, and to zoom in to see the magnified view.

Zoom

You can also switch views by clicking the Zoom button.

➤ Click the magnifying-glass pointer anywhere on the report. Or, click the Zoom button on the toolbar to display the whole page.

Zoom in on the data

The layout looks fine. Now you'll make sure that you have the data you want.

➤ Click anywhere on the report. Or, click the Zoom button on the toolbar.

Now you're looking at the magnified view again.

Move around the page

1   Use the vertical scroll bar to move up and down the page, and use the horizontal scroll bar to move from left to right.

2   Click the Two Pages button to change to a two-page view of the report. You might have to maximize the window to view the pages.

Two Pages

TIP   If you want your report to have wider margins, click Page Setup on the File menu, and then on the Margins tab, change the margins.

Printing a Report

When you print a report, you can print the entire report, you can specify a range of pages or individual pages you want to print, and you can specify how many copies you want to print. If you print more than one copy, you can have Microsoft Access collate the copies for you.

IMPORTANT   If you have a printer connected to your computer, you can print the Sales By Box report now. If you don't have a printer connected to your computer, you can skip to step 3.

Print a report from Print Preview

If you want to use the default print settings, you can also click the Print button on the Standard toolbar.

1   On the File menu, click Print.

The Print dialog box appears. You want to print one copy of the whole report, so you don't need to change any of the settings in the Print dialog box.

2   Click OK.

3   Close the Sales By Box report.

 TIP   When you double-click a report in the Database window, Microsoft Access opens it in Print Preview so that you can see how the report will look on the page before you print it. To print a report without opening it first in Print Preview, select the report in the Database window, and then click Print on the File menu or click the Print button on the toolbar.

Creating Mailing Labels

To create mailing labels, you use a Microsoft Access wizard. A *wizard* is like a database expert who asks you questions about the form or report you want and then builds it for you according to your answers. You use the Form Wizard to build forms and the Report Wizard to build reports. You can use the Label Wizard to create mailing labels.

Create mailing labels

After you examine the Sales By Box report, you decide to promote the two slowest-selling boxes by discounting them in a special mailing to all customers. You want to create mailing labels and print the labels sorted by postal codes. Because you just printed the Sales By Box report, the Database window still shows the list of reports.

1   In the Database window, click the New button.

The New Report dialog box appears.

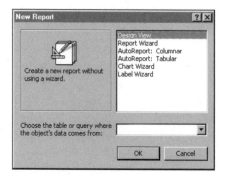

2 In the New Report dialog box, select Label Wizard.

3 Click the Choose The Table Or Query Where the Object's Data Comes From down arrow, and then select Customers.

The Customers table contains the names and addresses you want to print in the mailing labels.

4 Click OK.

The Label Wizard dialog box appears.

Select the mailing label size

You can choose from a wide range of label sizes, listed in either U.S. measurements (inches) or metric measurements. If you have label stock on hand, use the stock number to help you select the label size you want.

In the Label Type area, you can select the label paper type: sheet feed or continuous feed.

➤ Select Avery number 5260 (scroll down to find it), or the label stock you have available, and then click Next.

The Label Wizard displays a dialog box for formatting the text in your labels.

Choose the text font and color

You can use this dialog box to change the appearance of your mailing labels. For now, accept the default choices.

➤ Click Next.

Define the label text

1 In the Available Fields box, double-click the First Name field.

The field is added to the first line of your mailing label.

2 Press the SPACEBAR to add a space between first names and last names.

You'll type spaces and punctuation marks between the fields. These spaces and punctuation marks will appear on the label.

3 Double-click the Last Name field.

Microsoft Access adds the Last Name field to the first line of your mailing label, after the space you typed.

4 Press ENTER to move to the second line of the mailing label.

5   Add the following fields to the second, third, and fourth lines of the mailing label. If you make a mistake, select the line, and press the BACKSPACE key to remove the item from the mailing label.

Line	Field
Second	Street
Third	City, State/Province, and Postal Code fields in the third line. Type a comma between the City and State fields, and use a space between the State and Postal Code fields.
Fourth	Country

The Prototype Label box in the Label Wizard should look like this.

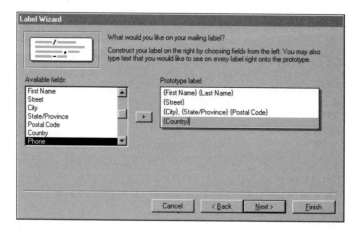

6   Click Next.

Sort the labels

You can sort the labels in the Label Wizard. When you select the field to sort in the Label Wizard, the wizard will sort the labels when they print. You want to sort the labels by postal code.

1   In the Available Fields list, select Postal Code, and click the single right-pointing arrow button between the two list boxes to have the Label Wizard sort by postal codes. Click Next.

2   The Label Wizard suggests the name of Labels Customers for the report. Accept that name by clicking Finish.

The labels appear as they will print on the page. Scroll through the labels.

TIP If the labels don't appear to be evenly lined up, the problem might be a mismatch between your printer driver and the label size or format. Try different label sizes.

Close the mailing label report

When you created the Labels Customers report, you saved the definition of the mailing labels, but not the actual names and addresses that print on the labels. The data that prints on the labels is stored in the Customers table. When Sweet Lil's adds a new customer, the customer information is added to the Customers table. The next time the Labels Customers report is printed, Microsoft Access will take the most current data from the Customers table to print the labels.

The report was automatically saved as Labels Customers when you created it, so you do not need to save it again.

 Close the Labels Customers report.

Your new report appears in the list of reports in the Database window. Now, whenever you need mailing labels for your customers, you can print this report.

 NOTE If you'd like to build on the skills that you learned in this lesson, you can do the One Step Further. Otherwise, skip to "Finish the lesson."

One Step Further: Creating More Complex Filters

It's spring 1997. In late 1996, Sweet Lil's launched a marketing promotion in Canada. Now, it's time to decide whether to expand the promotion for the United States by studying how successful the Canadian campaign is. Using filters allows you to quickly find and look at particular records. This exercise shows you more ways to specify information for your filter.

Identify new customers in Canada

Create a filter that shows Canadian customers added on or after November 15, 1996, the first day of the promotion.

1 Open the Customer Review form. Be sure that Form view is displayed.

You want to be in Form view because you use the Filter By Form button to create a complex filter.

Filter By Form

2 On the toolbar, click the Filter By Form button to begin building your filter.

The Filter By Form dialog box looks different, because you are building the filter in Form view.

3 Press TAB four times; the insertion point is between Address and Phone.

A down arrow appears to the right of the insertion point.

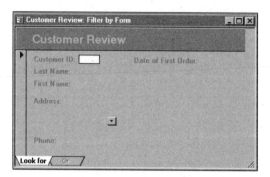

4 Click the down arrow, and select Canada.

Canada appears as a criterion in the Filter By Form dialog box. You could run a simple filter now by clicking the Apply Filter button, but for this exercise you'll add another, more complex criterion and a sort order.

Apply an Advanced Filter/Sort

1 On the Filter menu, click Advanced Filter/Sort.

The Customer ReviewFilter1 window opens, displaying the filter criteria you set in the previous steps. Next, you'll add criteria for Date Of First Order, and then sort the filtered records.

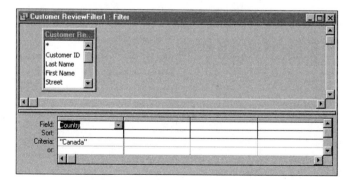

2 Press TAB to move to the next empty Field box in the criteria grid.

3 Click the down arrow for the empty Field box. In the drop-down list, scroll down, and then select Date Of First Order.

4 Click in the Sort box below Date Of First Order. Then, click the Sort down arrow and select Descending.

The records are sorted so that you see the newest customers (those that have the most recent date of first order) first. You want to see only those records for on or after November 15, 1996.

5 Under Date Of First Order, click in the Criteria box. Then, type the expression **>=15-Nov-96** and press ENTER.

The expression means "on or after November 15, 1996." After you enter the expression, Microsoft Access puts number signs (#) around the date, indicating that it is a date/time value.

6 On the toolbar, click the Apply Filter button to apply the filter.

Apply Filter

The filter is applied, as indicated in the navigation area at the bottom of the form. You can use the navigation buttons to see each of the individual records resulting from the filter, or you can switch to Datasheet view to see all the filtered records at once. You can apply advanced filters in either Form view or Datasheet view.

You can also click Datasheet View on the View menu.

7 On the toolbar, click the View down arrow, and select Datasheet View to see all the filtered records at once.

8 On the File menu, click Save.

9 On the File menu, click Close.

Finish the lesson

1 To continue to the next lesson, on the File menu, click Close.

2 If you are finished using Microsoft Access for now, on the File menu, click Exit.

Lesson Summary

To	Do this	Button
Apply a filter by using Filter By Selection	Select a criterion in Form view or Datasheet view, and then click the Filter By Selection button on the toolbar.	
Apply a filter by using Filter By Form	On the toolbar, click the Filter By Form button. Select criteria in the Filter By Form dialog box, and then click the Apply Filter button on the toolbar.	

To	Do this	Button
Set criteria for an advanced filter	In the criteria grid of the Advanced Filter dialog box, select a field in the Field box, and then type a criteria expression in the Criteria box below the Sort box.	
Sort records in a filter	In Datasheet view, click in a field, and then click the Sort Ascending or Sort Descending button. *or* On the Filter menu, click Advanced Filter/Sort. In the Criteria grid of the Advanced Filter dialog box, select Ascending or Descending in the Sort box below the field on which you want to sort.	
Open and preview a report	In the Database window, click the Reports tab, and then double-click the report you want.	
Switch between a magnified view of a report in Print Preview and a view of the whole page	Click anywhere on the report. *or* On the toolbar, click the Zoom button.	
Print a report	In Print Preview, click Print on the File menu, or click the Print button on the toolbar. *or* To print a report directly from the Database window, select the report. Then, either click Print on the File menu, or click the Print button on the toolbar.	
Create mailing labels	In the Database window, click the Reports tab, and then click the New button. Select Label Wizard, select the table or query that contains the data for the labels, and then follow the Label Wizard instructions.	

For online information about	Use the Office Assistant to search for
Specifying criteria	**Criteria,** and then click About Using Criteria In Queries Or Filters To Retrieve Certain Records
Using expressions	**Expression,** and then click What Is An Expression?
Printing reports	**Print reports,** and then click Print A Report

Controlling Database Growth

In this lesson you will learn how to:

- Use a Table Wizard to create a table.
- Add records using a table's datasheet.
- Design a new table.
- Add fields to a table.
- Set field properties.
- Create database relationships.
- Use primary keys to create links.

Organization is the key to a successful database; however, the importance of database organization becomes particularly clear when a database has to be expanded to incorporate new types of data. There are many ways to organize data. Photographs arranged in family albums, for example, are easier to find than those jumbled in a shoe box. A family album can, however, be organized by date or by holiday or even by subject.

In a Microsoft Access database, information is organized in *tables*, which are simply collections of data arranged in rows and columns. You can display database information in a variety of formats, but it's all stored in tables. The form used in Lesson 3, "Viewing Only the Information You Need," is one way of presenting data from one or more tables.

In this lesson, you'll learn how to create a table, define its fields, and add records to the table datasheet. You will also learn how to determine when you need a new database and how to create relationships within that database.

Understanding Tables and Databases

A database table contains data on the same subject or topic. One table might contain data about customers, such as each customer name, address, and phone number. Another table might contain data about candy, such as each bonbon's name, picture, and cost.

A Microsoft Access database is a collection of tables—or is at least one table— that you use to store related information. The tables in the Sweet Lil's database, for example, all contain data relating to different parts of Sweet Lil's business.

An important part of designing a database is deciding how to divide the data into tables and how those tables should be grouped into databases. Sweet Lil's database, for example, is made up of ten tables. Each of these tables describes a distinct entity.

Fields are covered in Lesson 1, "Viewing, Entering, and Customizing Data." In this lesson, you'll learn how to define the fields in a table, and you'll see how fields and records are displayed in tables.

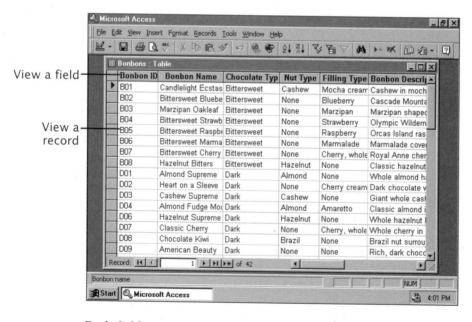

Each field corresponds to a column in a database table, and each field contains only one category of information. For example, each field in the Bonbons table contains a different category of information that describes a bonbon, such as the bonbon name, chocolate type, or filling.

Each record appears as a row in the table and contains all the data about each category. Each record in the Bonbons table, for example, contains all the data about a particular bonbon. Each record in the Customers table contains all the data about a particular customer.

Planning for Database Expansion

Sweet Lil's Chocolates is growing rapidly. More and more people are becoming customers, and more and more customers are using the toll-free order number. Most customers now want gift orders to arrive quickly, often overnight. To meet these needs, Sweet Lil's has to increase production and speed up delivery.

Two bottlenecks in producing and shipping the candy are the time it takes to get new supplies and the need for more shipping companies. To expedite communication with suppliers, Sweet Lil's will add supplier information to the corporate database. To meet its customers' requirements for faster delivery, the company will begin using two more shipping carriers so that customers have the option of air delivery.

Expanding Your Database by Using a Table Wizard

Microsoft Access can help you create a table by using a Table Wizard. Using a Table Wizard is a quick way to start a new database or to add a new table to an existing database. The Table Wizard may not capture every aspect of the new table or database, but you can always go back later and edit or change anything in the table.

Start the lesson

➤ If Microsoft Access isn't started yet, start it. Open the Sweet Lil's Lesson04 database. If the Microsoft Access window doesn't fill your screen, maximize the window.

If you need help opening the database, see Lesson 1.

Create a table by applying the Table Wizard

1 In the Database window, be sure that the Tables tab is in the front, and then click the New button.

The New Table dialog box appears.

2 In the New Table dialog box, select Table Wizard, and then click OK.

The Table Wizard dialog box appears.

3 In the Sample Tables list, scroll down, and then select Suppliers.

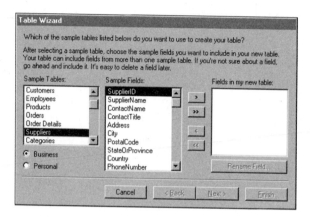

4 In the Sample Fields list, double-click each of the following fields to move the field to the Fields In My New Table list:

SupplierName   FaxNumber

ContactName   EmailAddress

PhoneNumber

5 Click Next.

Below the What Do You Want To Name Your Table area, the name "Suppliers" appears. You want to name your table Suppliers, so you don't have to make any change.

6 Be sure the Yes, Set A Primary Key For Me option is selected, and then click Next.

A primary key is one or more fields that uniquely identify each record in a table. It is usually easiest to let Microsoft Access set the primary key.

7 The next question you see asks, "Is your new table related to any other tables in your database?" You don't have any tables to relate the Suppliers table to now, so click Next.

8 Select the Enter Data Directly Into The Table option, and then click Finish.

Your new table opens in Datasheet view.

Changing a Table Design in Design View

Tables can be created by using the Table Wizard or when you are in Design view. Regardless of which approach you take, occasionally you will need to change a table design. These changes are always made in Design view.

The Suppliers table you created by using the Table Wizard captures the basic suppliers data that Sweet Lil's wants to store. You need to add two additional attributes: delivery time and ingredients. You will add these attributes to the table while it is open in Design view.

Add a field in Design view

View

The graphic on the View button changes to re- flect the most recent selection.

1 On the toolbar, click the View down arrow, and select Design View.

2 In the first empty row in the Field Name column, click to position the in- sertion point.

3 Type **Ingredients** and then press TAB.

The cursor is in the Data Type column. The default data type is Text.

4 Press ENTER to accept Text as the data type. Press ENTER again to move to the next row.

5 Type **DeliveryTime**

6 Press TAB to move the insertion point to the Data Type column. Click the Data Type down arrow, and then select Number.

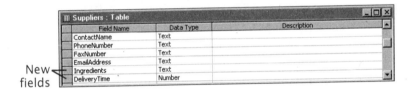

New fields

7 Close the Suppliers Table window.

8 A message appears, asking whether you want to save the changes to the design of the Suppliers table. Click Yes.

Adding Records in Table Datasheet View

The Datasheet view of a table is similar to the Datasheet view of a form. In Datasheet view, you can add to or look at your data. When you switch from Design view to Datasheet view, your records are reordered by the SuppliersID field—a special field known as a primary key. A *primary key* is the field or com- bination of fields that identifies a record as being unique. No two records can have the same value in their primary key field. Primary keys and multiple-field primary keys are discussed in more detail later in this lesson.

You use the View button on the toolbar to toggle between the available views and to select the view you want.

Add records

Because it is a primary key, the SuppliersID field is of the AutoNumber data type. When you open the Suppliers table in Datasheet view, you will see the word "AutoNumber," which lets you know that you don't have to fill in this field. In an AutoNumber-type field, Microsoft Access automatically numbers each new record. AutoNumber guarantees that each record has a unique value for that field. You need to add the other information about the new suppliers to the remaining fields.

 NOTE Microsoft Access puts an *input mask*—a control property that, in this case, helps speed up data entry—on the Phone Number field and Fax Number field to fill in the punctuation, so you type only the numbers.

1 In the Database window, double-click the new Suppliers table. The table opens in Datasheet view.

2 Press TAB to move to the Supplier Name field, and then type **Chocolate World**

As you begin typing, Microsoft Access gives the record an ID of 1.

3 Press TAB to move to the Contact Name field, and then type **Becky Rheinhart**

4 Press TAB to move to the Phone Number field, and then type **6175555460**

5 Press TAB to move to the Fax Number field, and then type **6175555459**

6 Press TAB to move to the Email address field, and then type **BecaR@chocko.com**

7 Press TAB to move to the Ingredients field, and then type **Chocolate**

8 To complete the record, press TAB to move to the Delivery Time field, and then type **5**

Save a record

The record you are working on is saved when you move to a new row. Before you move to another row, look at the record indicator in the field selector to the left of the SuppliersID field. The pencil symbol record indicator shows that you have added or changed data in the record but haven't saved the data yet.

Record — Indicator

You can move to the next record by clicking in the next row or by using the DOWN ARROW key. ➤ Press TAB to move to the next record.

When you move to the next record, Microsoft Access automatically saves the data in the previous record. You don't have to do anything else to save the record.

Add more records

1 Press TAB to move to the Supplier Name field, and then add the following two records to the Suppliers table.

When you enter new data, the pencil symbol reappears.

Supplier Name:	**Allfresh Nuts**	**Flavorly Extracts, Inc.**
Contact Name:	**Barney Cutter**	**Beverly Sims**
Phone Number:	**(313) 555-9987**	**(515) 555-9834**
Fax Number:	**(313) 555-9990**	**(515) 555-9888**
Email Address:	**BarneyC@nuts.com**	**BevS@Flavorly.com**
Ingredients	**Walnuts, Pecans**	**Lemon, Mint**
Delivery Time	5	7

2 Close the Suppliers Table window.

Designing and Creating a New Table

The first step in designing a new table is to determine the *key attributes*—what makes each item in the table unique—and what information is required about these items. It is also important to decide whether the new data requires creating a new database, rather than adding a table to the existing database. Creating a new database might be worthwhile if:

■ You have a large number of new records.

■ The information has a unique purpose in the organization.

■ Information gathering or dispersal creates networking or telecommunications issues.

Develop a new table

Sweet Lil's has decided that the Shipping Department information can be incorporated into the existing database. The information, however, requires adding a new table to accommodate the carriers data. For this table, the following list of attributes has been developed by the Shipping Department.

■ The name of and contact information for the shipping company

■ The type of carrier (air or land)

First, you open a new table.

1   In the Database window, be sure that the Tables tab is selected and the list of tables is in front, and then click the New button.

2   In the New Table dialog box, be sure that Datasheet View is selected, and click OK.

A blank datasheet that has 20 columns and 30 rows is displayed.

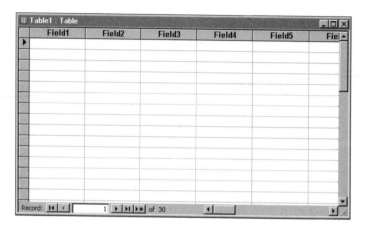

Choosing Appropriate Field Names

Fields are the basic building block of tables. It is important to give your fields appropriate names so that others can understand what the field is describing. You add fields to the new table by renaming the columns with the field names you want to use. Microsoft Access deletes any extra columns after you save the new table.

After you name your fields, you enter your data in the datasheet. Microsoft Access creates an appropriate data type and display format for the data you enter. The *data type* establishes what kind of data a field can hold, and the *display format* specifies how data is displayed and printed. When you create a table by using a Table Wizard, Microsoft Access assigns a data type and display format for all the fields based on the fields you selected from the list.

The following table shows examples of fields that have different data types and the data each field can hold.

Field	Data type	Data you might enter
Last Name	Text	Houlihan
Box Price	Currency	$18.75
Quantity on Hand	Number	500

Data types protect the accuracy of your data by restricting the type of information you can enter in a field. For example, you can't store a picture or a name in a field that has the Currency data type.

Now, you're ready to add the first field to your new table. Later, when you save the new table, Microsoft Access will create a primary key—one or more fields whose values uniquely identify each record in the table. You will use that primary key field to store an ID number for each carrier. To begin building your table, you'll first add data fields.

Name a field

➤ Double-click the default name Field1, and then type **Carrier Name**

A field name can contain up to 64 characters, including spaces. It can include any punctuation mark except a period (.), an exclamation point (!), an accent grave (`), or brackets ([ ]).

Carrier Name	Field2	Field3	Field4	Field5	Fiel

Table1 : Table

Name more fields

Next, you'll name additional fields.

You can select contiguous columns by dragging across their headers. You can resize all selected columns by double-clicking any header border except the leftmost header border.

1 Double-click the default name Field2, and then type **Air Delivery**

2 Position the pointer over the border between the fields Air Delivery and Field3. When the pointer changes to a two-headed arrow, double-click the border.

The Air Delivery column shortens to best fit the field name.

3 Double-click the default name Field3, and then type **Street Address**

4 Continue adding the following field names:

City Address

State Address

Postal Code

5 Resize column headers if you haven't done so already.

Your table should look like the following illustration.

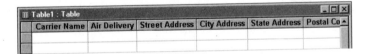

Carrier Name	Air Delivery	Street Address	City Address	State Address	Postal Co

Table1 : Table

Add records to the table

1 Click in the Carrier Name field for the first record, type **Wild Fargo Carriers** and then press TAB to move to the Air Delivery field.

Air Delivery is a field that will have a Yes/No data type. Yes will mean Air, and No will mean Surface. No will be the default for the Air Delivery field. Wild Fargo Carriers uses surface as its delivery method, so you type No. After you have entered a few records that have consistent data types, Microsoft Access will assign a data type to the field (which you can change in Design view).

2 Type **No** in the Air Delivery field.

3 Enter the following data for this record:

Street Address:	**410 N.E. 84th St.**
City Address:	**Chicago**
State Address:	**Illinois**
Postal Code:	**45123**

4 Add two more records to the carriers table:

Carrier Name:	**Grey Goose Express**
Air Delivery:	**Yes**
Street Address:	**100 Day St.**
City Address:	**New York**
State Address:	**New York**
Postal Code:	**12378**

Carrier Name:	**Pegasus Overnight**
Air Delivery:	**No**
Street Address:	**45908 Airport Way**
City:	**Dallas**
State:	**Texas**
Postal Code:	**78654**

Your table should look like the following illustration.

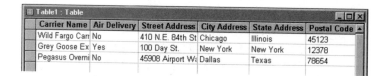

Carrier Name	Air Delivery	Street Address	City Address	State Address	Postal Code
Wild Fargo Carr	No	410 N.E. 84th St	Chicago	Illinois	45123
Grey Goose Ex	Yes	100 Day St.	New York	New York	12378
Pegasus Overni	No	45908 Airport Wa	Dallas	Texas	78654

Save the table

Save

1 On the toolbar, click the Save button. A Save As dialog box is displayed.

2 In the Table Name box, type **Carriers**, and then click OK.

Microsoft Access asks whether you want to create a primary key for the new table. Every table in your database should have a primary key. The primary key helps Microsoft Access search, find, and combine data efficiently.

3 Click Yes.

Microsoft Access creates a primary key for the table and saves the table as Carriers.

4 Double-click the field name ID at the top of the new primary key field. Type **Carrier ID** and then press ENTER.

The primary key field is named Carrier ID.

5 Close the table.

Create a data entry form

Although it is possible to enter data directly in tables, most data entry is done in forms because appropriately designed forms facilitate data entry and guarantee data validity. If no special formatting or controls are required for a data entry form, you can use Microsoft Access AutoForm to create a basic form.

1 In the Database window, select the Carriers table.

New Object

2 Click the New Object down arrow, and then select AutoForm.

Microsoft Access creates the form.

3 On the File menu, select Save As. A Save As dialog box is displayed.

4 Be sure that Carriers is highlighted in the New Name box. Click OK.

5 Close the newly created Carriers form.

Controlling Data Through Field Properties

Properties are used to control how Microsoft Access stores, handles, and displays data in the field. For example, to display numbers in a field as percentages, you would set the field's Format property to Percent.

Each data type is associated with a different set of properties. Fields that have Text and Number data types, for example, have a property called Field Size that sets the maximum size of data you can store in the field. Fields that have the Yes/No data type, on the other hand, don't have a Field Size property, because the values stored in a Yes/No field have a fixed size.

Another property you can set or change for most fields is the default control type. For example, in the Air Delivery field, your entry will always be either Yes or No, and it's easier to click a check box than type.

In the following exercise, you will set the Display Control property for the Air Delivery field to be a check box by changing the Display Control field property.

Set field properties

1   Make sure the Tables tab is selected, and double-click the Carriers table.

2   On the toolbar, click the View down arrow, and then select Design View.

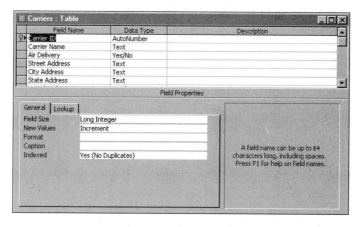

For fast, detailed information about any property, click in its corresponding property box, and press F1.

3   Click anywhere in the row for the Air Delivery field.

The field properties appear in the Field Properties sheet at the bottom of the table.

4   In the Field Properties sheet, click the Lookup tab.

The Display Control property is displayed on the Properties Sheet when the Lookup tab is selected and is set by default to Text Box.

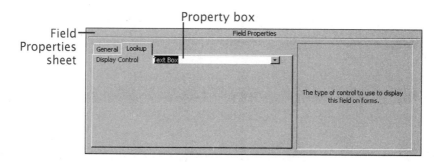

5 Click in the Display Control property box. Then click the down arrow that appears in the box, and select Check Box.

When you set the Display Control property to Check Box, the default control in the table and in all forms based on the table is a check box.

6 Switch to Datasheet view to see the new check box for the Air Delivery field. When Microsoft Access asks whether you want to save the table, click Yes.

7 Close the Carriers Table window.

Connecting a New Table to a Database

When you are expanding a database, it is important to understand how the new table will interact with existing tables. Creating the table is the first step toward incorporating the new data. To fully integrate the table, you need to build relationships or links to other tables.

There are two main ways of creating relationships: by using a lookup field and by defining relationships in the Relationships window. Relationships built in the Relationships window are generally more permanent and allow the database designer more control over the relationship behavior.

Understanding Relationships

See Lesson 5, "Keeping Database Information Reliable," for a discussion of primary keys.

Microsoft Access is used to create relational databases. Relational databases have become established as the most common form of database because they easily combine data from multiple tables simultaneously. After you create tables in your database and set each table primary key, you can create relationships between the tables. Relationships are used to collect data from several tables and place them in a single form, report, or query.

You can create two types of relationships in Microsoft Access: a *one-to-many relationship* or a *one-to-one relationship*. The most common type by far is the one-to-many relationship. In this type of relationship, one record in one table can have many related records in another table. For example, one customer can place many orders. Similarly, one record in a Customers table (called the primary table in the relationship) can have many matching records in an Orders table (called the *related table*).The *primary table* contains the field on the one side of the one-to-many relationship.

Related fields don't necessarily have to have the same name as the primary key fields to which they are related. However, related fields do have to contain matching data. In addition, related fields must have the same data type, with two exceptions; and if they have the Number data type, they must have the same field size.

NOTE There are two exceptions to the rule that related fields must have the same data type. The exceptions are (1) that you can match an Increment AutoNumber field with a Long Integer Number field and (2) that you can match a Replication ID number field with a Replication ID AutoNumber field. For example, the Carrier ID field in the Carriers table has the AutoNumber data type, and New Values is set to Increment. The Carrier ID field in the Shipping table has the Number data type, and its Field Size property is set to Long Integer.

Records in the Customers Table (the one side)...

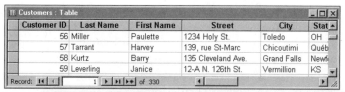

...can have more than one corresponding record in the Orders table (the many side).

In a one-to-one relationship, on the other hand, one record in the primary table can have only one matching record in the related table. The one-to-one type of relationship is less common than the one-to-many relationship; however, some circumstances require the one-to-one relationship. For example, Sweet Lil's might want to create a table of recipes for its bonbons. Each entry in the Bonbons table would have exactly one corresponding entry in the Recipe table.

 NOTE You can also create relationships between your tables to help ensure that the data in the relationship makes sense—for example, that you don't have orders in the Orders table that have no matching customer in the Customers table. For more details, see "Referential integrity" in Microsoft Access online Help.

Making Connections in Complex Relationships

You can easily create relationships with the Lookup Wizard, but it is not well suited for creating complex relationships. The Lookup Wizard is not the first choice when:

- Referential integrity is required.
- The primary key relies on more than one field.
- There is no direct link between the two tables.

In these situations, you should create the relationships in the Relationships window. When you create relationships in the Relationships window, you can join fields that have different names, and you can see the "big picture" of relationships in your database.

Before you can create a relationship in the Relationships window, the tables must contain matching fields. You relate the primary key field in the primary table (on the "one" side of the relationship) to a field that has a matching value in the related table (on the "many" side). The matching field is sometimes called a *foreign key*. If the related table doesn't contain a field that has data that matches the data in the primary key field in the primary table, you need to add the field to the related table so you can create the relationship.

Primary key ——— 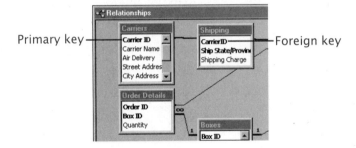 ——— Foreign key

After you create a relationship between two tables, you can't modify or delete the fields on which the relationship is based without deleting the relationship first.

Add tables to the Relationships window

In the relationship between the Carriers and Shipping tables in the Sweet Lil's database, the Carrier ID field is the matching field.

This is a one-to-many relationship. One carrier can have many different shipping charges, depending on the destination of the package, so the Carriers table is the primary table in the relationship. When you create the relationship between these two tables, you'll relate Carrier ID in the Carriers table to Carrier ID in the Shipping table.

Relationships

You can also click Relationships on the Tools menu.

Clear Layout

Show Table

You can also click Show Table on the Relationships menu.

1 On the toolbar, click the Relationships button.

The Relationships window opens.

 NOTE For this exercise, the Relationships window should be empty. If it is not, on the toolbar, click the Clear Layout button. Or, on the Edit menu, click Clear Layout. Then, click Yes.

2 On the toolbar, click the Show Table button.

The Show Table dialog box appears.

3 On the Tables tab, select the Carriers table, and then click Add.

4 Select the Shipping table, and then click Add.

A window of each table and its list of fields opens in the Relationships window.

5 On the Show Table dialog box, click the Close button.

Create a relationship between tables

1 In the Relationships window, drag the Carrier ID field from the field list in the Carriers table to the CarrierID field in the Shipping field list.

When you release the mouse button, the Relationships dialog box appears. Be sure that the matching field is listed for both tables. If it is not, you can click in the cell under either the Carriers or the Shippers header, and then click the down arrow to select the proper field.

2 Click the Create button.

3 The Carriers table is now related to the Shipping table. A line links the matching fields in the two tables. This relationship remains intact until you delete it. Your window should look like the following illustration.

For a demonstration of how to create a relationship between tables, double-click the Camcorder file named Creating Relationships in the Part5 Access Camcorder Files folder. See "Installing and Using the Practice and Camcorder Files," earlier in this book for more information.

4 Close the Relationships window.

When you close the Relationships window, a message asks whether you want to save changes to the Relationships layout. This decision affects only what is graphically displayed in the Relationships window. Any relationships you have created between tables remain in your database.

5   Click Yes to save the layout of the Relationships window.

The next time you open the Relationships window, you will see the display you just saved.

Delete and restore a relationship between tables

1   On the toolbar, click the Relationships button to see the layout of the Relationships window that you saved.

2   Click the line between the Carriers table and the Shipping table.

The line becomes thicker.

3   Press DELETE to delete the relationship.

A message appears, asking whether you want to delete the relationship.

4   Click Yes.

Microsoft Access erases the line between the two tables. They are no longer related.

5   Drag the Carrier ID field from the Carriers table to the CarrierID field in the Shipping table, and then click Create in the Relationships dialog box to re-create the relationship.

6   Close the Relationships window.

Creating Links by Using Multiple-Field Primary Keys

A table primary key can consist of one or more fields. If a table that has a multiple-field primary key is the primary table in a relationship, you must relate *all* the fields in its primary key to matching fields in the related table. To see why, look at the Shipping and Orders tables in the Sweet Lil's database. These two tables have a one-to-many relationship, and Shipping is the primary table.

The primary key for the Shipping table consists of two fields: CarrierID and Ship State/Province. Before Microsoft Access can correctly relate a shipping charge to an order, it must be able to find matching data for *both* fields because a shipping charge is based on both the carrier that the customer chooses and the destination of the order.

Relate a multiple-field primary key to matching fields

In the following exercise, you will create a relationship between the Shipping and Orders tables so that Microsoft Access can automatically look up an order's shipping charge.

Relationships

Clear Layout

Show Table

1 On the toolbar, click the Relationships button.

The Relationships window opens, showing the layout you last saved.

2 On the toolbar, click the Clear Layout button to give yourself a clean workspace.

The relationships do not change when you clear the layout.

3 Click Yes to proceed.

4 On the toolbar, click the Show Table button to open the Show Table dialog box.

5 In the Show Table dialog box, select and add both the Shipping table and the Orders table to the Relationships window. Then, close the Show Table dialog box.

6 In the Relationships window, drag the CarrierID field from the Shipping table to the Carrier ID field in the Orders table.

When you release the mouse button, the Relationships dialog box appears. Be sure that the Carrier ID field is listed for both tables. If it is not, you can click the cell under the Shipping heading or the Orders heading, click the down arrow, and then select the proper field.

7 Click the cell under Carrier ID for each table, and then click the list box down arrow to select Ship State/Province.

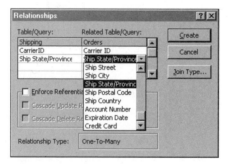

8 Click Create.

The Relationships window displays the relationship between the two tables. To see the relationship more easily, you can drag the Orders table farther away from the Shipping table and drag the border of the Orders table downward to show both fields without having to scroll.

9 Close the Relationships window. When Microsoft Access asks whether you want to save the layout, click Yes.

Because the tables are now related, Microsoft Access can use the values in both tables to find information.

See how your relationships work

You've created one relationship between the Carriers and Shipping tables and another relationship between the Shipping and Orders tables. You can see how the relationships work when you need information that requires data from more than one table.

See Lesson 7, "Getting An- swers to Ques- tions About Your Data," for more informa- tion about cre- ating queries.

You can use a filter to request information from the Sweet Lil's database; how- ever, when you use a filter, you can only set criteria and display selected data from one table. By using a query, you can take advantage of relationships be- tween tables by drawing on information from two or more tables. In the follow- ing exercise, you see how related tables are used in a query by using the Carrier ID and Ship State/Province fields in the Orders table to find the appropriate shipping charge for an order.

1 In the Database window, click the Queries tab to display the list of queries, and then click the New button.

The New Query dialog box appears.

2 In the New Query dialog box, double-click Simple Query Wizard.

The Simple Query Wizard dialog box appears.

3 In the Tables/Queries list, select Table: Orders. Then, in the Avail- able Fields list, double-click Order ID to add it to the Selected Fields list. The Simple Query Wizard dialog box should look like the follow- ing illustration.

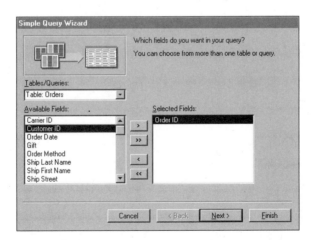

4 From the Carriers table, add the Carrier Name field to your Selected Fields list, and from the Shipping table, add the Shipping Charge field to your Selected Fields list.

Microsoft Access uses the relationships you created to join the tables in the query.

5   Click Next.

6   Be sure the Detail (Shows Every Field Of Every Record) option is selected, and then click Next.

7   Type **Carriers Query** as the title, make sure the "Open The Query To View Information" option is selected, and then click Finish.

The related data from all three tables appears in the Query window.

8   Close the Carriers Query window.

Microsoft Access has saved the query automatically, and the name Carriers Query appears in the list of queries in the Database window.

One Step Further: Controlling and Filtering Fields

In addition to assigning data types to fields, you can also control how fields behave by setting their properties. Now you will see how field properties are set, and how you can filter a table so that only selected values are displayed in the Datasheet view.

Set a field property

Field properties can be set to enforce business rules or procedures. For example, one of the rules that has been established at Sweet Lil's is that no order can be taken without a customer ID. To enforce this rule, the Required Property of the Customer ID field can be set to Yes.

1   In the Database window, click the Tables tab to display the list of tables.

2   Select the Orders table, and then click Design.

3   Select the Customer ID field.

4   In the Field Properties sheet of the Orders Table window, click in the Required property field.

5   Click the Required property field down arrow, and then select Yes.

When the Required property is set to Yes, if you try to leave the field blank, a warning message appears. You cannot add a record until you provide an entry for the Customer ID field.

Create a filter for a table

Filters can also be used to limit the records displayed in a table Datasheet view. Using a filter can be an easy way to locate selected records in a table. You will now filter the Orders Table to display only those orders placed on February 14, 1996.

1 Click the View down arrow, and then select Datasheet view.

2 Click Yes when asked if you want to save the Orders table, and then click Yes again to have the data tested against the new rule.

3 Click the Filter By Form button to display the Orders Filter By Form window.

Filter By Form

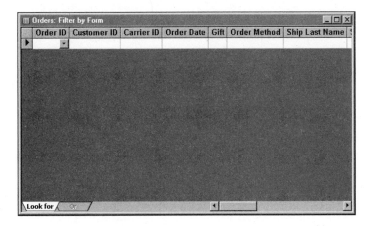

4 Click in the Order Date field, and then click the down arrow to display the list of data values.

Every value in the Order Date field is displayed.

5 Scroll down the list, and select the date 2/14/96.

#2/14/96# is entered as the filter criteria.

Apply Filter

6 Click the Apply Filter button.

Only the orders placed on Feb. 14, 1996, are displayed in the datasheet.

7 On the File menu, click Save.

8 Close the Orders table.

Finish the lesson

1 To continue to the next lesson, on the File menu, click Close.

2 If you are finished using Microsoft Access for now, on the File menu, click Exit.

Lesson Summary

To	Do this
Create a table	In the Database window, click the Tables tab, and then click New. Select Table Wizard, and follow the prompts.
	or
	In the Database window, click the Tables tab, and then click New. Select Datasheet View and click OK. Change the default field names to your own name, enter data for as many records as you choose, and then save the table. You can customize the table in Design view.
Add records to a table	Display the table in Datasheet view, and then type the data in the fields.
Add a field to a table	In the first empty row in Design view, type a field name in the Field Name column. Select a data type from the drop-down list in the Data Type column.
Set properties for a field	In the upper portion of the Design View window, click the row that defines the field, and then set the property in the Field Properties sheet in the lower portion of the window.
Get Help on any field property	Click in the property box, and then press F1.
Change a field name	Select the table in the Database window, and then switch to Design view. Move to the Field Name column, and then make your changes.

To	Do this	Button
Create a relationship between two tables	Open the table that will contain the lookup column. On the Insert menu, click Lookup Column. Follow the steps in the Lookup Wizard.	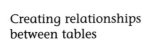
	On the toolbar, click the Relationships button to open the Relationships window, and then click the Show Table button on the toolbar. In the Show Table dialog box, select the primary table on the Tables tab, and click Add. Select the related table, and click Add. Close the Show Table dialog box. In the Relationships window, drag the common field from the primary table to the related table. In the Relationship dialog box, click Create.	
Delete a relationship between tables	Open the Relationships window. Click the line linking the tables, press DELETE, and then click Yes.	

For online information about	Use the Office Assistant to search for
Creating a table	**Creating a table**, and then click Create A Table
Adding fields to a table	**Adding fields**, and then click Add A Field (Column) To A Table In Datasheet View or click Add A Field To A Table In Design View
Changing a field name in a table	**Changing field name**, and then click Change A Field Name In A Table
Adding records to a table	**Adding records**, and then click Add New Data In Datasheet Or Form View
Setting or changing a table's primary key	**Primary key**, and then click Set Field Properties To Customize How Data Is Stored, Handled, Or Displayed
Setting the properties for a field	**Field properties**, and then click Set Field Properties To Customize How Data Is Stored, Handled, Or Displayed
Creating relationships between tables	**Relationships**, and then click Define Relationships Between Tables

Keeping Database Information Reliable

In this lesson you will learn how to:

Estimated time
45 min.

- Add a validation rule for a text box control.
- Create a combo box control.
- Change the tab order of controls on a form.
- Set a default value for a control.
- Force data entry of specific fields.
- Ensure that related tables always contain the correct data.
- Control data reliability by using a lookup field.
- Detect a many-to-many relationship and use a junction table.

One of the greatest challenges for database designers and administrators is making sure that the data is reliable. Customers, managers, government authorities, and the general public all can be affected by the information contained in an organization's database. In some instances, incorrect or invalid data is a minor irritation; in others, it can have dire consequences.

Database reliability is guaranteed through the use of system controls. Two of the most important system controls are data validation and referential integrity. *Data validation* is the set of procedures and techniques used to ensure that only data that passes a set of tests can be entered into the system. *Referential integrity* is a design technique that is employed to create more reliable databases. Referential integrity uses a system of cross referencing to create a database structure that is more likely to contain reliable data.

In this lesson, you will learn how to use form controls to extend the validation concepts discussed in Lesson 2, "Increasing Efficiency by Using Subforms." You will also learn how to evaluate the relationships discussed in Lesson 4, "Controlling Database Growth," and how to structure your tables so that they are related correctly.

Start the lesson

➤ If Microsoft Access isn't started yet, start it. Open the Sweet Lil's Lesson05 database. If the Microsoft Access window doesn't fill your screen, maximize the window.

If you need help opening the database, see Lesson 1.

Validating Data by Adding Form Controls

Any field that contains or accepts data on a form is actually a control. *Controls* are graphical objects that accept, display, or locate data. Microsoft Access is made up of objects; for example, tables, forms, queries, and reports are all objects. Controls are part of the objects that contain them. Controls are labels, text boxes, drop-down boxes, option buttons, toggle buttons, or object controls. In every lesson in this book, you use controls. When you use a wizard to create a form, the controls are created automatically. You can also build validation checks into *sections*, which are the basic parts of the Design window. You can also create new controls or modify existing controls by changing their properties while you are in Design view.

Building Validation Checks by Changing a Form Control Property

A common validation is to check whether data is within a range of acceptable values. For example, a company could have a business rule that limits the amount of credit granted to new customers. This rule could then be transformed into a validation check on a credit purchase field.

For a demonstration of how to add a validation check to a form control, double-click the Camcorder file named Adding A Validation Check in the Part5 Access Camcorder Files folder. See "Installing and Using the Practice and Camcorder Files," earlier in this book for more information.

Add a validation check

Sweet Lil's recently had a complete audit of its data-processing operations. One of the findings of the audit was that the company needs to increase its control over credit purchases. The auditor suggested several additions to the validation procedures to increase credit transaction control. One suggestion was to add a validation check on expiration dates.

You will now add a validation check to the Orders form. The validation check will prevent sales clerks from accepting expired credit cards.

1 In the Database window, click the Forms tab.

The Forms tab moves to the front.

2 Select the Orders form, and click the Design button.

The Orders form opens in Design view. Your screen should look like the following illustration.

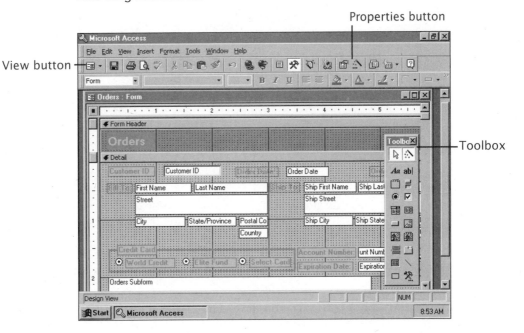

Properties button

View button

Toolbox

Properties

3 If the properties sheet is not open, click the Properties button to open it.

The properties sheet opens. The properties sheet displays the properties for the object that is selected. If the form is selected, the properties sheet displays properties that control the behavior of the form. If a control or section on the form is selected, the properties sheet will display the properties for the control or section, respectively.

4 In the Orders Form detail section, select the Expiration Date text box control, and then click the Data tab on the properties sheet.

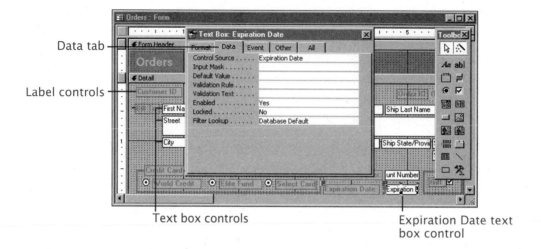

Data tab

Label controls

Text box controls

Expiration Date text box control

5 Click the box next to the Validation Rule property, type >=**now** and press ENTER.

This rule states that the expiration date on the credit card must be after the date indicated by the system date (today's date). The function, now (), which is built into Microsoft Access, returns the current date and time. When you press ENTER, the parentheses are entered automatically.

6 In the Validation Text property of the dialog box, click to position the insertion point, and type:

That is not a valid date. The credit card is either expired, or you have typed the wrong date. Check the date. If it is correct, reject the order.

7 Press ENTER.

8 Close the properties sheet.

Test your validation check

It is always a good idea to make sure any changes to object properties had the intended effect; in other words, you should always check your validation checks. In this exercise, you enter invalid data to see whether your validation rule works.

View

1 Click the View down arrow, and select Form View.

2 Click the New Record button to add a record.

Record 407 should be the current record.

New Record

536

3 Click in the Expiration Date field to position the insertion point, type **Jan-01-1990** and then press TAB.

The validation rule you typed appears as a message.

4 Click OK, change the date to a date after today's date, and then press TAB.

You need to change to a date after today's date to have the record accepted.

Save

5 Click the Save button to save the new version of the form, and then close the form.

A message box appears telling you that Access can't find a record in the table "Customers" with key matching field(s) "Customer ID". This is because you have not completely filled in this test record with data.

6 Click OK.

A message box tells you that your changes to the table will not be saved. This is a built-in control in Access; the control prevents you from entering data that is missing key information.

7 Click Yes.

Increasing Data Validity by Using a Combo Box Control

One way to increase the validity of your data is to allow data entry workers to select possible values from a list. By using value selection instead of typing records, you decrease the chances of typographical errors. One of the best ways to set up value selection is through a combo box. A *combo box* is a field that displays possible values from a drop-down list and lets you select the appropriate value. Combo boxes can be created by placing a combo box control on a form and setting the properties to determine the source for possible data values.

In many cases, the best way to list possible data values is to create a separate query that selects and arranges the data just the way you want it to appear in the list. Then you can use the fields in the query as columns in the list.

Queries are discussed further in Lesson 7, "Getting Answers to Questions About Your Data."

When operators take telephone orders for Sweet Lil's chocolates, speed and accuracy are their top priorities. To make their jobs easier, you plan to make several enhancements to the online form they use.

Currently, operators enter the customer ID number in a text box on the Orders form. You're going to replace the text box with a combo box that shows a list of customer names and ID numbers, so the operators can select the ID instead of typing it.

537

Customer ID
text box

 TIP If you want to change the text box into a label, a list box, or a simple combo box, select the control you want to change. Then, on the Format menu, click Change To, and click the control type you want.

Delete a text box

Before you can add the combo box, you need to make room for it by deleting the Customer ID text box and its label.

1   In the Database window, click the Forms tab, select the Orders form, and then click the Design button to open the Orders form in Design view.

2   If the Orders Form window is too small for you to see all the controls, resize the window by selecting a corner of the window and dragging the corner until the window is the appropriate size.

3   Click the Customer ID text box, and then press DELETE.

The Customer ID text box and its label are deleted. If the toolbox is blocking your view, you can move the toolbox by selecting its title bar and dragging the toolbox out of the way. You can also double-click the toolbox title bar. This will dock the toolbox and keep it out of the way.

Create a combo box bound control

One way to increase the validity of data entered through a combo box is by ensuring that the only choices the reader can select are valid ones. If the data selected in the combo box is to be entered into a table, the box must be bound to a field in either a table or a query so that Access can place the data correctly. A *bound control* is a control tied to a field in an underlying table or query. Your combo box on the Orders form should be bound to the Customer ID field in the Customer List query so that when an operator selects a customer from the form's combo box list, Microsoft Access will store the customer ID number in the bound field in the table.

In the following exercise, you use the Combo Box Wizard to create a bound combo box.

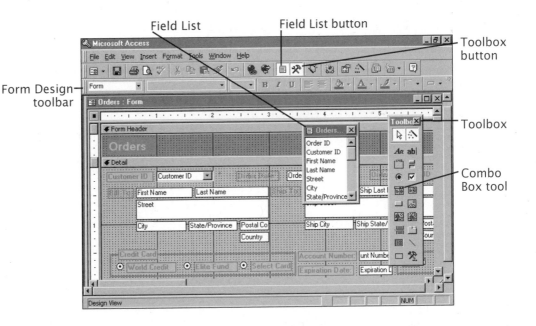

Field List

Field List button

Toolbox button

Form Design toolbar

Toolbox

Combo Box tool

Toolbox

Field List

Combo Box

1 Be sure that the toolbox and the field list are visible. If the toolbox isn't visible, click the Toolbox button on the Form Design toolbar. If the field list isn't visible, click the Field List button on the Form Design toolbar.

2 Be sure that the Control Wizards tool is selected in the toolbox. If it's not, select it.

3 In the toolbox, click the Combo Box tool.

Now when you drag the Customer ID field from the field list, Microsoft Access creates a combo box that's bound to the field.

4 Drag the Customer ID field from the field list to just above the First Name field on the form.

When you release the mouse button, the Combo Box Wizard appears.

Create a combo box list

The Combo Box Wizard guides you through the creation of the combo box list for your form.

1 In the first Combo Box Wizard dialog box, be sure the I Want The Combo Box To Look Up The Values In A Table Or Query option is selected, and then click Next.

2 In the View area, select the Queries option, and then select the Customer List query. Click Next.

3 On the Available Fields list, double-click the Customer ID field, double-click the Last Name field, and then double-click the First Name field. Click Next.

These will be the columns in your combo box.

4 Double-click the right edge of each column header to adjust the column width to its best fit. Click Next.

5 Select Customer ID as the column that contains the data you want to store in your table. Click Next.

6 Be sure that the Store That Value In This Field option is selected, be sure Customer ID is displayed in the box to the right, and then click Next.

7 Customer ID is the default label for your combo box. This is the label you want, so click Finish.

The Orders form has a combo box bound to the Customer ID field. Your form should look like the following illustration.

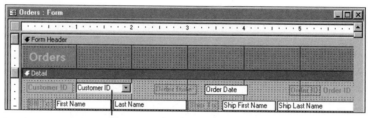

New combo box

8 Close the field list.

Use the combo box

You can see how using the combo box simplifies looking up customer IDs. Now when a new order is taken, all the operator has to do is select the customer's name, and the customer name and address are filled in automatically

1 Click the View down arrow, and then click Form View.

2 Click the Customer ID down arrow, and select the name Arlene Grant.

The customer ID number appears in the Customer ID field.

Improving Data Entry Accuracy by Controlling Tab Order

Good screen design is integral to ensuring valid data. Data entry screens that follow a logical order—or that mirror paper source documents—can increase accuracy and streamline data.

The order form used by the Sweet Lil's sales clerks is an example of good screen design. The fields are well-designated and follow a logical pattern. The customer details are grouped in one area, and the shipping details are grouped in another area. Finally, the credit information is in a separate section. The current process for moving between fields on the online form, however, does not follow this pattern. You will change the tab order of the Orders form so that when the sales clerks use the form, the fields will be presented in a more logical order. The *tab order* of a form is the order in which the insertion point moves through fields when you tab from field to field in Form view.

Change tab order

Now when you open the Orders form in Form view the Order Date is the first field selected. To make the Customer ID field the selected field whenever you open the form, you can change the tab order of the Orders form.

When you create a new control, Microsoft Access puts the new control last in the tab order, regardless of where you placed that control on the form. You'll edit the tab order so that the new Customer ID combo box you just created is first in the tab order, not last.

1   Click the View down arrow, and click Design View.

2   If the Customer ID combo box control is not highlighted, select it by clicking anywhere on the control.

3   On the View menu, click Tab Order.

The Tab Order dialog box appears.

4   Scroll down in the Customer Order list of controls until you see the Customer ID control at the bottom of the list.

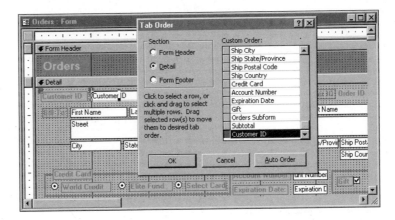

5   Place your mouse pointer in the column to the left of the Customer ID control. When the pointer becomes a right-pointing arrow, click once to select the field.

541

6 Click and drag the Customer ID control to the top of the list.

7 Click OK.

8 Switch to Form view to test the tab order.

    The Orders form opens; the Customer ID is selected.

9 Save the Orders form.

Improving Validity by Setting a Default Control Value

Another way to improve the reliability of the data in your database is to set default values. If you know that certain data will always be the same, setting a default will help you avoid incorrect data entry. Default values can be created through the Default Value property of a control. You can set the Default Value property either to an expression or to a constant value, such as text or a number.

Display today's date in a text box

The date a Sweet Lil's order is taken will always be the date on the Order form. You want to give the Order Date box a default value so the operators don't have to type the date themselves. In this case, you'll set the value equal to an expression that includes the Date function. The expression will be entered in the property sheet of the Orders form.

Properties

1 Click the View down arrow, and click Design View.

2 Click the Order Date text box to select it. If the properties sheet isn't displayed, on the Form Design toolbar, click the Properties button to display the Order Date control properties.

3 In the Default Value property box on the Data tab, type the expression **=Date( )** and then press ENTER.

4 Close the properties sheet.

5 Switch to Form view.

    Because Microsoft Access enters the default value when you start a new record, you need a new record to check your property setting.

New Record

6 Click the New Record button at the bottom of the form to move to a new blank record.

    A new record appears; today's date is in the Order Date text box.

7 Close the form. When asked whether you want to save the changes, click Yes.

Improving Validity by Using Field Properties

Although form control properties are an excellent way to improve validity of data, they are not the only tools at your disposal. Another way to increase the reliability of your data is by setting properties for fields in the table. Setting field properties has the advantage of affecting that particular field in each and every form that uses that field. For example, the validation rule you set for the Expiration Date control on the Orders form could have been set for the Expiration Date field in the Orders table. Setting the rule for the field guarantees that the rule is followed by any control based on the Expiration Date field.

Validating Records by Applying the Required Property

One field property that is useful in guaranteeing valid records is the Required property. The *Required property* means that records cannot be accepted without data in that field. A field without any data has a value of *null*. If the Required property is set to Yes, null values are not allowed.

Occasionally you will want to capture a record even though it is missing some information. If the data in a particular field is not crucial to the validity of the record, the Required property for that field should be set to No.

Set a Required property

One field that should be required is the Ship Postal Code field in the Orders form. Without the Ship Postal Code, the order is not valid. In the following exercise, you change the Required property of the Orders table Ship Postal Code field to Yes.

1   In the Database window, click the Tables tab.

2   Click the Orders table to select it, and then click the Design button to open the table in Design view.

3   Click in the Ship Postal Code field to select it.

4   In the Field Properties sheet, change the Required field to Yes by clicking in the field and selecting Yes from the list

From now on, you cannot save a record that has a null value in the Ship Postal Code field. Your Orders table should look like the following illustration.

543

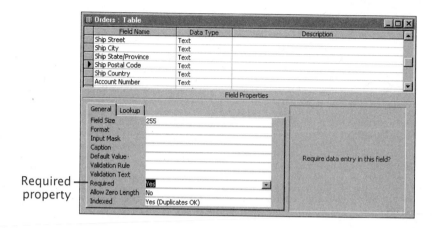

Required
property

5 On the Orders table, click the Close button.

A message appears, asking whether you want to save the changes.

6 Click Yes.

A message appears, asking whether you want to check the existing data to be sure it adheres to the new validation rule. If you don't check the data, you might leave null value records in this field.

7 Click Yes.

If any records violate the rule, another message appears to warn you.

NOTE You shouldn't have any invalid data; however, if you do, the message will ask you if you want to continue checking against the new rule. Answer No to end the test. Then close the table without saving the changes, find the records that are missing the required data, and enter values for the required field. Then complete the above steps again.

Test the Required property

To verify that the Required property has been established, you try to enter an order without a postal code.

1 In the Database window, click the Forms tab, and then double-click the Orders form to open it in Form view.

In the Orders form, the first field selected is Customer ID.

2 Use the New Record button on the navigation bar to start a new record.

3 Select 1 from the Customer ID field list.

Customer 1 is Rita Hanson.

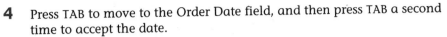

4 Press TAB to move to the Order Date field, and then press TAB a second time to accept the date.

The insertion point moves to the Order ID field.

5 Enter 417 for the Order ID.

6 Press TAB three times to move to the first blank Ship To field. Fill in the following Ship To information. Press TAB to move through the fields.

Field	Value
Ship To First Name	**Orson**
Ship To Last Name	Jones
Ship To Street Address	**123 Burnside**
Ship To City	**Chicago**
Ship To State	**Illinois**
Ship To Postal Code	Leave blank
Ship To Country	**USA**

7 Use the following details to fill in the remaining fields.

Field	Value
Credit Card	**World Credit**
Account Number	**123 78429**
Expiration Date	**11/30/98**
Gift	**No**
Box ID	**ALLS**

When you click in the subform to enter the Box ID, a message box indicates that the Ship To Postal Code field cannot have a null value.

8 Click OK, type **32123** in the Ship To Postal Code field, and complete the entry for the Box ID.

9 Close the Orders form.

Validating Records by Creating Referential Integrity

One of the best ways to make sure your data is valid is to use relationships between tables. Database relationships are generally built on rules or policies of the organization. When tables are related to each other, you can guarantee that changes in one table will affect the data in the related table. This is accomplished through referential integrity. Referential integrity is a system of

For a demonstration of how to enforce referential integrity, double-click the Camcorder file named Enforcing Referential Integrity in the Part5 Access Camcorder Files folder. See "Installing and Using the Practice and Camcorder Files," earlier in this book for more information.

Linking tables is discussed in Lesson 6, "Getting and Working with External Data."

rules that ensure that relationships between records in related tables are valid and that you can't accidentally delete or change related data.

Before you can use referential integrity, several conditions must be met. First, the matching field from the primary table must be a primary key or have a unique index. Second, the related fields must have the same data type. Finally, both tables must belong to the same Microsoft Access database. If the tables are linked, they must be in Microsoft Access format. The database in which the linked tables are stored must be open to set referential integrity. Referential integrity can't be enforced for linked tables from databases in other formats; that is, you can't enforce referential integrity for an Access Database when it contains linked tables that are in Microsoft Excel, Paradox, dBase, TXT, or any format other than Microsoft Access.

Referential integrity increases the validity of your data by enforcing the following rules.

■ You can't enter a value in the foreign key field of the related table if that value doesn't exist in the primary key of the primary table. However, you can enter a null in the foreign key, specifying that the records are unrelated. For example, you can't assign an order to a customer that doesn't exist, but you can assign to no one by entering a null in the Customer ID field.

■ You can't delete a record from a primary table if *matching* or corresponding records exist in a related table. For example, you can't delete a customer record from the Customers table if there are matching orders for that customer in the Orders table.

■ You can't change a primary key value in the primary table if that record has related records. For example, you can't change a carrier's ID in the Carriers table if there are shipments assigned to that carrier in the shipping table.

Guarantee validity by creating referential integrity

One standard business rule is that a customer cannot be removed from the database if there are pending orders. Sweet Lil's would like to implement this rule by applying referential integrity to the relationship between the Customers table and the Orders table. In this exercise, you will set referential integrity through the Relationships window.

1 In the Database window, click the Tables tab.

2 On the toolbar, click the Relationships button to open the Relationships window.

Relationships

The Relationships window is a workspace for adding tables and creating relationships. The workspace can be cleared to make it easier to see the relationships you are creating. The relationship you want is the one connecting the Customers and Orders tables.

Show All Relationships

3 Click the Show All Relationships button to display all the database relationships in the Relationships window.

4 Maximize the Relationships window.

5 Double-click the line connecting the Customers table to the Orders table. The Relationships dialog box appears.

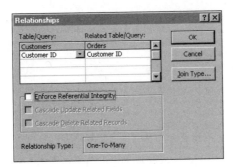

6 Select the Enforce Referential Integrity check box.

7 Click the Join Type button.

The Join Properties dialog box appears. In the Join Properties dialog box, you can change the type of relationship. In this case, you want to show all records in both tables where the two fields are equal, which is the default selection.

8 Click OK to close the Join Properties dialog box.

9 Click OK to close the Relationships dialog box.

Understanding Cascade Updating and Deleting

After you have established referential integrity, you can use it to increase the validity of your data by using the Cascade Update Related Fields and Cascade Delete Related Fields commands. These commands ensure that changes you make in the primary table will ripple through to the corresponding records in the related tables.

NOTE If the primary key in the primary table is an AutoNumber field, setting the Cascade Update Related Fields check box has no effect; you can't change the value in an AutoNumber field.

You can set the Cascade Update And Delete properties when defining a relationship, or you can set these properties later by using the Relationships dialog box. If the Cascade Delete Related Records check box is selected, any time you delete records in the primary table, Microsoft Access deletes related records in the related table. For example, if the Customers table is a primary table,

547

anytime you delete a customer record from the Customers table, all the customer's orders are automatically deleted from the Orders table. In addition, records in the Order Details table, which is related to the Orders records, are also deleted. When you use the Cascade Delete Related Records option, Microsoft Access warns you that related records might also be deleted.

Keep primary keys consistent by using Cascade Update Related Records

The core of Sweet Lil's business is, of course, the boxes of candy. If the business does not focus on identifying the boxes correctly, all the information in the database is at risk. In this exercise, you use the Cascade Update command to ensure that the Box ID fields in the Boxes table, the Box Details table, and the Orders Detail table are consistent.

1   In the Relationships window, click the line connecting the Boxes table and the Box Details table to select it.

  The line thickens.

2   Double-click the line.

  The Relationships dialog box appears.

3   Be sure that the Enforce Referential Integrity check box is selected, and then click the Cascade Update Related Fields check box to select it.

4   Click OK.

  The Relationships dialog box closes. The Boxes table has a 1 next to it, indicating that this is the "one" side of a one-to-many relationship. The Box Details table has the infinity symbol placed next to it, indicating that this is the "many" side of the relationship.

5   Repeat steps 1 through 4 to establish the relationship between the Boxes and Order Details tables.

Ensure data validity by Using Cascade Delete Related Records

Sweet Lil's wants to be sure that when customers are deleted all open orders are removed as well. This will ensure that no orders are open for customers that are no longer valid. You can ensure that the records are deleted by setting the Cascade Delete Related Records property.

1   In the Relationships window, double-click the line between the Customers and Orders tables.

  The Relationships dialog box appears.

2   In the Relationships dialog box, select the Cascade Delete Related Records check box.

When the Cascade Delete Related Records box is selected for this relationship, any changes to the primary table (Customers) will ripple through to the related table (Orders).

3   Click OK to accept the change you have made to the relationship.

4   Close the Relationships window, and click Yes to confirm that you want to save changes to the layout of the Relationships window.

5   Click the Restore button on the database window.

Make sure Cascade Delete is working

1   In the Database window, double-click the Customers table to open it.

2   Select record 5.

3   On the toolbar, click the Delete Record button.

A message appears, stating that you are about to delete related records.

Delete Record

4   Click No to continue, and then close the Customers table.

Protecting Data Integrity by Using a Lookup Field

Sweet Lil's has developed a table for carriers. The objective in building the new table was to speed up shipments to customers and from suppliers. To speed up shipping, you will add a field that will keep track of the coverage area for each carrier. There are only three different designations for coverage area: Domestic, International, or Both. To accomplish this, you will create a lookup field that will list each option. This will speed up data entry and protect data integrity by allowing the user to select from a list and limiting the data that is entered in the field to the three available choices.

Create the Lookup field

In the following exercise, you will create a lookup field that lists the coverage options for carriers. The Lookup Wizard will create a combo box control in the Carriers table so that employees can select a name from a list instead of typing it.

1   In the Database window, click the Tables tab, and then double-click the Carriers table.

The Carriers table will contain the lookup field, and the lookup field will display names from a list that you will type.

2   On the Insert menu, click Lookup Column.

The Lookup Wizard starts, and the first dialog box appears. You want the new field (the lookup column) to display values that you will type in, so you select the second option.

549

3   Click Next.

The Lookup Wizard asks how many columns should be in your lookup field. Leave the default number of columns.

4   Click in the cell below the Col 1 heading, type **Domestic** and press TAB.

The insertion point moves to a new blank cell.

5   Add values for International and Both, and then click Next.

The Lookup Wizard asks what label you would like for your lookup column.

6   Type **Coverage** and then click Finish. The Carriers table appears in Datasheet view, and the new lookup column is added to the table. Now Sweet Lil's employees can select a coverage value in the table quickly by clicking the down arrow and selecting a name from the list. In addition, when a form is created that uses the Carriers table, the Coverage field will automatically be a combo box on the form.

7   Click the Coverage field down arrow. Your screen should look like the following illustration.

See "Increasing Data Validity by Using a Combo Box Control" earlier in this lesson for a discussion of how to create a combo box control without creating a lookup column.

Coverage	Carrier ID	Carrier Name	Air Delivery	Street Address	City /
	1	Wild Fargo Carriers	☐	410 N.E. 84th St	Chica
Domestic	2	Grey Goose Express	☑	100 Day St.	New \
International	3	Pegasus Overnight	☐	45908 Airport W;	Dallas
Both	(AutoNumber)		☐		

A lookup field ensures data integrity by providing a list of values.

8   Select Domestic as the coverage for the first record, International for the second record, and Domestic for the last record.

9   Close the Carriers table, and then click Yes to save your changes.

Understanding Many-to-Many Relationships

One-to-one and one-to-many relationships are discussed in Lesson 4, "Controlling Database Growth."

When you evaluate a relationship between two tables, it's important to look at the relationship from both sides. You might think at first that you have a one-to-many relationship when you actually have a many-to-many relationship. A *many-to-many relationship* occurs when one record in either table can have more than one matching record in the other table. In those cases, because you don't know which table should be the primary table, you need a third table that links the two tables before you can create the relationships.

The Boxes table and Bonbons table are a good example of a many-to-many relationship. At first glance, you might think that boxes and bonbons have a one-to-many relationship because one box can contain many different types of bonbons. But take a look at the relationship from the bonbons side. One type of bonbon can be used in more than one box.

You'd have a problem if you tried to create a one-to-many relationship between the Boxes table and the Bonbons table: which would you make the primary table in the relationship? Suppose you made the Boxes table the primary table. You'd add a Box ID field to the Bonbons table to hold the matching values. But when you got to a record for the Bittersweet Blueberry bonbon, you'd have to enter box IDs for both the All Seasons box and the Alpine Collection box, because the Bittersweet Blueberry bonbon is in both boxes. If you enter two box IDs, Microsoft Access can't match the Bittersweet Blueberry record to the right boxes—you can have only one value in each matching field. The same thing happens if you try putting a Bonbon ID field in the Boxes table.

The solution is to create a *junction table,* a table that acts as a bridge between two other tables and that contains the primary keys of the two tables you want to relate. In a junction table, you can add a field that doesn't exist in either of the original tables but that gives you additional information relevant to both the other tables. In the Sweet Lil's database, the junction table is called Box Details. The primary key of the Box Details table consists of Box ID and Bonbon ID—the primary keys of the two tables you're trying to relate. The Box Details table also contains a Quantity field, which tells you how many of each bonbon are in a box.

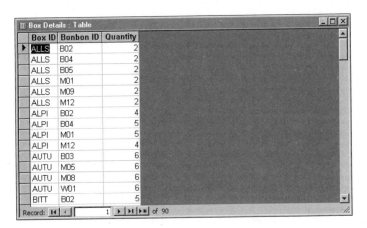

 NOTE   If you'd like to build on the skills that you learned in this lesson, you can do the One Step Further. Otherwise, skip to "Finish the lesson."

One Step Further: Exploring Junction Table Relationships

When you create a junction table, you don't add fields to it that really belong in one of the two related tables. For example, you might be tempted to add the Box Name field to the Box Details table. But that field is already in the Boxes table; it shouldn't be repeated. The only fields that belong in the Box Details table are those needed to define the link (Box ID and Bonbon ID) and any field whose data describes the relationship between the records in the other two tables. The Quantity field qualifies because its data relates to both the other tables—it tells how many of each bonbon are in each box.

View junction table relationships

The Boxes table has a one-to-many relationship with the Box Details table, and so does the Bonbons table. The Box Details table serves as a junction table between the two tables involved in the many-to-many relationship. Use the Relationships window to see how the junction table serves as a bridge between the Boxes table and the Bonbons table.

Relationships

Clear Layout

Show Table

1   In the Database window, click the Tables tab. Then, on the toolbar, click the Relationships button to open the Relationships window.

2   On the toolbar, click the Clear Layout button, and then click Yes.

Clearing the layout gives you an empty space for working; it has no impact on the relationships.

3   On the toolbar, click the Show Table button.

The Show Table dialog box appears.

4   Add the Bonbons table, the Box Details table, and the Boxes table to the Relationships window.

5   Close the Show Table dialog box.

You can see the links between the tables.

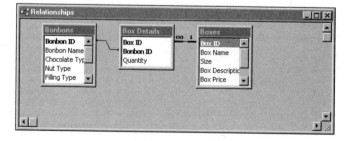

6   On the File menu, click Save.

7   Close the Relationships window.

Finish the lesson

1 To continue to the next lesson, on the File menu, click Close.

2 If you are finished using Microsoft Access for now, on the File menu, click Exit.

Lesson Summary

To	Do this	Button
Change the properties of a form control	Open the form in Design view. Select the control, and click the Properties button to open the properties sheet.	
Create a validation rule for a form control	Type the rule in the control's Validation Rule property on the properties sheet.	
Create a combo box control	Open a form in Design view. Select the Combo Box tool in the toolbox. Drag the field from the field list to a place on the form to start the Combo Box Wizard.	
Change the tab order for a form	Open the form in Design view. Select a control, and use the Tab Order command from the View menu to change the order of moving through fields on a form.	
Set the default value for a field	Open the table in Design view, and select a field by clicking its Field Name. In the Field Properties Default Value property, type the value you want as the default for all new records added to the table thereafter.	
Create a Required field	Open the table in Design view, and then select the field you want to require by clicking its Field Name. Click in the Field Properties Required Property field, and select Yes from the drop-down list.	

To	Do this	Button
Enforce referential integrity	In the Database window, click the Relationships button. Double-click the line connecting the two tables. Select the Enforce Referential Integrity check box.	
Establish Cascade Update Related Records	In the Database window, click the Relationships button. Double-click the line connecting the two tables. Select the Enforce Referential Integrity and Cascade Update Related Fields check boxes.	
Establish Cascade Delete Related Records	In the Database window, click the Relationships button. Double-click the line connecting the two tables. Select the Enforce Referential Integrity and Cascade Delete Related Fields check boxes.	
Insert a lookup field	Open a table in Datasheet view. On the Insert menu, select Lookup Column to start the Lookup Wizard. Select values from a table or query, or add your own. Follow the wizard prompts, and then click Finish when done.	

For online information about	Use the Office Assistant to search for
Creating validation rules	**Creating validation rules,** and then click Define Validation Rules To Control What Values Can Be Earned Into A Field
Changing tab order	**Changing tab order,** and then click Change Tab Order In A Form
Establishing default values	**Default values,** and then click Define A Default Value That Is Automatically Entered In A Field Or Control
Referential integrity	**Referential integrity,** and then click What Is Referential Integrity?
Cascade updates or cascade deletes	**Cascade update,** and then click Why Should I Use Cascading Updates Or Cascading Deletes?
Creating relationships between tables	**Relationships,** and then click Define Relationships Between Tables

Getting and Working with External Data

Estimated time
35 min.

In this lesson you will learn how to:

- Link your database to a table created in another database management program.
- Work with data in a linked table.
- Import a file from Microsoft Excel.
- Use a hyperlink to connect a form to a table.

In ideal conditions, a database is constructed quite logically using a single tool or a set of related tools, such as those offered by Microsoft Office. In the real world of business computing, however, systems are often constructed using a variety of tools, and data is usually stored in a variety of formats. This is particularly true in organizations that have a long history of computer use.

To accommodate this variety of formats, Microsoft Access databases can incorporate data from many different software packages. For example, Microsoft Access can use data stored in Microsoft Excel, Lotus 1-2-3, dBASE, Microsoft FoxPro, Paradox, Microsoft SQL Server, HTML, or a text file.

In this lesson, you'll learn how to attach a table from a different database format to your Microsoft Access database and how to use Microsoft Access to work with data in a table. You'll also learn how to share data between your Microsoft Access database and outside sources, such as an external database.

Gathering Data from External Sources

When you *import,* or pull in, data into your Microsoft Access database, Microsoft Access copies the data from its source into a table in your database. You can import data from these file formats:

- A spreadsheet file, such as a Microsoft Excel version 3.0 or later file or a Lotus 1-2-3 file in a .wk1 or .wk3 format

- A text file, such as a file you might create in a word-processing program or a text editor

- A file in another database format, such as a Microsoft FoxPro version 2.*x* or later file, a Paradox version 3.*x* or later file, a dBASE III or later file, a Microsoft SQL Server file, or another Microsoft Access database file, just to mention a few

You also have the choice of linking to files in any of these formats. A *link* is a connection between your Microsoft Access database and the external table, which can also be another Microsoft Access table. A linked table isn't copied into your Microsoft Access database; the table stays in its original file format. That way, you can use Microsoft Access to work with the data, and someone else can still use the table in its original program.

In this lesson, you'll start by linking a table, which is stored in a common database format known as a DBF (the Database File format used by dBASE, FoxPro, and other programs) file to the Sweet Lil's database. Later, you'll import the same data.

Start the lesson

➤ If Microsoft Access isn't started yet, start it. Open the Sweet Lil's Lesson06 database. If the Microsoft Access window doesn't fill your screen, maximize the window.

If you need help opening the database, see Lesson 1.

Getting Connected Through an External Table

If you link an external table to your Microsoft Access database, you can view and update the data even if others are using the data in the table's source program. You can create Microsoft Access forms and reports based on the external table. You can even use a query to combine external data with the data in your Microsoft Access tables. See Lesson 7, "Getting Answers to Questions About Your Data," for information about using queries to combine data from different tables.

One of the first business functions Sweet Lil's converted to electronic processing was a simple database of fixed assets. Most processes in the organization have been converted to the new systems; however, the company still maintains a fixed assets register table in an older file format. The Assets table was created using dBASE IV, a database management program. The data is stored in a file format known as DBF. The Accounting Department is anxious to have the table incorporated into the larger database; however, the data must remain in DBF format because other systems are still using DBF.

Link an external table

To integrate the table of fixed assets without changing the file format, you will link the data to Sweet Lil's database.

Look In Favorites

1 On the File menu, point to Get External Data, and then click Link Tables.

The Link dialog box appears.

2 Click the Look In Favorites button, and then double-click the Part5 Access Practice folder.

3 In the Files Of Type list, select dBASE IV.

The dBASE IV file, Assets.dbf, appears in the list of files. Assets.dbf was copied to your Part5 Access Practice folder when you copied the practice files to your hard disk.

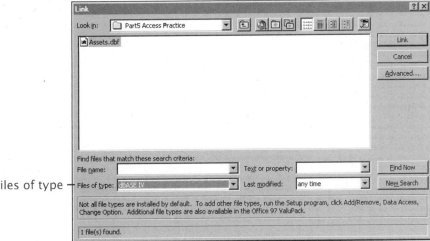

Files of type

4 Click Link.

Microsoft Access links the table to your database, and then the Select Index Files dialog box appears. An index file indicates the order for displaying records in a DBF file. This file does not have an associated index file, so you cannot include one in the link.

5   Click Cancel.

A message indicates that the table was successfully linked.

6   Click OK, and then close the Link dialog box.

The Assets table is listed in the Database window along with the other tables in the Sweet Lil's database. The symbol identifies the table as a linked dBASE table.

dBase table symbol ———

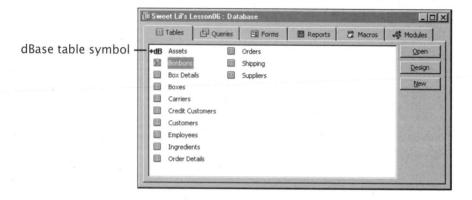

Incorporating a Linked Table

Now that the external table is linked to your Microsoft Access database, you can use it much as you would a regular Microsoft Access table. You can't change the structure of a linked table (that is, you can't add, delete, or re-arrange fields), but you can reset the field properties in Design view to control the way Microsoft Access displays the data. You can also use field properties to give a field a default value or to check new data entered in a field. You can edit data in the linked table, and if the linked table is edited by another program, the changes will appear in your database.

Open a linked table

➤   In the Database window, double-click the Assets table.

The table opens in Datasheet view. The table should look like the following illustration.

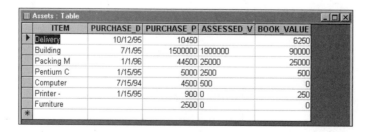

Change a field property

You decide you would the like to see the data in the Book_Value field displayed as currency.

View

The graphic on the face of the View button changes according to the current selection.

1 On the toolbar, click the View down arrow, and click Design View.

A message indicates that you can't modify some properties of a linked table, and asks whether you want to open the table anyway.

2 Click Yes.

The Assets table opens in Design view.

3 Click in the selection column to the left of the Book_Value field.

The properties of the Book_Value appear in the Field Properties sheet in the lower pane of the window. The Hint box beside the Field Properties listing says that the Data Type property can't be modified in linked tables. But you can still modify how Microsoft Access displays the data by setting the field's Format property.

4 In the Field Properties sheet, click in the Format property box.

The Hint box displays information about how to set the Format property.

5 Click the Format property down arrow, and then select Currency.

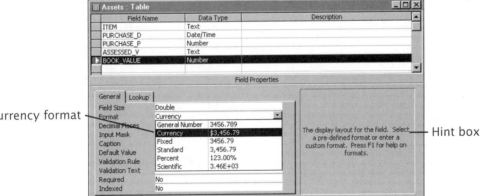

6 Switch to Datasheet view. In the message box that appears asking if you want to save, click Yes.

The data is reformatted.

7 Close the Assets table.

Importing a Table

The Accounting Department has decided to convert all its old files to Microsoft Access files. One of the files used by the Accounting Department is a spreadsheet that keeps track of employee payroll deductions. This file was created in Microsoft Excel. The Accounting Department is going to update these records in Microsoft Access; the file can be imported into Sweet Lil's database. Remember that when you link a table, the data retains its original file format. When you import a table, the data is converted to Microsoft Access format.

Import a table

1   On the File menu, point to Get External Data, and then click Import.

The Import dialog box appears.

2   In the Files Of Type list box, select Microsoft Excel.

The Payroll file is displayed in the list of files.

3   Double-click the Payroll file.

The Import Spreadsheet Wizard opens.

4   Click the First Row Contains Column Headings check box indicating that you want to use the column headings as field names, and then click the Next button.

5   Click the In A New Table option indicating that you want to save the data in a new table, and then click the Next button.

6   This dialog box allows you to specify whether fields are indexed. You do not need to make any changes to the suggestions made by Microsoft Access, so simply click the Next button to continue.

7   Select the Choose My Own Primary Key option.

The Employee ID field will be selected as the primary key.

8   Click Next to go to the last dialog box.

9   Press DELETE to erase the default name, and type **Payroll**

10   Click Finish, and then click OK to close the successful importing acknowledgment message box.

In the Database window, the imported Payroll table is added to the list of tables.

Working with Data in the Imported Table

The data in the imported table is now part of your Microsoft Access database, but you want to change some aspects of the table. You can customize the table's design, just as you can customize a table you created yourself.

Change properties

In this exercise, you customize the tables.

1 In the Database window, click the Design button to open the Payroll table in Design view.

2 In the YTD Insurance field, click the Data Type down arrow, and then select Currency.

3 On the toolbar, click the View down arrow, and then select Datasheet View.

A message indicates that you need to save the table.

4 Click Yes.

A message box indicates that you might lose some data and ask whether you want to continue.

5 Click Yes.

Your table should look like the following illustration.

Employee ID	First Name	Last Name	YTD Insurance
1	Mary	Culvert	$722.55
2	Jerome	Woods	$542.36
3	Nora	Bromsler	$450.25
4	Frederick	Mallon	$893.52
5	Adrienne	Snyder	$542.36

6 Close the Payroll table.

Adding Hyperlinks to Your Database

For a demonstration of how to add a hyperlink, double-click the Camcorder file named Adding A Hyperlink To A Database in the Part5 Access Camcorder Files folder. See "Installing and Using the Practice and Camcorder Files," earlier in this book for details.

One of the most important recent changes in computing is the growth of the Internet or, more specifically, the World Wide Web. The *Internet* is a complex system of interconnected networks that spans the globe. Many organizations share information with their suppliers, consumers, and the general public by creating a permanent presence on the Internet. Anyone interested in the company or its products can view the site by using a type of software known as a *browser*.

In Microsoft Access, it is very easy to connect your database to other resources, including the Internet. Access now includes hyperlinks as a data type that can be stored in a table. A *hyperlink* is a way of "jumping" from one object to another. You can think of a hyperlink as a trail that leads from your database to data stored in another location. The trail's destination can be another object in your database, another Office document, or an Internet site. In this lesson, you will learn how to create a hyperlink to another object in the database.

Microsoft Office and Intranets

Using hyperlinks to connect Microsoft Office documents is an excellent way to develop a corporate intranet. An *intranet* is an internal communications system that makes use of the World Wide Web protocol to exchange information from desk-to-desk or across the world.

Sweet Lil's is in the process of improving internal office communications. The company is establishing links to make it easier to move between the forms in its database. For example, the Human Resources manager would like to be able to quickly move between the Employees form and the Payroll table. This type of link is established by inserting a hyperlink in the form in Design view.

Connect two forms by using a hyperlink

The Human Resources manager wants to be able to check an employee's payroll deductions while she is viewing the employee's other records. Although she is aware that you can create a form that ties the data together, she believes that this would create an overly complex form. You decide to insert a hyperlink in the Employees form to tie the two forms together.

In this exercise, you will insert a hyperlink that can open the Payroll table from within the Employees form.

1 In the Database window, click the Forms tab.

2 Select the Employees form and then click the Design button to open the form in Design view.

Insert Hyperlink

3 On the toolbar, click the Insert Hyperlink button.

The Insert Hyperlink dialog box appears.

The Link To File Or URL box creates hyperlinks to other documents or to the Web.

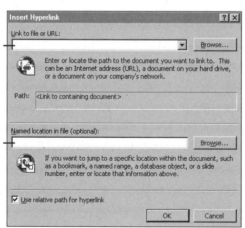

The Insert Hyperlink dialog box is used to create hyperlinks within or external to your database.

The Named Location In File box creates hyperlinks to locations within your database.

Connecting a Microsoft Access Table to the World Wide Web

Connecting a form or report to the World Wide Web (WWW) is very similar to connecting to an object in the database. Both use hyperlinks to make their connections. The only real differences are the type of address that is inserted in the hyperlink, and how the insertion is made. Although Microsoft Office hyperlinks can use either a Universal Naming Convention path or a Universal Resource Locator (URL) path, hyperlinks to the WWW must be made through a URL.

The location a hyperlink leads to can be either a Universal Naming Convention Path (UNC) or a Universal Resource Locator (URL). UNCs are written \\server\share\path\filename, and are used more frequently for communications within an organization. URLs generally start with a protocol (which is like an area code), such as http, for accessing the site. The protocol is then followed by the identifier (which is like a phone number) for the organization that maintains the Internet site. For example, http://www.msn.com opens the Microsoft Network site.

With the development of the intranet as a new medium for conducting internal business, many organizations have begun allowing people outside the organization to have limited access to the organization database through "firewalls" that segregate data made available to the public World Wide Web from data available only to members of the organization. Microsoft Access is well-designed to accommodate presentation of data through the Internet.

World Wide Web documents are viewed using a browser such as the Microsoft Internet Explorer. Browsers display documents that include commands for a special programming language called the *Hypertext Markup Language* (HTML). HTML documents can be created by using such programs as Microsoft Word Internet Assistant or Microsoft FrontPage. HTML files can be read by any word-processing package, but they are filled with commands that Web browsers use for displaying graphics and managing hyperlinks.

When a customer anywhere in the world fills in a field on Sweet Lil's Candy Order page, a command is sent through the World Wide Web to Sweet Lil's. When Microsoft Access receives the command, it is processed just as if a sales clerk had issued it in Sweet Lil's home office. In effect, Sweet Lil's Web page allows customers to place orders just as they once could by mail or by calling on the phone. The advantage is that they can do it from anywhere in the world, and any time of the day or night. Sweet Lil's is now open 24 hours a day, worldwide!

4 Next to the Named Location In File box, click the Browse button.

The Select Location dialog box appears. This is where you select the object to which the hyperlink will lead.

5 Be sure the Tables tab is selected, and then scroll through the list of tables until Payroll is displayed.

6 Click the Payroll table to select it, and then click OK.

The table name appears in the Insert Hyperlink dialog box.

7 Click OK.

A Table Payroll label is added to the form. If the label is too small, resize it by dragging the handles to the right until the full text is displayed. You can also reposition the field.

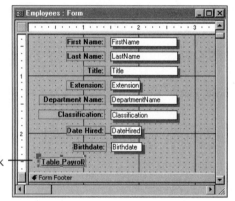

The new hyperlink

Test your new hyperlink

In this exercise, you test the hyperlink.

View

1 Click the View down arrow, and then click Form View.

2 Click the new Payroll Table hyperlink.

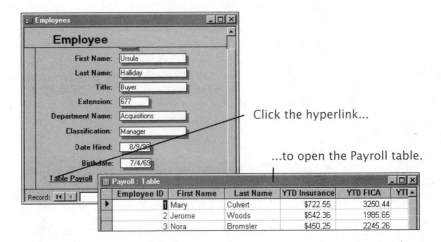

Click the hyperlink...

...to open the Payroll table.

The Payroll table opens in Datasheet view.

3 Close the Payroll table.

4 Close the Employees form.

5 When the dialog box asks if you want to save your changes, click Yes.

 NOTE If you'd like to build on the skills that you learned in this lesson, you can do the One Step Further. Otherwise, skip to "Finish the lesson."

One Step Further: Hyperlinking to an Office Document

Sweet Lil's has adopted Microsoft Office as its standard set of tools for creating applications and has chosen to use Office documents to build the corporate intranet. Every month, the Credit Department uses Microsoft Word to write letters to credit customers who are late in making payments. The Accounting Department wants to view those letters in the Credit Customer form for accuracy.

NOTE In the Insert Hyperlink dialog box, you can create a hyperlink to any file you can browse to. Whether you are on a network, an intranet, or the WWW, you can make a connection just as easily as you are connecting to your local hard drive in these exercises.

In the following exercises, you will modify the design of the Credit Customer form to include a command button that hyperlinks to the Microsoft Word file containing the credit letter.

Add the command button

Control Wizards

Command Button

Properties

1   In the Database window on the Forms tab, select the Credit Customer form, and click the Design button to open the form in Design view.

2   In the toolbox, make sure the Control Wizards tool is *not* selected, and then click the Command Button tool.

3   Drag a rectangle on the form below the current fields to create the command button.

A new command button appears on the form.

4   If the properties sheet is not already open, on the toolbar, click the Properties button.

5   Click the All tab, and type **View Credit Letter** for the Caption property.

Establish the hyperlink

Builder

1   Click in the Hyperlink Address property. Click the Builder button.

The Insert Hyperlink dialog box appears.

2   Click the Browse button next to the Link To File Or URL combo box, and then in the Part5 Access Practice folder, select the Credit Letter file. (Hint: Change the Files Of Type to Documents.) Click OK.

The path to Credit Letter.doc appears in the Insert Hyperlink dialog box.

3   Click OK to return to Design view.

4   Close the properties sheet.

Open the credit letter

1   On the Form Design toolbar, click the View down arrow, and click Form View.

The Credit Customer form opens in Form view.

2 Click the View Credit Letter command button.

Microsoft Word opens, and the credit letter is displayed.

3 Close Microsoft Word, and then close the Credit Customer form and save your changes.

Finish the lesson

1 To continue to the next lesson, on the File menu, click Close.

2 If you are finished using Microsoft Access for now, on the File menu, click Exit.

Lesson Summary

To	Do this	Button
Link an external table	Open the database. On the File menu, point to Get External Data, and then click Link Tables. Navigate to the file you want to link, and then click the Link button.	
Change field properties of a linked table	In Design view, click the field name and then click the property you want to change in the Field Properties sheet in the lower half of the window. The Hint box text will let you know whether the property can be changed.	
Import a table	Open the database. On the File menu, point to Get External Data, and then click Import. Select the file type and double-click the filename. Follow the instructions of the Import Spreadsheet Wizard for Excel and text files.	
Insert a hyperlink from a form to another Microsoft Access object in the current database	Open the form in Design View. Click the Insert Hyperlink button to open the Insert Hyperlink dialog box. Click Browse next to the Named Location In File box. Select the object by opening the appropriate sheet (table, query, form, report, macro, or module), and double-clicking the object's name. Click OK in the Insert Hyperlink dialog box.	

For online information about	**Use the Office Assistant to search for**
Importing or linking data	**Importing or linking data,** and then click Import Or Link Data
Inserting hyperlinks	**Inserting hyperlinks,** and then click Add A Hyperlink To A Form, Report, Or Datasheet

Getting Answers to Questions About Your Data

In this lesson you will learn how to:

Estimated time
45 min.

- Create a query based on a table or on another query.
- Set criteria to extract a set of related records.
- Sort data and hide a field in a query.
- Create a query that shows related data.
- Create a query using related tables.
- Join tables in a query.

The raw data stored in a database is factual. When organizations first begin using a database, they generally focus on creating systems that will accurately and quickly retrieve this data. A more sophisticated use of databases moves beyond retrieving data to converting that data into information. *Information* is processed data.

The power of database systems is their ability to respond quickly to day-to-day business changes. Frequently, organizations need to look at their data from different angles. Before calling your customers about a marketing campaign, you might want to create a list of selected names and phone numbers. To review sales trends, you might want to find out how many orders you received in a specific month. To facilitate express orders of supplies, you might want to quickly locate the name and phone number of a business contact.

Relational databases are commonly used for developing business systems because they are so adaptable. A well-designed database contains a table for each key section of the organization. The result is a system that provides extraordinary flexibility in making data into information.

In Microsoft Access, you can find the information you want by creating a fundamental database analysis tool: the query. A *query* is a tool that brings together data from multiple tables to answer a question or perform an action on the data. In this lesson, you will create a variety of queries that select the data you want. You'll also calculate total values using a query, and you'll use a query to answer a "what if" question.

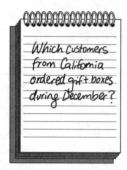

Customer	State/Province	Gift	Order Date
Adams, Cathy	CA	Yes	23-Dec-95
Fogerty, Sam	CA	Yes	09-Dec-95
Harkin, Rory	CA	Yes	03-Dec-95
Kennedy, Brian	CA	Yes	10-Dec-95
Kimball, Mary	CA	Yes	23-Dec-95
Kimball, Mary	CA	Yes	02-Dec-95
Kumar, Andrew	CA	Yes	19-Dec-95
Lopez, Maria	CA	Yes	10-Dec-95
Olembo, Julia	CA	Yes	15-Dec-95
Pence, Stephen	CA	Yes	23-Dec-95

Which customers from California ordered gift boxes during December?

In Lesson 4, "Controlling Database Growth," queries were previewed when relationships were created between tables. In this lesson, you learn to create queries and refine your requests for more specific data.

Understanding Queries

A query is a way to define a particular group of records. A query can also manipulate records and show you the results. Think of a query as a request for a particular collection of data, such as "Show me the names and phone numbers for our carriers, and show me their shipping charges." A query is made up of records that were created from fields from various tables.

You use queries in much the same way that you use tables. You can open a query and see its results in a datasheet. Queries can be the basis for forms or reports. You can also use a query to update tables; that is, you can update the data in the query results, and then save the updated data to the originating table.

Because queries are so flexible, you might find that you use them more often than tables in day-to-day operations. You can use a query to sort data or to view a subset of the data in your database. You can also use the query to perform analysis. For example, instead of wading through all the customers in the Customers table, a regional sales manager could look at only the customers in his region and see information about their purchases at the same time. He could then manipulate the records to see what effect a 10 percent increase in purchases would have on his commissions.

Datasheet of the Ingredient Source query

Category	Type	Contact Name	Source ID
Chocolate	Fudge	Becky Rheinhar	1
Chocolate	Bittersweet	Becky Rheinhar	1
Chocolate	Dark	Becky Rheinhar	1
Chocolate	White	Becky Rheinhar	1
Chocolate	Milk	Becky Rheinhar	1
Nut	Brazil	Barney Cutter	2
Nut	Cashew	Barney Cutter	2
Nut	Almond	Barney Cutter	2

Record: 1 of 24

The query shows data from the Ingredients table...

Ingredients : Table

Category	Type	Source ID
Chocolate	Milk	1
Filling	Mocha cream	3
Filling	Peanut butter	3

Suppliers : Table

SuppliersID	Supplier Name	Contact Name	Phone Numbe	Fax Numbe
1	Chocolate Worl	Becky Rheinhar	(617) 555-5460	(617) 555-545
2	Allfresh Nuts	Barney Cutter	(313) 555-9987	(313) 555-999
3	Flavorly Extract	Beverly Sims	(515) 555-9834	(515) 555-988

Record: 1 of 3

...with data from the Suppliers table.

For more information about using filters, see Lesson 3, "Viewing Only the Information You Need."

Queries are similar to filters in that both can be used to select data. Queries, however, are more powerful than filters. Filters select data from one table; queries can extract data from many different tables. You can also save a query and use it again, and you can use an existing query to build a new query.

Using queries, you can approach the same information in many different ways. For example, you can use the same tables to create one query that shows which customers bought which products, another query that shows which products sell best in Europe, and another that shows product sales sorted according to postal codes. You don't have to store the product information three times for the three different queries—each piece of information is stored in its table only once.

Creating Queries

In Microsoft Access, you can create a query by using the Simple Query Wizard. When you first start creating queries, using a wizard is the best approach, because a wizard will guide you through the process. After you have selected the data you want to examine, you can modify the query to focus on the particular information you want. You should plan your query—that is, decide what data you want to use— before you begin using the Simple Query Wizard, because you want to select only the data you need to answer your question.

Start the lesson

▶ If Microsoft Access isn't started yet, start it. Open the Sweet Lil's Lesson07 database. If the Microsoft Access window doesn't fill your screen, maximize the window.

If you need help opening the database, see Lesson 1.

Generating a List by Creating a Query

You're in charge of a telephone survey of Sweet Lil's customers in your sales region. Your region is New York State, so you'll use a query to get a list of the names and phone numbers of the New York customers. The information you need is stored in the Customers table.

Create a query

In the following exercise, you create a query for the New York customers.

1 In the Database window, click the Queries tab.

2 Click the New button.

The New Query dialog box appears.

3 In the New Query dialog box, double-click Simple Query Wizard.

The Simple Query Wizard appears.

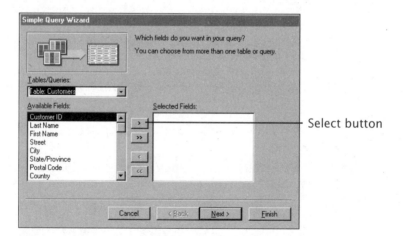

Select button

4 Click the Tables/Queries down arrow, scroll up, and then select Table: Customers.

The Customers table fields are displayed in the Available Fields list. You use this list to select the fields you want your query to display.

You can also select the Customer ID field and use the Select button (>) to move the field to the Selected Fields column.

5 Double-click the Customer ID field.

The Customer ID field moves to the Selected Fields list.

6 Add the Last Name, First Name, State/Province, and Phone fields to the Selected Fields box by selecting the field and then clicking the Select button.

The Selected Fields list now has five fields displayed. You have defined the query; now you just need to save it before you put it to work.

Name and save a query

In this exercise, you name and save the query.

1 In the Simple Query Wizard, click Next.

A dialog box in which you define the query's name appears.

2 In the What Title Do You Want For Your Query box, type **NY Customers** and then click Finish.

The results of the query are displayed in Datasheet view so you can see whether the query is correctly defined. The name of the query appears in the title bar. Microsoft Access automatically saves the query and adds it to the list of queries in the Database window.

Modifying Queries in Design View

After you have created the basic structure to select the data you want to work with, you can make the modifications by opening the query in Design view and dragging fields from the upper portion of the Query window to the design grid in the lower portion. You place the fields in the design grid in the order you want them to appear in the datasheet. Microsoft Access then assembles the SQL commands required to perform your query.

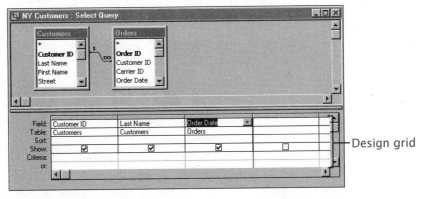

Design grid

You can also use the Query window to create a query, but it is faster to use the Simple Query Wizard.

The Query window can help you build on an existing query. Often, one question leads to another, and you will find that you want to keep changing a query. For example, you might start by finding all your customers from California. Then, by making small changes in the query design grid, you can find all the California customers who ordered gifts, and finally, all the California customers who ordered gifts in December. And you can keep refining the query until you get it just right.

Setting Criteria to Focus Your Queries

The current query displays records for all customers in the Customers table. But you're interested only in the customers from New York State, so you'll set criteria to limit the query to records for customers in New York State.

Expressions in filters are discussed in Lesson 3, "Viewing Only the Information You Need."

You set criteria for a query using an *expression*, a formula that specifies which records Microsoft Access should retrieve. For example, to find fields with a value greater than 5, you'd use the expression >5. The symbol > means "greater than." You use an expression in a query the same way you use an expression in a filter.

In these exercises, you'll specify criteria to limit the query, and then you'll run the query.

View

The graphic on the View button changes to reflect the current selection.

Specify criteria

1 Click the View down arrow, and then click Design View.
2 In the State/Province column in the design grid, click in the Criteria row.
3 Type **NY** and press ENTER.

When you press ENTER, Microsoft Access automatically places quotation marks around what you typed. The quotation marks indicate text. If your criteria is a number, it is not enclosed in quotation marks.

Run your query

For a demonstration of how to set the criteria for a query, double-click the Camcorder file named Setting Query Criteria in the Part5 Access Camcorder Files folder. See "Installing and Using the Practice and Camcorder Files," earlier in this book for more information.

▶ Click the View down arrow, and click Datasheet View to check the query results. Your query should look like the following illustration.

Customer I	Last Name	First Name	State/Province	Phone
12	Herron	Tom	NY	(212) 555-3944
13	Hernandez	Jim	NY	(212) 555-4893
16	Silverman	Frank	NY	(914) 555-2480
22	James	Carol	NY	(212) 555-2904
25	Zahoor	Ali	NY	(212) 555-2455
79	Kanter	Nate	NY	(718) 555-8503
95	Kwiatkowski	Andrew	NY	(716) 555-5686
104	Mason	Andrea	NY	(914) 555-2904
105	Wolensky	Joseph	NY	(516) 555-2077
136	Hollins	Samantha	NY	(607) 555-0860
170	Hines	Roger	NY	(212) 555-0496
191	Hooper	Robert	NY	(212) 555-9348
196	Cannon	Tamara	NY	(315) 555-4924

NY Customers : Select Query

Record: 1 of 21

Microsoft Access displays a list of the customers in New York State and their phone numbers; these are the fields that you specified in the Simple Query Wizard.

Add more criteria

Now you have a list of customers in your sales region. But you want to call only your most recent customers: those who have customer IDs greater than 200. In this exercise, you'll add another criterion to the query to find these customers.

1 Click the View down arrow, and click Design View.

2 In the Criteria row in the Customer ID column, type the expression **>200** and press ENTER.

By adding this criterion, you're telling Microsoft Access, "Find customers who have customer IDs greater than 200 and who live in New York State." Your query should look like the following illustration.

Find customers who have Customer IDs greater than 200...

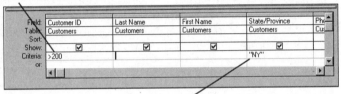

...and who live in New York.

3 Click the View down arrow, and click Datasheet View to switch to Datasheet view and see the list of the customers you're going to call.

Improving the Appearance of a Query

You can make your query more effective and easier to use, you can arrange records in a more convenient order, and you can modify the query results so that selected fields are hidden.

Sorting Records

For more sorting examples, see Lesson 3, "Viewing Only the Information You Need."

Sorting the records makes it easier to find specific information in your query. For example, to find a phone number for a specific customer, you can list the customers in alphabetical order.

Sort records alphabetically

1 Click anywhere in the Last Name column.

Sort Ascending

2   On the toolbar, click the Sort Ascending button.

All the records in the query results are sorted according to customer last name. Your query should look like the following illustration.

Customer I	Last Name	First Name	State/Province	Phone
310	Brownlee	Jason	NY	(914) 555-0931
249	Gunther	Paul	NY	(212) 555-4934
298	Hendricks	Louise	NY	(516) 555-2067
280	Kahn	Juliet	NY	(212) 555-9424
374	Knutson	Jean	NY	(518) 555-6207
343	Mitchell	Sandy	NY	(607) 555-9679

Record: 1 of 8

Hiding Fields

Occasionally, you have to include a field for the query to generate the correct information, but you don't want to include that field in the query results. For example, in the NY Customers query, you don't want the State/Province field in the datasheet because all the records have the same value, NY. This field must be included in the Design view of the query, because you use the field to set the criteria, but you can use the Show check box in the design grid to hide this field so that it doesn't appear in the datasheet.

Hide a field

1   Click the View down arrow, and click Design View.

2   In the Show row in the State/Province column, click the check box to clear it. Your query should look like the following illustration.

Clear the State/Province Show
check box to hide the column.

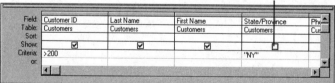

The query will use any criteria or sort information in this field, but it will not show the field in the datasheet.

3   Click the View down arrow, and click Datasheet View.

The State/Province field no longer appears in the query results.

4   Close the NY Customers query window. If prompted to save your changes, click Yes.

Bringing Data Together by Using a Query

When you create a query that gathers information from more than one table, Microsoft Access needs a way to determine which records are related. Microsoft Access uses matching values in equivalent fields in two tables to correctly associate data in different tables. To create a relationship between two tables, you draw a join line between two matching fields in the Relationships window. The *join line* is a graphic image that indicates the database has issued the commands needed to create a relationship. In most cases, the primary key from one table is joined to a field in another table that contains the matching values.

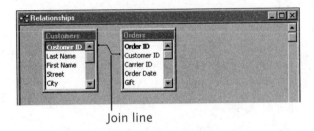

Join line

Creating relationships between tables is discussed in Lesson 4, "Controlling Database Growth."

You can use the relationships you've already developed to create queries that draw data from throughout your database.

Create a query using related tables, and add a field to the query

Lillian Farber, the president of Sweet Lil's, is analyzing the company's orders for November, and she wants a list of all orders placed in that month. She wants to know the order IDs, the customer names, and the dates of the orders. The information that Lillian Farber needs is contained in two different tables: the Orders table and the Customers table. In this exercise, you create a new query by using these tables in the query design grid.

1   In the Database window, click the Queries tab if it is not already in front, and then click the New button.

   The New Query dialog box appears.

2   In the New Query dialog box, double-click Design View.

   The Query window opens, and the Show Table dialog box appears.

3   On the Tables tab in the Show Table dialog box, double-click the Orders table, and then double-click the Customers table.

4   On the Show Table dialog box, click Close.

   Field lists for the Orders table and the Customers table are shown in the Query window. A join line automatically appears between the Customer

ID fields in the two tables. This is because a relationship was created in the database. Your query should look like the following illustration.

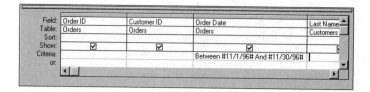

5 In the Orders table field list, double-click the Order ID, Customer ID, and Order Date fields.

The three fields appear in the design grid.

6 In the Customers table field list, double-click the Last Name field.

The Last Name field appears in the design grid.

7 On the File menu, click Save.

8 Name the query Order Information, and then click OK.

Fine-tune and test the query

In this exercise, you use an expression to select records for the month of November. This expression includes the Between...And operator.

1 In the Criteria row in the Order Date column, type **Between 1-Nov-96 And 30-Nov-96** and then press ENTER.

The format of the date changes, and number symbols (#) automatically appear around the dates.

2 To size the column to its best fit, double-click the right border at the top of the Order Date column in the design grid.

The column is resized to show the complete expression, as shown in the following illustration.

3 Click the View down arrow, and click Datasheet View to see the orders for November. Your query should look like the following illustration.

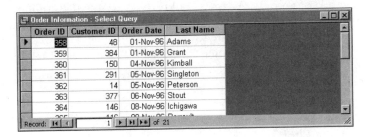

4 Save the query again, and then close the Order Information window.

Relating Tables by Applying a Query

It is impossible to anticipate all the possible information requirements when designing tables and relationships. Fortunately, queries can draw data from tables that do not have predefined relationships.

If you build a query from tables that do not have a relationship but do have a field with the same name and data type, a temporary relationship is developed between the tables. In this temporary relationship, at least one of the join fields must be a primary key. This relationship exists solely for the purposes of the query. The Query window will automatically display a join line between the tables, indicating that the matching fields will relate the data for the query.

If no relationship exists between the tables you want to use, and they do not have fields with the same name and data type, Microsoft Access will not create a relationship when you add the tables to a query. You can still use related data by joining the tables in the Query window when you create the query. Relationships built in the Query window, however, are not permanent. The reason: relationships require memory for storage. Microsoft Access was designed to allow temporary relationships to be built for query purposes without requiring that the relationship be saved. Just as with any relationship, for the join to work in a temporary relationship, the tables must contain fields with matching data in the primary and foreign keys.

 NOTE When you draw a join line between two tables in the Query window, the join applies to that query only. If you want to use the same two tables in another query, you'll need to join them again in the new query.

Join two tables in a query

The Ingredients table lists categories and types of ingredients that bonbons are made of, and it contains a field called Source ID that identifies where the ingredient is purchased. The Suppliers table has information about Sweet Lil's ingredient suppliers, and the table contains a field called Suppliers ID. You can join these two fields in a query because they contain matching data.

In this exercise, you create a quick way to look up the contact names for Sweet Lil's suppliers.

1   In the Database window, click the Queries tab, and then click the New button.

The Suppliers table was added in Lesson 4, "Controlling Database Growth."

2   Double-click Design View, add the Ingredients table and the Suppliers table to the query by selecting them and clicking Add, and then close the Show Table dialog box.

3   From the Ingredients table, drag the Category field to the SuppliersID field in the Suppliers table.

A join line indicates a relationship between the two fields that associates the data correctly between the two tables. Your query should look like the following illustration.

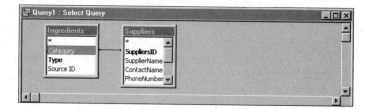

You realize that the tables should be linked on the Source ID field rather than the Category field, so you need to delete the join line and re-make the join linking on the Source ID field.

4   Click on the line between the Ingredients and Suppliers tables in the QBE (query by example) grid, and, after the line thickens, press DELETE.

The join line is removed.

5   Drag the Source ID field from the Ingredients table to the SuppliersID field in the Suppliers table.

The line connects the two fields.

6   In the Ingredients table field list, double-click the Category and Type fields to add them to the design grid.

7   In the Suppliers table field list, double-click ContactName to add it to the grid.

8   In the Ingredients table field list, double-click Source ID to add it to the grid.

9 In the Source ID column, click in the Sort box, click the down arrow, and then select Ascending.

You have sorted the fields in the order you want them to appear in the query results.

Check the query datasheet

1 Click the View down arrow, and click Datasheet View to view the results.

Your query should look like the following illustration.

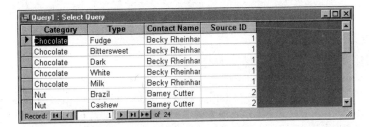

2 Scroll through the records to see the information in the Contact Name field change according to which supplier (Source ID) is used.

3 Close the query. When Microsoft Access asks whether you want to save changes, click Yes.

The Save As dialog box appears.

4 In the File Name box, type **Supplier Contacts** and then click OK.

Print the query datasheet

You decide it would be useful to have a paper copy of the query results. In this exercise, you use the Print command to print the datasheet.

1 In the Database window, double-click the Supplier Contacts query.

The Supplier Contacts query opens in Datasheet view.

2 On the File menu, select Print.

The Print dialog box appears. You can select to print multiple copies or to set up your printer if it is not properly configured.

3 Click OK to print the datasheet to your printer.

4 Close the query.

NOTE If you'd like to build on the skills you learned in this lesson, you can do the One Step Further. Otherwise, skip to "Finish the lesson."

581

One Step Further: Refining Queries

You can also display the bottom values for a field by sorting the field in descending order or see only a percentage of the returned values by selecting one of the percentage values from the Top Values list.

A well-designed query is both specific enough to contain all relevant information and flexible enough to be applied to a variety of situations. Two easy ways to add value to a query are to add a field caption, which helps ensure that data is described completely, and to use the Show Top filter, which limits the information that is returned. If the query is used as the basis for a form, the field caption is used to label the data. If a field caption is not available, the name of the field from which the query extracted data is used as a label. For example, consider the NY Customers query. The query does not locate just any customers, it locates customers who are in New York. However, if this query is used to build a form, the data would be labeled Customer ID, because the field does not have a caption.

Set properties for a field

You want to be certain that your NY Customers query accurately describes exactly what is being displayed. You decide to include a caption for the Customer ID field, so that any form using the query will accurately describe the data in its default caption property. In the following exercise, you will set the Field Caption property to New York Customers.

1 Open the NY Customers query in Design view.

2 Select the Customer ID field by clicking inside the Field row of the first column.

Properties

3 On the toolbar, click the Properties button to open the Field Properties sheet.

4 To add a caption to the Customer ID field, click in the Caption field.

5 Type **New York Customers**

6 Close the Field Properties sheet.

Display only the top five values

You also decide that this query would be more useful if it limited the values displayed to five customers at a time. In the following exercise, you will use the Top Values property to limit the query.

Top Values

1 Click the Top Values down arrow, and then click 5.

2 Switch to Datasheet view to see the changes.

Only the records with the five highest Customer ID numbers are displayed.

3 Close the query, and when Microsoft Access asks if you would like to save changes, click Yes.

Finish the lesson

➤ If you are finished using Microsoft Access for now, on the File menu, click Exit.

Lesson Summary

To	Do this	Button
Create a query	In the Database window, click the Queries tab. Click New, and then double-click Design View or Simple Query Wizard.	
Add a field to a query in the Query Design view	Double-click the field in the upper portion of the Query window.	
Save and name a new query	On the File menu, click Save. In the Save As dialog box, type a name, and then click OK.	
Set criteria	In the query design grid, enter criteria in the Criteria box for any field in the query.	
Sort the records in a query	In the design grid, click the Sort box of the field you want to sort, click the down arrow, and then select Ascending or Descending. *or* In Datasheet view, click in the column you want to sort, and then click the Sort Ascending or Sort Descending button on the toolbar.	
Hide a field in a query	In the design grid, clear the Show check box under the field you want to hide.	
Find a range of data	In the design grid, enter criteria using the Between...And operator.	
Join tables in a query	Use the Show Table dialog box to add the tables to the design grid. The two tables must contain fields with matching data. Drag the matching field from one table, and then drop it on the matching field in the other table.	

For online information about	Use the Office Assistant to search for
Creating queries	**Creating queries,** and then click Create A Query
Adding or deleting fields and tables in a query	**Modify a query,** and then click Design Or Modify A Query
Joining tables in a query	**Joining tables,** and then click Join Multiple Tables And Queries In A Query
Setting criteria in a query	**Criteria,** and then click About Using Criteria In Queries Or Filters To Retrieve Certain Records
Changing field properties	**Field properties,** and then click How Field Properties In A Query And Its Underlying Table Or Query Are Related

Exploring the Microsoft Outlook Environment

Estimated time
25 min.

In this lesson you will learn how to:

- Explore the different Outlook folders.
- Create new Outlook items.
- View the contents of folders.

In today's business world, keeping track of all the information that crosses your desk can almost be a full-time job. In a typical work environment, you might have different types of vital information stored in many different places. For example, you might keep track of your schedule in a desk calendar or a daily planner. You might use electronic mail, or *e-mail*, to communicate with your co-workers and colleagues, in addition to keeping their phone numbers and addresses in an address book. You probably store important documents on your computer's hard disk, or print and keep paper copies in file cabinets in your office. And, if you are like many people, you have a few sticky notes or lists posted around your desk to remind you of other things you need to do, like pick up groceries or call a client.

Microsoft Outlook is a desktop information manager that you can use to organize, find, and view all of the above information. With Outlook, you can schedule appointments for yourself or coordinate meetings with a group. You can send messages and documents to other users to share information, or view and arrange your own e-mail messages and other files without leaving the program. You can maintain a daily task list to keep track of all the things you need to accomplish. You can even create notes and reminders for yourself, right on the Desktop. All of these functions are fully integrated with one another,

587

and with Microsoft Office 97 so that you can manage each day's workload using a single program.

Setting the Scene

As you work through the exercises in this book, imagine that you are the Operations Coordinator for the Margo Tea Company, a rapidly growing organization that specializes in the sales and distribution of quality teas from around the world. In addition to maintaining your own schedule, e-mail messages, task list, and personal contacts, you are responsible for organizing meetings between employees and assigning tasks to your co-workers when appropriate. In this lesson, you'll take your first steps toward using Outlook to do your daily work—you'll familiarize yourself with the work environment and learn how to explore the different information areas within the program.

Creating a Profile

Before you can start using Outlook, you must have a user profile. Your profile contains information about customized options that you can use while you are working in Outlook, including your password and a list of the available information services. Your default profile will probably be set up for you by your system administrator.

Before you begin, it is strongly recommended that you perform the following steps to create an additional profile for a fictional person, Shawn Davis. Creating this profile will give you a clean environment in which you can practice performing tasks. In addition, what you see on your screen will more closely match the illustrations in this book as you work through the lessons.

IMPORTANT   If you have not installed the Part6 Outlook Practice files, refer to "Installing and Using the Practice and Camcorder Files," earlier in this book.

Modify Outlook startup settings

Microsoft Outlook

1   Double-click the Microsoft Outlook shortcut icon on the Desktop.

The Information viewer appears, and the Inbox folder opens. The Office Assistant appears in the lower-right corner of your screen, and the Welcome To Microsoft Outlook! Help balloon appears.

2   Click OK in the help balloon.

The Help balloon closes, and a message appears asking if you want to use Word as your e-mail editor.

3 Click No.

4 On the Tools menu, click Options.

The Options dialog box appears.

5 Be sure that the General tab is selected.

6 In the Startup Settings area, click the Prompt For A Profile To Be Used option button, and then click OK.

The next time you start Outlook, you will be prompted for a user profile.

7 On the File menu, click Exit And Log Off.

Create a practice profile

1 Double-click the Microsoft Outlook shortcut icon on the Desktop.

The Choose Profile dialog box appears.

2 Click New.

The Inbox Setup Wizard starts.

3 Verify that the Use The Following Information Services option button is selected, and then verify that only the Microsoft Mail check box is selected.

Microsoft Mail should be the only information services selected for the purposes of Part 6 of this book. If any other check boxes are selected, click them to clear them.

4 Click Next.

5 In the Profile Name box, type **Shawn Davis** and then click Next.

6 Click Browse

The Browse For Postoffice dialog box appears.

7 Double-click your hard disk, double-click the Office 97 6in1 Step by Step folder, double-click the Part6 Outlook Practice folder, and then click the Wgpo0000 folder. Click OK and then click Next.

This is the path to the practice postoffice you installed on your hard disk as part of the practice files.

8 Select the name Shawn Davis from the list of names, and then click Next.

9 Type **password** in the Password box, and then click Next.

In the remaining steps, you create a practice personal address book associated with the Shawn Davis profile so that entries you add to the practice personal address book are not mixed up with your real personal address book. You also create a practice personal folder file, or set of Outlook folders, for the same reason.

Once you are done with the lessons in Part 6, see "Installing and Using the Practice and Camcorder Files" earlier in this book for information on how to remove the Shawn Davis profile.

10 In the path box, select the text "mailbox.pab," type **shawnd.pab** and then click Next.

11 In the path box, select the text "mailbox.pst," type **shawnd.pst** and then click Next.

12 If a screen appears containing option buttons, verify that the Do Not Add Inbox To StartUp Group option button is selected, and then click Next. If this screen does not appear, skip this step.

13 Click Finish. Click Cancel to close the Choose Profile dialog box.

Starting Microsoft Outlook

When you start Outlook, the Information viewer is the first area you see. This is the main window you use to view and work with all types of information in Outlook. By default, the Information viewer shows the contents of the Inbox folder when you first start Outlook. The Inbox folder contains messages that are sent to you from other users.

To begin working through this lesson, you start Outlook by choosing the Shawn Davis profile. A user profile contains information about customized options that you can use while you are working in Outlook, including your password and a list of the available information services. You can also use your own profile for these exercises, but it is recommended that you use the Shawn Davis profile so that the exercises and illustrations in the book will match what you see on your screen.

Start Outlook

To learn more about the Office Assistant, refer to the "An Introduction to the Office Assistant" section later in this lesson.

1 On your Desktop, double-click the Microsoft Outlook shortcut icon.

Outlook starts. The Choose Profile dialog box appears.

2 Click the down arrow, and then click Shawn Davis.

For the purposes of this book, you'll use the Shawn Davis profile.

3 Click OK.

The Information viewer appears, and the Inbox folder opens. The Office Assistant appears in the lower-right corner of your screen, and the Welcome To Microsoft Outlook! Help balloon appears.

4 Click to clear the Show These Choices At Startup check box, and then click OK.

The Help balloon closes.

Maximize

You can also double-click the title bar to maximize the window.

5 Click the Maximize button on the Microsoft Outlook window.

Your screen should look similar to the illustration below. A "Welcome to Microsoft Outlook!" message from Microsoft may also appear in the Inbox.

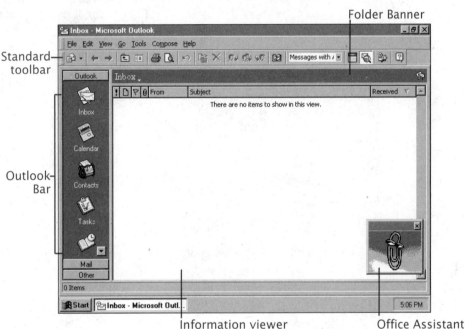

Folder Banner

Standard toolbar

Outlook Bar

Information viewer

Office Assistant

> **IMPORTANT** For the purposes of this book, the Office Assistant will not appear in the illustrations. If you want to hide the Office Assistant temporarily to match the illustrations, use the right mouse button to click the Office Assistant, and then click Hide Assistant. If the Office Assistant is in your way but you want to leave it on to help guide you, simply drag it to another area on the screen.

591

An Introduction to the Office Assistant

While you are working with Microsoft Office 97, an animated character called the *Office Assistant* pops up on your screen to help you work productively. The Office Assistant offers help messages as you work. You can ask the Office Assistant questions by typing your question, and then clicking Search. The Office Assistant then shows you the answer to your question.

You can close any Office Assistant tip or message by pressing ESC.

You will sometimes see a light bulb next to the Office Assistant—clicking the light bulb displays a tip about the action you are currently performing. You can view more tips by clicking Tips in the Office Assistant balloon when the Office Assistant appears. In addition, the Office Assistant is tailored to how your work—after you master a particular skill, the Office Assistant stops offering tips.

Clippit, an Office
Assistant, in action

The Office Assistant appears in the following situations:

- When you click the Office Assistant button on the Standard toolbar.
- When you choose Microsoft Outlook Help on the Help menu or when you press F1.
- When you use certain features. For example, you might see the Office Assistant when you are importing or exporting files with the Import And Export wizard.

  The Office Assistant is a shared application—any settings that you change will affect the Office Assistant in other Office 97 programs. You can customize the Office Assistant in two ways. You can:

Office Assistant

Determining when you want to see the Office Assistant

You can use the right mouse button to click the Office Assistant, and then click Options to open the Office Assistant dialog box. You can then define when you want the Office Assistant to appear and what kind of help you want it to offer.

Changing your Office Assistant character

You can use the right mouse button to click the Office Assistant, and then click Options to open the Office Assistant dialog box. Click the Gallery tab to select another Office Assistant character.

Set up your Inbox for this lesson

For the purposes of this lesson, and to more closely match the illustrations, you should drag messages from the Part6 Outlook Practice folder into the Inbox to simulate receiving mail. Normally, messages you receive appear automatically in the Inbox.

1   Click the Start button, point to Programs, and then click Windows Explorer or Windows NT Explorer.

2   In the left side of the window, titled All Folders, click drive C.

3   In the right side of the window, titled Contents Of, double-click the Office 97 6in1 Step by Step, and then double-click the Part6 Outlook Practice folder.

The contents of the practice folder appear.

4   Double-click the Lesson 1 folder

The messages used in this lesson appear.

5   Click an open area in the taskbar with the right mouse button, and then click Tile Horizontally. If you are using Windows NT, click Tile Windows Horizontally.

The Exploring-Lesson 1 and Inbox-Microsoft Outlook windows are tiled horizontally, or arranged one on top of the other. Your screen should look similar to the following illustration.

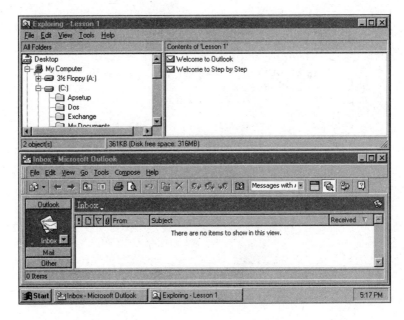

6   In the Exploring-Lesson 1 window, on the Edit menu, click Select All.

593

7   Drag the selected files to the Information viewer area, in the Inbox-Microsoft Outlook window.

The Practice files are copied.

8   Click the Close button on the Exploring-Lesson 1 window.

9   Click the Maximize button on the Inbox window.

Navigating in Outlook

To work efficiently in Outlook, you first need to find the information you want. *Items*, or units of information, such as messages, appointments, or tasks, can be stored in many different folders within Outlook. You must be able to locate and open the correct folders to display the items you need.

When you install Outlook on your computer, an *information store*, or container for a series of folders, is created on your hard disk automatically. This information store, Personal Folders, contains the built-in folders for your personal use in Outlook. Folders in Outlook are arranged in three *groups*: Outlook, Mail, and Other. Each of these groups contains several built-in folders that are either created automatically when you install Outlook, or are included as part of the Windows 95 or Windows NT operating system.

The Outlook group contains folders that are specific to Outlook's personal information management functions, including folders for your schedule and a list of important contacts. The Mail group contains those folders that are specific to e-mail functions, including folders where you can read your mail or store copies of messages you have sent to others. The Other group provides access to the other folders and documents you work with, whether they are stored on your computer's hard drive or on an office network. Some folders appear in more than one group. For example, the Inbox and Deleted Items folders can be accessed from the Outlook group or from the Mail group. The following table describes the built-in folders for each group.

Group	Folder	Description
Outlook	Inbox	Stores the e-mail messages that you receive.
	Calendar	Displays an appointment book where you can keep track of your schedule.
	Contacts	Stores the names, phone numbers, and addresses of the people with whom you correspond and work.
	Tasks	Displays a to-do list of your personal and business tasks.
	Journal	Displays a history of your recorded activities in a timeline format.
	Notes	Stores general information, such as ideas, grocery lists, or directions, in one location.

Group	Folder	Description
	Deleted Items	Temporarily stores the items that you delete until you permanently delete them or quit Outlook.
Mail	Inbox	Stores the e-mail messages that you receive.
	Sent Items	Stores copies of the e-mail messages that you send.
	Outbox	Holds e-mail messages that you send until they are delivered to recipients.
	Deleted Items	Temporarily stores the e-mail messages that you delete until you permanently delete them or quit Outlook.
Other	My Computer	Provides access to other drives, folders, and files on your computer.
	My Documents	Stores documents created using other Microsoft Office 97 programs, such as Microsoft Excel or Microsoft Word.
	Favorites	Stores shortcuts to important Internet addresses.

Switching Folders Using the Outlook Bar

The Outlook Bar is the thick vertical bar that appears to the left of the Information viewer. Icons for the available folders in Outlook appear on the Outlook Bar; each icon acts as a shortcut to the designated folder. The folder icons are also arranged in their respective groups, separated by shortcut bars labeled with the name of each folder group. You can switch between groups by clicking the appropriate shortcut bar. The following illustration shows the default folder selection when you start Outlook.

Open different folders

In this exercise, you use the Outlook Bar to switch between folders to familiarize yourself with the different Outlook groups.

1 Be sure that the Inbox folder is currently open.

"Inbox" should appear in the Folder Banner, and a "Welcome to Microsoft Office 97 Professional 6-in-1 Step by Step!" message and a "Welcome to Microsoft Outlook!" message should appear in the Information viewer.

2 On the Outlook Bar, click the Calendar icon.

Calendar appears, and the current date appears in the Folder Banner. Your screen should look similar to this illustration.

Calendar

The current date on your screen might be different from the date in the illustrations in this book, depending on when you start the exercises.

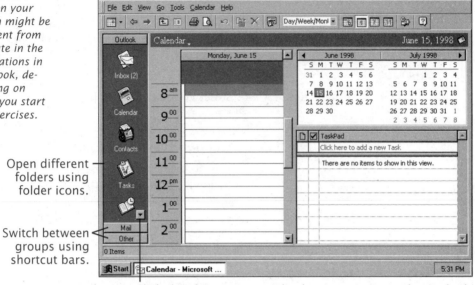

Open different folders using folder icons.

Switch between groups using shortcut bars.

Click this down arrow to display more icons in the Outlook group.

3 On the Outlook Bar, click the down arrow above the Mail shortcut bar.

The list of icons scrolls upward to display more icons in the Outlook group.

If you did not maximize the Inbox window, click the down arrow several times to see the Journal icon.

4 On the Outlook Bar, click the Journal icon.

Journal appears in the Information viewer. The current month appears above the timeline, and the current day is selected in the timeline display. Your screen should look similar to this illustration.

Journal

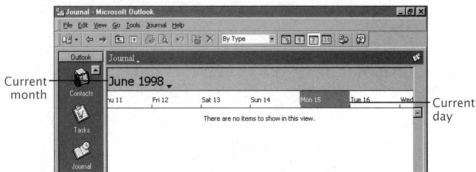

Current month

Current day

Switch folder groups

In this exercise, you use the shortcut bars to display the different groups of folder icons on the Outlook Bar.

1 On the Outlook Bar, click the Other shortcut bar.

Icons for the folders in the Other group appear on the Outlook Bar. Journal still appears in the Information viewer because you have not selected another folder yet.

My Computer

You might notice a similarity between the My Computer folder contents and Windows Explorer or Windows NT Explorer.

2 On the Outlook Bar, click the My Computer icon.

The available drives for your computer appear in the Information viewer. Your screen should look similar to the following illustration.

You may have more available drives, depending on your network configuration.

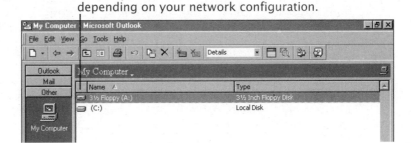

3 On the Outlook Bar, click the Mail shortcut bar.

Icons for the folders in the Mail group appear on the Outlook Bar. My Computer still appears in the Information viewer.

Deleted Items

The Deleted Items folder should be empty, unless you have deleted items recently.

4 On the Outlook Bar, click the Deleted Items icon.

The Deleted Items contents appear in the Information viewer. You can open the Deleted Items folder from either the Mail group or the Outlook group.

5 Click the Outlook shortcut bar.

Icons for the folders in the Outlook group appear on the Outlook Bar.

6 Click the Inbox icon.

The contents of the Inbox folder appear in the Information viewer. You can open the Inbox folder from either the Mail group or the Outlook group. The number of unread messages in a folder appears in parentheses next to the Inbox.

Creating Notes to Store Information

You can easily create new items of any kind in Outlook. In fact, you do not even need to be in the appropriate folder before you create a particular kind of item; you can add a contact or a note from Calendar, or start a new message while viewing your contact list.

New Appointment

NOTE The New button appears on the toolbar in each Outlook folder, but the picture on the button, its full name, and the item it creates change depending on which folder is open. For example, in Calendar, the New button is called the New Appointment button and it creates a new appointment for your schedule.

In the following exercises, you'll practice the basic skills necessary to create new items by creating an electronic note, one of the many item types in Outlook. You will learn more about creating other types of items, such as appointments, in subsequent lessons. You'll also learn about the different ways to view various types of items in your Outlook folders.

You have probably used sticky notes or scrap paper to jot down those pieces of information that don't really belong anywhere else—the confirmation number for an airline reservation, perhaps, or a reminder to yourself to pick up your dry cleaning in the afternoon. If you accumulate a lot of these notes, however, you might find it difficult to locate a particular one; you might misplace or even lose notes if they are scattered around your work area. With Outlook, you can create electronic versions of these notes and store them in your Notes folder so that they are always in one secure, convenient location. You can also keep important notes open on your Desktop as you work, just as you might post a sticky note on the edge of your monitor to remind you throughout the day of something important.

Create an electronic note

In this exercise, you create a note to remind yourself that it is your turn to bring refreshments to the weekly team meeting.

Notes

New Note

1 On the Outlook Bar, click the Notes icon.

The Notes folder opens, and a sample note may appear in the Information viewer. The New button displays a picture of a note.

2 On the Standard toolbar, click the New Note button.

A blank note appears.

3 Type **Bring bagels for tomorrow's meeting!**

The text is immediately saved—changes to a note are saved automatically. Your screen should look similar to the following illustration.

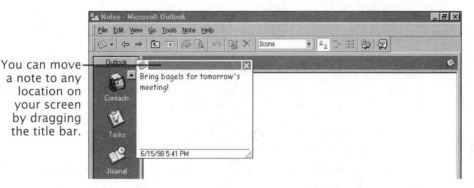

You can move a note to any location on your screen by dragging the title bar.

Close

4   Click the Close button on the note.

The note closes and a note icon appears in the Information viewer.

> **TIP**   You can change the color of your notes to suit your taste or to help color-code notes on particular topics. On the Tools menu, click Options. On the Tasks/Notes tab under Note Defaults, click the Color down arrow, and then select a color from the list. To change the size or the font of your notes, click the appropriate down arrows in the Note Defaults area and make your changes. You can also use the right mouse button to click individual notes, point to Color on the shortcut menu, and then click a color name.

Viewing Folder Contents

Just as you can switch between folders to display different types of items, you can apply different *views* to the items in those folders so that the information appears in a way that is most useful to you. Each folder in Outlook comes with a different set of standard views depending on the type of items contained in the folder. For example, you can display your scheduled appointments in a daily, weekly, or monthly format in Calendar. In your Inbox, you can display messages organized by the name of the person who sent them, or in a timeline according to when they were received. You can easily select a different view for a folder by choosing a menu command or by clicking a drop-down arrow on the Standard toolbar. You can also create your own custom folder views by modifying the existing views or by designing your own unique view.

You will learn more about AutoPreview in Lesson 3, "Reading and Organizing Messages."

The first time you start Outlook, the Inbox folder opens by default, and the Messages With AutoPreview view is applied to the contents of the folder. AutoPreview allows you to see the first three lines of new messages so that you can quickly scan your messages and decide which ones need your attention first. After you have read a message, the AutoPreview text for that message is no longer shown in the Information viewer. In the following exercises, you will experiment with the standard views in different folders, so you can see a variety of ways to display your information.

Change the Inbox folder view

In this exercise, you apply standard views to the contents of the Inbox folder to display your messages by sender, and then by the received time.

Inbox

You can also point to Current View on the View menu, and then select a view name.

1 On the Outlook Bar, click the Inbox icon. Be sure that the current view is Messages With AutoPreview.

The name of the current view appears in the Current View box on the Standard toolbar.

2 On the Standard toolbar, click the Current View down arrow.

A list of the available views appears.

3 Click By Sender.

The By Sender view is applied to your Inbox. Your screen should look similar to the following illustration.

Sender category

Click the plus sign button to expand a category.

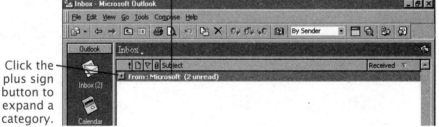

4 Click the plus sign button next to the "From: Microsoft" category.

The category expands to show the "Welcome to Microsoft Office 97 Professional 6-in-1 Step by Step!" and the "Welcome to Microsoft Outlook!" message from Microsoft. If you receive any other messages from Microsoft, they will appear under the "From: Microsoft" heading.

The Standard toolbar buttons change to reflect the current view.

5 On the Standard toolbar, click the Current View down arrow.

The list of available views appears.

6 Click Message Timeline.

The Message Timeline view is applied to your Inbox. The messages from Microsoft appear in the timeline when they were received. In this case, the messages were received when you copied them to the inbox. Your screen should look similar to the following illustration.

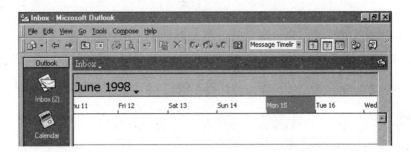

7 On the Standard toolbar, click the Current View down arrow, and then select Messages With AutoPreview.

The default view is reapplied to your Inbox.

Change the Calendar folder view

The default view for Calendar is Day/Week/Month, and when you first open Calendar, your schedule appears in a single-day format. A weekly format and a monthly format are available as subsets of the Day/Week/Month view, and can be applied by clicking the appropriate toolbar button. In this exercise, you apply standard views to the Calendar folder to display your schedule in weekly and monthly formats.

Calendar

1 On the Outlook Bar, click the Calendar icon.

The contents of the Calendar folder appear in single-day format.

2 On the Standard toolbar, click the Week button.

The current week appears in Calendar, and the current date is selected. Your screen should look similar to the following illustration.

Week

You will learn more about adding items to Calendar in Lesson 4, "Organizing Your Schedule Using Calendar."

The current week and date are also
selected in the Date Navigator

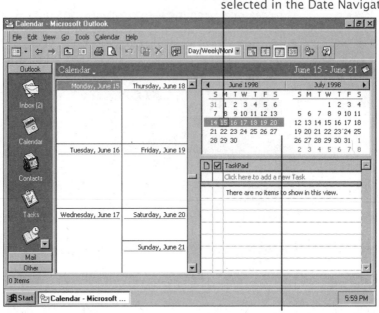

Date Navigator

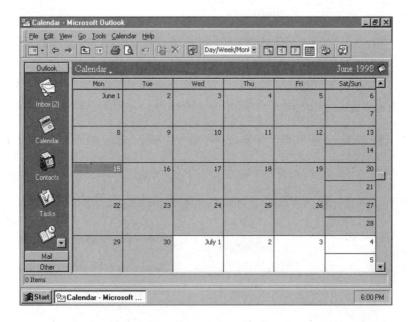

3 On the Standard toolbar, click the Month button.

Month

The current month appears in Calendar, and the current date is selected.
Your screen should look similar to the following illustration.

Day

4 On the Standard toolbar, click the Day button. Be sure to click the Day button and not the Go To Today button. The Day button has the number 1 on it.

Calendar returns to single-day view, and the current date appears.

Adding Folders to the Outlook Bar

As you have seen, it is very easy to move between all your important folders with the Outlook Bar and shortcut bars. By using My Computer in the Other group, you can view the contents of any folder on your computer or on the network. If there are particular folders that you use frequently, you can create shortcuts directly to those folders, and add new shortcut icons and even new groups to the Outlook Bar.

Create a new group on the Outlook Bar

In this exercise, you add a folder group for current projects to the Outlook Bar.

1 Use the right mouse button to click the Other shortcut bar on the Outlook Bar.

2 Click Add New Group.

A new shortcut bar, New Group, appears below the Other shortcut bar.

3 Type **Current Projects**, and then press ENTER.

The highlighted text is replaced as you type, and the new name appears on the shortcut bar.

4 On the Outlook Bar, click the Current Projects shortcut bar.

There are no folders in the Current Projects group yet.

Create a new folder

You have just been asked to give a presentation on time management to this month's management conference. In this exercise, you create a folder on your hard disk to store your notes and documents for the upcoming conference.

1 In the Outlook Bar, click the Other shortcut bar.

The folders in the Other group appear.

2 On the Outlook Bar, click the My Computer icon.

The available drives for your computer appear in the Information viewer.

3 In the Information viewer, double-click drive C.

The contents of drive C appear.

4 On the File menu, point to New, and then click Folder.

The Create New Folder dialog box appears.

5   In the Name box, type **Conference**, and then click OK.

The new folder is added as a subfolder of drive C. Your screen should look similar to the following illustration.

Conference folder

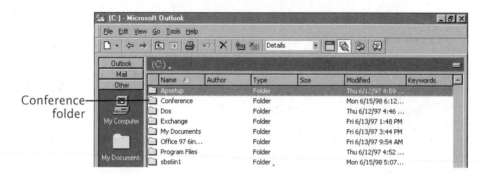

Add a folder shortcut to the Outlook Bar

In this exercise, you add the Conference folder to the Current Projects group on the Outlook Bar so that you can find it immediately.

1   In the Information viewer, click the Conference folder.

2   On the Outlook Bar, click the Current Projects shortcut bar.

3   Drag the Conference folder onto the Outlook Bar, below the Current Projects group heading.

An icon for the Conference folder appears in the Current Projects group. Your screen should look similar to the following illustration.

Shortcut icon

Remove a group from the Outlook Bar

After you have finished working with a group of folders, you can remove those folder shortcuts from the Outlook Bar. In this exercise, you remove the Current Projects group and the folder shortcut it contains.

IMPORTANT Removing folder shortcuts from the Outlook Bar will not delete the folders themselves from your hard disk. Folder groups deleted from the Outlook Bar are not sent to the Deleted Items folder.

You can also use the right mouse button to remove individual shortcut icons from a group.

1 Use the right mouse button to click the Current Projects shortcut bar.

A shortcut menu appears.

2 Click Remove Group.

You are prompted to remove the group.

3 Click Yes.

The group, and the folder shortcut it contains, are removed from the Outlook Bar.

Finish the lesson

Delete

1 To continue to the next lesson, click the Conference folder, and then click the Delete button.

2 In the Confirm Folder Delete dialog box, click Yes.

3 On the Outlook Bar, click the Inbox icon.

4 If you are finished using Outlook for now, on the File menu, click Exit And Log Off.

IMPORTANT If you use the Exit command, you are logged off the server computer, but not other messaging applications, such as Microsoft Mail. By using the Exit And Log Off command, you are logged off all messaging applications.

Lesson Summary

To	Do this	Button
Start Outlook	On the Desktop, double-click the Microsoft Outlook shortcut icon. Select a profile, and then click OK.	
Open folders	On the Outlook Bar, click the folder icon you want.	
Switch between folder groups	On the Outlook Bar, click the shortcut bar for the group you want.	
Create an electronic note	In the Notes folder, click the New Note button, and then type the text of your note.	

To	Do this	Button
Change the folder view	On the Standard toolbar, click the Current View down arrow, and then select a view.	
Display a single day, a week, or a month in Calendar	Click the Day, Week, or Month button.	
Delete an item	Select the item. On the Standard toolbar, click the Delete button.	
Create a new group on the Outlook Bar	Use the right mouse button to click bar on the Outlook Bar. Click Add New Group. Type a name for the new group, and then press ENTER.	
Add a folder to the Outlook Bar	In the Information viewer, select the folder you want to add. Drag the folder onto the Outlook Bar where you want it to appear.	
Remove a group from the Outlook Bar	Use the right mouse button to click the group shortcut bar, and then click Remove Group. Click Yes.	
Quit Outlook	On the File menu, click Exit And Log Off.	

For online information about	Use the Office Assistant to search for
Moving around in Outlook	**Moving around in Outlook,** and then click Move Around In Outlook
Viewing contents of My Computer	**My Computer contents,** and then click Show The Contents Of My Computer
Creating new folders for items	**Creating new folders,** and then click Create A Folder For Items
Changing folder views	**Changing folder views,** and then click Change The View
Creating shortcuts on the Outlook Bar	**Outlook Bar shortcuts,** and then click Create A Shortcut On The Outlook Bar For A Folder

Creating and Sending Messages

Estimated time
30 min.

In this lesson you will learn how to:

- Create and address new messages.
- Enter and edit message content.
- Format text.
- Check message spelling.
- Send messages.
- Recall messages.

With Microsoft Outlook, it's easy to communicate information quickly to others in your organization. For example, if you want to give a co-worker a memo, you could print the memo, and then leave it on her desk. If your co-worker is in another building or a branch office, you could fax or mail the memo to her. However, if you use Outlook, you can send the memo using electronic mail, or *e-mail*, or as a fax, without leaving your computer. You can also receive e-mail messages and faxes from your co-workers directly on your computer, in your Inbox.

Sending your messages using electronic mail is a particularly efficient way to communicate. You can use e-mail for anything you might use the postal service or telephone for, such as sending reports, new hire announcements, or correspondence regarding a project. If you need to send copies of your message to other people, you can easily add more recipients to your message or forward it to others. After a message is sent, the recipient gets it within

607

seconds or minutes, depending on how fast it is processed. Sending e-mail over a network of computers allows you to communicate exclusively online, saving both time and paper.

Not only can you exchange e-mail messages with others in your organization, but you can also send messages to and receive messages from people all over the world by using the *Internet*. The Internet is a vast system of linked computers, a worldwide "network of networks," that connects educational institutions, research organizations, businesses, government entities, and millions of private individuals. E-mail is the most commonly used service of the Internet. Anyone with a computer and a modem or a network connection can use the Internet through an Internet access provider or Internet service provider, such as The Microsoft Network. Internet access providers supply the link between the Internet user and the Internet supercomputers.

Start Outlook

In this exercise, you start Outlook using the Shawn Davis profile.

1   On the Desktop, double-click the Microsoft Outlook shortcut icon.

    Outlook starts. The Choose Profile dialog box appears.

2   Click the down arrow, and then click Shawn Davis.

    For the purposes of this book, you'll use the Shawn Davis profile.

3   Click OK.

    The Information viewer appears, with the Inbox folder open.

4   On the Outlook Bar, click the Mail shortcut bar.

    You will only be working with the Mail group in this lesson.

Creating Messages

When you create a new message using Outlook, a blank form called the Mail Form appears. This form serves as a template to help you compose your message and identify the recipients.

Start a message

In this exercise, you create an e-mail message.

1   Be sure that the Inbox folder is open and that the messages appear in Messages With AutoPreview view.

2   On the Standard toolbar, click the New Mail Message button.

    A blank message appears. Your screen should look similar to the following illustration.

New Mail
Message

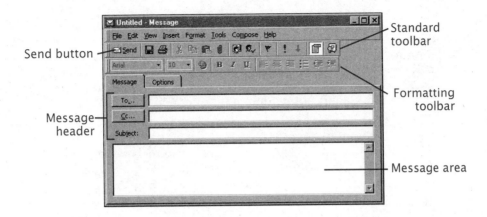

 IMPORTANT If your blank message looks different than the above illustration, you might have Microsoft Word set as your e-mail editor. This feature allows you to use Microsoft Word tools to edit and format your e-mail messages. If Word is being used, you may see additional toolbars and controls on your e-mail editor. You can turn off the Word option and use the default editor instead by performing the following steps:

1 Close the message window.

2 On the Tools menu in the Outlook window, click Options.

3 Click the E-mail tab.

4 Clear the Use Microsoft Word As The E-mail Editor check box, and then click OK.

Addressing Messages

Before you start writing the text of your message, you address it by entering recipient names in the To area located at the top of the *message header*. This is similar to a paper memo where the recipients are identified at the top of the first page. In Outlook, you identify recipients using the *Address Book*, the central location where the names of all the users to whom you can send messages are stored. The Address Book can include more than one address list.

The *global address list* contains a directory of all users in your company or organization. A company's global address list might include the names of all employees in a single building, as well as the names of all employees at several out-of-state branch offices. Every user in your company has access to the global address list, but depending on how your mailbox is configured, your global address list might look different from other users'. The system administrator creates and maintains the global address list for your organization on the server so that all users' computers are linked together.

In addition to your global address list, your Address Book contains a *personal address book*. If you send messages to someone who isn't listed on the global address list for your organization, such as a client who works for another company, you can add that name and e-mail address to your personal address book. Because only you have access to your personal address book, you are responsible for adding entries and maintaining it.

Finally, your Address Book contains an Outlook Address Book which lists e-mail addresses for your business and personal contacts from the Contacts folder. Any time you enter an e-mail address for a contact, the Outlook Address Book is automatically updated to include that information.

For the purposes of this book, you have also created a *postoffice address list* by installing the practice files. The postoffice address list is typically created by the system administrator, and contains the names and e-mail addresses of a particular group of users; usually, these names are a subset of the names in an organization's global address list. In this case, the names are fictitious names of the employees of the Margo Tea Company. In the following exercises, you will address messages using these fictitious names rather than sending messages to your real co-workers.

Address a message using the postoffice address list

As the Operations Coordinator at the Margo Tea Company, you need to arrange a meeting with members of the Sales and Production departments to discuss this year's line of gourmet teas. You decide to notify employees of the meeting via e-mail using Outlook. In this exercise, you insert the names of the appropriate employees in your message header using the Address Book.

If your computer is only connected to the practice workgroup postoffice, you won't see a global address list.

1 In the message header, click the To button.

The Select Names dialog box appears containing names from your Address Book. The global address list for your organization appears by default. Therefore, your Select Names dialog box will look different from the following illustration.

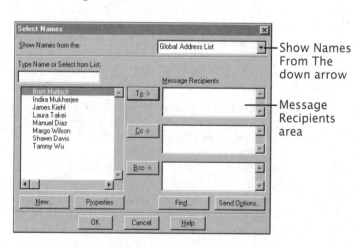

2 Click the Show Names From The down arrow, and then select Postoffice Address List.

The names of the Margo Tea Company employees appear.

3 In the list, click Laura Takei, and then click the To button.

Laura Takei appears in the To box in the Message Recipients area to the right of the list.

4 Click OK.

Your message appears again with Laura Takei's name in the To box in the message header. Your message should look similar to the following illustration.

Underlined recipient names have been checked against the names in your Address Book.

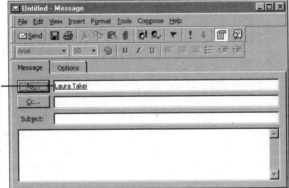

Check Names

NOTE When you address a message, you can also simply type a recipient name, or part of a recipient name, into the To box on the message form. Before you send the message, the names you type are checked against the Address Book names automatically and exact matches are underlined in the To box. If more than one match is found, a red wavy line appears under the name. Click the wavy-underlined name to see a list of possible matches. You can also check names manually by clicking the Check Names button on the Standard toolbar.

Send a copy to another recipient

You're addressing your message to those recipients you want to attend the meeting. If there are other people that you want to inform about the meeting, you can send them a copy. For the purposes of this exercise, you address a copy of the message to yourself, using your profile name, Shawn Davis. Normally, you would not send yourself a copy of a message because a copy of every message you send is automatically stored in the Sent Items folder.

The abbreviation "Cc" stands for "carbon copy" or "courtesy copy."

1   Click the Cc button.

The Select Names dialog box appears.

2   Click the Show Names From The down arrow, and then select the Postoffice Address List.

The names of the Margo Tea Company employees appear.

3   Click Shawn Davis, and then click the Cc button.

Shawn Davis appears in the Cc box, in the Message Recipients area.

4   Click OK.

Your message appears again, with Shawn Davis in the Cc box.

> **NOTE**   You can also send a blind copy of a message. A blind copy (Bcc) is similar to a copy, except that only the blind copy recipient and the sender are aware that the message included the blind copy recipient. To view the Bcc box in the message header, on the View menu, click Bcc Field.

Add names to your personal address book

In this exercise, you add several names from the postoffice address list to your personal address book, because you communicate with those people frequently and you want to be able to find their e-mail addresses more quickly.

Address Book

1   On the Standard toolbar, click the Address Book button.

The Select Names dialog box appears.

2   Click the Show Names From The down arrow, and then select Postoffice Address List.

The names of Margo Tea Company employees appear.

3   Use the right mouse button to click James Kiehl.

A shortcut menu appears.

To select a name, you can also click the Properties button, and then click the Personal Address Book button in the Add To area.

4   Click Add To Personal Address Book.

James Kiehl is added to your personal address book. Although you do not see the results immediately, you will check your personal address book in the next exercise.

5   Click Indira Mukherjee, hold down CTRL, and then click Tammy Wu.

When the desired names do not directly follow one another in the list, you hold down CTRL to select them.

6   Use the right mouse button to click one of the selected names.

A shortcut menu appears.

7   Click Add To Personal Address Book.

Indira Mukherjee and Tammy Wu are added to your personal address book.

Address a message using your personal address book

In this exercise, you add a name from your personal address book as a message recipient.

1 Click the Show Names From The down arrow, and then select Personal Address Book.

The names you added to your personal address book—Indira Mukherjee, James Kiehl, and Tammy Wu—appear.

2 Select Indira Mukherjee, and then click To.

Indira Mukherjee appears in the To box under Message Recipients.

You can also double-click a name to add it to the To box.

3 Click OK.

Indira Mukherjee appears in the To box.

Add an Internet address to your personal address book

Entries in your personal address book can include recipients who use another e-mail or messaging system outside your company. A common way to send e-mail to someone outside your company is by using the Internet.

In this exercise, you add the Internet address for Debbie Abdul, the Account Executive in charge of the Margo Tea Company advertising campaign, to your personal address book.

1 On the Standard toolbar, click the Address Book button.

The Select Names dialog box appears.

2 Click the New button.

The New Entry dialog box appears.

3 Under Select The Entry Type, click Other Address.

4 In the Put This Entry area, be sure that the "In The Personal Address Book" option button is selected.

You do not need to open your personal address book to add names to it.

5 Click OK.

The New Other Address Properties dialog box appears.

You can also use an alias, such as "Debbie at work," for a Display Name.

6 In the Display Name box, type **Debbie Abdul**, and then press TAB.

This is the way the name will appear in your personal address book.

7 In the E-mail Address box, type **dabdul@fitch_mather.com**, and then press TAB.

The fictional e-mail address for Debbie Abdul is added to your personal address book.

8 In the E-mail Type box, type **Internet**

This specifies the type of e-mail address you are adding. Your dialog box should look similar to the following illustration.

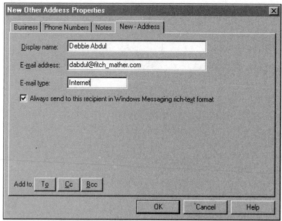

9 Click OK.

The new address is added to your personal address book, and Debbie Abdul appears in the To box in your message header.

Entering and Editing Message Content

You can also type your message subject and text before you identify the message recipients.

Now that you have identified the recipients of your message, you can finish the message by entering a subject, and then typing the message itself in the blank area located at the bottom of the Mail Form. The message area expands as you type, so your messages can be brief or lengthy. Adding a message subject helps recipients identify the message topic, since the subject appears in the message header in recipients' Inboxes.

You can enter and edit text in your message just as you would using a word processor. In Outlook, you can use the BACKSPACE key or the DELETE key to delete text, and move or copy text by dragging and dropping. You can also reverse an action by using the Undo command on the Edit menu.

Enter and edit the message text

In this exercise, you type the subject of your message and then add the main content of the message. You'll start off by inviting everyone to the meeting to discuss this year's product line, and then you'll make changes to the text.

1 Click in the Subject box, and then type **Product Line Meeting**

2 Press TAB to move the insertion point to the message area, and then type **We need to discuss the new porduct release schedule. Let's order boxed lunches and meet in her office Tuesday at noon.**

Be sure that you type the word "product" incorrectly as "porduct" so you can spell-check it later.

You can also drag to select text.

3 Double-click the word "boxed" to select it, and then press the DELETE key.

4 Double-click the word "her," and then type **Margo's**

5 Click in front of the word "Tuesday," type **next**, and then press the SPACEBAR.

Your message should look similar to the following illustration.

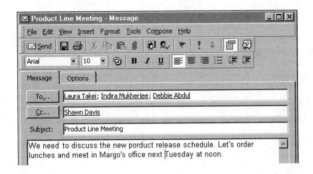

Checking the Spelling of Messages

You can use the spell checker in Outlook to identify and correct spelling errors in your messages before you send them. It is a good idea to check the spelling of all your outgoing messages, whether or not you think you made any mistakes. When you start the spell checker, your message is checked from the beginning of the message, no matter where the insertion point is placed. If you don't want to check the spelling for the entire message, you can select part of it, even a single word. The text in the Subject box is also checked for spelling, but recipient names are ignored.

If the spelling of a word isn't recognized when you check your message, you can correct the word contained in your message by selecting the correctly spelled word from a list of suggestions. If the spelling of a word is correct as is, but the spell checker does not recognize it, you can either add the word to the dictionary, or ignore the word and continue the spell check. In addition to misspelled words, duplicated words are recognized, and the second word can be deleted using the spell checker. The buttons used in the Spelling dialog box are described in the following table.

Use this button	To
Ignore	Ignore only that occurrence of the word.
Ignore All	Ignore all instances of the word in the message.
Change	Change only that occurrence of the word.
Change All	Change all instances of the word in the message.

Use this button	To
Add	Add the word to the dictionary for future reference.
Suggest	Display a list of proposed spellings or words.
Options	Set options for spell checks.
Undo Last	Reverse the last spell-check change.
Cancel	Cancel the spell check.

Spell check your message

In this exercise, you check your message for spelling, especially since you deliberately made a spelling error in the previous exercise.

1   On the Tools menu, click Spelling.

The spell checker starts. The Spelling dialog box appears and the word "porduct" is not recognized by the dictionary. A suggested word appears in the Suggestions box.

2   Be sure that the word "product" is selected in the Suggestions box, and then click Change.

The word is corrected in your message, and the next unrecognized word, "Margo's," appears in the Change To box.

3   Click Ignore.

The word "Margo's" is a valid name. A message appears indicating that the spell check is complete.

4   Click OK.

 TIP   To have all messages automatically checked for spelling before they are sent, click Options on the Tools menu in the Outlook window, click the Spelling tab, and then select the Always Check Spelling Before Sending check box.

Formatting Text

In Outlook, you can format the text in your messages to help emphasize your ideas and create interest. For example, you can choose from a series of *fonts* to create a different look, or you can format text as bold, italic, or underlined. These text characteristics, or attributes, are also known as *rich text format*. When you create a message in rich text format, the text attributes can be recognized by different programs so that you can send formatted messages even to users who might not have Outlook. You can also add bullets to highlight and separate the main points of your message, or change the color of the text.

To format text, you first select the text you want to format, and then apply the formatting. If you do not select any text before you format, the formatting you define will be applied to any text that you type after the insertion point. Only the text in the message area can be formatted.

You can use the buttons on the Formatting toolbar to change text attributes, such as bold, italic, underline, and text color. Or you can use the Font command on the Format menu to change the appearance of the text. You can also change text formatting and paragraph formatting. Paragraph formatting includes alignment, indentation, and bullets.

Add text

At the Margo Tea Company, you want all of your messages to be interesting and effective. You decide to experiment with text and paragraph formatting in your message about the upcoming product line meeting. In this exercise, you add some information about the meeting agenda to your message. You will format this text in the next two exercises.

1 Press CTRL+END to move the insertion point to the end of your message text, and then press ENTER twice.

The insertion point moves to a new line.

2 Type the following text, pressing ENTER after each line.

Our agenda will include:

Reviewing the existing product line

Drafting a schedule for new product releases

Approving a new label design

Format text

In this exercise, you use buttons on the Formatting toolbar to change the appearance of the text you just typed.

1 Triple-click the line "Our agenda will include:" to select it.

2 On the Formatting toolbar, click the Italic button.

The text is italicized.

Italic

3 Select the text "Reviewing the existing product line" through "Approving a new label design."

4 On the Formatting toolbar, click the Bold button.

The text is formatted as bold.

Bold

Font Color

5 On the Formatting toolbar, click the Font Color button.

A color palette appears.

6 Click Green, the fifth color in the top row.

The text is formatted with the color green.

 NOTE You must have a color printer to print text in color. If you use a black and white printer to print colored text, the text will appear in shades of gray.

Format the paragraph

In this exercise, you use buttons on the Formatting toolbar to format several lines of text.

1 Be sure that the text "Reviewing the existing product line" through "Approving a new label design" is selected.

Bullets

2 On the Formatting toolbar, click the Bullets button.

Bullets are added in front of each new paragraph of text.

3 On the Formatting toolbar, click the Increase Indent button.

The text is indented to the right.

Increase Indent

4 Click anywhere in the text.

The selection is cleared. Your message should look similar to the following illustration.

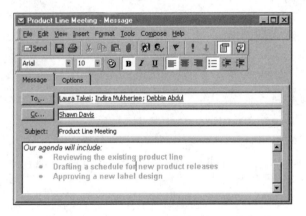

TIP You can automatically sign all of your e-mail messages with a particular phrase or selection of text. For example, your signature text could be "Shawn Davis, Operations Coordinator." To do this, click AutoSignature on the Tools menu. The AutoSignature dialog box appears. Type in the text and format the text using the Font and Paragraph buttons. Select the Add This Signature To The End Of New Messages check box if you want to add the signature to new messages. When done, click OK. Click the Insert Now button if you want to insert the signature in the current message.

Creating a Reusable Message Template

Using Microsoft Word 97 as your e-mail editor, you can edit your Outlook messages and modify their appearance. For example, suppose you want to send a weekly message to the members of your project team, containing a table that lists this week's meeting agenda items. You can create an original message template or modify an existing Outlook message template and save the changes with a new name.

To select an existing template to modify, verify that the contents of your Inbox appear in the Information viewer. On the Compose menu, click Choose Template. A list of all the available Outlook templates appears in the Choose Template dialog box. (You can also access the list of templates from the Calendar menu in Calendar, the Contacts menu in Contacts, the Tasks menu in Tasks, and so on. The Choose Template command appears on each of these menus.) Select a template from the list and click OK to open it.

To enable WordMail tools, click Options on the Tools menu. On the E-mail tab, select the Use Microsoft Word As The E-mail Editor checkbox. After you have opened a template, use the message tools and WordMail tools to modify the template to suit your needs. For example, you can use Word 97 to create a table in the message area, and use the regular message formatting tools to change its appearance. When you have finished designing your template, you can save it with the rest of the Outlook templates.

To save an original template, on the File menu, click Save As. Save the template in the Program Files\Microsoft Office\Templates\Outlook folder. Type a name for the new template, such as "Meeting Agenda," in the File Name box. Finally, be sure to click the Save As Type down arrow and select Outlook Template (*.oft). Your original template will be stored with the rest of the Outlook templates. You can use an original template at any time by clicking the Choose Template command on the Compose menu, and then double-clicking the template you want to use.

Sending Messages

Now that you have addressed and composed a message, you are ready to send it. When you send a message, it is moved to your Outbox folder, where it is temporarily stored, usually for a few seconds, until it's delivered to the recipient or recipients. Message recipients do not need to be present to receive a message; the message is delivered to and stored in their Inboxes until they log on to Outlook and open the message. If your e-mail message cannot be delivered because of a network problem or an incorrect address, you will receive a notification message from the server. Before you send your e-mail message, you can select several options that will affect its delivery.

Tracking Sent Messages

If you want to make sure that your message was successfully sent, or if you want to know when the message was opened by the recipient, you can select a *tracking* option. Depending on the tracking option you assign, a notification is sent to you when the recipient receives a message, when the recipient opens the message, or both. A notification message informing you that a message has been delivered is also called a *Delivery Receipt*. A notification message indicating that a message has been read by the recipient is called a *Read Receipt*. Assigning tracking options to your messages is similar to using registered mail. Tracking can be useful if your message is time-sensitive.

IMPORTANT Any options you select on the Options tab in a message apply only to that message.

You can check the tracking results for a message you have sent by reading the receipts from your system administrator, or by opening the copy of the message in your Sent Items folder. The Tracking tab records the message status for each recipient.

NOTE You can also conduct a vote with a message; the voting results are maintained on the Tracking tab. You can learn about setting voting options on an outgoing message in the "Conducting a Vote with a Message" section in Lesson 3, "Reading and Organizing Messages."

Set tracking options for a message

In this exercise, you set the tracking options for your message to make sure all the recipients successfully receive and read it. Since you are sending your message to fictional users in this exercise, you will receive an Undeliverable Receipt from the system administrator.

1 Click the Options tab, and then maximize the message.

Your message should look similar to the following illustration.

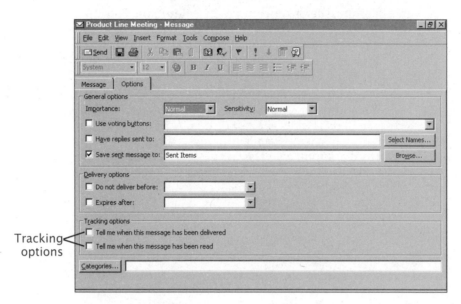

Tracking options

2 In the Tracking Options area, select the Tell Me When This Message Has Been Delivered check box.

You will be notified when the recipients receive this message.

3 In the Tracking Options area, select the Tell Me When This Message Has Been Read check box.

You will be notified when the recipients open this message.

4 Restore the size of the message window.

TIP If you want to set tracking options for all outgoing messages, on the Tools menu in the Outlook window, click Options. On the Sending tab, select the Tell Me When All Messages Have Been Delivered check box and/or the Tell Me When All Messages Have Been Read check box, and then click OK. You can also process receipts automatically so that tracking information is recorded on the Tracking tab and receipts are deleted after they have been processed. To do this, on the Tools menu, click Options. Click the E-mail tab, and then select the options you want in the Settings For Automatic Processing Of Mail area.

Assigning Priority to Messages

You can also assign a priority to a message so that the recipient can determine its importance before opening it. By default, messages are sent with a normal priority, but you can mark them with a low or a high priority, depending on their importance. For example, you want the recipients of your message regarding the product line meeting to know that it requires immediate attention, so you assign it a high priority.

After you send a message, recipients are able to identify the priority level by looking at the message header in their Information viewers. Messages with a high priority level are indicated with a red exclamation point next to the message header, while messages with a low priority have a blue downward-pointing arrow. Normal priority messages do not have a symbol next to the message header. The priority symbols are listed in the following table.

Symbol	Priority level
! ✉	High priority
↓ ✉	Low priority

Assign high priority to a message

In this exercise, you assign high priority to your message because you want to emphasize the importance of the upcoming product line meeting.

Importance: High

➤ On the Standard toolbar, click the "Importance: High" button.

The message is assigned a high priority and the text in the Importance box on the Options tab changes to High.

Message Flag

 TIP If you are sending a message that requires further action—for example, a message that the recipient must respond to—you can also attach a message flag to draw attention to the message. On the Standard toolbar in the Mail Form, click the Message Flag button, and then select a flag message. You will learn more about message flags in Lesson 3, "Reading and Organizing Messages."

Send your message

Now that you have set all the delivery options for your message, you are ready to send it.

➤ On the Standard toolbar, click the Send button.

After a moment, your message is sent and a copy is created in the Sent Items folder. Because you addressed a carbon copy to yourself, a new message also appears in your Inbox.

TROUBLESHOOTING You should receive several receipts from your system administrator, including a Delivery Receipt indicating that your message was received by the recipients in your workgroup, and an Undeliverable Receipt for the fictitious Internet address. If you receive a message stating that you have no transport provider, click OK; this means that your network has not been set up for Internet messaging.

Recalling a Message

Occasionally, you might want to retrieve a message you've sent. For example, suppose you have sent someone a message containing incorrect information or addressed a message to the wrong person. With Outlook, you can recall messages you have sent as long as the recipient has not yet opened the message. If a recipient has already opened your message, it cannot be retrieved.

When you recall messages, you can choose to simply delete your unread message from the recipient's Inbox or replace the original message with a different one. Either way, the recipient of the original message is notified that it was recalled.

Replace a message

You just remembered that you will be out of the office all day on Tuesday to attend a seminar, and therefore won't be able to hold the product line meeting. In this exercise, you recall your original message and request a meeting on a different date.

Sent Items

1 On the Outlook Bar, click the Sent Items icon.

The contents of the Sent Items folder are displayed in the Information viewer.

2 Double-click the Product Line Meeting message in the Information viewer.

A copy of your sent message appears.

3 On the Tools menu, click Recall This Message.

A message appears, prompting you to delete or replace the existing message from the recipients' Inboxes.

4 Click the Delete Unread Copies And Replace With A New Message option button, and then click OK.

Your original Product Line Meeting message appears.

5 In the message, double-click the word "Tuesday," and then type **Thursday**

6 On the Standard toolbar, click the Send button.

The replacement message is sent. On the copy of the message in your Sent Items folder, a note appears in the Comment area above the message header, reminding you that you attempted to recall the message. Your screen should look similar to the following illustration.

New
Comment
icon

Comment
area

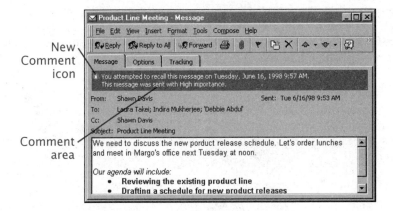

7 Click the Close button on the message window.

Copies of both the original message and the replacement message are displayed in your Sent Items folder.

IMPORTANT If you choose to replace a recalled message, you must specifically send the replacement message. If you do not resend a replacement message, the original is simply deleted from the recipients' Inboxes.

View the replacement message

Since you did not open the carbon copy of the message you sent to yourself, the replacement message is delivered to your Inbox in place of the original. In this exercise, you use AutoPreview to make sure that the corrected replacement message is in your Inbox.

1 On the Outlook Bar, click the Inbox icon.

The contents of your Inbox appear.

2 Be sure that Messages With AutoPreview is the current view.

The name of the current view appears in the Current View box on the Standard toolbar. Your screen should look similar to the following illustration.

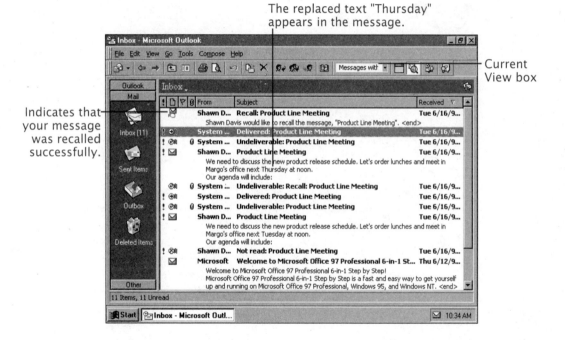

The replaced text "Thursday" appears in the message.

Indicates that your message was recalled successfully.

Current View box

Finish the lesson

Follow these steps to delete the practice messages you used in this lesson, so that you have a clean Inbox folder to work with in the next lesson. You will learn more about deleting items in Lesson 3, "Reading and Organizing Messages."

1 Be sure that the contents of the Inbox are displayed.

2 On the Edit menu, click Select All.

The contents of your Inbox are selected.

Delete

3 On the Standard toolbar, click the Delete button.

The messages are deleted.

4 To continue to the next lesson, on the Outlook Bar, click the Inbox icon.

5 If you are finished using Outlook for now, on the File menu, click Exit And Log Off.

Lesson Summary

To	Do this	Button
Start a message	In the Inbox folder, click the New Mail Message button.	
Address a message	Click To, and then select an address list. Select recipient names, and then click To.	
Send a carbon copy	Click Cc, select recipient names, and then click Cc.	
Add names to your personal address book from another address list	In the Address Book, use the right mouse button to click a name. Click Add To Personal Address Book.	
Add an Internet address to your personal address book	In the Address Book, click New, click Other Address, and then click OK. Type a Display Name, an E-mail Address, an E-mail Type, and then click OK.	
Enter and edit message text	In the message area, type your text. To edit, place the insertion point where you want to edit, and then type new text or use BACKSPACE to delete text.	
Spell check a message	On the Tools menu, click Spelling, and then accept or reject the changes.	
Format text	Select the text you want to format. On the Formatting toolbar, click the appropriate buttons for the formatting effects you want to apply.	

To	Do this	Button
Track sent messages	On the Options tab, select the options you want in the Track-ing Options area.	
Assign a high or low priority to a message	On the Standard toolbar, click the "Importance: High" button or the "Importance: Low" button.	
Recall a message	On the Outlook Bar, click the Sent Items icon. Open the mes-sage you want to recall. On the Tools menu, click Recall This Message. Select Delete Unread Copies Of This Message and click OK.	
Recall and replace a message	On the Outlook Bar, click the Sent Items icon. Open the mes-sage you want to recall and re-place. On the Tools menu, click Recall This Message. Select De-lete Unread Copies And Replace With A New Message and click OK. Edit the message and resend the message.	

For online information about	Use the Office Assistant to search for
Creating messages	**Creating messages,** and then click Create A Message
Sending messages	**Sending messages,** and then click Send Mes-sages
Using the Address Book	**Address book,** and then click About the Ad-dress Book
Adding e-mail addresses	**Adding e-mail addresses,** and then click Enter An E-mail Address For A Contact
Tracking messages	**Tracking messages,** and then click Track When Messages Are Delivered Or Read
Setting importance level	**Setting importance level,** and then click Set The Importance Level

Reading and Organizing Messages

Estimated time
35 min.

In this lesson you will learn how to:

- Locate and read messages.
- Reply to and forward messages.
- Organize messages.
- Create and manage folders.
- Conduct a vote with messages.

You probably have already received messages from other people, or at least are aware that messages have been sent to you. Now, you need to be able to locate them, and then read them. In addition to reading your messages, you need to find out what you can do with them after you read them. For example, you can reply to or forward messages to share information with others. You can also store messages about a specific project in a separate folder or delete messages that you no longer need.

At the Margo Tea Company, you have received several messages concerning the new product line meeting. In this lesson, you'll learn how to quickly respond to your messages so that you can be prepared for the upcoming discussion. You'll also organize the messages in your Inbox so that you can quickly file and later find the information that you need.

Start Outlook

1   On the Desktop, double-click the Microsoft Outlook shortcut icon.

Outlook starts. The Choose Profile dialog box appears.

2   Click the down arrow, and then click Shawn Davis.

For the purposes of this book, you'll use the Shawn Davis profile.

3   Click OK.

The Information viewer appears, with the Inbox folder open.

4   On the Outlook Bar, click the Mail shortcut bar.

You will only be working with the Mail group in this lesson.

Set up your Inbox for this lesson

For the purposes of this lesson, and to be able to complete the following exercises, you must drag messages from the Part6 Outlook Practice folder into the Inbox to simulate receiving mail. Normally, messages you receive appear automatically in the Inbox.

1   Click the Start button, point to Programs, and then click Windows Explorer or Windows NT Explorer.

2   In the left side of the window, titled All Folders, click drive C.

3   In the right side of the window, titled Contents Of, double-click the Office 97 6-in-1 Step by Step folder and then double-click the Part6 Outlook Practice folder.

The contents of the practice folder appear.

4   Double-click the Lesson 3 folder.

The messages used in this lesson appear.

5   Click an open area in the taskbar with the right mouse button, and then click Tile Horizontally. If you are using Windows NT, click Tile Windows Horizontally.

The Exploring–Lesson 3 and Inbox–Microsoft Outlook windows are tiled horizontally, or arranged one on top of the other. Your screen should look similar to the following illustration.

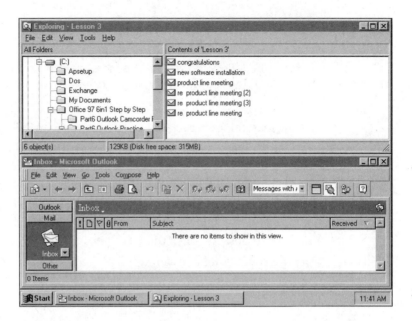

6 In the Exploring–Lesson 3 window, on the Edit menu, click Select All.

7 Drag the selected files to the Information viewer area, in the Inbox–Microsoft Outlook window.

The practice files are copied, and you are ready to start the lesson.

8 Click the Close button on the Exploring–Lesson 3 window.

9 Click the Maximize button on the Inbox window.

Locating and Reading Messages

After you start Outlook, you can start working with your messages in the Information viewer. You can easily identify and manage your incoming messages because they are automatically placed in the Inbox folder.

You can readily distinguish between messages in the folder contents list by reading the message header. The message header identifies the sender, the subject, and when the message was sent. Messages that have not been opened appear in bold type, while messages that have been opened are in regular type. In addition, the number of unread messages in a folder appears next to the folder name in parentheses, in both the Outlook bar and in the Folder List.

TIP When you receive incoming messages, a message icon appears on the taskbar. If Outlook is not the active window, you can quickly open your Inbox by double-clicking the message icon.

Explore your mailbox folders

In this exercise, you open your built-in folders to view where different messages are stored. You can review the message you sent about the Product Line Meeting and find out if any messages are located in any other folders in your Inbox.

1   On the Outlook Bar, click the Deleted Items icon.

If you have deleted any messages recently, they will appear in the Deleted Items folder.

2   On the Outlook Bar, click the Outbox icon.

The Information viewer should show no messages stored in the Outbox because you have not sent any messages recently.

3   On the Outlook Bar, click the Sent Items icon.

Any messages you have sent appear.

4   On the Outlook Bar, click the Inbox icon.

The practice items in your Inbox appear in the Information viewer.

Open a message

In this exercise, you open the Product Line Meeting message so you can read it.

1   In the Information viewer, double-click the Product Line Meeting message from Shawn Davis.

A copy of the message you sent in Lesson 2 opens. In the header, you can see the name of the sender, the date and time it was sent, and the message recipients' names. Your message should look similar to the following illustration.

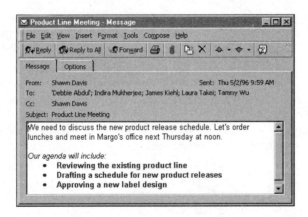

You can also click Close on the File menu.

2 On the Product Line Meeting–Message window, click the Close button. The message closes.

Browsing Through Messages Using AutoPreview

By default, the messages in your Inbox appear in Messages With AutoPreview view. With AutoPreview, the first three lines of text are displayed for all new, unopened messages. You can preview the message contents at a glance and decide which of your new messages you should open and read first. If a message is short enough, you do not even need to open it to read the entire message. After you open a message, the message header no longer appears in bold type, and the first three lines of text are no longer displayed.

 TIP If you want AutoPreview text to appear for both unread and read messages, on the View menu, click Format View. In the AutoPreview area, click the Preview All Items option button, and then click OK. To turn off AutoPreview, click the No AutoPreview option button.

As you look in the Information viewer, you can also see that icons appear to the left of messages. Different kinds of messages have different icons associated with them to help you identify them. For example, an icon for an e-mail message with an attachment looks like an envelope with a paper clip, while a Delivery Receipt icon looks like a postage meter stamp with a green arrow. These icons can also help you determine which messages need your immediate attention. Some of the different icons used to identify messages in the Information viewer are listed in the following table.

Icon	Description
✉	Standard e-mail with normal priority
❗✉	E-mail with high priority
↓✉	E-mail with low priority
✉ 𝔔	E-mail with an attached file
⊕	Postmark for Delivery Receipt
⊘	Postmark for Undeliverable Receipt
⊘	Postmark for read messages
⊗	Postmark for unread messages
✉	E-mail message that you have replied to
✉	E-mail message that you have forwarded
✉	E-mail message with comment or note in the message header

633

In the Information viewer, columns divide the message header by priority, item type, message flag, attachment, sender, subject, received date, and size. By default, messages are sorted by date, with the most recent message at the top of the list. You will learn how to sort your messages differently later in this lesson.

 NOTE Your Inbox might have more or fewer messages than in the illustrations in this lesson. If your messages appear in a different order, click the Received column button in the Information viewer until your Inbox messages are sorted by date.

Most of your unread messages are responses to the Product Line Meeting message that you sent. Because you have not read these messages, they are in bold type, and the first three lines of text are displayed below each message header. You can now review and read your new messages. When you open a message, it appears as a Mail Form, which is very similar to the Mail Form you use to compose and send messages.

Read an entire message

With AutoPreview, the first three lines of Laura Takei's response to your Product Line Meeting message are visible, but the message continues past the range of AutoPreview. In this exercise, you open Laura's message so you can read it in its entirety. When you open a message that is a reply or a forward, the original message text is appended to the bottom of the message by default.

You can also click Open on the File menu.

1 Double-click the "RE: Product Line Meeting" message from Laura Takei.

The message opens. The complete message text appears.

2 Scroll downward, as necessary, to read the entire message.

Following Laura Takei's reply is the text of your original message.

Browse through messages

Instead of opening and closing each message individually, you can quickly browse through them by opening a message, and then clicking the Next Item or Previous Item buttons on the Standard toolbar. In this exercise, you browse through your messages, including the replies to your Product Line Meeting message.

Previous Item

1 On the Standard toolbar, click the Previous Item button until the message from Brett Matlock appears.

The title of the message is New Software Installation.

2 Click the Previous Item button again.

The previous message, a Congratulations message from Margo Wilson, appears.

Next Item

3 On the Standard toolbar, click the Next Item button three times, until the message from Indira Mukherjee, responding to the Product Line Meeting message, appears.

4 Click the Next Item button again.

A reply from James Kiehl appears.

5 On the message window, click the Close button.

The messages you have opened and read no longer appear in bold type, and no longer show any message text in AutoPreview.

Flagging Messages for Action

Suppose you need to follow up on an issue that was brought to your attention by a particular message, such as reviewing an attached report or placing a conference call to the sender. You do not have to follow up on the message immediately, but you don't want to forget to do it later, either. With Outlook, you can *flag* a message in your Inbox with a reminder to follow up on the issue at another time. If you want, you can add a specific due date to the message flag. You can also attach flags to the messages that you send to others to alert them that an action item is included in your message, and needs their close attention. When a recipient receives a message with a flag, a note about the purpose of the flag appears in the comment area above the message header.

You can choose from a predetermined list of message flags, such as "Call" or "No Response Necessary." If the existing flags in Outlook do not meet your needs, you can also create your own. If a message contains a flag, a red flag icon appears in the message flag column in the Inbox. Once you have followed up on a message, you can mark its flag as completed; a gray flag icon appears in the message flag column to indicate a completed follow-up.

Flag a message

In this exercise, you flag the message from Brett Matlock because you want to remind yourself to call him and ask about Outlook training for all employees.

1 Double-click the New Software Installation message from Brett Matlock.

The message opens.

2 Maximize the message.

You must maximize the message to see the entire Standard toolbar on the Mail Form.

Message Flag

3 On the Standard toolbar, click the Message Flag button.

The Flag Message dialog box appears.

4 Click the Flag down arrow.

A list of message flags appears.

5 Select Call.

6 Click the By down arrow.

A drop-down calendar appears; the current date is selected.

7 Click Today.

The current date appears in the By box.

8 Click OK.

A note about the message flag appears in the comment area above the message header. Your message should look similar to the following illustration.

Comment area—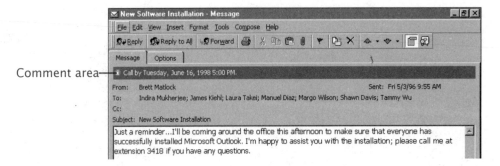

9 Click the Close button on the message window.

A red message flag appears in the message flag column. Your screen should look similar to the following illustration.

Message flag—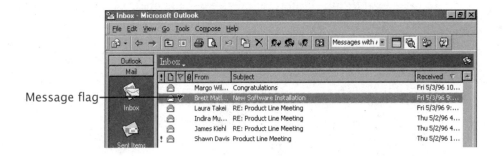

NOTE If you have maximized a message, all your messages will appear maximized from that moment on. Similarly, if you restore a message, all messages will appear restored until you choose differently.

Flag a message as completed

Suppose you just called Brett and asked him your question. In this exercise, you mark the message with a completed flag to remind yourself that you have taken care of the issue.

Message Flag

If you want to remove the message flag, click Clear Flag.

1   Double-click the message from Brett Matlock.

2   Click the Message Flag button.

The Flag Message dialog box appears.

3   Select the Completed check box, and then click OK.

A note is added to the comment area, including the time and date that the message was flagged as completed.

4   Click the Close button on the message window.

A gray flag appears in the message flag column.

Responding to Messages

Suppose you want to respond to a message you have received or pass message information along to somebody else. You could create a new message, add the recipient and the subject, and then try to recall the details of the original message that you want to discuss. A much faster way to respond, however, is to select or open a message, and then use a toolbar button to direct the message back to the sender or to a new recipient. Your reply is added above the original message text. In the Mail Form, the names of the message response buttons appear directly on the buttons in the Standard toolbar.

Replying to Messages

When you *reply* to a message, you can either respond only to the person who sent the original message or include all the carbon copy recipients listed in the original message. For example, if your team lead sends a message inviting everyone on the team to a lunch meeting, you can inform the lead and your fellow team members that you cannot attend, all in a single message. Reply messages are identified by the letters "RE" in the subject area.

Reply to a recipient

In this exercise, you reply to Laura Takei's message regarding the lunch orders for the Product Line Meeting.

1   Click the "RE: Product Line Meeting" message from Laura Takei.

You do not need to open a message to reply to it.

Reply

2 On the Standard toolbar, click the Reply button.

A Mail Form appears. The To and Subject boxes are automatically filled in, with the subject preceded by "RE:" Notice that Laura's message appears below the message area where you will type your text.

The insertion point automatically appears in the message area.

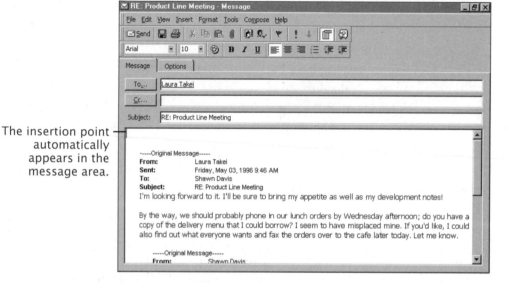

3 Type **Thanks for your help! Drop by my desk and I'll give you copies of the menu and the order form.**

4 On the Standard toolbar, click the Send button.

Your reply is sent to Laura Takei. The message icon in the Information viewer changes to indicate that you have replied to the message.

Message icon indicates that you have replied to the message.

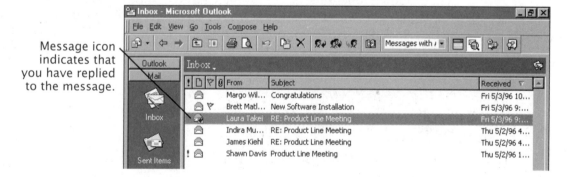

5 Double-click the "RE: Product Line Meeting" message from Laura Takei.

The message opens, and a note appears in the comment area, recording the date and time of your reply.

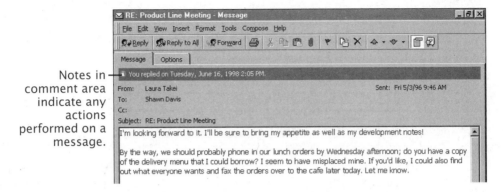

Notes in comment area indicate any actions performed on a message.

6   Click the Close button on the message window.

Reply to All

> **NOTE**   If you want to reply to all the original recipients of a message, click the Reply To All button on the Standard toolbar.

Forwarding Messages

Sometimes you receive messages that you think another person should also see. Or, you might not be the best person to reply to a message. When this happens, you can *forward* a copy of the message to a new recipient, rather than retype the message or show a printout of the message to the person who needs to see it. You can forward a message to several people, or add Cc and Bcc recipients, just as you can when you create a message. Keep in mind that just as you can forward messages that you receive from other people, others can forward your messages to whomever they want; therefore you should exercise caution when forwarding confidential information.

Forwarded messages are similar to replies in that the original message is appended at the end of the message. If you want to precede the message with text, you can type your own message before the appended text. For example, you can type background information on a forwarded message so that the recipient can handle the message without asking you why you are forwarding it. Forwarded messages are identified by the letters "FW" in the subject area.

Forward a message

In this exercise, you forward the message about recent sales figures from Indira Mukherjee to Margo Wilson, since Margo has the most current profit information.

1   Double-click the "RE: Product Line Meeting" message from Indira Mukherjee.

2   On the Standard toolbar, click the Forward button.

A Mail Form appears with the Subject box filled in.

Check Names

You can also press CTRL+K to check names.

3 In the To box, type **margo**

4 On the Standard toolbar, click the Check Names button.

The name Margo Wilson appears automatically after it is checked against the Address Book.

5 Click in the message area, and type **Since you have the most current profit reports, could you get them to Indira for her meeting presentation? Thanks!**

6 On the Standard toolbar, click the Send button.

Indira's message is forwarded to Margo Wilson. A note is added to the comment area on the original message, with the date and time the message was forwarded.

7 Click the Close button on the original message window from Indira Mukherjee.

The message icon in the Information viewer changes to indicate that you have forwarded the message. Your screen should look similar to the following illustration.

Message icon indicates the message has been forwarded.

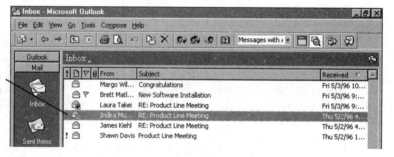

Organizing Messages

Although you can let your messages accumulate in your Inbox, you'll find that organizing your messages will allow you to find them more quickly later. You can organize your mail folders in several ways depending on your preferences and work habits. For example, you can create folders for different types of messages, and then move your messages into the appropriate folders. In addition, you can delete messages or save them on your hard disk.

Sorting Messages

When your Inbox contains several messages, you can organize the messages by arranging them according to specific criteria, or *sorting* them. The information in the message header is used to sort messages by column, such as sender, subject, and received date. Other columns in the message header show the message type, and whether or not there is a priority or attached file associated with the message.

Depending on the type of information in the column, messages can be sorted in ascending or descending order. An ascending sort lists data from A to Z, from the lowest to the highest number, or from the earliest to the latest date. A descending sort lists data from Z to A, from the highest to the lowest number, or from the latest to the earliest date. By default, messages in your Inbox are sorted by date, in descending order so that the most recent message appears at the top of the list. A down arrow in a Received column heading indicates that messages are sorted in descending order while an up arrow indicates an ascending sort. The following illustration shows the default sort for a typical Inbox.

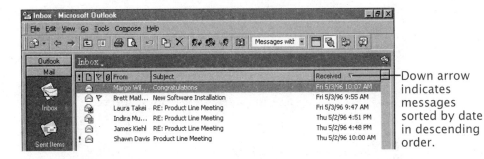

Down arrow indicates messages sorted by date in descending order.

To quickly change how your messages are sorted, you can click a column heading. For example, if you click the Received column heading, the messages are sorted in ascending order to show the oldest message at the top of the list. You can have different sort orders for different folders.

Sort messages

In this exercise, you experiment with sorting to find a good way to organize the different types of messages contained in your Inbox.

By default, the From column is sorted by first name, and then by last name.

1 In the Information viewer, click the From column heading.

The messages in your Inbox are sorted in ascending order by sender. Your screen should look similar to the following illustration.

Up arrow indicates an ascending sort for this column.

2 Click the From column heading again.

The messages are sorted in descending order by sender.

The letters "RE" and "FW" are not taken into account when you sort.

3 Click the Subject column heading.

The messages are sorted in ascending order by subject.

4 Click the Subject column heading again.

The messages are sorted in descending order by subject.

TIP You can modify the way usernames are listed in your personal address book. For example, if the From column is sorted based on first names, you can change the properties to sort by last names. To do this, on the Tools menu, click Services, select Personal Address Book, click Properties, and then click the Last Name option button. However, you cannot modify the way usernames appear in the global address list; the sort order is set by your system administrator.

Grouping Messages

For a demonstration of how to group messages, double-click the Camcorder file named Grouping Messages in the Part6 Outlook Camcorder Files folder. See "Installing and Using the Practice and Camcorder Files," earlier in this book for more information.

You can sort messages, one category at a time, by clicking the different column headings in the Information viewer. However, if you want to sort messages using more than one category at a time, you can group them into well-defined categories. You can group messages by up to five criteria at once. For example, you can group messages to sort by sender, then by subject, and then by date. By grouping messages, you set the level of detail that you want to use to display your messages in any folder.

Grouped messages are organized in an outline form using the grouping categories you select, with the first sort farthest to the left in the Information viewer. A plus sign (+) indicates that a category is collapsed and any information below it is hidden. A minus sign (-) indicates that the category is expanded. If there are any unread messages in a category, the number of unread messages appears in parentheses next to the category heading.

Group messages

As the Operations Coordinator, you want to organize your Inbox so that you can easily find information about your different projects. In this exercise, you group your messages.

Group By Box

You can also group messages by clicking Group By on the View menu, and then selecting the grouping and sorting criteria you want to apply.

1 On the Standard toolbar, click the Group By Box button.

The Group By box appears below the Folder Banner in the Information viewer. Your screen should look similar to the following illustration.

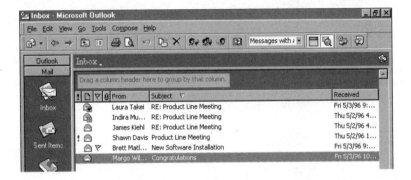

2 Drag the Subject column header into the Group By box.

The messages in your Inbox are grouped by subject in descending sort order. Your screen should look similar to the following illustration.

Down arrow indicates a descending sort.

Collapsed categories

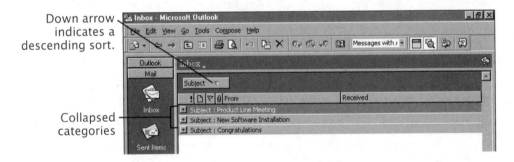

3 Click the plus sign (+) next to the "Subject: Congratulations" category.

The category expands and the message from Margo Wilson appears.

4 Click the minus sign (-) next to the "Subject: Congratulations" category.

The category collapses and the message is hidden.

5 Click the plus sign (+) next to the "Subject: Product Line Meeting" category.

The category expands to show four messages with the subject "Product Line Meeting." The messages are sorted in descending order by received date, based on the default settings. Your screen should look similar to the following illustration.

643

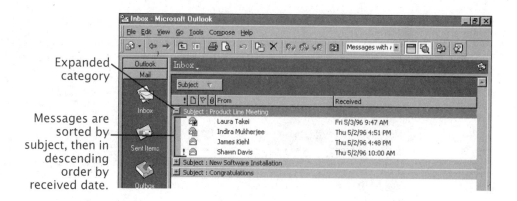

Expanded category

Messages are sorted by subject, then in descending order by received date.

TIP   If you hide the Group By box, your messages will still be grouped.

Modify grouping criteria

In this exercise, you change the way the messages are grouped in your Inbox by adding another grouping criterion to the Group By box.

The Importance column heading is identified by an exclamation point (!) on it.

1   Drag the Importance column heading into the Group By box, and place it to the right of the Subject heading.

Your messages are grouped first by subject in descending order, and then by importance in descending order. Your screen should look similar to the following illustration.

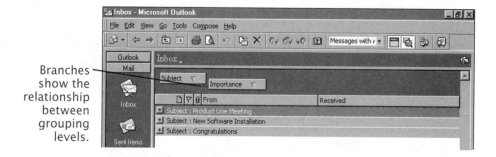

Branches show the relationship between grouping levels.

2   Click the plus sign (+) next to the "Subject: Product Line Meeting" category.

The category expands to show two importance grouping categories, "Importance: High" and "Importance: Normal."

3   Click the plus sign (+) next to the "Importance: High" category.

A Product Line Meeting message from Shawn Davis with high priority appears.

4   Click the plus sign (+) next to the "Importance: Normal" category.

Three messages about the product line meeting with normal priority appear. Your screen should look similar to the following illustration.

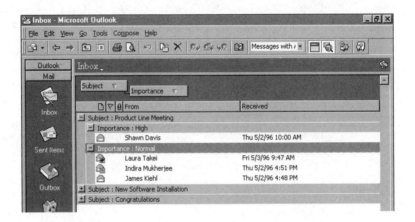

    TIP   You can create a personal view based on the groupings in your Inbox. To do this, choose the groups and sorts you want to apply to your messages, type a new view name in the Current View box on the Standard toolbar, and then press ENTER.

Restore the original view

You can also restore the default view by dragging the group column headings back into the message header.

In this exercise, you cancel the grouping in your Inbox by reapplying the default view, Messages With AutoPreview.

1   On the View menu, point to Current View, and then click Messages With AutoPreview.

A message appears, asking if you want to save or discard the current view settings.

2   Be sure that the Discard The Current View Settings And Reapply The View "Messages With AutoPreview" option button is selected, and then click OK.

The groups are removed, the Group By box is hidden, and the Messages With AutoPreview view is reapplied to your Inbox.

TROUBLESHOOTING If you accidentally save changes to a standard view, you can easily reset it. On the View menu, click Define Views. In the Views For Folder box, select the view you want to restore, and then click Reset.

Displaying Specific Files by Using Filters

If you want to display only certain messages in a folder, you can apply a *filter* to it. Any messages that do not match the filter conditions are hidden temporarily. For example, if you want to show only messages from your manager in your Inbox, you can filter the messages by sender. This can be especially useful if you receive many messages in the course of a day, and you need to find individual messages quickly.

When a filter is applied to a folder, the words "Filter Applied" appear on the Folder Banner and on the status bar in the lower-left corner of the screen. If a view includes a filter, it is applied to the folder first, before any other criteria. For example, if messages in a folder are sorted or grouped, and a filter is applied, the messages are filtered first and then sorted or grouped. You can easily remove the filter to show all messages again. Filtering messages is similar to sorting and grouping messages, except that the messages you filter out are hidden from view.

Filter messages

In this exercise, you apply a filter to your Inbox so that only the messages related to the product line meeting are visible.

1 Be sure that the contents of your Inbox appear in the Information viewer.

2 On the View menu, click Filter.

The Filter dialog box appears.

3 In the Search For The Word(s) box, type **meeting**

4 Click the In down arrow and select Subject Field And Message Body.

The filter will search for the word "meeting" anywhere in a message.

5 Click OK.

The filter is applied, and only messages about the product line meeting appear in the Inbox. Your screen should look similar to the following illustration.

Remove the filter

Now that you have viewed your test messages, you want to remove the filter.

1   On the View menu, click Filter.

The Filter dialog box appears.

2   Click Clear All and then click OK.

The filter is removed and all the messages appear in the Inbox again.

Printing Messages

Any message in any folder can be printed. You can print several messages at once, as well as print more than one copy of a message. When you print multiple messages, you can print one message per page or print them all in a row on the same page(s).

You can also print messages with attachments, such as other documents, if your computer recognizes the file format and if the original application used to create the attachment is installed on your computer.

IMPORTANT   You must have a printer installed to complete the following exercise. If you don't have access to a printer, skip to the "Working with Folders" section.

Print a message

In this exercise, you print the message from Margo Wilson, because you want to have a hard copy of the message to post in your office.

1   Click the Congratulations message from Margo Wilson.

You do not need to open a message in order to print it.

2   On the Standard toolbar, click the Print button.

Print

NOTE   The Print button can be used to quickly print messages using the last print settings. To modify the print settings, on the File menu, click Print.

Working with Folders

If you have received numerous messages that deal with a specific topic, such as a particular project, you can place those messages into their own folder. When you are finished with the project, you can easily delete the folder to streamline your work environment.

You can also display the folder list by clicking the Show/Hide Folder List button on the Standard toolbar.

You can create your own personal folders in Outlook, and then move or copy messages into them. You can also create a subfolder within a folder, such as your Inbox, to further organize your messages. All of your personal folders are shown in the Folder List. You can click the plus sign (+) next to a top-level folder to display subfolders.

You can easily delete any folders that you create. However, when you delete an entire folder, you also delete all the subfolders and items it contains. Just as with messages, if you accidentally delete a folder, you can recover the folder and its contents from the Deleted Items folder before you log off from Outlook. Built-in folders, such as the Inbox folder and Sent Items folder, cannot be deleted.

Create a folder

In this exercise, you create a subfolder in your Inbox folder to store messages concerning the upcoming Product Line meeting.

1 Be sure that the contents of your Inbox appear in the Information viewer.

You can also point to Folder, and then click Create Subfolder.

2 On the File menu, point to New, and then click Folder.

The Create New Folder dialog box appears.

3 In the Name box, type **Product Line**

This is the name for your new folder.

4 Click in the Description box, and then type **Messages regarding the Margo Tea Company product line**

5 Be sure that the Create A Shortcut To This Folder In The Outlook Bar check box is selected, and then click OK.

The Product Line subfolder is created and a shortcut icon to the subfolder appears in the Mail group on the Outlook Bar.

6 Scroll down to see the Product Line shortcut icon in the Mail group.

Your screen should look similar to the following illustration.

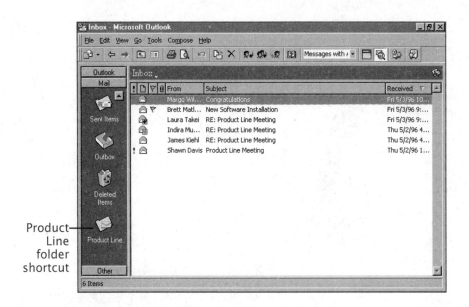

Product—
Line
folder
shortcut

View the Folder List

In this exercise, you display the Folder List to see the relationship between the new subfolder and your other Outlook folders.

1   On the Folder Banner, click the word "Inbox."

The Folder Banner List appears.

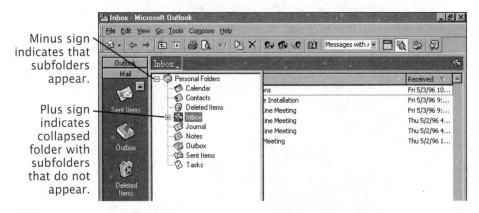

Minus sign
indicates that
subfolders
appear.

Plus sign
indicates
collapsed
folder with
subfolders
that do not
appear.

2   Click the plus sign (+) next to the Inbox folder.

The Product Line subfolder appears. Your screen should look similar to the following illustration.

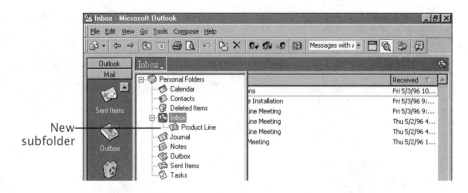

3 . Click the word "Inbox" again on the Folder Banner.

The Folder List closes.

Move a group of messages to a folder

Now that you have a folder for storing messages related to the Margo Tea Company's product line, you can move messages into it. In this exercise, you sort messages by subject, and then move the appropriate messages to the Product Line subfolder you created.

1 Be sure that the contents of your Inbox appear in the Information viewer, and then click the Subject column heading.

The messages are sorted in ascending order by subject.

2 Drag the "RE: Product Line Meeting" message from Laura Takei onto the Product Line shortcut icon on the Outlook Bar.

The message is moved to the Product Line folder.

Hold down SHIFT to select multiple consecutive messages; hold down CTRL to select multiple non-consecutive messages.

3 Repeat step 2 to drag the other messages about the product line meeting into the Product Line folder.

4 On the Outlook Bar, click the Product Line shortcut icon.

All messages regarding the upcoming product line meeting are now located in one folder.

TIP You can have incoming messages with a particular subject or sender moved to a specific folder automatically, if you are using Outlook with a Microsoft Exchange Server. To do this, on the Tools menu, click Inbox Assistant, and then click Add Rule. Select options in the dialog box to determine when you want to apply the rule, what message conditions you want to be used, what you want to happen to the message, and any exceptions to the rule.

Deleting Messages

When you have finished reading and taking actions, such as replying to or forwarding messages, it is a good idea to decide whether you want to save or delete your messages. If you save all the messages that you receive, they will require a lot of storage space, and they will be harder to organize. If you no longer need a message, you should delete it.

Because deleted messages are moved to the Deleted Items folder temporarily, if you change your mind about deleting a message, you can still retrieve it. By default, messages will remain in the Deleted Items folder until you choose to delete them permanently or empty the entire folder.

Delete a message

In this exercise, you delete messages that you no longer need from your Inbox.

1 On the Outlook Bar, click the Inbox icon.

2 Click the Congratulations message from Margo Wilson.

You do not need to open a message to delete it.

Delete

3 On the Standard toolbar, click the Delete button.

The message is moved from the Inbox folder to the Deleted Items folder.

Delete a folder

Now that the product line meeting has taken place, and all the issues have been addressed, you don't need to keep the messages relating to it anymore. In this exercise, you delete the Product Line subfolder from your Inbox.

Folder List

1 On the Standard toolbar, click the Folder List button.

The Folder List appears to the left of the Information viewer. Your screen should look similar to the following illustration.

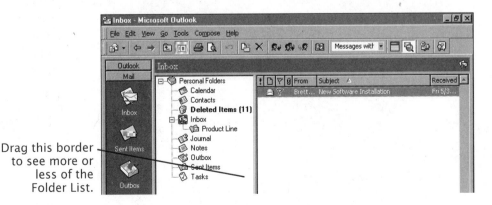

Drag this border to see more or less of the Folder List.

651

2   In the Folder List, click the Product Line subfolder.

3   On the Standard toolbar, click the Delete button.

The Product Line folder and its contents are placed in the Deleted Items folder.

4   Click the plus sign (+) next to the Deleted Items folder.

The folder expands to show the deleted Product Line folder within the Deleted Items folder.

5   On the Outlook Bar, use the right mouse button to click the Product Line shortcut icon.

A shortcut menu appears.

6   Click Remove From Outlook Bar.

A message appears, asking you to confirm the deletion.

7   Click Yes.

The folder shortcut is removed from the Outlook Bar.

8   Click the Folder List button again to hide the folder list.

Folder List

Empty the Deleted Items folder

In this exercise, you delete the contents of the Deleted Items folder.

1   On the Outlook Bar, click the Deleted Items icon.

The items that you deleted earlier appear in the Deleted Items folder.

2   On the Outlook Bar, use the right mouse button to click the Deleted Items icon.

A shortcut menu appears.

You can also click Empty "Deleted Items" Folder on the Tools menu.

3   Click Empty "Deleted Items" Folder.

A message appears, asking you to confirm the deletion of all items and subfolders.

4   Click Yes.

The contents of the Deleted Items folder are permanently deleted.

TIP   You can set the Deleted Items folder to empty automatically each time you exit from Outlook. On the Tools menu, click Options. On the General tab, select the Empty The Deleted Items Folder Upon Exiting check box, and then click OK.

Conducting a Vote with a Message

Suppose you want to conduct a quick, informational survey of your co-workers. For example, you want to know what everyone thinks about adopting a new company recycling program. You could walk around the office asking everyone's opinion of the program, record their answers, and add up the results, but this would be fairly time-consuming. With Outlook, you can conduct a vote using an e-mail message. Recipients simply click a button to indicate a response, and the results are tabulated for you in the copy of the original message located in your Sent Items folder.

In the following exercises, you ask several co-workers to participate in a community fund-raiser, and then use the voting options in Outlook to collect their responses.

 IMPORTANT Because this section requires you to collect voting results, you'll need to recruit some help from at least two other people on your network who are willing to cooperate by reading and responding to your message. If your computer is only connected to the practice workgroup postoffice, use names from the Postoffice Address List to address your message.

Create a new message

In this exercise, you create a message and address it to several co-workers.

New Mail Message

1 On the Outlook Bar, click the Inbox icon.

2 On the Standard toolbar, click the New Mail Message button.

A blank Mail Form appears.

3 Click the To button.

4 Click the Show Names From The down arrow, and then select Global Address List.

The names of people in your organization's global address list appear.

You can hold down CTRL to select multiple non-consecutive names.

5 Select the names of the people helping you with this exercise, click To, and then click OK.

6 In the Subject box, type **Walk For Kids**

7 In the message area, type **I'm looking for volunteers to join me in this year's 10-K walk to benefit local schools. Would you like to be a member of the Margo Tea Company corporate team?**

Add voting buttons to your message

In this exercise, you include voting buttons in your message so that recipients can respond easily.

1 Click the Options tab.

2 In the General Options area, select the Use Voting Buttons check box.

Sample button text appears in the list box to the right.

3 Click the button text down arrow to display the different text options.

4 Click the "Yes; No; Maybe" option button.

A Yes button, a No button, and a Maybe button will appear on the message in the recipients' mailboxes.

5 Be sure that the Save Sent Message To check box is selected, and that Sent Items appears in the Save Sent Message To box.

The survey responses will be tracked on your copy of the original message located in your Sent Items folder.

6 Click the Send button.

The message with voting buttons is sent to your co-workers.

IMPORTANT To complete the next exercise, be sure that the recipients respond to the message by opening it in their respective Inboxes, and clicking Yes, No, or Maybe. The recipients are then prompted to send their responses back to you. A note is added to each recipient's message in his or her mailbox. If you addressed your message to practice workgroup postoffice names, skip this exercise.

Track survey results

When you send out a voting message, the recipients' responses are delivered to your mailbox and their answers, such as "Yes", "No", or "Maybe", appear in the Subject column so that you can assess the responses at a glance. However, if you are tracking a large number of responses, you can also check your copy of the original message in the Sent Items folder. All voting responses are recorded in a single place. In this exercise, you review the responses to your survey in your Inbox folder and in your Sent Items folder.

1 On the Tools menu, click Check For New Mail.

This ensures that all responses have been delivered to your Inbox. Your screen should look similar to the following illustration.

Responses appear in the Subject column.

The names and responses on your screen will be different from those in this illustration.

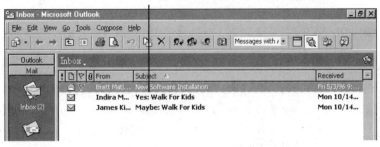

2   Open and close each response.

You must open voting messages to record their results on the Tracking tab on the original message.

3   On the Outlook Bar, click the Sent Items icon.

The contents of the Sent Items folder appear. Your screen should look similar to the following illustration.

Icon indicates that information has been added to the Tracking tab on the message.

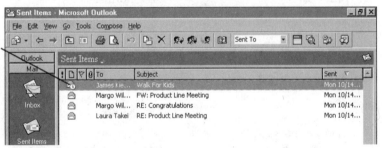

4   Double-click the "Walk For Kids" message.

5   Click the Tracking tab.

The reply totals appear in the comment area, and the message status for each recipient is displayed. Your message should look similar to the following illustration.

Reply Totals

Individual responses

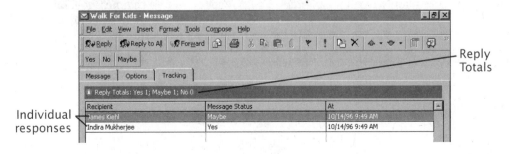

6   Click the Close button on the "Walk For Kids" message.

Finish the lesson

You can also click the Delete button.

1   Select the practice messages you used in this lesson in your Inbox folder, Sent Items folder, and Deleted Items folder, and then press DELETE.

2   To continue to the next lesson, on the Outlook Bar, click the Calendar shortcut icon in the Outlook group.

3   If you are finished using Outlook for now, on the File menu, click Exit And Log Off.

Lesson Summary

To	Do this	Button
Open a message	Double-click the message.	
Browse through multiple messages	Open a message, and then, on the Standard toolbar, click the Next Item button or the Previous Item button.	
Flag a message	Open the message. On the Standard toolbar, click the Message Flag button. Type your message flag text. Select a due date, if necessary, and then click OK.	
Flag a message as completed	Open the message. On the Standard toolbar, click the Message Flag button. Select the Completed check box and then click OK.	
Reply to a message	Click or open the message. On the Standard toolbar, click the Reply button.	
Reply to all recipients	Click or open the message. On the Standard toolbar, click the Reply To All button.	
Forward a message	Click or open the message. On the Standard toolbar, click the Forward button.	

To	Do this	Button
Check names	Type a recipient name. On the Standard toolbar, click the Check Names button.	👤✓
Sort messages in a folder	In the Information viewer, click the column heading for a category.	
Group messages in a folder	On the Standard toolbar, click the Group By Box button. Drag the column headings you want to group by into the Group By box.	▤
Reset the current view	In the Current View box on the Standard toolbar, select the name of the view you want to apply. Discard the current view settings.	
Print messages	Click the message. On the Standard toolbar, click the Print button.	🖨
Create a new folder	Select the location for your folder. On the File menu, point to New, and then click Folder. Type a name and description for the new folder, and then click OK.	
Delete a message	Select the message you want to delete. On the Standard toolbar, click the Delete button.	✕
Conduct a vote with a message	Create a new message. On the Options tab, select the Use Voting Buttons check box. Select or enter text for the buttons, select a location where the results can be tabulated, and then send the message.	

For online information about	Use the Office Assistant to search for
Replying to messages	**Replying to messages,** and then click Reply To A Message
Forwarding messages	**Forwarding messages,** and then click Forward Messages
Grouping messages	**Grouping messages,** and then click About Groups
Printing messages	**Printing messages,** and then click Print
Sorting messages	**Sorting messages,** and then click Sort A List Of Items
Flagging messages	**Flagging messages,** and then click About Message Flags
Voting using messages	**Voting using messages,** and then click Ask Others To Vote In A Message

Organizing Your Schedule Using Calendar

**Estimated time
30 min.**

In this lesson you will learn how to:

- Create and edit appointments.

- Set recurring appointments.

- Add events to your calendar.

- Print your schedule.

Keeping track of all the appointments you make can be difficult. Is the team meeting on Thursday or Friday? Ten o'clock or two? Many people use an appointment book, a desk calendar, or a daily planner to keep track of their schedules. In Microsoft Outlook, Calendar acts as an electronic appointment book. You can use Calendar to record appointments, set reminders for upcoming appointments and events, and even coordinate meetings electronically with other people.

In Calendar, you can view your appointments for a single day, a week, or a month at a time. You can create a task list to help you monitor your progress on various projects, schedule tasks at specific times, and then cross them off as you complete them.

As the Operations Coordinator for Margo Tea Company, it is vital that you manage your time efficiently. In this lesson, you'll learn how to keep your own schedule up to date in Outlook, and you'll use Calendar to record all of your business and personal appointments. After you have mastered these skills with your own schedule file, you can begin coordinating schedules with other people.

Start the lesson

In this exercise, you start Outlook using the Shawn Davis profile, and then switch to the Calendar folder.

1 Start Outlook using the Shawn Davis profile.

2 On the Outlook Bar, click the Calendar icon.

The contents of the Calendar folder appear in the Information viewer. The current date appears in the Folder Banner.

IMPORTANT When you install Outlook, a sample appointment and a sample task are automatically added to your Calendar on the date the program is installed. These items will be placed on different areas of your Calendar depending on when you install Outlook and create your profile.

Creating and Editing Appointments

When you open your Calendar folder, the Day view of your schedule appears by default. Day, Week, and Month views are available to help you keep track of scheduled appointments. In Day view, the appointment area resembles a lined daily planner. Each day is divided into 30-minute time slots in which you can enter appointments. By default, the workday starts at 8 A.M. and ends at 5 P.M. The time slots outside this workday period appear shaded. In Week and Month views, the appointment areas resemble a calendar grid.

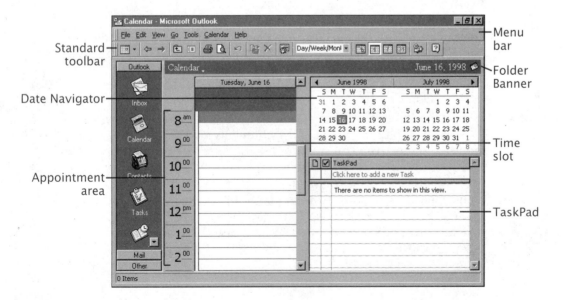

The Date Navigator appears to the right of the appointment areas in Day and Week views. The Date Navigator shows the current calendar month and either the previous or following month, depending on how you move from date to date. You can use the Date Navigator to scroll to different dates so that you can add future appointments or refer to past ones. Bold dates indicate that at least one appointment is scheduled for that date. Below the Date Navigator is the TaskPad, which displays tasks.

You want to add the upcoming meetings to your schedule. You also want to schedule some personal appointments and make sure that they do not interfere with your work as Operations Coordinator.

Navigating in Calendar

In Day view, the easiest way to change dates is by using the Date Navigator. The months in the Date Navigator appear as small calendars, and you can simply click a date to display that date's appointments. You can also use the scroll bar at the top of the Date Navigator to display different months.

Change the date

Changing the year to 1999 for these exercises prevents confusion with your real appointments.

For the purposes of this lesson, you will change the year to 1999 so that your Calendar will match the illustrations in this book. In this exercise, you practice changing dates using different navigation methods.

1 On the Go menu, click Go To Date.

The Go To Date dialog box appears.

2 Be sure that the text in the Date box is selected, and then type **5/14/99**

You can type dates in any style—such as 5-14-99 or May 14, 1999—to change them.

3 Click OK.

The appointment area and the Date Navigator display the date Friday, May 14, 1999.

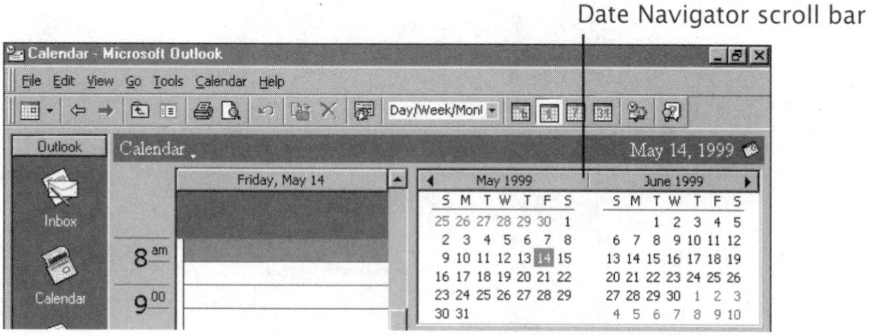

Date Navigator scroll bar

You can also click the name of a month to display a list of months to switch to.

4 On the Date Navigator scroll bar, click the right arrow.

June 1999 and July 1999 appear in the Date Navigator, and June 14 is selected. When you change months, the selected day of the month stays the same.

5 Click the left scroll arrow four times.

February 1999 and March 1999 appear, and March 14 is selected.

6 In the Date Navigator, click February 16.

The date changes to Tuesday, February 16, 1999.

Adding an Appointment to Your Schedule

It's very easy to add appointments to your schedule in Calendar. You can select a block of time in the appointment area, and simply type the appointment details into the time slots. Or, if you want to schedule a more detailed appointment, you can open an appointment form and enter the information. In the following exercises, you will create appointments using two different scheduling methods.

Add an appointment

In this exercise, you add an appointment to your schedule by typing the appointment description directly into the appropriate time slot.

1 In the appointment area, drag the pointer over the time slots from 11:00 A.M. to 12:30 P.M. to select them.

Three time slots are highlighted.

2 Type **Product Line meeting**, and then press ENTER.

The new appointment appears. Your screen should look similar to the following illustration.

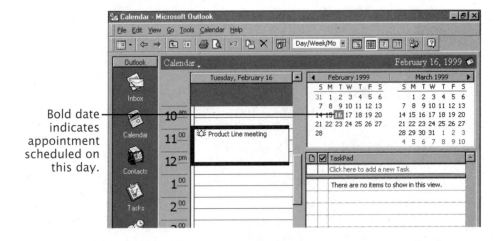

Bold date indicates appointment scheduled on this day.

Create a detailed appointment

In this exercise, you use the New Appointment button to add a more detailed appointment to your schedule.

1　In the appointment area, drag to select the 2:30 P.M. to 4:00 P.M. time period.

You are creating an appointment with a 90-minute duration.

New Appointment

The New Mail Message button in the Inbox becomes the New Appointment button in Calendar.

2　On the Standard toolbar, click the New Appointment button.

A new appointment form appears. The time period you selected is converted into start and end times on the form. Your screen should look similar to the following illustration.

Start Date box ———　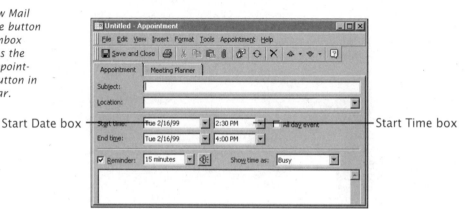　——— Start Time box

3　In the Subject box, type **Team strategy meeting**, and then press TAB.

The insertion point moves to the Location box.

4　In the Location box, type **Conference Room B**

5　Click the Start Time down arrow.

A list of times in half-hour increments appears.

You can also enter a new time by typing the number in the Start Time box.

6　Select 3:30 P.M.

The new start time for the meeting is entered, and the end time changes from 4:00 to 5:00 to preserve the 90-minute duration of the meeting.

663

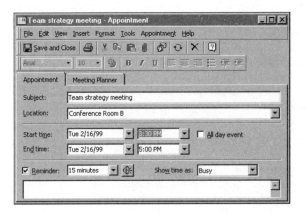

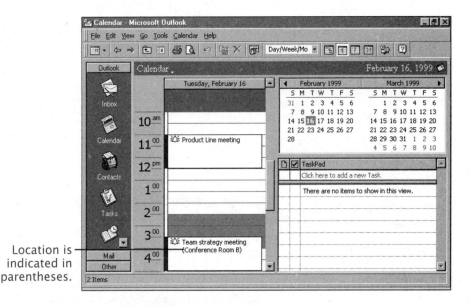

Location is indicated in parentheses.

7 On the Standard toolbar, click the Save And Close button.

The appointment is added to your schedule. Your screen should look similar to the following illustration.

Editing Appointments

You can quickly and easily change an appointment in Calendar. For example, you can move an appointment to a new date or time, or change its duration. You can schedule several similar appointments by copying an appointment to the Clipboard, and then pasting it to another date. You can also set appointments to recur over a long period of time. You can select and edit an appointment directly in the appointment area, or, if you want to make detailed changes to an appointment, you can open the appointment form. You can use the Delete button to cancel an appointment.

Outlook includes an *Autodate* function that makes it even easier to select dates and start and end times for your appointments. The Autodate fields are text-sensitive, which means that instead of typing "12:00 P.M." in the Start Time box, you can type "noon," and Calendar will recognize and insert the appropriate time. In the same way, you can type text such as "next Wednesday" to insert the appropriate date.

IMPORTANT When you enter Autodate text in date fields, the selected dates correspond to the date and time set on your computer, not necessarily the date you are working on in Calendar. For example, although you are scheduling appointments for 1999 in this lesson, if you typed "this Tuesday" as a start date in the appointment form, the start date would be entered as Tuesday of the current week on your system.

As Operations Coordinator for Margo Tea Company, you have many different responsibilities. You need to make frequent changes to your schedule to accommodate the needs of both your co-workers and your outside clients.

Change an appointment

In this exercise, you make changes to an appointment in the appointment area.

1 Click the "Team strategy meeting" to activate it.

Blue top and bottom borders appear on an active appointment and the mouse pointer changes to an insertion point.

2 Double-click to select the word "Team."

The text is highlighted.

3 Type **Campaign**, and then press ENTER.

The text is replaced as you type.

4 Point to the top border of the "Campaign strategy meeting" appointment.

The pointer changes to a two-headed arrow.

5 Drag the top border up one time slot to 3:00 P.M.

The appointment start time changes to 3:00 P.M. The duration is now two hours.

6 Point to the bottom border, and then drag the bottom border up two time slots to 4:00 P.M., and then press ENTER.

The appointment duration changes to one hour. Your screen should look similar to the following illustration.

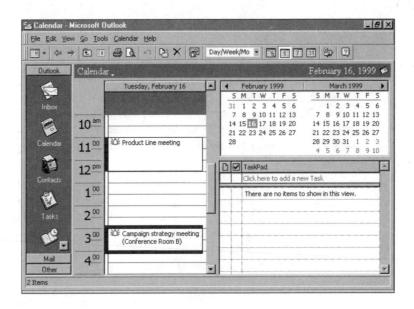

Add information to an appointment

In this exercise, you modify an appointment by opening the appointment form.

1 Double-click the "Product Line meeting" appointment to open it.

The "Product Line meeting" appointment entry form appears.

2 Click in the Location box, and then type **Margo's Office**

3 In the Start Time box, select the current text, "11:00 A.M."

4 Type **noon**, and then press ENTER.

The time is entered as 12:00 P.M. The end time changes to 1:30 P.M.

5 Click the End Time down arrow.

A list of end times and durations appears.

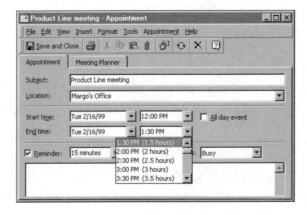

6 Scroll up, and then select "1:00 P.M. (1 Hour)."

The end time and duration are changed.

7 On the Standard toolbar, click the Save And Close button.

The start and end times of the "Product Line meeting" appointment change, and a location is added to the appointment.

Move an appointment

In this exercise, you use the Date Navigator to quickly move an appointment to a different day.

1 Position the pointer over the left border of the "Campaign strategy meeting" appointment.

The pointer changes to a four-headed arrow.

2 Drag the appointment onto February 12 in the Date Navigator.

The appointment is moved to Friday, February 12, 1999, and that date appears in the appointment area. The start time, 3:00 P.M., and the end time, 4:00 P.M., do not change. Your screen should look similar to the following illustration.

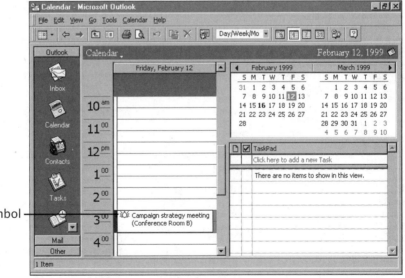

Reminder symbol

Setting Reminders

You can set a reminder for any appointment. When you have set a reminder, a message appears to notify you of the upcoming appointment. You can set the timing on a reminder to control how far in advance of the appointment it appears. The following illustration shows a sample reminder message.

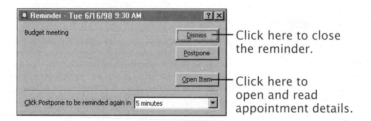

Click here to close the reminder.

Click here to open and read appointment details.

A reminder is automatically set for each new appointment you create; the default timing on a reminder is 15 minutes. When an appointment has a reminder, a reminder symbol appears with the appointment description in the appointment area.

Change a reminder

In this exercise, you change the timing for the reminder for the "Product Line meeting" so that you will get the reminder early and have enough time to set up your presentation materials.

1 In the Date Navigator, click February 16.

The date changes to Tuesday, February 16, 1999. The "Product Line meeting" appointment appears.

2 Double-click the "Product Line meeting" appointment.

The appointment form opens.

You can also type a number into the Reminder box to set the timing.

3 Be sure that the Reminder check box is selected, and then click the Reminder down arrow.

A list of timing increments appears.

4 Select 30 minutes.

5 On the Standard toolbar, click the Save And Close button.

The reminder is set for 30 minutes before the appointment.

NOTE The time setting for a reminder does not appear anywhere in the appointment area. To check a time setting, you need to open the appointment form.

Setting Tentative Appointments

You can use Calendar in Outlook to view your co-workers' schedules, and to coordinate meetings and appointments with them. You can set or change user access *permissions* to your schedule at any time, which gives you control over who has access to your schedule. The different access permissions control the ability of your co-workers to view or change part of your schedule. You will learn more about setting access permissions and using Outlook over a network in Lesson 5, "Coordinating Schedules with Other Users."

Suppose you want to remind yourself of an appointment, but you're not really sure that you'll be able to keep it. For example, a friend has invited you to lunch, but you think you might need to stay in the office to attend a project meeting. You can schedule *tentative* appointments that are listed in your schedule, but do not appear when others use your Calendar. You can finalize tentative appointments in your schedule or change them to another time if a colleague schedules a conflicting priority appointment. Tentative appointments appear in light blue in your schedule.

Make an appointment tentative

In this exercise, you make the "Campaign strategy meeting" appointment tentative because you are not sure that the invitees outside of your company will be able to attend.

1   In the Date Navigator, click February 12.

The date changes to Friday, February 12, 1999. The "Campaign strategy meeting" appointment appears.

2   Double-click the "Campaign strategy meeting" appointment.

The appointment form opens.

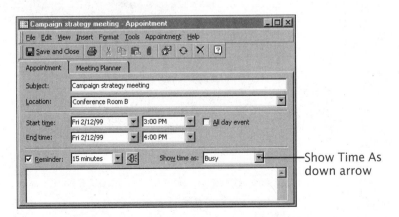

3   Click the Show Time As down arrow, and then select Tentative.

The appointment will appear as tentative in your schedule.

4 On the Standard toolbar, click the Save And Close button.

The "Campaign strategy meeting" appointment appears in light blue in your schedule. Your screen should look similar to the following illustration.

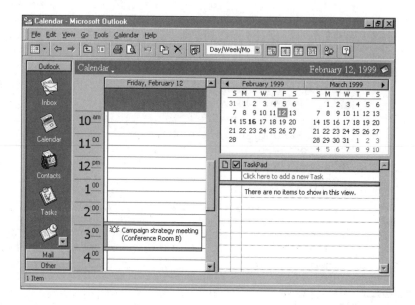

Making Appointments Private

You can coordinate schedules with others by allowing them access to your Calendar, but still protect your own confidential information. You can designate your personal appointments as *private* so that they cannot be read by other Outlook users. A private appointment appears as a busy time in the scheduled time slots when others view your schedule, but the details of the appointment are not visible.

Schedule a private appointment

In this exercise, you schedule a dentist appointment. Because this appointment is personal in nature, you want to designate it as private.

1 Be sure that Friday, February 12, 1999, appears in the Information viewer.

2 Drag to select the 10:30 A.M. to 11:30 A.M. time period.

3 Type **Dentist**, and then press ENTER.

The appointment is added to your schedule.

4 Use the right mouse button to click the "Dentist" appointment.

A shortcut menu appears.

5 Click Private.

A key symbol appears, indicating that the appointment is private. Your screen should look similar to the following illustration.

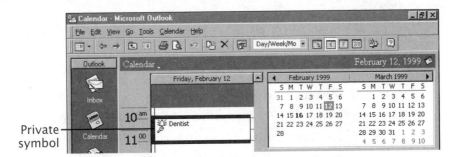

Private symbol

Scheduling Time Out of the Office

In addition to recording your busy times, you can mark specific time periods or appointments to indicate that you are actually out of the office at that time. When other users view your schedule, they will know that you are definitely unavailable during those periods. Out of office times appear in purple in your schedule.

Mark an appointment as out of office

In this exercise, you set the "Dentist" appointment to show that you are out of the office so that any co-workers who view your schedule know that you are not available at that time.

1 Double-click the "Dentist" appointment.

The appointment form opens.

2 Click the Show Time As down arrow.

A list of display options appears.

3 Select Out Of Office.

4 On the Standard toolbar, click the Save And Close button.

The appointment appears in your schedule with a purple border, indicating that you will be out of the office at this time.

Setting Recurring Appointments

As your team continues its work on developing and marketing Margo Tea Company's new product, you want to schedule a weekly meeting to monitor everyone's progress and make sure that each team member is kept up to date on the project's status. You can schedule recurring appointments in Calendar so that you do not have to enter the meeting information each week.

Set a recurring appointment

In this exercise, you schedule a recurring bi-weekly appointment with the product line team.

1 In the Date Navigator, click February 15.

2 Select the 9:00 A.M. to 10:00 A.M. time period.

3 Type **Team update**, and then press ENTER.

The appointment is added to your schedule.

4 Double-click the "Team update" appointment.

The appointment form opens.

Recurrence

5 On the Standard toolbar, click the Recurrence button.

The Appointment Recurrence dialog box appears.

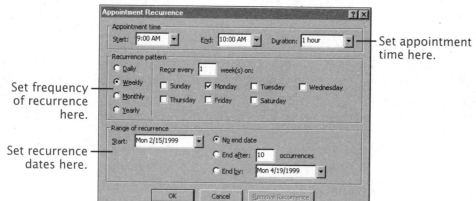

Set frequency of recurrence here.

Set recurrence dates here.

Set appointment time here.

6 In the Recurrence Pattern area, be sure that the Weekly option button is selected and that 1 is selected in the text box between Recur Every and Week(s) On.

7 In the Recurrence Pattern area, be sure that the Monday check box is selected, and then select the Wednesday check box.

The "Team update" appointment is set to recur twice a week, on Monday and Wednesday mornings from 9:00 A.M. to 10:00 A.M.

8 In the Range Of Recurrence area, click the End By option button.

You use this option to set a specific end date for the recurrence.

9 In the End By box, select the current text, and then type **6/16/99**

The appointment will recur until Wednesday, June 16, 1999.

10 Click OK.

The recurrence information appears on the Appointment tab of the "Team update" appointment form. Your screen should look similar to the following illustration.

Recurrence information

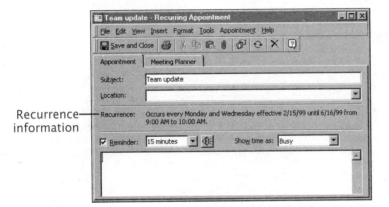

 Save and Close

11 On the Standard toolbar, click the Save And Close button.

The appointment form closes. A recurring symbol appears with the appointment description in the appointment area. Your screen should look similar to the following illustration.

Recurrence symbol

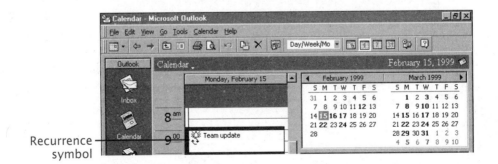

NOTE You can also change an existing appointment to a recurring appointment. Simply open the appointment form, and then click the Recurrence button on the Standard toolbar.

Cancel an appointment

In this exercise, you cancel one of the recurring "Team update" appointments because you will be out of the office at a seminar all day.

1 In the Date Navigator, click February 17.

The date changes to Wednesday, February 17, 1999.

2 Click the "Team update" appointment to activate it.

Delete

3 On the Standard toolbar, click the Delete button.

A message appears, asking if you want to delete all instances of the recurring appointment or just one.

4 Be sure that the Delete This One option button is selected, and then click OK.

Only the "Team update" appointment on February 17 is canceled.

IMPORTANT You cannot delete an appointment by pressing DELETE on your keyboard. You must first select the appointment, and then use the Delete button on the Standard toolbar.

Adding Events

You can add an *event*, such as a seminar or a vacation, to your schedule by using the Event command or by simply typing the event information into the *banner* that appears at the top of the appointment area. When you add an event, a message appears in your schedule on the date of the event, but the event is not scheduled for a particular time.

You can also insert annual events, such as holidays or birthdays, in your schedule. An annual event will recur automatically in your Calendar each year.

Add an event

In the previous exercise, you canceled one of your appointments with the product line team because you plan to be out of the office that day. In this exercise, you add a two-day seminar to your schedule as an event.

1 Be sure that Wednesday, February 17, 1999, appears in the Information viewer.

2 On the Calendar menu, click New Event.

A blank event entry form appears.

3 In the Subject box, type **Personal Empowerment Seminar**, and then press TAB.

4 In the Location box, type **Convention Center**

5 Be sure that Wed 2/17/99 appears in the Start Time box and that the All Day Event check box is selected.

6 Click the End Time down arrow.

A calendar appears.

7 Select February 18.

The End Time is set for Thu 2/18/96.

8 Clear the Reminder check box.

Since you will be out of the office to attend the seminar, you won't be there to receive a reminder.

9 On the Standard toolbar, click the Save And Close button.

The event appears in the banner at the top of the appointment area. Your screen should look similar to the following illustration.

Event appears in banner.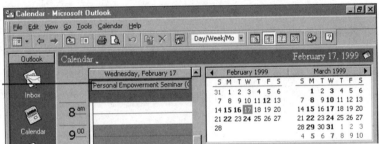

Importing Holidays

In Outlook, holidays are considered all-day annual events. You can easily add holidays to your schedule by importing them from one of the holiday folders included with Outlook. Each folder contains a package of holidays observed by a specific country or by a religious group. For example, July 4, Independence Day, is included in the United States folder, while Passover is included in the Jewish Religious Holidays folder. When you import holidays from one of these folders, the name of the holiday appears in the Subject box on the event form, and the religion or country of origin appears in the Location box. You can import any combination of holidays you choose.

Import a set of holidays

In this exercise, you import the set of holidays located in the United States folder to add them to your calendar.

675

1 On the Tools menu, click Options.

The Options dialog box appears, and the Calendar tab is active.

2 Click Add Holidays.

The Add Holidays To Calendar dialog box appears.

3 Be sure that the United States check box is selected, and then click OK.

The holiday files are imported.

4 Click OK to close the Options dialog box.

5 In the Date Navigator, click February 14.

Valentine's Day, a United States holiday that occurs on February 14, appears in the event banner at the top of the appointment area. Your screen should look similar to the following illustration.

Text in parentheses indicates where holiday is observed.

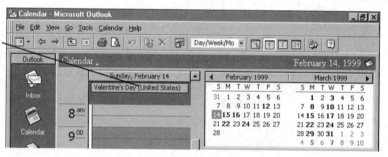

Delete

TIP You can delete individual holidays from your Calendar or delete them all at once. To delete holidays, on the Standard toolbar, click the Current View down arrow, and then select By Category. Click the plus sign next to Categories: Holiday, select the holidays you want to delete, and then click the Delete button.

Printing Schedules

You can print a copy of any portion of your schedule file so that you can carry the information with you or incorporate it into a report. You can determine how the printed copy appears on the page by choosing from a variety of page layouts. You can also change the attributes of the printed text, such as the font size.

NOTE You cannot hide private items when you print your schedule. If you do not want private items to appear in the printed copy, you can filter them out before you print. To do so, on the View menu, click Filter, and then click the Advanced tab. Click the Field button, point to Frequently-used Fields, and then click Sensitivity. Click the Value down arrow, select Private, click OK, and then print your schedule.

While you are attending the Personal Empowerment Seminar as a representative of Margo Tea Company, you want to have a printed copy of your schedule at hand so that you can refer to the rest of your appointments for the week and write down any new appointments immediately, instead of waiting until you return to the office.

Print a schedule

In this exercise, you choose a print setting, and then preview and print one week of your schedule.

1 On the File menu, click Print.

The Print dialog box appears; it is set to print the current schedule date, February 14, 1999, by default.

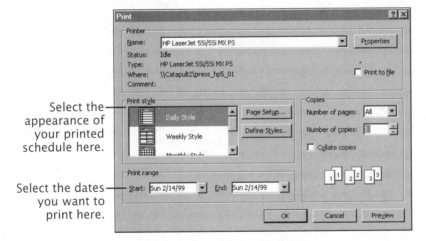

Select the appearance of your printed schedule here.

Select the dates you want to print here.

2 In the Print Style area, select Weekly Style.

A week of your schedule will be printed on a single page.

3 In the Print Range area, click the Start down arrow.

A small calendar appears.

4 Click February 15.

5 In the Print Range area, click the End down arrow, and then click February 21.

6 Click Preview.

The Print Preview window opens. Your screen should look similar to the following illustration.

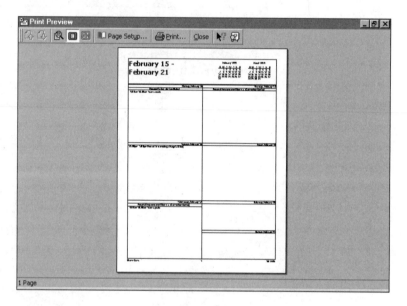

7 Click the Print button.

The Print dialog box appears again.

8 Click OK.

A copy of your schedule for the week of February 15 through February 21, 1999, prints.

Customizing Your Calendar Display

You can customize most of the Calendar options. For example, you can set the default display so that the workday in the appointment area starts at 9:00 A.M. instead of 8:00 A.M., or change it so that the work week starts on Tuesday. You can change the dimensions of the appointment area to display more appointment text or show a different number of months in the Date Navigator.

At Margo Tea Company, the typical workday begins at 8:30 A.M. and ends at 5:30 P.M. You want to change the Calendar settings to reflect your workday. You also want to resize the appointment area to view your appointments in more detail.

Change Calendar default options

In this exercise, you change the start and end times of your workday.

1 On the Tools menu, click Options.

The Options dialog box appears, with the Calendar tab in front.

2 In the Calendar Working Hours area, click the Start Time down arrow.

A list of available times appears.

3 Select 8:30 A.M.

4 Click the End Time down arrow, select 5:30 P.M., and then click OK.

The change does not take place until you leave the Calendar folder, and then return to it.

5 On the Outlook Bar, click the Inbox icon.

The contents of your Inbox appear in the Information viewer.

6 On the Outlook Bar, click the Calendar icon.

The current date appears in the Information viewer, and the workday begins at 8:30 A.M.

Resize the appointment area

In this exercise, you resize the appointment area so that more space is available for appointment details.

1 Position the pointer over the right border of the appointment area until the pointer changes to a two-headed arrow.

Your screen should look similar to the following illustration.

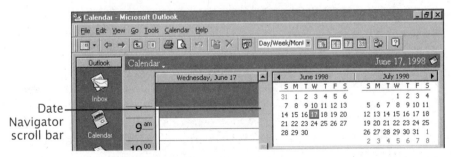

Date Navigator scroll bar

2 Drag the appointment area border to the right until a gray line appears in the middle of the Date Navigator, and then release the mouse button.

The appointment area has doubled in width, and the Date Navigator contains only the current month. Your screen should look similar to the following illustration.

679

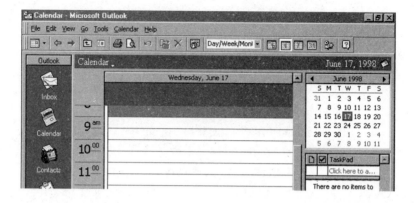

 TIP To display multiple consecutive days in the appointment area, hold SHIFT and click the adjacent days you want to see in the Date Navigator. To display non-consecutive days, hold CTRL and click the appropriate dates in the Date Navigator.

Finish the lesson

Follow these steps to delete the practice appointments you created in this lesson.

1 On the Go menu, click Go To Date.

2 Type **2/15/99**, and then click OK.

3 Click the "Team update" appointment, and then click the Delete button.

A message appears, asking if you want to delete all occurrences of this appointment.

4 Click the Delete All Occurrences option button and then click OK.

The appointments are deleted.

5 Delete the "Dentist" appointment and the "Campaign Strategy meeting" on February 12, 1999, and the "Product Line meeting" on February 16, 1999.

6 Delete the Personal Empowerment Seminar event on February 17, 1999.

7 On the Tools menu, click Options. On the Calendar tab, reset the Start Time to 8:00 A.M., the End Time to 5:00 P.M., and then click OK

8 On the File menu, click Exit And Log Off.

Lesson Summary

To	Do this	Button
Change the date	On the Go menu, click Go To Date. Type the new date, and then click OK.	
Add an appointment to your schedule	On the Standard toolbar, click the New Appointment button. In the appointment form, type the appropriate information.	
Edit an appointment	Double-click the appointment in the appointment area. Make changes in the appointment form.	
Move an appointment	Drag the appointment to a new date in the Date Navigator.	
Change a reminder	Open the appointment form. Click the Reminder down arrow, and then select a new timing increment.	
Make an appointment tentative	Open the appointment form. Click the Show Time As down arrow, and then select Tentative.	
Make an appointment private	Use the right mouse button to click the appointment in the appointment area, and then click Private.	
Schedule time out of the office	Open the appointment form. Click the Show Time As down arrow, and then select Out Of Office.	
Schedule a recurring appointment	Open the appointment form. On the Standard toolbar, click the Recurrence button. Choose a recurrence pattern and range.	
Add events	On the Calendar menu, click New Event. Type in the appropriate information.	
Import holidays	On the Tools menu, click Options. On the Calendar tab, click Add Holidays, select the holiday folders from which you want to import, and then click OK.	

To	Do this
Print schedules	On the File menu, click Print. Select a print style and the date or dates you wish to print, and then click OK.
Change Calendar default options	On the Tools menu, click Options. On the Calendar tab, make the changes you want, and then click OK.

For online information about	Use the Office Assistant to search for
Creating appointments	**Creating appointments,** and then click Schedule An Appointment, Meeting, Or Event
Editing appointments	**Editing appointments,** and then click Edit An Appointment
Setting reminders	**Setting reminders,** and then click Set An Appointment Reminder
Changing the free and busy time	**Free and busy times,** and then click Change The Free/Busy Time Of A Calendar Item
Setting recurring appointments	**Recurring appointments,** and then click Make An Appointment Recurring
Scheduling events	**Scheduling events,** and then click Schedule An Appointment, Meeting, Or Event

Coordinating Schedules with Other Users

Estimated time
25 min.

In this lesson you will learn how to:

- View other users' schedules using the Meeting Planner.
- Send meeting requests.

The Calendar in Microsoft Outlook helps you organize your schedule. In addition, you can use Calendar over a network to coordinate meetings with the other people in your office. You can use the *Meeting Planner* feature to review your schedule along with the schedules of your co-workers, and to schedule meetings at mutually available times. You can also use *AutoPick* to quickly determine an acceptable meeting time and location. You can send out meeting requests via e-mail and receive responses in your Outlook Inbox. You can also change meeting dates and times, and easily inform attendees of the changes without creating and addressing a new meeting request.

Everyone involved with Margo Tea Company's new product line is hard at work on his or her piece of the project. As the Operations Coordinator, you need to schedule meetings with the entire team so that everyone can be kept informed on the products and the advertising campaign as they develop. In this lesson, you'll learn how to view your co-workers' schedules using the Meeting Planner, and you'll also learn how to request meetings in the Calendar folder, and add meetings to your schedule.

IMPORTANT Because this lesson explores the interactive aspects of the Calendar folder in Outlook, you'll use your own profile and work with your own schedule. You will not be able to complete the exercises as written if you are not using Outlook in a networked environment with a global address list, such as an organization. You'll need to recruit some help from one or two other people on your network to complete the exercises. Find at least one person on your network who will cooperate with your practice meeting and requests.

Start Outlook

In this exercise, you start Outlook and switch to the Calendar folder.

If you receive a reminder for an appointment during this lesson, click the Dismiss This Reminder option button.

1 Start Outlook using your own profile name.

You should use your own profile for this lesson so that you can work with other people on your network.

2 On the Outlook Bar, click the Calendar icon.

The contents of your Calendar folder appear in the Information viewer; your schedule for the current date appears.

Scheduling a Meeting

In the Calendar folder, you can see all your appointments in some detail and display them a day, a week, or a month at a time. But what if you want a more graphical representation of your schedule, where you can see your free and busy times at a glance? You can use the Meeting Planner to view your schedule, and others' schedules, in a timeline format. With the Meeting Planner, you can easily see the times that are blocked off on your schedule for existing appointments and the times that are available for new meetings or appointments.

View your own schedule

In this exercise, you display the Meeting Planner to look over your entire schedule, and then check specific details for an appointment.

 IMPORTANT This lesson will be the most useful and interesting if you and your co-workers have appointments scheduled. If you don't have any appointments on the current date, you can add some, or move to a date in the future when you and your co-workers have appointments. You can switch to any future date by using the Date Navigator or the Go To Date command on the Go menu.

Plan A Meeting

For consistency, the illustrations in this lesson will continue to use the Shawn Davis profile that was used in the previous lessons.

1 On the Standard toolbar, click the Plan A Meeting button.

The Plan A Meeting dialog box appears. The current date appears in the Meeting Planner grid, and the time periods during which you have an appointment or a meeting scheduled are marked with a solid line, but no details are shown. Your screen should look similar to the following illustration.

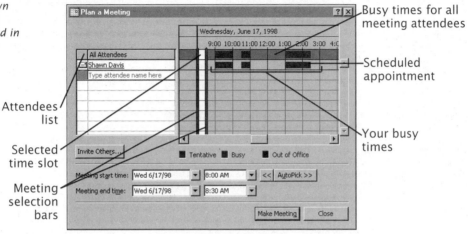

Attendees list

Selected time slot

Meeting selection bars

Busy times for all meeting attendees

Scheduled appointment

Your busy times

You cannot use the right mouse button to click busy bars in the darker "All Attendees" line at the top of the grid.

2 Use the right mouse button to click a busy time slot.

The appointment time and description appear. Your screen should look similar to the following illustration.

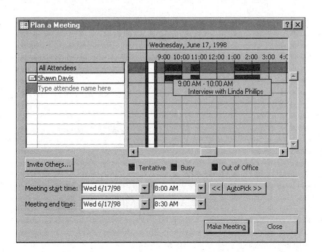

Viewing Other People's Free and Busy Times

In the Plan A Meeting dialog box, you can see at a glance when your schedule is open for new appointments. But how can you find out when other people are available so that you can set the time and date for a meeting? Using Outlook and with access to your network, you can easily view your co-workers' schedules and determine the best time for a meeting.

By default, although your co-workers can view your free and busy times, they cannot read the details of your appointments and tasks. If you want certain people to be able to see more details about your schedule, you can grant them different levels of access permissions, as long as they are using Outlook with a Microsoft Exchange Server.

Your name always appears in the Attendees box located next to the Meeting Planner grid. To add names to the Attendees box and display their schedules, you can type in their names or choose them from your organization's global address list.

 NOTE Most Microsoft Schedule+ files are compatible with Outlook files, so if some of your co-workers have not yet upgraded to Outlook, you will still be able to exchange scheduling information with them. If you do not have a global address list, skip this exercise.

Display another person's schedule

In this exercise, you display your co-workers' schedules in the Meeting Planner grid.

1 In the Plan A Meeting dialog box, click Invite Others.

The Select Attendees And Resources dialog box appears. Names from your organization's global address list are shown, in addition to your own name.

2 Select the names of the people working with you on this lesson, and then click Required.

The names appear in the list of required attendees.

3 Click OK.

The names of your co-workers appear in the All Attendees list, and each attendee's busy times are marked in the Meeting Planner grid. Busy times appear in blue, tentative appointments in light blue, and out-of-office appointments in purple.

TIP If you want to coordinate a meeting with a colleague in another time zone, you can display an additional time zone in your Calendar. This is useful if members of your organization are working in satellite offices nationwide, for example, and you occasionally need to schedule meetings or conference calls. To display a second time zone, on the Tools menu, click Options, and then click the Calendar tab. Click Time Zone. Select the Show An Additional Time Zone check box. In the Label box, type a description, such as Northwest District. Click the Time Zone down arrow, select the zone you want to use, and click OK. You can quickly switch to the second time zone in Day view by using the right mouse button to click the blank space above the appointment area, and then clicking Change Time Zone.

Requesting a Meeting

The AutoPick function is the easiest way to schedule a meeting with several of your co-workers. When you use AutoPick, you do not need to look at each person's individual schedule to determine free and busy times. You select your attendees, the location, and any equipment you need, and specify a duration for the meeting. Then, you use AutoPick to search the schedules of attendees for the first available time that meets all your requirements.

When you select attendees for a meeting, you can decide to make them required attendees or optional attendees. Optional attendees are informed of the meeting but are not required to attend. The meeting request they receive is similar to a carbon copy. If you name any optional attendees, you can check their schedules for available times using AutoPick. But even if you don't, all optional attendees receive a carbon copy of the meeting request message, so they can choose to attend if they wish.

If schedules for locations and other resources are maintained on your network, you can also select a meeting location and request specific equipment using the Meeting Planner. A *resource* can be a conference room, an overhead projector, a VCR, or any other equipment you might need at a meeting. If you select a resource, this information will also appear on the meeting request form.

After you select a meeting time with AutoPick, you can send a message to each of the attendees, asking whether he or she is available. Although you could switch to the Inbox and send out messages inviting people to the meeting, you can create and send a meeting request form without leaving the Calendar folder using AutoPick.

Schedule a meeting using AutoPick

In this exercise, you use the AutoPick function to quickly find a convenient time and schedule a meeting with required attendees. For the purposes of this exercise, you will not select any optional attendees, locations, or resources.

For a demonstration of how to schedule a meeting, double-click the Camcorder file named Scheduling A Meeting in the Part6 Outlook Camcorder Files folder. See "Installing and Using the Practice and Camcorder Files," earlier in this book for more information.

1 Be sure that the Plan A Meeting dialog box is active and that the names of the people working with you on this lesson appear in the All Attendees list.

The date and time selected in the Meeting Planner grid correspond to the current date and time on your computer.

2 Click the Meeting End Time down arrow.

A list of times and durations appears.

3 Select the time that corresponds to a two-hour duration.

The time you choose will vary depending on the current time on your computer. In the Meeting Planner grid, the meeting selection bars move to enclose a two-hour time period.

You can also drag the meeting selection handles to change the meeting duration.

4 Click AutoPick.

The meeting selection bars appear around the first two-hour time period available for all attendees. Your screen should look similar to the following illustration.

The button to the left of the AutoPick button, with the left-pointing arrows, searches for available times earlier than the selected date.

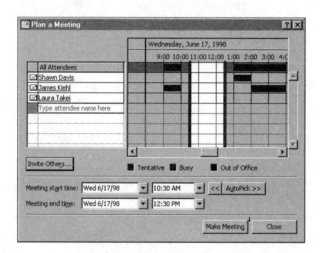

5   Click Make Meeting.

A blank meeting request form, which is very similar to the appointment form, appears. The names of your co-workers appear in the To box, and a note appears in the Comment area at the top of the form, informing you that invitations to this meeting have not yet been sent. Your screen should look similar to the following illustration, if you maximize the meeting request form.

This note appears until you send the meeting request. →

The time and date selected by AutoPick appear here automatically. →

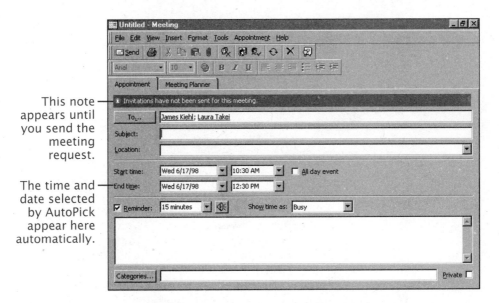

6   In the Subject box, type **Ad campaign update**

7   In the Notes area at the bottom of the form, type **Now that we have some feedback from Debbie Abdul, let's meet and review our project schedule.**

8   Be sure that the Reminder check box is checked.

You want each attendee to receive a reminder for the meeting when it comes up in his or her schedule.

9   On the Standard toolbar, click the Send button.

The meeting request is sent, and the meeting is added to your schedule in the appropriate time slots. Your screen should look similar to the following illustration.

If the first available meeting time you found using AutoPick is on a different date, click that date in the Date Navigator to see the meeting.

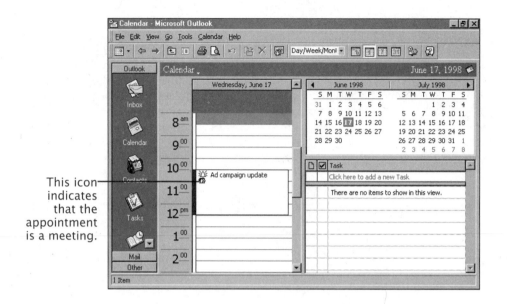

This icon indicates that the appointment is a meeting.

TIP Suppose you need to plan a meeting with a group of individuals, each of whom has a very tight schedule. You could use AutoPick, but what if the next available date it finds is three months away? In situations like this, it is often easier to organize a meeting by selecting a specific time in the Meeting Planner. If other users of your network have given you access to their schedules, you can view the details of their appointments and ask them to reschedule items if your meeting takes precedence.

Viewing Responses to Meeting Requests

After recipients respond to the meeting requests you've sent out, you can view the responses without leaving the Calendar folder. The Meeting Request tab in the appointment form displays the list of meeting attendees and their responses to your request. You can also view other users' schedules on the Meeting Planner tab and invite additional meeting attendees, if you wish.

When you send a meeting request, the invitees can respond in three ways: Accept, Decline, or Tentatively Accept. When they receive a meeting request, they click one of these option buttons to send their decision back to you. They can also choose to add a text message to their response. You can view these messages in your Inbox in Outlook, or track the responses on the Meeting Planner tab for the meeting appointment in your Calendar. When your co-workers accept or tentatively accept a meeting request, the meeting is automatically added to their schedules.

Verify attendee responses

In this exercise, you open the "Ad campaign update" meeting appointment and double-check the information on the Meeting Planner tab.

IMPORTANT Be sure to ask your co-workers whom you've recruited for this lesson to send responses to your meeting request so that you can complete this exercise.

1 Double-click the "Ad campaign update" meeting appointment.

The appointment form opens. The number of responses you have received appears in the Comment area at the top of the form.

2 Click the Meeting Planner tab.

The Meeting Planner tab appears, and the Show Attendee Status option button is selected. The responses from your co-workers are listed in the table. Your screen should look similar to the following illustration.

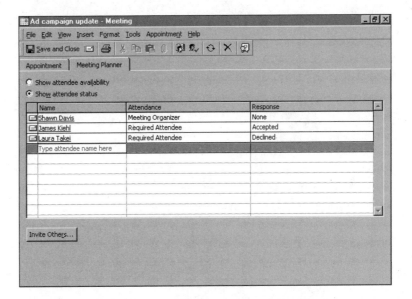

3 Click the Show Attendee Availability option button.

The Meeting Planner grid appears. A blue bar between the selected time slots for a name indicates that the meeting has been added to the schedule for that person. Your screen should look similar to the following illustration.

691

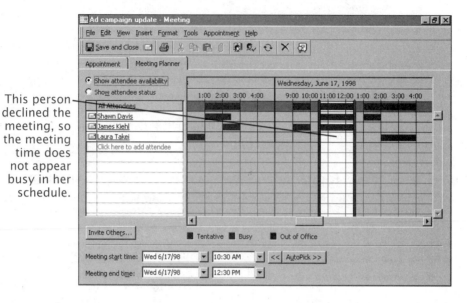

This person declined the meeting, so the meeting time does not appear busy in her schedule.

4 Use the right mouse button to click the blue bar for a name in the meeting time slot.

The meeting time and the text "Ad campaign update" appear.

If you requested a meeting location, it also appears when you click the blue bar using the right mouse button.

5 Click anywhere to cancel the selection, and then close the appointment form.

TIP You can transform a regular appointment into a meeting by opening the appointment, and then inviting attendees using the Meeting Planner tab.

Changing Meeting Times and Locations

Sometimes you will find that, although the schedules look clear for a meeting time when you view them in the Meeting Planner, something might have come up or people you invited might have other appointments they haven't added in Outlook. When someone declines a meeting or asks if you could reschedule it, you can easily make changes.

Reschedule a meeting

In this exercise, you change the time for a meeting and notify attendees.

1 Position the mouse pointer over the left move handle on the "Ad campaign update" meeting.

The pointer changes to a four-headed arrow.

2 Drag the meeting to have it start two hours later.

A message appears, asking if you want to send an update to meeting attendees to inform them of the change.

3 Click Yes.

A new meeting request form, addressed to the co-workers who are helping you with this lesson, appears. The new meeting start and end times appear in the appropriate boxes, and the text of your original message is appended to the new form.

4 Select the text in the Notes area, and then type **Sorry, change in schedule!**

5 On the Standard toolbar, click the Save And Close button, and then click Yes to send the message.

' The new meeting time is sent to your co-workers. They can accept or decline the request, but this is not necessary to complete this lesson.

 TIP You can check attendees' free and busy times in the Meeting Planner grid before you reschedule a meeting.

Finish the lesson

Follow these steps to delete the practice items you created in this lesson.

 IMPORTANT Because you are logged on to Outlook with your own profile, be sure you delete only the practice appointments and messages you added or created during this lesson.

Delete

1 In the Calendar folder, delete the meeting you scheduled in this lesson. Do not notify meeting attendees of the change.

2 In your Inbox, delete messages you created in this lesson.

3 If you are finished using Outlook, on the File menu, click Exit And Log Off.

Lesson Summary

To	Do this	Button
View your schedule in the Meeting Planner	Switch to the Calendar folder. On the Standard toolbar, click the Plan A Meeting button.	
View other users' schedules	In the Plan A Meeting dialog box, click Invite Others. Select and add names from one of the address lists and then click OK. View their schedule.	
Select a meeting time during which each required attendee is available	In the Plan A Meeting dialog box, be sure that the names of all attendees appear in the All Attendees list and then click AutoPick.	
Request a meeting	In the Plan A Meeting dialog box, be sure that the time you want is selected, and then click Make Meeting. Type a subject and any other necessary information in the meeting request form, and then send the message.	
Track meeting request responses	Double-click the meeting appointment in your schedule. Click the Meeting Planner tab, and then click the Show Attendee Status option button.	
Reschedule a meeting	In your schedule, position the pointer over the move handle for the meeting appointment. Drag the meeting to a new location. Click Yes to notify attendees of the change. Type any additional information in the meeting request form, and then send the message.	

For online information about	Use the Office Assistant to search for
Meeting planner	**Meeting planner,** and then click Meeting Planner
Responding to meeting requests	**Responding to meeting requests,** and then click Respond To A Meeting Request Or Notification

Matching the Exercises

Windows 95, Windows NT, and Office 97 have many optional settings that can affect either the screen display or the operation of certain functions. Some exercise steps, therefore, might not produce exactly the same result on your screen as is shown in this book. If your screen does not look like an illustration at a certain point in a lesson, a note in the lesson might direct you to this appendix for guidance. Or, if you do not get the outcome described in the lesson, you can use this appendix to determine whether the options you have selected are the same as the ones used in this book.

NOTE Since each computer system is configured with different hardware and software, your screen display of icons, folders, and menu options might not exactly match the illustrations in this book. Such system differences should not interfere with your ability to perform the exercises in the book.

Installing Windows 95 Components

The exercises in this book assume a "Custom" setup of Windows 95, with all components installed. If Windows 95 was installed on your computer under a "Typical," "Portable," or "Compact" setup, you might not have all the components necessary to complete the lessons. If you are missing one or two components, such as an accessory, you can easily add it.

Add or remove Windows 95 components

Regardless of which setup option you chose, you can add or remove components later, after Windows 95 is installed and running. You do not have to run the Setup program again. You can add or remove Windows 95 components with Add/Remove Programs in Windows 95 Control Panel.

1 Double-click the My Computer icon.

2 In the My Computer window, double-click the Control Panel icon.

3 In the Control Panel window, double-click the Add/Remove Programs icon.

The Add/Remove Programs Properties dialog box appears.

4 Click the Windows Setup tab to make it active.

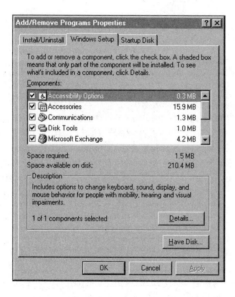

5 In the Components list box, double-click a component group, such as Accessories.

The list box displays the detail components in the group. Some groups might only contain one component.

6 Click the check boxes corresponding to the components you want to add or remove.

A clear check box indicates that the component is not installed or will be removed. A checked box indicates that the component is already installed or will be added. A grayed box indicates that some, but not all, of the components are installed or will be added.

7   Click OK to return to the Windows Setup tab to select another component group.

8   Once you are done making your selections, click OK in the Add/Remove Programs Properties dialog box.

If you are adding a component, you might be prompted to insert one or more of the Windows 95 Setup disks. If you originally installed Windows 95 from a network location, you may be prompted to type the path for the network location where the Windows 95 steup files are stored. Follow the directions on your screen to add the component.

Using the Default Windows 95 Settings

Windows 95 makes it easy for you to configure your Desktop to suit your working style and preferences. However, the exercises in this book assume that all Windows 95 options are at their default settings. Even when an exercise changes an option setting, the "Finish the Lesson" procedure usually resets the setting to the default.

You can easily change your Windows 95 options to match the illustrations in the exercises.

Show or hide toolbars

You can toggle the toolbar on and off in the My Computer and Windows Explorer windows. The toolbar setting can be different for each window that you open.

1   On the My Computer or Windows Explorer window, click the View menu.

If the Toolbar command is checked, this indicates that the toolbar is currently showing. If it is not checked, the toolbar is hidden.

2   On the View menu, click Toolbar to show or hide the toolbar.

Change window sizes

If your window sizes appear different from the exercise illustrations, you can change their sizes.

1   Position your mouse pointer on any edge of the window whose size you want to change.

The mouse pointer changes to a double-headed arrow.

2   Drag the edge of the window in or out to make the window smaller or larger.

Restore windows

If a window is filling the entire screen and you want to see other parts of the Windows 95 Desktop, you can restore the window.

Restore

1   Bring the maximized window to the top of your Desktop by clicking its name on the taskbar.

2   On the maximized window, click the Restore button in the upper-right corner of the window. Be sure that you don't click the Close button to the right of the Restore button.

The window is restored to its previous, smaller size.

Change views

If you are seeing a different view of files in a My Computer or Windows Explorer window, you can change the view. The views can be different for each My Computer window that you open.

1   In the My Computer or Windows Explorer window for which you want to change the view, click View.

2   On the View menu, click the view you want: Large Icons, Small Icons, List, or Details.

Arrange icons on the Desktop

If your Desktop icons appear jumbled, or in a different order than what you expected to see, you can arrange your icons.

1   Use the right mouse button to click an empty area of the Desktop.

2   On the pop-up menu, point to Arrange Icons, and then click By Name.

The icons are arranged by name on your Desktop.

3   Use the right mouse button to click an empty area of the Desktop again.

4   On the pop-up menu, point to Arrange Icons, and then click Auto Arrange to arrange your icons.

Arrange icons in My Computer or Windows Explorer

If the icons in a My Computer or Windows Explorer window appear jumbled, or in a different order than what you expected to see, you can arrange your icons. The icons can have a different arrangement for each window that you open.

1   In the My Computer or Windows Explorer window, click the View menu.

2   On the View menu, point to Arrange Icons, and then click By Name.

The icons are arranged by name on your Desktop.

3   On the View menu, point to Arrange Icons again, and then click Auto Arrange.

Hide filename extensions in My Computer or Windows Explorer

If the filenames in My Computer or Windows Explorer include three-letter extensions, you can hide the extensions for file types that are registered.

1   In the My Computer or Windows Explorer window, click the View menu.

2   On the View menu, click Options.

3   On the Options dialog box, click the View tab.

4   On the View tab, click Hide MS-DOS File Extensions For File Types That Are Registered.

5   Click OK.

Open cascading My Computer windows

If only one My Computer window appears, even as you are opening new folders, you can set your display to open a new window for each new folder.

1   In the My Computer window, click the View menu, and then click Options.

2   In the Options dialog box, be sure that the Folder tab is active.

3   On the Folder tab, click Browse Folders Using A Separate Window For Each Folder, and then click OK.

Installing Windows NT Components

The exercises in this book assume a "Typical" setup of Windows NT. If Windows NT was installed on your computer under a "Portable," "Custom," or "Compact" setup, you might not have all the components necessary to complete the lessons. If you are missing one or two components, such as an accessory, you can easily add it.

Add or remove Windows NT components

Regardless of which setup option you choose, you can add or remove components later, after Windows NT is installed and running. You do not have to run the Setup program again. You can add or remove Windows NT components with Add/Remove Programs in Windows NT Control Panel.

1   Double-click the My Computer icon.

2   In the My Computer window, double-click the Control Panel icon.

3   In the Control Panel window, double-click the Add/Remove Programs icon.

The add/Remove Programs Properties dialog box appears.

4 Click the Windows NT Setup tab to make it active.

5 In the Components list box, double-click a component group, such as Accessories.

The list box displays a detailed list of components in the group. Some groups might only contain one element.

6 Select or clear the check boxes corresponding to the components you want to add or remove.

7 Click OK to return to the Windows NT Setup to select another component group.

8 Once you are done making your selections, click OK in the Add/Remove Programs Properties dialog box.

If you are adding a component, you might be prompted to insert the Windows NT CD-ROM. If you originally installed Windows NT from a network location, you may be prompted to type the path for the network location where the Windows NT setup files are stored. Follow the directions on your screen to add the component.

Using the Default Windows NT Settings

Windows NT makes it easy for you to configure your Desktop to suit your working style and preferences. However, the exercises in this book assume that all Windows NT options are at their default settings. Even when an exercise changes an option setting, the "Finish the Lesson" procedure usually resets the setting to the default.

You can easily change your Windows NT options to match the illustrations in the exercises.

Show or hide toolbars

You can toggle the toolbar on and off in the My Computer and Windows NT Explorer windows. The toolbar setting can be different for each window that you open. You can show or hide the toolbar on your screen to match the illustrations in this book.

1 On the My Computer or Windows NT Explorer window, click the View menu.

If the Toolbar command is checked, the toolbar is currently showing; if it is not checked, the toolbar is hidden.

2 On the View menu, click Toolbar to show or hide the toolbar.

Change window sizes

If the size of your windows appear to be different from the exercise illustrations, you can adjust them.

1 Position your mouse pointer on any edge of the window whose size you want to change.

The mouse pointer changes to a double-headed arrow. You can change the window size horizontally by dragging on a side edge, or vertically by dragging on the top or bottom, or both at the same time by dragging on a corner.

2 Drag the edge or corner of the window in or out to make the window smaller or larger.

Restore windows

If a window fills up the entire screen and you want to see other parts of the Windows NT Desktop, you can restore the window to its previous size.

1 Bring the maximized window to the top of your Desktop by clicking its button on the taskbar.

Restore

2 On the maximized window, click the Restore button in the upper-right corner.

The window is restored to its previous, smaller size.

Change views

If the way files appear in a My Computer or Windows NT Explorer window are different from the illustrations in the book, you can change the view. The views can be different for each My Computer window that you open. You can change the view on your computer to match the illustrations in this book.

1 In the My Computer or Windows NT Explorer window for which you want to change the view, click the View menu.

2 On the View menu, click the appropriate view: Large Icons, Small Icons, List, or Details.

Arrange icons on the Desktop

If your Desktop icons appear jumbled, or in an order other than what you expected, you can arrange them.

1 Use the right mouse button to click an empty area of the Desktop.

2 On the shortcut menu, point to Arrange Icons, and then click By Name.

The icons are arranged by name on your Desktop.

3   Use the right mouse button to click an empty area of the Desktop again.

4   On the shortcut menu, point to Arrange Icons, and then click Auto Arrange to arrange your icons.

Arrange icons in My Computer or Windows NT Explorer

If the icons in a My Computer or Windows NT Explorer window appear jumbled, or in an order other than what you expected, you can arrange them. The icons can have a different arrangement for each window that you open.

1   In the My Computer or Windows NT Explorer window, click the View menu.

2   On the View menu, point to Arrange Icons, and then click By Name.

     The icons are arranged by name in your window.

3   On the View menu, point to Arrange Icons again, and then click Auto Arrange.

Hide filename extensions in My Computer or Windows NT Explorer

If the filenames in My Computer or Windows NT Explorer include three-letter extensions, you can hide the extensions for file types that Windows NT recognizes. For example, Windows NT automatically recognizes file types with a .doc extension as being WordPad files.

1   In the My Computer or Windows NT Explorer window, click the View menu.

2   On the View menu, click Options.

3   On the Options dialog box, click the View tab, if necessary.

4   On the View tab, select the Hide File Extensions For Known File Types check box.

5   Click OK.

Open cascading My Computer windows

You can set up your display so that a new My Computer window appears every time you open a new folder. You can also browse through folders using a single window that changes each time you open a new folder.

1   In the My Computer window, on the View menu, click Options.

2   In the Options dialog box, be sure that the Folder tab is active.

3   On the Folder tab, click the Browse Folders Using A Separate Window For Each Folder option button, and then click OK.

Troubleshooting: Error Displayed When Double-clicking any Write File

You might encounter the following error message after double-clicking any Write file, including the History practice file in Part 1.

"Unable to read from C:\Windows, it is opened by someone else."

This error occurs when Write files (files with the .WRI extension) are not properly associated with the Write program. Because WordPad replaced Write in Windows 95, we can associate Write files with WordPad. After doing so, when you double-click a Write file it will open in WordPad. This resolves the error noted above.

Set Write Files to Open in WordPad

1   Click Start. On the Start menu, point to Programs, and then click Windows Explorer.

2   In the left window of Windows Explorer, click the hard disk (C:). Now in the right window, find the Office 97 6in1 Step by Step folder and double-click it.

3   In the right window, find the Part1 Windows Practice folder and double-click it.

4   In the Part1 Windows Practice folder (now in the right window), click the History practice file once to select the file.

5   Now hold the SHIFT key down and with the right mouse button click the History practice file. This will cause an extended version of the context-sensitive pop-menu to appear.

6   On the pop-up menu, click Open With. In the Open With dialog box, scroll to the bottom of the list of programs and click WORDPAD.

7   Click the Always Use This Program To Open This Type Of File check box, and then click OK. WordPad will automatically open the History document after you complete step 7.

Now whenever a Write file is double-clicked in My Computer or Windows Explorer, WordPad will start and will open the file.

Matching the Illustrations of Word 97

Microsoft Word makes it easy for you to set up the program window to suit your working style and preferences. If you share your computer with others, previous users might have changed the screen setup. You can easily change it back so that the screen matches the illustrations in the lessons. Use the following methods for controlling the screen display.

If you change the screen display as part of a lesson and leave Microsoft Word, the next time you open Microsoft Word, the screen looks the way you left it in the previous session.

Display or hide toolbars

If toolbars are missing at the top of the screen, previous users might have hidden them to make more room for text. You can easily display the toolbars that contain the buttons you need in the lessons.

You can also hide specialized toolbars that you no longer need so that you can see more text on the screen. However, most of the lessons require that the Standard and Formatting toolbars appear.

1 On the View menu, point to Toolbars.

2 In the Toolbars menu, click toolbar names to add check marks for the toolbars you want to see; click toolbar names to clear the check marks for the toolbars you want to hide.

Display the ruler

If the ruler is missing from the top of the screen, previous users might have hidden it to make more room for text. Although the ruler is not required in all lessons, it is usually displayed in the illustrations. To display the ruler, do the following.

  On the View menu, choose Ruler.

If the vertical scroll bar does not appear

If you do not see the vertical scroll bar, a previous user might have hidden the scroll bar to make more room for text. You can easily display it again.

1 Click the Tools menu, and then choose Options.
2 Click the View tab to display the view options in the dialog box.
3 In the Window area, click the Vertical Scroll Bar check box. A check mark appears in the check box to indicate that it is selected.
4 Click OK.

If the Word program window does not fill the screen

A previous user might have made the Microsoft Word program window smaller to allow quick access to another program. You can enlarge the document window by doing the following.

Maximize

➤ Click the Maximize button in the upper-right corner of the Microsoft Word title bar.

If the right edge of the Microsoft Word window is hidden so that you cannot see the Maximize button, point to "Microsoft Word" in the title bar at the top of the screen, and then drag the title bar to the left until you see the Maximize button.

If the document does not fill the space that Microsoft Word allows

The last time Microsoft Word was used, the user might have displayed the document in a smaller size to get an overview of a document. To see your document at the normal size, use the Zoom button on the Standard toolbar.

Zoom

➤ Click the Zoom down arrow, and select 100%.

If you see the top edge of the page on the screen

The last person to use Microsoft Word might have worked in Page Layout view, which displays one page of text on the screen. Return to Normal view for the lesson.

Normal View

➤ Click the Normal View button to the far left of the horizontal scroll bar.
or
On the View menu, select Normal.

If spaces appear before periods when moving text

A previous user might have preferred not to use the Smart Cut And Paste feature. Because all the lessons after Lesson 1 assume that this feature is active, you can turn this feature back on.

1 From the Tools menu, choose Options.
2 Click the Edit tab to display the Edit options in the dialog box.
3 Click the Use Smart Cut And Paste check box.
4 Click OK.

If you see words in brackets

If you see {TIME...} or {SYMBOL..} or {DATE...} in the document, you are looking at the codes that instruct Microsoft Word to insert a certain type of information. You can hide the codes and view the information that Microsoft Word inserts to replace the codes without changing the document in any way.

1 From the Tools menu, choose Options.
2 Click the View tab to display the view options in the dialog box.
3 Click the Field Codes check box to clear it.
4 Click OK.

If you see "¶" in the document

You are viewing the paragraph marks that indicate the end of paragraphs. You might also be viewing other nonprinting symbols that mark spaces or locations where the TAB key was pressed. These symbols do not appear in the document when it is printed. Many users work with the symbols on all the time. If you prefer to hide the nonprinting symbols, you can do so without affecting the document in any way. Some of the instructions in the lessons require you to locate a specific paragraph mark in the document. In this case, be sure to click the Show/Hide ¶ button on the Standard toolbar to display paragraph marks and other nonprinting symbols.

Show/Hide ¶

➤ To hide the symbols, click the Show/Hide ¶ button on the Standard toolbar.

Returning Microsoft Word to Its Original Settings

A fast way to ensure that your results match those described in the lessons is to create a special Word shortcut on your desktop that you use only when you are working through the Step By Step lessons. By making a minor modification to this new shortcut you can reset many options to their original "out-of-the-box" state. Do not, however, use this special shortcut for doing your regular work in Microsoft Word.

1 Create a shortcut by locating the WINWORD.EXE file and dragging it to the desktop.

Use the Find command on the Start menu to help you locate this file if you are not sure where it is on your computer.

2 Use the right mouse button to click the new shortcut, and on the shortcut menu, click Properties.

3 Click the Shortcut tab.

4 Click the Target line, and press END to move to the end of the line.

5 Press the SPACEBAR and type /a

6 Click OK to return to the desktop.

7 Consider giving your new shortcut a new name by clicking the Rename command on the shortcut menu and typing a new name, such as "Word Reset" or some other name to distinguish it from other shortcuts you might already have on the desktop.

8 Double-click the new shortcut to start Word from the desktop.

One fast way to confirm that you are working in Word with original settings in effect is to click the File menu and verify that no filenames appear at the bottom of the File menu.

Changing Other Options in Word 97

If you are not getting the results described in the lessons, follow the instructions in this section to verify that the options set in your program are the same as the ones used in this book.

Review each of the following dialog boxes to compare settings for those options that users change most often and that are most likely to account for different results. You can view these dialog boxes by choosing the Options command from the Tools menu. Then you click the tab corresponding to the options you want to see.

View Options

Click the View tab to change options that affect the appearance of the document window. Here are the View settings used in this book. The first illustration displays the settings to use when a document is in Normal view. The second illustration displays the settings to use when a document is in Page Layout view.

Normal View options

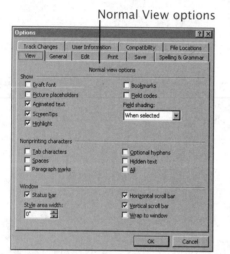

Page Layout View options

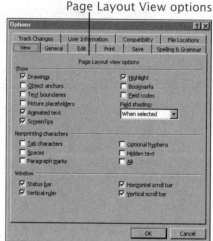

General Options

Click the General tab to change options that affect the operation of Microsoft Word in general. Here are the General settings used in this book.

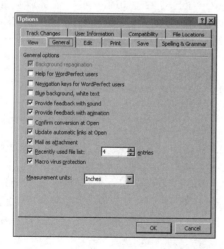

Edit Options

Click the Edit tab to change options that affect how editing operations are performed. Here are the Edit settings used in this book.

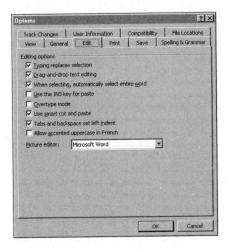

Print Options

Click the Print tab to change options that affect how printing operations are performed. Here are the Print settings used in this book.

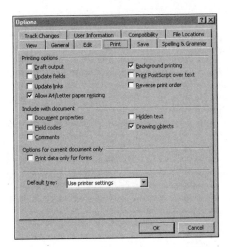

Save Options

Click the Save tab to change options that affect how your documents are saved to disk. Here are the Save settings used in this book.

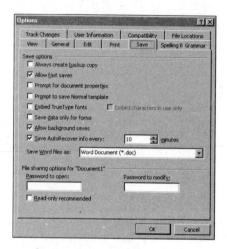

Spelling & Grammar Options

Click the Spelling & Grammar tab to change options that affect how the spelling and grammar features work. Here are the Spelling & Grammar settings used in this book.

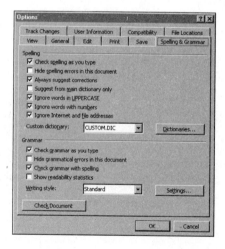

AutoFormat, AutoCorrect, and AutoText Options

To review AutoFormat, AutoCorrect, or AutoText options, you can click any of these commands on their respective menus. In any of the dialog boxes, click the Options button to display the AutoCorrect dialog box. Click the appropriate tab to review the specific options that affect how the AutoFormat, AutoCorrect, and AutoText features work.

AutoFormat

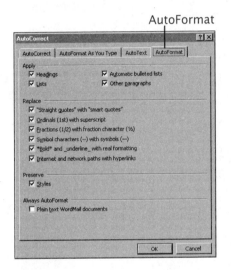

AutoCorrect

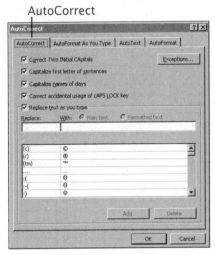

AutoFormat As You Type

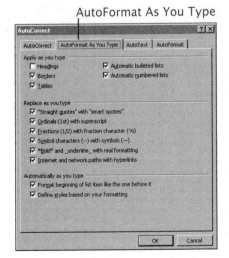

AutoText

Matching the Illustrations of Excel 97

Microsoft Excel makes it easy for you to set up the program window to suit your working style and preferences. If you share your computer with others, previous users might have changed the screen setup. You can easily change it back so that your screen matches the illustrations in the lessons. The following methods can help you control the screen display.

If you change the screen display as part of a lesson and leave Microsoft Excel, the next time you open Microsoft Excel, the screen looks the way you left it in the previous session.

Display toolbars

If toolbars are missing at the top of the screen, previous users might have hidden them to make more room for text. You can easily display the toolbars that contain the buttons you need in the lessons.

1   On the View menu, point to Toolbars.

2   In the Toolbars menu, click toolbar names to add check marks for the toolbars you need.

   Most of the lessons require that the Standard and Formatting toolbars appear.

Hide extra toolbars

To use specific features in some of the lessons, additional toolbars appear in the program window. If, after completing the lesson, you no longer want these toolbars to appear, you can use the Toolbars shortcut menu to hide toolbars you do not want to see. However, most of the lessons require that the Standard and Formatting toolbars appear.

1   Use the right mouse button to click any toolbar.

2   On the shortcut menu, click the name of the toolbar you do not want to see.

If the vertical or horizontal scroll bars do not appear

If you do not see the vertical or horizontal scroll bars, a previous user might have hidden the scroll bars to make more room for data. You can easily display them again.

1   On the Tools menu, click Options.

The Options dialog box appears.

2   Click the View tab to display the view options in the dialog box.

3   In the Window Options area, select the Vertical Scroll Bar and Horizontal Scroll Bar check boxes.

If either or both of these check boxes were previously selected, skip to step 4.

4   Click the OK button.

If the Microsoft Excel program window does not fill the screen

A previous user might have made the Microsoft Excel program window smaller to allow quick access to another program. You can enlarge the document window by doing the following.

Maximize

➤   Click the Maximize button.

If the right edge of the Microsoft Excel window is hidden so that you cannot see the Maximize button, point to "Microsoft Excel" in the title bar at the top of the screen, and then drag the title bar to the left until you see the Maximize button.

If your chart on a chart sheet does not fill the window

A previous user might have displayed charts at a smaller size. To see your chart at full size, use the Sized With Window command on the View menu.

➤   On the View menu, click Sized With Window.

If the document does not fill the space that Microsoft Excel allows

A previous user might have displayed the workbook in a smaller size to get an overview of a worksheet. To see your workbook at the normal size, use the Zoom Control down arrow on the Standard toolbar.

➤   Click the Zoom Control down arrow, and then select 100%.

715

If the sheet tabs do not appear in your workbook

A previous user might have hidden the sheet tabs to see more of the worksheets. To view the sheet tabs, you use the Options command on the Tools menu.

1 On the Tools menu, click Options.

2 In the Options dialog box, click the View tab.

3 In the Window Options area, select the Sheet Tabs check box, and then click OK.

If you see number signs rather than numbers in your practice files

If you see number signs (#) instead of numbers in your practice files, your column width might not be wide enough. To display the numbers, you resize the columns.

➤ Select the affected columns, and then double-click the column header border between two of the selected columns.

If gridlines do not appear in your workbook

A previous user might have hidden the gridlines to see a cleaner view of the data. To view the gridlines again, you use the Options command on the Tools menu.

1 On the Tools menu, click Options.

2 In the Options dialog box, select the View tab.

3 In the Window Options area, click the Gridlines check box, and then click OK.

If your columns are identified by numbers instead of letters

A previous user might have changed the reference style to R1C1. To change to the A1 reference style, you use the Options command on the Tools menu.

1 On the Tools menu, click Options, and then click the General tab.

2 In the Settings area, click the R1C1 reference style check box, and then click OK.

If the Workbook Properties dialog box appears when you save a document

A previous user might have turned on the Workbook Properties option. To turn the Prompt For Workbook Properties option off again, use the Options command on the Tools menu.

1 On the Tools menu, click Options, and then click the General tab.

2 Clear the Prompt For Workbook Properties check box, and then click OK.

Changing Other Options in Excel 97

If you are not getting the results described in the lessons, you can follow the instructions in this section to verify that the options set in your program are the same as the ones used in this book.

Review each of the following dialog boxes to compare settings for those options that users change most often and that are most likely to account for different results. You can view these dialog boxes by clicking the Options command on the Tools menu. Then click the tab corresponding to the options you want to see. The following illustrations show the option settings used in this book.

View options

Click the View tab to change options that affect the appearance of the document window.

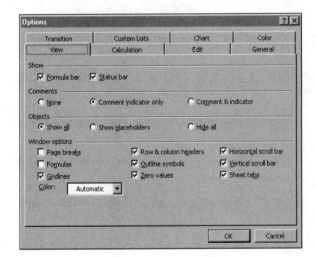

717

Calculation options

*Click the Calcu-
lation tab to
change options
that affect the
calculations of
your formulas.*

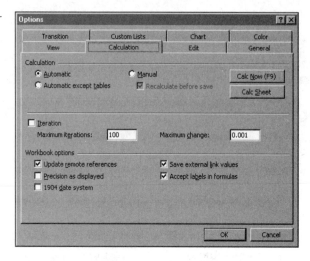

Edit options

*Click the Edit
tab to change
options that af-
fect how editing
operations are
performed.*

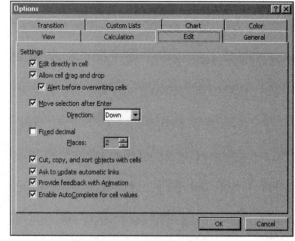

General options

Click the General tab to change options that affect the operation of Microsoft Excel in general.

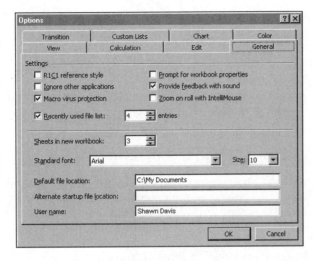

Chart options

Click the Chart tab to change options that affect how charts appear in Microsoft Excel. (Chart tab options are available only when a chart is active.)

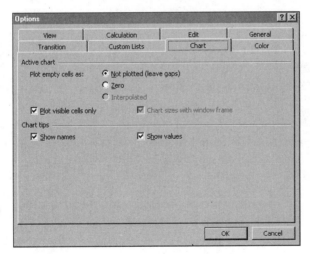

Matching the Illustrations of Outlook 97

Outlook makes it easy to set up the program window to suit your working style and preferences. If you share your computer with others, previous users might have changed the screen setup. You can easily change it back so that your screen matches the illustrations in the lessons. The following methods can help you control the screen display.

If you change the screen display as part of a lesson and leave Outlook, the next time you open Outlook, the screen will look the way you left it in the previous session.

If the filenames in the Open dialog box have extensions

A previous user might have changed a display option in Windows Explorer or Windows NT Explorer to see filename extensions, such as .doc for Microsoft Word files. To hide the extensions, you can change the setting in Explorer, the file management program in Windows 95 and Windows NT version 4.

1 On the Start menu, point to Programs, and then click Windows Explorer or Windows NT Explorer.

2 On the View menu, click Options, and then click the View tab.

Be sure that you click the View menu in Explorer, and not in Outlook.

3 Select the Hide MS-DOS File Extensions For File Types That Are Registered check box for Windows 95 or select the Hide File Extensions For Known File Types check box for Windows NT.

4 Click OK, and then close Explorer.

Display toolbars

If toolbars are missing at the top of the screen, previous users might have hidden them to make more room for text. You can display the toolbars that contain the buttons you need.

➤ On the View menu, point to Toolbars, and then click the name of the toolbar you need.

Most of the lessons require that the Standard toolbar appears.

Hide extra toolbars

To use specific features in some of the lessons, additional toolbars appear in the program window. If, after completing a lesson, you no longer want these toolbars to appear, you can use a shortcut menu to hide toolbars you don't want to see. However, most of the lessons require that the Standard toolbar appears.

1   Use the right mouse button to click any toolbar.

A shortcut menu appears.

2   On the shortcut menu, click the name of the toolbar you do not want to see.

If the Outlook program window does not fill the screen

A previous user might have made the Outlook program window smaller to allow quick access to another icon on the Desktop. You can easily enlarge the window by clicking a button.

➤   On the program window, click the Maximize button in the upper-right corner of the title bar.

If the right edge of the Outlook window is hidden so that you cannot see the Maximize button, point to "Microsoft Outlook" in the title bar at the top of the screen, and then drag the title bar to the left until you see the Maximize button. You can also double-click anywhere on the title bar to maximize the window.

If the Folder List appears

A previous user might have chosen to display the Folder List to view a hierarchy of all the folders on the computer. In the lessons in this book, you are prompted to display the Folder List only when it is necessary to complete an exercise. You can hide the Folder List using a toolbar button.

Folder List

➤   On the Standard toolbar, click the Folder List button.

The Folder List button is a toggle button; you can click it to hide or display the Folder List.

If the Date Navigator does not display two months

A previous user might have resized the appointment area in Calendar to make room for more appointment text. You can resize it by dragging the border of the appointment area.

1   In Calendar, position the pointer over the border between the Date Navigator and the appointment area.

The pointer changes to a two-headed arrow.

2   Drag the border to the left until it stops in the first third of the appointment area.

The Date Navigator displays two months.

If Word is installed as the e-mail editor

A previous user might have installed Word as the Outlook e-mail editor. This feature allows you to use Microsoft Word tools to edit and format your e-mail messages. If Word is being used, you may see additional toolbars and controls on the form that you use to compose messages. You can turn off the Word option and use the default editor instead.

1   On the Tools menu in the Outlook window, click Options.

2   Click the E-mail tab.

3   Clear the Use Microsoft Word As The E-mail Editor check box, and then click OK.

Using the Default Views

Each of the Outlook folders on your computer—Inbox, Calendar, Contacts, Tasks, Journal, Notes, and so on—comes with a selection of predesigned views that you can apply to display information differently. For the lessons in this book, it is assumed that the default view is applied to each Outlook folder at the beginning of a lesson; during the exercises, you may be asked to switch or modify views. The following table lists the default views for each of the Outlook folders.

Folder	Default view	Other settings
Inbox	Messages With AutoPreview	
Calendar	Day/Week/Month	Single day displayed
Contacts	Address Cards	
Tasks	Simple List	
Journal	By Type	Week displayed
Notes	Icons	
Deleted Items	Messages	
Sent Items	Sent To	
Outbox	Sent To	

Day

NOTE   To apply a different view to a folder, on the Standard toolbar, click the Current View down arrow to display a list of the available views for that folder, and then click the view you want to use. In the Calendar folder and the Journal folder, you can display a single day or a week by clicking the corresponding Day or Week button on the Standard toolbar.

absolute cell reference A cell address in a formula that does not change when copied to another cell. An absolute reference has the form A1.

accessories Basic programs included with Windows 95 and Windows NT that assist you with your everyday work on the computer—for example, WordPad and Paint. Accessories also include utilities that help you use your computer's telecommunication, fax, and multi-media capabilities more easily. System tools are accessories that help you manage your computer resources. Games are also included as part of your Windows 95 or Windows NT accessories.

active cell The selected cell in a worksheet. The active cell is surrounded by a heavy border and is identified by the cell address.

active window In a multiple-window environment, the window that is currently selected and whose contents will be affected by all mouse actions, commands, and text entries.

anchor point The point that remains stable as the text grows and shrinks during editing; for example, a top anchor point with a left text alignment allows the text to grow right and down as it normally would when you type. A top center anchor point would allow the text to grow left, right, and down.

application *See* program.

argument The information that a function uses to produce a new value or perform an action. For example, a new value is returned when the SUM function adds the argument (A6:A12). An argument consists of numbers, references, text, operators, arrays, or error values.

attributes The features of an object, such as color, shadow, and pattern.

AutoCorrect A feature that replaces common misspellings as you type with the correct spelling.

AutoFormat A feature used to format a range of cells with a predefined set of attributes.

AutoLayout Ready-made placeholders for titles, text, and objects such as clip art, graphs, and charts.

automatic word selection A selection option that makes it easier to select multiple words. Place the pointer anywhere in a word and drag to select the entire word.

AutoShapes toolbar A toolbar that contains tools for drawing common shapes such as stars, banners, flowcharts, connectors, and action buttons.

baud rate The speed at which a modem can send or receive information. Baud rate can be confused with the more accurate measuring of modem speed in bits-per-second (bps).

binary file   A file type that is encoded using only the binary digits 0 and 1. Binary files are usually programs, graphics, or complex documents, and are readable only by a computer.

bit   A binary digit. The smallest unit of information a computer can handle. A bit can have the value 0 or 1, and is represented physically as a single pulse sent through a circuit, or a single spot on a disk. A group of 8 bits is called a byte.

bitmap   A collection of bits that make up a dot pattern or graphic image. Bitmaps with a BMP extension are the default file type for the Paint accessory.

boot   To start a computer.

bound   A property of fields or controls in an Access object, such as a form or report. A bound field or control will be updated when the data that the field or control is bound to changes.

bound control   A control tied to a field in an underlying table or query.

bullet   A mark, usually a round or square symbol, often used to add emphasis or to distinguish between items in a list.

byte   A unit of information consisting of 8 bits. Typically the equivalent of a single character, number, or punctuation mark.

cascading menu   A menu that opens another menu. Cascading menus are indicated by an arrow next to a menu item. By pointing to the item, you open a new menu.

CD-ROM   A compact optical disc, similar in appearance to an audio CD, that can store over 500 MB of information. A CD-ROM drive is needed to read the data on a CD-ROM.

cell   The basic unit of a table or worksheet. The intersection of a row and a column forms one cell. You type text, numbers, or formulas into cells. Each cell is named by its position in the row (1, 2, 3) and column (A, B, C). For example, cell A1 is the first cell in column A, row 1.

chart   A graphic representation of worksheet data. Values from worksheet cells are displayed as bars, lines, or other shapes. Common chart types are pie, bar, line, and area.

click   To press the primary mouse button once.

Clipboard   The temporary holding place for text or other objects that have been cut or copied in a program.

collapse   To reduce the number of rows displayed in a view by showing only categories or by eliminating responses.

color scheme   The basic set of eight colors provided for any slide. The color scheme consists of a background color, a color for lines and text, and six additional colors balanced to provide a professional look to your presentation. You can apply color schemes to slides and to notes pages.

column   A vertical section of a worksheet or table. In Microsoft Excel, there are 256 columns in a worksheet. In Excel, columns are usually identified by letters (A–Z, AA–AZ, BA–BZ,... IA–IV).

column break   The line that identifies the end of a column and the beginning of another column.

comment   [1] In Word, a feature you can use to add comments to a document. Comments appear in a document when you point to comment flags with the mouse. [2] A note that explains, identifies, or comments on the information in a specific cell or range of cells.

comparison operators   The criteria used to search for records that are equal to, less than, or greater than a specific value, or for records that are between two values.

constrain keys   Keys such as CTRL and SHIFT that when held down constrain how an object is drawn. Using these keys can constrain an object to expand from its center or its sides, top, or bottom.

context-sensitive help   A type of online help used to identify any screen element in a window or to provide relevant information about the current operation.

control   An object such as a text box, a list box, or a command button that adds functionality to a program, displays information, or allows the user to control a program.

Control Panel   The set of Windows 95 or Windows NT programs you can use to change system, hardware, software, and Windows 95 or Windows NT settings.

copy   To duplicate information from one location to another, within a file, to another file, or to a file in another program. Copied information is stored on the Clipboard until you cut or copy another piece of information.

crop   To cut away parts of a graphic.

crosstab query   A query that displays summarized values from a single field and rearranges the values into rows and columns.

cursor   *See* insertion point.

cut   To remove selected information from a document so you can paste it to another location within the file, to another file, or to a file in another program. The cut information is stored on the Clipboard until you cut or copy another piece of information.

database   A collection of data related to a particular topic or purpose, such as a database of customer information. Can also refer to a type of program, such as

725

Microsoft Access, that you can use to organize and manipulate detailed lists of information.

data points   The individual values plotted in a chart and represented by bars, lines, pie slices, dots, and other shapes.

data source   The file that contains the variable information for a merge document.

data type   The attribute of a field that determines the kind of data the field can contain.

data validation   The process of checking if the data being entered meets a specific set of criteria.

default   A predefined setting that is built into a program and is used when you do not specify an alternative setting. For example, a document might have a default setting of 1-inch page margins unless you specify another value for the margin settings.

descending   A method of ordering a group of items from highest to lowest, such as from Z to A. *See also* sort.

Desktop   The entire Windows 95 or Windows NT screen that represents your work area. Icons, windows, and the taskbar appear on the Desktop.

destination   A document or program into which an object is embedded or linked.

detail report   A report that provides a more narrow view of a set of data.

dialog box   A box that displays additional options when a command is chosen from a menu.

dimmed   The grayed appearance of a command or option that is unavailable.

disk   A round, flat piece of flexible plastic (floppy disk) or inflexible metal (hard disk) that stores data. The disk is coated with a magnetic material on which digital information can be recorded. To protect this material, disks are enclosed in plastic or metal casings.

disk drive   A hardware mechanism that reads information from or writes information to a hard disk, floppy disk, CD-ROM, or network drive.

document   Any independent unit of information, such as a text file, worksheet, or graphic object, that is created with a program. A document is saved with a filename by which it can be retrieved.

double-click   To press the primary mouse button twice rapidly. Double-clicking an object performs the default action.

download   To transfer a file from a remote computer to your local computer. This can be done with computers linked on a network or through telecommunication.

drag   To hold down the mouse button while moving the mouse.

drag-and-drop   A mouse technique for directly moving or copying a set of information from one location to another. To drag an object, position the pointer over the object, hold down the mouse button while you move the mouse, and then release the mouse button when the object is positioned where you want it.

electronic mail   Notes, messages, and files sent between different computers that use telecommunication or network services. Also referred to as *e-mail*.

e-mail   *See* electronic mail.

embed   To insert an object from a source program into a destination document. When you double-click the object in the destination document, the source program opens and you can edit the object. *See also* link.

endnote   An explanatory comment reference inserted at the end of a section or document.

expand   [1]To display all subordinate entries in an outline or in a folder. [2]To display a list of all documents in a view.

Explorer   *See* Windows Explorer *or* Windows NT Explorer.

export   The process of converting and saving a file to be used in another program. *See also* import.

expression   A formula that calculates a value. You can use expressions in forms, reports, tables, queries, macros, and modules.

extension   *See* file extension.

field   An area in a table or form in which you can enter or view specific information about an individual task or resource. On a form, a field is an area where you can enter data.

file   Any independent unit of information, such as a text document, a worksheet, or a graphic object, that is created using a program. A file is saved with a filename by which it can be retrieved.

file extension   A period and up to three characters at the end of a filename. The extension can help identify the kind of information a file contains. For example, the extensions CMD and BAT indicate that the file contains a batch program. The file extension is an optional addition to the filename.

file format   The format in which data is stored in a file. Usually, different programs, such as Microsoft Word or Microsoft Excel, have different file formats.

filename   A name used to identify a file. Depending on the file system, a filename can be 1 to 255 characters long, including spaces, acceptable punctuation marks, and an optional extension of 1 to 3 characters.

file server *See* server.

file type The category designation of a file object. File types include bit map, text, or spreadsheet. The file type is usually reflected in the MS-DOS filename extension.

filter A set of criteria you can apply to records to show specific tasks, records, or resources. The tasks, records, or resources that match your criteria are listed or highlighted so that you can focus on just the information you want.

folder A container in which documents, program files, and other folders are stored on your disks. Formerly referred to as a *directory*.

font A family of type styles, such as Times New Roman or Arial. Effects, such as bold or italic, and various point sizes can be applied to a font. *See also* point.

footer The text or graphics printed at the bottom of every page in a document.

footnote An explanatory reference inserted at the bottom of a page that provides additional information on some text that is designated with a reference mark.

foreign key A field in a related table that contains the values that match the related fields in the primary key in the primary table.

form A Microsoft Access database object on which you place controls for entering, displaying, and editing data.

format [1] The way text or cells appear on a page. [2] To prepare a disk to record or retrieve data. Formatting a disk usually erases any information the disk previously contained.

Format Painter A feature that picks up an object's format and applies that format to another object.

formula A sequence of values, cell references, names, functions, or operators that produces a new value from existing values. A formula always begins with an equal sign (=).

function A built-in formula; a named and stored procedure that performs a specific operation and returns a value. Functions begin with a function command and are followed by a set of parentheses. Inside the parentheses is the argument, which can be a set of cell references, a range, numbers, text, or other functions. Some functions do not use an argument.

grid An invisible network of vertical and horizontal lines that covers a PowerPoint presentation slide. The grid automatically aligns objects to the nearest intersection of the grid.

handles Small black squares located in the lower-right corner of selected cells or around selected graphic objects, chart items, or text. By dragging the handles, you can perform actions such as moving, copying, filling, sizing, or formatting on the selected cells, objects, chart items, or text.

hanging indent   A paragraph indent in which the first line is flush with the left margin and subsequent lines are indented.

hard disk   *See* disk.

hard page break   A marker in a document that forces the succeeding text to start on a new page.

hardware   The physical parts of a computer system, such as the monitor, keyboard, and printer.

header   The text or graphics printed at the top of every page in a document.

HTML (HyperText Markup Language)   A set of rules used to format World Wide Web pages. HTML includes methods of specifying text characteristics (bold, italic, etc.), graphic placement, links, and so on. A Web browser, such as Internet Explorer, must be used to properly view an HTML document.

hyperlink   An object, such as a graphic or colored or underlined text, that represents a link to another location in the same file or in a different file. When clicked, the new location or file is displayed. Hyperlinks are one of the key elements of HTML documents.

I-beam   *See* insertion point.

icon   A small graphic that represents a Windows 95 or Windows NT element, such as a program, a disk drive, or a document. When you double-click an icon, the item the icon represents opens.

import   To convert a file that was created in another program. *See also* export.

indent   The distance between the left or right edge of a block of text and the page margin. A paragraph can have a left, right, and first-line indent. Indents can also be measured relative to columns in a section, table cells, and the boundaries of positioned objects.

insertion point   The blinking vertical bar that marks the location where text is entered in a document, a cell, or a dialog box. Also referred to as a cursor.

Internet   A worldwide "network of networks," made up of thousands of computer networks and millions of commercial, education, government, and personal computers, all connected to each other. Also referred to as the Net.

intranet   A self-contained network that uses the same communications protocols and file formats as the Internet. An intranet can, but doesn't have to, be connected to the Internet. Many businesses use intranets for their internal communications. *See also* Internet.

join line   A line between fields displayed in field lists in the Microsoft Access Relationship window or the Query window that indicates how the fields are matched between the tables.

729

junction table A table that provides a link between two tables that have a many-to-many relationship. The junction table provides the relationship between the two tables.

kerning The space between a pair of letters.

key field *See* primary key.

kilobyte (KB) One thousand bytes or, more precisely, 1024 bytes.

landscape The horizontal orientation of a page. *See also* portrait.

leading The space between lines of text. The term *leading* comes from early type-setting, when thin bars of lead were set between lines of type to adjust the spacing.

link [1] *See* hyperlink. [2] To copy an object, such as a graphic or text, from one file or program to another so that there is a dependent relationship between the object and its source file. Also refers to the connection between a source file and a destination file. Whenever the original information in the source file changes, the information in the destination file is automatically updated.

linked object An object created in another application that maintains a connection to its source. A linked object, unlike an embedded object, is stored in its source document, where it was created. You update a linked object within its source application.

macro A series of commands stored as a group so they can be treated as a single command.

marquee A moving dotted line that surrounds your selection.

master document A holder for subdocuments displayed in an outline structure. A master document is usually a long document divided into smaller documents.

master text The formatted placeholder for the main slide text on the Slide Master. The master text controls the font, color, size, and alignment of the main text object as well as its placement on the slide.

maximize To expand a window to occupy the full screen. *See also* minimize; restore.

megabyte (MB) One million bytes.

memory The primary storage in a computer, which is measured in bytes, kilobytes (K or KB), and megabytes (MB).

merged document Material (often a form letter) in which customized information is combined with repetitive or boilerplate text.

Microsoft Exchange   The Windows 95 and Windows NT program you can use to send and receive electronic mail, faxes, and files on a network or online service. Microsoft Exchange acts as a central "post office" for all messaging activities.

The Microsoft Network   The built-in online service included with Windows 95 and Windows NT.

minimize   To contract a window to an icon. This can be reversed by double-clicking the icon. *See also* maximize; restore.

modem   A hardware device that converts digital computer information into audio signals that can be sent through phone lines. These signals are received and converted back to digital signals by the receiving modem.

multimedia   A program or system that incorporates the use of a variety of visual and audio elements, such as, sound, video, graphics, and music.

multiple selection   Selecting more than one object by using the SHIFT+click method or by dragging the selection rectangle. When you flip, rotate, or resize a multiple selection, all objects in the multiple selection react together.

My Computer   The Windows 95 and Windows NT program that you can use to browse through your computer's filing system, and to open drives, folders, and files. You can also use My Computer to manage your files and your filing system, by moving, copying, renaming, and deleting items.

network   A system of multiple computers that uses special networking programs to share files, software, printers, and other resources among the different computers that are connected in the network.

network drive   A shared folder or drive on the network that you have mapped to your computer. A network drive is represented by a network drive icon. You can use this icon to open and use the files and folders stored in that drive.

Network Neighborhood   The Windows 95 and Windows NT program you can use to explore the network to which your computer is connected.

nonprinting characters   The characters such as tab characters, paragraph marks, spaces, and breaks that do not appear in a printed document. Nonprinting characters can be displayed to aid in formatting.

null field   A field containing no characters.

object   A table, chart, graphic, equation, or other form of information you create and edit. An object can be inserted, pasted, or copied into any file.

one-to-many relationship   A relationship in which a record in the main database can be related to one or more records in a detail database. *See also* one-to-one relationship.

one-to-one relationship   A relationship between two tables in which a value in a related table exists in a primary table. The value can occur only once in the related table. *See also* one-to-many relationship.

online   Connected to a network or connected to your Internet service provider's server.

operating system   The software used to control application processing and hardware resources, such as memory, disk space, and peripheral devices.

operator   A symbol used for simple math calculations. For example, the operators for addition and subtraction are the plus sign (+) and the minus sign (-).

Pack And Go   A wizard that makes it easy to compress your presentation onto a disk. Use the Pack And Go Wizard to prepare a presentation for use on another computer.

page break   A break that determines the end of a page and the beginning of the following page. Documents contain automatic page breaks (also referred to as soft page breaks) based on the margins. Manual page breaks (also referred to as hard page breaks) are inserted to break a page at a specific location.

page footer   Text or graphics that appear at the bottom of every page of a report.

page header   Text or graphics that appear at the top of every page of a report.

palette   A box containing choices for color and other special effects you use when designing a form, a report, or other object.

paste   To insert cut or copied text into a document from the Clipboard.

paste special   To insert cut or copied text or graphics with a special format (for example, BMP and RTF for graphics and text, respectively).

path   The location of a file within a computer filing system. The path indicates the filename preceded by the disk drive, folder, and subfolders in which the file is stored. If the file is on another computer on a network, the path also includes the computer name.

PivotTable   An interactive worksheet table that summarizes data using a selected format and calculations. It is called a PivotTable because you can rearrange the table structure around the data.

pixel   Short for "picture element." The smallest graphic unit that can be displayed on your screen. All the images displayed on a computer screen are composed of pixels. *See also* bitmap.

placeholder   A reserved object to place information. In PowerPoint, each place-holder is surrounded by a dotted line with a message telling you to click and type your text or to double-click to open an embedded application.

point   A typographical unit of measurement, often used to indicate character height, line thickness, and the amount of space between lines of text. There are ap-proximately 72 points to an inch. Abbreviated "pt." *See also* font

pointer   The representation of the mouse position on the Desktop. You move the pointer on the Desktop by moving the mouse on a smooth, horizontal surface. The pointer changes shape depending on the action.

pop-up menu   A menu that lists shortcut commands that directly relate to the action you are performing. Many pop-up menus are accessed by clicking desktop and program elements with the right mouse button.

portrait   The vertical orientation of a page. *See also* landscape.

PowerPoint Animation Player   A special application that is designed to display the full range of PowerPoint's special effects over the Internet. You can distribute the Player freely.

PowerPoint Viewer   A special application that is designed to give electronic slide shows for those who are going to be running slide shows on computers with-out PowerPoint. You can distribute the Viewer freely.

Presentation Conference   A wizard that makes it easy to present a slide show over a network or the Internet on two or more computers at the same time.

primary key   One or more fields in a table that hold values that can uniquely identify each record in the table.

Print Preview   A view that displays your document as it will appear when you print it. Items, such as text and graphics, appear in their actual positions.

print range   A set area of the worksheet to be printed.

program   Computer software, such as a word processor, spreadsheet, presenta-tion designer, or relational database, designed to perform a specific type of work.

program file   A file that stores detailed computer instructions that make a pro-gram operational.

properties   The information about an object, including settings or options for that object. For example, you can look at the properties of a file for information such as the file size, file type, and file attributes.

protocol   A communications standard—such as TCP/IP, used on the Internet and intranets, or NETBEUI, used in Microsoft networks—that ensures reliable trans-mission among the computers and other components on a network.

query   A database object that represents the group of records you want to view. A query is a request for a particular collection of data.

Quick View   A resource in Windows 95 and Windows NT that allows you to browse through and view the files on your computer without opening the programs that created each file. Documents can be opened directly from Quick View for editing.

random access memory (RAM)   The computer's memory, which can be accessed randomly rather than sequentially. RAM allows the computer to store and retrieve information without searching sequentially from the beginning of a location.

range   Two or more adjacent cells on a sheet. You identify a range by the upper-left corner and lower-right corner cell addresses, separated by a colon or by two dots, for example, A1:B10 or A1..C5.

read-only   An attribute of a disk volume, folder, or file stored on a shared, network computer that is made available to other users on the network. An item designated as read-only allows users to view files, but not edit the files.

read-only memory (ROM)   Memory containing instructions or data that can be read but not modified. Permanent startup programs and other essential information are stored in ROM.

record   A set of information that belongs together and describes a single item in a table or query.

Recycle Bin   The Windows 95 and Windows NT program that holds files, folders, and other items you have deleted. Recycle Bin is represented by an icon on the Desktop. Until Recycle Bin is "emptied," you can recover items you have deleted or placed in Recycle Bin.

reference   A cell address used in a formula.

reference mark   A number or character indicating that additional information is located in a footnote or endnote. By default, reference marks for footnotes are Arabic numerals and reference marks for endnotes are roman numerals.

referential integrity   Rules that are used to preserve the valid relationships between related tables.

relative cell reference   In formulas, a reference to the address of another cell in relation to a cell that contains a formula. *See also* absolute cell reference.

Required property   A property that can be set for a field that will not accept null values.

restore   [1] To expand a minimized application by double-clicking it or to return a window to its previous size. [2] To recover information previously deleted.

rich text format (RTF)   A text formatting standard that makes it possible to transfer formatted documents between programs.

row   [1] A horizontal section of a worksheet. Rows are usually identified by numbers. [2] The data in all the cells in a single row of a list. A row is called a record when the list is used as a database.

rule   A line or border.

ruler   A graphical bar used for measurement that's displayed in a document window. You can use the ruler to indent paragraphs, set tab stops, adjust page margins, and change column widths in a table.

save   The function that stores information residing in memory in a designated place, under a designated name on one of your computer's disks.

ScreenTip   A brief description that appears when the pointer is positioned over an object.

section   A part of a document separated from the rest of the document with a section break. You can use sections to change the page setup, headers and footers, and column formatting in different parts of the same document.

section break   A line that identifies the end of a section and the beginning of the following section. Section breaks are used to format different parts of a document—for example, columns or headers and footers.

selection bar   In Word and WordPad, an invisible area at the left edge of the document window used to select text quickly with the pointer.

selection box   The gray slanted-line or dotted outline around an object that indicates it is selected. Selecting and dragging the selection box moves the object.

server   [1] A central computer on certain types of networks to which all computers on the network are connected, and through which users can obtain shared network resources. [2] Software that provides resources to a computer or program that requests it.

shortcut   An easily accessible icon that represents and points to a program, folder, or file stored elsewhere on the computer. You can place a shortcut on your Desktop, Start menu, or Programs menu.

shortcut menu   A menu of commands that opens when you use the right mouse button to click. The commands listed in the menu vary depending on what element you right-click.

smart cut and paste   A cut and paste feature that makes sure words are correctly spaced after using the Cut and Paste commands.

soft page break   A marker inserted automatically in a document to indicate where a full page ends and a new page begins. The locations of soft page breaks are automatically adjusted when material is added to or deleted from a document.

software   Internal computer programs that instruct the computer on what to do. There are two basic categories of software: operating systems and programs.

sound card   The printed circuit board that you can install in your computer to generate and record sound files.

source   [1] In a Web page, the text page that displays all HTML tags. In Internet Explorer, the source for the displayed Web page can be seen by choosing Source from the View menu. [2] The document or program in which the file was originally created. *See also* destination.

split bar   The double line that indicates where a window is split.

split box   The solid box at the end or top of a scroll bar that users drag to split a document window in two, so that each half can be scrolled independently. Users can split a window vertically, horizontally, or both.

spreadsheet   A type of program into which data can be entered in columns and rows. The program can then be used to perform calculations, maintain a database, and create graphic presentations representing the data.

Start button   The command button that by default is located in the lower-left corner of the screen on the taskbar of Windows 95 and Windows NT. The Start button serves as the starting point from which all Windows 95 or Windows NT programs, activities, and functions begin.

Start menu   The menu that presents commands that are a starting point for all work you do on your computer, such as starting a program, opening a document, finding a file, and getting help. You open the Start menu by clicking the Start button displayed on the taskbar.

status bar   The bar at the bottom of the screen that displays information about the currently selected command, the active dialog box, the standard keys on the keyboard, or the current state of the program and the keyboard.

style   [1] A named collection of text formatting choices, such as font, size, leading, spacing, and alignment, that can be applied to change the appearance of text. Body Text, Headline, and Subhead are examples of styles that are often used. Styles are stored in a document or template. [2] A variation in the appearance of a character, for example, italic, bold, shadow, outlined, or normal.

style area   The vertical area on the left edge of a document in which the style name of each paragraph appears.

subfolder   A folder that is located within another folder. All folders are subfolders of the root folder.

subform   A form within a form.

tab order   A form property that controls how the cursor moves between fields when you press TAB.

table One or more rows of cells commonly used to display numbers and other items for quick reference and analysis. Items in a table are organized into rows (records) and columns (fields).

taskbar The bar located at the bottom of the default Windows 95 or Windows NT Desktop. The taskbar includes the Start button as well as buttons for any programs and documents that are open.

template A special kind of document that provides basic tools and text for shaping a final document. Templates can contain text, styles, glossary items, macros, and menu and key assignments.

tick mark A small line that intersects an axis and marks off a category, scale, or data series. The tick mark label identifies the tick mark.

title bar The bar at the top of a window that displays the name of the document or program that appears in that window.

toolbar A bar below the menu bar of Windows-based programs that displays a set of buttons used to carry out common menu commands. Toolbar buttons can change, depending on which window or view is currently selected. Toolbars typically can be moved or docked at any edge of a program window.

transitions The effects that move one slide off the screen and the next slide on during a slide show. Each slide can have its own transition effect.

trendline A graphic used to study problems of predictions such as future sales. Also called a regression analysis.

typeface The unique style of a set of printed characters in a document. The typeface includes attributes, such as font, size, and appearance.

upload To transfer a file from a user's local computer to a remote computer. A transfer can be done with computers linked on a network or through telecommunication.

virus A program that attaches itself to another program in computer memory or on a disk, and immediately spreads from one program to another or remains dormant until a specified event occurs. Viruses can damage data, cause computers to crash, and display offending or bothersome messages.

Web *See* World Wide Web.

Web address The address to a file on the Web such as an HTML page. The Web address or URL (Uniform Resource Locator) consists of a protocol, host name, path, and filename. For example, http://www.microsoft.com/office/default.htm. *See also* path.

Web browser Software that interprets and displays documents formatted for the World Wide Web, such as HTML documents, graphics, or multimedia files.

Web page   A document on the Web, formatted in HTML. Web pages usually contain links that you can use to jump from one page to another or from one location to another. *See also* link.

Web site   A collection of Web pages at the same location.

widow   The last line of a paragraph forced to the top of the next page of text.

wildcard   Special character used in place of any other characters. An asterisk (*) takes the place of one or more characters; a question mark (?) takes the place of one character.

window   A separate rectangular part of the screen identified by a border. A window represents an open object and displays information. Multiple windows can be open at the same time.

Windows Explorer   The Windows 95 program you can use to browse through, open, and manage the disk drives, folders, and files on your computer. In a network system, you can also use Windows Explorer to view and open shared folders on other computers on the network. You can use Windows Explorer to manage your files by moving, copying, renaming, and deleting files.

Windows NT Explorer   The Windows NT program you can use to browse through, open, and manage the disk drives, folders, and files on your computer. You can also use Windows NT Explorer to view and open shared folders on other computers on the network. You can use Windows NT Explorer to manage your files and your filing system by moving, copying, renaming, and deleting files.

wizard   A tool that guides you through a complex task by asking you questions and then performing the task based on your responses.

WordArt   A feature used to create unique and creative effects with text. Using WordArt, you can display text at angles and in a variety of patterns and shapes.

wordwrap   In a word processing program, a feature that causes a word to automatically move to the next line when the word exceeds the margin limits.

workbook   A Microsoft Excel document in which you can store other documents. A workbook can include multiple worksheets and chart sheets.

worksheet   A set of rows, columns, and cells in which you store and manipulate data. Several worksheets can appear in one workbook, and you can switch among them easily by clicking their tabs with the mouse.

World Wide Web   The collection of available information on the Internet that is connected by links so that you can jump from one document to another. Also referred to as the Web, WWW, and W3.

Index

Index

J

join line, 577, 579, 580
Journal folder, *594*
Journal icon, *596*
Journal window, *596*
junction tables, 551–52
justified text, 176

K

Keep Lines Together option,
    199–200
Kerning option, *173*
key attributes, 515–16
keyboard shortcuts. *See also specific*
    keys
    copying, 109
    cutting, 102
    deleting, 138
    deleting files/folders, 111
    moving among slides, 366
    opening Start menu, 11
    pasting, 103, 109
    switching between programs,
        84–85
    undoing commands, 140
keywords. *See* file properties

L

labels. *See* cell labels; mailing
    labels; text labels
Label Wizard, 500–503
landscape orientation, 222
Language dialog box, *412*
Large Icons button, *99*
Last Tab Scroll button, *243*
Las Vegas Lights option, *174*
Leaders, 186–87
left-aligned text, 176
left indent marker, 181
letterhead, preprinted, 145
Letter Paper format, 392
Letter Wizard, 132, 143–48
Letter Wizard dialog box, *144, 145,*
    146, 147
lines. *See also* join line
    creating blank, 148
    drawing freehand, 440
    green, wavy, 135, 155, 206

lines, *continued*
    keeping together, 199–200
    orphan, 200
    red, wavy, 132, 155, 206
    spacing
        in document paragraphs,
            189–90
        in presentations, 408–9, 417
    widow, 200
Line Spacing command, 408
Line Spacing dialog box, *408*
Line tool icon, *92*
Link dialog box, *557*
linking, 556–58, 567
list boxes, 14, *14, 16*, 473, *473*
List button, *99, 152, 153*
lists. *See also specific lists*
    selecting values from, 474
logos. *See* graphics
Look In box, 152
Look In Favorites button, *143, 152,*
    153
lookup fields, 549–50, 554
Look Up Reference dialog box, *416*
Lookup Wizard, 523
low priority symbol, *622*

M

magnification
    adjusting document, 158, 166,
        174–75
    viewing entire page width, 191
Magnifier button, *197*
magnifier pointer, 196–97, 204
Mail Form, *609, 611*
Mail group, 594
    folders in, *595*
mailing labels, 500–503, 506
Map Network Drive button, *99*
Marching Black Ants option, *174*
Marching Red Ants option, *174*
margin markers, 430–32
margins
    adjusting page, 223
    adjusting presentation master,
        430–32
    report, 499
    setting document, 220–21, 234
    setting presentation, 435
    setting worksheet page, 302, 312

master placeholders. *See also spe-*
    cific placeholders
    editing, 425
    formatting text in, 426–28
masters, 419. *See also* Notes Master;
    Slide Master; Title Master
    hiding objects from slides, 434
master subtitle placeholder, *423*
master text
    adjusting indents in, 429–32
    formatting, 426–28, 435
master text placeholder, *422*
master title placeholder, *422, 423*
Maximize button, 17, *18*
Media Player, *76*
Meeting Planner feature, 683
meeting request form, *689*
meetings, scheduling, 684–93, 694
menu bars, 11
menus, 4–5. *See also* cascading
    menus; pop-up menus; *spe-*
    cific menus
    closing, 11, 23
    customizing, 48–52
    opening, 11, 12, 23
Merge And Center button, *272*
message boxes, *116*
Message Flag button, *622, 635*
message header, 609
Message icon, *638*
messages. *See* e-mail
Messages With AutoPreview view,
    599, 600
Message Timeline view, 601
Microsoft Access
    relationships in, 521–22
    starting, 457–59
    window, *79*
Microsoft Access dialog box, *457*
Microsoft Bookshelf, 415–16, 418
Microsoft Excel
    document icon, *98*
    window, *79*
Microsoft FrontPage, 310
Microsoft Outlook
    closing, 605, 606
    modifying startup settings,
        588–89
    opening documents with, 155
    opening files with, 316
    starting, 590–91, 605

Index

IMPORTANT—READ CAREFULLY BEFORE OPENING SOFTWARE PACKET(S). By opening the sealed packet(s) containing the software, you indicate your acceptance of the following Microsoft License Agreement.

MICROSOFT LICENSE AGREEMENT

(Book Companion CD-ROM)

This is a legal agreement between you (either an individual or an entity) and Microsoft Corporation. By opening the sealed software packet(s) you are agreeing to be bound by the terms of this agreement. If you do not agree to the terms of this agreement, promptly return the unopened software packet(s) and any accompanying written materials to the place you obtained them for a full refund.

MICROSOFT SOFTWARE LICENSE

1. GRANT OF LICENSE. Microsoft grants to you the right to use one copy of the Microsoft software program included with this book (the "SOFTWARE") on a single terminal connected to a single computer. The SOFTWARE is in "use" on a computer when it is loaded into the temporary memory (i.e., RAM) or installed into the permanent memory (e.g., hard disk, CD-ROM, or other storage device) of that computer. You may not network the SOFTWARE or otherwise use it on more than one computer or computer terminal at the same time. For the files and material referenced in this book which may be obtained from the Internet, Microsoft grants to you the right to use the materials in connection with the book. If you are a member of a corporation or business, you may reproduce the materials and distribute them within your business for internal business purposes in connection with the book. You may not reproduce the materials for further distribution.

2. COPYRIGHT. The SOFTWARE is owned by Microsoft or its suppliers and is protected by United States copyright laws and international treaty provisions. Therefore, you must treat the SOFTWARE like any other copyrighted material (e.g., a book or musical recording) except that you may either (a) make one copy of the SOFTWARE solely for backup or archival purposes, or (b) transfer the SOFTWARE to a single hard disk provided you keep the original solely for backup or archival purposes. You may not copy the written materials accompanying the SOFTWARE.

3. OTHER RESTRICTIONS. You may not rent or lease the SOFTWARE, but you may transfer the SOFTWARE and accompanying written materials on a permanent basis provided you retain no copies and the recipient agrees to the terms of this Agreement. You may not reverse engineer, decompile, or disassemble the SOFTWARE. If the SOFTWARE is an update or has been updated, any transfer must include the most recent update and all prior versions.

4. DUAL MEDIA SOFTWARE. If the SOFTWARE package contains more than one kind of disk (3.5", 5.25", and CD-ROM), then you may use only the disks appropriate for your single-user computer. You may not use the other disks on another computer or loan, rent, lease, or transfer them to another user except as part of the permanent transfer (as provided above) of all SOFTWARE and written materials.

5. SAMPLE CODE. If the SOFTWARE includes Sample Code, then Microsoft grants you a royalty-free right to reproduce and distribute the sample code of the SOFTWARE provided that you: (a) distribute the sample code only in conjunction with and as a part of your software product; (b) do not use Microsoft's or its authors' names, logos, or trademarks to market your software product; (c) include the copyright notice that appears on the SOFTWARE on your product label and as a part of the sign-on message for your software product; and (d) agree to indemnify, hold harmless, and defend Microsoft and its authors from and against any claims or lawsuits, including attorneys' fees, that arise or result from the use or distribution of your software product.

DISCLAIMER OF WARRANTY

The SOFTWARE (including instructions for its use) is provided "AS IS" WITHOUT WARRANTY OF ANY KIND. MICROSOFT FURTHER DISCLAIMS ALL IMPLIED WARRANTIES INCLUDING WITHOUT LIMITATION ANY IMPLIED WARRANTIES OF MERCHANTABILITY OR OF FITNESS FOR A PARTICULAR PURPOSE. THE ENTIRE RISK ARISING OUT OF THE USE OR PERFORMANCE OF THE SOFTWARE AND DOCUMENTATION REMAINS WITH YOU.

IN NO EVENT SHALL MICROSOFT, ITS AUTHORS, OR ANYONE ELSE INVOLVED IN THE CREATION, PRODUCTION, OR DELIVERY OF THE SOFTWARE BE LIABLE FOR ANY DAMAGES WHATSOEVER (INCLUDING, WITHOUT LIMITATION, DAMAGES FOR LOSS OF BUSINESS PROFITS, BUSINESS INTERRUPTION, LOSS OF BUSINESS INFORMATION, OR OTHER PECUNIARY LOSS) ARISING OUT OF THE USE OF OR INABILITY TO USE THE SOFTWARE OR DOCUMENTATION, EVEN IF MICROSOFT HAS BEEN ADVISED OF THE POSSIBILITY OF SUCH DAMAGES. BECAUSE SOME STATES/COUNTRIES DO NOT ALLOW THE EXCLUSION OR LIMITATION OF LIABILITY FOR CONSEQUENTIAL OR INCIDENTAL DAMAGES, THE ABOVE LIMITATION MAY NOT APPLY TO YOU.

U.S. GOVERNMENT RESTRICTED RIGHTS

The SOFTWARE and documentation are provided with RESTRICTED RIGHTS. Use, duplication, or disclosure by the Government is subject to restrictions as set forth in subparagraph (c)(1)(ii) of The Rights in Technical Data and Computer Software clause at DFARS 252.227-7013 or subparagraphs (c)(1) and (2) of the Commercial Computer Software — Restricted Rights 48 CFR 52.227-19, as applicable. Manufacturer is Microsoft Corporation, One Microsoft Way, Redmond, WA 98052-6399.

If you acquired this product in the United States, this Agreement is governed by the laws of the State of Washington.

Should you have any questions concerning this Agreement, or if you desire to contact Microsoft Press for any reason, please write: Microsoft Press, One Microsoft Way, Redmond, WA 98052-6399.

The
Step by Step
Practice Files CD

The enclosed CD-ROM contains timesaving, ready-to-use practice files that complement the lessons in this book. It also contains Camcorder files, which are "movies" showing how to do certain tasks. To use the practice files and Camcorder files, you'll need Microsoft Office 97 Professional Edition and either Microsoft Windows 95 or Microsoft Windows NT version 4.

Before you begin the *Step by Step* lessons, read the "Installing and Using the Practice and Camcorder Files" section of the book. There you'll find detailed information about the contents of the CD and easy instructions telling how ot install the files on your computer's hard disk.

Please take a few moments to read the License Agreement on the previous page before using the enclosed CD.

Register Today!

Return this
Microsoft® Office 97 Professional 6-in-1 Step by Step
registration card today

Microsoft® Press
mspress.microsoft.com

OWNER REGISTRATION CARD   **1-57231-703-5**

Microsoft® Office 97 Professional 6-in-1 Step by Step

FIRST NAME MIDDLE INITIAL LAST NAME

INSTITUTION OR COMPANY NAME

ADDRESS

CITY STATE ZIP

( )

E-MAIL ADDRESS PHONE NUMBER

U.S. and Canada addresses only. Fill in information above and mail postage-free.
Please mail only the bottom half of this page.

**For information about Microsoft Press®
products, visit our Web site at
mspress.microsoft.com**

Microsoft·*Press*